Acclaim for th

"Oberon Zell! Who better to write a young Wizard's Grimoire than this living legend from the magickal world? Here is the man who recreated living unicorns, who traveled to the remote South Seas in search of genuine mermaids, who created the Church of All Worlds. If there is anyone who can bring magick to life for a million aspiring Wizards, it is Oberon. I recommend him to any publisher who wants to catch the rising tide of youthful interest in benevolent magick." **—Amber K**

Author: *Pagan Kids' Activity Book* (Horned Owl 1995)
True Magick: A Beginner's Guide (Llewellyn 1985)

"Oberon Zell-Ravenheart is, in my opinion, one of the most intelligent and creative people in modern Paganism. He has been doing this as long or longer than almost anyone else. He has been personally involved with many important historic events in the creation of the Earth-based spirituality that is important to so many people today. And he has the unique distinction of being probably the most influential male in the Goddess movement! He is the perfect man to teach young apprentice Wizards how to find their place in the world. He can help them to use magick in a responsible and respectful way.

"Oberon is a gifted storyteller, a powerful magician, and he is young at heart. He loves what he is doing and he will unselfishly offer to share what he has learned with those who are ready for it. I have known Oberon, or known of him, since 1969, and I am eagerly looking forward to his book and to what I can learn from it! Viva Oberon!" **—John Sulak**

Co-Author: *Modern Pagans* (RE/Search 2001)

"I have known Oberon Zell for a number of years and have had the pleasure of being in ritual with him. He is a pioneer, leader, and visionary among Pagans and within the magickal community. One of the founders of the Church of All Worlds, he also pioneered *Green Egg,* which was the premier Pagan publication. His work contained therein was thought-provoking, scholarly, and challenging.

"Oberon is an experienced writer and Wizard; he brings years of practice, expertise, and highly principled, scholarly care to this endeavor." **—Dana D. Eilers**

Author: *The Practical Pagan* (New Page 2002)
Pagans and the Law (New Page 2003)

"I'm excited to have been asked to contribute to Oberon Zell-Ravenheart's *Grimoire for the Apprentice Wizard.* There is no more important task than the awakening of wonder, magic and love for the inspirited Earth in the greater culture. And no one more ideal to pull it off than Oberon.

"There is a trend reflected in the interest in Harry Potter and Tolkein—with boys 8-18 experiencing a growing hunger for things heroic and vital. There's never been a better opportunity for affecting and inspiring them. They're looking for alternatives, for role models and inspiriteurs.

"Oberon has the talents as well as experience to make it happen, the way he brought together a church, a movement...and our Grey Council. He awakens a fire in every young person he comes into contact with, having long lived the life

enchanting art, writings and talks are themselves a magical manifestation, and his influence on our community is legendary." **—Jesse Wolf Hardin**

Author, *Kindred Spirits: Sacred Earth Wisdom*
(Swan•Raven 2001) Earthen Spirituality Project

"I'd heard about Oberon's diligence in the magickal community since day one as a Witch over 18 years ago. I finally had the joy of meeting this wonderful gentleman and Elder in our community recently, who has obviously filled his life, spirit, and mind with all manner of magickal information, and more importantly, practical applications. The idea of his helping young men along the Path of Beauty is nothing short of brilliant.

"For too long Wicca has been mistaken as being a woman's art, and indeed many books direct their writings to that audience. In so doing we have cut off the God, and made many men, both young and old, feel isolated and somewhat out of the loop. A book of this nature helps balance our Wheel, with honor, respect and gratitude as guides (not to mention a heaping dose of fun and fulfilling activities). **—Patricia Telesco**

Author: *Advanced Wicca* (Kensington Citadel 2000)
Charmed Life (New Page 2000) and 40+ other titles

"I couldn't imagine someone more appropriate to write this book than Oberon Ravenheart. I have worked with him personally for over 25 years, and have found him to be an excellent teacher, craftsman, artist, scholar, and general creative genius. The boys who read this book will be lucky to have him as a mentor. His ability to organize information into nifty charts and easy-to-access language remains unequaled in the magickal community." **—Anodea Judith**

Author: *Wheels of Life* (Llewellyn 1987)
Eastern Body-Western Mind (Celestial Arts 1997)

"To those who study the occult, in particular, Witchcraft, the name of Oberon Zell-Ravenheart is internationally-known and respected. He is a genuine Wizard, and he has written this book for any person wishing to become one. Perhaps, as some have written, Oberon Zell-Ravenheart is the real Albus Dumbledore to aspiring Harry Potters!

"As a handbook and guide for becoming a Wizard, this is as near perfect and honest a book as one will find today...a great service to the occult community.

"Oberon has written a classic on Wizardry. This is his masterpiece. One of the pioneers of Paganism in the United States, his lifetime of learning and information is shared with readers from all walks of life. The lessons in this fine book are accurate, honest, and entertaining.

"If you want to become a Wizard, this is the book to start with, and learn from. This *Grimoire* is must-have reading for readers interested in true magick.

"Highly recommended. Congratulations to the author for writing a classic, and congratulations to New Page Books for publishing it for readers." **—Lee Prosser**

Ghostvillage.com review
(from *Fate Magazine*, 3/19/2004)

Grimoire for the Apprentice Wizard
Edited by Lauren Manoy
Typeset and formatted by Oberon Zell-Ravenheart
Cover illustration and design: Jean William Naumann
Printed in the U.S.A. by Book-mart Press

To order this title, please call toll-free 1-800-CAREER-1 (NJ and Canada: 201-848-0310) to order using VISA or MasterCard, or for further information on books from Career Press.

The Career Press, Inc., 3 Tice Road, PO Box 687,
Franklin Lakes, NJ 07417
www.careerpress.com
www.newpagebooks.com

Library of Congress Cataloging-in-Publication Data

Zell-Ravenheart, Oberon, 1942-
Grimoire for the apprentice wizard / by Oberon Zell-Ravenheart.
p. cm.
Includes bibliographical references and index.
ISBN 1-56414-711-8 (pbk.)
1. Magic. 2. Wizards. I. Title.

BF1611.Z45 2004
133.4'3—dc 222003060780

Grimoire for the Apprentice Wizard

Oberon Zell-Ravenheart
and the Grey Council

New Page Books
A division of The Career Press, Inc.
Franklin Lakes, NJ

Foreword: The Grimoire and the Grey Council

By Raymond Buckland

A great number of us have been wanting—longing—to board the Hogwarts Express and to travel to an academy that teaches the really exciting things in life. Things such as magick, herbal lore, divination, conjuring, and so on. In a word, we have been wanting to learn WIZARDRY. It's one thing to read about the experiences of someone else—even such a fascinating person as Harry Potter—but it's quite another thing to be able to go through the whole magickal educational process yourself. To enter such a school and know that your teachers are the very finest Wizards and Witches in the world would be awe-inspiring. So, how to do this? How to find and attend such a Wizard's academy?

You'll be happy to know that you don't have to wait for a special invitation to be delivered, be it by owl mail or otherwise. You don't even have to be the child of a Wizard or Witch. In fact you can even be a regular Muggle child and still get into this school. *(It has been rumored that even some grown-up Muggles have been so attracted to it that they, too, have slipped in!)* Where is this school? It's right here in your hands. The Course in Wizardry—at least the Apprentice Level of the course—is contained in this book. That's like suddenly discovering that there's a home study branch of Hogwarts Academy! Here may be found seven major courses, plus an appendix and bibliography, put together by the Grey Council of Wizards for *you* to study and learn.

Members of the Grey Council are living, breathing, famous Wizards and Witches of the present day. They are not "made up" or in any way invented by an author. They are alive and real and have been practicing their various crafts for up to forty or fifty years. When Harry Potter was first taking the Hogwarts Express to Hogwarts Academy, he was shown the trading cards of Witches and Wizards that came in the Chocolate Frogs packs. Ron Weasley introduced him to these, showing such famous personalities as Merlin, Paracelsus, Morgana, Circe, Cliodna, Ptolemy, Dumbledore, and Hengist. These were actually a mixture of real Witches and Wizards and those of fiction and legend. But in this book there are only real ones.

I have known Oberon Ravenheart for over 30 years. He is one of the pioneers of Paganism in the United States. I can't think of a better, more qualified person to write a handbook for apprentice Wizards. Oberon *is* a Wizard (he always has been!). With his many decades of experience he, more than anyone, is uniquely qualified to write this book, having been teaching for the majority of his life. His name is greatly respected in all of the varying fields of Paganism and Witchcraft. He is truly an Elder…of Paganism, Witchcraft, and Magic.

As a member of the Grey Council, I am perhaps typical of your teachers, so let me tell you a little about my background. I was first attracted to these subjects more than fifty years ago. *(Half a century! How time flies!)* What I wouldn't have given to have had access to just such a book as you are now holding in your hands, back in those early days. But such knowledge was hard to come by then. I had to dig and search; follow up ancient clues and long-lost trails. I had to beg and borrow, and to apprentice myself to the few knowledgeable mages I was able to find. Over the years I learned to use a crystal ball, to read tarot cards, to heal with my hands, to make use of herbs and potions, and to do many other things not normally taught or made available.

Over forty years ago I was initiated into a Witches coven. I learned spells and charms and I learned to do magick. It was a long, sometimes hard road I traveled. But it was very satisfying and, in practicing what I was taught, I was able to bring aid, happiness, and comfort to many others. Along the way I became a teacher myself and was thus able to pass on what knowledge I had so painstakingly acquired.

The other members of the Grey Council—those who are now, through this book, *your* teachers—have similar backgrounds to mine. We have all dedicated our lives to the magickal arts and to making our knowledge available to those ready and willing to accept it . . .those such as *you*.

This is a *grimoire*. The word comes from the old French word meaning "grammar." It is, indeed, a grammar of magick. In other words, it explains exactly how magick is performed: how it is planned, prepared for, put together, and *very carefully* worked. You wouldn't expect to be able to learn a foreign language without doing some study. You would need to learn new words and how to put them together so that they made sense. You would need to know occasional alternate words that could be used, and the correct way to pronounce them. If you didn't do this study, no one would understand you. In other words, it wouldn't be working. Well, so it is with magick. By learning the grammar—the grimoire—you will be able to not only make yourself understood (to the elements, the spirits, the animals, trees, plants, and all other aspects of nature—plus, of course, to other Wizards), but you will be able to show that you are fluent in the language—that you are a master of it. This translates into becoming a master Wizard, a magician recognized by his peers (those of equal standing) as competent and knowledgeable.

In so many subjects in everyday school, you sometimes find yourself wondering "Why do I have to learn this?" "What use is this to anyone?" You resist doing the work, the study, the homework. But with the *Grimoire for the Apprentice Wizard*, all that is changed! You will find yourself eagerly looking forward to the next step, and the one after that, and the one after that! Study will become a joy. You won't want to stop. Imagine learning such things as Foundations of Magick, Magickal Skills, The Soul of Nature, Tools of Magick, Wizardly Regalia, Spellcraft, Conjury, Magickal Bestiary, and so on and so on. What wonderful titles! What wonderful subjects! Wortcunning; Mathemagicks; Skrying. New words and ancient teachings. This is not just a book *about* Wizardry; it's a book *of* Wizardry!

Let this book take you on a journey. It opens on Wizardry—concerning Wizards, becoming a Wizard, foundations of magick, magickal skills, etc. It introduces you to ideas and concepts, then leads you along the secret path that wends its way through the sometimes fearsome appearing trees of the forest of ancient knowledge. Along the way you learn that all is not as it seems. What many people take as frightening, or scary, you will learn to be safe, inspiring, and power-enabling. The path through the woods goes on and on, but the deeper it goes, the more interesting you will find it. This is a little like venturing into the Forbidden Forest near Hogwarts. That is a place where "secrets are kept and mysteries can be unraveled."[1] There will be temptations along the way, yes. There will appear to be some short-cuts. But where do they really lead? The safest route is with your guides, with the Grey Council. You will not be led astray. Stay on the path and do what they suggest. Remember, Hagrid was not afraid of the forest, because he knew it and knew of its inhabitants. So with the Grey Council. We know the safest routes and will guide you safely.

In all the many wonderful and powerful instructions given in this course of Wizardry, there are two things that I would urge you to always bear in mind. The first is to *always* consider the results of your actions. The second is to accept the responsibility for those actions.

By considering the results of your actions I mean that you should always look ahead to see how what you do might affect other people. You've heard of the "domino effect," I'm sure. If you stand up a long line of dominoes, whether in a straight line or a long, curving pattern, when you knock down the first one it will hit against the second which will then fall. In falling, that second one will hit the third, and knock it against the fourth, and so on, until the whole line—no matter how long it is—has been knocked over as a result of your pushing against that first one. This works not only with dominoes but with just about everything. It works with magick too. When you do magick that affects one person, that action may then, in turn, affect a whole number of other people. It might not be obvious, at first, just how this reaction will progress. But that is where the outstanding Wizard shows his superiority. He will have thought through his actions and will ensure that what is designed to work on one person will not adversely affect another. You won't be doing negative magick—no Wizard worth his pointed hat does negative magick—so there should be little chance of you accidentally harming others. But it always behooves you to *think things through*.

As to taking responsibility for your actions, that should really be unnecessary to say. We should all, always, take responsibility for what we do. Never try to blame someone else for your mistakes. So if something goes wrong—especially magically—own up to it being your fault and immediately do all that you can to correct it. That is the Wizard's way.

How powerful can you become? Forget that word "power" if you can. Let's instead ask, how *effective* can you become? The answer is very effective indeed. Let me give you an example. Back in the middle of the twentieth century (yes, this is a little bit of history—but very interesting) Europe was in the throes of a war that was to develop into a world war. It was the second of its kind and would destroy many lives and disrupt most of the world for many generations. In Great Britain, a small band of Witches and Wizards saw the threat of the enemy poised to launch itself across the narrow English Channel and to attack England. A powerful woman magician, whose name was Dion Fortune, organized a magickal program bringing together Britain's most powerful Witches and Wizards. This program was designed to turn back the advancing tide of the enemy. The group was comprised of the most powerful of a wide variety of types of magickal people. There were Witches, Wizards, magicians, adepts (highly skilled experts) of different traditions. But they all faced a common enemy. They worked together to build a great magickal wall that would not only stop the enemy invasion but would actually turn them away and make them simply stop trying. The magick was performed on a number of occasions, working up to a major effort at one of the most powerful times of the year. The result was that the enemy stopped, turned around, and went away! The war was not over, but the immediate threat of invasion was removed. This was a mighty work of magic. It is to be hoped that you will never have to face such a menace. But know that the magick you are to be taught in this book not only works, but can work powerfully enough to change history!

Welcome to this unique course of magick, and know that you are setting your foot on the first step along the path that will take you out of the ordinary and into the special world of Wizardry.

—Raymond Buckland
Nov. 11, 2003

[1] *The Magical Worlds of Harry Potter,* David Colbert (Lumina Press, Wrightsville Beach, 2001)

Acknowledgements

Although many Wizards throughout history seem to have lacked significant feminine companionship and influences, I have been blessed with many wonderful women in my life. So first of all I would like to extend my acknowledgement and appreciation to my wife and soulmate over the past 30 years: Morning Glory. Next, I wish to appreciate Liza Gabriel, my magickal partner and co-conspirator. Thank you each for your love and support during our adventurous times together. And to all my other women friends and lovers over the years: thank you each for bringing the Goddess into my life and work—particularly in Her aspect as Muse.

Next, I thank the other members of the Grey Council—wise ones, friends, compatriots, peers, and fellow journeyers on these magickal paths who have advised and contributed to this *Grimoire:* Ray Buckland, Jesse Wolf Hardin, Jeff "Magnus" McBride, Katlyn Breene, Trish Telesco, Raven Grimassi, Donald Michael Kraig, Nelson White, Ellen Evert Hopman, Fred Lamond, Todd Karr, Luc Sala, Nybor, Abby Willowroot, Ian "Lurking Bear" Anderson, Lady Pythia, and Amber K.

Thanks also to some of other fine folks not currently on the Council, whom I've consulted in various phases: Dragon Singing (mathemagicks, laws of magick), Julie Epona (ethics), Craig Parsons-Kerins (physics), Haramas (Egyptian), Farida Ka'iwalani Fox (the Elements), Diane Darling (Elven Chess), Jack Griffin (role-play gaming), Bryce Kuhlman, Anodea Judith (rituals, chakras), Bob Gratrix, Isaac Bonewits (laws of magick), David Birtwell and Christian Chelman (conjury), Paul Moonoak (rites of passage), Sheila Attig (study of magick), Leigh Ann Hussey (sabbats), and Diana Paxson (Norse). The willingness of these people to review these writings and/or offer their expertise has been a great contribution to this work!

I thank Georgio, Laurie, Mike, Ron and all the wonderful people at New Page Books for believing in me and this project before I even began it. I thank Abby Willowroot and Lauren Manoy for help in editing the text for my intended readership. And I thank Wolf Dean Stiles-Ravenheart for setting me up with a new computer and scanner, and teaching me Photoshop.

I also wish to thank those who have been Mentors and Teachers to me throughout my life—particularly my father, Charles Zell, Mr. Teske, Capt. Bennings, Robert Anson Heinlein, Gale Fuller, Deborah Letter-Bourbon, Carolyn Clark, and Mama Julie. By the same token, I wish to acknowledge my son, Bryan, and my stepson, Zack—my first Apprentices in magick and Wizardry. This book really began for you, and I only wish you could have had it sooner…

And I offer my humble gratitude to all the great Wizards and Shamans who have gone before, and left us a legacy of Magick stretching back to the Age of Ice and Stone.

Ad astra per magicae artes...

Oberon Zell
OZ

9/21/2003

Oberon Zell-Ravenheart

Grimoire for the Apprentice Wizard

Ah, young Wizard-to-be, welcome to the world of Magick and Mysterie! I, Oberon Zell-Ravenheart, will be your mentor and guide on your path towards becoming a true Wizard. Also contributing to your studies will be other members of the Grey Council—the legendary fellowship of Mages, Sages and Wise Ones. Someday, perhaps, you too will become part of this company. For Wizardry is traditionally passed from Master to Student through a program of Apprenticeship. This *Grimoire* will be your handbook for the first part of your journey. It's for you alone—and those you trust absolutely. Keep it safe, and keep it secret—these Mysteries must not fall into the wrong hands! And if you wish to further your studies in the Arcane Arts, come to the online **Grey School of Wizardry** at *www.GreySchool.com.*

Table of Contents

Preface: A Wizardly Soliloquy

We are the makers of magic. And we are the tellers of tales. —Willy Wonka

HUMANS ARE STORY-TELLERS. We live within our stories. We are all beings of myth and legend—and future generations will sing songs and tell tales of us just as we sing songs and tell tales of the Argonauts, the Knights of the Round Table, and the Merry Men and Maids of Sherwood Forest. We come into this world bearing dreams of former lives, and we each create our own story as we grow, learn, travel, and share our lives and dreams with others. And so each of us lives out our own personal mythology.

The main difference between a Wizard and others is that the Wizard *knows* the importance of stories and myths, and seizes the power to tell the story in a way that shapes the future. All Wizards are storytellers—and their stories tell us who we are, where we came from, and where we are going.

In the legendary saga of The Hero's Quest, the Wizard's role is to mentor the young Hero, teaching him to see beyond the appearances of the world. He helps the hero learn to perceive the patterns which underlie and connect all things. Just think of the way Obi-Wan Kenobi teaches Luke Skywalker about The Force, and you get the picture.

The Wizard is also the one who explains the situation to the Hero before sending him out upon his Quest. At the point in the Story where it comes time for the Hero to take up his Mission, the Wizard takes him aside and tells him what he will need to know. The Wizard explains what's going on in the world that a Hero is needed; what forces are gathering; what journey must be undertaken, and to where; what powers must be confronted and overcome; and what must be done to restore the Balance of the world.

Imagine, if you will, that you are sitting around a campfire at the edge of the Uncharted Lands. With your companions, you have journeyed far and are weary. Now the old man who has accompanied you here gets up and places another log on the fire. Gripping in one hand a staff as tall as he is, with a glowing crystal atop, he waves his other hand over the flames, which suddenly blaze up in bright sparkling colors. Now that he has your attention, he says something like this:

"This is a place between the Worlds, and this is a time outside of Time. It is not by mere chance that you have come here this night, for there is a larger purpose, a grand design, a great task that awaits you:

"For this is a time long prophesied, when the opposing forces of Evolution and Entropy have come to a head. The world has fallen out of alignment, and the eternal balance of Light and Dark has become disrupted. The Dark Lord has begun to extend his domain of death into the world of the living.

"This has happened before, and you know the legends of such previous times. But each time the cycles bring these opposing forces into confrontation again, the stakes get higher. Now they have reached the ultimate: We stand on the threshold of planetary illumination, or planetary annihilation. The outcome is by no means certain.

"It is for this very mission that you have been born on Earth in this lifetime. You have been guided to this very place, on this very night, for this very purpose. At such momentous times as these, the forces of Life and Death call forth their eternal champions. It is your destiny to be the noble Heroes of your time—a time that will be sung of in all future ages.

"Your Mission, should you choose to accept it, is to journey to the Fortress of Ultimate Darkness. There you must confront the Dark Lord and restore the Great Balance... If you fail, the world will be plunged into a new age of darkness. If you succeed, the conscious lifestream of Earth will be free to make the greatest leap in evolution since the first lobe-finned fish crawled out of a stagnant pool onto dry land.

"But be warned: The Dark Lord is immensely powerful. He is supported by legions of armies, and his influence is felt in every facet of the world.

You cannot hope to defeat him by force of arms, for the deadliest weapons ever conceived are his own. And he also controls the wealth of empires, with power to buy and sell the very Earth you stand upon. He is the father of lies and deceit, and can turn even your own parents against you. You must learn his weaknesses, and make them your own strengths: love, compassion, magick, purity of heart and nobility of soul. Your life has prepared you for this Quest.

"For yours is a magickal journey. You will gather Companions, courageous, heartfull and true, and they will come through for you when all seems lost. You will be betrayed by ones you have trusted. You will learn painful and valuable lessons, teaching you what you will need to know for each leg of your journey."

Through the night the old man shares stories and songs with you and your companions. One by one, the others drift off to sleep, but you stay awake listening in wonder to the tales of magick and mystery. It seems as if your world has suddenly grown far bigger than you ever imagined.

In the morning, all are breaking camp and packing to leave this place. Plans are being made, and maps are being consulted. No wisp of smoke betrays the fire of the night before. Other than the ring of stones, left for succeeding travelers, there is no sign of your presence. You are still talking alone with the old man, who tells you:

"Here's the great secret of the Hero's Quest story: As the Hero journeys along his path—the Glory Road, as it's called—all those he encounters and interacts with have each their own scripts. They all know who they are, and what role is theirs to play. Only the Hero has no script, and must make it up as he goes along. For he is the only one in motion in the story—as he goes from station to station picking up clues. Each encounter is both a test and a preparation for the next. And only in this way can his training be accomplished and his destiny be fulfilled.

"However, there are other paths…."

As you stand in reflection by the dead campfire, the old man goes over to bid farewell to the rest of the Company: "I have no more to tell you; nor can I accompany you further. My own path leads elsewhere. I can only advise you to follow the Path of the Heart...."

And the Companions head off down their path, and into legend. Watching them pass, the old man then turns and begins walking away down a different path. You feel as if a Presence stands behind you, holding aloft a torch in each hand, illuminating each of the ways unwinding from this place of decision.

You look as far as your Vision can reach down the paths that lie before you. You feel the Winds of Destiny blowing through your soul. And then you turn and follow the Wizard.

The Script is being written….

The Calling

by Jesse Wolf Hardin, of the Grey Council

You are *called*.... Make no mistake about it! Called by Earth and Spirit to live a more intense, magickal life. Called to pay any price—and reap every reward—in the pursuit of Truth and Adventure. Called to heighten your six senses and develop every possible skill, all in service to a deep and destined purpose.

It's an irresistible siren's call, echoing out of the caves of our ancient tribal past as well as those unseen folds of the future. It pulls at the heart, makes the skin tingle, and stirs the feet to dance. It beckons you to leap over the walls of convention and habit, to escape to the world of your dreams and fulfill your most heroic mission. At times it's but a quiet prodding like a silk-winged fairy gently whispering in your ear. Other times the call is a roar so loud that you're surprised everyone in the world can't hear.

It's possible you've felt a little different from those around you ever since you were a child. You likely experienced things more intensely than other kids, crying longer, laughing louder—loving, playing, and trying harder. Being "normal" never seemed like much of goal to you. Unlike those friends and classmates who chose to numb-down in order to fit in, you preferred your own special loneliness to the dulled world of the *mundane.* You never stopped believing in miracles and magick, even as you became expert at exposing illusions and lies. No matter where you herald from, your "home" is the state of Wonder.

The fact that you are reading this Grimoire now tells not only about your curiosity, but your heart. It is a testament to your vision and determination, and makes you part of an unbroken lineage of the enchanted and engaged, the caring and called. You are a direct descendant of the first two-leggeds to ever consecrate and celebrate this inspirited Earth, and a direct outgrowth of three and a half billion years of ecstatic evolution. And you will, in your own time, be one of the teachers and Elders to pass on the baton—the magic wand—to the coming generations of apprenticing Wizards and wise ones. Yes, the enlivened universe is calling you...demanding, in return, your focus and attentions, ritual and follow-through.

To be called is to be *destined*—destined to fulfill an essential and meaningful purpose, destined to employ your power and practices in service to a crucial cause. But unlike "Fate," Destiny requires our conscious and willful participation. Every day is yet another chance to fudge and slack, to deny our sacred calling or avoid the responsibilities of our mission. And likewise, every moment is a decisive moment—another opportunity to make magic happen, to spread love and do good deeds...to fulfill our Destiny and fully live up to our heroic Wizard's creed.

Introduction

The scientists of today may well have been regarded as Wizards in centuries past. In essence, the best Wizards have been those who have had keen minds, and have been able to free their thoughts from everyday struggles and ponder on the bigger issues of life. This ability was prized in the old world of villages and other small communities, as it was recognized as making the community better able to survive various calamities and ills.

—Anton & Mina Adams,
The World of Wizards, p. 6

, Oberon Ravenheart, am a practicing Wizard. In my long and interesting life, I have been (and am) many things: counselor, teacher, writer, lecturer, artist, priest, magician, ritualist... I have been trained and initiated into several different traditions of magick and Witchcraft, and am considered an Elder throughout the magickal community. But the title with which I most identify, and the one which those who know me most readily use in describing me, is *"Wizard."*

A Wizard is not a Priest or representative of any church or religion, but an *adept* ("expert") in the realms of Magick, *arcane* ("secret") lore, mysticism, philosophy, and knowledge in a wide variety of areas. Wizards were the first scientists—*science* means "knowledge," and *wizardry* means "wisdom." Some of the most prominent scientists (like Thomas Edison) are referred as "Wizards" in their biographies. In fact, the main difference between a Wizard and a scientist even today is that most Wizards don't work in institutional laboratories, and don't get paid by government or corporate grants!

"Wizard" is a *profession,* like teacher, doctor or lawyer. And just like a scientist or a teacher, a Wizard can be whatever religion he chooses (or none at all!). Throughout history, Wizards have existed and functioned perfectly well within whatever religious structure was around at the time. There have been (and are) very renowned Jewish Wizards (King Solomon was said to be the greatest of all!), Christian Wizards, Moslem Wizards, Buddhist Wizards, Hindu Wizards, Taoist Wizards... well, you get the idea.

I am writing and compiling this book—this *Grimoire*—for you and future generations of young people who dream of becoming Wizards. Through entering my daily life, you, as my Apprentice, will be introduced to a number of people—historical, mythic, and living—who comprise the *Grey Council,* the secret network of Wizards, Mages and Sages that spans all of history and includes wise and magickal people of many cultures and traditions. This *Grimoire* includes many contributions from other members of the Grey Council, as we pass on to you what we think you will need to know.

Grimoires

Grimoires, or "Black Books" as they were commonly called, came into wide circulation and usage in Europe in the Middle Ages and Renaissance times—over 500 years ago. Ideally, they were supposed to have been hand-copied from generation to generation from even older books. Every Wizard and Magician had his collection of favorite grimoires, and so did many doctors and noblemen. In fact, these were some of the first books to be printed when the printing press was invented. Many of these are beautifully illustrated with old woodcuts. Much of the material in those grimoires dates from around 100-400 CE, and comes from Hebrew and Latin texts of *Hermetic* lore (Hermes is the Greek god of magick).

Grimoires (from the Old French word for "grammar") are basically magickal handbooks—you might even say "cookbooks"—giving precise instructions for various spells and rituals, including what to wear, what tools to use, and what charms and incantations to say at certain astrological times and hours. They contain recipes for oils, incenses and potions, and descriptions for making magickal tools, *talismans, amulets* and *sigils* (I'll explain all these later). They instruct the magician in how to prepare for certain rituals with fasting and other purifications. And these old grimoires also describe the various "families" of gods, spirits, demons, angels, and other magickal beings that may be summoned and consulted by following the instructions.

This particular Grimoire has been created especially for you, as an Apprentice Wizard. In it we of the Grey Council will be introducing you to the basics of Wizardry and Magick. Through these pages, you will become a Wizard-in-training just as if you were sitting with me in my cluttered study—filled with arcane instruments, occult secrets and mysterious volumes of forgotten lore. Here you will meet weird creatures and grotesque monsters. You will study ancient artifacts and strange contraptions. You will brew foul-smelling potions, create awesome spells, and conduct magickal rituals. And you will learn to perform astonishing special effects and magical illusions to mystify and amaze your friends.

How to Use This Book

Here are a few notes about my writing style. First, you will notice that when I refer to some important historical person, I will often list after their name their dates of birth and death, like: (1475-1520). If such dates are obviously during the *common era* of our Western civil calendar (in which the current year I am writing is 2003), I will often leave them at that. If they are very early on, however, I may specify "common era" by noting "CE" after the date—as in "376 CE." This means the same as when other writers use "AD" (for *anno domini*—"year of our Lord" in Latin—referring to the "Christian Era"). In the same way, for dates *before* the common era, I will add "BCE," just as others might use "BC" (for "before Christ"). You will find this same usage in many magickal and scientific writings, so I thought you'd like an explanation. I've done the best I could here, but sometimes we just don't have any precise records of a person's year of birth or death, so the following customary notes have been adopted: "c." stands for *circa,* meaning "about." "fl." means "flourished," indicating the time during which someone was most famous. "b." and "d." means "born" and "died." For rulers, "r." indicates the period of their reign.

Also, I would like to mention my pronunciation guides. Like many who read a lot, I acquired most of my vocabulary from books. In many cases, however—especially regarding foreign words and names—the written words gave me no clear idea of how to pronounce them. So I will include simple phonetic keys to pronunciation for words that might have confused me when I was your age. Here is an example: (pro-NUN-see-AY-shun). The syllable (SIL-a-bull) in all capital letters is the one which gets the emphasis (EM-fa-sis). And since many magickal terms come from older languages than English (especially Latin and Greek), I will frequently include a little translation when I first introduce such words, such as *polyhedron* (Gr. "many-sided").

I have organized this entire Grimoire as a 7-year course of study in Wizardry for Junior High through High School level. Each of the Courses includes six or seven Classes, and each Class contains a number of Lessons. The Table of Contents provides a Study Guide in outline form. When I need to refer to another Lesson, I could do it the long way, like: Course 3: 'Practice;' Class VI: 'Correspondences;' Lesson 2: 'The Magick Circle.' But this is far too complicated, and will get old very fast! So instead I will abbreviate, like so: See 3.VI.2: 'The Magick Circle.'

Multiple Interpretations

As we go through all these teachings, it is important to realize that in many cases there are multiple and sometimes contradictory interpretations of symbols. Since symbols represent things, different traditions often have differing symbology. For instance, while most cultures view the Sun as the very quintessence of masculinity, the Sun is regarded as female in Japanese Shinto (the Goddess *Amaterasu*).

In this Grimoire, materials have been gathered from many sources, and the members of the Grey Council, who are advisors and contributors, come from a wide variety of backgrounds and traditions. While there is a remarkable unity among us throughout all these teachings, occasionally there are differences between our respective symbolic associations. There's nothing wrong or bad about this, it's just that people are coming from different *paradigms* (models). An important principle widely accepted among magickal people is that there is *no* "One True Right and Only Way!" In many cases, I will call such disagreements to your attention, and indicate key differences in symbology. For example, while I associate the Wand with Air and the *Athamé* (knife) with Fire, in Ceremonial Magick, the Wand is considered a tool of Fire, and the Dagger represents Air.

Also, just because of space limitations, I have had to make some tough decisions here. Wizardry is a vast subject—encompassing every culture on Earth and at least 4,500 years of history. Like many Wizards, I have a huge library of thousands of volumes. I can't possibly cover all of it in this one book—or even a passing mention of most of it. So I'm focusing almost exclusively here on the Western Wizardry heritage. I'm not teaching (or even recommending) you to practice in Native American, African, Caribbean, Asian, Tibetan, Hindu, Middle Eastern, etc. traditions. After you complete the course of study I am offering here, you will have the rest of your life to pursue further studies in other areas of your choosing.

...and so we begin...

Course One: Wizardry

Class I: Concerning Wizards

A wizard can turn fear into joy, frustration to fulfillment.
A wizard can turn the time-bound into the timeless.
A wizard can carry you beyond limitations into the boundless.
—Deepak Chopra (*The Way of the Wizard*)

1. Introduction: What is a Wizard?

> *In the 16th and 17th centuries—the height of popularity of the village magician—it applied to a high magician but also to various popular magicians, who were known by other names as well: cunning men, cunning women, charmers, blessers, sorcerers, conjurers and witches. After 1825, Wizard became almost exclusively synonymous with Witch, but this usage died out during the 20th century. Modern Witches do not use the term.*
> —Rosemary Guiley (*Encyclopedia of Witches and Witchcraft*, p. 389)

Here is how the word "Wizard" is defined in the dictionary:

IZARD—FROM ANGLO-SAXON *WYSARD* (m.), "wise one." A usually solitary practitioner of magick and repository of arcane knowledge. A loremaster. 1. a sage. 2. a magician; conjurer; sorcerer. 3. a person exceptionally gifted or clever at a specified activity (as in "computer wizard"). Usually—but not necessarily—a specifically masculine term. Wizards have also been referred to as "Natural Philosophers."

In traditional tribal cultures we find *shamans,* or medicine men and women, who are both gifted and learned in talents and skills of *augury* (foretelling the future), herbalism, hypnosis, psychic work, and sorcery. They are the village teachers, magicians, spirit guides, healers, and midwives. Among some of the Celtic tribes of Western Europe, such shamans were known as *Wicce*—an Anglo-Saxon word meaning "shaper"—from which comes our present term "Witch." In Renaissance days, men practicing "witchcraft" were more often called "Wizards." The term *Wizard* first appeared in the 15th century, and was used for both wise men and wise women. In the 20th century, most people only knew of Wizards from stories and fairy-tales. The most famous of these were J.R.R. Tolkein's *The Lord of the Rings,* featuring Gandalf the Wizard, and Mary Stewart's *The Crystal Cave* (and other books), about Merlin. Indeed, during those years, many people forgot that Wizards had ever really existed at all! But a few of us still remained, although largely in remote areas hidden from public view.

In the ways that Guiley noted, Wizards in recent centuries seem to have served pretty much as male counterpart of the village Witch as she is commonly described by modern practitioners of the Craft: A magickal shaper of reality; a Shaman of pre-Christian European tradition. In Medieval and Renaissance times, Witches specialized in herbalism and midwifery, and were mostly women. Modern Witches may be both men and women, and their workings today are directed primarily towards healing, both of people and the Earth.

> *Virtually every village or town in Britain and Europe had at least one wizard, who usually was respected and feared by the local folk. The wizard specialized in a variety of magical services, such as fortune-telling; finding missing persons and objects; finding hidden treasure; curing illnesses in people and animals; interpreting dreams; detecting theft; exorcising ghosts and fairies; casting spells; breaking the spells of witches and fairies; making amulets (charms); and making love philtres (potions). Because he was deemed the diviner of the guilty in crimes, the word of the wizard often carried great weight in a village or town.* —Guiley, p. 389

Lesson 2: My Life as a Wizard

Now, I have lived about as rurally as it's possible to get, having spent eight years (1977-'85) living in a 5,600-acre homesteading community in the Misty Mountains of Northern California. My lifemate, Morning Glory, and I moved into a completely undeveloped wilderness, where we built our own houses and barns, developed our springs, planted gardens and orchards, dug a pond, raised livestock—all without electricity, telephones, television, or even radio.

During that time, I served my community in the traditional capacity of rural Wizard, pretty much as

Rosemary Guiley described. I created and conducted rituals of all kinds, from individual *divinations* ("readings"), initiations, *handfastings* (marriages), baby blessings, healings, house-blessings, protections, and *exorcisms*—to large seasonal rituals for the entire community of about a hundred families, and even larger public events in the nearby town of Ukiah. I also taught in the little community school and mentored a number of the kids as they grew up.

But our real Work from 1979–84 was raising unicorns. And when we traveled around the country exhibiting our living unicorns, our natural scene was Renaissance Faires, where my appropriately costumed *persona* ("character") was that of Wizard (as Morning Glory was an Enchantress). When we did interviews for TV, magazines, and newspapers that were not associated with the Faires, we presented ourselves as "Naturalists," which seemed pretty much the mundane equivalent.

Medieval Wizard drawn by Gillot, engraved by Toullain

What was it that drew me to Wizardry as a way of life and encouraged me to choose a title that hardly anyone used in these modern times? Simply put, it's the mythology of it all! My favorite mythological references come from fantasy and science fiction literature, as well as classical mythology. Such authors as J.R.R. Tolkien, Mary Stewart, Marion Zimmer Bradley, Ursula leGuin, Peter Beagle, and T.H. White have deeply infused my concept of what a Wizard is with their depictions of the likes of Merlin and Gandalf, with whom I immediately identified upon reading those tales.

But for me, the greatest appeal of both the historical and mythological Wizards with whom I identify is that they were engaged in shaping the greater *paradigm* ("model") of the society around them. Wizards, let's face it, are natural-born meddlers! Alchemists, inventors, king-makers, prophets, seers, spellcasters, loremasters, teachers, initiators, magicians, visionaries—Wizards are perpetually engaged in world-transformation, trying to make the world a better place for everyone. This is the "Great Work." Wizards do not think small! And Wizards know that the best way to predict the future is to create it. So, in the tradition of all the Wizards who have gone before me, my wizardly "Great Work" has been that of transforming and guiding the society in which I find myself into a new phase of social, cultural, and conceptual evolution. Virtually everything I have done in my life has been towards this end—including this Grimoire.

Lesson 3: Between the Worlds of Magick and Mundane

Wizards have also impressed with their intense belief in several levels of reality—that of the ordinary world, the extraordinary world of fairies, elves and other spirit entities, the hierarchy of the angels, and the realm of the higher being. Many Wizards have attempted to rise above Earthly concerns and focus on the spiritual worlds, forging links between the world of the living and that of the dead. Angels and the fairy folk are also believed to be the allies of various Wizards. Communication with beings from other dimensions has been taken seriously, and studied in depth.

—Anton & Mina Adams
(*The World of Wizards*, p. 7)

One of the most basic understandings of Wizardry is that we live not just in a *Uni*verse, but in a *Multi*verse of many worlds. Now, a "world" is not merely the same thing as a planet (though planets are also referred to as worlds—especially those that may be inhabited). A world can be any realm or state of existence that we may inhabit or even imagine. We may speak geographically of the Old World (usually meaning Europe) or the New World (the Americas). Or we may divide societies into those of the Western World (Western Europe, North America, and Australia) or the Eastern World (Eastern Europe, the Middle East, and Asia). Politically, nations today are seen as belonging to the Free World, the Communist World (which used to be much bigger, during the Cold War), or the Third World. We may even talk historically of the Ancient World, or the Modern World—or even the World of Tomorrow!

But there is also the World of Music, the World of Art, and the Wide World of Sports. There is the World of Science, the World of Computers, and the Animal World. There are literary worlds—such as the World of Middle-Earth, or the World of Harry Potter. And there are the Worlds of the Imagination, the Worlds of Myth, the Worlds of Dreams, the Worlds of Magick.... It is these worlds in particular that are frequented and inhabited by Wizards, Witches, magicians, and other magickal folk—as well as elves, dragons, unicorns, faeries, gods, and spirits. This Grimoire you are holding will be your guidebook to the Worlds of Magick.

The wonderful Harry Potter books of J.K. Rowling present a *mythos* (that is, a foundation story) that says: "Beyond the borders of the mundane

("Muggle," as she calls it) world, there is another world—a world full of magick, and magickal people. This is a world of very different rules and principles, where Imagination, Hope, Dreams, and Love have real power to change and transform." And the thing is—as everyone who reads these books secretly hopes and suspects—this is true! This is my world; and if you wish to make it so, it can be yours.

I used the word "mundane" just now, to distinguish the ordinary, everyday, so-called "normal" world from the World of Magick. We call that world "Mundania"—and the people who live only in that world and know no other, we sometimes call mundanes or mundys. These words are not intended to be taken as insults, nor should they be used in that way. It is only a way of acknowledging that there are, indeed, different worlds.

There is no single name for the World of Magick. It has been called many names by many peoples. Mostly, magickal folk just refer to specific places—such as a particular magickal gathering-place, sanctuary, retreat center, forest, mountain, canyon, stone circle, and so on. Such places are often said to be "between the worlds." Therefore, magickal folks—such as Wizards, Witches, and Shamans—are also known as "Walkers Between the Worlds." For we are at home in any world, and frequently travel between them in the pursuit of our Work and Mission.

Our universe is embedded in an infinitely larger and more complex structure called the multiverse, which as a good approximation can be regarded as an ever-multiplying mass of parallel universes. Every time there is an event at the quantum level—a radioactive atom decaying, for example, or a particle of light impinging on your retina—the universe is supposed to "split" or differentiate into different universes. —Roger Highfield (*The Science of Harry Potter,* pp. 18-19)

3. Glossary: "Wizards and Witches and Mages—oh my!"

Now would probably be a good time to explain some of the different kinds of magickal folks. These terms can be confusing to the unfamiliar, so here is a brief little Glossary. (Also, one essential companion to this Grimoire must be a good dictionary!) An important thing to understand here is that these categories are not mutually exclusive, and any given individual may embody a number of them...indeed, a capable Wizard may be known by most of these terms! The primary distinction between "Wizards" and "Sorcerers" is around the issue of service: Wizards desire above all else to be *of* service; Sorcerers desire above all else to *be* served. Wizards (like Gandalf) bend all their efforts and magick towards making the world a better place—for everyone, and for all future generations. Sorcerers (like Sauron and Saruman) bend all their efforts and magick towards the singular goal of ruling the world—conquering, subduing, controlling and even enslaving everyone else.

Obviously, these desires and goals are diametrically opposed. Fortunately for all of us, the very nature of these distinctions supports the ultimate good, as Wizards cooperate and work with others, while Sorcerers are in ultimate competition (especially with each other), cannot trust anyone, cannot be trusted *by* anyone, and in general do not play well with others. As Gandalf said to Saruman, "There is only one Lord of the Rings, and he does not share power!"

Wizard: This is from the Anglo-Saxon *wysard:* "wise one." A Wizard is a lore-master, especially of *arcane* (that is, lost or secret) knowledge (hence popular usage such as "computer wizard"). A Wizard is also a magickal practitioner; however, the word is rarely used today to describe a practitioner of Wicca (or Witchcraft)—or a member of any particular faith. Indeed, most (but not all) Wizards tend to be solitary, though they may belong to a Wizardly Council or Order. The most famous Wizard of legend was Merlin. While the vast majority of Wizards throughout history have been men, there have been a few women Wizards as well—such as Maria the Jewess and Hypatia of Alexandria.

Vizier: This title comes from Arabic, meaning, "bearer of burdens," and was given to the chief minister and adviser under the King. The most famous Vizier of ancient Egypt was Imhotep (yes, the "Mummy"), who was the Vizier of Pharaoh Djoser, and the world's first recorded Wizard. The title often became synonymous with "Court Wizard," especially when a Vizier was also renowned for his Wizardry—such as Imhotep, Merlin, or Dr. John Dee.

Mage: This term is often used as a synonym for "Wizard," especially in a complimentary sense. A Mage may also be called a *Magus,* which means a master of the magickal arts. The ancient *Magi* (like the "Three Wise Men" in the Bible) were Zoroastrian Priests originating in Media and Persia (now Iran). The Persian word *magu* is the root of the word *magic*. This term became *magos* in Greek, and later *magus* in Latin; eventually coming to be used for wise and powerful magicians of any sort.

Sage: A Sage is an elderly person of sound judgment, who has achieved wisdom through reflection and experience. The term is used for a savant, an expert, a scholar, and a learned philosopher or teacher, such as Lao-Tzu or Socrates. *Sagacity* means wisdom, and wise counsel is called "sage advice." Although Sages are usually considered to be men, *Saga* was a common Latin term for a Sorceress in the Middle Ages, and some wise women today identify themselves as Sages.

Mystic: A Mystic (from Greek *mystai,* meaning someone who has been initiated into secret Mysteries) is a person whose profound spiritual or "otherworldly" experiences have given them a deep intuitive comprehension or vision of hidden truths and awareness. Such experiences are usually indescribable and therefore beyond rational human understanding and explanation.

Druid: The Druids were the priest class, the highly trained, intellectual elite of the Celtic tribes. They included both men and women.

Bard: In ancient Celtic tradition, Bards were part of the Orders that were headed by the Druids. Bards were the poets, musicians, and singers of the epic songs and tales that conveyed the history and lore of the people. At a time when very little was written down, a Bard was expected to memorize enormous amounts of poetry, songs, and stories.

Magician: Simply, any practitioner of the magickal arts. There are performance Magicians who create seemingly "impossible" illusions and feats with sleight-of-hand ("prestidigitation") and special effects. And there are Ceremonial Magicians who create elaborate rituals designed to alter and transform the consciousness of themselves and others.

Alchemist: *Alchemy* was the forerunner of modern chemistry, blending Egyptian metallurgy with Greek philosophy and Middle Eastern mysticism. The goals of Alchemists were the discovery of the "Philosopher's Stone" that would transform "base metals" into gold and the "Elixir of Life" that would heal all ills and allow one to live forever.

Sorcerer/Sorceress: *Sorcery* implies some sort of supernatural power over people and their affairs. People who wield such magickal charm or influence are called *Sorcerers* (or Sorceresses in the case of women). This term has a generally negative connotation, implying evil or "black" magick. The most famous Sorceress of legend was Circe (SUR-see). In Homer's *Odyssey*, she turned Odysseus's men into pigs.

Enchantress/Enchanter: Unlike sorcery, *enchantment* has very positive connotations. Enchantresses are "bewitching," fascinating, charming, sexy women whose magick brings delight and pleasure to others. The word is often used as a compliment for particularly attractive and charismatic Witches and Gypsies. A man who embodies those characteristics may be known as an *Enchanter,* though this term is rarely used for men.

Soothsayer: Literally, "truth sayer." An old word for prophets, visionaries, seers, and fortunetellers. The word could be used for anyone who predicts the future. Another word meaning the same thing is *Mantis* ("Diviner"), as in the insect known as the Praying Mantis. The many techniques of divination are called "The Mantic Arts," and practitioners are called "-mancers."

Seer: This term dates from the 14th century and means "one who sees." A Seer is a person credited with extraordinary moral and spiritual insight, who predicts events or developments. The term may be used for anyone who practices *divination* (magickal techniques for finding lost information or predicting the future) especially by concentrating on a glass or crystal globe (*scrying*). Other words for Seer are Sibyl and Oracle.

Necromancer: Someone who conjures up the spirits of the dead to speak with them and learn hidden knowledge and secret information, and to foretell the future. Today people who do this are usually called *Mediums* or *Channels.* Necromancy is a form of divination.

Cybermancer: This word refers to "Computer Wizards"—particularly "hackers" and those who specialize in seeking out and obtaining obscure information through sophisticated Internet search techniques. Another name for this is **Technomage,** from the science-fiction TV series *Babylon 5.*

Scott Fray

Prophet: Prophets are usually divinely inspired preachers, who often speak on behalf of the Gods and Goddesses themselves. They are great teachers, known for compelling religious visions and revelations—often completely transforming their societies. Abraham, Moses, Jesus, and Mohammed are considered the great Prophets of Judaism, Christianity, and Islam.

Philosopher: From the earliest beginnings in ancient Greece, Philosophers have sought to understand the underlying principles and nature of "life, the universe, and everything." They seek to apply wisdom, knowledge, and reason to every aspect of life and society, and they are particularly known for being great teachers. Since philosophy includes *metaphysics* (the nature of reality and the origins of everything), Wizards are often also referred to as "Natural Philosophers."

Shaman: The spiritual leaders in traditional tribal cultures are the Shamans, or medicine men and women, who are both gifted and learned in talents and skills of divination, herbalism, hypnosis, psychic work, and sorcery. In some places these may be called "Witch Doctors." They are the village teachers, magicians, spirit guides, healers, and midwives. In particular, the Shaman uses altered states of consciousness (often aided by certain sacred medicine plants) to control psychic phenomena and travel to and from the spirit realm. The term originates with Siberian shamans, and specifically refers to Tibetan, Siberian, Mongolian, Inuit, and others.

Cunning Man/Woman: "Cunning" comes from the Old Norse *cunna* ("to know") and the Old English *kenning* ("wise"). This term was applied to the resident magicians and healers of small English towns and villages ever since the late Middle Ages. They were also called *wise man* or *woman, Wizard, conjurer, sorcerer, charmer, blesser, peller* ("expeller"), *white Witch* and recently, *hedge Witch.* Like traditional tribal Shamans, these country "White Witches" possess magickal healing powers and provide cures, remedies, charms, spells, and divination—usually for a modest fee. Most were old people, who claimed their title by heredity or through supernatural encounters.

Tungusik (Siberian) Shaman

Witch: In Medieval Europe and Britain, "Cunning Women" were often called *Wicce*—an Anglo-Saxon word meaning "shaper"—from which we get our term "Witch." This word, in turn, comes from Middle High German *wicken* ("to conjure"). Modern Witches include both men and women, and much of their magick is directed towards healing, of people and the Earth. Many Witches also practice *divination* and magickal techniques for the evolution of consciousness.

Cunning Man

Wicca: *Wicca* is a modern subset of traditional Witchcraft emphasizing its aspect as a Pagan mystery religion. Wiccan rites—held at the full (and sometimes dark) Moons and the Solstices, Equinoxes and Cross Quarters—celebrate an annual God and *perennial* ("ever-living") Goddess through the phases of the Moon and the cycle of the seasons. Wiccan ethical principles temper personal freedom with personal responsibility. The Wiccan *Rede* ("counsel") states: "As it harms none, do as you will."

Pagan: *Paganism* (meaning "of the country") is a collection of diverse spiritual paths which are rooted in or inspired by *indigenous* (native) and *Classical* (ancient Egyptian, Greek, Roman, etc.) traditions worldwide. Paganism is often referred to as "The Old Religion"—meaning pre-Christian. Pagans believe in the interconnectedness of all life, *animism* (everything is alive), *pantheism* (everything is Divine), *polytheism* (there are many gods and spirits), and *immanent divinity* (divinity is within everyone—expressed by some as "Thou art God/dess"). Pagans value diversity, good works, living lightly on the Earth, individual freedom, personal responsibility, and equality between men and women. Many (but not all) magickal folk identify their spiritual practice as "Pagan."

Priest/Priestess: A man or woman dedicated to the service of the Gods—often concentrating on a single manifestation or aspect (such as a Priest of Apollo, or a Priestess of Aphrodite). They may also serve a community of worshippers. Priestly tasks can include maintenance of temples and altars, administering of sacraments, conducting and presiding over rites and rituals, pastoral counseling, etc. They may also serve as a direct channel for the spirit and voice of their chosen Deities.

Warlock: I left this one for last, as it is a word very rarely used in the Magickal community. This old term of insult comes from Old English *waer-loga:* "traitor" or "liar." It once described a Witch who betrayed others to the Witch hunters, and it is often used erroneously by Mundanes to refer to male Witches. Today, some Wiccans may use the term for an initiated Witch who turns against the Craft.

Lesson 4. Rules of Wizardry

(The following comes mostly from Julie Epona)

With every new thing you have learned in Life there has been a set of Rules. In Kindergarten you learned to share and not to push. In soccer or baseball you learned the rules of the game; the boundaries and how to keep score. In math you have learned how to manipulate numbers and in your language classes you have learned the rules of spelling and punctuation.

In Magick and Wizardry there are also Rules. Some will be quite obvious, like the result of successfully crossing home-plate. Other rules will be more difficult to understand and apply, like the rules of commas and "i before e." Rest assured that with experience will come greater understanding.

One final note before we begin discussing these rules. You must clearly understand the difference between real Magick and Illusion. Illusion is a craft of the entertainer, like dance or music. The Illusionist can make elephants dance or tigers disappear. Magick is the art and science of manipulating probability. The Wizard controls his life and changes his destiny through interaction with the Universe within all of its dimensions.

Here is a list of rules for Magick and Wizardry:

- Magick is real.
- Know yourself.
- The best way to predict the future is to create it.
- Question authority.
- Magick is both an art and an experimental science.
- Be watchful of what you do and say.
- Intention controls Results.
- Don't invoke what you can't banish.
- Always consider the options.
- The job isn't done until you've put away the tools and cleaned up the mess.
- Keep silent regarding a Magickal work for 24-hours, lest your analysis create doubt, thereby weakening the Intention that binds your spell.

Write these down in your journal and commit them to memory. These rules need to become as integral to your life as knowing which hand you use to hold your fork. Now, we will discuss each rule in turn.

Magick is real. The things you accomplish with your spells, incantations, and invocations will affect your future. The beings that you call forth within your Magick Circle exist within the Spirit Realm. Magick is real; it is not a metaphor. The symbols and correspondences you will learn are tools to enable you to control your Reality.

Know yourself. Socrates once told his students that "an unexamined life is not worth living." As you travel the path of the Apprentice, you will maintain your Magickal Journal. Your notes and observations will enable you to learn who you truly are and what you truly want. Through meditation and focus you will learn why you respond to events and things in specific ways. As you learn more about yourself, you will gain the knowledge you need to change and become the Wizard you want to be.

The best way to predict the future is to create it. It is human nature to want to know what is about to happen. Many people throughout history and in our current time have turned to psychics and forms of divination to learn what lies ahead. The Wizard has the power to create the future he wants. To manifest what you desire will enable you to predict your future.

Question authority. "Why" is a very powerful word. As an Apprentice you must question "why" something is done, and "why" it is done in a certain way. Understanding "why" leads to a clearer understanding of "how." Your ability to question why something is being asked of you or expected of you will protect you. Questioning can and must be done with respect for the teacher. However, you must always be willing to stand up and say "no" when someone gives you an instruction that goes against what you know to be your best interest. Your ability to question will protect you from others who wish to manipulate you.

Be certain you understand "why" before you act. Respect those who have come this way before, and learn from them. But if they say, "It can't be done," chances are it *can* be done or there is another way of achieving the same goal. I say, if it works for you, use it. If it doesn't, don't use it.

Magick is both an Art and an experimental science. Some people, like some artists, are naturally good at magick. However, with practice, someone who is not as good as others can easily become better than those who put no effort into the work. Remember that authors, writers, and lecturers try to share magick the best way they can. But that doesn't mean it will work perfectly for you. Experiment and use what others say as a guide, not as a law.

Intention controls results. A Wizard's most powerful tool is his intention, his will to manifest what he desires. If the desire is for knowledge, then an intention of becoming a diligent student will enable you to obtain the desire. However, if your intention is to ace the test without the necessary study, your results will probably be disappointing. With Magick it is extremely important to be very clear on your intention before you start the Working.

Be watchful of what you do and say. Magick happens all the time, not just when you are in a ritual.

Don't invoke what you can't banish. We have already established that Magick is real. The Elementals, Deities, and Spirits do exist and will be present when called. Some are friendlier than others; all have their own agendas, which may not be the same as yours. It is very important that you can send your visitors back to their realm, before you invite them into yours.

Always consider the options. There are always options, various ways to act or not to act. Since Magick operates within the greater laws of the universe, it remains true that for every action there is an equal and opposite reaction. Your analysis of the options to any given situation must include an understanding of the consequences, to the best of your ability. Sometimes, a third or fourth option is better than the either/or selection people think are their only choices. The corollary is to always think before you act.

The job isn't done until you've put away the tools and cleaned up the mess. This is true whether you're doing your math homework, building a model, or casting a spell. Your task is not complete until you have put everything in its place and returned your space to its neutral state. A Magick Circle left in disarray will drain the focus from your working and undo what you have worked to create.

Keep silent regarding a magickal work for 24-hours, lest your analysis create doubt, thereby weakening the Intention that binds your spell. As we have discussed, your intention will control your results. Once your working is complete and the space has been returned to its proper state, then you need to keep silent about what you have done. Analysis can lead to doubt that will degrade your intention and focus, thereby reducing the positive energy flowing into your spell. You should immediately record what you did and how you felt in your Journal. Wait 24-hours, then discuss your working with those you trust. After this waiting period you can begin to explore what results you can observe and analyze how you accomplished the working, with an eye toward making the working stronger then next time.

As you travel the path of the Apprentice these Rules will strengthen and protect you. Learn them well.

Task: Your Magickal Journal

Here is your first task in your studies as a Wizard's Apprentice: Acquire a blank Journal or diary to write in. You will be able to find blank notebooks or diaries with distinctive covers—sometimes even little pad-locks—in many gift stores, especially metaphysical ones. Try to purchase one with a hard cover, so that it will hold up well over time. Don't put anything special on the outside cover to indicate what your magickal journal is, but on the inside, copy this bookplate design and glue it to the first page, filling in your magical name (see Class II) in the blank space, as well as the date you begin using it

In your magickal journal, I want you to write something just about every day. Just like a "Captain's Log," start each entry with the date, and the time of day. Mention how the weather is, and where you are. Later, you will be able to look back and perhaps connect mood with weather, or begin to note synchroni-cities between events in the natural world and your inner world. Including location and parts of your environment will sharpen your powers of observation, and activate envisioning skills later. You might also note differences between day and night musings.

Write what's happening in your life, and how you feel about it. Write down your dreams when you wake up (although later we'll talk about having a special "Dream Journal" just for dreams). Write about your discoveries and insights. Write about your friends and family. Record your adventures, family trips, Summer vacations. Write what makes you happy, and what makes you sad. Write poetry and draw pictures. Write down your magickal spells and experiments, and later on, note the results. When you fill up one volume, note the final date on the bookplate, put it away in a safe place, and get another.

6. Recreational Reading (Fiction)

As you study these lessons, you might also enjoy some recreational reading about Wizards and Wizardry. The following fantasy stories and series are favorites among members of the Grey Council, and they contain much authentic wizardly wisdom:

Susan Cooper—*Over Sea, Under Stone* (1965); *The Dark is Rising* (1973); *Greenwitch* (1974); *The Grey King* (1975); *Silver on the Tree* (1977)

Diane Duane—Young Wizards series: *So You Want to be a Wizard* (1996); *Deep Wizardry* (1996); *High Wizardry* (1997); *A Wizard Abroad* (1999); *The Wizard's Dilemma* (2002); *A Wizard Alone* (2002); *The Wizard's Holiday* (2003)

Lyndon Hardy—*Master of the Five Magics* (1984); *Secret of the Sixth Magic* (1988); *Riddle of the Seven Realms* (1988)

Tamora Pierce—Circle of Magic: *Sandry's Book* (1997); *Tris's Book* (1998); *Daja's Book* (1998; *Briar's Book* (1999); —The Circle Opens: *Magic Steps* (2000); *Street Magic* (2001); *Cold Fire* (2002); *Shatterglass* (2003)

T.H. White—*The Sword in the Stone* (1963)

Class II: Becoming a Wizard

"You're a Wizard, Harry—and a thumpin' good one, I'd wager! —once you train up a little. Didja ever make anything happen? Anything you couldn't explain—when you were angry, or scared?"
—Hagrid (from *Harry Potter and the Sorcerer's Stone*—the movie)

1. Introduction: What a Wizard Needs to Know

I ASKED SOME MEMBERS OF THE GREY Council to make a list of what they thought a Wizard ought to know and be able to do. Here are some of the answers. These things are true of all the Wizards I know. To learn all this is a lifelong quest, but for you it will begin here, with your Apprenticeship.

A Wizard should...

Be a constant student of life;
See the Divine in Nature and Nature in the Divine;
Not say a word and be clearly heard;
Lead without force and teach without pride;
Take the most mundane things and surroundings, sense their inner magick and be able to open that window for others;
Stare into the dark infinity of the night sky and feel it as an awesome source;
Love the beauty of paradox and be always be able to see the cosmic humor in the darkest times;
Be a shapeshifter to blend in or be invisible if needed... and make those around feel safe, and heard;
Maintain his calm center and clear mind when all about him is chaos;
Open his inner eyes and really see;
Say "I don't know..." and realize that is great wisdom, that is okay;
Have compassion for all beings, and know when to be a healer and when to be a witness;
Know that the secrets of magick are bestowed upon the open-hearted;
Speak to the Gods and know he is heard;
Cast a sphere of protection and light;
Make up his own mind , walk his own path and never follow another blindly;
Know the courage and power of nonviolence and the swift strength of a keen mind;
Conjure a tale or myth that the moment requires to be understood;
Know the plants and creatures of the wild enough call them friends and allies;
See the God and Goddess within all and everyone;
Have a spirit that glows in the dark.

—Katlyn Breene

A Wizard should be able to master self-control, share freely, keep their environment clean, design their lives, create sacred space, respect the beliefs and truths of others, take care of their own basic needs, work effectively with and without magical tools, face challenges with confidence, create music, create art, walk responsibly on the Earth, listen as well as speak, exercise good judgment, take responsibility, grant kindness, design a ritual, write a poem, balance accounts, build a wall, help the vulnerable, comfort the dying, take orders, give orders, shun ego reactions, act alone, cooperate in a group, solve dilemmas, analyze a new problem, do menial tasks cheerfully, program a computer, cook a healthy meal, fight efficiently, avoid Witch wars, cultivate a generous spirit, live courageously and die gallantly. Elitism is for the insecure.

—Abby Willowroot

Above all else, a Wizard knows himself—what drives him, and his weaknesses, for without this knowledge, he is not a Wizard at all. —Rev. Pete Pathfinder Davis

Lesson 2: Your Apprenticeship; my Mentorship

It is a common magickal saying that: "When the Student is ready, the Teacher will appear." But, like all Great Truths, the opposite is also true: When the Teacher is ready, the Student will appear. Long before there were ever schools, and still today in many fields, people learned their crafts by becoming Apprentices to Masters. For one who has spent a lifetime learning and mastering an art, a craft, a trade, or a profession, the time comes when he or she begins looking for a *protégé* (PRO-te-zhay), or successor who will wish to carry on the Work into the next generation. At that point, a Master turns towards teaching, and accepts students—and, hopefully, Apprentices.

The word *mentor* comes from the ancient Greek story of Odysseus (o-DESS-ee-us), as told in *The Odyssey* by Homer. *Mentor* was the name of his loyal friend and advisor, and the teacher of his son, Telemachus (tel-EM-a-kus). So a mentor came to mean a wise and loyal advisor, a teacher and coach. And it is especially used to mean an older person who offers the kind of guidance and counsel a boy or girl needs to make the transition from childhood, through adolescence, and into the responsibilities of adulthood.

When I was young, I had several mentors who were very important to me and who helped guide me during the most important choices and transitions I had to make. I directed my primary studies towards psychology, sociology, anthropology, history, archaeology, and comparative religions. These were the fields in which I majored, and they became the basis for my professional career in the mundane world for many years. And, along with my continuing explorations of science and natural history, these studies led me into Wizardry.

Being an Apprentice Wizard

And so, in writing this Grimoire, I am taking on the role and responsibility of mentorship for you, as it had been given to me in my youth. There is a very important saying among magickal people: "What goes around comes around." When we truly understand this, we automatically want to pass on the gifts we have been given, when it comes our turn to do so. And so it is.

In olden days, Apprentices would often leave home and go to live with the Master. Like Arthur with Merlin, or Dick Grayson at Wayne Manor, they might live in the same house, as a "Ward." Sometimes they would live with other apprentices or students in a Guild Hall, Studio, or (as at Hogwarts) a student dormitory in a special school. You, of course, will be living at your own home. But when you are reading this book, I'd like you to imagine you are sitting right here with me in my study, or working beside me in my garden, or joining me in a walk through the forests, across the fields, along the seashore. Or maybe we will just be lying on our backs on a hillside, looking up at the stars....

So, now that you have started your apprenticeship, what is it we are going to expect of each other? Well, you can expect of me that I will provide you these lessons in an organized and systematic order. You can count on me to give you the most honest, reliable, and responsible information I know. I will be your teacher, and your mentor. After all, my greatest hope is that you will carry on my Work, add to it, and, in your turn, pass the torch to the next generation....

As for what I expect of you...first of all, I expect you to pay attention. I expect you to take care of yourself, and treat others well. I expect you, in fact, to be excellent to each other! I expect you to study and learn these Lessons. And write something in your magickal journal just about every day.

Lesson 3: Your Family

(mostly by Patricia Telesco)

During this time in your life, it is very important to get along with your family. Magickal paths may come and go, but family is forever. Honoring your parents can be hard and sometimes frustrating, but it's worth it and it's a way of giving back something to your family that's very Wizardly—that is, respect! I'm hoping you will have a good enough relationship with your own parents that you can talk with them about all this. Of course, if your parents are like Harry Potter's horrible aunt and uncle, that may not be easy! Few of us are lucky enough to be born into magickal families. In fact, we even have a name for magickal children born to Mundy parents: We call them "Changelings." I was a Changeling myself. So, if you also are a Changeling, here are a few tips to help you communicate with your folks:

Consider your family's background—find the things that are similar to Wizardry, and focus on those in your talks with your parents. There'll be plenty of time to hash out the differences later. Whatever you do, don't show up for talks with Mom and Dad in a robe and waving a wand! I suggest one of mom's favorite sweaters and your hair combed. If you want them to take your choice seriously, look like a serious young adult.

Be likewise respectful of your friends' families,

knowing that your choice to be a Wizard is a private and personal one. It's one with which not everyone is going to be comfortable, and sometimes no matter how excited you may be, it's best to keep mentions about that part of your life for appropriate times and places.

If the worst thing happens and your parents say "no" to this book and to your magickal interests, know that being a Wizard begins in your mind, heart, and spirit. No one can change what you *are.* They might delay your studies a bit, but that's all. In your home, your parents are still #1, and accepting their decision with maturity will usually impress them. Try revisiting the idea in six months or a year. Even Rome wasn't built in a day, and allaying parental misgivings can take time, but persistence can pay off.

But if you can keep your grades up at school (I *know* you're smart!), and you can manage to stay out of too much trouble (well, that may be a bit harder, of course), hopefully your folks will let you hang out with your magickal friends. You'll have this book, and they'll probably have some others, and these books will give you all kinds of ideas for things to do together.

Lesson 4: Your Magickal Names

As a Wizard, you will acquire several names at different phases of your life. Your first name is the one your parents gave you when you were born. If you were born into a magickal family, it may even have been given to you in a special naming ceremony, or *seining* (baby blessing). This is your birth-name, and the one by which your parents and close family will always know you. In all tribal societies, and in the magickal community, a second name is given at the first Rite of Passage, from childhood into adolescence (traditionally on or between your 11th and 13th birthdays). There are many variations of such rites, but they commonly include an ordeal, or challenge.

> *On the day the boy was thirteen years old, the Wizard Ogion returned to the village, and the ceremony of Passage was held. The Witch took from the boy the name his mother had given him as a baby. Nameless and naked he walked into the cold springs of the river Ar where it rises among rocks under the high cliffs. He crossed to the far bank, shuddering with cold but walking slow and erect as he should through that icy, living water. As he came to the bank Ogion, waiting, reached out his hand and clasping the boy's arm whispered to him his true name.*
>
> *Thus was he given his name by one very wise in the uses of power.*
>
> — Ursula LeGuin (*A Wizard of Earthsea,* p. 14)

The name you receive upon this Rite of Passage is your first magickal name, or, as it is sometimes called, your *circle name.* It is the name by which you will be known among other magickal folk, but not among Mundanes. If it is given to you ritually by a mage, it may also be your *soul-name* or *true name.* Usually around the same time you will also acquire a *use-name,* or nickname, by which you will be known to your friends. Later, as you go forward through life on a magickal path, you will acquire other names among other circles of people. If you receive Initiation into various magickal Orders, Circles, or Traditions, you may be given a new circle name each time, to be used only among those people. Since most people in the magickal community also move in the mundane world (going to school, having jobs, etc.), many have a common magickal use-name that serves them in both communities—such as Star, Dragon, or Wolf.

The magickal name chosen by members of the original Order of the Golden Dawn was often just their family motto. Today, however, most magickal people pick a name that is deeply meaningful to them personally, and to their spiritual direction. The search to find such a name can be time-consuming, involving, and powerful to those who do it.

Until you actually undergo a Rite of Passage or magickal Initiation, you cannot receive a true magickal name from me or anyone else. Later on, I will offer you a Quest to find a True Name for yourself. This will be a deep journey of discovery into your own essential identity and destiny, and may take awhile to fulfill. But right now, at this beginning of your apprenticeship, I recommend that you consider taking a magickal use-name, with which you will personally identify and be known by among your closest friends.

Quest: Choose Your Magickal Use-Name

Many people in the magickal community choose use-names based upon things of Nature. Especially popular are *totems*—that is, those animals with which they feel the closest kinship. For many years (1979–94) my use-name was Otter. In the Bestiaries in 6.I and 7.III of this Grimoire, you can find lists of both natural and magickal creatures, and their attributes. If you feel a greater kinship with plants than with animals, you might wish to take a green name, such as a tree, herb, or flower. There are also minerals, places, stories, and so on that you can draw from. This chart gives a few examples out of countless possibilities.

Colors: You can also add a color to any name—like "Greywolf," "Silverflame," or "Whiteoak." See 1.III.7: "The Colors of Magick" for color attributions.

Combining: Any of these names (or others you may come up with) can be combined into one name,

Animals:	Plants:		Others:
Badger	Ash	Jasper	Dark
Bear	Aspen	Rock	Fire
Buffalo	Branch	Stone	Flame
Cougar	Bud	**Attributes:**	Heart
Crow	Cypress	Binder	Light
Dragon	Fir	Bringer	Lore
Eagle	Forest	Cutter	Moon
Fox	Herb	Dancer	Ocean
Gryphon	Leaf	Finder	Rain
Hawk	Oak	Flyer	River
Horse	Root	Healer	Sea
Moose	Rowan	Lover	Snow
Otter	Seed	Jumper	Sky
Phoenix	Thorn	Mender	Spark
Raven		Runner	Star
Robin	**Minerals:**	Singer	Storm
Spider	Amber	Walker	Sun
Tiger	Crystal	Weaver	Tempest
Wolf	Jade	Wise	Way

like author Starhawk, or used as two or even three, like the late actor River Phoenix; or author Silver Ravenwolf. You can get names like "Snowcat," "Seawolf," "Stardancer," or "Skywise" (from *Elfquest*). Use your imagination!

Numerology: Another consideration is your magickal number. This is taken by adding up all the numbers in your birthdate (including all four digits in the year), and then adding them again, until you get a final single-digit number. This is your birth number. Many magickal folks believe that your name should have the same number. See 6.III.3: "Numerology;" "Quest: Your Lucky Number."

A Naming Ceremony

When you have finally chosen a magickal name for yourself, you should write it into the following spell (and in your Magickal Journal). Then stand in front of a mirror, look yourself in the eye, and say:

I name myself ________________________.
________________________ do I know.
I am now ________________________.
And what I say three times is so!
By all the powers of land and sea,
By all the might of Moon and Sun,
As I do will, so mote it be;
Seal the spell and be it done!

Lesson 5: The School of Magick & Wizardry

Much of your life right now probably revolves around going to school. Unfortunately, your school probably isn't very much like Hogwarts! But it can be, for you—a lot more so than you might think. After all, school means studying, and you now have this Grimoire to study, right along with your regular textbooks. And school means having teachers. I'm betting that you probably have at least one really good teacher in your school—and through this Grimoire, you also have me, and the other Wizards of the Grey Council.

Get to know your favorite teachers; stay after class and talk to them. You may be surprised at how cool some of them can be when you get to know them... I know, because I have taught in public school myself (and have also worked as a school counselor), and I know many magickal folks who work as teachers in schools all over the world. They never make a point of revealing themselves, but they're out there—and you can find them, if you just look carefully.

And best of all, school means having friends. It used to be that kids like you (and me) were the weirdos in school. The really cool kids were the jocks and cheerleaders—they were "in," and we were "out." They had the best parties, and we were never invited. But all this has changed. There are many, many people now in the worldwide magickal community—and many of us have kids. They're known as "Magikids," and they go to school, just like you do. I'm betting that there's at least one right in your own class. They won't be too hard to find—just look for the magickal jewelry (especially pentacles). And if you wear a pentacle too, they'll find you. And now that you are my Apprentice, you have an "in." If they're part of the magickal community, their parents may already know me or have read some of my writings. If you become friends with them, you will form the nucleus of your own magickal circle.

At the time of this writing, there is no residential School of Witchcraft and Wizardry like Hogwarts where you can go. It is one of my fondest hopes to change that... There are, however, currently a number of online courses available—especially in Witchcraft. There are even a few special Summer Camps for Magikids run by real Witches and Wizards. And you should certainly check our own online **Grey School of Wizardry** at: *www.GreySchool.com.*

Regarding Harry Potter

—by Susan Morris, aka Chasomdai

I've read some very nasty fundamentalist articles calling the Harry Potter series a Satanic threat, claiming it was written to steal the souls of children or lure them away from mainstream religions. To teach them that Witches are "good" (this usually includes a diatribe on the "evil" of Witches,) so they are more likely to become Witches. Such writers demonstrate their own ignorance and bigotry, which says far more against them than against Harry Potter or Witches.

While the Harry Potter books are considered by

most Witches and Wizards to be very positive and fun, they really don't present any religious concepts at all, and should not be associated with the religion of Wicca or Paganism. The stories do present some of the myths about Witches and Wizards in a positive way; but they still present the stereotypes instead of the truth. Most people know that real Witches and Wizards don't really fly on broomsticks, of course. But many Witches are concerned that impressionable children might confuse the fantasy of Harry Potter with real Magick and Witchcraft.

Of course, general values that true Witches and Wizards hold are presented—Harry Potter is a good kid who eventually wins out. But the Harry Potter stories should not be considered as anything more than delightful works of fiction.

Lesson 6: Being a Magikid in the Public School

Studies: The foundation of Wizardry is rooted in knowledge of many things, and one of the most obvious characteristics of any Wizard is an intense curiosity about almost everything. Being in school gives you a great opportunity to discover and explore some of these fields. History and the natural sciences are especially important, as are geography and literature. And if you can find it offered, of course world mythology will surely be one of your favorites!

Drama and Performance: There are several places in the public school system where Magikids like you can find a perfect fit. The very best is the drama department. Long, long ago, clear back in the Stone Age, everything happened around the campfire. Making music and telling stories (and acting them out) around the fire eventually turned into both theater and ritual. And so the Theatre has always been the heart of magick. Try out for every school play.

If you don't get an acting part, join the stage crew. Work on props, costumes, makeup, sets—anything to become part of the theater. Did you ever notice, when they roll the credits at the end of a movie, the list of actors is fairly short, but the list of all the rest of the crew and people it took to produce that movie goes on and on and on? There's a whole World there, and it's full of magick! In fact, that's probably the place where you'll find most of the other Magikids also....

In this Grimoire, you'll be learning a bit of performance magick (called *conjury*) along with all the rest. You can put on your own little magick shows, and create your own magickal *persona* (character), and everyone will be delighted. You can even learn a string of jokes, and do a stand-up comedy routine (my first Apprentice and stepson, Zack, has made quite a career out of this!). I also recommend very highly learning to juggle! Juggling is such an important wizardly skill that many old writings do not even distinguish between jugglers and magicians. In fact, the Magician card of the tarot is also called "The Juggler."

Art: If you have any artistic abilities, take all the art classes you can. Learn drawing, painting, sculpture, woodcarving, pottery, weaving, sewing, jewelry making. Make your own sigils, amulets, pentacles, wands, chalices, robes, altar figures. Offer your artistic services for school posters, playbills, drawings for the school paper, etc. Artists are highly appreciated in the magickal community—as well as in the theater. There is always a demand for magazine and book illustrations, jewelry, posters, T-shirts, figurines, and other things like that. In fact, being an artist (I create jewelry and sculptures of Gods and Goddesses) is the main way I support my family!

Music: Music has always been a very important part of magick. *Bardcraft* was regarded as the foundation of all Druidry, and the power of the ancient singers, bards, and minstrels could topple tyrannical kings. If you have any musical abilities whatsoever (which I, regrettably, have not), then by all means work to develop these. Learn to play a musical instrument (especially the guitar). Join the school band, or sing in a chorus or choir. Learn traditional songs—especially ballads. Write your own poetry, and set it to music. You can find lots of wonderful inspiration from currently available tapes and CDs.

On Science and Magick: Being a Wizard means that you will work with forces and effects that have not, thus far, been validated by mainstream science. That doesn't mean that you should automatically believe in *anything* that sounds cool and strange, nor does it mean that you should dismiss science as the limited view of narrow minds. Science is a very powerful systematic use of our minds to learn things. It is, however—and this is the part that is generally not taught or admitted in our schools—a limited set of tools.

Science works very well for studying phenomena that lend themselves to experimentation. That is, the kinds of things where you can carefully control the conditions under which the experiment happens and where you have access to all the information about what happens to the thing you are studying. But science doesn't work very well for studying complex, chaotic systems, or phenomena that are very rare and only appear under unusual conditions that can't be created in a laboratory. The history of science is filled with examples of real things (like meteorites, ball lightning, continental drift, unicorns, or giant squids) that were declared by the leaders of mainstream science "not to exist," because these leaders had never seen them and couldn't figure out an explanation for how they *could* exist. Once evidence to explain these phenomena was discovered, they were finally "admitted" to be real by scientists who had denied their reality for years.

In the early 20th century, a mathematician named Gödel actually proved that it is *mathematically inevitable* that the Universe will contain things that are true but cannot be proven. Wizards work with such forces and phenomena. So be a critical thinker and be interested in learning about how the world works, and also keep an open mind about things that seem to be true even though we don't understand how…yet.

Task: Create Your Personal Altar

To begin any kind of magickal practice, you will need to create a personal altar in your room. This will be a place to display your magickal tools, and it will be the center of much of your magickal practice. Personal altars are as varied and as individual as the people who have them. There is no really "wrong" way to make one. Any flat horizontal surface can be made into an altar. Many magickal folk use a small table (square, round, or rectangular), a bureau, dresser or cabinet, the top of a TV, or even one shelf of a bookcase (mine is like that—though our large Ravenheart Family Altar is on the mantle over our fireplace). If you have very little space, a particularly convenient way to make a personal altar is a triangular shelf attached to the walls in a corner of your room. An altar can be any size you find convenient, but I recommend one at least two feet wide and a foot deep. Once you have a suitable altar space, you will need an altar cloth. A decorated silk scarf or large handkerchief is ideal, but any piece of pretty material you like will do. If you check your local metaphysical store, you will probably find some lovely altar cloths with magickal designs printed on them. For color-coded magick, you will want to have appropriately colored altar cloths.

There are a few things that go on almost every altar. First, you should have something to represent each of the Elements (Earth, Air, Fire, and Water). Earth may be represented by a crystal, a geode, a little cup of salt, a *pentacle,* bread, fruit, or even a small potted plant. Air might be represented by a feather, a *thurible* (incense burner), a bell, a flute, or a dried butterfly. Water is usually contained in a cup, or *chalice*—but a seashell, starfish, or piece of coral also makes a lovely representation of this Element. Water in your chalice should never be allowed to get stale, but should be refreshed regularly—especially before any working. Fire is universally represented by a red votive candle in a red jar, but a piece of red lava, coal, charred wood, or a polished red stone or gem will also serve. Even a little figurine of a red dragon can be used for Fire. Your magickal tools—such as your wand, *athamé* (ritual knife), jewelry, medicine pouches, *amulets, talismans,* etc. should also be kept on or around your altar. If you have a lot of such stuff, you might want to fasten a branch or deer antler above your altar from which you can hang things on chains and cords.

> ***NOTE:*** *NEVER leave a candle burning on your altar when you are not in the room! I've known of several magickal folks whose homes burned down from untended altar candles! Also make sure that there is nothing above your candle that could possibly catch fire—including another shelf, curtains, etc. You should have your altar set-up checked by your mom before lighting any candles on it.*

Next, your altar should have some representation of Spirit. This may be in the form of a crystal ball or statues or pictures of Gods and Goddesses, which you can make yourself or buy at a metaphysical store. Don't try and crowd your altar with such images—one or a matched set of two will do nicely. (I make such altar statues, and I have a very nice pair of young God and Goddess figures that I designed just for you!). Another way to represent Spirit is to have a mirror at the back of your altar, which will reflect your own face when you do your workings. After all, the Divine Spirit is always within you! Your altar is a little home for Spirit/God/Goddess to dwell with you as an honored guest. Treat Them so, and They will honor you in kind. If you wish to establish an Altar to a particular deity, consider this carefully. Take the time to study Them, learn Their attributes and symbols. We'll talk more about this later on….

And finally, your personal altar should have representations of yourself and your loved ones. Photos are the most common way to include them, but some folks use little animal figures to represent themselves and family members—especially those who strongly identify with particular *Totem* critters. Such representations are particularly used in working healing magick. Other decorations may be added as you like. Pretty stones (especially ones with natural holes through them), crystals, fossils, bones, meteorites, shells, acorns, etc. that have the kind of energy you want can be arranged decoratively. Remember, however, that your altar is a sacred space, and never casually put mundane objects (like your hairbrush, a can of soda, or your wallet) on a consecrated altar! Keep your altar clean and fresh.

When you have it all set up, do a little Rite of Consecration. Light the candle and incense (if you are using them), and say:

This altar now be sacred space
Of Spirit and of Mystery
May Magick dwell within this place
And all upon it blessed be!

Lesson 7: Progression and Advancement

Initiations

The word *initiation* means "beginning." An Initiation is a formal rite of passage ritual for admitting a new member into an existing group. Most college fraternities and sororities have Initiation rituals, and so do some youth groups, as well as street gangs. Some Initiations feature challenges and ordeals, and the tougher the ordeal the greater is the subsequent sense of belonging to the group. Many magickal traditions work in groups—variously called covens, lodges, orders, circles, groves, nests, hearths, etc.—and most of these have Initiation rituals. But the minimum age of admission to these magickal groups is normally 18, as responsible groups do not accept minors. Don't try and run in magick until you can walk!

Initiation can be a magickal metamorphosis, opening the door to expanded consciousness and awareness of the next stage of your spiritual and magickal evolution. It can so transform you that your concept of personal and worldly reality is forever altered. Initiation is more than the handing down of "secrets" and wisdom. It can also be a way of saying to the Universe: "I am ready to be witness to the unveiling of the Mysteries as revealed in my own life. I open to and accept the challenge to be taught through experience."

Degrees and Grades

Some magickal groups also have a number of degrees, or grades (like school), which acknowledge stages in spiritual development and magickal training. You may already be familiar with the colored belt system in Oriental martial arts; magickal degrees are similar. The number of such degrees varies from group to group. Some magickal societies feature ten or more degrees, but the most common number is three. Each system has its own name for these. In Druidry, the three grades are *Ovates, Bards,* and *Fili.* In Witchcraft the usual degrees are *Initiate, Priest/ess,* and *High Priest/ess.* The Craft Guilds acknowledged *Apprentices, Journeymen,* and *Masters.* The tradition of Wizardry that I am offering you here recognizes *Apprentices*, *Journeymen,* and *Adepts.*

Some foolish people see attaining such degrees as a goal in itself and may even try and collect them by cheating! But true magickal folk know that we can receive our degrees of training, knowledge, wisdom, competence, and compassion only when we have truly earned them. They may come in various and wondrous ways—in flashes of vision and understanding, in unexpected good fortune, and just the way you know that your life is on the right track through magickal *synchronicity* (that is, "lucky coincidences"). This Grimoire will provide you with the tools for a complete Apprenticeship program, and when you complete it, you may qualify as a Journeyman Wizard. As you are taking your lessons through this book, rather than in person, there is no way for me to evaluate your progress through this Apprenticeship, and therefore no way for me to bequeath any magickal degrees upon you. If you ever decide someday to join a magickal group, Lodge, or Order, you will still have to qualify according to their program. But if you learn these lessons well, I expect you'll do just fine! And perhaps someday we may meet in person....

Class III. Foundations of Magick

"Any sufficiently advanced science is indistinguishable from magic." —Arthur C. Clark

1. Introduction: Perspective, Reverence, and Humility

(By Bob Gratrix)

BECOMING A WIZARD IS A TRICKY thing. Some who are attracted to the idea of becoming a Wizard want to gain power or to impress others. But a true Wizard starts from the understanding that any human being, no matter how knowledgeable and powerful, is still just one small and temporary being in a Universe that is currently thought to be about 14.1 billion years old and about 88 *quadrillion* miles across.

As his or her knowledge grows, a Wizard sees more and more that the proper relationship to the vast and mysterious Universe is awe, humility, and reverence. It is astounding, beautiful, and precious that we humans have consciousness and are able to grow as we do into such complex personalities, to accumulate knowledge and skills such as Wizardry.

To be a Wizard is to acknowledge that *everything is alive* and *everything is connected.* We'll talk more about that later. What that means is that the proper orientation to everything, including other people, is respectfulness and humility. A true Wizard doesn't lord over other people or seek attention just because he or she has gained a little knowledge. Always remember that however much we learn, however skilled we become in the art of Wizardry, what we do not know will always be vastly more than what we do

Life is, among other things, a process. Out of the state of our beings we experience and observe that a cycle of change and transformation is at work, a shared state of being and becoming. A Wizard is at the work of creation, and his tools are essentially those of perception, self-knowledge, and natural law. A Wizard's fingers can touch the heartbeat of Life itself and know both its powers and frailties, the careful balance that exists in all growing things. Within that knowing lies the potential for transformation and acceleration of the natural processes that are at work. These transformations are the essence of magick and creation, they are life affirming and courageous acts that can bring changes both great and small. It is the ability to speak the magickal incantations that banishes torment from the troubled, the ability to see and levitate that which is falling down, the energy and insight to remove that which blocks the flow of what Life is at work at. It is for all this and so much more, a Wizard creates rituals so any number of others may share in an expression of their humanity and dignity before these life forces.

Our lives are our most intimate works of creation, and like sculptors we hold fine images of just whom we would represent to the world. We have some idea of our highest vision of our Self, a familiarity with the glorious gift that we carry into the world and our hope to revel in all that we are beneath this golden Sun. While we are at this creative work, if we are to continue to grow, we must step back from time to time to see how we are shaping up. We need to see what needs to be changed next in our personal evolution. We need to look deeply into the concepts and beliefs that we have accepted as true and challenge those ideas with what we now know of ourselves, making whatever adjustments are supported by our self-examination. We look for patterns that define the themes that are working their way through us, to see who we are and what we are becoming. We look for patterns in our behaviors and perspective that bind us to what we are manifesting. And we use these same powers of examination and reception outwardly, so that the essence of that which surrounds us can be recognized for exactly what it is.

Lesson 2: Seeing and Thinking like a Wizard

The real voyage of discovery consists not in seeking new lands but in seeing with new eyes.
—Marcel Proust

If you've seen models or pictures of a brain, you know that there are two halves—the *cerebral hemispheres.* The left side of the brain (which controls the right side of the body, and the right hand) is all about logical, rational thinking. Mathematics, written language, speech, mechanics, science, and politics are all associated with the right brain, and so we "see" all this stuff with our "left eye." Scientists, mathematicians, mechanics, accountants, and politicians are all said to be very "left brain."

The right side of the brain, on the other hand (ha!) is all about intuitive, mystical awareness. Art, pictures, symbols, music, singing, poetry, magic, dreams, visions, and psychic experiences are all associated with the right brain, and so we "see" all this stuff with our "right eye." Artists, musicians, mystics, and poets are said to be very "right brain." The right brain controls the left hand.

Try closing one eye and holding your head still,

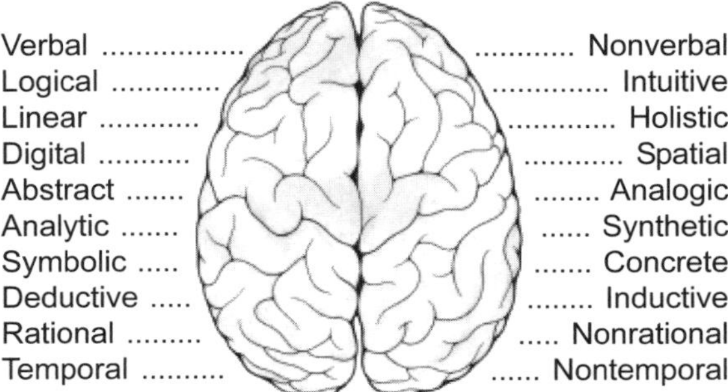

and look at a scene with many complex layers (like a roomful of people or trees in a woods). Or try looking at 3-D pictures through those special 3-D glasses only one eye at a time. Seen through only one eye, everything seems flat, rather than three-dimensional. You lose all sense of perspective. In the larger sense of things, that's how most people "see" everything. And what they see *is* the "mundane" world.

Going in With Both Eyes Open

One of the main distinctions between Wizards and others is a special way of looking at the world, and seeing beyond the surfaces. Some people call this "thinking outside the box." Most people really "see" with only one eye—either the left or the right. That is, they filter all their perceptions and experience through one side of the brain *or* the other. A Wizard "sees" with both eyes, using and integrating both sides of the brain at once. And so a Wizard has a sense of perspective that most people simply cannot imagine (and the word imagine means "see an image in your mind"). When you "see" that way, patterns appear to you that no one else can see (in fact, they'll tell you that you're just seeing—or imagining—things). It's like those clever *stereogram* pictures that look like just a mess of little colored dots and squiggles, until you unfocus both your eyes just right—and then suddenly a whole 3-D image leaps out at you. The mind of a Wizard looks at everything that way. We might even call this "holographic perception."

There's a saying that, "In the land of the blind, the one-eyed man is King." In the Kingdom of Magick, the one-eyed man is blind. These lessons are to teach you to always see with both eyes....

Quest: Binocular Visualizations

These little exercises will help you focus your perception, inner vision, and magickal imagination. Before you do each one, you should rub your palms vigorously together until they are charged with heat. Then place them over your open eyes, allowing the energy to be absorbed into your eyes.

1. Third Eye: Stand about 6" back from a mirror, and gaze into your reflection with both eyes open. At first you will see two eyes, of course. But go into soft focus eye mode and slowly the two eyes will merge into one—a "third eye!"

2. Floating Sausage: Point your index fingers at each other about 6" in front of your open eyes. Bring your fingertips together and gaze at the contact point with soft focus. Soon you will see a "sausage" appearing between them. Slowly separate your fingertips until the "sausage" appears to be floating in space. Bring it into clear focus and hold it steady for a couple of minutes without straining.

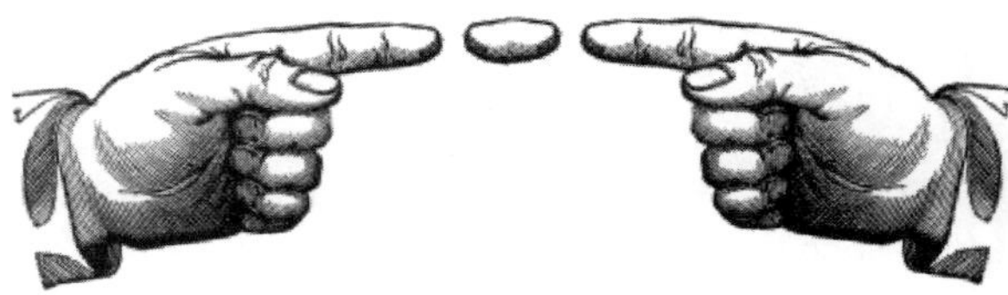

3. 3-D Cube: Use the same technique of soft focus and allow these two images to float together until there are three. The middle one will be in 3-D.

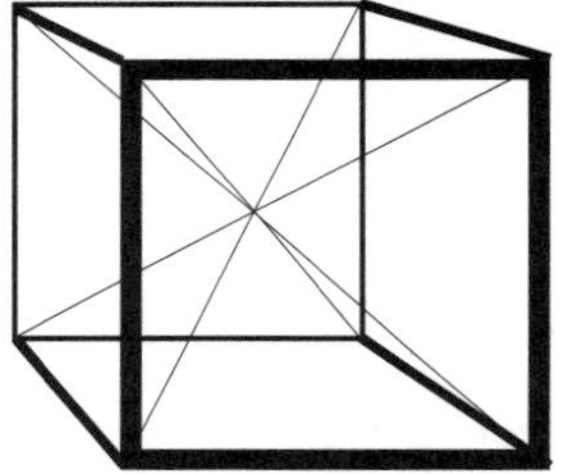

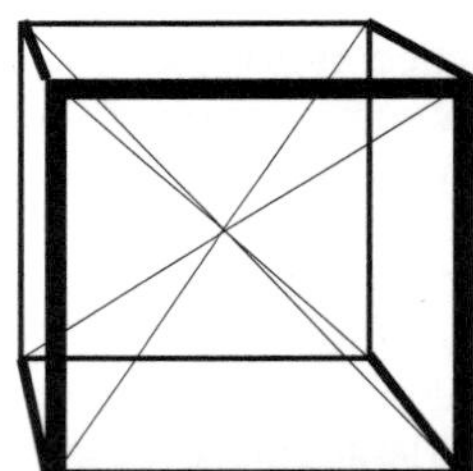

4. "3-D Photo:" Now look at these two photos in the same way, and allow them to merge into a single 3-D image! Practice until you can hold the 3-D effect

5. Stereogram: Now look at this mess of little squiggles and see if you can perceive the 3-D image hidden within. To do this, you will need to use both eyes *and* both sides of your brain in synch! Such images are called SIRDS (Single Image Random Dot Stereograms) and you can view many more of them at: *www.nottingham.ac.uk/~etzpc/sirds.html.*

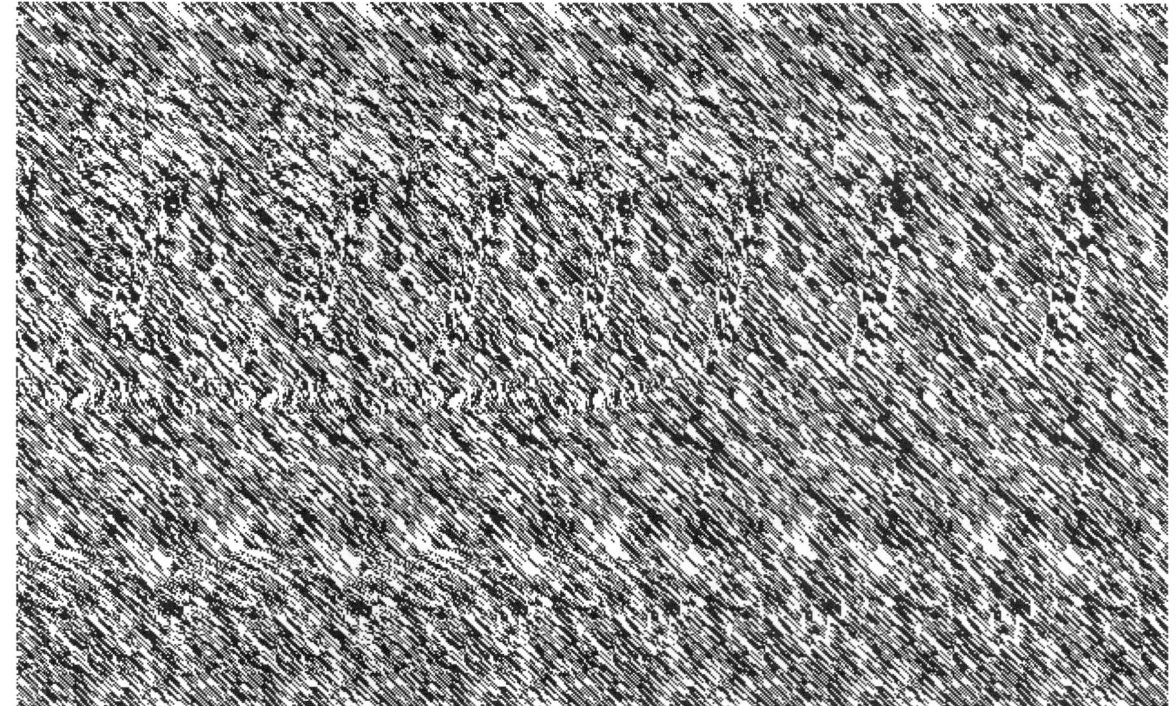

Quest: Listening Like a Wizard

A major wizardly skill is mastering stillness and becoming aware of the subtle sound clues that the natural world provides us. Wizardly hearing attunes you to the magickal world. Wizards listen, not just with our ears, but with all our senses, making ourselves aware of many things that are invisible to others. There are many layers of sound all around us, even when it seems to be silent. Feeding all these layers of sound and the information the sounds contain to your conscious mind increases your power and gives your spellwork a richer, more robust texture.

Try this right now: Relax your mind and listen. What do you hear first? Next? What else? How are the sounds inter-related? As you listen, your mind will begin to tune into many sounds and impressions that usually go unnoticed. The more you practice this, the more it will become natural for you to absorb the subtle sounds and energies all around. You will tune into the feeling of a breeze on your skin and other tactile sensations, as your sense of touch learns to listen. Even in a city, the sounds of Nature are everywhere, mingled with the sounds of civilization. Listen with your senses, your intuition, and your wizardly curiosity.

Later, try taking a little "Listen Quest" in Nature. This could be your own backyard, by the sea, or in the woods — some place that is very familiar or beloved. Listen until a plant or a tree, an aspect of Nature, or an animal appears or otherwise makes itself known, perhaps only in your thoughts. Listen until the spirit of that animal, plant, or thing (it could be a rock or a waterfall) has called to you. Once you "hear" this message, then leave an offering of thanks—cornmeal, a shell, some fruit, a song, or a prayer.

Lesson 3: Magick Is Always Power and Change

Magick is what we call various ways of making changes in ourselves and the world by means that cannot be explained by currently accepted theories and understandings of science and society. Of course, many technologies that we now take for granted—such as television, cell phones, microwaves, computers, the Internet, video games, holograms, X-rays, sonograms, MRI (magnetic resonance imaging), etc.—would have totally seemed like magick only 100 years ago! As far as most people are concerned, they still are magick, because their actual workings are incomprehensible to most users.

And, ironically enough, many things that are now widely considered to be in the realm of "magick"—such as telepathy, astral projection, mediumship, and other psychic phenomena—were considered to be "scientific" (as in "The Psychic Sciences") only a hundred years ago. Some of the greatest founding fathers of the Scientific Revolution were also alchemists, astrologers, and magicians. There has always been a continual reshuffling back and forth between the realms of science and magick as theories and fashions change.

And Wizardry has always happily embraced both. Both sides of the brain—both eyes wide open.

The word *magick* itself somes from the Zoroastrian priests of ancient Persia, who were called *Magi.* The Magi were famous for their powerrs of healing and divination—especially astrology. They believed that the cosmos was both alive and Divine, and they revered the planets, stars, and other heavenly bodies. The "Three Wise Men" who brought gifts to the newborn Jesus in Bethlehem were Persian Magi.

> *The Persian word* magus *(meaning 'priest' and 'fire worshipper') was adapted into Greek as* magos *(meaning a 'wise one,' 'wizard' or 'juggler'). Demonstrations, feats or traits 'of a Wizard' were said to be* magikos, *and it was this Greek root that was westernized into* magic *and* magical.
> —Tom Ogden (*Wizards & Sorcery,* p. 129)

Glossary of Magickal Concepts

Okay, now it's time for another little mini-glossary. The following words and concepts are going to be important to understanding the following Lessons:

Paradigm: A *paradigm* is a philosophical model or world-view by which other things are understood. For instance, as silly as it seems now, throughout the Middle Ages the widely held paradigm of the solar system was that the Earth was in the center, and the Sun, Moon, planets, and stars all revolved around us on a series of concentric transparent crystal spheres, like different-sized light bulbs on spinning glass eggshells. Everything that people experienced and believed in had to somehow fit that paradigm, and anything that couldn't be made to fit had to be ignored—or outlawed.

Meme: *Memes* are units of ideas. These are "mental genes" that people pass on, ideas or paradigms that seem to fight to ensure their own existence. This word was coined by Richard Dawkins of Oxford University in his 1976 book, *The Selfish Gen*.

Analogy: An *analogy* is a comparison between two different things (called *analogs*) by noting some point of similarity. We'll say, this is like that, only different. Most riddles are based on analogies, such as "A box without hinges, lock or lid, yet golden treasure inside is hid." The answer is "egg," and the analog is a treasure chest. Because Wizards see hidden patterns, many things can be viewed this way as analogs, and so Wizards often seem to others to be "speaking in riddles."

Metaphor: A *metaphor* is a comparison in which one thing is said to *be* another (rather than just be *like* another). We say, this *is* that. Metaphors enable us to see things in whole new ways and open up new possibilities. When Shakespeare said "All the world's a stage," he gave us an important perspective to see ourselves as actors in a cosmic drama.

Allegory: *Allegories* are teaching stories in which characters, things, and happenings in the story stand for other things in real life. Fables are very popular allegories in which animals represent different types of people. *Paradigms, analogies, metaphors,* and *allegories* are all different kinds of conceptual maps we draw in our minds. The important thing to remember here is that the map is not the territory—and the menu is not the meal! Many people do not get this, but Wizards do.

Paradox: A *paradox* is something that seems to be self-contradictory and therefore absurd, but may in fact point to a deeper or hidden truth. One of the most famous examples is the time travel paradox: If you went back in time and accidentally killed your mother when she was a child, then she wouldn't grow up to have you; and you wouldn't exist to later get into the time machine and go back to kill her. But if you didn't kill her, then she *would* have had you, and you *would* have gone back in time.... In the case of Wizardry, paradox is most often invoked when we say that for a Great Truth, its opposite is also true. The classic example is: "As Above, So Below."

Synchronicity: *Synchronicity* means literally the same as *coincidence*—a simultaneous occurrence (two things happen together at the same time). But while coincidences are just random, synchronicities reveal hidden patterns and meanings. What we call *luck* is really about synchronicity. Often when you are on the right track in your life, synchronistic events occur as signposts of divine guidance.

Synthesis: A *synthesis* is the putting together of separate parts to form a whole. Particularly, it refers to a union in which opposites (the *thesis* and *antithesis*) are reconciled.

Hologram: A *hologram* is an image in which every tiny part contains the essence of the whole—like the DNA in each of our cells that contains the pattern of our entire being.

Template: A *template* is a pattern or cutout that can be placed over, held against, or traced around to reveal or impose a matching pattern in something else. Some of my favorite patterning templates are those special glasses that turn double images into 3-D, as in movies and comic books.

Synergy: *Synergy* is the result of bringing together and combining separate things so that the whole is greater than the sum of the parts, and something completely new appears. A good example is water. Its separate parts are oxygen and hydrogen, two flammable gases that explode when ignited. But when they are combined in a molecule of H_20, the result—water—is a completely unique new substance that can exist as solid, liquid *and* gas all within 100°C.

Gestalt: *Gestalt* is a German word meaning "shape" or "form." This word is used to describe integrated patterns of mental concepts that produce a synergistic new paradigm. New ideas are pretty much always the result of gestalt thinking.

Epiphany: An *epiphany* is a sudden revelation, when all the pieces come together into a *gestalt*, and you see something in a way you'd never thought of before. In ancient Greece, this word was used to describe the appearance or manifestation of a god, and people still tend to say, *"Omigod!"* when they have an epiphany.

Lesson 4: The Origin of Magick

Magick began with the taming of Fire. When we first learned how to actually *make* Fire, we took a quantum leap in our mastery of the world that separated us from all other creatures, and set us on the path of Humanity. We became the very first living creatures that could intentionally create something out of nothing — something very powerful, which would do our bidding. Fire kept the cave bears, dire wolves, and saber-tooth tigers away from our caves and camps. Fire drove game animals into our traps and ambushes; even the mighty mammoth quailed before the torches of our hunters (you would too if you were covered in long flammable hair!). These same torches illuminated for us the secret passages of caves that no other seeing creature could explore, and allowed us to paint on cave walls magickal pictures of animals, stars, people, symbols—and images of Shamans, the first Wizards. These paintings were probably among the earliest spells ever cast.

Fire lit the darkest nights and kept us warm during ten-thousand-year-long winters. Fire roasted our meat, cooked our vegetables, melted ice, boiled water, dried salmon, tanned hides, hardened our wooden spear-points, and baked our first clay pottery. Gathered around our hearths and campfires, we sang our first songs, chanted our first chants, made our first music, danced our first dances, told our first stories, and performed our first plays. All our magick—and all our culture—came first from the Fire. And Fire made us both human and powerful.

Cave of The Three Brothers, France, 14,000 BCE

Lesson 5: What is Magick?

Over the years, just about every magickal practitioner and writer has taken a shot at defining and explaining what magick is. Most agree that magick involves the manipulation of reality towards a desired end by methods that cannot be explained by the current scientific paradigm. Some consider psychic phenomena as the basis of magick. Here are a few of the most popular and interesting definitions:

Magick is...

"...the Highest, most Absolute, and most Divine knowledge of Natural Philosophy, advanced in its works and wonderful operations by a right understanding of the inward and occult virtue of things; so that true Agents being applied to proper Patients, strange and admirable effects will thereby be produced."
—The *Lemegeton of King Solomon* (1500 CE)

"...a science and an art comprising a system of concepts and methods for the build-up of human emotion, altering the electrochemical balance of the metabolism, using associative techniques and devices to concentrate and focus this emotional energy, thus modulating the energy broadcast by the human body, usually to affect other energy patters, whether animate or inanimate, but occasionally to affect the personal energy patterns." —Isaac Bonewits

"...the science and art of causing change to occur in conformity with Will." —Aleister Crowley

"...the conscious application of imagination and focused attention to bring about a desired goal through visualization" —Ellen Evert Hopman

"...coincidence control." —Oberon Ravenheart

"...probability enhancement." —Anodea Judith

Lesson 6: Magick as Probability Enhancement

While all of these definitions are true, and each helps to a fuller understanding, my personal favorite is Anodea's. It offers us a real key as to what we're doing when we practice magick. We are shifting the *probabilities* (or "odds") from one outcome to another. All events that have not yet come to pass have some degree of probability that they may or may not occur. We can express such probabilities in terms of percentages, as when we say, "There's a 50% chance of rain tomorrow," or "The odds against that happening are ten to one." In such a statement, there are two factors: the *probability* and the *improbability.* If the odds are ten to one against, the *probability* is one and the *improbability* is ten. But the thing is, in such a case, if you do it ten times, then the improbability drops to one, and the probability goes up to ten. Once more, and the improbability becomes a *virtual certainty.* Even if the odds are a million to one against, like in winning the lottery, if more than a million people play, then at least one is virtually certain to win. This is why there are so many coincidences and synchronicities. In an infinite multiverse, all improbabilities must be finite. Nothing we can imagine is truly impossible. The only real question is, what are the odds?

In this context, doing magick as "probability enhancement" consists of increasing the odds (probabilities) in favor of our desired outcome. It's like piling rocks on the high end of a seesaw until the balance shifts, and the other end goes up. Every bit helps—not only large boulders, but even small pebbles and grains of sand; it just takes more of them. When both ends of the seesaw are off the ground and level, the balance is 50:50, and it hinges on the *fulcrum* (balance point). At that point, it doesn't take much to tip the balance one way or another—or even to pivot the whole thing into a different alignment entirely.

The trick is to find the *cusp.* A cusp is an intersection between fields of alternative probability. At such places the potential as to which of these alternatives the probability wave will collapse into is in delicate balance—things could easily go either way. At a cusp, it takes little energy to move between the intersecting states, and "probability enhancement" by a Wizard can have very large impact because of a domino effect of probabilities changing outward through space and time like ripples in a pond as a result of the change he induces through his practice of magick.

Archimedes, a great Wizard and inventor of ancient Greece who discovered many principles of mechanics, said: "Give me a lever long enough, a fulcrum, and a place to stand, and I will move the world!" This is a basic principle of Wizardry, and we will return to it frequently in these lessons, as we create *levers,* recognize *fulcrums,* and find a place to stand....

Lesson 7: The Colors of Magick

In almost every discussion about magick, the first thing that comes up is the issue of "black" or "white." Of course psychic energy itself—like electricity—has no "color." There is no black or white, not even gray; it is morally neutral. But we can *use* that energy for many purposes—just as we can use electricity. It's the *use* of that energy that we are talking about here when we say "magick." And it can be used for good, evil, or anything else the practitioner wishes to use it for. The purpose for which it is used is determined by the ethics of the practitioner. Throughout history, there has been an unfortunate tendency to over-simplify the use of magick (and far too many other aspects of life) into just two choices: "good" and "evil." And these have been traditionally expressed as "white" and "black." Certainly these distinctions are valid for many practitioners who do, in fact, choose between such simple alignments. But most Wizards are more complex than that, and we see magick in terms of a rainbow spectrum of hues for many purposes.

In fact, the use of colors in magickal workings has acquired traditional associations with the Elements (Earth, Air, Fire, Water, Spirit), the planets, and the purposes of the spells. In the tables of correspondence that you will find in this Grimoire, you will see listed in every grouping the appropriate associated colors. These may be used for the colors of candles, robes, lights, altar cloths, wall hangings, and even *talismans* and other objects used in the spell. Correspondences of colors and purposes are not absolute, however, and may vary somewhat among different cultural traditions. There are also overlaps where some colors may blend into one another.

Here is a basic spectrum of colors of Magick as used by myself and many other magickal folk:

Red—(Fire) Physical work, as in healing of people and animals. Also physical passion and sexuality. Red is the power color. Red is the color of fire, inspiration, vitality, pride, anger, bravery, strong emotions, purification, arid places, aggressive music (especially drumming like a heartbeat), and lightning storms. Red is the best color to ward off danger. Use it for stability, grounding, prosperity, and physical health.

Orange—Pride and courage; heroism and attraction; kinship and prosperity (as in a good harvest). Orange is attuned to warmth, friendship, abundance, spirit, will, principles, theory, and alertness. Like gold, it is associated with passionate music, the rustle of Autumn leaves, and natural sounds at dusk or just after a storm. Use orange for fluidity of movement, pleasure, and connection.

Yellow—(Air) Mental work; meditation, will, intellect, and communication. Another version of gold, yellow is the color of friendship, goodness, and faith. Golden yellow is the color of charm, trust, Summer, bright sounds such as children's laughter, and upbeat music. Pastel yellow tends more towards Spring, psychic endeavors, and creativity. Yellow is a terrific color to improve balance, self-esteem, charisma, divination, and creativity. Use it also for strength of will, vitality, purpose, and effectiveness.

Green—(Earth) Vegetation, as in gardening and herbalism; fertility and prosperity. Hope, joy, delight, growth, and change are all aspects of green. Forest green is connected with fertility, the body, courage, and classical music or wilderness sounds. Ivy green represents the emotional aspects, coping with grief, cliffside ponderings, and hushed music or silence. Pale green, as in the color of new grass, aids the healing process. Use green also for balance in relationships, compassion, and self-acceptance.

Blue—(Water) Emotional work; love, peace, and protection. Considered the color of wisdom, thoughtfulness, and celestial regions, blue shares Friday and the planet Venus with green (as in aqua, or blue-green). A feeling of youthfulness fills this color. Blue is an excellent hue for peacefulness and profound reflection. Use it also for harmony, creativity, communication, and resonance.

Indigo—Perception, imagination, illusion, and the ability to see patterns. Wizardry in general. Indigo is associated with nightmares, hallucinations, and madness. Indigo shading to ultraviolet is often called "the color of magick." This is a popular color for Wizard's robes—often emblazoned with stars, moons, and other astronomical symbols.

Violet (Purple)—Power, wealth, and good fortune. Considered the color of royalty, purple represents judgement, industry, and religious thought. Violet is the color of spirit, etheric realms, higher esoteric learning, ancient wisdom, and deeper Mysteries. Use violet as your focus specifically for spiritual centering and meditation, as well as expanded consciousness and cosmic awareness.

Brown—Everything to do with animals of all kinds, especially animal communication. Brown is the most common color of fur and feathers and represents all things soft and fuzzy. Brown is for "horse whisperers," animal trainers, pet psychics, and all people who seem to have an uncanny ability to communicate with animals.

Black—Blighting or binding; protection. As the color of night, black represents foreboding, fortitude, and consistency because of the need to "make it through the darkness." Black is sometimes used as a protective color for magickal tools—especially handles and wrappings. It is also used when trying to banish a bad habit, turn negativity, or make drastic life changes. Black is also, of course, the color of Sorcery and the "Dark Arts."

White—Blessing, or anything you want! The color of purity, white represents friendship, sincerity, divinity, transformation and singular focused sounds such as a gong or bell. White is the color of the Goddess, and so used in all forms of blessings.

Gold—Masculine energies; strength, leadership, vitality. Gold represents adolescence, joy, fruitfulness, and nobility. Men of magick often prefer tools, amulets and jewelry made of gold, bronze, or brass.

Silver—Feminine energies; intuition, insight, dreams, psychic gifts, and divination. Silver represents women's Mysteries and magicks, secrets, and Witchcraft. Witches' jewelry is made of silver or sometimes copper (the metal of Venus).

Lesson 8: Color-Coded Wizardry

Throughout history and legend, a number of "Schools," Orders, and specialized practices of magick and Wizardry have been designated. Many of these have distinguished themselves by colors such as listed above. Much as the students of Hogwarts are entered into the respective Houses of Gryffindor (red), Ravenclaw (blue), Hufflepuff (yellow), or Slytherin (green), the work and teachings of these schools have focused on such color-coded categories of practice.

Wizards following those schools have consequently adopted those colors also, so we have Red Wizards, Green Wizards, White Wizards, Black Wizards (these tend to be sorcerers), and so on. Grey Wizards (or, as some call themselves, "Rainbow Wizards") are non-specialized, being adept in many areas. Some Witches have also adopted color identifications—particularly white and green. And similar colors are also accorded to Faeries.

Quest: Choose Your Color

As you begin your Apprenticeship, I would like you to consider these colors of Wizardry, and choose for yourself which color you feel most connected with. Check 1.IV.3: "Color-Coded Practices" for more information on them. This will become your starting point, and you will thus become an Apprentice (Color) Wizard. Using your magickal name, you will be known as "(Name) the (Color)"—like Gandalf the Grey. Now go to the section of this *Grimoire* (Courses 5 and 6: "Spectrum") that deals with that color, and study those lessons. Later, as you advance in your mastery of Wizardry, you will be able to claim additional colors....

The 12 Colors of Wizardry

Color	Practice	Element	Direction
	1. Arts & Practices		
YELLOW	Divination	Air	East
RED	Alchemy	Fire	South
BLUE	Healing Arts	Water	West
GREEN	Wortcunning	Earth	North
	2. Magicks & Wizardries		
GREY	Lore Mastery	Knowledge	Center
WHITE	Ceremonial	Spirits/Soul	Above
BLACK	Sorcery	Matter/Energy	Below
CLEAR	Mathemagicks	Numbers	Everywhere
	3. Sciences & Disciplines		
AQUA	Meditation	Inner	Northwest
ORANGE	Conjury	Outer	Southwest
BROWN	Beast Mastery	Life/Death	Northeast
VIOLET	Cosmology	Time/Space	Southeast

Task: Make Your Color Tabard

When you have selected which color of Wizardry you would like to start with, you should make a *tabard* of that color. A tabard is a simple over-the-shoulder draping that Wizards wear when doing particular kinds of magick. Here's how to make yours:

First, measure your own height. You'll find as we go on that many personal objects and items of clothing in Wizardry are based on your own individual "measure." This makes them very specifically yours, and they become invested with your own identity. Now, go down to your local fabric store and purchase a piece of material about two inches longer than your measure (the extra is for hemming).

Look in the section of printed cotton that covers the range of colors you want, and find an appropriate print that you like. For instance, if you pick green as your color, you might find something with a leafy pattern. If you pick brown, you could get something with a design of animals. Or if you pick red or blue, you might find something that looks like fire or water. But if you pick white, there should be no printed design on it at all.

Take your material home and lay it out on the floor. Fold it in half the long way, so it is the length of your body. Then fold it back into thirds. Now unfold one of those thirds, so you have a section 2/3 long, and one that is 1/3 long, and put a little mark on the first centerfold at the one-third point. Now take a pair of scissors and carefully cut/slice the centerfold of the 2/3 section right up to the 1/3 mark, but no further. Your should now have a basic tabard, which will look like this:

Trim off any unprinted edging, and hem it up along all the cut edges to complete your tabard. You wear it over your shoulders with the two long sections hanging down in front.

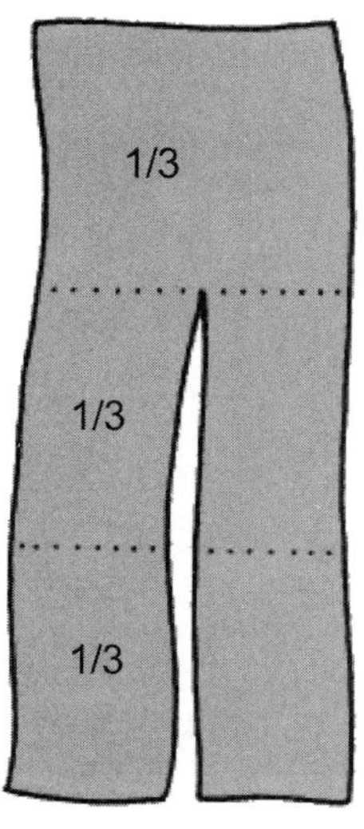

Quest: Self-Dedication

If you are serious about entering into an Apprenticeship to Wizardry, I offer you this rite of Self-Dedication. First, hand-copy the words of this rite onto a piece of parchment paper. Write your own magickal Use-Name in the first line. Next, prepare your space so you will not be disturbed. Take a shower or bath, and put on your color tabard. Then light a candle on your personal Altar, and turn out all other lights in the room (this is best done in the evening, when it is dark outside). Now place a round mirror (a makeup mirror will do nicely) on your Altar, and position yourself so you can see your face reflected in it. Looking yourself in the eyes, read aloud the words of the Rite, while taking them into your heart:

A Rite of Self-Dedication

(by Saraluna and Katlyn)

Hear me Ancient Ones, Guides,
Guardians and Powers,
It is I, (your name, or magickal Use-Name)
In this sacred space I open myself
In this sacred place and in this time I am changed,
I align my soul to its greatest purpose.
I call upon Spirit to witness my dedication
And acknowledge my ever-deepening connection.
I call upon the Old Ones, the Ancestors,
The Elements, and the Web that connects us all

Hear now my solemn Vow of Dedication:
Here, in this holy and perfect moment,
I pledge my path to Living Magick.
I accept the wisdom that all things have meaning
And all beings are my teachers.
From this moment onward, I declare myself
A Vessel of Spirit
A true Seeker of the Way of the Wizard
A Weaver in the Sacred Web of Life

I shall honor the Sacred Journey before me
With every cell of my being,
With every breath, step, and action.
May I hold the light of truth
As I quest toward my highest visions.
May I always see the Divine in Nature
And Nature in the Divine
I shall walk the Path of the Wizard
In Perfect Love and Perfect Trust.
So mote it be!

When you have finished, roll your hand-written pledge into a little scroll, and tie it with a piece of ribbon. Keep it at the back of your Altar, behind the mirror. Every now and again, pull it out, unroll it, and read it to remind yourself of what you have pledged.

Class IV: Magickal Arts

"Magic, when well-done, is considered entertainment.
"The practice and rehearsal of magic, when well-done, can be meditative. When done together well, they are meditainment. *Magic is my meditation and entertainment for an audience of one; me. When I enter into a state of meditainment, the world vanishes and I am deep in the reflection of the mirror of self.*
"Disciples of many inner traditions have explored active meditations like walking and dancing as ways to explore the inner world, to make contact with the deep, hidden wisdom inside each of us. Meditation is a practice. For us, our magic is our practice." —Magnus

1. Introduction: Magick in Fact and Fiction

OR MANY PEOPLE, THE IDEA OF magickal practice comes mostly from stories, TV shows, and movies—in which Witches, Wizards, and Sorcerers hurl firebolts, make things disappear (or become invisible), instantly change their hair color or physical appearance, transform into animals, bring to life inanimate objects, clean house without raising a finger, teleport instantaneously from one place to another, read minds, levitate, and engage in colorful magickal battles full of weird special effects—and all with a wave of the hand, a twitch of the nose, or the twinkling of an eye.

Real-life magickal practices are somewhat different. They run the gamut from simple spells and charms—mostly concerned with individual healings, blessings, transformations, and other small workings; divinatory readings; shamanic ecstatic practices used for healing and journeying; through "Circle Work" involving raising group energy for healings, community service, weather working, and other such; to larger group workings to heal and save the planet—such as protecting endangered forests, peoples, and species.

And some of those practices shown in the movies actually do have real-life analogs—though they may not be quite as dramatic as they are made to appear with Hollywood special effects! It's like with a laser: in movies you always see a beam of light going from the laser to the target; but in real life, lasers only show a dot on the actual target—the beam itself is invisible. And so it often is with real magick.

In this Class, I will introduce you to some of the main types of magick. Later, I'll show you how to do them yourself.

Lesson 2: Types of Magick

Magickal work and practices are often distinguished into two main types, commonly referred to as "High Magick" and "Low Magick."

High & Low Magick: Theurgy & Thaumaturgy

High Magick (also called *theurgy,* meaning "working things pertaining to the gods"), which often calls upon the aid of friendly spirits and gods, is associated with religion. Theurgy refers to the use of magick to effect changes in the magician's own internal reality. Theurgy is not concerned with service to others, but rather in one's own personal enlightenment, self-actualization, and *apotheosis* ("becoming Divine"). The focus is on prayers, invocations, and meditations. Theurgic magic was highly developed by the Neo-Platonists, adherents to a philosophical and religious system developed in Alexandria, Egypt, in the 3rd century CE that was based on a blend of the doctrines of Plato and other Greek philosophers, Oriental mysticism, Judaism and Christianity. Plato believed in a morally neutral natural magic, like electricity, the use of which was up to the practitioner.

Thaumaturgy ("wonder-working"), on the other hand, is the use of magick to effect changes in the reality of the outer world. As it is concerned with the scientific and technical aspects of such workings, this is what we call "Practical Magick." Thaumaturgy is also often referred to as Low Magick or sorcery—especially when it is provided in the service of others. All forms of *folk magick*—which served the villages and common people—became known as Low Magick. Over time, much of the traditional lore and practices of folk magick declined in popular use, regarded as superstitions.

In Greece, Low Magick (called *mageia,* "sorcery") had acquired an unsavory reputation for fraud by the 5th century BCE. Practitioners were not members of the priesthood but individuals who claimed to have magical powers and would help clients for fees. Such people still practice widely, advertising in the papers and working out of botanicas and reading rooms. Most of the laws against the practice of "fortune-telling" and the like are about this. The very lowest form of this magick is *goeteia,* which in the classical world was practiced by persons who cast spells, "howled" incantations, and concocted potions.

Witchcraft

In traditional tribal cultures throughout the world we find *shamans,* or medicine men and women, who are both gifted and learned in *divination*, herbalism, psychic work, and sorcery. They are the village teachers, magicians, spirit guides, interpreters of dreams, spell-casters, healers, and midwives. Among some of the Celtic tribes of Western Europe, such shamans were known as *Wicce* (WEE-cheh)—an Anglo-Saxon word meaning "shaper"—from which we derive our present term "Witch."

During the centuries of persecution at the hands of the Inquisition and others, many of these village Witches were horribly tortured and killed, along with many people in the communities they served. The 20th century revival of Witchcraft (often called simply "the Craft") can be mostly attributed to Gerald Gardner, a British Witch who became public after the repeal of the British anti-Witchcraft laws in 1951. One of Gardner's initiates, Doreen Valiente, created beautiful *liturgy* (rites, rituals, and prayers), including the much-beloved "Charge of the Goddess," which states: "If that which you seek you find not within you, you will never find it without. For behold, I have been with you from the beginning, and I am that which is attained at the end of desire."

Witchcraft can therefore be defined as the practice of magick as it relates to pre-Christian European Shamanism. The arts of Witchcraft today include herbalism, divination, magick, ceremonial ritual, healing, potions, and spirit-world contact. Based on scholarly reconstruction, imagination, and some inherited traditions, Witchcraft (also called Wicca by some) is now emerging as a distinct spiritual tradition and way of life for entire communities as well as the solitary practitioner. Modern Witches are both men and women—indeed, most of the founders of the major modern *Traditions* (or "denominations") of Witchcraft have been men. But there tend to be more women than men in most covens, and some groups, such as the Dianics, are entirely female. The vast majority of women in the magickal community today are Witches, though there are women involved in all other branches and traditions of Magick as well.

The Witch by Hans Weiditz (1532)

Hypnosis and Guided Meditation

From the Greek word *hypnos* (sleep), *hypnosis* is a sleep-like trance induced by repeated commands and mental concentration in which the subject acts only on the suggestions of the hypnotist. In such a state, subjects are sometimes able to recall long-forgotten memories and experiences, and hypnosis is a useful tool in various kinds of therapy. The word *hypnosis* was coined in 1843 by Dr. James Braid, who used a common technique of having his patients gaze steadily at a bright object. Medical hypnosis can be used to induce *anesthesia* (without feeling) for everything from tooth extractions to minor surgery.

Hypnosis has also been called *mesmerism* after Friedrich Anton Mesmer (1734-1815). He thought the effects were produced by a kind of invisible energy, or fluid, which passed from the hypnotist to the subject. Comparing this force with that of a magnet, Mesmer called it "animal magnetism."

Hypnosis seems to awaken the same kind of right-hemisphere consciousness we experience in dreams. In this state, all critical faculties go right out the window. Hypnotized subjects are incredibly suggestible—believing anything they are told by the hypnotist, and acting accordingly. Old-time stage hypnotists often used such suggestion to make people believe they were animals, and people would run around the stage on all fours barking like dogs to the amusement of the audience. This is because of the very different types of logic used by the different brain hemispheres.

Our left brain—in which we experience normal waking consciousness—operates with *deductive logic,* reasoning from the specific to the general. This is the kind of scientific problem-solving thinking made famous by Sherlock Holmes and modern detectives. Our right brain, however, works on *inductive logic,* reasoning from the general to the specific. This is the kind of thinking we often call "suspension of disbelief," as when we are dreaming, or utterly absorbed in a movie or novel. No matter how bizarre and preposterous a thing might happen, we just don't ever think to go, "Hey, waaiit a minute—that's not possible!" In inductive logic we just take whatever comes up as a given, and fill in all the blanks to back it up. And under hypnosis, our left brain consciousness is suppressed, and we operate out of our right brains. This is called the "Theory of Relative Psychic Exclusion."

Hypnotism has been known from ancient times and practiced as a secret technique of magick. Many enchantments and bewitchments have been accomplished through hypnosis—and post-hypnotic suggestion, wherein a previously hypnotized subject continues to act unawares on commands received while in trance.

Guided Meditations are scripted visualizations in which a person in a light hypnotic trance is told a story in the second person ("You are walking along a path, and you come to a…"). It's almost like going on a role-playing game adventure. Such guided meditations can be used to take you to places both real and imaginary—such as forgotten experiences of your early childhood. As such, this is a very useful technique in modern psychotherapy. There are whole books and tapes of such scripts, used to help people in many ways.

Lesson 3: Color-Coded Magickal Practices

In Class III, Lesson 7: "Color-Coded Wizardry," I listed several categories of magick and Wizardry according to their associated colors. Practitioners specializing in one of these areas may be known by that color, as Gandalf the Grey. Here is a bit more about these color-coded practices—in order of their position in the Spectrum. Later on in this Grimoire, I'll have a whole Class on each of them.

Meditation (Aqua Magick) (5.I)

Meditation is the basis of most of the Eastern disciplines of magick and Wizardry. I'm sure you have seen Masters meditating in movies, especially those involving martial arts. Properly used, meditation opens the door to individual growth and personal advancement. Of all the techniques of advancement in the psychic and spiritual fields, meditation is by far the most effective.

Healing (Blue Magick) (5.II)

Healing refers to all forms of magickal arts and practices devoted to curing diseases, relieving aches and pains, promoting tissue regeneration, restoring vitality and fertility, etc. Throughout history, healers have been the folk doctors, nurses, and midwives—especially in rural and "primitive" communities without access to officially licensed physicians and pharmacists.

Wortcunning (Green Magick) (5.III)

Herbalism is the lore and art of knowing and using the magickal, medicinal, and other properties of plants. The old word used for the knowledge of the secret properties of herbs is *Wortcunning* ("herbal wisdom"), and this has always been a particular study of Witches.

Divination (Yellow Magick) (5.IV)

Divination is the art of foretelling or predicting the future; or discovering things that are lost, hidden, or secret. Although not all seers were Wizards, all Wizards are expected to be seers. Many ancient peoples were completely obsessed with divination and would hardly make a move without consulting diviners, seers, oracles, or prophets. Unusual occurrences, such as disturbing dreams and *omens,* were also given divinatory meanings—this is where we get our word *ominous.* Over the ages, seers have devised many techniques of divination—called the *Mantic Arts* (from *mantis,* meaning "diviner").

Illusion (Orange Magick) (5.V)

Also called stage magic and performance magic, this area deals with "miraculous" illusions and special effects. Illusion magick is often divided into two categories: *legerdemain* (conjuring) and *prestidigitation* (sleight-of-hand). Designed to amaze and mystify onlookers, the arts of Illusion originated with the first Shamans. Special effects have been used in enhancing the theater of ritual since the first campfire was lit. Various types of performance, such as magic acts, acrobatics, juggling, puppetry, and fire-eating all came from such rituals.

Alchemy (Red Magick) (5.VI)

Alchemy is the magickal art and science of transformation and transmutation. Alchemy was the forerunner of modern chemistry, originating in Alexandria, Egypt, during the 1st century CE, when Egyptian metallurgy was fused with Greek philosophy and Middle Eastern mysticism. Medieval Alchemists pursued three basic objectives: the Transmutation of "base metals" (particularly lead) into gold and silver; the discovery of the Elixir of Life that would heal all ills and bestow immortality; and the creation of the *homunculus,* an artificial man.

Beast Mastery (Brown Magick) (6.I)

Beast Mastery concerns everything to do with animals of all kinds—especially animal communication. Beast Masters include "horse whisperers," animal trainers, pet psychics, and all people who seem to have an uncanny ability to communicate and work with animals. Beast Mastery includes knowledge of zoology and the lore of Totems. Beast Masters seek to know the names of all animals, as well as how they evolved, what they eat, their behaviors, lifestyles, mating rituals, and languages.

Cosmology (Violet Magick) (6.II)

The great bowl of the night sky—the Celestial Sphere—that surrounds our tiny world has always been a subject of magickal and Wizardly studies. "Connecting the dots" of the stars to form constellations elevated our earliest myths and legends into the heavens. The fixed position of the Pole Star amid the celestial rotation gave us a firm bearing in all seasons. The movements of the Sun, Moon, and planets through the signs of the Zodiac gave us our calendar, our first way of keeping time, and our earliest form of effective Divination.

Mathemagicks (Clear Magick) (6.III)

The Pythagorean Mysteries laid the foundation for all mathematics, particularly arithmetic, geometry, and music. Their motto was: "All is Number." According to Pythagoras, everything in the Universe is based upon the same fundamental "blueprints" created by geometric patterns that repeat over and over in an endless dance of sound, light, and color. These patterns form a matrix of grid energy derived from a central source. They create the entire natural world and allow us to experience duality, emotions, linear time, and all the reality we experience.

Ceremonial Magick (White Magick) (6.IV)

Ceremonial Magick, originating in the 17th and 18th centuries within secret magickal orders, is based upon both the Qabalah and the Hermetica, along with Neo-Platonism and Oriental doctrines. In its highest sense, Ceremonial Magick is a transcendental experience that takes the magician into mystical realms and into communication with the Higher Self. It awakens the magician to the God within.

Lore Mastery (Grey Magick) (6.V)

Lore means "teachings," and Lore Mastery is the primary attribute of the Wizard. Throughout history, Wizards have studied and collected books and writings containing the wisdom of the ages, and many have assembled important libraries and museums. Lore mastery is all about knowing *arcane* (hidden) secrets and esoteric mysteries known to very few others. It is said that "knowledge is power," and much of a Wizard's true power comes from his vast knowledge. Lore, however, is more than merely secrets and mysteries. A very important body of lore concerns myths and legends; a Lore-Master is also a storyteller, who can always come up with a tale to make any point.

Sorcery and Demonology (Black Magick) (6.VI)

The simplest form of Low Magick is *sorcery,* in which a physical act is performed to achieve a result. Sorcery forms the bulk of folk magick, and is often referred to as "Black Magick" or "the Dark Arts." Sorcery is also sometimes called *sympathetic magick,* based on the principle that all things are linked together by invisible bonds (the "Law of Sympathy"). *Demonology* is a form of sorcery popular in the Middle Ages and Renaissance, in which the aid of demons was enlisted by the magician. Although thought to be easier to control than angels, demons could be dangerous and malicious, and the old grimoires contained detailed instructions for conjuring and controlling them. Another form of "Black Magick" is *Necromancy,* in which the spirits of the dead are conjured up for consultation.

Black Magick itself is not necessarily evil, any more than any other color. But while all magickal folk practice some forms of sorcery, few actually identify themselves as Sorcerers. Those who do are generally engaged in attempting to control others and rule the world. The primary distinction between a Sorcerer and a Wizard thus lies in the realm of service: A Wizard desires to be of service *to* others; a Sorcerer desires to be served *by* others. Often, powerful Wizards and Sorcerers will find themselves standing in opposition as each other's *nemesis* (ultimate enemy).

Lesson 4: A Brief History of Magick and Wizardry in the Western World

Magick is universal. There is not a single culture or society on Earth that does not practice it and have its own special classes of practitioners. Every tribe and village in every land has its Shamans, Sorcerers, "Witch Doctors," and Medicine Men/Women. In Asia, India, China, and throughout the Far East, magick has been raised to a high art. However, along with the magick of tribal peoples, Far Eastern magick is beyond the scope of this book and will have to be deferred to a later edition.

Among the great classical pre-Christian civilizations of the Mediterranean and Middle East, the ancient Egyptians, Hebrews, Babylonians, Persians, Greeks, Romans, and Druids had magickal systems that greatly influenced the later development of magick in the Western World, and it is this heritage that I wish to present here.

Egypt (2700–50 BCE)

In Egypt, the Pharaohs were considered divine kings in possession of innate magickal abilities. As in many systems, there were two classes of magicians.

The most esteemed were the trained Priests, professional magicians who acted as substitutes for the Pharaoh in the performance of all necessary magical services. These included the *Viziers,* or Court Wizards, such as Imhotep and Dedi of Dedsnefru. The second class was the *lay magicians,* the equivalent of folk magicians, healers, and Wizards. The Egyptian god of Magick was Thoth, or Tehuti, depicted as a baboon or an ibis. From Egyptian magick came the concept of the power of sacred names, which greatly influenced European magick during the Middle Ages and Renaissance.

Hebrews (1630–587 BCE)

Although strict Judaic law prohibited all practices of divination and sorcery, two of the greatest figures in the Old Testament—Moses and Solomon—are also famed as among the greatest Wizards of all time. Moses is said to have established a secret magickal school called the Tabernacle Mysteries. The first five books of the Bible (the *Pentateuch*) are known to Jews as the *Torah* ("Law") and were believed to have been written by Moses himself. With their elaborate rules and detailed instructions, it is thought that they were intended as symbolic allegories and parables. The keys to their symbolism, as taught by the Tabernacle Mysteries, constitute the Jewish *Qabalah.*

King Solomon commanding the Djinn; Jacobus de Teramo, 1473

Solomon was King of Israel in the 10th century BCE and the builder of the Great Temple. Renowned for his wisdom and wealth, and his long and prosperous reign, Solomon flourished in legend as a master Wizard. Talmudic legends tell how the wise monarch exercised dominion over the beasts of the field, the birds of the air, and assorted demons and supernatural spirits by the power of his magick ring. It was said he employed demons in building the Temple, and from them and other inhabitants of the invisible world he secured much of his wisdom. *The Key of Solomon* and other magickal texts were attributed to him. According to Jewish Talmudic scholars, Solomon mastered the mysteries of the *Qabalah.* He was also famed as an alchemist and necromancer.

Babylonia (612–538 BCE)

The name *Babylon* means "Gate of the Gods." The Babylonians specialized in astronomy, astrology, and mathematics. We still use their numbering system today. They kept precise records of planetary motions and cosmic events—such as eclipses, comets, novas, planetary retrogrades, etc. They also devised countless varieties of mystic sigils, amulets, charms, and talismans that continue to be used by modern magicians. The Babylonian priesthood was educated and secretive. They believed that all illness came from displeasing the Gods. Long and complex rituals were performed only for wealthy and socially prominent people, by high-degreed priests of the state Temple. "Low" temples were available for cult statues, where the deity resided and received worship.

Persia (539–331 BCE)

The word *magick* itself comes from the Zoroastrian priests of ancient Persia, who were called *Magi.* They reached their greatest renown during the time of the Persian Empire (539–331 BCE). Followers of Zoroaster (born c. 570 BCE), the Magi were famous for their powers of healing and divination—especially astrology. They believed that the cosmos was both alive and divine, and they revered the planets, stars, and other heavenly bodies. They also honored the four Elements—Earth, Air, Fire, and Water. Ahura Mazda was the Zoroastrian god of goodness, wisdom, and truth, and was opposed by the evil Ahriman. Zoroastrian beliefs had a profound effect on Judaism—especially concerning matters of the Afterlife—and these ideas passed over into Christianity. Zoroastrianism continues today in the faith of the Parsees of India and Iran.

Greece (480–323 BCE)

The Greeks developed a system and philosophies of magick, which were greatly influenced by concepts

imported from Egypt, the Middle East, and Asia. The Greek god of Magick was Hermes, giving us the name of Hermetic magick. Like the Egyptians, the Greeks envisioned magick as divided into two classes: High and Low. Throughout the Greco-Roman world, the most influential forces were the Oracles, dedicated to various Gods. At these ancient sites, specially trained priestesses would deliver notoriously ambiguous responses to questions. Also during this period, various forms of divination were in constant use, most notably that of examining the *entrails* (guts—especially the liver) of slaughtered livestock to discern the will of the gods. Greece was also the home of several significant initiatory mysteries, the most famous being those of Eleusis, which enacted the story of the grain goddess Demeter, her daughter Kore the flower-maiden, and Hades Lord of the Underworld, who abducts Kore each Fall to become Persephone, his bride and Queen.

The Druids (600 BCE–500 CE)

Throughout Gaul and the British Isles, the educated priest caste of the Celtic peoples was the Druids. *Dru* means "Truth," as in "Truth-Knower." The title may also have a connection to oak and is sometimes said to mean "oak priest." Druids regarded fire and water as the original building blocks of creation, and trees as sacred along with stones, animals, birds, plants, and the unseen spirits of the Otherworld. They honored the Gods and Goddesses of the Celtic peoples and celebrated the Cross Quarter festivals of Beltaine, Lughnasadh, Samhain, and Imbolg. Both men and women, their skills included codifying laws, dispute resolution, the bardic arts, healing, sacred story-telling, genealogy, mathematics, astronomy, divination, philosophy, politics, teaching, administering justice, ritual, and magickal work. Druids legitimized and presided over the crowning of the High Kings of Ireland at Tara.

Druids cutting sacred mistletoe in the oak forest

The Celtic culture originally coalesced in eastern Europe (Black Sea area, Danube basin), moving ever westward. For a thousand years or more, the Celtic religion and culture covered most of Europe, from the Western shores of France and Brittany to the Black Sea, and from Germany to northern Spain and northern Italy. The Druids and their religion were thus the spiritual foremothers and forefathers of Europe as we know it. They were heavily persecuted under Roman rule, but the Romans never got to Ireland or north of the Antonine wall in Scotland, and Druids persisted in many areas. Bardic schools continued well into the 17th century.

Rome (735 BCE–455 CE)

A principal Roman god of Magick was Mercury, the messenger of the gods. The Romans used sorcery and counter-sorcery to defeat rivals and advance them politically and materially. Though sorcery was popular with the public, the private practice of it was greatly feared by those in authority, and harsh laws were passed against it. The Cornelian Law proclaimed: "Soothsayers, enchanters, and those who make use of sorcery for evil purposes; those who conjure up demons, who disrupt the elements, who employ waxen images destructively, shall be punished by death." These same attitudes were preserved in the Medieval Christian Church.

Medieval Europe (455–1400 CE)

Because magick connected people to their pre-Christian Pagan beliefs and traditions, the Christian Church worked diligently to separate magick from religion. The use of magick by the people was prohibited, while the Church itself adopted what it found useful and systematically banned the rest. In western Europe, most villages had healers, herbalists, and midwives. These practitioners, called Witches, were frequently women. Their arts were called Low Magick (humble, accessible) as opposed to High Magick (exalted, elite) such as Alchemy. Such women, who continued to follow the Old Ways, were targeted for persecution by the Church's *Canon Episcopi,* issued c. 900: "Some wicked women are perverted by the Devil and led astray by illusions and fantasies induced by demons, so that they believe that they ride out at night on beasts with Diana, the pagan goddess, and a horde of women. They believe that in the silence of the night they cross huge distance.... They say that they

Diana's commands and on certain nights are called into her service."

Despite the Church's bans on magick, alchemy flourished in Europe from the 7th to the 17th centuries. Based on the *Hermetica,* alchemy traced its origins to ancient Egypt. When Arabs conquered Egypt in the 7th century, they adopted Egyptian alchemy and carried it into Morocco and Spain. Less than 200 years later, Spain was the center of alchemical studies. Soon this science was spread throughout Europe. From about the 8th to 16th centuries, various forms of Medieval magick emerged from a renewal of Neo-Platonism, Qabalistic, and Oriental doctrines brought back to Europe by the Crusaders. Medieval magick coalesced as a system in the 12th century. The Knights Templar, formed in 1118, developed a magickal system learned from the Johannites sect in Jerusalem.

Magicians of Europe were learned men, scholars, physicians, and alchemists. Their magick consisted of intricate procedures involving dress, consecrated tools, magical symbols, and sacred names of power to summon and banish various spirits. The unspeakable name of the Hebrew God, Yahweh, known as the *Tetragrammaton* ("four letters:" YHVH), became the most potent name.

Magicians and Wizards were not troubled much by the Church until the 13th century, with the establishment of the Inquisition. In the 13th and 14th centuries, Aristotelian philosophy gained favor over Platonic philosophy. Under Aristotelian thought, no natural magick exists in the world; therefore magick must be either divine or demonic. By the 15th century, magicians—seen as competitors to the Church—were harassed and hounded, though never to the same degree as sorcerers and Witches, who were brutally tortured and executed by the thousands for heresy. The centuries of persecution—from 1227 to 1736—are remembered by magickal folk as "The Burning Times."

The Renaissance (1400-1605 CE)

The term "Wizard" first came into use in 1440 and was at that time applied to both wise women and wise men. Virtually every village or town in Britain and Europe had at least one Wizard, who was usually both respected and feared by the local folk. The village Wizard specialized in Low Magick, offering a variety of mag-ickal services, such as fortune-telling, finding missing persons and objects, finding hidden treasure, curing illnesses in people and animals, interpreting dreams, detecting theft, exorcising ghosts and Faeries, casting spells, breaking the spells of Faeries and malevolent Witches, and making lucky charms and love potions. As the diviner of the guilty in crimes, the word of the Wizard often carried great weight in a village or town.

Medieval magick reached a peak in the Renaissance in the 16th century under Cornelius Agrippa von Nettesheim and Paracelsus in Europe, and John Dee and Robert Fludd in England. Agrippa's *De Occulta Philosophia* ("On the Occult Philosophy") dealt with divine names, natural magick, and cosmology. Paracelsus stressed the Hermetic doctrine of "As above, so below," which holds that the microcosm of the Earth reflects the macrocosm of the Universe. Fludd, a Qabalist, attempted to reconcile Neo-Platonic and Aristotelian philosophies and relate them to the Qabalah.

During the Renaissance, the Wizard as High Magician was an intellectual who pursued alchemy and the Hermetic wisdom. They studied and followed the teachings of Agrippa, Paracelsus, Dee, the Neoplatonic philosophers, and others. Wizards read the Grimoires, invoked spirits in ceremonial rituals, and scryed in crystals. Often such High Magick Wizards served as special counselors and advisors (*viziers*) to noted royalty. Queen Elizabeth I was served by John Dee as "Court Wizard" and advisor. With his partner, Edward Kelly, Dee developed the system of *Enochian* magick, a language comprised of calls for summoning spirits and traveling in the astral planes.

The Age of Reason (1605-1900 CE)

In the 16th and 17th centuries, the word "Wizard" applied to high magicians and also to various popular magicians, who were known by other names as well: cunning men and women, charmers, blessers, sorcerers, conjurers, and Witches. But in the mid-17th century, Wizardry of both folk and High Magick began to decline in prestige, retreating from urban centers to the countryside. In 1662, the Royal Academy of Science was founded in England. This was the beginning

From title page of Christopher Marlowe's The Tragicall Historie of the Life and Death of Doctor Faustus, *1631*

of the separation of Magick from the Mundane World, as the Academy redefined the disciplines, casting out all that they deemed "unscientific" and therefore "false." Astronomy was separated from astrology, physics from metaphysics, and chemistry from alchemy. With this division, the left hemisphere of human experience was severed from the right, and Western civilization became blind in one eye.

In the magickal world, the 17th and 18th centuries witnessed a popularity of secret magical orders, such as the Freemasons and Rosicrucians. Their rituals were based on the Hermetica, Mystery schools, the tarot, interpretations of the Qabalah, and astrology. Various Grimoires, containing detailed instructions for magickal rites, circulated widely. The most important of these, still used today, is the *Key of Solomon,* in existence as early as the 1st century CE. During the 17th and 18th centuries, modern Ceremonial Magick had its beginnings. This is a complex art of dealing with spirits. It requires a rigorous discipline and has an intellectual appeal. Ceremonial magicians derived power from the Judeo-Christian God through the control of spirits, usually demons. They believed demons were easier to control than angels. In its highest sense, Ceremonial Magick is a transcendental experience that takes the magician into mystical realms and communication with the Higher Self.

High Magick enjoyed a great revival of interest at the beginning of the 19th century with the publication of Francis Barrett's *The Magus* (1801). The revival was greatly influenced by Eliphas Levi, whose explanation of how magick works in *Dogma and Ritual of High Magic* (1856) has had a lasting impact on the thinking of magicians. Levi put forth three Laws of Magic: Willpower, Astral Light, and "As above, so below." Other factors contributing to the rise of ceremonial magick were Spiritualism and Theosophy, both involving communication with spirits and the dead. Folk-magick Wizardry continued to be predominantly a rural phenomenon. After 1825, the word Wizard became almost synonymous with Witch, but its usage later declined during the 20th century.

Modern Times (after 1900)

Perhaps the greatest system of Western Ceremonial Magick was devised by the Hermetic Order of the Golden Dawn, founded in England by three Rosicrucians in the late 19th century. The Golden Dawn expanded upon Levi's writings, adding a fourth Law, Imagination, without which the Will was ineffective. The Golden Dawn had a great influence on Aleister Crowley, thought by some to be the greatest magician of the 20th century. His major contribution to Magick was the popularization of Rabelais' *Law of Thelema:* "Do what thou wilt shall be the whole of the law." Another magickal group which has influenced modern magick is the *Ordo Templi Orientis* (O.T.O.—the "Order of the Temple of the Orient"), founded at the beginning of the 20th century by a German, Karl Kellner, and devoted to Tantric sex magic. The 1950s saw the public emergence of Witchcraft, spearheaded by Gerald Garner, an Englishman who published several books, devised various rituals, and initiated numerous Witches.

In the final third of the 20th century there occurred a great Renaissance of Magick, Witchcraft, and Paganism. From the 1960's onward, many new magickal groups were founded, and the numbers of practitioners swelled from hundreds to millions. Vast numbers of books on various aspects of magick were produced, supporting an entire new industry of "occult" publishers and bookstores. And finally, at the dawn of the 21st century, Wizardry once more came into public recognition with the publication of the *Harry Potter* books and films, and the brilliant *Lord of the Rings* movies.

Class V: Magickal Talents

1. Introduction: Gifts and Talents

LIKE MANY OF YOU, I WAS NOT BORN into a magickal family. But I was a natural mageborn, and I was always seeking my magickal heritage. As a young Wiz-kid, I became quite obsessed with the whole idea of magickal talents and psychic abilities. I read a lot of mythology, fairy tales, science fiction and fantasy, and in those stories, characters often had, like Superman, "powers and abilities far beyond those of mortal men." Long before I found others like myself or the magickal community, I began studying everything I could find about psychic phenomena. And as I learned about each of those talents that had been cataloged, I began to practice trying to develop them in myself. Since I had no teacher in those days to instruct and train me in the Magickal Arts, I had to make up my own exercises and training programs, and I was much more successful with some than with others.

2. Glossary: A Catalog of Psychic Talents

There are many varieties of psychic talents and phenomena. Almost everyone experiences some of these occasionally in their lives. The more gifted or trained you are, the stronger these abilities may manifest. In many cases, such talents come into effect around the time of puberty, when they may become quite strong. This is the best time to begin an Apprenticeship in Magick, and among magickal folk, this may be a time for a Rite of Passage.

The *scientific method* requires systematic observation, study, theories, and experiments that can be tested and reproduced. This presents a problem when examining the psi-sciences, as it is difficult to "make" telepathy occur on demand, under controlled circumstances. Psi-abilities are very real but usually manifest best when manifesting organically.

Here is a list of some of the most important psychic Gifts and talents. While I've never heard of anyone being able to do all of them, many people can do one or more—and as a Wizard's Apprentice, you can learn to do a number of these. I'll offer you some exercises like those I used to do, and if you practice, I think you'll be amazed at what you'll be able to do.

Empathy— "Feeling" someone else's emotions, or another's physical pain and/or symptoms. *Empaths* come in two flavors: *receiving* and *projecting.* Receiving empaths "pick up" what others are feeling. When others around you are happy or sad, so are you. Projecting empaths "infect" others with their own emotions. If you're a projecting empath, when you're happy or sad, so is everyone else around you. While essential for compassion and healing, Empathy is important to learn to control, as it is easy for an empath to lose your sense of boundaries—not knowing where you leave off and others begin.

Telepathy— This word means literally "remote feeling," which would seem to make it the same as empathy. But *telepathy* is the word used for direct mind-to-mind communication of thoughts and images, rather than just feelings. Telepathy involves "hearing" the thoughts of others ("mind reading"), or being able to project your thoughts to others.

Psychokinesis (SY-ko-kin-EE-sis)— "Mind moving." Moving or influencing objects without touching them physically. This is one of the rarest and most difficult psi-talents. When it occurs over some distance, it may be called *telekinesis* ("remote motion"). This sometimes spontaneously appears in cases of troubled teens during puberty, in homes with much dissonance or abuse (see *Poltergeist*).

Pyrokinesis (PY-ro-kin-EE-sis)— "Fire moving." Starting or controlling fires by force of mind alone. People who can do this are known as *Firestarters.*

Poltergeist (POL-ter-gyst)— This word means "noisy ghost." It refers to spontaneous *psychokinesis* and mysterious noises that often seem like hauntings. These phenomena are commonly (though not always) associated with adolescents going through major and traumatic psychological changes—especially around puberty and sexuality—when psychic powers may rage completely out of control.

Healing— The ability to reduce pain and inflammation, facilitate tissue regeneration, and other healing. Usually done with a "laying on of hands."

Clairsentience (klair-SEN-tee-ence)— "Clear awareness." The ability to sense or be aware of things beyond the "normal" range of perception. Each type of "clear sensing" has a name:

Clairvoyance— "Clear vision." The ability to "see" things that are not in sight or cannot be seen. Sometimes this word is used for particularly keen insight.

Clairaudience— "Clear hearing." The ability to "hear" things that are not within hearing range or cannot normally be heard. Also the sensitivity to pick up inner voices or subtle audio input.

Clairkinesthesia (klair-kin-es-THEE-zha)— "Clear touching." The ability to "feel" a sense of physical touch and pressure from nothing present.

Clairolfaction—"Clear smelling." The ability to smell, or be aware of, scents and perfumes that are not physically present, or from other dimensions.

Clairgustance—"Clear tasting." The ability to taste, or be aware of, flavors that are not physically present, or from other dimensions.

Psychometry (sy-KOM-e-tree)—The ability to know the history of a personal object by vibrations and touch. Psychics who work with the police are often *psychometrists* who can "see" a crime or identify a criminal from touching a murder weapon or other associated object. Psychometry is also used by some advanced psychics and healers who have the ability to read disease or physical symptoms in a person's body, even in persons they have never met, by touching an object that has been handled or worn by the person. When reading objects in this way, the psychic often "feels" the symptoms in his own body.

Precognition (pre-kog-NI-shun)—"Fore-knowledge." Knowing or sensing that something is going to happen before it actually comes to pass. This may occur in "True Dreams" or waking visions. Often the precognitive messages are jumbled, and there is not real clarity of the experience that is to come, just of its "flavor."

Déjà vu (DAY-zha-VOO)—"Already seen." The eerie feeling of having "been here before." A sudden uncanny sense of recognition of a place or events that you have no conscious knowledge of ever having visited or experienced previously. Some instances of *déjà vu* might be the result of "remembering" precognitive dreams. And sometimes people will jokingly say *"Vujà Dé!"* to mean "I have never been anywhere even remotely like this before!"

Astral Projection— Traveling "out of the body." This is also called *transvection.* This may be as in a dream, where you travel to some distant place or dimension. Or it may be an experience of rising out of your body and looking down on it, as often happens in near-death experiences.

Dreamwalking—Entering someone else's dream as a conscious visitor. The dreamer may or may not see and remember the dreamwalker.

Teleportation—"Remote transportation." Disappearing from one place and instantly reappearing somewhere else. The transportation of matter through space by converting it into energy and then re-converting it back into matter at the terminal point, like the transporters in Star Trek. This can also manifest as the person's astral body appearing elsewhere.

Levitation—Literally, the opposite of *gravitation,* as in anti-gravity. Lifting yourself or other objects off the ground unsupported by physical means. Levitation is a popular Illusion for performance magicians.

Possession—Entering into someone else's mind, whereby you see and hear through his senses. A possessing entity (whether human or otherwise) may or may not "take over" and control the body of the one possessed—with or without his knowledge. When this is done with animals, it is called "Borrowing."

Time Travel—Projecting your consciousness into the past or future—generally by entering into the mind of someone in that time. You might travel through time with a familiar, or as yourself.

Channeling—Deliberately pulling your own consciousness out of "the driver's seat," and allowing another consciousness to possess and speak through you while you have no awareness. People who do this regularly are called *Mediums* or *Channels.* Some work primarily with spirits of the dead, and some with non-human entities, such as animal spirits or space aliens.

Invisibility—The ability to not be noticed or seen by others. Many call it "cloaking." Another way of becoming invisible is by "sidestepping" in space.

Shape-Shifting—Temporarily "becoming" some other person or creature by mimicking their physical appearance, movements, behavior, speech, and vocalizations—even to the extent that others perceive you as that being. This might include dressing up in an animal costume and walking on all fours, or sitting on your haunches and howling at the moon. Sometimes shape-shifting may be accomplished through possession ("borrowing"), telepathy, or empathy—actually "entering into" the subject. *"Were-"* creatures, such as werewolves, are shape-shifters who may or may not be conscious of their alter-form. Those who become animals deliberately may be called *animorphs* or *animages.*

"The Voice"—A powerful "tone of command" that elicits instant unthinking compliance from others. The "Bene Gesserit" of *Dune* are an excellent example. Military officers and police are particularly trained in the use of The Voice, as are strong Mages and High Priest/esses.

Lesson 3: Meditation and Visualization

When I was a boy, I used to practice memorizing the layout of spaces, such as the interior of my house, a stretch of sidewalk, or a familiar part of the woods. Then, while holding that image firmly in my mind, as if it were a map, I would close my eyes and walk through the space, "seeing" and navigating it according to my memory. As I came to where I visualized various objects should be, I would stop and reach out to touch them. If they weren't where I expected them to be, I would open my eyes, go back to my starting point, and begin over. This was one of my earliest exercises in *visualization,* an essential magickal skill. I recommend you try it…

Here are a few more exercises to practice that will help you develop some of the psychic talents described above. Don't try these all at once; you don't even have to do all of them. But if you are interested in learning how to do some of these things, and if you have any natural Gifts in these areas, these exercises will help you. And remember, the more you practice, the better you'll become!

Body Control

Take every opportunity to practice body control in your everyday life. If you feel tired, force yourself to go on just a little longer before resting. If you feel hungry, don't eat for an extra half-hour. If you feel thirsty, don't drink for awhile. Practice walking a balance beam. Take gymnastics. Do handstands, somersaults, and backflips. Learn to juggle balls and spin fire. Become a good dancer.

When I was a boy in school, I would practice holding my breath, using the big clock on the wall to time myself. I practiced constantly, and eventually I got so I could go four minutes without breathing. As I was still growing at the time, these exercises increased my lung capacity tremendously. Now, 50 years later, I can still swim underwater the entire length of an Olympic-size swimming pool, and I can stay down for longer than anybody else when diving for abalone off the Califia Coast.

Another kind of body control is mastering your facial muscles. I practiced for hours in front of mirror to learn how to raise and lower my eyebrows independently, wiggle my ears, dilate my nostrils, achieve certain emotional expressions, etc. All good actors practice in this way, and you should, too.

Meditation

Meditation is the most important foundational skill to learn, as it will help you to be able to do many other things. I'm sure you have seen Masters meditating in movies, especially those involving martial arts. What you are trying to do in meditation is to completely "center" yourself into a still and focused place where you are perfectly balanced and in tune with your body and your surroundings. From this center point, you will then be able to move in any direction in mind and body—even through time and between dimensions.

Sit or lie in a comfortable position and relax your body completely. Then observe yourself carefully to note any muscles that start to become restless. Allow such muscles to consciously relax, and do the same for any other groups of muscles—but don't fall asleep! Complete and total relaxation is your goal. Use a timer, starting off with five minutes the first day, then increase your meditation period another five minutes each day until you can completely relax for half an hour.

When you are able to do this, go to 5.1: "Meditation" for further instructions and exercises…

Lesson 4. Seeing & Reading Auras

When you have become skilled at meditation and visualization, you will be ready to learn to see *auras.* Auras are the fields of *biomagnetic energy* that emanate from and envelop all living things. Like the Earth Herself, each of us is a living field generator. Since we're not spinning on our axis like the Earth, our field poles are not generated by rotation, but are more like those of a magnet. One pole, called the *Crown Chakra,* is at the top of our heads, right at the juncture of the three large skull bones (frontal and parietals) that come together there (when we are babies, this point is actually an open hole!). The opposite pole—called the *Root Chakra*—is at the base of our spine, right at the tip of our tailbone.

Just like the Earth's *magnetosphere,* with its Van Allen Belts, our auras form several layers, based on energy levels. The first layer, extending about an inch out from our skin, is called the *etheric body.* Because it is the densest layer, it is also the easiest to learn to see. The next layer is called the *astral body*, and it extends another several inches further. Beyond the astral body are the *mental* and *spiritual* bodies. These are very high-energy and elastic, and their limits can vary under differing circumstances.

Perhaps you know of the *Aurora Borealis,* or "Northern Lights" that fill the skies of northern countries with brilliant, shimmering ethereal "curtains," "spears," and dancing "flames" of rainbow-colored light. Around the South Pole, these are called *Aurora Australis,* or "Southern Lights." These awe-inspiring displays are caused by the ionization (stripping away the electrons) of particles from the Solar Wind as they are sucked into the circular "event horizons" of the

Earth's magnetic field around the magnetic poles. This is just like what happens inside a fluorescent light, including a "black light." Your etheric body, then, is equivalent to the Earth's auroras. And if you learn how to look for it, it can be just as visible.

Magickal Exercise: Seeing Auras

The aura around the head is called the *nimbus;* around the whole body it is called the *aureole*. Have a friend sit in front of a blank wall or curtain—something tan, beige, or off-white is best. Have the lighting be low, with the light source out of your view (a few candles can work well). Sit about ten feet back, settle yourself into a light meditative state, and stare blankly at your friend's "third eye"—right between the eyebrows. As you do so, open your eyes wide and let them go into a soft focus, as if you are actually focusing on a spot about halfway between you. You may find this easier to do by hanging a white thread from the ceiling at this distance, and focusing on it. Breathe smoothly and maintain your off-focus. After a bit, you will begin to see a clear light outlining your friend's head, as if they were glowing softly. But if you shift your focus to try and see it more clearly, it will disappear. The trick is to not look directly *at* the aura, but rather catch it at the edges of your vision.

Practice this awhile until you can do it easily. Then try the same thing under differing lighting, different backgrounds, and with different people. Eventually, you will be able to see auras around anyone—in school, on the bus, in restaurants and theatres. And when you can see auras around people, you will be able to see them also around pets, plants, and especially trees (which have enormous auras!)

What you will have learned to perceive in this way is the etheric aura. As your perceptions improve, you can also learn to detect the energy that radiates into the astral body and beyond. You may be able to see it flowing, ebbing, wavering, and shimmering like the Earth's Aurora. With practice, you may become able to see colors, which can indicate a person's emotional or physical condition. Any state of the individual's being causes reactions in the aura. Emotional states will primarily affect the color. Physical conditions not only affect color, but also cause peculiarities in the patterns of the aura, such as ragged edges or holes over injuries or sore spots. Learning to see these patterns will be of great use if you become a Healer.... (See 5.II.4: "Auric Healing.")

Seeing the colors of auras takes considerably more skill than merely perceiving a glowing light around someone. And such colors, when they are perceived, will be very individual to the perceiver. You and a friend may both learn to see aura colors, but they may seem to be different to each of you. This is normal. With time and practice, you will learn your own system of what these colors mean to you.

> ***NOTE:*** *Don't feel bad if you simply cannot manage to "see" these auras, no matter how much you try. Just as some people are color-blind, or tone-deaf (as I am), we may develop some senses more strongly than others. After all, what we sense and experience really occurs in our brains, not actually in our eyes and ears. You may find that you can sense auras in other ways—"feeling" them, perhaps, or "hearing" a hum around people....*

Magickal Exercises: Controlling your Aura

Seeing the auras of others is a passive exercise. Now here are some exercises for you to actively expand and contract your own aura.

Hold your hand out in front of you, back towards you and fingers spread wide, as if you were pushing something away. Use the same technique you have just learned to see the aura of your hand and fingers. Now start breathing intensely, rapidly in and out, through your nose. Without changing your position, tense your muscles, and stare at your aura as if your eyes could emit laser beams. As if you are turning up a burner on the stove, focus your intention on "pumping up" your aura, so that it seems to "burn" brighter and brighter. Visualize the auras lengthening from your fingertips, extending like the flames of a blowtorch as you level your hand and point your fingers away. Then, when you have extended them as far as you can, suck in a deep breath, and retract them back to the normal glow as you slowly close your fingers into a loose fist. Practice this over and over. If you have friends to work with, you should each take turns practicing pumping up, extending, and retracting your auras while the other watches. This will help each of you learn to both see and control your auras.

Tractor beams and repulsor beams: When you have practiced this technique enough to get good at it, you will be ready to try projecting psychic *tractor beams* and *repulsor beams*. It's just a matter of extending and retracting your aura. As you forcefully extend it, use it to push against (repulse) anything before it. And as you retract it, use it to suck in (attract) stuff in the same way. Also, for practice, try just reaching out with your aura and "tapping" someone on the shoulder; see if you can get them to turn around!

Candle flames: Light a candle in a darkened room, and practice using your auric tractor and repulsor beams to affect the flame. Make it flicker, flare up, or die down. As you get better at this, keep moving the candle further and further away from you, until you can affect the flame from across the room.

Smoke weaving: I attend quite a few magickal gatherings where the campfire is the center of all activity (more on this later, in the Classes on "Back to Nature" and "Rites and Rituals"). Around such campfires, the smoke can often become a problem as it drifts into our faces. When the smoke begins to drift to my side of the fire, I use both hands to weave and shape it away from me, and to direct it straight up. To do this, I spread all my fingers, extending their auras. Like a potter shaping clay on a wheel into a tall vase, I wave my finger auras against each wisp of smoke, brushing, patting, smoothing, and redirecting its flow. This can become like dancing. And I have a policy about this: Anytime anyone notices what I'm doing, and asks me about it, I show them how. Most people, I've found, can learn this fairly easily.

Cloud busting: This is really part of Weather-Working, which will be discussed further in 4.I.5: "Thaumaturgy: Sympathetic Magick." Large-scale weather-working should not be done casually, as there can be unforeseen consequences. But I've found that small-scale cloud-busting is pretty harmless, so I will explain it here. If it's a cloudy day and you'd like it to clear up, say, for a picnic, the first thing is to find some little patch of blue sky somewhere (this is called "sailor's breeches")—or even a place where the cloud cover seems a bit less solid. Reach toward that weak spot in the clouds with both hands, and visualize extending your aura as far as you can in a long repulsor beam. It may take years of practice to be able to reach it all the way up to the clouds, but it can be done. Hold your hands back to back, fingers extended, then "pry" the clouds apart as if they were piles of cotton right in front of you. As the clouds open and the blue patch becomes larger, just keep pushing the edges of the opening wider until the sun shines through.

Shielding: You can also learn to "harden" the outer shell of your auric field into a psychic shield. This is done in pretty much the same way as projecting an auric repulsor field. But instead of making it into a single tight beam, move your hands, palms flattened and fingers spread wide, up, down, and all around your body at arms' length, while visualizing that you are shaping and pressing against the inside of an impenetrable shell all around yourself. Like the Earth's Van Allen Belts, this shell will protect you from any incoming psychic energy—and it can even be developed into a "cloaking field" to make you invisible.

Cloaking: Psychic invisibility does not mean that you can stand in the middle of a room jumping up and down and waving your arms and no one can see or photograph you. Being invisible means that you become so inconspicuous that people simply do not notice that you are there at all. Their gaze will pass right over you, sliding off your aura like it was Teflon, or reflected elsewhere as a mirror. Afterwards, they will not remember your having been present. In addition to "hardening" your auric shell into a cloaking field, there are two opposite tricks of invisibility that Wizards use; both involve your *gaze.*

The first works best with total strangers, as on the street or in a crowd. In this trick, you gaze intently at

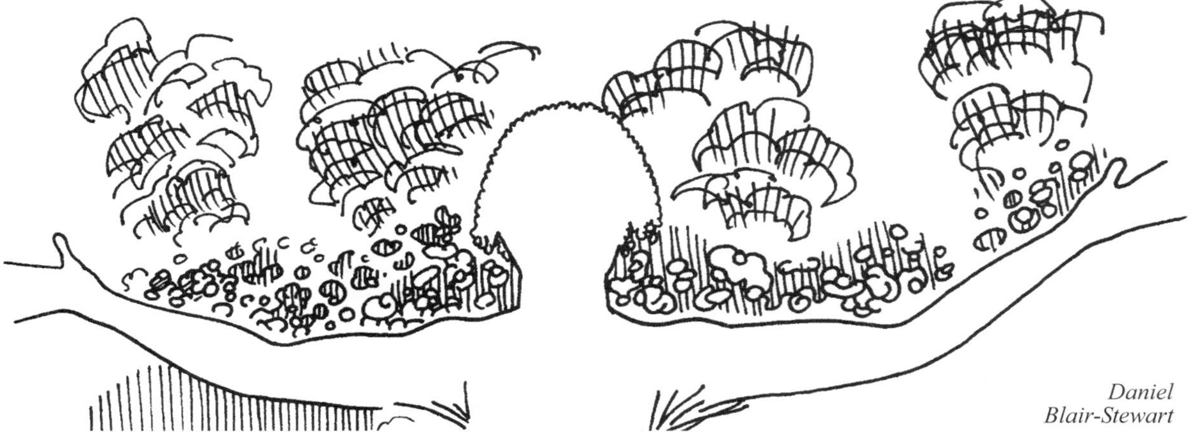

Daniel Blair-Stewart

the other person, locking eyes briefly with them. Usually they will blink and look elsewhere almost instantly just to avoid your gaze. And as soon as they do, drop your eyes and turn away, and you will become invisible to them. They simply will have erased you from their mind.

The second trick of invisibility is just the opposite, though it also works best in a crowd—like at a party. If there is someone who knows you whom you don't want to see you, the most important thing is to not let him or her catch your eye. Look anywhere else, but avoid looking at them, or even closely enough where they can see your eyes. With your cloaking field up, you can slip right past them and they'll never notice you were there.

Lesson 5: Psychokinesis

When I was a boy, I read about people who could move things around by the power of their minds (called *psychokinesis*) and I determined that I was going to learn to do this, too. I practiced over and over with flipping coins and tossing dice. I would hold the coin or die with the face I wanted up, and stare hard at it until that face was burned into my mind. I always chose the "head" on the coin, and the six on the die. Then, I would hold that image focused in my mind, and repeat the word *heads* or *sixes* silently to myself as I tossed the coin or die. Eventually, over several years, I got quite good at this. So good, in fact, that my younger brother and sister refused to toss a coin or play any games involving dice with me! They insisted I "cheated." But I'd practiced long and hard to develop this skill, just like my brother practiced shooting baskets.

However, there is great wisdom in the Hogwarts prohibition against using Magick around Muggles—especially to gain an advantage over them. If you do, they may come to resent you and make life difficult for you. This sort of behavior has gotten people burned at the stake! For many beginners, the impulse to "be powerful" often interferes with ever getting a true handle on what power actually is, and how to use it wisely or well. Never forget the super-hero's credo: "With great power comes great responsibility" (—Stan Lee, *Spiderman*).

Magickal Exercises: Psychokinesis

Here are a few more little exercises you can try to develop your psychokinetic abilities. Remember: Practice is everything!

Spinners: Spinners are very easily made. Take a small piece of paper, about two inches square, and fold it in half both ways, so it is only one inch square. Then unfold it, and refold it diagonally from corner-to-corner both ways. Open it out and re-shape it along the folds with the diagonal folds high and the cross folds low, like this:

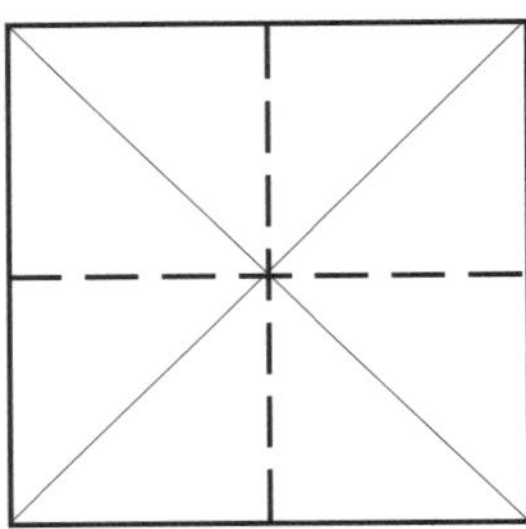

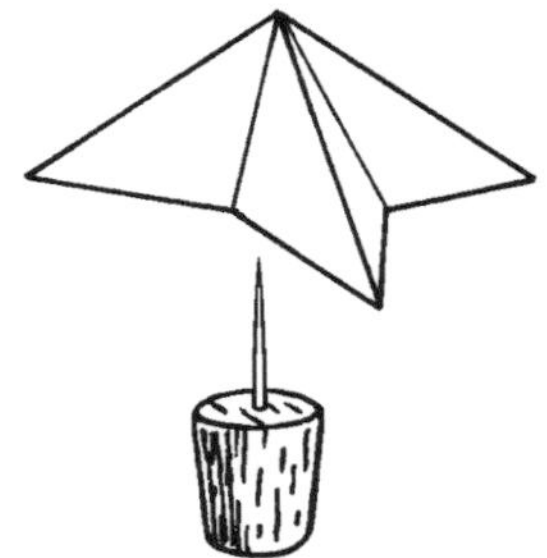

Now get a bottle with a cork in it (like a wine bottle), and stick a sewing needle eye-end into the cork, with the point up. Balance your folded paper on the point of the needle so it spins freely. This is your spinner.

Set your spinner up on a table in front of you, and concentrate on making it spin by the force of your mind alone. Be careful not to blow on it; breathe through your nose only! Concentrate long enough and hard enough, and you should be able to get it moving. See how fast you can make it spin. Then make it stop and spin in the opposite direction.

Plasma Generators: These are high-voltage generators used to create electrical sparks. *Plasma*—which consists of ionized gas (in which the atoms have been stripped of electrons)—is the fourth *state* of matter (the other three being solid, liquid, and gas). This is the same stuff as in the Earth's auroras and the Sun's *corona.* Plasma generators are used in plasma balls—those clear globes that house little electrical storms and are often found in trendy gadget stores. I highly recommend getting one of these things—they are both very cool Wizard balls (like a *palantir*) and useful devices for developing and honing your psychic skills. Make sure the one you get has a sliding scale for variable settings.

In a darkened room, set your plasma ball on a table, at a low enough setting that there are no lightning bolts—just a faint glowing cloud of sparkling octarene-colored plasma. Now bring one finger slowly up to the glass until a single electrical bolt arcs from the generator to the glass. This will indicate that you have the right setting.

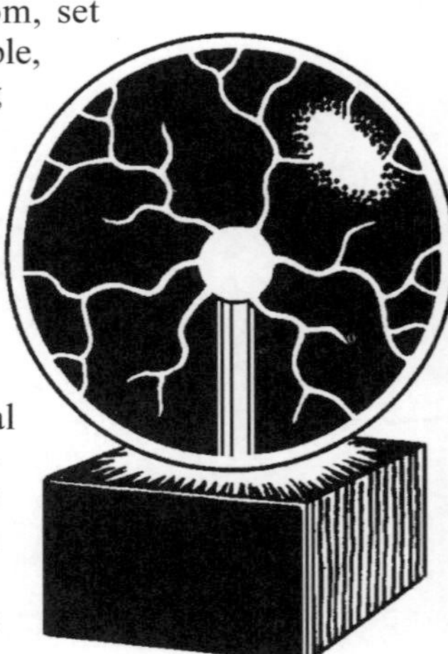

The exercise here

is to focus your attention on the plasma ball to make electrical bolts come towards you over a distance. Hold your face about a foot from the plasma ball, keep your hands out of the way, and "think" a bolt of lightning into hitting the glass aimed straight for your third eye (the center of your forehead). See how often you can call these bolts forth to you. Now the really fun part of this exercise is when you get someone else to sit on the opposite side, and do exactly the same thing. You can have a little contest to see who can bring the most bolts to their side! When you touch the glass with a finger, or the palm of your hand, you will notice a radiance around it, like an aurora. This is called a *Kirlian field,* and is a kind of way of making part of your aura visible—the way iron filings make a magnetic field visible.

Tubiflex worms: *Tubiflex worms* (also called "sludge worms") are commonly sold in pet shops as live food for tropical fish. These tiny thin worms are red because their blood, like that of mammals, contains iron-rich hemoglobin. Because hemoglobin can hold more oxygen than the body fluids of most pond animals, tubiflex worms can live in water that does not have much oxygen. Tubiflex worms live packed together in a mass, make tubes in the mud, and spend all their time eating muck with their heads stuck in

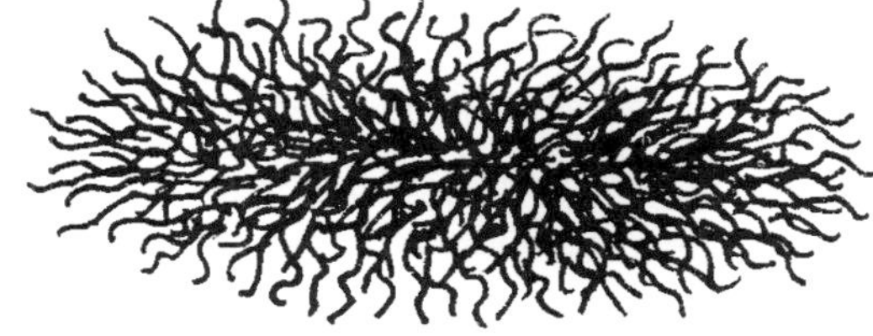

the bottom of the pond and their tails waving above in the water. If part of a worm is eaten or broken off, it can regrow that part.

Buy an once or so of tubiflex worms at your neighborhood pet store, and dump them into a round, shallow bowl of water, like a punchbowl. (If you are doing this at home, be sure and ask your mom first!) If your tap water is treated, you should use bottled water or (best) pond water. The worms will stick together in a single squirming mass.

Because of the high concentration of iron in their blood, tubliflex worms are particularly sensitive to electromagnetic fields. Try moving a magnet around the outside of the bowl, and watch how the worms react. You will find you can affect them with the magnet, just as if the worms were iron filings. But this squirmy-wormy mass can also be manipulated psychically! Concentrate on the mass of worms, just as with the plasma, and form it into a ball, a donut, a cross, a star—even send out tentacles and extensions in different directions. You will be amazed at how responsive the worms can be to your thoughts.

> ***NOTE:*** *If you want to keep your tubiflex worms more than a few days, you will need to provide them some food. They don't eat much. A half- teaspoon of muck from a fish or duck pond, a horse trough, a fish tank, a rain gutter, or even a bit of garden dirt will serve. And when you are done with your worms, you should release them into a pond—or feed them to your fish.*

Lesson 6: Telepathy and Clairvoyance

The first Gift I discovered as a child was that of telepathy. I could often "hear" the thoughts behind conversations. Sometimes when people were talking to me I could not even distinguish what was coming from their mouth, or what was coming from their minds. When I was very young, before starting school, I lived in a big Victorian house with my mother, my aunt, and my grandmother. My grandfather had died right about the time I was conceived (in fact, I was really him reincarnated), and my father was in the South Pacific fighting World War II. So my whole world revolved around these three women. And I heard their thoughts just as clearly as their words. But I had no way of knowing there was anything unusual in this; I thought everybody communicated this way.

One night, after I had gone upstairs to bed, I woke up with my head full of voices. I got out of bed and crept to the stairwell, where I saw that the big living room was full of people; my folks were having a party. I had never heard so many voices all talking at once, and it seemed overwhelmingly loud to me. So I cried out, "Be *QUIET!"* And as all heads turned to me there on the stairs, behind the banister, I saw that all their mouths had stopped moving. But their voices seemed even louder than before; I was still hearing their thoughts! I clapped my hands over my ears, ran upstairs to my bed, and hid under the covers. Eventually I was able to sleep. And when I woke, I no longer heard people's thoughts as voices in my head—which

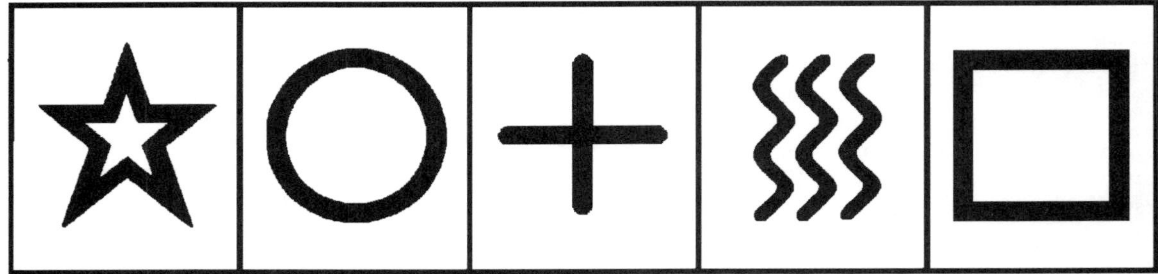

probably made it much harder for my mother, aunt, and grandmother to communicate with me!

Over the years, I sometimes had brief "flashes" of spontaneous telepathic communication—especially in romantic situations. But something in my mind had acted to protect me, and "shut off" that open gateway that had allowed the thoughts of others to just come pouring uncontrollably into my head. As a teenager, I heard about scientific experiments in telepathy that were being conducted by the Rhine Institute at Duke University. Remembering my earlier experiences, I set out to duplicate these experiments to recover my childhood talent.

Magickal Exercises: Telepathy and Clairvoyance

Thought transference actually occurs more commonly than most people realize. How many times have you found yourself talking with someone, and one or the other of you will say: "That's just what I was about to say!" Or you'll be thinking or talking about someone, and the phone rings, and it's him. My lifemate, Morning Glory—who is a famous Witch and Enchantress—and I have often heard ourselves saying the exact same words at the exact same moment from opposite sides of a crowded room. And people go: "Wooo—stereo Ravenhearts!"

Two of the experiments developed by the Rhine Institute are fairly easy to do. I recommend you try them. If you do them often enough, you may find that your performance will improve with practice. However, experiments in telepathy obviously require at least one other person, so you will need to find a friend who is also interested in magick, so you can practice together. These are perfect exercises to do over an Internet chat line.

Zener cards: Zener cards were developed in the late 1920s through a collaboration of Dr. Karl Zener (Duke University) and J.B. Rhine (Harvard). Zener cards are well-suited to developing and experimenting with psychic skills. They are like psychic exercise equipment. There are five different standard symbols in a deck of Zener Cards, and five cards of each symbol for a total of 25 cards per deck. To make your own set, copy the cards on this page onto card stock and cut them out. You will also need to make recording charts, numbered 1–25, with two spaces after each number: one for the sender, and one for the receiver.

Sit in a quiet room out of direct view of your partner. One of you (the sender) shuffles the deck and focuses on each card for a few moments, writing it down on the chart. The other person (the receiver) says which symbol they sense the sender is focusing on. The sender should then write that response next to the first. The sender should not tell the receiver whether they are right or wrong. Do this little exercise often, and keep records. Over time, you may find that one of you is a better sender and the other a better receiver.

"Far-Seeing" drawings: In a similar manner to using Zener cards, try transmitting drawings by telepathy. Laboratory experiments using this technique were called "Far-Seeing," and they were used to train spies! To do this, you and your friend should be in separate rooms or even separate houses (you can keep in touch by phone or computer). Each of you should be sitting at a desk, in a quiet room, with a pad of drawing paper and pencil or charcoal. One of you (the sender) will draw a simple picture of anything you want (tree, house, person, animal, whatever…). Draw it with your *left hand*, and concentrate strongly on the image as you draw it. At the same time, the other person (the receiver) should relax, close his eyes, and allow an image to form in his mind. Then, after a few moments, the receiver should draw whatever he thinks of—also with his left hand. Then you should take turns and switch. Later, compare notes and see how close you've come; you might be surprised! As with all these exercises, practice will improve your performance.

Songs: Another similar exercise can be done with songs. To do this you really do need to be in separate houses. As with the drawings, the sender should think of a catchy popular tune, chant, or jingle known to both of you, and start singing it. The best kind are those ones you just can't get out of your head (they're called "Pepsis" because they're used for advertising). Then the receiver opens his mind to let the song in—and after a while you check with each other and see how you did.

Class VI: Perchance to Dream

Sleep is actually a Ceremony, a remarkable essential Ceremony in which we participate over and over again, for our entire lives, along with all other sentient beings. As a matter of fact, the Universe itself participates in this Ceremony of restful 'letting go,' gently creating the appropriate backdrop for our Sleep by turning down the earth's lights and turning on the Heaven's Nightlights, quieting the daily noises and most of the Earth's creatures, and often seeming to still even the very air and waters around us. Many native peoples still believe that the Dream World to which we travel when we sleep and regenerate ourselves, physically, emotionally, and spiritually, may well be a truer 'reality' than the everyday world in which we generally function. —Hel

1. Introduction: Dreaming

RE DREAMS REALLY IMPORTANT, TELLing you things that could be to your advantage, or are they simply "late-night movies" to entertain your unconscious mind while your conscious rests? You average seven dream periods each of up to 45 minutes duration—every night of your life. Dreaming is vital to the state of your well being. People who have their dream periods interrupted over extended periods develop emotional stress. Dreams are complex, well-orchestrated and imaginative productions arising from our unconscious, or "super-conscious" mind. When you consider this source, the importance of dreams becomes clear. For many people, the dream state is the only medium available for the higher (or deeper) mind to communicate with the conscious mind. The least you can do is try and understand with the message is!

All men dream: but not equally. Those who dream by night in the dusty recesses of their minds wake in the day to find that it was vanity: but the dreamers of the day are dangerous men, for they may act their dream with open eyes, to make it possible. —T. E. Lawrence

Those who dream by day are cognizant of many things which escape those who dream only by night. —Edgar Allan Poe (1809-1849)

Lesson 2. The Gates of Horn and Ivory

It is said that dreams may come in through either of two gates—the Gate of Horn or the Gate of Ivory. Dreams that come through the Gate of Ivory—which is most dreams—are about your own internal matters. Mostly, these are the ways your mind sorts out, processes, and files the ongoing events, experiences, and thoughts of your life. There are numerous fascinating little "dream dictionaries" available that list various symbols encountered in dreams—along with interpretations of their meanings. I will give you a few examples below, but interpretations of dream imagery and symbolism will vary from person to person, and are not always universal. And while the images and occurrences in such dreams may be of deep personal significance to you, it is important to understand that they are about you, and not about others.

Dreams that come through the Gate of Horn, on the other hand, are "True Dreaming." These tend to fall into two categories: Dreams that are remembrances of past things forgotten, and dreams that are foretellings of things to come. Things forgotten that may be remembered in dreams include events and experiences from your past lives, your infancy, and your childhood—all that happened to you before you acquired speech in your current incarnation. Or if you have been unconscious—as in an accident, surgery, or UFO abduction—memories of what happened during that period may come through in dreams.

Dreams of things to come can be important visions that foretell positive things in your life—such as meeting your True Love, or achieving some great accomplishment. Or they can be warnings of some terrible disaster to be avoided. Many people have cancelled their travel reservations on the basis of such dreams of dire foreboding, and have thus avoided the crashing of trains, planes, and automobiles, or the sinking of ships. Such catastrophes where many people die tend to create such a "disturbance in the Force" that the ripples, like those of a stone tossed into a pool, flow backwards in time as well as forwards, and perturb the Dreaming Itself.

Keep a special *dream diary* beside your bed, and first thing upon awakening write down as much as you can remember of your dreams—especially the vivid ones. Note also the date and any special emotional "impressions" you may feel. Over time, as you re-read these entries, and note which dreams may have come true, you will learn to recognize and distinguish between the Gates of Horn and Ivory.

If you have difficulty remembering your dreams, try this simple exercise: Take a piece of sticky-back blank label paper, and write on it in bold permanent

A Dictionary of Dream Symbols

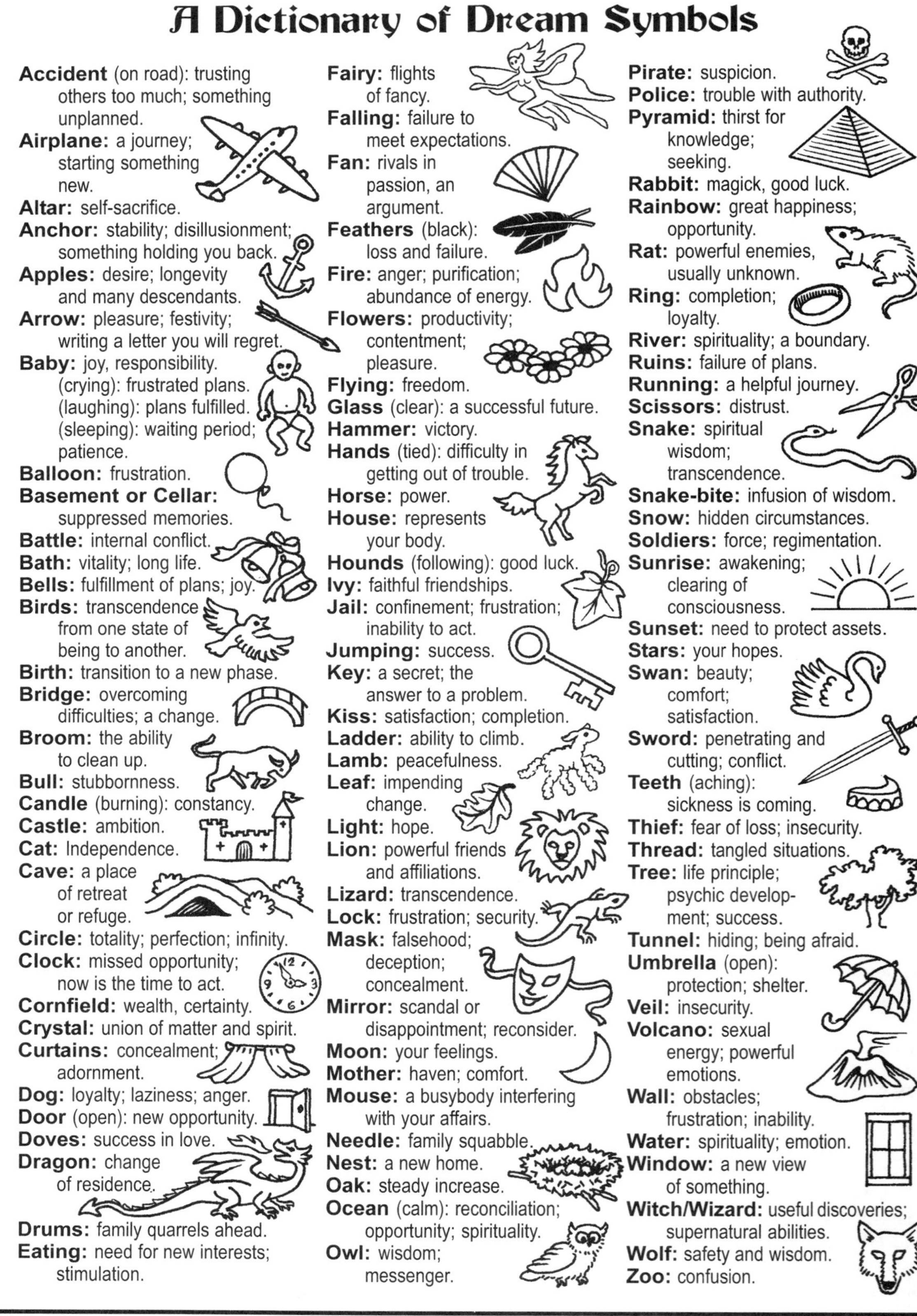

Accident (on road): trusting others too much; something unplanned.
Airplane: a journey; starting something new.
Altar: self-sacrifice.
Anchor: stability; disillusionment; something holding you back.
Apples: desire; longevity and many descendants.
Arrow: pleasure; festivity; writing a letter you will regret.
Baby: joy, responsibility. (crying): frustrated plans. (laughing): plans fulfilled. (sleeping): waiting period; patience.
Balloon: frustration.
Basement or Cellar: suppressed memories.
Battle: internal conflict.
Bath: vitality; long life.
Bells: fulfillment of plans; joy.
Birds: transcendence from one state of being to another.
Birth: transition to a new phase.
Bridge: overcoming difficulties; a change.
Broom: the ability to clean up.
Bull: stubbornness.
Candle (burning): constancy.
Castle: ambition.
Cat: Independence.
Cave: a place of retreat or refuge.
Circle: totality; perfection; infinity.
Clock: missed opportunity; now is the time to act.
Cornfield: wealth, certainty.
Crystal: union of matter and spirit.
Curtains: concealment; adornment.
Dog: loyalty; laziness; anger.
Door (open): new opportunity.
Doves: success in love.
Dragon: change of residence.
Drums: family quarrels ahead.
Eating: need for new interests; stimulation.
Fairy: flights of fancy.
Falling: failure to meet expectations.
Fan: rivals in passion, an argument.
Feathers (black): loss and failure.
Fire: anger; purification; abundance of energy.
Flowers: productivity; contentment; pleasure.
Flying: freedom.
Glass (clear): a successful future.
Hammer: victory.
Hands (tied): difficulty in getting out of trouble.
Horse: power.
House: represents your body.
Hounds (following): good luck.
Ivy: faithful friendships.
Jail: confinement; frustration; inability to act.
Jumping: success.
Key: a secret; the answer to a problem.
Kiss: satisfaction; completion.
Ladder: ability to climb.
Lamb: peacefulness.
Leaf: impending change.
Light: hope.
Lion: powerful friends and affiliations.
Lizard: transcendence.
Lock: frustration; security.
Mask: falsehood; deception; concealment.
Mirror: scandal or disappointment; reconsider.
Moon: your feelings.
Mother: haven; comfort.
Mouse: a busybody interfering with your affairs.
Needle: family squabble.
Nest: a new home.
Oak: steady increase.
Ocean (calm): reconciliation; opportunity; spirituality.
Owl: wisdom; messenger.
Pirate: suspicion.
Police: trouble with authority.
Pyramid: thirst for knowledge; seeking.
Rabbit: magick, good luck.
Rainbow: great happiness; opportunity.
Rat: powerful enemies, usually unknown.
Ring: completion; loyalty.
River: spirituality; a boundary.
Ruins: failure of plans.
Running: a helpful journey.
Scissors: distrust.
Snake: spiritual wisdom; transcendence.
Snake-bite: infusion of wisdom.
Snow: hidden circumstances.
Soldiers: force; regimentation.
Sunrise: awakening; clearing of consciousness.
Sunset: need to protect assets.
Stars: your hopes.
Swan: beauty; comfort; satisfaction.
Sword: penetrating and cutting; conflict.
Teeth (aching): sickness is coming.
Thief: fear of loss; insecurity.
Thread: tangled situations.
Tree: life principle; psychic development; success.
Tunnel: hiding; being afraid.
Umbrella (open): protection; shelter.
Veil: insecurity.
Volcano: sexual energy; powerful emotions.
Wall: obstacles; frustration; inability.
Water: spirituality; emotion.
Window: a new view of something.
Witch/Wizard: useful discoveries; supernatural abilities.
Wolf: safety and wisdom.
Zoo: confusion.

marker the word: "**REMEMBER.**" Stick it to a drinking glass full of water, and place the glass beside your bed. Just before you lay down and close your eyes to sleep, take a drink. As you do, think to yourself: *"When I awake and take another drink from this glass, I will remember my dreams."* Then go to sleep. In the morning, when you wake, take a drink from the glass right away, and as you do, the memory of your dreams will come flooding back. Quickly take notes in your dream diary, writing down all the details you can remember. Don't worry about trying to get everything in perfect order—just jot down everything you can think of as it comes to you. Over time, you will get better and better at this.

Lesson 3. A Dictionary of Dream Symbols

"Dream Dictionaries" have been around since ancient times. They were very popular in classical Greece and in the Roman Empire. Here are a few of the most common symbols you may encounter in your dreams, along with popular interpretations. But don't take these interpretations too seriously, as everyone's dreams are individual. Each of us has our own unique personal symbology, based on our life experiences. Therefore, you must analyze and interpret the symbols in your dreams from the standpoint of your own personal feelings about them.

Lesson 4. Nightmares

Nightmare means literally a monstrous black spirit-horse that carries us away on a terrifying and uncontrollable ride through dark and scary places. Nightmares are like a stuck replay, with added dramatization and special effects, of experiences too frightful to think of in our waking state. In very young children, such nightmares may be remembrances of a tragic death in their previous life. Especially if they died by violence, these "night terrors" can be so frightening that they cause *insomnia* (the inability to sleep).

Throughout my own early childhood, I was haunted by nightmares in which I kept reliving my last death. I had died of a heart attack, and I experienced this as if I was falling backwards down a bottomless well, with the world I knew shrinking into a smaller and smaller circle until it was gone from my sight, and I kept falling endlessly through total darkness...until I awoke as a baby in my new life.

Another source of nightmares can be traumatic experiences in this current life. Children (and even adults) who have been exposed to violence or abuse; lived through tragic accidents or fires—especially if others have died; or who have had severe and life-threatening illnesses or experienced other traumas will have nightmares in which they will continue to relive these horrors—often symbolically.

Particularly frightening nightmares are sometimes caused by a disconnection between the brain and the body as one is falling asleep or just awakening. The Japanese, who have long known of this phenomenon, call it *kanashibari*, and Western researchers refer to it as "sleep paralysis." About 4% of all people experience it regularly, and 40-60% at least once. Some hear disturbing sounds and incoherent voices. Others hallucinate evil supernatural beings and creatures. Most find themselves unable to move or speak and feel a weight on their chest. Also common are sensations of levitation, flying, and passing through spiral tunnels—all with a great sense of dread and terror.

Kanashibari nightmares often involve shadowy demonic creatures, such as the Dementors of Harry Potter's world, or the Ringwraiths of *Lord of the Rings.* Many such creatures have been identified in myth—such as *succubi* and *incubi* who lie upon sleepers and have sex with them, or ugly old hags, goblins, and ghosts that squat on a sleeper's chest and choke them. The *Lethifold* is a floating black cloak that envelops and suffocates its victims. And the fire-eyed black demon-horse we call the *Nightmare* is common to many cultures. Many "alien abduction" experiences may be explainable as kanashibari.

The best antidote to all types of nightmares is to learn to seize control of your dreams, through *lucid* ("clear") *dreaming* (see following). You can wield spells and powers to combat these monsters of the dark, just as in a video game. In fact, a video game is a very good way to visualize The Dreaming when you are having nightmares!

Anti-Nightmare spell: Hang a "dreamcatcher" or a small wreath of gray feathers over your bed to prevent nightmares and bring restful sleep. A pyramid-shaped crystal under your bed will protect you from psychic attack in your sleep. Hang up a red onion and place mugwort under your pillow to keep away evil spirits. Then set a magick Circle of Protection around your bed each night before you go to sleep, like this:

Stand in the middle of your bed and hold up a small mirror, such as a makeup mirror, facing outwards, so that the walls of your bedroom are reflected. Turn around *deosil* (clockwise) in a complete circle, and visualize a circular reflective wall spreading outward from the mirror in your hand, as if you are on the inside of a mirrored Christmas tree ornament. As you do this, say:

Circle of Light surround my bed;
All fears of night gone from my head.
May peaceful dreams come unto me;
As I do will, so mote it be!

Another charm against nightmares goes like this:

Thou evil thing of darkness born
Of tail and wing and snout and horn,
Fly from me from now till morn!
—Valerie Worth

Lesson 5: Lucid Dreaming

There is another world we may enter through dreams, which is sometimes called the *Dreamtime,* or *The Dreaming.* This is a psychic realm we share with all other dreamers, both human and non-human, and it has its own established landscapes and geographies. Within The Dreaming are the countries of Faerie, the Afterworlds of all faiths, the realms of gods, spirits, and ancestors, and all the fantasy worlds of myth and story. And within The Dreaming, you can be or do anything you can imagine. When you have learned to clearly visualize anything you want, you will be ready for the next step. This is called *lucid dreaming.* The idea is to be conscious in your dreams, so you can go places you want, do things intentionally, and remember them when you wake.

When you go to bed at night, use the skills you have already learned of meditation and visualization. Lie down, close your eyes, put yourself into a meditative trance, and begin to visualize that you are walking along a path. As you go along, various things will begin to appear that you are not visualizing intentionally. As this happens, you will be entering The Dreaming. Stay conscious, but let these unbidden visions come. When you are fully in the World of Dream, hold your hands up in front of your face. Turn them around; open and close your fingers. As long as you can keep seeing your hands and controlling them, you will be control of your dream-self.

Another important part of lucid dreaming is to visualize and hold images of your wand, athamé, and other magickal tools. Try to see yourself wearing your magickal robes in your dreams (see 3.III.3). This will help you maintain your dream-persona as a Wizard. In this state of lucid dreaming, you can become the most powerful magician you can imagine. Use your wand and other tools in your dreams. Just like in a video game, you can transform things, hurl fireballs, levitate, and develop all the martial arts skills of the characters in *The Matrix.* You will be able to challenge and defeat your nightmares, and enjoy wonderful adventures. My own favorite thing to do in lucid dreaming is levitation and flying: I "pull myself up" to float about a foot off the ground, and then I "swim" through the air exactly as if I was swimming underwater—sometimes just at room level, and sometimes soaring like an eagle high above the treetops. Every time, I study how I do this very carefully, hoping that one day I will be able to carry this skill back into the Waking World!

The whole trick here is to remain conscious. As with every discipline, the main thing is practice—do this every night, and you will get good at it. Time can be stretched within The Dreaming so that a few hours asleep can seem like days or longer. And if you practice your magickal skills in The Dreaming, where you have all the time in the world, you will also increase your magickal abilities in the Waking World.

Lesson 6: Journeying and Dreamwalking

As you master the skill of lucid dreaming, you will eventually be able to set a course within The Dreaming to particular Astral realms, places, times and dimensions—such as Faerie, the Afterworlds, historical eras, or even the lands of myth and fantasy. This is called *shamanic journeying.* You will be able to fly to such places by levitation, or even transport yourself instantaneously by teleportation. You will be able to seek out, meet, and converse with anyone you wish—living or dead, real or imaginary—including dragons, totems, spirits, Gods, and Goddesses.

But beware! Some of these places and encounters can be very dangerous and can trap the unskilled, unprepared, or unwary. There are places that you really do not want to go! Do not attempt such journeys until you have mastered control of your own dreambody. And when you have achieved such mastery, after years of practice, you may become a *Dreamwalker*—able to enter the dreams of others. But this is a great Power, and hence a great Responsibility, and not for the novice Apprentice. It is an ability used by Shamans and psychic healers.

When I was young, before I had acquired any discipline in my psychic abilities, I would sometimes find myself apparently accidentally dreamwalking in someone else's dream, as the images and symbols clearly did not belong to me. The most common of these "wrong dreams" were ones involving large numbers of snakes—often poisonous ones. These seemed clearly intended to be someone's worst nightmares, as if they belonged to Indiana Jones. Trouble was, I really *liked* snakes, and I was always finding them and bringing them home to keep in my terrariums (we still have a couple of large boas). So I wasn't at all scared to have them crawling all over me in my dreams—even biting me. I would laugh in these dreams, knowing that the Sandman had really mixed up! Later, I learned that in traditional dream symbolism, snakes represent "spiritual wisdom; transcendence into a state of wisdom." And snakebites in a dream mean "an infusion of wisdom." So maybe there was a good reason for them to be in my dreams after all....

Lesson 7: Dream Discovery

Dream discovery is a specific kind of lucid dreaming whereby you set an intention to dream about a specific thing—usually in order to solve a problem, gain an insight, design a symbol, or visualize a project (such as a painting, sculpture, music, etc.). I have used this technique to create unicorns, conceptualize statues I intend to sculpt, make architectural designs, plan magazine and book layouts, and create logos for various groups—such as the wizardly logo you see here.

One of the most famous instances of dream-discovery was that of the ring structure of Benzene. Until Kekule made the discovery, molecular structures in chemistry were conceived as linear (being in a straight line). This, however, did not explain many properties of Benzene. Kekule was trying to figure out a structure—without much success—when the solution came to him in a dream. He described this experience to an assembly of scientists who had met to commemorate his discovery:

> *"...I turned my chair toward the fireplace and sank into a doze. Again the atoms were flitting before my eyes. Smaller groups now kept modestly in the background. My mind's eye sharpened by repeated visions of a similar sort, now distinguished larger structures of varying forms. Long rows frequently rose together, all in movement, winding and turning like serpents; and see! what was that? One of the serpents seized its own tail and the form whirled mockingly before my eyes. I came awake like a flash of lightning. This time also I spent the remainder of the night working out the consequences of the hypothesis."*
>
> —Madhukar Shukla, "The Discovery of the Benzene Ring"

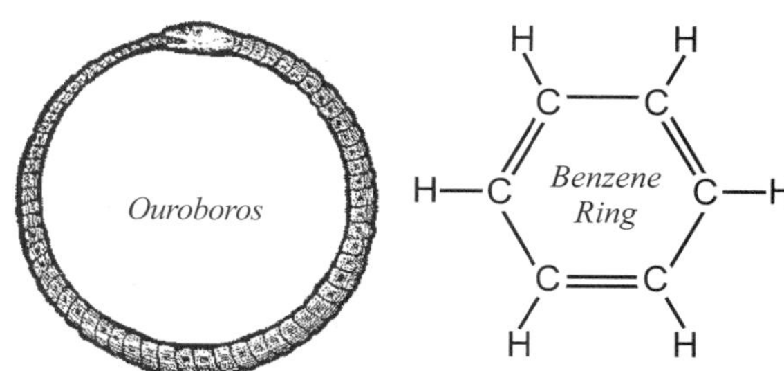

First, you must become completely obsessed with the discovery you are trying to make. Read everything you can find about it; search the Internet (go to *www.Google.com*); question everyone you know about the subject. Then, from all you have gathered together, start collecting symbols, pictures, photos, news clippings, and any other visible images you can copy or print out. Write or draw some ideas yourself, and include these. Cut them all out and spread them over a large table or the floor. Shuffle and rearrange these into patterns and designs until you are happy with the overall arrangement. Take plenty of time with this. Then get some scissors and glue sticks and paste your arrangement of pieces onto a large sheet of cardboard as a collage. Don't worry if the design comes out looking a little different as you paste it up; that's also part of the process.

Before you go to bed, spend a while staring at your collage, trying to memorize every detail. You should be able to visualize it clearly in your mind when you close your eyes. Put a notepad and pencil beside your bed, along with a glass of water. Write down a specific question on a piece of paper (parchment is best for this and all such spells), and place it under your pillow along with a little "dream-pillow" sachet of *artemesia* herb. Then, in the same way you learned earlier to remember your dreams, just before you lie down to sleep, take a drink, making an affirmation as you do so that all the pieces will come together in your dreams, and you will see the solution you are looking for. And you will remember it when you awaken and take another drink of water.

If you would like to further empower a prophetic dream, you can align yourself with the lunar aspect, as the Moon is the ruler of sleep and dreams. The best time is when the Moon is waxing and almost full, ideally on a night of the week related to what you are trying to discover (see 3.VI.5: "Table of Correspondences: Planets"). You might also take a warm, relaxing bath before going to bed, adding a few drops of the following oils to your bath water: lavender, rosemary, peppermint, thyme, and powdered poppy seeds. While you are taking your bath, burn some of the following lunar incense in your bedroom: camphor, powdered aloeswood, jasmine, pulverized cucumber seeds, and powdered white sandalwood (all in equal parts).

Class VII: Patterns of Magick

"Look for the beauty in the pattern. There are no coincidences at this level of complexity."
—David Deutsch

1. Introduction: Pattern Recognition is a large part of the game

GREAT PART OF WIZARDLY SEEING and thinking is pattern recognition. That is, looking at a bunch of trees, and seeing a Forest. Or, as in stereograms, looking at a bunch of squiggles and seeing a three-dimensional scene. This kind of perception is also basic to science. It has helped us to understand and create theories about the way the Universe works. Every time someone makes an important breakthrough in perception and sees "the Whole Picture," it's an epiphany. It's like finding a bunch of puzzle pieces all mixed up together, with some right side up and others upside down. Our job is to sort them out, turn them around, find ones that have similarities, and fit them together piece by piece until a picture emerges.

The ultimate goal of science is to discover a single grand "Theory of Everything," one where all the pieces of all the different puzzles can be assembled into one giant picture, with no pieces left over. Scientists call this idea The Unified Field Theory, but they still haven't worked it out. The main problem is including and accounting for Life and Consciousness, and so far there are no equations for this.

Magickal folks and geniuses see patterns where others do not. In 1831, Charles Darwin looked at the variety of finches in the Galapagos Islands and saw the pattern of the evolution of life as a branching tree. In 1953, James Watson, Francis Crick, Maurice Wilkins, and Rosalind Franklin looked at organic nucleic acids and conceived the double spiral pattern of the DNA molecule.

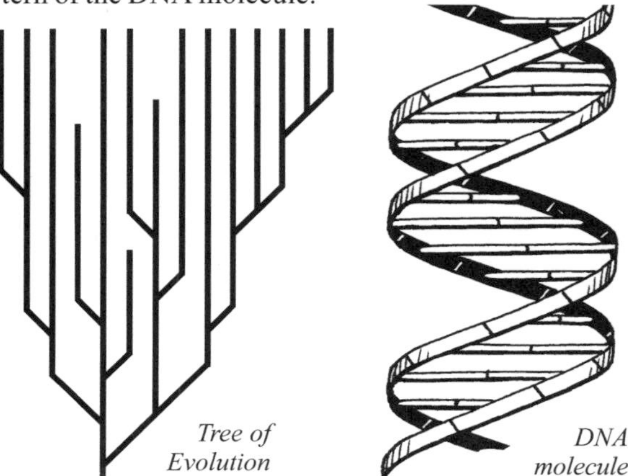

Tree of Evolution *DNA molecule*

Nature has symbols too, found in many underlying patterns of structure. One of the most important is the spiral. It is found everywhere from the DNA molecule in your body, through the arrangements of leaves and seeds in plants and flowers, the shells of snails and the chambered nautilus, tornadoes and hurricanes, all the way up to the shapes of galaxies. Wherever you look, the spiral or another pattern is present. We'll discuss some of these patterns in more detail later on, in Course 2, Class I: "Natural Mysteries."

However, sometimes our minds can get overly enthusiastic, and we perceive patterns that aren't really there. In 1877, Giovanni Shaparelli looked at markings on the surface of Mars and his mind organized them into a pattern of lines, which became famous as "the Martian canals." Only when we sent Mariner space probes to Mars to take photos we discovered that there were no canals there at all. No lines were found of any kind, just craters, lava fields, mountains, and deserts, similar to those on the Moon. We also found red iron rust, polar ice caps, enormous vol-canoes, vast canyons, and ancient riverbeds—and recently, frozen oceans of ice just beneath the surface.

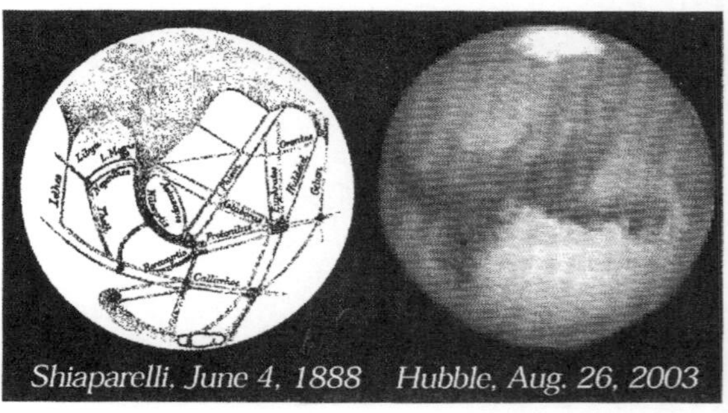

Shiaparelli, June 4, 1888 Hubble, Aug. 26, 2003

Another famous creative pattern visualization is in the designs that have been seen in the heavens—the patterns of star constellations. Stars are scattered across the sky randomly (having no pattern at all) from our perspective. But ancient peoples drew lines between various bright stars as if they were "connecting the dots" and came up with stick-figure pictures that they named after characters and creatures in their favorite myths and stories. And all of us, including modern astronomers, still refer to those imaginary patterns as if they represented reality!

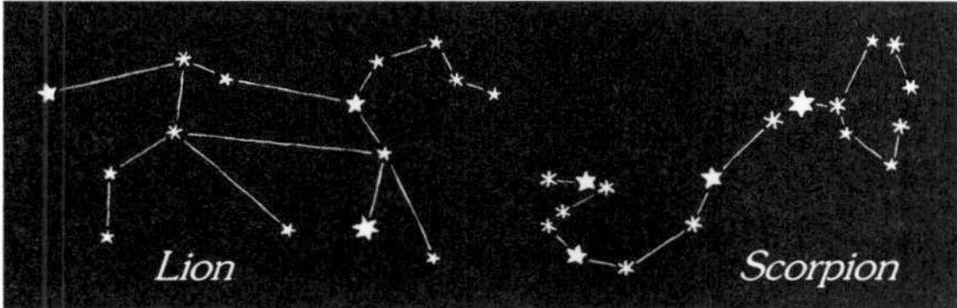

Such symbolic false patterns are called "optical illusions," and if we understand the principles of how they work, we can create our own, with hidden meanings deliberately imbedded in them (as with the constellations). Here are a few examples:

Lesson 2: Patterns, Divination, and the Holographic Universe

Most forms of divination begin with creating a random distribution of elements, and then attempt to make some magickal sense out of them by finding or creating patterns. When we flip a coin to get heads or tails, it is random. In cartomancy (card reading, as in tarot), the first thing we do is shuffle the deck. Dice, runestones, knucklebones, yarrow stalks, and oracle stones are "thrown" by scattering them. Some systems use a set background template (pattern) like a dartboard, where various sections are assigned meanings, and whatever falls within certain sections attains the significance or meaning of that section.

In the mundane world, it's sort of like deciding where to take a vacation by closing your eyes and sticking a pin into a map! Wherever the pin lands is assigned the definition of "Holiday Destination." Horoscopes are charted that way, with the positions of the planets and stars falling into various "houses." Tarot card readings are laid out according to a particular spread design.

Task: Make a Divination Box

Here's a simple divination system you can create:

Find a shallow 8-1/2"x11" box or box lid, like the ones notepaper comes in. Take a piece of paper the same size and fold it into four sections. In the upper right section, write the word "**YES**." In the upper left, write "**MAYBE**." In the lower left, write "**NO**." And in the last section, write "**DUNNO**."

Unfold the paper and place it in the box so you can see the writing. Next, on another piece of paper, write some simple question for which an answer could be "yes" or "no."

Find a special small stone or crystal you particularly fancy. Now, hold that stone cupped in your hands and shake it up good while you repeat the question over and over. When you are ready, toss the stone into the box. Whatever space it lands in gives you your answer.

Practically all systems of magickal divination are based on this simple principle; some systems are just a lot more elaborate and complex than others. You could divide that paper into as many sections as you want, in any shapes you want, and write anything you want in the sections. And you could use dice instead of stones, with the numbers giving added "weight and meaning" to the sections they land in. No matter how complex you make it, the principle is the same.

The reason for these patterning templates—and why they actually seem to work for us—is that the Universe (and the Multiverse as well) is basically *holographic.* Have you ever thought about the structure of atoms? Atoms are like tiny solar systems, with their electrons orbiting the nucleus like planets orbit the Sun. Every cell in our bodies is a miniature version of our entire selves; and we, in turn, are cells in the greater body of Mother Earth. In a hologram, every tiniest particle (the *micro-cosmos*) contains the essence and template of the whole (the *macro-cosmos*). This most fundamental principle of Magick is stated in the opening words of *The Emerald Tablet* of Hermes Trismegistus: *"That which is above is like that which is below and that which is below is like that which is above, to achieve the wonders of the one thing."* This is usually simply stated: *"As above, so below; as below, so above."* Modern Wizards add: *"As within, so without; as without, so within."* And so, the macrocosm of larger events is reflected in our little microcosmic model; and by manipulating the microcosm, we affect the macrocosm.

A Note on Great Truths

—by Ian "Lurking Bear" Anderson

There are numerous mentions of "Great Truths" whose opposites are also true in this book. This idea sounds sort of Zen-like, but it comes to us from a European physicist of the 20th century:

> *"There are trivial truths and there are Great Truths. The opposite of a trivial truth is plainly false. The opposite of a Great Truth is also true."*
> —Niels Bohr

Niels Bohr was an important figure in the development of *quantum physics.* To help get a grasp of Great Truths, try these pairs of ideas on for size and see how each one is true:

Everything is connected. Everything is separate.
There are no accidents. Everything is an accident.
All is joy. All is sadness.
There is no objective reality. All reality is objective.
The universe is pure material. The universe is pure spirit.

These things can be simultaneously true because the nature of the Universe is paradoxical. (Is this a Great Truth too? Think about it.)

Task: Infinity Mirrors

> *You can use two mirrors like this, if you know the way of it: you set them so that they reflect each other. For if images can steal a bit of you, then images of images can amplify you, feeding you back on yourself, giving you power.*
> *And your image extends forever, in reflections of reflections of reflections, and every image is the same, all the way around the curve of light.*
> *Except that it isn't.*
> *Mirrors contain infinity.*
> *Infinity contains more things than you think.*
> *Everything, for a start.*
> *Including hunger.*
> *Because there's a million billion images and only one soul to go around.*
> *Mirrors give plenty, but they take away lots.*
> —Terry Pratchett (*Witches Abroad,* pp. 50–51)

A great way to experience the holographic universe is to stand between two large mirrors, and see your reflection repeated again and again, endlessly into infinity. It gives you a new perspective.

I once visited an art exhibit that had a cubical room you could enter, with mirrors covering all four sides, plus the floor and ceiling. Of course, you took your shoes off and went in with just socks on your feet. There were light bulbs at each of the eight corners. When you closed the mirrored door and stood in the center, all that you could see was your own reflection, from all angles, and the lights like stars, repeating and receding over and over forever. It was an amazing experience!

You can get the general idea in your own home, if you set up a couple of mirrors facing each other on either side of a hallway, and stand between them. The trick is to not have them both flat against the wall, but have one slightly angled so you can see the image of one mirror reflected in the other as well. You can also experience something of this effect in clothing stores, where they have little recessed mirrored alcoves. Doing this will expand your wizardly perceptions!

Heaven above
Heaven below
Star above
Star below
All that is above
Also is below
Grasp this and rejoice!
—Alchemical text

Lesson 3: Surfing the Synchronicity Wave

Meaningful *synchronicities* of "lucky coincidences" are especially noticed by Wizards and other magickal folk. Often when you are on the right track in your life, synchronistic events occur as signposts of cosmic approval or divine guidance. When there seem to be a lot of synchronicities piling up, it's time to pay attention! I like to think of synchronicities like waves in the ocean. Most of them are just little "coinky-dinks" (as I call small random coincidences), like the little surface waves and ripples that lap against the shore—nothing to get excited about, just the normal background flow.

But when several such coinky-dinks fall together, a larger wave rises out of the sea of probabilities. Then

Daniel Blair-Stewart

we pay attention, put on the templates of our special "3-D sunglasses," and look out to sea. Because it might be that This Means Something! Often something Big, and if we're paying attention, like a surfer paddling out there beyond the breakers on his boogie board, we can see that wave coming, we can position ourselves to catch it, and when it rises beneath us, we can use its momentum and power for a wild ride.

This is what we call surfing the synchronicity wave. The rule here is simple: Pay attention! Stay alert, and notice everything. You are developing a skill. Just like a detective in a movie, or a tracker in the wild, how good you are at this skill depends on how well you observe every little detail. Fitting the clues together will point your way towards recognizing the larger pattern, the synchronicity that is more than just random, minor, overlapping events.

> Abby Willowroot says: *"I tend to view Synchronicity as a kind of sacred* entrainment *with the Universe and its pulse. When you are 'in the flow,' synchronicities happen frequently. The more you 'push the river,' the less frequently they happen. It seems like the difference between making magic and being magically in tune and allowing magic to flow through you, as you direct it."*

Lesson 4: Glossary of Metaphysical Concepts

Just as in the science of physics, the realm of metaphysics also has its own vocabulary. Here are a few important terms and concepts you should know:

Metaphysics: "Beyond physics." The study and philosophy of the relationships between perceived reality and the deeper, underlying universal reality and principles. The word was originated by Aristotle to describe his books that came after his work on physics.

Mundane: "Worldly." Commonplace, ordinary, nonmagickal. Used to refer to "normal" reality, as opposed to altered or enhanced states of perception.

Sacred: Especially imbued with the essence of divinity, or considered to be so imbued.

Profane: The opposite of *sacred.*

Occult: "Hidden." This term refers to all the mysterious and secret arts, studies, knowledge, practices, and groups—especially those that are not understood, unpopular, and often condemned by *Mundanes.* In astronomy, an object is "occulted" when it disappears behind something else.

Mysteries: Things that can only be known through experience, and cannot be communicated verbally or in writing. Such are often conveyed as part of an Initiation.

Initiation: A ritualized transformational experience that introduces one to a new reality. A rite of passage into a mystical society or religion.

Esoteric: Hidden, implicit, experiential, and "inner."

Exoteric: Obvious, explicit, explainable, and "outer."

Arcane/Arcana: Secret, mysterious. Another word for all things esoteric and occult. *Arcana* are things that are arcane in nature. Arcana is the plural of *arcanum* —Latin neuter form of *arcanus*: Knowledge usually considered for Initiates only, as in the Mysteries.

Paranormal: "Alongside the normal." Outside the range of the normal. Unusual or "supernatural." Not explainable by current scientific principles.

Supernatural: That which apparently goes beyond experience or existence in the natural world, or cannot be explained through known natural laws or forces. Miraculous.

Anomaly/Anomalous: Something unusual, abnormal, inconsistent, contradictory, or improper.

Archetype: The basic pattern, or idea, in the collective unconscious from which all things in the same class are representations.

Path: A method, system, or approach to magickal or mystical knowledge.

Adept: "Arrived" or "attained." Expert. One who has studied and achieved much and has become highly skilled in magick or mysticism. To be adept at something means you're "good at it."

Mystic: One who pursues the philosophical and spiritual side of magick.

Enlightenment: A state of deep and total awareness, experiencing constant connectedness with all and everything. Some people experience at times a united state that gives a hint of what enlightenment is.

Lucidity: A state of enhanced awareness, when an exceptional understanding of the deep essential nature of things, people and events and their connectedness is experienced, usually with clairvoyance or telepathic faculties.

Avatar: A deity incarnate in human form, such as Christ, Buddha, or Krishna. A person regarded as an exemplary representation of some kind.

Macrocosm: "Big world." The world without. The Universe all around us.

Microcosm: "Little world." Traditionally, the microcosm is the human being seen as a miniature representation of the larger Universe.

Aura: "Invisible breath or emanation." Auras are the fields of *biomagnetic energy* that emanate from, envelop, and interconnect all living things, within and without

Astral: "Of the stars." *Astral* refers to the invisible universe and fields of living energies, consciousness, and magick. The shadowy realms and alternate realities in which magickal practitioners operate. Astral realms and regions (such as the

Dreaming) are perceived and accessed through right-hemisphere techniques of meditation, visualization, hypnosis, and dreaming.

Astral body: A body of living energy corresponding to and surrounding the physical body.

Astral projection (or travel): Separating your *astral body* from your physical one to journey in the *astral realms*. Extension of one's point of reference beyond the limits of the physical body, usually with an accompanying image of the body as a vehicle.

Wraith: A projected astral body.

Totem: An animal or natural object that is taken as the symbol or ancestor of a person or group of people.

Ghost: The spirit of a dead person that is bound to the mortal realms for some reason, such as untimely death, unfinished business, or concern for loved ones.

Fetch: The collective astral projection of a coven or other magickal group. May be used by an individual as a sort of "astral familiar."

Familiar: A non-human being, especially an animal, with whom one has an empathic psychic bond. Such a creature serves as a magickal partner, guide, or teacher.

Elemental: A localized focus or manifestation of the collective spirit of any of the four material Elements. These are called: *Gnomes* (Earth), *Undines* (Water), *Sylphs* (Air), and *Salamanders* (Fire).

Mana: A Polynesian term for power, or psychic energy. One's personal power, charisma, strength, force, mojo, etc.

Bioplasma: A more technical word for *mana.*

Biomagnetic: Living energy, likened in Nature to the non-living energies of electricity and magnetism.

Biocurrents: Electrochemical energy currents generated by living cells. Called *orgone energy* by Wilhelm Reich.

Morphogenic: "Shape-producing." In 1981, biologist Rupert Sheldrake postulated the existence of biological *morphogenic fields* that govern the behavior of species. These fields possess very little energy themselves, but are able to take energy from another source and shape it. The field acts as a geometrical influence, shaping behavior. Invisible, intangible, inaudible, tasteless, and odorless, morphogenic fields are built up through the accumulated behaviors of species' members.

Chakras: Energy centers of the astral body that are associated with parts of the physical body. The seven major ones are associated with areas along the spine and with the central nervous system. From bottom to top, these are: 1. Root; 2. Sex; 3. Solar Plexus; 4. Heart; 5. Throat; 6. Third Eye; and 7. Crown. We also have small Chakras in our hands and feet.

Entity: A conscious being, spirit, living creature, or personification.

Incarnate: "Enter into flesh." To have or take on a body.

Discarnate: "Without a body."

Ecstatic/Ecstasy: Intense joy or delight. A state of emotion so intense that one is carried beyond rational thought and self-control. The trance, frenzy, or rapture associated with mystic or prophetic exaltation.

Geas (pronounced gaysh): A charge or commitment that is laid on a person to fulfill some specific task.

Bane: Bad, evil, destructive.

Brutch: An area of psychic distortion in local space/time, such as the "Bermuda Triangle."

Cusp: A transitional phase point or intersection in time, space, and function. In astrology, the intersection of two signs or houses. A cusp is an intersection between fields of alternative probability. At such places the potential as to which of these alternatives the probability wave will collapse into is in delicate balance—things could easily go either way.

Lesson 5: Advanced Studies

The following Lessons are more advanced. I have included them here because they are foundational, and this Course is all about the foundations of Magick. But if your head is already beginning to hurt with all these studies, you can skip this section and maybe return to it later, when you are ready for it. Because some of the following is highly technical, I've consulted with Craig M. Parsons-Kerins, a software engineer and martial artist living in Massachusetts. He has a bachelor's degree in physics with work towards a master's degree. He is a member of Mensa and the Triple Nine Society, and has been in the Craft for 20 years, with a specific focus on British Traditional Craft.

A. Symmetry

The appreciation of forms and patterns dates back to the early days of civilization or even to our predecessors. Simple forms of symmetry are recognized by animals and even by computers. Symmetric forms appear in cave paintings and have been used throughout the ages to express religious beliefs. Other forms like circular shapes were the basis of designs for items in practical use. Repetitions of identical units have been used in applied art (like rugs) and in early architecture. It was the Greeks, however, who defined the concept and used it in various contexts in science, architecture, the arts, and in many ways of everyday life. The name itself comes from the Greek word *symmetria*, or "same measure."

Our inclination to symmetry may have deep biological origins. Recent studies indicate we are likely to choose symmetrical mates over asymmetrical ones.

This most probably played an important role in our evolution through the notion that symmetrical individuals are less likely to carry genetic defects. Our external appearance, like the appearance of most animals, has one form of symmetry called *mirror* or *reflection* symmetry, a feature important in moving forward along a straight line between two points in space (and pursue prey). It is not surprising, therefore, that symmetry is related to somehow feeling right—to our appreciation of balance, equilibrium, and, consequently, longevity.

A collection of objects can also display a symmetry of a different kind if they are ordered in certain periodic fashion. Implicit in this form of symmetry is the satisfaction of having returned to origins where we have been before, whether it be in space or in time. At the same time, perhaps it is also less exciting than a disordered state because of its predictability.

B. Parity: The Force and the Flow

I'm sure you've seen the *Star Wars* movies. The most important single theme running throughout the entire saga is that of *The Force.* In the original movie, *Star Wars Chapter 4: A New Hope*, Obi-Wan Kenobi explains The Force to young Luke Skywalker: "The Force is what gives the Jedi his power. It's an energy field created by all living things. It surrounds us and penetrates us. It binds the galaxy together." This is a true and profound insight as far as it goes, but "The Force" is only one half of the equation. The other half is equally important. Throughout all aspects of Nature and cosmology there runs a strong "Principle of Parity." This means that everything includes its opposite, or mirror image. In science, Newton's Third Law of Motion states that "For every action, there is an equal and opposite reaction." In Oriental Taoism, this concept is called "Yin and Yang," illustrated by this symbol: It is the Sacred Balance that is at the core of all things.

The Yin-Yang is a circle divided into two nested teardrops, representing the unity of apparent opposites. The Yin represents the dark, death, the hidden, Winter, and female side of the cosmos, while the Yang symbolizes the light, life, activity, Summer, and male. Each side contains the essence of the other in the form of a small circle, a little nucleus, or seed of the opposite.

"The Force" is also expressed as two opposites: the Light Side vs. the Dark Side (Good and Evil). But unlike the movie theme of the Light energy of "The Force" overcoming the Dark Side in *Star Wars*, in Nature and Magick they are inseparable. The two sides dance together in Taoism—and in magick. This is why we often say that for a Great Truth (like "As Above, so Below"), its opposite is also true. Left/right, dark/light, matter/energy, space/time, positive/negative, active/passive, life/death, creation/destruction, inner/outer, up/down, hot/cold, expansion/contraction, male/female, God/Goddess: These dual aspects are all examples of two halves of greater wholes. They are complimentary opposites, in which each pole implies the existence of the other. In fact, it is a good exercise when you see one thing, to try and also see what its complimentary opposite must be. Say, "On the one hand…and on the other hand."

The complimentary opposite of "The Force" is not the Dark Side of the Force (which is, after all, just half of The Force itself). It is "The Flow." The "energy field created by all living things" is counterbalanced by the energy field of non-living things. These two energies penetrate each other in great simultaneous ebbs and flows like the ocean tides. The Force is carrying us actively forward through time, evolving, expanding, coming together—tending towards increasing and higher energies, ever-greater complexity, consciousness, and Divinity. While at the same time, the Flow (called entropy in physics) is flowing passively in the opposite direction, devolving, contracting, coming apart—tending towards decreasing and lower energies, dissipation, unconsciousness, and oblivion.

The Cosmos may be seen as a great whirling, spiraling Dance of these eternal Partners through Time and Space. They are embodied in the Hindu Goddess Kali Ma, who dances both life and destruction.

C. Fields, Shields and Auras

A *field* is an *elliptical* (egg-shaped around two centers) spheroid of energy emanating from and surrounding a power source, called a *field generator.* Familiar examples of this are magnetic fields; they are generated by magnets, and by the Earth; electromagnetic fields, generated by electrical motors; and gravitational fields, generated by massive objects such as planets and stars. These fields are everywhere; even the tiniest objects such as molecules, atoms, and subatomic particles all have their own fields, no matter how small.

Physical reality is not only matter and energy; fields are real, but they are non-material. Fields are not a form of matter; rather, matter is energy bound within fields. Fields interrelate and interconnect matter and energy within their realm of influence. Several kinds of fundamental fields are recognized by scientists: the gravitational and electromagnetic fields of physics, the matter fields of quantum physics, and morphic fields of biology.

Field generators create fields through *polarity*—a negative/positive (or north/south) pole at opposite ends creates a continuous flow of energies and particles between them. These flows follow lines of force that can be traced in various ways. For instance, if you lay a bar magnet down on a piece of paper and sprinkle iron filings around it, you will see the filings line up along the magnetic lines of force to map out the magnet's entire field. Try this and then visualize this same pattern regarding every other kind of field.

Other than with magnets, most fields are created by rotational friction. The negative/positive poles occur at the *axis of rotation*. The Earth's gravitational field is aligned with its axis of rotation, which is the North Pole in the middle of the Arctic Ocean and the South Pole in the middle of Antarctica. But the inner core of the Earth rotates at a slighted different angle and speed, and its poles—called the magnetic poles—are what a compass points to, as these are the negative/positive poles of Earth's magnetic field.

Gravitational fields are infinite in extent, though they lose strength over distance, but other fields have very limited ranges. It is these limited fields that may be "hardened" into *shields*. The Earth's magnetic field (called the *magnetosphere*) reaches out to about 15,800 miles, but it "hardens" into a compact layer 1,975 miles overhead to become the inner Van Allen Belt. This ring-shaped belt is created by a portion of the magnetosphere being driven back towards the Earth by the Solar Wind—charged particles from the Sun coming towards the Earth and interacting with the magnetosphere. The radiation belts consist of such particles moving through the magnetosphere and being deflected by the field (a charged particle moving in a magnetic field undergoes an acceleration due to a force generated by the object's movement). This is the Earth's shield, and it protects us from cosmic radiation by absorbing and disbursing the incoming particles:

Like the Earth Herself, each of us is a living field generator. The fields that emanate from and surround our bodies are called our *Auras*. Because we're not rotating on our axis like the Earth, our field poles are more like those of a magnet. One pole, called the *Crown Chakra,* is at the top of our heads, right at the juncture of the three large skull bones (*frontal* and *parietals*) that come together there (when we are babies, this point is actually an open hole!). The opposite pole—called the *Root Chakra*—is at the base of our spine, right at the tip of our tailbone.

D. Morphogenic Fields

The concept of *morphogenic* ("shape-creating") fields was first proposed in the 1920s. It was revived in 1968 by Rupert Sheldrake, a former Cambridge University biologist. Sheldrake says that every living thing contributes its experience to a collective "memory pool." The field acts as a template, shaping behavior. Morphogenic fields are built up through the accumulated behaviors of species' members and act as a template, shaping behavior.

When events happen, similar events are more likely to happen because a morphogenic field has been created. With morphogenic fields, the evolution of behavior becomes much easier to explain. Spiders of a particular species are linked into a morphogenic field for creating the appropriate kind of web. The morphogenic field will change, based on the experiences of individual spiders. Thus these experiences can be passed down to future generations. Gradually, the best fields become the strongest ones, and the animals follow these guidelines automatically. This works like evolution. However, unlike physical evolution, the organizing principle lies outside the animal. In addition, it can learn from experience and can pass on much more complicated things, such as having a mental model of a web. Because there is a link between the structure of the animal and the structure of the morphogenic field, spiders will automatically latch onto fields appropriate to their own species.

Morphogenic fields explain the way Nature remembers things. An overlap of creativity and routine behavior shapes the way different life forms behave, and this evolutionary learning process is essentially retained as a collective, species-wide memory. Thus every life form has some impact on the behavior of every other life form, particularly those within its own species. And there is a greater field ("The Force") that binds together all humans, and beyond that, all life forms.

Many of our magickal rituals are designed to "tap into" the morphogenic field at various stages, such as "getting in touch with" our ancestors or the Spirits of Nature in order to draw upon their wisdom. This is why some magickal groups jealously guard their ritual secrets—they wish to keep the morphogenic field that they have created very specific and concentrated in order to have very specific and concentrated results. If too many people get the "coven secrets" and make modifications to the ritual structure, then the morphogenic field becomes diffuse and ill-defined, making the thoughtform harder to focus on specific tasks; the magick "loses its kick."

Course Two: Nature

Course Two: Nature

Class I: Natural Mysteries

The most beautiful experience we can have is the Mysterious. It is the fundamental emotion which stands at the cradle of true art and science. —Albert Einstein

1. Introduction: Life, the Universe, and Everything

HROUGHOUT THE AGES, WIZARDS, philosophers, and scientists have sought to understand the Great Mysteries of Life, the Universe, and Everything. Wizards work with energy, which is information. It organizes itself into patterns, and does not exist except in dynamic relationships. By being able to sense and understand these patterns, the Wizard can position himself to be moved in a desired direction by the unfolding flow of events and still be able to alter the unfolding flow through his conscious participation.

The Nature of the Secret

In the ninth discourse of the *Bhagavad-Gita,* it is said that the Great Secret of the Universe, of Life itself, had several characteristics that would mark it as a true secret. First, the secret had to be *intuitional*; that is, capable of being known by anyone wishing to know it and not dependent upon outside teaching or being revealed by an adept. Second, it had to be *righteous*; that is, lawful, within the bounds of the cosmos, according to universal principles. And third, it had to be *pleasant beyond measure;* that is, the secret had to be life-enhancing and exceed the pleasures of earthly existence. Here, in two easy lessons, is the essence of that Secret:

Lesson 2. Everything is Connected to Everything Else

We are part of the sea and the stars.
We are part of the winds of the south and the north
We are part of mountain, moon and Mars,
And the Ages have sent us forth.
—William Ernest Henley, 1845

All of it—every atom in every cell in your body; you and all your family, friends, and neighbors throughout the world; every living creature and plant upon the face of the Earth; every planet, moon, and comet in the solar system; every star in the Milky Way galaxy; every galaxy in the vast and infinite Universe—all are connected into one great Web of Unity, one great Universal "Internet" of Space and Time, Matter, and Energy.

There is one light of the sun, though it is interrupted by walls, mountains, and infinite other things. There is one Intelligent Soul, though it seems to be divided. All things are implicated with one another. The Spirit that bonds us all as One is holy. Everything on Earth, under the heavens, is connected with every other thing. All the different things in the world are coordinated and combined to make up the same universe.
—Marcus Aurelius (161-180 CE)

Humankind has not woven the Web of Life. We are but one thread within it. Whatever we do to the Web, we do to ourselves. All things are bound together. All things connect. —Chief Seattle

And this interconnection and interpenetration of everything with everything else provides the basis for all Magick, according to the First Law of Magick: the Law of Sympathy, which says that all things are linked together by invisible bonds. This means that, just like with a spider web, any action that touches one thread affects the entire web. As conservationist John Muir once said, "You cannot pluck a flower without touching a star."

Lesson 3: "It's Alive!"

> *There is no matter as such! All matter originates and exists only by virtue of a force.... We must assume behind this force the existence of a conscious and intelligent Mind. This Mind is the matrix of all matter.* —Max Planck,
> Nobel Prize–winning father of quantum theory

Just as everything is connected to everything else in one great web, Wizards know also that the whole thing is alive. Your body is composed of several trillion cells, each a living system itself, but together comprising the greater synergic unity that is you. All these living cells are made of molecules, which in turn are composed of atoms. And atoms are made up of protons, electrons, neutrons, and a whole host of sub-atomic particles that we keep discovering.

In the same way, you and I and every other person, creature, tree, and flower are cells in the greater living body of Mother Earth—or Gaea, as many call Her. And the living Earth is only one of countless bodies of all sizes—planets, moons, asteroids, comets, meteorites, planetoids, and planetesimals—that make up our solar system. Our entire solar system itself is like a giant atom or cell, with the Sun as its nucleus. And ours is only one of a hundred billion star systems that make up the great spiral form of our galaxy, all revolving in a vast whirlpool vortex about the enormous black hole at its center. And the expanding spiral shape of our galaxy is exactly the same as the spiral of a chambered nautilus seashell, a pinecone, the dance of a honeybee, and the solar wind that blows radiation through our solar system. All these systems have their own lives and all are also linked into each other like Russian nesting dolls, each one fitting perfectly within the next larger one. And there is no end to it. Through the Hubble telescope, we are just now beginning to discern that the uncountable numbers of galaxies throughout the universe are not scattered randomly, but are clustered in vast bubble-like structures that look a lot like cells....

And here's the really mind-boggling part: Where there is life, there is consciousness. Even the tiniest living organism has awareness, or *sentience,* through which it seeks food, avoids discomfort, reproduces itself, and makes innumerable choices between this and that in the course of its life. Such sentience pervades every living creature—from a single-celled amoeba with no brain or nervous system, to a great sperm whale with the largest brain on the planet. It is such sentience that distinguishes an entity from an object.

The lowliest bug has its own little agenda. It demonstrates its sentience by investigating its world with intense interest and curiosity, by making continual choices based upon its preferences. And most importantly, things matter to it; it *cares.* It cares whether it lives or dies, whether it eats or goes hungry, and whether it reproduces. It hides from predators and defends itself when attacked. It actively hunts for food and mates by seeking and following interesting clues. And if it's a mother, it very likely protects its young. When you think about it, this sentience drives the very heart of evolution.

Lesson 4: The Balance

> *"The world is in balance, in Equilibrium. A Wizard's power of Changing and of Summoning can shake the balance of the world. It is dangerous, that power. It must follow knowledge, and serve need. To light a candle is to cast a shadow...."* —Ursula K. LeGuin,
> *A Wizard of Earthsea,* pp. 43–44

All things in the world, the many worlds, the Universe, and the Multiverse, are in a state of *equilibrium.* This means a cosmic Balance, in which every action has its equal and opposite reaction. Light balances darkness, positive balances negative, anti-matter balances matter, and so on. Herein lies another secret of Wizardry: A Wizard always stands at the balance point in the middle, and looks both ways equally. The Wizard must look at the energy flow behind and ahead through his point of balance in the present in order to make choices that do not shake the balance of the world and cause the Wizard harm from the turbulence. I put this principle into action constantly in my own life. When I consider any amount of time over the past, for example, I automatically consider the same amount of time into the future—whether it's years, decades, centuries, millennia, or geological aeons.

Lesson 5: The Circle of Life

One of the most important distinctions between the magickal view of life and the mundane view concerns the great Circle of Life. The mundane view of time is linear—that is, seeing time as moving forward in a straight line, from beginning through middle to end. But to magickal people, and particularly Wizards, all of Time moves in cycles, and what goes around comes around again. This is especially obvious in the Circle of Life—the journey of every living being from birth, through life, to death, and around again to rebirth. As we see the Wheel of the Year turn through the seasons—from the new birth of Spring, through the ripening of Summer, to the harvest of the Fall, to the barrenness of Winter, and around to Spring again—so turns the Circle of Life for each of us.

Such life circles are never closed, but are open-ended instead. They're not so much like a ring, but more like a coiled spring—a spiral, an open helix, like the DNA molecule that gives the blueprint for all life. Each time we come round, we are a bit further along in the course of evolution. That evolution is one not only of body, but also of soul, for each time around, consciousness is increased. Inanimate stones are crumbled by bacteria into soil, out of which grows grass and vegetables. Herbivores eat the plants, and so the spirit of vegetation ascends to the level of animals. Carnivores eat the herbivores, and the herbivore spirit moves another notch up the food chain. In each lifetime, we gain experience and learn lessons, and our wisdom and consciousness grow ever greater. However, what comes around in the course of evolution is not ego consciousness, the sense of self the student has in this incarnation. The consciousness that is eternal and evolving is collective, a field shared by all beings. One of the things a Wizard does is to "tune in" to that extra-personal web of relationships and information, benefiting every time from his exchange and identification with it.

Just as we grow from a tiny embryo in our mother's womb into a baby, a child, an adolescent, and finally a mature adult, so has Mother Earth grown through all the ages of life from single-celled organisms through simple *invertebrates* (creatures without backbones), to complex animals with skeletons and sophisticated nervous systems. The entire evolution of life on Earth can be seen as the embryological development and maturation of a single vast creature: Mother Earth Herself. We call Her "Gaea," as She was named by the ancient Greeks, and we are part of Her body and Her life. Our souls and Hers are One—like tiny droplets of rain are all still One with Water everywhere.

There is a famous expression that describes this Great Truth: *"Ontogeny recapitulates phylogeny."* This translates as: "The development of the individual re-traces the development of the species." Only *phylum* really means a much broader category than "species." *Chordates,* the phylum of which we are a part, includes all animals with backbones, as well as some simple creatures with only a basic "spinal cord" and no bony spine to contain it. But each of us, as we grow from a tiny embryo, goes through all the developmental stages of all our ancestors, from being a single cell through having gills, a tail, and being covered with fur—and all before we are born! And in the same way, our individual development mirrors that of Gaea Herself, repeated endlessly in each generation as we, like She, evolve towards ever-greater consciousness.

Lesson 6: The Cycles of Time

To a Wizard, it is clear that Time does not move in a straight line, but in spiraling Cycles. The hands of the clock go around, but move forward one hour in each turning. The days of the week come around again, but move forward through the months. The seasons turn through the great Wheel of the Year, and Spring always follows Winter—but the years roll forward down the centuries and aeons. All things appear to move through Time in circles, but every circle is part of a larger circle, which is also moving, and so nothing stays in the same place. Nor does it just go forward. The next larger cycles carry us forward one loop for each turning.

On a cosmic level, those spiraling cycles continue.... The Earth turns from day to night and the Moon circles around. But the Earth and the Moon are also circling the Sun through the seasons—along with all the other planets, moons, comets, and the rest. But this doesn't bring us around to the same place each year, because the solar system is also circling around the galaxy, along with all the other star systems. Of course, the galaxy itself is also moving through the cosmos...and so it goes.

Here are some of the Cycles of Time that we have charted. Some of them are very regular, almost like clockwork. Others may seem far less regular, and indeed we are still trying to determine a formula for them.

Geological Ages (37 million years)

The longest Cycles we have experienced in the history of life on Earth are those we call *Geological Cycles* (*Ge* was the original Greek name for Gaea, Mother Earth, and all sciences and magicks having to do with the Earth—such as *ge*ology, *ge*ography, *ge*omancy, *ge*ophysics—begin with *ge*). Like the ages of a person, from infancy through childhood, adolescence, maturity, middle age, and old age, the Ages of the living Earth have been charted and given names. Based mostly on the names of locations where rocks and fossils of those periods were first found, here are the names and lengths of time (millions of years = "my"; millions of years ago = "mya"; and "ya" = years ago) of the Geological Ages, beginning with the first one in which complex living organisms appeared. This is called the Cambrian Era, and all time before it is simply referred to as "Pre-Cambrian."

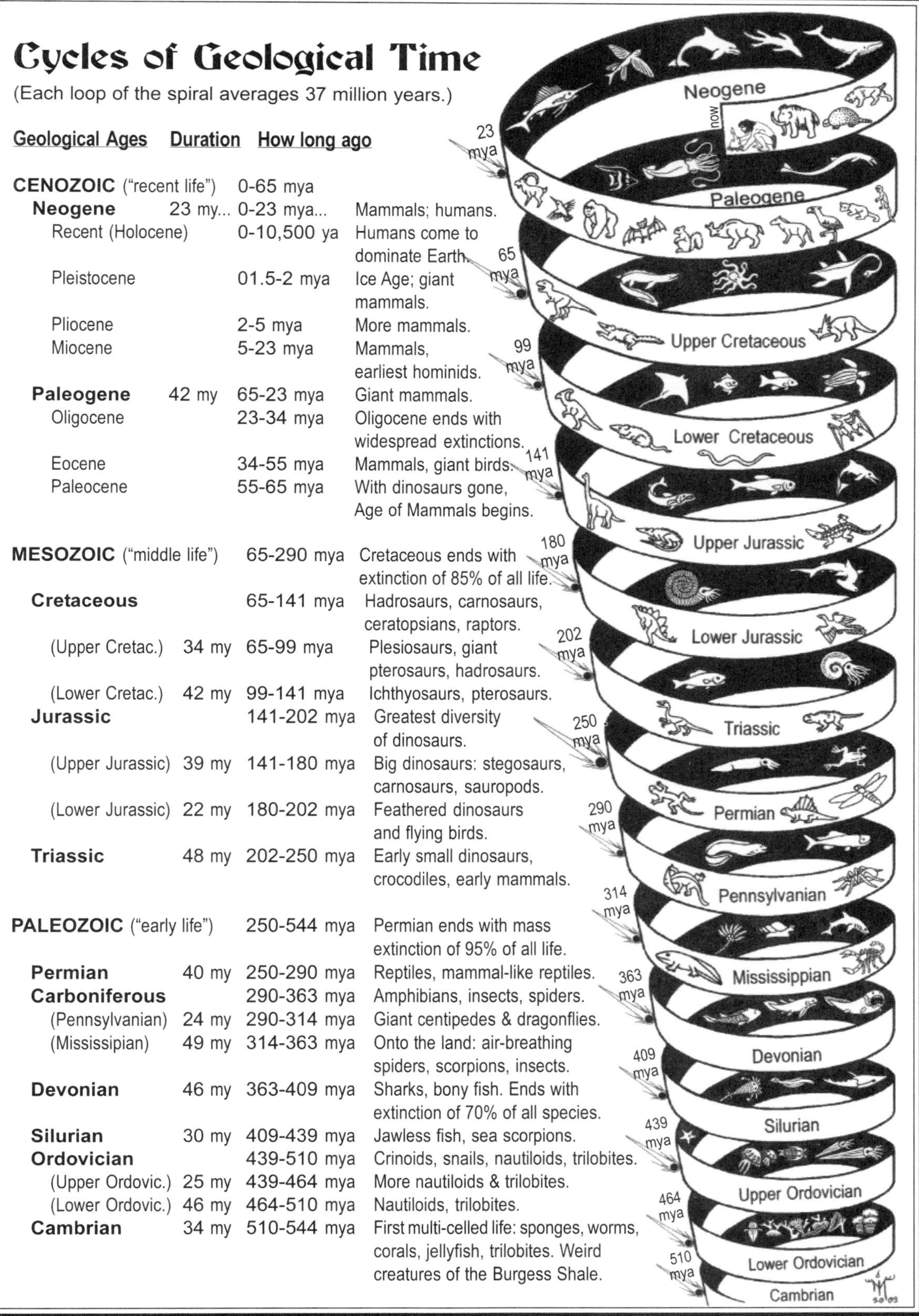

Cycles of Geological Time

(Each loop of the spiral averages 37 million years.)

Geological Ages	Duration	How long ago	
CENOZOIC ("recent life")		0-65 mya	
Neogene	23 my...	0-23 mya...	Mammals; humans.
Recent (Holocene)		0-10,500 ya	Humans come to dominate Earth.
Pleistocene		01.5-2 mya	Ice Age; giant mammals.
Pliocene		2-5 mya	More mammals.
Miocene		5-23 mya	Mammals, earliest hominids.
Paleogene	42 my	65-23 mya	Giant mammals.
Oligocene		23-34 mya	Oligocene ends with widespread extinctions.
Eocene		34-55 mya	Mammals, giant birds.
Paleocene		55-65 mya	With dinosaurs gone, Age of Mammals begins.
MESOZOIC ("middle life")		65-290 mya	Cretaceous ends with extinction of 85% of all life.
Cretaceous		65-141 mya	Hadrosaurs, carnosaurs, ceratopsians, raptors.
(Upper Cretac.)	34 my	65-99 mya	Plesiosaurs, giant pterosaurs, hadrosaurs.
(Lower Cretac.)	42 my	99-141 mya	Ichthyosaurs, pterosaurs.
Jurassic		141-202 mya	Greatest diversity of dinosaurs.
(Upper Jurassic)	39 my	141-180 mya	Big dinosaurs: stegosaurs, carnosaurs, sauropods.
(Lower Jurassic)	22 my	180-202 mya	Feathered dinosaurs and flying birds.
Triassic	48 my	202-250 mya	Early small dinosaurs, crocodiles, early mammals.
PALEOZOIC ("early life")		250-544 mya	Permian ends with mass extinction of 95% of all life.
Permian	40 my	250-290 mya	Reptiles, mammal-like reptiles.
Carboniferous		290-363 mya	Amphibians, insects, spiders.
(Pennsylvanian)	24 my	290-314 mya	Giant centipedes & dragonflies.
(Mississipian)	49 my	314-363 mya	Onto the land: air-breathing spiders, scorpions, insects.
Devonian	46 my	363-409 mya	Sharks, bony fish. Ends with extinction of 70% of all species.
Silurian	30 my	409-439 mya	Jawless fish, sea scorpions.
Ordovician		439-510 mya	Crinoids, snails, nautiloids, trilobites.
(Upper Ordovic.)	25 my	439-464 mya	More nautiloids & trilobites.
(Lower Ordovic.)	46 my	464-510 mya	Nautiloids, trilobites.
Cambrian	34 my	510-544 mya	First multi-celled life: sponges, worms, corals, jellyfish, trilobites. Weird creatures of the Burgess Shale.

Here's a simple *mnemonic* (memory trick) with which you can memorize all those names in order by their first initials COSDC.PTJC.PEOMPPR. Say, "**C**amels **O**ften **S**it **D**own **C**lumsily. **P**erhaps **T**heir **J**oints **C**reak. **P**ossibly **E**arly **O**iling **M**ight **P**revent **P**ermanent **R**heumatism." That is: **C**ambrian, **O**rdovician, **S**ilurian, **D**evonian, **C**arboniferous; **P**ermian, **T**riassic, **J**urassic, **C**retaceous; **P**aleocene, **E**ocene, **O**ligocene, **M**iocene, **P**liocene, **P**leistocene, **R**ecent. Learn this and you will certainly impress your science teachers!

Each of these ages is distinguished from those before and after by a change in Gaea's layers of rock, as if they are chapters in a book. And the fossils in each layer are also quite distinct. You can go to a place like the Grand Canyon, where many millions of years of these layers have been cut through and exposed in the cliff faces, and you can see that they are clearly separate. Something happened at the end of each age that brought that age and its life forms to an end. Take a look over the chart, and notice the duration of each of those ages. There is a definite cycle here, averaging 37 million years for each age.

As our solar system orbits the center of the galaxy in a 200-million-year circle dance, the journey takes us up and down through the galaxy's equatorial dust plane about every 37 million years. Many scientists are now considering that this may be the factor behind the cycle of mass extinctions that have occurred just about that often throughout the history of life on Earth. Perhaps the dust disturbs the outer shells of debris surrounding our solar system in the form of the Kuiper Belt and the Oort Cloud, dislodging comets and asteroids and sending them plunging through the orbits of the inner worlds—and sometimes crashing into ours.

Historical Eras (various durations)

As with the history of life, human history has also been divided into eras, primarily based on the types of materials used for making tools and weapons. Generally speaking, since the appearance of modern "Cro-Magnon" humans, these eras are described as follows, although there is often some overlap between them. It is important to note, however, that the existence of these eras does not mean that everyone in the world moves from one to the next at the same time; there remain a few cultures in the world even today who are still living pretty much in the Stone Age!

Historical Era / Materials	Time Period	Duration
Plastics, Silicon, Synthetics (Space)	1950 -future	50+ yrs.
Age of Steel (Roman/Christian Era)	50 BCE-1950 CE	2,000 yrs.
Iron Age (Classical Era)	1500-50 BCE	1,450 yrs.
Bronze Age ("Golden Age")	3000-1500	1,500 yrs.
Copper Age (City Building)	5000-3000	2,000 yrs.
Neolithic (new stone) (farming)	8500-5000	3,500 yrs.
Upper Paleolithic (Ice Age)	40,000-8500	30,000 yrs.

Zodiacal Aeons (2,167 years)

While the historical eras listed above follow a linear rather than cyclic pattern, some of them can be overlaid approximately with the Astrological Ages, corresponding to the 12 signs of the Zodiac. These astrological ages or "Aeons" are based on the *precession of the equinoxes* (equinox means "equal night"). The equinoxes are the two times a year (March 21 and Sept. 21) when the day and night are equal in length. But more precisely, the equinoxes are the imaginary points in the heavens where the extension of the Earth's equator (called the *celestial equator*) intersects the *plane of the ecliptic* (also called simply "the ecliptic": the equator of the solar system, and apparent path of the Sun against the constellations of the Zodiac). The Earth's *axis of rotation* (a line going straight through the poles) is inclined at an angle of 23½ degrees from the ecliptic, which is why we have seasons, as each hemisphere (North and South) in turn faces more towards the Sun or away from it.

These two planes (the celestial equator and the ecliptic) intersect at two points. These are the *Vernal* (Spring) and *Autumnal* (Fall) *Equinoxes* (Figure 1).

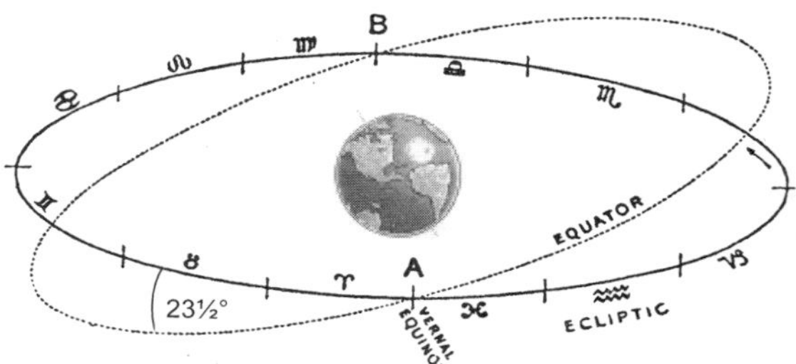

Figure 1: The Ecliptic and the Celestial Equator showing the Vernal (A) and Autumnal (B) Equinoxes

When the ancient Babylonians devised the Zodiacal calendar in the 2nd millennium BCE, they used the heliacal rising of Aries on the Vernal Equinox to mark the beginning of the year. "Heliacal rising" is the rising of a constellation just before the Sun. However, Aries no longer rises with the Sun on the Vernal Equinox due to the *precession of the equinoxes.*

The precession of the equinoxes, also known as the Platonic Year, is an apparent westward movement of the equinoxes caused by the slow wobbling of the Earth's polar axis. Just like a spinning top wobbles when it slows down, so does the Earth. It rotates on its own axis, but at the same time the axis describes a slow circle in the sky. This circle has a radius of 23½° and takes 26,000 years to complete.

Today the North Pole points to the star Polaris; in 12,000 years it will point to Vega in the constellation Lyra (Figure 2).

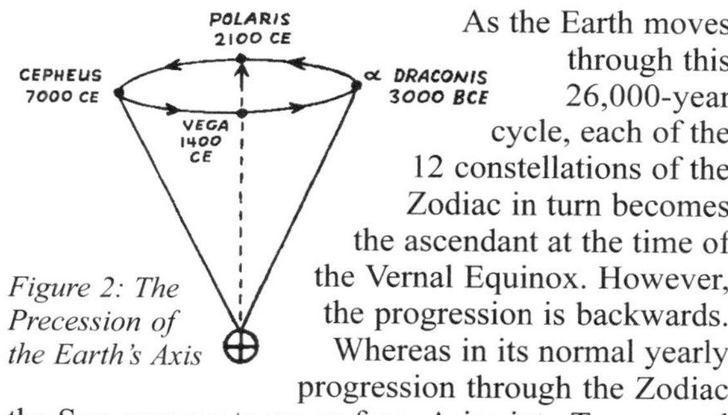

Figure 2: The Precession of the Earth's Axis

As the Earth moves through this 26,000-year cycle, each of the 12 constellations of the Zodiac in turn becomes the ascendant at the time of the Vernal Equinox. However, the progression is backwards. Whereas in its normal yearly progression through the Zodiac the Sun appears to move from Aries into Taurus, and so on, the equinoxes move in the opposite direction.

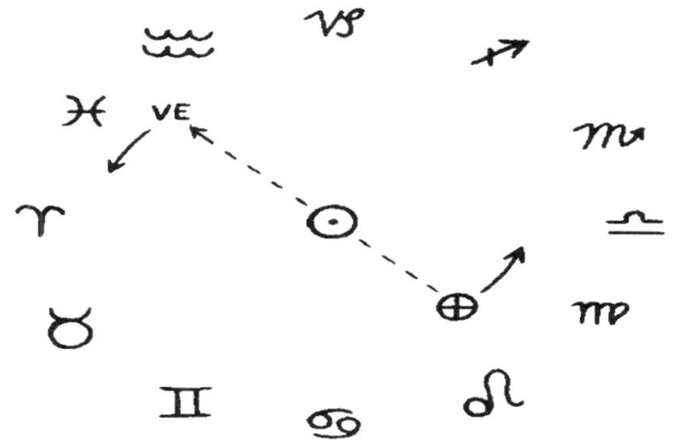

Figure 3: The yearly apparent movement of the Sun through the Zodiac, showing the present position of the Vernal Equinox

Because it takes 26,000 years for the Earth to complete one precessional wobble, it follows that the Sun will rise on the Vernal Equinox in each sign for 30 degrees, or 2,167 years. Each such period constitutes a World Age, or Zodiacal Aeon, named for the sign ascendant at the time of the Vernal Equinox. Here are the Signs and time periods since the Ice Age, including the next Aeon of Aquarius. I have also indicated the approximately corresponding historical ages:

Aeon	Sign	Years	Overlapping Historical Ages
Aquarius (water)	♒	2012-4179	Space Age: galactic diaspora
Pisces (fishes)	♓	155 BCE-2012 CE	Roman/Christian Era (Dark Ages 450-1450)
Aries (ram)	♈	2322-155 BCE	Iron Age / Age of Heroes (Classical)
Taurus (bull)	♉	4489-2322	Bronze Age / Golden Age (cattle)
Gemini (twins)	♊	6656-4489	Copper Age (city building)
Cancer (crab)	♋	8823-6656	New Stone Age (farming)
Leo (lion)	♌	10,990-8823	Old Stone Age / Ice Age

Religious Epochs (500 years)

Another interesting cycle in human history has moved in approximately 500-year periods, or *epochs.* These epochs have witnessed the successive prominence of major religions, usually initiated by visionary Prophets. On the next page is a list of these epochs and some of their Prophets.

Renaissances (60 years)

Just about every sixty years, with remarkable regularity over the past few centuries at least, there has occurred a Renaissance ("re-birth") in Western civilization. Each of these periods has seen a similar flowering of the arts, poetry, music, literature, drama, culture, sciences, spirituality, and "utopian" communities. Why do these cycles occur every sixty years? Perhaps that is the average lifetime for a perpetually recurrent generation of "Cultural Creatives" to live, change the world, die, and be reborn over and over…the very meaning of *renaissance.* Here are the dates for each of these that I have mapped, with projections for the next couple:

Renaissances

Dates	Popular Name
2080s	The Diaspora
2020s	The Awakening
1960s	The Psychedelic Sixties
1900s	*Fin de Siecle* ("End of Cycle")
1840s	Transcendentalist Movement
1780s	The American Revolution
1720s	The Age of Enlightenment
1660s	The Scientific Revolution
1600s	The English Renaissance
1540s	The Age of Exploration
1480s	The Italian Renaissance

There are many more cycles I haven't listed here, such as wars (20 years) and sunspots (11.1 years). Indeed, dozens of smaller cycles have been noted with time periods of 18.2 years, 9.6 years, 9.2 years, 8 years, and 5.91 years. Some cycles are actually speeding up (or collapsing). For thousands of years the *Schumann Resonance* or pulse ("heartbeat") of the Earth has been 7.83 cycles per second. The military have used this as a reliable reference since its discovery. However, since 1980 the frequency of this resonance has been slowly increasing. It is now more than 12 cycles per second!

Much of the time these various cycles, moving at different frequencies like the hands on a clock, seem independent. But just as the clock hands and the calendar will all come together at the stroke of midnight on New Year's Eve, sometimes a whole bunch of different cycles will all match frequencies at the same time. We call such a time "The Year of the Jackpot"—a term coined by science fiction writer Robert Heinlein from the way the rotating symbols line up in a casino slot machine. In such a "Jackpot" time, the coincidence of many cycles acts to cause a high peak "Synchronicity Wave"—like a temporal

Religious Epochs

Approx.	Religion	Founding Prophets	Key Events
c.2000	Gaian Earth Religion	Zell (1942), Lovelock (1919)	Gaea Thesis 1970
c.1500	Protestantism (Germany)	Martin Luther (1483-1546)	Reformation 1517
c.1000	Roman & Orthodox Church	Pope Leo IX (1002-1054)	Great Schism 1054
c.500 CE	Islam (Arabia)	Mohammed (570-632)	Hejira (flight) 622 CE
1st century	Christianity (Roman Empire)	Jesus (4 BCE-29 CE)	Crucifixion 29 CE
c.500 BCE	Buddhism (India)	Buddha (490-410 BCE)	Sutras
	Confucianism (China)	Confucius (551-479 BCE)	Analects of Confucius
	Taoism (China)	Lao Tzu (6th century BCE)	Tao-Te Ching
	Pythagorean Mysteries	Pythagoras (580-500 BCE)	Parthenon in Athens 438 BCE
	Zoroastrianism (Persia)	Zoroaster (628-551 BCE)	The Gathas
c.1000	Judaism (Israel)	Solomon (970-928 BCE)	Great Temple in Jerusalem
c.1500	Monotheism (Hebrews)	Moses (1668-1548 BCE)	10 Commandments 1628 BCE

tsunami ("tidal wave"). At these times the powers of magick are greatly augmented, and—like a surfer riding a huge breaker—magicians and Wizards of all types can accomplish amazing things that would be more difficult at any other time. These dawning years of the 21st century are such a time, and 2012 is the next "Jackpot" year.

Lesson 7. Time Traveling

Imagine you are walking along a path through a rolling countryside. Sometimes the path takes you into deep valleys, with forests on either side of you. You cannot see to the sides, and you cannot see far ahead. But you have a map that you are following, and landmarks along the way are marked on the map. Eventually, your path brings you to the top of a hill. From there, you can look back over the path you've already traveled; and you can look ahead over the path yet before you—as far, at least, as the next hilltop. So, from this high vantagepoint, you take out your notebook and draw a new map of the road ahead. You mark on it the rivers, forests, rocky outcroppings, villages, deserts, swamps and other features you will have to pass or cross to reach that distant peak.

This is how our path through Time appears to a Wizard. As the various Cycles of Time turn and turn again, each time we come round to the same season, it is like coming to the top of the next high hill. And if we know how to look out, that vantage point allows us to see the next cycle—the path through the valley to the top of the next hill. Throughout the ages, many Prophets, Seers, and visionaries have viewed the coming ages from such peaks of history's synchronicity waves and cycles. They have left recorded prophecies—which may be seen as "roadmaps of time." But while the visions of such seers as Nostradamus, Edgar Cayce, and Mother Shipton have provided intriguing "maps" of the times from their days to ours, they have only been able to see to the top of the next peak from where they stood. And that peak is where we now stand. Those prophetic maps are now obsolete and can chart our path no further. It is now time for the making of new maps, and the charting of a new future—a future that we can create through Wizardry. Let me tell you a little story about changing the future by magick…

In the middle of the 20th century, when I was a young man, most people in the world believed unquestionably that a global nuclear *holocaust* (destruction by fire) was inevitable and *immanent* (due any moment). Every movie about the future made in those days pre-supposed that civilization would soon be destroyed in a nuclear war, and any survivors would be battling hideous mutants in the radioactive ruins. This conviction ran so deep that in 1960, when George Pal made an excellent movie of H.G. Wells' novel, *The Time Machine,* he naturally had to include a nuclear war as the time traveler journeys into the future. But an important part of that story is showing the temporal "odometer" on the dashboard of the time machine, indicating the date. So Pal had the time traveler make a stop just as the great nuclear holocaust was being unleashed. And the date on the dial read: "1966"—only six years from the release of the film!

But when 1966 arrived, we didn't have a nuclear war. Instead, something happened that changed our future forever. That September a new TV show premiered—with a completely new vision of the future in which there had been no holocaust, and a united humanity was traveling among the stars. This show, as I'm sure you have guessed by now, was *Star Trek.* Its creator, Gene Roddenberry, is said to have explained his intention as: "I'm trying to present a new vision of the future that will be so compelling that people will choose it over a global nuclear holocaust."

And so he did—one of the greatest acts of magick in our time. Nearly forty years, six TV series (all continuing in syndication), and ten movies have created a future that has inspired both our imagination and our technology towards the exploration of space, and gave us the greatest Mission Statement of magickal intent ever articulated: "To explore strange new worlds; to seek out new life and new civilizations; to boldly go where no one has gone before!"

So mote it be. True Wizards know that the best way to predict the future is to create it.

Lesson 8. The Great Work

Lesson 8: The Great Work

"To find the Absolute in the Infinite, in the Indefinite, and in the Finite, this is the Magnum Opus, the Great Work of the Sages."
—Albert Mackey, *Morals and Dogma*

And so now we come in this course to The Great Work. According to the Hermetic Order of the Golden Dawn, the objective is "to obtain control of the nature and power of one's own being." But this is only the first step. Ultimately the Great Work is to aid, abet, and foster the evolution of consciousness into the next quantum leap. In Eastern traditions this is called Enlightenment. It is a full awakening of the spirit, in which one experiences with every fiber of one's being the full connection with all other Beings, throughout all of Time and Space. It is the integration of both brain hemispheres into simultaneous consciousness, rather than the normal alternation of one or the other. In Wizardry, we call this *Apotheosis*—literally, deification, or "becoming Divine."

The Awakening

Just as each of us awakened into consciousness as an infant, so too is Gaea Herself poised on the threshold of a planetary Awakening. This might come about as a kind of universal telepathy. But I think the emergence and rapid evolution of the Internet is already providing the seeds of a technological vehicle of global consciousness through which this Awakening will inevitably manifest. I believe that the two-handed coordination required for modern computer consoles is stimulating not only a re-awakening of the dormant right brain hemispheres of humanity, but a full synchronization of both forms of mentality into a new ambidextrous consciousness that will be able to sustain the awakened mind of Gaea. And as with the awakening of consciousness in our own minds, as the billions of neurons in our brains linked up synergistically, just so shall we all participate in the Awakening of Gaea Herself—and our full Apotheosis.

Scientist/philosopher Teilhard de Chardin (1881–1955) envisioned just such an awakening of universal consciousness as the "Omega Point"—the ultimate fulfillment of the entire purpose of creation and evolution. This would be the point in time when the individual consciousnesses of all living beings on Earth coalesce into a single collective consciousness. He said: "We are faced with a harmonized collectivity of consciousnesses to a sort of superconciousness. The Earth not only becoming covered by myriads of grains of thought, but becoming enclosed in a single thinking envelope, a single unanimous reflection" (*The Phenomenon of Man*, 1955).

The Diaspora

We stand at a great crossroads in evolution; perhaps the most critical in the entire history of Life. The very technology that presently threatens all life on this planet could alternately be used to build starships to carry our children throughout the galaxy. Perhaps humans are also intended to be the spores of Gaea. Reproduction is an essential function of all living systems, and this applies no less to a living planet.

I believe that before the end of this century, we will see the beginnings of the great *Diaspora* of humanity out into the stars. Diaspora means "scattering," or "dispersion"—particularly of a people with a common origin, such as the Jews after the Romans destroyed Jerusalem in 70 CE. But the root of the word, *speirein,* means "to sow," as in the planting of seeds. Establishing space colonies, terraforming the barren surfaces of the Moon, Mars, or Titan—"flying Mother Nature's silver seeds to a new home…" as Neil Young sings—may be one of the most important purposes for the evolution of a technological species.

And perhaps one day seedlings of Gaea will be planting new roots in distant soil beyond the farthest star….

Class II: The Soul of Nature

I am a paradise of deep wilderness,
The soul of Nature and life of the Divine
Fragrant and fertile is my body,
Touch me in the petals of every sweet blossom.
Through abundance you shall know me.
I am thy oasis, pouring forth the waters of life
—Katlyn Breene, "A hymn from the heart of the Living Goddess"

1. Introduction: Personifications

MY FAVORITE SEQUENCE IN DISNEY'S original *Fantasia* (1940) was Beethoven's "Pastorale Symphony," enacted against a tapestry of Greco-Roman mythology by centaurs, unicorns, pegasi, and a tipsy Bacchus. There appeared, for the first time on film, several of the old Gods: Jupiter, Vulcan, Diana…

At the very end, when Nox draws Her veil of night over the Arcadian landscape, and the thin crescent of the new moon appears against the stars, and the camera closes in to reveal Diana standing on a cloud, flanked by a deer, and Diana draws the bow of the moon and shoots a meteoric arrow across the sky… Well, that got me; I was hooked! Eventually I even created a statue inspired by that image.

Understand that these various personalizations of natural forces are just that. As Death so often says in Terry Pratchett's *Discworld* novels, "I AM AN ANTHROPOMORPHIC PERSONIFICATION." (That is, the representation of an idea in human form.) From millennia of observation, we have found that natural forces behave "as if" they actually *are* such embodied creatures like Disney's unicorns, deities, and centaurs. Understanding and interacting with these anthropomorphized forces works better for most Wizards when they think of the forces in this way.

Lesson 2. The Cosmic Family of Nature

One of the most important teachings of all tribal peoples is that all living beings—along with the Earth, Sea, Sky, Sun, and Stars—are part of one great Family. Many teachings echo the Native American Lakota expression: *Mitakuye Oyasin!* —"All my relations." In the creation myths and other stories of all peoples throughout the world we find tales of connectedness, of how the original cosmic Parents came into being, and engendered the world and everything in it. Two of the greatest archetypes of universal parentage are Mother Nature and Father Time.

Mother Nature *(Natura)*

I am the beauty of the green Earth,
And the white Moon among the stars,
And the mystery of the waters,
And the desire of human hearts.
Call unto your soul: Arise and come unto me!
For I am the soul of Nature
That gives life to the universe.
From me all things proceed,
And unto me all things must return.
—Doreen Valiente, "The Charge of the Goddess"

Mother Nature is the eldest and greatest aspect of the Goddess, the all-encompassing embodiment of Universal Life. Her cosmic energy coalesces into Matter-Mater—the Mother of all forms. The words *matter* and *mater* literally mean "Mother." Dion Fortune once commented that all goddesses are manifestations of the One Great Goddess whose identity is the universal feminine spirit of Nature.

Nature is the very essence of diversity. She represents both Darkness and Light and her worship is the reconciliation of opposites. The search for Balance is the goal of her people, and it is achieved by the acceptance of multiple paths and truths.

The First Lesson of the Goddess is . . .
"All life is sacred."

The Second Lesson of the Goddess is . . .
"There is only one race . . . the human race."

Medieval alchemists made continual references to "Dame Nature" as the source of all life, sustenance, and knowledge. She is so universally known that she has even been used in TV commercials to sell margarine, with the famous slogan; "It's not *nice* to fool

Mother Nature!" She is truly the Mother of All Mothers! And Mother knows best!

Father Time *(Chronos)*

This thing all things devours:
Birds, beasts, trees, flowers;
Gnaws iron, bites steel;
Grinds hard stones to meal;
Slays king, ruins town,
And beats high mountain down.
—Gollum's riddle,
from *The Hobbit,* by J.R.R. Tolkien

The ancient Greeks personified Father Time as the Titan *Chronos,* from which we get words like *chronometer* (clock) and *chronology* (time-line). As Time devours all, Chronos was said to have devoured his own children. Gaea, their Mother, was furious over this, and she hid the 12th child from him when it was born, substituting a rock wrapped in a baby blanket. Raised secretly in a cave, when the last child (named Zeus) was grown, he cut Chronos open and released his eleven brothers and sisters. After the great Battle of the Titans (the *Titanomachia*), these became the familiar Gods and Goddesses of Olympus.

The Romans called Chronos *Saturn,* and identified him as the God of both Time and the Harvest. Shown in a black hooded robe and carrying a reaper's scythe and an hourglass, Saturn became known as the Harvester of Souls—or the Grim Reaper. Rome celebrated a huge festival in his honor every year at the time of the Winter Solstice, the shortest day of the year, which marked the turning of the yearly Wheel of Time into the New Year. This week-long festival was called *Saturnalia*, and it is the origin of most of our customs around Christmas and New Year's. Saturn was often depicted as departing at this time, to be replaced with the newborn Sun Child of the coming year. I'm sure you will recognize this Saturnine imagery!

The Star Goddess *(Nyx & Astra)*

Hear ye the words of the Star Goddess
The dust of whose feet are the hosts of heaven
She whose body encircles the universe...
—Doreen Valiente, "The Charge of the Goddess"

The Star Goddess is the personification of the night sky, with all the stars. The Egyptians called her *Nuit;* to the Greeks she was *Nyx;* to the Romans *Nox* (from which we get the words *equinox* and *nocturnal*); and we call her Night. The Milky Way is said to be the milk of her breasts expressed across the heavens to nourish life on all the infinite worlds. She is the spirit and body of our galaxy. Of her are born star systems and planets including, of course, our own Earth.

Of course, many individual stars and constellations are also named for goddesses (as well as gods). Such a star goddess in ancient times was *Astraea,* or *Astra,* whose name gives us the generic word for "star," as in *astra*l, *astro*nomy, and *astro*naut. The daughter of *Themis,* Goddess of Harmony, Astraea was said to have lived on Earth in the legendary Golden Age. But as humans grew more violent, the gods abandoned the Earth and retreated to the heavens. Patient and hopeful, Astraea was the last of the immortals to leave the world of men.

The original name *Astra* is the root of many names for the Goddess of the Evening Star, or, literally, "Eastern Star:" *Ishtar, Esther, Aster, Asherah, Aphrodite, Astarte*—and *Eostre*, goddess of the fertile Spring, whose Festival is *Ostara* or Easter, celebrated at Spring Equinox. The Eastern Star, however, is actually a planet: Venus (the Roman name for this goddess). All these variations of her name still share the same attributes: love, beauty, sex, and fertility. And her symbol is the seven-pointed star. Because it is visible before any other stars can be seen, this is the "Wishing Star" of the child's spell-poem:

Star light, star bright,
First star I see tonight;
I wish I may, I wish I might,
Have the wish I wish tonight.

Father Sun *(Sol)*

One of the most powerful and universal representations of divine masculinity is the Sun God. He was called *Ra* by the Egyptians, *Helios* by the Greeks, and *Sol* by the Romans. As the blazing heart at the core of our solar system, Sol supplies all the energy for life on Earth. Plants convert sunlight into food, which nourishes animals. And the burning of organic materials to warm our bodies and cook our meals only releases the sunlight stored within. Thus, Sol is truly the Father of us all, as Gaea is our Mother.

Some of the many sun gods worshipped throughout the world have included *Apollo* in Greece—brother of Artemis, the Moon Goddess; *Lucifer,* the lightbringer; *Lugh* of the Celts; and *Horus* and *Aten* in Egypt. One of his oldest names is *Bel*—meaning "bright" or "brilliant." This is seen in the Canaanite *Ba'al;* the Celtic *Belenos;* and *Balor* of the Flaming Eye. Bale-fires are still lit throughout Ireland at his great festival of *Beltaine* (May Day), marking the beginning of Summer.

Hail to the Sun God,
He's a really fun God!
Ra! Ra! Ra Ra Ra!

Sister Moon (*Luna*)

Luna is the Roman name for the Lady in the Moon. From the earliest times, most human cultures have considered the Moon to be feminine. In ancient Greece she was called *Artemis, Diana,* or *Selene.* She is *Hina* in Hawaii and *Ixchel* in old Mexico. She was *Arianrhod* to the Welsh and *Heng-O* in Taoist China. She is often said to be either the sister or the wife of the Sun God.

Luna has three faces, corresponding to the three phases of the Moon—waxing, full, and waning. She is thus identified as the Triple Goddess—Maiden, Mother, and Crone, corresponding to the ages of women. And as the Moon controls both the tides of the sea and the tides of women's bodies, she is seen as a goddess of Magick and mystery, and worshipped by Witches everywhere, who gather in her name at the full Moons (and sometimes in the dark of the Moon).

The Moon was born from the Earth four billion years ago, before there were any living creatures on our world. A Mars-sized planetoid smashed into the early molten Earth, knocking a great mass out of the opposite side, which coalesced into the Moon. Her birthplace is now the basin of the Pacific Ocean. Thus Luna, though airless, dry, and lifeless, is truly Earth's sister world.

When I gaze upon the full Moon, I think of all the people I know and love throughout the world, and know that they too are looking up at her face at the same time. I visualize the full Moon as a great mirror in the sky (which, in fact, she is), and I send my love reflecting from her to all those I care about.

Pray to the Moon when she is round
Good luck with you will then abound
And what you seek for shall be found
On land, or sea, or underground.

Lesson 3. Mother Earth & Her Children

Mother Earth (*Gaea*)

"Of Earth I sing, eldest of all
And Mother of the Gods..."

So begins the Homeric Hymn to Gaea, the Earth Mother. *Gaea* (Latin *Gaia*) is the name given by the ancient Greeks to the primordial planetary goddess worshipped by humanity since the dawn of the Stone Age. In Hesiod's *Theogony* (the ancient Greek creation story) Gaea was created by Light and Love from the primal cosmic Chaos. Her first offspring was *Ouranos,* the Heavens. Fertilized by the cometary arrows of *Eros* (Love), Gaea gave birth to all the world's plants, animals, Titans, Gods, Goddesses, and, of course, humanity. So Gaea is the Mother of us all. The Romans called her *Terra,* from which we get words like *terrestrial* and *terra*-forming. Every culture on Earth has had a name for her, and many of them—such as the Peruvian *Pachamama*—are a variant of "mama," the first word of most human babies.

Throughout the world, even small children intuitively recognize Mother Earth. She is the oldest and most universally acknowledged religious archetype in all of human experience. In the few images of Gaea that come down to us from ancient Greece, she appears enthroned, or as a beautiful and mature woman with wild hair, emerging from the opening Earth. The very rocks and stones were called "the bones of Gaea."

Photos taken from space since the 1960s have awakened people the world over to our Earth as a whole entity. This awareness has caused the name of Gaea to re-emerge, this time into natural science, in the form of "The Gaia Thesis," which asserts that our planet is a single living organism.

"Gaia" by Susan Seddon-Boulet

Task: Make an Ice-Age Matrika

Matrikas, or "little mothers," were made for more than 20,000 years during the last Ice Age. Found across the Eurasian continent from Spain to Siberia, they are so similar in style that they could have all been made by the same artist. When I decided to become a sculptor in 1973, the first image I set out to reproduce was the oldest of these (30,000 years!), the "Venus of Willendorf," shown here. Try making one yourself for your altar. First, of course, you will need clay. If you have access to a kiln (like at school) and can have it fired, you can use regular ceramic clay. Otherwise, I recommend air-drying clay, like "Mexi-Clay." I prefer red clay, in either case. These figures don't usually have lower arms, and the faces are generally featureless. Dry her or fire her, and you will astound future archaeologists!

The First Children of Gaea

The first Children of Gaea are what we call the three great "Kingdoms (or Queendoms) of Life." These are Plants, Animals, and Fungi, the basic divisions of all multi-cellular organisms. From the point of view of our magickal personifications, these manifest as five: two sets of twins—the Green and the Red—and one loner, the Grey.

The crucial difference between plants and animals resolves to a single atom in a complex molecule of the circulatory fluids. In plants, that atom is magnesium, making the molecule appear green. We call it *chlorophyll,* and it conveys the power of photosynthesis—turning light and water into sugar. In animals, the equivalent atom is iron, making the molecule appear red. We call it *hemoglobin,* and it allows our blood to extract oxygen from the air. So the Spirits of vegetation are green, and those of animals are red. Having neither chlorophyll nor hemoglobin, the color of the Spirit of fungi, like some mushrooms, is a pale grey. All of these are intimately inter-related and interdependent upon each other

The cycle of the turning seasons is called the *Wheel of the Year.* Mythically, the main characters in this annual drama are Mother Earth, Father Sun, and their children: the leafy Green Man and flowery Maid, and the hornéd Red Man and furry Maid. (NOTE: When we say "Red Man," this has nothing to do with Native Americans….) The seasonal round is the story of their births, courtship, marriage, pregnancy, maturation, death, and rebirth—all enacted as a great dance in the Circle of Life. (See "The Wheel of the Year," Course 4, Class VI.)

The Green Maid *(Flora)*

For she will bring the buds in Spring
And laugh among the flowers.
In Summer's heat her kisses are sweet;
She sings in leafy bowers.
She cuts the cane and gathers the grain
When fruits of Fall surround her.
Her bones grow old in Wint'ry cold;
She wraps her cloak around her.
—Hope Athern, "The Lady's Bransle"

Flora
by Katlyn

Green Goddess is more than a salad dressing! She is by far the eldest daughter of Gaea, for the first green algae appeared in the oceanic womb of Mother Earth more than 2½ billion years ago. Her Latin name, *Flora,* has been given by scientists to the entire Queendom of plants. She is usually shown with a face of flowers. Spilling forth from her bounteous cornucopia, flowers, fruits, and vegetables are especially associated with the Green Goddess, as they are the *ova* (eggs) of plants.

Like the Green Man, the Green Maid also undergoes the annual vegetation cycle of birth, life, death, and rebirth—from the planting through the harvest, and back again to the season of planting. In the Eleusinian Mysteries of ancient Greece, the Maiden Goddess of Spring flowers was called Kore ("daughter"), and her Mother, Demeter, was goddess of all the vegetative world—especially the grains. The Roman name for her, Ceres, gives us our word *cereal.*

As the embodiment of the flowering of all Nature, Flora was called the secret patron of Rome, without whose help the city would die. Her festival was the *Floralia*—April 28–May 3.

The Green Man *(Florus)*

Oh, he will call the leaves in the Fall,
To fly their colors brightly!
When warmth is lost he paints with frost,
His silver touches lightly!
He greets the day in the dance of the May,
With ribbons wound about him!
We eat his corn and drink from the horn—
We would not be without him!
—Artemisia, "The Lord's Bransle"

Florus, the Green Man, is the masculine aspect of the vegetable kingdom. He came into being with the first sexual differentiation of plants into male and female around 300 million years ago, in the form of the earliest seed-bearing plants, or conifers. Florus is the pollinator, and seeds and grains are associated with him. As the garden god, he is a generous spirit of vegetative fertility who teaches us nurturing and sharing, providing bread, juice, and wine from his body and blood for our tables and sacraments. He is also the forest god, providing safety and refuge, nuts and berries, homes and habitats for all the wild creatures. In all his attributes, he remains consistently benevolent, though he is considered a guardian of the forest.

The essential characteristic of the Green God is his annual vegetation cycle of death and resurrection, and so his rites have been at the heart of many of the ancient initiatory mysteries. Initiates accompanied the Green God at harvest as he died and journeyed through the Underworld, eventually to be reborn in the Spring. Thus he became the Initiator, as well as the spirit guide, accompanying the soul on its journey through the Underworld to eventual rebirth.

The Green Man has been most particularly identified with those plants, such as grains and grapes, whose fermented juices provide intoxicating alcoholic beverages. Thus his spirit directly influences mortals by affecting their very consciousness. I refer to him by his Latin name, *Florus,* although he is much better known throughout the Western world as Jack, a name that comes from the ancient Greek *Iacchos,* whom the Romans called *Bacchus,* the god of wine and ecstasy. Jack is an English nickname for John, as in John Barleycorn, whose famous song tells of the growing of barley and the brewing of whiskey. In ancient Egypt he was *Osiris;* in the Middle East he was called *Tammuz;* and in Africa he is still called *Ochosi. Kokopeli* is his Native American name.

In Spring, when he is just raising his little green head out of the forest floor, we call him Jack-in-the-Green, or Jack O'Green. He may be found in early Summer surveying his congregation as the flower Jack-in-the-Pulpit. The fruit-flavored brandies fermented in late Summer are called Applejack, Bootjack, or Smokejack. At *Samhain,* or Summer's end, we carve his empty pumpkin skull into a spooky Jack O'Lantern, to stand guard on All-Hallows Eve and scare away unfriendly spirits. And through the bitter cold of Winter, his ghostly spirit reminds us of his continuing presence as Jack Frost decorates our windows with beautiful crystal designs. We see his familiar leafy "foliate face" engraved on ornate buildings and in gardens.

Task: Make a Green Man Mask

Here's a cool mask you can make that will put you in touch with the Spirit of the Green. Masks are an ancient form of shape-shifting. You might not feel any different at first wearing a mask, but everyone else sees only the mask and relates to you as the face you show. There are many occasions besides Halloween when it can be fun to wear a Nature Spirit mask. Parties, plays, rituals, celebrations, and Renaissance Faires all provide opportunities to put on another face.

A wonderful Green Man mask can be made quite easily. First, go to a craft or costume store and buy a cheap blank mask for the upper half of your face. The mask should not cover your nostrils, lips, or chin. If you cannot find one exactly right, you can always get a full-face mask and cut off the part below the nose and cheeks with scissors. Also cut the eye holes larger *(Fig. 1).* Also at craft stores, you can find plastic leaves of all kinds and sizes. Buy a batch of fairly large ones, with a few smaller ones thrown in. You will also need a tube of clear silicon glue, such as is used for aquarium cement, and a heavy-duty stapler.

Fig. 1

Starting at the outside edges of the mask, glue and then staple a complete border of the largest leaves into place, with stems pointing toward the center—which will be right between your eyebrows. Be sure to staple from the inside, so the flat side of the staples will be against your skin, and not the points *(Fig. 2)*! Then glue the next layer of leaves over the first (staples are used only on the outermost layer), and further inward, making sure to position them carefully around the eye holes. (Clamp them until the glue sets.) Continue another layer inward with smaller leaves, and finally place one just the right size and shape over the nose. You will now have a classical Foliate ("leafy") Face—the most common image of the Green Man! (Girls may do the same thing with plastic leaves and flowers to make a Flora mask.)

Fig. 2

The Red Maid *(Fauna)*

(by Morning Glory Zell-Ravenheart)

Fauna is the Latin name for the Queendom of the Animals. She is the wife of Faunus, and the feminine personification of the Spirit of all Animals, including, of course, human beings. She is called the Red Maid because of the red blood coursing through the veins of animals. Fauna is the Lady of the Beasts—*Potnia Theron* in Latin.

Other animals may experience her in their own unique perceptions, but humanity first began to worship her around the end of the Paleolithic and the beginning of the Neolithic period, from 12,000-6,000 BCE. Possibly this coincided with the beginning of agriculture and animal domestication. She is known in many forms to many people in agricultural and hunter-gatherer cultures around the world. Her names are legion: *Artemis, Diana, Epona, Bendis, Hathor, Despoina, Astarte, Lakshmi, Ma Ku, White Buffalo Woman...* She is usually pictured as a powerful (and often bare-breasted) woman standing either between two animals or holding onto an animal in each hand. Sometimes she is shown riding on an animal, such as a tiger.

Fauna's rites are often associated with lunar worship and may seem somewhat contradictory on the surface. She is the protector of young animals and wild nature; but on the other hand she eats meat, and blood is her sacrament. This is because she is the Goddess of *all* the animals, both predator and prey. Ancient hunters prayed to her for luck on the hunt, and farmers prayed to her for increase of the flocks. Maybe nowadays we should call on her to help us save endangered species!

The Red Man *(Faunus)*

He shall wake the living dead—
Cloven hoof and hornéd head,
Human heart and human brain,
Pan the Goat-God comes again!
Half a beast and half a man—
Pan is all and all is Pan!
—Percy Bysshe Shelley,
"The Goat-Foot God"

Faunus is often called the Horned One—*Pan* and *Cernunnos* (which means "horned one") being his most common names. He is the masculine personification of the Spirit of all animals, and thus he wears their crown of horns.

Forest faun by Oberon

Faunus is the god of fields, shepherds, and prophecy. He is also the leader of the *fauns,* the Roman branch of the Greek *satyrs.* Fauns and satyrs resemble humans except for having goat's feet, tails, pointed ears, and short horns. In different places, the horns of the Red Man would be those of whatever animals most impressed the people: deer in Europe, buffalo in the Americas, and Antelopes in Africa and Asia. The father of the satyrs in Greece was Pan, whose name means "all." The ancient scholars of Alexandria believed that Pan personified the natural world, and the word *pantheism* comes from this idea, that All is God and God is All.

Pan's positive side is the laughing, lusty lover and musician; this aspect was called *Pangenitor,* the "all-begetter." But like all of Nature, Pan has a shadow side as well. In this form he is called *Panphage,* the "all-devourer," and as such he is the fierce protector of the wilderness. The word *panic* itself derives from Pan, for in this form he causes irrational wild fear.

The Grey One *(Micota)*

Micota is the Latin name for the Queendom of Fungi. The fungus group includes mushrooms, molds, and slime molds. The first fungi appeared on Earth over a billion years ago. Unlike Flora, Micota cannot make turn inorganic substances into food, but can only live off of other living things—either as *parasites* ("one who eats another's food") on the living, or *saprophytes* ("growing from decay") on the dead. Mushrooms are only the tiny fruits poking up from intricate networks of fibers that spread underground over huge areas. These fibers are called *mycelium,* and they very much resemble the nerve fibers in the human brain. Some of these mycelia networks are so huge that they are, in fact, the largest living things on Earth. The Spirit of Micota is vast and deep!

Mushroom god stones from Columbia

Many fungi are intimately involved with humanity, and mushrooms especially have a long history both as food and shamanic medicines. Some people believe that humans gained consciousness through eating certain magick mushrooms that grew on the dung of cattle and caribou whose herds provided sustenance for early nomadic tribes on every continent. Throughout the world, many Mystery rites and Initiations have involved eating these mushrooms and journeying into other worlds of The Dreaming.

> ***NOTE:*** *While some mushrooms are delicious, others are so deadly poisonous that a tiny bite can kill you. Many of the most dangerous look so much like harmless varieties that only an expert can tell them apart. So you should never just go gathering and eating wild mushrooms unless you are with an expert mushroom hunter!*

Lesson 4. Nature Spirits *(Devas)*

Deva is a *Sanskrit* (from India) word for Spirit. It is the root of such words as *divine, divinity, divination,* and even *devil*. Nature Spirits of all kinds are called Devas. They are the personifications of various places and aspects of inanimate Nature. Devas may manifest themselves through such things as animal and insect noises, a rising wind, or the sudden presence of a flock of birds. Devas can be seen stimulating growth, bringing color to flowers, hovering over beautiful sites, playing in waves and waterfalls, dancing in the wind and sunlight. Their work is the evolution of beautiful and responsive forms of life.

Nymphs

In ancient Greece, such devas in feminine aspect were called *nymphs,* a word meaning a young girl, bride, or nurse. They are invested with magickal charm, beauty, and often supernatural powers. As the female spirits of the pulsing life of Nature, the nymphs were often the companions of the lustful Satyrs. Nymphs belong to the oldest and deepest layers of Greek mythology, populating seas, rivers, springs, trees, forests, and mountains. An important traditional role of nymphs was to look after heroes in their youth. Indeed, many of the Greek heroes had nymphs as mothers or nurses.

Oceanids are nymphs of the ocean, the daughters of Oceanus.
Nereids are another family of sea nymphs; the daughters of Nereus, the wise old man of the sea.
Naiads are the nymphs of running water—rivers, streams, and springs.
Oreads or **Orestiads** are mountain nymphs.
Dryads and **Hamadryads** are forest and tree nymphs. Each has her own tree, and they live and die with their trees.

Faeries

The word *Faerie* (or *Fairy*) comes from the Latin *fata* ("fate"). The Fates were three goddesses who visited newborn children to determine their destiny. This word became *fay* in old English, meaning enchanted or bewitched, and *fay-erie* (faerie) meant both a state of enchantment and an enchanted realm. There are many kingdoms of faeries, with quite different origins and characteristics. Some—such as elves and pixies—are believed to have originally been ancient races of flesh-and-blood people. Then there are the Nature faeries, who are devas very much like the Greek nymphs. Many Nature faeries manifest as the spirits of particular flowers or other plants, much as dryads and hamadryads. As such, they often appear to have wings of flower petals, or of butterflies or other insects. Some are associated with mushrooms, especially those that grow in a ring.

Most faeries have powers of some kind, and can bring good luck or ill. Some are kindly, and others quite wicked, but all of them are tricksy and need to be treated with the utmost respect! Thus it is customary to refer to them as "the good people," "good neighbors," or "gentry" so as not to offend them. It is also a good idea to leave offerings of milk and honey out for them.

Faeries by Katlyn

Class III: The Elements

Earth, Water, Fire and Air—
Put 'em together in a garden fair;
Put 'em in a basket bound with skin...
When you answer this riddle you'll only begin!
—Incredible String Band

Introduction: Mama Julie's Lessons

NE OF MY FAVORITE TEACHERS WAS Mama Julie, matriarch of the Tower Family. I studied Magick with her over twenty years ago, in the early '80s. She is long dead now, but I remember her lessons most fondly. The most important thing I learned from her was to approach all my magickal studies and experiences through the four Elements. That is, she taught me to sort the world and everything in it into those categories, and then to completely immerse myself into learning and experiencing everything I could in each of those areas. Now I pass these lessons on to you…

The ancient Mithraic Mysteries held that a person must master all of the four Elements before he can attain spiritual enlightenment and wisdom. He must successfully undergo Initiations of Earth, Water, Air, and Fire—each of which challenges a different aspect of one's nature.

Lesson 2. The Elements

Credited to the 5th century BCE Sicilian philosopher Empedocles, the concept of four (or five) Elements as the basis of all life and being in the Universe was an essential teaching of Aristotle (384-322 BCE) and the Pythagorean Mysteries of ancient Greece, and this system has figured prominently in the magicks of all Western systems, from the Middle East, Egypt, Greece, Rome, Hermetics, and Alchemy to modern occultism, Witchcraft, and Wizardry. It is the most widely used conceptual model in the world, and is the foundation of the Enochian magickal system, as well as the tarot, astrology, the seasons, and the Magick Circle. Simply stated, the four Elements are Earth, Water, Fire, and Air. Furthermore, each Element is imbued, as is everything in the Universe, with the non-physical Essence of the Divine, which we generally call *Spirit*. Just as each person is a unique manifestation of the Divine, so is every rock, every tree, every mountain, every river. So Spirit is often considered to be the Fifth Element—distinguishing living beings from inanimate objects.

Although modern chemists have adopted the word "elements" to refer to the 100+ different kinds of atoms, that was not the original meaning or intention of this term. Rather, the *Elements* as the ancients (and magickal folk throughout history) have understood them are what Mundanes call the *states* of matter. Everything in the Universe is composed of matter, energy, or some combination of the two. All material things—those that are made of matter—can exist in any of four states: *solid, liquid, gas,* and *plasma*, and with the addition or subtraction of *energy* by various means (such as adding or reducing heat or pressure) they can transition from one state to another. We usually think of H_2O water, for instance, in its liquid state. But when energy (in the form of heat) is removed from it, it can be frozen solid into ice; or it can be boiled away into gaseous vapor if energy is added. Its component atoms of hydrogen and oxygen can be ionized (stripped of electrons) as fiery plasma, such as we see in the Auroras. This is why a simple burning candle is the most perfect of all magickal tools—it contains all four Elements simultaneously. The solid waxen candle itself is Earth; the liquid melted wax is Water; the gaseous smoke is Air; and of course the glowing flame is Fire.

The importance of the concept of Elements in magick is through the correspondences (analogies) of each with many things. Plato (427-347 BCE), for instance, divided all beings into four groups: Earth=beasts, Water=fish, Air=birds, and Fire=stars. Medieval alchemists and magicians assigned Elemental associations to various gems and minerals, heavenly bodies, directions and seasons, plant and animal species, geometrical shapes, the internal and external parts of the human body, and human personality traits. In each of us, these represent physical existence (Earth), compassion and emotion (Water), intellect and communication (Air), and transformation and creativity

(Fire). All of these associations have been neatly organized into tables of correspondence. See Course 3, Class VI: "Correspondences."

In working magick, magicians, Witches, and Wizards summon the subtle forces of the Elements and their guardian spirits, the Elementals. We consecrate our tools and ritual objects with the Elements by touching or passing them through each substance—such as salt, dirt, or crystals for Earth, a cup of Water, the smoke of burning incense for Air, and a candle flame for Fire. When a Magick Circle is cast, each Element or its symbol is placed at the corresponding Quarter, and its guardian spirit is invoked.

Lesson 3. Elementals

Elementals are spirit beings, which personify each of the four Elements. They are similar enough to the devas and other Nature spirits I described in the previous Class that some people just refer to all Nature spirits as "Elementals." However, properly speaking, the Elementals are specifically associated only with their particular Element, not with places or species.

While some magicians believe in the literal manifestations of Elementals described below, others believe that these descriptions are just the way that Elementals manifest in our minds' eye as we interact with them while in deep states of trance or meditation. Shamanic practitioners from native cultures throughout the world use drumming, dancing, and other means of going into trance to enter an *alternate reality* within themselves, where they encounter figures such as these. Others have had experiences where they are really quite certain they have seen figures just as described here in the outer, waking world. The main point here is that *Spirit is everywhere* and the spirits in rocks and mountains, for example, have different character and qualities than do the spirits in rivers and oceans.

Paracelsus (1493-1541) classified the four families of Elementals as follows:

Earth Elementals— Gnomes. These are usually depicted as squat little men with big boots, long beards, and tall pointy hats—looking exactly like those "garden gnome" statues. Female gnomes are called *gnomides.* They are often confused in the popular imagination with dwarves, who are really quite different. Gnomes live in tunnels underground and in caves, and they are the guardians of gems, minerals, and other hidden treasures in the Earth. The word *gnome* derives from the Greek *genomus* (earth-dweller). The king of the gnomes is Gob, and so his subjects are also called *goblins.*

Kathryn White

Water Elementals— Undines. These appear very much like our popular images of mermaids, graceful and lovely, with fishy tails and webbed fingers, and living in all waterways—oceans, rivers, streams, waterfalls, lakes, ponds, springs, and fountains. Unlike mermaids, however, undines can readily morph into or out of an entirely liquid form. They may rise from the water draped in mist, but cannot exist long apart from it. For they don't just *live in* water; they are *made of* water—especially splashing waves. *Undine* comes from the Latin *unda* (wave). The ruler of the undines is Neksa.

Air Elementals— Sylphs. These are slender and delicate little flying creatures, often confused with faeries. They ride the winds, gather clouds, and shape snowflakes. Female sylphs are called *sylphids. Silphe* is Greek for "butterfly," and sylphs may often be camouflaged amid flocks of flying insects. The wings of sylphs are usually shown as transparent, like dragonfly wings. The leader of the sylphs is Paralda.

Howard Wookey (1928)

Fire Elementals— Salamanders. Elemental salamanders are not the same things as the little colorful amphibians (which are actually named after the Elementals, not the other way around, because the amphibians are sometimes seen crawling out of burning logs where they have been hibernating in the Winter), but they are often similarly depicted. Elemental

Paracelsus (1536)

Salamanders are fiery dragon-lizards that live in flames. These are also the kinds of Elementals most easily seen, when you gaze deep into the heart of a blazing fire. Like Fire itself, Salamanders are very dangerous. Their name comes from the Greek *salambe* (fireplace). The Salamanders are ruled by a magnificent flaming dragon-spirit called Djin (JIN).

Lesson 4. Earth

I am the Earth around you
I am the heartbeat within you
I am the ground below you
I am all that I am!
—Abbi Spinner

Solid Earth is the foundation upon which everything in our world is built. As products of the evolution of life on planet Earth, we are the literal children of the Earth. Many ancient cultures viewed the life-giving land beneath their feet as a goddess, whom the Greeks called Gaea. Earth, which provides us with our food, is the flesh and bones of our bodies and the bones of the living Earth are the rocks that lie beneath our feet. Geology means "the study of Gaea" in Greek, and is the science of understanding the history of Gaea's bones and body as they have formed, changed, grown, and transmuted over 4.3 billion years. Like the three main tissue layers of our bodies (*endoderm, mesoderm,* and *ectoderm*), stone comes in three main types: *igneous, sedimentary,* and *metamorphic.* Igneous rock is formed quickly from molten lava that has cooled and solidified. It includes intrusive and extrusive forms (e.g., granite and basalt). Sedimentary rock is laid down slowly in layers of mud and sand on the bottoms of lakes and seas (this is where fossils are found). And metamorphic rock started out as igneous or sedimentary, but has been changed under geologic pressure.

Molecules are made up of atoms of the chemical elements, and they have geometric forms. That means that the molecules of a particular substance, under the right circumstances, can be fit together like a puzzle to form extremely regular solids we know as *crystals.* This is common knowledge: Table salt makes cubic crystals, water makes complex six-sided crystals we call snowflakes, and so forth. Crystals have long been viewed as magickal in nature, and magicians ranging from Brazilian shamans to Australian aboriginal healers to Dr. John Dee, the court magician of Queen Elizabeth I of England, have all used them as an important part of their magickal tool kit Different kinds of crystals are used for different things. Those considered most magickal are those that appear translucent, or (best) transparent.

The most common kind of crystal we see throughout the world is the quartz crystal, which can be clear or variously colored, depending on the trace minerals mixed in with the silicon that quartz is made from. Now, the most fascinating thing about quartz is that it is *piezoelectric.* That is, under certain kinds of pressure, it will produce an electric charge. This is why quartz was the basis of the old-time crystal radios; and this is why modern computers can run on silicon chips. Quartz can communicate an energetic charge—which makes it useful for a magician.

I have climbed mountains and cliffs, walked through deserts, searched for fossils, and studied geology. I have even experienced earthquakes! In my sculpture, I work directly with Earth in the form of clay. Of all of my connections with Earth in its Elemental form, my favorite activity has been spelunking, or cave exploring. If you live in any part of the world were there are natural caves, I highly recommend you visit them. Every cave is unique and beautiful—from spectacular limestone caves with stalacTites (hanging down from the ceiling, like the letter "T") and stalagMites (growing up from the floor, like the letter "M"), to eerie lava caves with formations like frozen black water. Many caves are open to the public, with guided tours; these are well worth the price of admission! If you would like to explore "wild" caves, you might be able to join a local spelunking society for some amazing underground adventures.

Quest: Coming down to Earth

—by Farida Ka'iwalani Fox

Let us start with the Earth. Go outside somewhere where it is quiet and you can be undisturbed. Find a comfortable spot and take a moment to stand there. Feel the contact your feet make with the ground. Be aware of your weight as it is supported by the Earth; feel the force of gravity upon your body.

Now focus your attention on your breathing. As you exhale, visualize openings in the soles of your feet and imagine that you are sending roots down into the cool and nourishing Earth. With each exhalation, let those roots sink deeper until it seems as if you cannot move from the spot. As you are becoming more firmly established in the Earth, imagine that you are releasing the tensions and stresses of your life—simply breathe them out and visualize them running down your body, into your roots, and out into the Earth.

As you breathe in again, begin to draw up into yourself the nutrients that are in the Earth Herself. Think of such qualities as steadfastness, endurance, stability. In this simple exercise you are reconnecting with the foundation of your life. You are grounding yourself. Let yourself enjoy this connection. You may actually feel something like an electrical current running into your feet and legs. This would be a good time to reflect upon the graciousness of our planet who receives not only our personal toxins, but also the excessive pollution of our modern life. Our gratitude for the purification work of the Earth is helpful.

You can end this little exercise by taking a walk on the Earth, being very aware of each step you take. Imagine an interchange between you and the Earth. As you make contact with each step, you bless one another. This activity of consciously walking and breathing becomes a very real relationship between you and the planet who is our Mother and our physical home. Enjoy it!

Lesson 5: Water

I am the Water around you
I am the pulse of life within you
I am the ocean flowing through you
I am all that I am!
—Abbi Spinner

All water is one Water, contiguous and indivisible. Water sustains us, and Water unites us. Water is a universal medium, a universal solvent, and a universal electrical conductor. And so Water shared is Life shared. Water is the one essential ingredient that makes life possible, as well as that which unites all life. For Water is indivisible. You can pour a pitcher of it into several glasses, then pour them all back together again, and the Water is unchanged. Earth's water cycle carries water vapor into the sky via evaporation, returns it to the land as rain, flows down to the oceans as rivers, and back to the sky again through the endless great Round River. In the process that Water passes through the bodies of every living creature—drunk in, peed out; absorbed through roots, transpired through leaves, in and out, throughout and about. Our bodies are 85% water, and the plasma of our blood is chemically contiguous with the ancient waters of the oceanic womb where life began. Moreover, Water's property of electrical conductivity makes it the medium of our bioenergetic consciousness.

Water has a remarkable and unique property: It expands when it freezes, making its solid form lighter than its liquid, and allowing ice to float. Were it not so, the Earth's oceans would long ago have frozen solid from the bottom upwards. Astronomers have located water ice on the Moon, Mars, and possibly Mercury. The rings of Saturn are mostly ice. One of Jupiter's moons, Europa, seems to be covered with a watery ocean beneath a frozen surface, where many think life may exist. Water is everywhere in the cosmos—and house-sized snowballs are constantly falling upon the Earth from space, at the rate of 5–30 every minute! Water is not just *on* Earth, Mars, Europa, and all the rest—it is *falling* upon all these worlds in a continual hailstorm that permeates all of space!

In my own exploration of the Elements, Water has always been very special to me. I learned to swim almost at the same time I learned to walk. I grew up by Crystal Lake in Illinois, a beautiful lake where I spent every Summer swimming in the clear water. I have done bodysurfing and water-skiing. I took up SCUBA diving, and in 1984, I led a diving expedition to the Coral Sea in search of mermaids! (But that's another story....) So if you don't already know how to swim, I urge you to do so.

Quest: The Sweet Water of Life

(by Farida Ka'iwalani Fox)

Water is reflective and quiescent without being necessarily passive. It is receptive and always seeks its own level, flowing easily around and over obstacles. These are qualities we may wish to cultivate at times when life seems unyielding and barren. Our bodies are 90% liquid, and our earliest prenatal experience of existence was one of floating in a watery chamber—our mother's womb. The development of the fetus repeats the biological shapes of ancestral life-forms whose homes are in the water. For the first nine months of our existence we are at ease and comfort in the gentle rocking motion of the amniotic fluid. We can return to that state of grace by increasing our awareness of Water.

Take a short visit to a body of water anywhere—the lake, the river, the ocean, a pool, even a plastic wading pool in the backyard—or your bathtub. Allow yourself to get into the water quickly, so that you can feel the contrast of coolness as it covers your skin. Let yourself float quietly for a few moments to experience that sense of buoyant support of this, our long-ago home. Consider, as you are being tenderly rocked and massaged by the cool liquid, that the very core of your cellular memory-banks are being gratefully reminded of their origins. If you are in a creek or streambed, you might like to experience sitting like a boulder in the middle of the current to feel the power of the water as it rushes around you. Perhaps you will allow the current to dislodge you from your spot and move you into the flow of the stream. While you are floating in the water you may even find that tears arise spontaneously. Consider that your own inner water has risen to meet and exchange blessings with the same element outside your body: water seeking itself. There's something miraculous in that ability.

Before leaving your visit to the Water, silently thank and bless the Spirit of Water that has so kindly and mercifully extended itself to you.

Lesson 6: Air

I am the Air around you
I am the breath of life within you
I am the wind blowing through you
I am all that I am!
—Abbi Spinner

We have moved in our study from the most dense and material of Elements, Earth, to the most gaseous and permeable, Air. Air may be the most difficult of the Elements to discuss, simply because of its quality of invisibility. We have a mystified attitude about Air—that it is insubstantial and perhaps untrustworthy. We may even make the mistake of thinking it is the least powerful of the four Elements, because it seems to lack materiality. But Air is the one we are most immediately and vitally dependent upon. One may survive over a month without food, and several days without water. Body temperature may drop for hours before life is threatened. But we can live only a few *minutes* without air. Life on our planet is dependent upon the oxygenation process. It is impossible to consider our relationship to Air without considering our breath, the taking in of oxygen, and the releasing of toxic by-products of the living processes.

In my immersion in the experience of each of the Elements, I have built and flown rubber-band-driven model airplanes and many kinds of kites, joined the Civil Air Patrol as a boy to fly in small planes, and gone up in a hot air balloon. I have taken many airplane flights all over the world. I have even bungee-jumped off a high bridge over a deep canyon. I have faced the ferocity of Air in a Missouri tornado and a Florida hurricane. But there is much more I have yet to do in this Element. I still want to experience skydiving, ultralite flying, and hang gliding. I want to go up in the air on a huge kite pulled by a motorboat....

Quest: Breathing the Wind

(by Farida Ka'iwalani Fox)

How might you begin conscious interaction with this subtle and yet powerful Element? One blustery day of Winter, take a walk on some windy promontory, where you can enjoy both the sweeping view and the sweeping gusts of fresh air. Take some time to observe the effect on nearby trees and plants. Perhaps you can discern a pattern to the wind in the way that the trees' branches billow and wave. Or, sitting on a grassy slope, you may perceive the air movements by observing the rippling, waving prairie around you. Air motion, in its swirls and eddies, waves and troughs and circular forms, is not unlike the ocean, whose waters flow, rush, and ripple. Weather patterns and the great ocean currents are extensions of each other: currents of air and currents of water, affecting one another in an inevitable way. Is there a deeper, hidden Mystery here?

After observing and contemplating the attributes of Air in the natural setting, turn your attention to yourself and *your* interaction with this Element. Perhaps the joyous play of the wind will inspire you to swoop and dip and twirl, dancing with the wind for your partner, and feeling the rush of the air on your face, the freedom of leaping and running through space! Allow yourself this freedom, to dance the Dance of Life, and allow movement to lift you, to give you wings, to lighten your heart.

Now turn to your breath. Much can be learned by studying your own breathing process. Notice how you are breathing at different moments during the day. You may find a correlation between your mental/emotional state, the quality of your breath, and the quality of your life. Take a normal but full breath, in and out, through your nose. Notice that when you are upset or agitated your breath is more rapid and noisy. When you are calm and peaceful, your breath is also. It is possible to control, to some extent, the emotional atmosphere around you through controlling your breath. Take now another breath and, as you inhale, be aware of the breath as it passes through your nostrils. Feel it fill completely and naturally the vessel of your body, knowing that it carries all that you need at this moment for your renewal. Release it slowly and gently, allowing whatever tensions you may have experienced today to disperse with the exhalation.

It is not necessary to expend great effort on this exercise, nor is it supposed that the more noise and intensity you produce, the more effectively you are breathing. The breathing process is with us from the beginning to the end. As taught by slower cultures, breathing is meant to be enjoyed. Let us begin with our conscious connection with the Element Air by learning to enjoy breathing and learning to notice what effect different types of breathing may produce in our emotional state.

Lesson 7: Fire

I am the Fire around you
I am the spark of life within you
I am the flame burning through you
I am all that I am!
—Abbi Spinner

Fire has always held a special fascination for us, since our ancestors first mastered its use, setting our first foot on the road to becoming human. Fire meant not only warmth and light, but also the difference between life and death. Fire plays a special role in the relationship between man and the Otherworlds, between inner and outer reality. Fire is an Elemental force of Nature, but it is also the natural bridge between the worlds, linking the natural and the supernatural, the sacred and the mundane.

In our modern world, Fire is everywhere. It drives our cars, gives us electricity, and propels our planes. It is the central active principle in our world of combustion and incandescence. Light, directly related to Fire, is becoming more and more the basis of our communication networks. In magickal symbolism, Fire stands for movement, action, release of energy, and transformation. It has been said that Fire is locked in wood; hence trees, wands, or sticks represent its potential. The power of Fire is to burn, to consume, to radiate heat and light. Transformation comes in realizing that something can rise like the Phoenix from the ashes of its self-consummation. Thus Fire can act as an agent of transformation in ourselves and society. Fire is a good place to burn away your anger and problems, and help improve your personal energy. The heat of Fire can be associated with qualities like passion, ardor, fervor, intensity. Through the action of light and radiance, these qualities can be transmuted to a higher octave of themselves as compassion, caring, commitment, intention, purpose, and resolve.

In my personal journey through the Elements, Fire has been a very important part. I can use flint and steel, a firebow, or a magnifying glass to light a fire without matches. I have built more campfires than I can count and learned to cook various meals over them. I have learned how all the different kinds of wood burn. Every Winter Solstice it is my task to build and light the Yule fire. I have also fought forest fires that burned on the land where I lived for many years. And in making ceramic sculptures, I have worked with the intense fires of the pottery kiln. I have also walked barefoot over burning coals in several different traditions of firewalking—but I warn you not to try this without expert supervision of an experienced teacher!

Quest: The Fires of Transformation
(by Farida Ka'iwalani Fox)

Whenever you find yourself deeply concerned over something, resolutely determined to follow a course of action, committed to a cause, or making and carrying out decisions, you can assume that the Fire Element is at work in your life. Frequently you may see Fire manifesting as anger, and you are frightened by the uncontrollable behavior that can result in irretrievable loss. It is helpful to remember that one purpose of angry feelings is to impel you to take action, to move out of a bad situation.

On the other hand, you may feel passive and indifferent about people and events. Boredom and coldness may seem to be your major responses to life. In this case, Fire is lacking, and while seeking it out, you may also want to consider that there may be a core of deep hurt at your center that has caused you to dampen down your inner Fire. At other times, you may be consciously aware of personality traits you would like to change. You may find yourself plagued with envy or jealousy, frequently tormented by fears, indecision, and anxiety. The glacial quality of depression may have frozen the heat of anger (and life as well) into a bleak and meaningless inner landscape.

At these times, how may Fire serve you? How may you invoke the presence of this Element into your life in a safe yet intimate manner? Assuming you have access to a fireplace or open fire pit, make an appointment with the spirit of Fire. Lay in your tinder and wood for burning with care (see following: "Building the Campfire"). This fuel is the nourishment you provide for feeding the fire. You would do the same for any other creature committed to your care. When you are ready to ignite the materials, think for a moment of the miracle that is about to happen. With the strike of a match, the flame will spring into being. You may want to greet the flame with a blessing, such as "Blessed be, thou creature of Fire." Watch as the little salamanders eagerly lick the meal you have prepared for them. Observe the nature of Fire as it gains strength and crackles merrily—or snaps angrily. Imagine that the popping and snapping is a form of communication. What might Fire be saying to you? Tell the Fire your deepest secrets, your hidden desires and passionate longings. Watch the directions of the dancing flames. As time passes and the Fire matures, gaze into the glowing coal caverns. What shapes do you see there, in that fantastic Fire world?

Allow yourself to view your own passions. Do they consume you with rage and fury, or do they radiate warmth and light that sustains you and others around you? Does this trait tell the truth about who you really are at the center of your being? Does it reflect the Divine Light within you? Or is it a lie and a pretense, reflecting what you or someone else might *think* you are? Would you be willing to sacrifice that which holds you back? Would you be willing to throw your fear into the Fire—or your jealousy, distrust, or self-hatred?

Write on a slip of paper a quality that you believe you would be better off without and ask the Fire to take it and burn away the pain and unhappiness it has caused you. Or, even more powerful, choose an item from among your personal possessions that symbolizes the quality you wish to transform, and give it to the Fire. But be sure to visualize what will come in its place. As the old jealousies, angers, and hidden shame are consumed, the True Self, compassionate and forgiving and radiant, is able to shine brightly, a beacon light for all to see.

Task: Make a Fire-Pot

A very impressive fire-pot can be made with a cauldron-shaped ceramic bowl. A small iron caldron, with the traditional three feet, would work also, but only if the rim is level and unbroken by a handle, as you will need to be able to cover it tightly with a pot lid to put the fire out. Collect all the candle ends you can find, or just use candle wax you can buy in a store.

You should first lay in a layer of sand, so the bottom won't get too hot. Then tear up a bunch of cotton rags into small pieces, mush them together, and stuff them into the pot. Old tee shirts or towels are excellent. Melt the candle ends or wax in a separate (disposable) pot or saucepan, which you can pick up cheap at Goodwill. Then carefully pour the molten wax over the mushed-up rages in the pot, until it's pretty full, with a few pieces of rags sticking up. Let the wax harden, and you will have a perfect fire-pot; when you light the rags, they will act just like the wick of a candle, only making much more flames. Always put something under it when it's burning, like a trivet, flat stone, or ceramic dish, as the bottom may get hot enough to burn wood or cloth. Be sure to keep a pot lid of the right size handy as this is the only way you can put out the fire—never try to blow it out!

Another much simpler kind of fire-pot is just filled with wood alcohol, which can be lit for a dancing blue flame. You should add some Epsom salts to give stability to the fire.

Lesson 8: Spirit

I am the Spirit around you
I am divinity within you
I am the light shining through you
I am all that I am!
—Abbi Spinner

The Fifth Element is Spirit. It is this that animates us and gives us consciousness. Just as Water exists throughout the galaxy in the form of ice and rains down upon all the worlds and moons, so does Spirit permeate all the Elements and brings them to life. Consider: Your spirit encompasses every cell and part of your body—even the minerals of your bones and the water in your cells and blood. All the Elements except Spirit are identical in a body that has died as they were when it was living. The only difference is the lack of Spirit—but that difference is everything.

Just so does each level of Spirit encompass all the Elements within its consciousness. The Spirit of Gaea, the living Earth, includes and interpenetrates us and every other living creature—as well as the waters, the rocks, the air, and the fires of our planet. And the Spirit of Gaea is encompassed within the greater Spirit of the solar system, which in turn is encompassed within the Spirit of our galaxy…and so on, both Above and Below.

The evolutionary journey of your own Spirit has already traveled billions of years, through all your ancestors back to the dawn of life. But, just like the water in your blood and cells, all Spirit is One—even when seemingly contained in separate vessels. Here is a little Vision of Spirit I had many years ago:

All living creatures are like cups of various sizes and shapes, with which the Waters of Life are scooped from the Well of Souls. And all the cups are emptied back into the pool when they are broken at death. New cups are continually being fashioned of living clay and are dipped in their turn into the same well to be filled. But it is rare that a new cup will scoop up exactly the same batch of molecules as had been contained in a former cup. Usually, there will be a considerable mix.

And so it is that a person may have bits of "past life" memories of several other people, as well as assorted animals, or that a human-sized cup could contain a number of birds and other small animals, but at most, only a fraction of a single whale. And in the proper balance of Nature, each new generation replaces the previous, so that the number of each kind of cup remains approximately constant.

What do you suppose happens when one species proliferates greatly at the expense of others? When there are no more cups of Mammoth, Cave Bear, Megatherium, Saber-Tooth, Dodo, Moa, Sperm Whale, Thylacine, Condor, or countless others, but the cups labeled "Human" are being produced by the geometrically increasing billions? In that case, I believe, the human soul-stuff would become increasingly diluted with other decimated species, and all the vanished animals would return in human form.…

And the lost souls of dinosaurs became dreams of dragons.…

Class IV: Back to Nature

1. Introduction: Getting Out There

Y MOST IMPORTANT TEACHER HAS always been Nature Herself. From the time I was a little kid, I have always spent as much time as I could alone out in the woods. I would climb up into trees in the Spring and sit so still that the birds would get used to me being there, so I could watch them build their nests, lay their eggs, hatch, and feed their babies. I would go out into meadows where I saw deer grazing, and sit quietly under a certain tree day after day until they learned to ignore my presence, and would come within a few feet of me. I would climb out of my bedroom window on the nights of the full Moon, and wander among the Children of the Night. As I mentioned in my Lesson on Water, I grew up near a crystal clear lake, and I rigged up an air pump and hose so I could stay underwater for long periods and watch fish making their little nests in the sandy bottom and laying their eggs. And from my mid-30s through early 40s, I lived for eight years in the middle of 5,600 acres of undeveloped land in the Misty Mountains of NorCalifia, with no electricity, radio, television, or telephones, and raised wild animal babies, foraged for wild foods, and experienced the turnings of the seasons from the Earth to the Stars. I consider the foundations of my Wizardry to be rooted in such experiences, and I strongly encourage you also to get out into Nature as often as possible. There is only so much you can learn from books!

Lesson 2. Giving Back: Wizards as Earth Warriors

—by Jesse Wolf Hardin

Wizards draw power from the spirits and entities of the sacred, living Earth. In turn, we're each called to do all we can to restore, nourish, and celebrate the natural world...as well as defend her from the destructive tendencies of our own human kind. By "responsibility" I don't mean "obligation," but rather, the "ability to respond!" And that's what we Wizards do best: respond to the needs of the immediate moment, including its many dangers and threats—with a potent combination of instinct and intuition, insight and empathy, passion and skill, assertive action and applied magic.

We give back to the Earth by ritually acknowledging the land where we hold our Circles, but also through hands-on service such as tree planting and wilderness restoration...and by guarding the places of power, the forests that surround our sacred groves, the plants and animals that are our teachers. This is best accomplished three different ways:

1. By a community or circle getting together to purchase a special piece of land, replant it, re-sanctify it, and setting up a land trust or land use agreements that can help to protect it in the future.

2. By deeply loving and committing to a favorite park, nearby river or forest—visiting it regularly, bonding to it and its resident spirits, getting in touch with its will and needs, and committing to its integrity and well-being. This can include cleaning up trash left by others, planting native seeds along streambeds, and putting up a fight if anyone ever tries to pave over, degrade, or destroy it.

3. By personally resisting the destruction and development of every remaining wild and magickal place—through educational outreach, art and articles, petitions, lawsuits, creative public demonstrations, and civil disobedience actions.

Like Wizardry, ecology is the practice of relationship and the directing and balancing of energies, and environmentalism is rooted as much in ecospirituality as science. The great American conservationist John Muir acted out of a clearly mystical relationship with nature. Aldo Leopold reinvented the land ethic not through any brilliant conclusions, but as a result of the magickal epiphany he called being "one with the mountain." Redwoods heroine Julia Butterfly writes that it was her spiritual connection to the tree she called "Luna" that allowed her to stay a hundred feet up in it for so many months while besieged with police loudspeakers, loggers' saws, and Winter storms that assaulted her tiny aerial platform.

True Wizardry is not just inspiration and the ability to make things happen. Nor is it simply our reward; it is our assignment. It's part of the "great work," long shouldered by the generations of Wizards and seekers, Earth lovers and Earth warriors. It includes the always vital practices of awakeness and wonder, sentience and sensuality, perceptivity and awe. Of grounding and connecting, revering and celebrating, protecting...and championing. Of our taking any risk and paying any price, in order to do what this precious Earth—and our flawless hearts—tells us is right.

Lesson 3. Camping Out

If it is possible for you to go to summer camp or join the Boy Scouts, I urge you to do so. If your folks are up for it, perhaps you can take family camping trips to national parks. But staying in a cabin, trailer, or RV doesn't count as camping out! If you have any friends who live on a farm or in the country, see if they would like to hold a campout in their woods. But even if none of these are a possibility for you, maybe you can at least pitch a tent in your backyard this Summer, and sleep out under the stars. Consider camping to be a basic assignment of your Apprenticeship in Wizardry!

Shelter and Bedding: First off, you will need to get a tent, sleeping bag, and pad. I have camped out in everything from large trash bags and "tube tents" to big fancy multi-room tents. Of all these, my favorites are simple dome tents with rain flys, which come in various sizes, are lightweight and compact, and can be set up by one person in a few minutes. You should also have a large enough plastic tarp to spread under your entire tent as a groundcloth, and another to cover your woodpile in case of rain.

Next, a good sleeping bag is essential. You should get a rectangular one that opens out completely into a large comforter, rather than a "mummy bag" that just opens halfway down one side. Personally, I hate those nylon down bags, as I don't like the feel of nylon against my skin, and the down flattens out under your body, so you get no insulation against the ground. I prefer a cotton flannel lining and crushed foam insulation, which is very lightweight, even if not so compact. But check out several kinds and find one you like. Don't forget a pillow—if nothing else, you can just take a zippered pillowcase and stuff it with clothes or grass....

Finally, you're going to really need some comfortable padding under you, as even the smallest pebbles, roots, and twigs can make your sleep miserable! The best pads I've seen roll up tight and compact, but fluff up with air when they're unrolled. But if you're not going to have to carry stuff very far, any kind of foam pads can work. Air mattresses are popular, but I find them to be heavy to carry, hard to inflate, and they often deflate during the night and you end up lying on the rocky ground anyway. In some places, you can also make nice padding by gathering pine bows and covering them with a thick layer of grass.

Gear and Supplies: You will need a few basic tools and equipment. Important gear should include a knife and eating utensils (I still have my old Boy Scout knife, with multiple tools, including a fork and spoon)—although if you know how to use chopsticks, you can easily make some on the spot. But you will at least want a spoon, plate, bowl, and cup. You should also have a covered pot and a frying pan. You can pick up nifty little "mess kits" at any camping supply store, that include all this stuff neatly nested together. However, avoid *aluminum* cookware and utensils! Get these of steel, even though it may be a bit more expensive. Aluminum ions in food will damage your neurons. A little grill to put over the cook fire can be very useful, too. And don't forget a lighter for the fire!

Other essential camping stuff includes a basic first aid kit (with antibiotic cream and bandages!), a flashlight (especially one that also converts to a camping light), toilet paper, a small folding camp shovel to dig a latrine, a compass, binoculars, camera, good bug spray, strong sun block, a notebook and pen, watch, towel, metal mirror, zip-lock plastic baggies of various sizes, a ball of heavy twine, nylon rope, and maybe even fishing gear. Don't forget personal hygiene stuff like soap (for hands and dishes), hairbrush, toothbrush, and toothpaste. And always bring along trash bags for cleaning up. I make several check lists for different seasons and types of camping, just so I don't forget anything essential.

And, of course, you will need to have enough food and water. This could be simple granola, nuts, and dried fruit, or more elaborate meal stuff if you don't mind packing it along. If you bring canned goods, don't forget a can opener! You should plan on a gallon of water for each day. If you are going to be hiking any distance to get to your campsite, you will also need a backpack to carry everything in.

Clothing: What clothing you will need will, of course, depend on climate, weather, and how long you will be out. I always like to pack a compact rain poncho and a fold-up wide-brim hat. Have good hiking shoes, extra socks and underwear, light stuff for the day, and warmer stuff for night. My Wizard's cloak (see 3.III: "Wizardly Regalia") comes in handy for keeping warm around the campfire, as well as being a fine blanket when I sleep.

> ***IMPORTANT:*** *Never go hiking or camping alone! Always go with a buddy. That way, if anything should happen to either of you, there will always be someone to help—or to go for help.*

Lesson/Task 4: Pitching Camp

> *The ideal site has trees, water, grass-covered ground, gently sloping terrain, protection from severe weather, and a view. The possibility of finding all of these in one campsite is quite remote, but the more of them you can get in one site, the better it will be. Avoid natural hazards in picking any campsite.*
>
> (*Boy Scout Fieldbook,* 1978 edition, p. 50)

Choosing your campsite and deciding just where to pitch your tent involves several considerations. First, you should pick a spot for your tent that is as level as possible, with more level area nearby for a campfire. If the slant of the ground is too steep, you'll wake up in the morning outside your tent! However, if there is any chance of rain, you will want to pitch your tent on enough of a gentle slope to provide water drainage. In such case, you should also dig a small drainage trench all around your tent, with a channel leading away downhill. Another important thing to consider is the other life forms in your camping area. Learn to recognize poison ivy, poison oak, nettles, brambles, thistle, cactus, and other nasty plants, and avoid camping anywhere near them! Also, make sure you are not pitching your tent on top of an ant colony—especially (in some parts of the U.S.) fire ants.

Trees are important for shade, as the sun hitting your tent in the morning will turn it into an oven. I call that a "bake-awake" tent. Because you will most likely be pitching your tent in the evening, make sure that you note where the sun is setting, and realize that it will be coming up in the opposite direction—the East. This is the side where you want to make sure there are plenty of shady trees. However, unless you are camping somewhere there is no chance of rain or heavy winds, you should not pitch your tent directly *under* a tree, as leaves will continue to drip water for a long time after a rain, and heavy branches can come down in a windstorm.

Avoid large roots or rocky outcroppings in your tent space. Before you pitch your tent, you'll want to carefully clear out all the rocks, pebbles, branches, twigs, pinecones, and the like. Then lay down a large plastic ground cloth to keep out moisture from underneath. And I recommend laying a little piece of carpet or Astroturf right in front of the tent door to wipe your feet on before you come inside.

Never leave food outside your tent, even in ice chests, as animals will get into it. I've seen raccoons, wild pigs, and even ants utterly destroy the next morning's breakfast supplies—to say nothing of what bears can do. Most animals will be deterred by keeping your food inside your tent, but if you are camping in bear country, you should hang it high in a bag at the end of a long nylon rope suspended over an overhanging branch some distance from your tent. Tie the other end of the line to a lower branch, and you can raise or lower your stash as needed.

When you break camp to leave, be sure to restore the area to the condition in which you found it. Pick up and pack out any artificial debris—paper, cans, bottles, etc.—even if it's not yours. Except for trampled grass, there should be no trace of your having camped there. However, in some places it may be okay to leave the fire-pit for the next campers; check if there is a question.

Lesson 5: Lesson/Task: Building the Campfire

There is just no substitute for sitting around a campfire late into the night with your closest friends. As I said back in 1.III.3: "The Origin of Magick," Fire was our first Magick—and it always calls us back to the Source. Because you're in training to become a Wizard, you should learn how to build the campfire, as that task tends to fall to the Wizard if there's one around!

Make the Firepit: First, choose your site well. Make it in the open, with no tree branches hanging overhead that could catch fire! There must be a 10' diameter circle of clear space all around the fire, scraped to dirt or sand, and free of anything burnable. The size of the fire-pit, and the seating area around it, will depend on how many people are included. In the center of the area, hollow out a little depression, at least two feet in diameter for the smallest one-person fire (bigger as needed). Pile the dirt around the edges to make a small crater. If there are any rocks in the area, pile them into a wall around the fire-pit, packing the loose dirt into the spaces between them. If there are no rocks, make the crater a little deeper, with a higher dirt bank around it. The crater-shape of the fire-pit will act as a lens to keep the flames and smoke directed upwards, the way the parabolic mirror behind the bulb of a flashlight focuses the beam.

Build the Fire: Now go out and gather a sufficient pile of dead wood (never cut or break off any living wood for a fire!). Don't bother with anything green or rotten, as all you will get is smoke. You will want resinous pine for the small kindling, and hardwoods for the actual fuel. See the following for the lore of different woods for fires. Break it into appropriate-sized lengths, and stack most of it outside the fire circle, sorted by size, so you can easily select what you need to burn. If you can't break it easily underfoot, it's too green to burn. If there is any likelihood of rain, cover your woodpile with a plastic tarp.

If the ground is very wet, you should lay a floor of sticks, tree bark, or stones. Then lay a bed of dry leaves, pine needles, or (the very best) dry birch bark from a dead tree. This is your *tinder.* If everything else is wet, split open a dead branch, and you will find it dry on the inside. Slice up a number of "feathers" with your knife, leaving the shavings attached.

Cover the tinder with a little pile of small dry sticks; pine is excellent. This is the *kindling.* Then, having chosen your larger sticks carefully for burning qualities, place them in a "teepee" shape, starting with the smaller and adding longer and thicker sticks around them—always keeping a point in the center. This point will direct the flames upward and maximize both the light and heat that radiates outward to the circle. Don't build it too high at first— just enough to get things started.

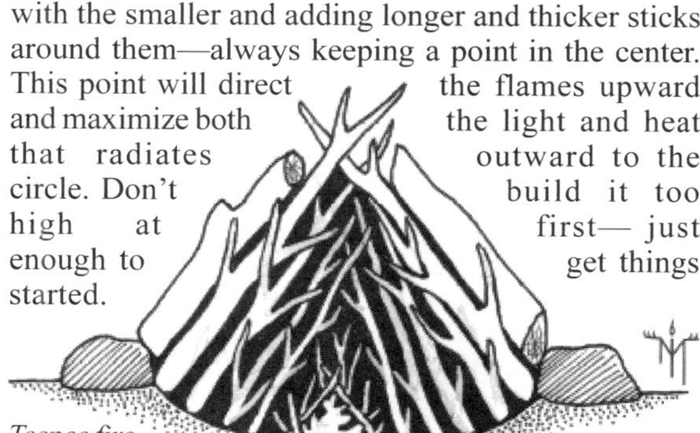
Teepee fire

6. Lesson/Task: Fire Without Matches or Lighter

If you'd like to learn some real Wizardry, here are a few ways to make a fire without matches or lighter: Marking a spark is easy; the trick is getting a fire from the spark! You will need special tinder: bone-dry, finely-divided organic material to catch the spark, ignite readily, and blaze into hot flame. Try mouse nests, birch bark curls, dry weed tops, cedar bark, scraped lint from cloth or cardboard, charred cloth, or cotton insulation from your jacket or sleeping bag.

> ***IMPORTANT:* Never *leave a fire burning unattended*—*or even smoking! Make sure that the last person to go to bed puts out the fire completely, with sprinkled water and dirt, until there are no glowing coals or smoke.***

Flint & Steel: Flint, quartz, or other very hard rock will spark when you strike it a glancing blow from your steel knife. Catch the spark in your tinder; then hold it in your cupped hands and blow gently on the bright spot from below until it bursts into flames. Learn to recognize flint, and if you come across a piece when you are hiking, stick it into your pocket.

Lens: A magnifying glass can be used to focus the Sun's rays onto tinder and ignite it. You can even use eyeglasses, binoculars or a camera lens!

Log cabin fire for heat

To light your campfire, open up a few little spaces between the logs so you can get into the dry tinder at the bottom of the fire on the windward (up-wind) side, and light it at several points. Blowing on the flames will help it catch—especially if you can come up with a hollow pipe, reed, or tube of some kind to blow through. Once the tinder gets burning, you're pretty much set. Now, all you have to do is add fuel at just the right rate to keep the fire going the way you want it to be. You should place each new log carefully—there is a whole art form to this! And have handy a poking stick to help you rearrange the logs as they burn and fall.

Quest: Know Your Neighborhood Ents

As you might know, the Ents in Tolkein's *Lord of the Rings* are the guardians and herders of the trees. Like many Nature spirits, they are each identified by their species of tree. So here's a magickal Quest for you: Learn to identify the different kinds of trees in your area. Pick up a little guidebook to local trees, and learn the names, leaves, and general shapes of at least 13 of them. Make a notebook collection of a leaf and seed from each tree you learn, along with a simple outline drawing of its general shape.

And here is some traditional lore of firewoods, along with drawings of the leaves of each tree:

13 Logs for the Fire

Oak logs will warm you well
That are old and dry;
Logs of pine will sweetly smell
But the sparks will fly.

Birch logs will burn too fast,
Chestnut scarce at all;
Hawthorn logs are good to last—
Cut them in the Fall.

Holly logs will burn like wax,
You may burn them green;
Elm logs like to smouldering flax,
No flame to be seen.

Beech logs for Winter time,
Yew logs as well;
Green Elder logs it is a crime
For any man to sell.

Pear logs and Apple logs,
They will scent your room.
Cherry logs across the dogs
Smell like flower of broom.

Ash logs, smooth and grey,
Burn them green or old.
Buy up all that come your way—
Worth their weight in gold.

—Translated from the Gaelic by Standish O'Grady

Lesson 7: Woodcraft

Woodcraft refers to all the skills that can enable you to go into the wilderness and survive for months at a time. You may never have to resort to them for survival, but I think a good Wizard should know these things; I do. When it comes down to basic survival, your most important woods tool is your knife. Get a good one, and keep it honed to razor sharpness. Keep it folded or sheathed when not in use, and avoid nicking the edge or breaking the point.

There are several excellent handbooks for camping and wilderness survival, which will tell you everything you need to know. I highly recommend you get one of these and take it with you on every camping trip. My favorite is the 2nd Edition *Boy Scout Fieldbook,* published in 1967 and 1978. Later versions, unfortunately, seem to have dropped much of the woodcraft and wilderness survival lore.

Snakes

There are only four kinds of poisonous snakes in North America, and you should learn to readily identify any of them. Three are *pit vipers,* and they all share common features: triangular heads, thin necks, thick bodies, and diamond-shaped markings all down their backs. These are water moccasins, copperheads, and rattlesnakes. There is only one species of copperhead and one of water moccasin, but there are eight different species of rattlers in the U.S.

Copperhead

Water Moccasin

Rattlesnake

The fourth kind of North American poisonous snake is an *elapid,* related to cobras. This is the coral snake, of which there are two virtually indistinguishable species—Eastern and Western. They are brightly colored in bands of red, yellow, and black, and they look almost identical to the pretty scarlet king snake. There is a simple rule to tell them apart, based on the order of colors of their bands: "Red and yellow, kill a fellow; red and black, venom lack."

Scarlet King Snake

Coral Snake

If you are at all unsure of whether a snake you encounter may be one of the poisonous variety, *don't mess with it!* Don't try to pick it up, kill it, or hurt it in any way. Just stay out of its way, and it'll stay out of yours. Rattlesnakes even give you a warning buzz, which you'll recognize instantly once you've heard it! Make plenty of noise when you walk through the woods, and carry a walking stick to poke the bushes ahead of you.

Camp Cooking

Every woodsman should know a few basic meals that can be prepared in the wild and cooked over a campfire. A camp cooking fire is built very differently than a fire made for sitting around, as it is designed to maximize heat, not light. Most cookfire designs use a narrow trench cut in the ground, where layer after layer of larger and larger sticks are laid in the same direction and burned down to coals. One excellent design uses an X-shaped trench, so that air can circulate through the fire. Pots and pans can be rested on the bank above the trench, or on stones. Or build your cookfire between two logs, like so:

Cooking fire

Making Shelter

The experienced woodsman should be able to make survival shelters completely from scratch. The easiest kind to make are those that take advantage of natural objects such as caves, overhangs, cliffs, rock faces, large trees, downed trees, or large roots. Starting with any of these, you can build a lean-to by propping long logs, branches, or other downed trees against them. Thatch the roof with layers of leafy boughs and branches for protection from rain. Large evergreen trees often have a tent-like interior (or even burned-out hollows in the case of redwoods) that can be added to and adapted into a cozy shelter.

Deadfall lean-to

Task: Make a Personal Survival Kit

Every good woodsman (and every good Wizard who goes out into the woods) should assemble a personal survival mini-kit. I made my first one when I was a boy and always kept it with my camping gear, in my pocket when I was hiking. Here's a basic plan, adapted from the *Boy Scout Fieldbook:*

First, get a waterproof container, small enough to fit into your pocket, but big enough to hold all this stuff. Perfect ones with clear plastic tops are available in the fishing section of sporting goods stores. Assemble the following items and arrange them so they fit neatly together in the box: (1) mini-lighter; (2) penlight; (3) emergency candle; (4) compass; (5) magnifying glass; (6) whistle; (7) single-edged razor blades or X-Acto knife; (8) nylon fishing line, 25-lb. test; (9) fishhooks of various sizes, plus sinkers, flies, and spinners; (10) wire, 5-10', light and flexible for snares; (11) adhesive tape, 1" wide, 16" long; (12) small notepad and ball-point pen; (13) aluminum foil, 4 sheets 12" square, to make drinking and cooking utensils; (14) bandages of various sizes; (15) iodine tablets to purify water; (16) needles and nylon thread for repairs; (17) several zip-lock sandwich baggies.

If you have more room, you might think up more stuff on your own. For instance, I cut up some tin cans to make little arrowheads, creased lengthwise for strength. They took up hardly any space, and if I'd needed to (which I never did), I could have made a whole set of bow-and-arrows with them and the fishing line. I also keep a little snakebite kit and some Sting-Kill, separate from my first aid kit. Finally, include a checklist of everything in your survival kit, so you can replace things you may use up.

Lesson 8: Foraging

In the places where I have lived over the past 25 years, wild blackberries grow in profusion, ripening in late July and into the Fall. I dearly love to go out gathering berries, which I find to be a profound meditational experience. Given the heat of the season, I just wear a pair of shorts and sandals. I consider it my own little martial arts discipline to give the berries a sporting chance to do me injury. My challenge is to maneuver carefully, be aware of where each thorny branch awaits a misstep, reach through the protective tangle of sharp points, and pluck forth the juiciest, must succulent treasures from the bramble dragon's toothy maw. I seldom emerge completely unscathed; I regard the inevitable scratches as honorable battle scars.

You have heard romantic tales of "The Great Hunt" in which bands of ancient hunters went out to bring down mammoths, cave bears, seals, buffalo, wild boar, and deer to feed the Tribe. Many stories and movies have depicted these hunts as the greatest of adventures, with the carcasses being carried back slung on poles, and roasting on a spit over a roaring fire. But there is another, far more important side of those old "hunter-gatherer" societies that often gets overlooked—the gatherers! Even in those cultures most devoted to hunting, 80% or more of the food actually eaten comes from *gathering,* not hunting!

Modern shopping styles of men and women are often compared to hunting and gathering. Men go into stores as hunters: They have a specific quarry in mind, they go straight to it, they nab their prey, and arrive home with a triumphant cry of "I got it!" Women, on the other hand, tend to approach shopping as gatherers: They wander up and down the aisles, poking through shrubbery, pulling up roots, turning over rocks, looking for nothing in particular, but sticking whatever looks tasty into their basket.

But I'm much more of a natural gatherer than a hunter. After all, how did our ancestors learn which plants, leaves, seeds, berries, roots, fruits, nuts, mushrooms, and even bugs were good to eat, or medicinal, and which were poisonous? How did they learn to turn inedible things like acorns or grains into food? While the hunters were working on better spearpoints, bows and arrows, bear traps and mammoth pits, the gatherers were learning the foundations of agriculture, herbalism, medicine, pharmacology, and alchemy. The gatherers—both men and women—became the tribal Shamans, the first Wizards. They not only discovered all the edible and medicinal plants, but have passed down their knowledge through the ages in guidebooks called *herbals.*

Quest: Forage for Wild Foods

Edible wild plants are found all over the world, in all seasons. There are fruits, nuts, berries, roots, grains, saps, and greens—all ripe for the picking. All you have to do is learn to recognize them and know how to prepare them. Get a guidebook of edible wild plants for your area, along with recipes. Any bookshop or camping supply store will have guides to the edible plants in your area. Then go out and see how many you can find and harvest. Prepare them in a meal, and serve it to your family or magickal friends. Foraging for wild food is a real Quest—especially bringing enough back to share with others, eat with cereal, and bake into pies. Wear appropriate protective clothing, and carry a bucket or basket. It's especially fun to go out with friends—chatting, singing, snacking, joking, and laughing together as gatherers have done since the dawn of time.

Personally, I love walking through the wilderness at different times of the year and finding tasty food growing all around me. As I forage for wild things to eat (and bring home), I feel deeply connected to my shamanic ancestors over these many thousands of years. Some plants, however, are poisonous or inedible. An important rule is: ***Never eat anything that tastes bitter or bad!***

Lesson 9: Predation

Many perfectly respectable and highly admired animals are natural predators, and our human history has always included hunting as well as foraging. I personally prefer not to kill reptiles, birds, and mammals—for food or any other reason. But I don't believe it is necessarily *wrong* to do so, in a humane and responsible fashion, any more than it is for a wolf. What to eat is a choice each individual needs to make for themselves.

Tracking: Whether you are tracking them for dinner, or just to take their picture, you should learn to recognize the foot tracks, droppings, and other signs of many different animals in your neighborhood. When I come to a mud flat, a beach, or a snowfield where there are various animal tracks, I take it as a matter of pride to be able to identify many if not all of them—noting details like whether they were running or walking, how many, what they were doing.... Deer not only leave hoofprints; they also make trails that you can follow through the woods. Also look for other signs along animal trails—such as trampled grass, broken branches, scuffed bark on trees, bits of fur clinging to thorns.... Below are the tracks of some common animals in North America; see if you can spot any of them on your next campout.

Fishing: The water and its food sources are our natural heritage. In lakes, streams, and tidepools at the seashore, we can find abundant delicious food in the form of clams, mussels, snails, crayfish, crabs, abalone, conchs, and fish. Many of these are very easy to catch and harvest—especially clams and mussels, which just don't run away! Crayfish and crabs are best hunted at night with a flashlight, when they tend to congregate in large numbers in shallow water. Just grab 'em in the middle, behind the claws, and toss 'em into a bag or bucket.

Fish may require a bit more work. If you're fishing for food rather than sport, forget all the conventional rods and tackle. Little fish can sometimes be herded into shallow water and grabbed or netted. Bigger fish can be corralled in a *weir* of rocks or wooden stakes and speared with barbed gigs you can easily make from forked tree branches—hold the spear quietly just under the surface of the water, then jab swiftly at a single fish. Spear fish at night, when they will be attracted and immobilized by a flashlight beam.

Fish gig

Fish that live in deeper water require hooks, lines, and sinkers to get the bait to the fish. A kit containing such supplies takes up very little space in your gear and is well worth bringing along on any camping trip. You can tie the line to an improvised pole made from a branch, or you can just dangle it from your hands. Live bait is best—especially worms, grubs, caterpillars, and large bugs (all of which can be found under rocks and dead wood). For best results, first "chum" the area by sprinkling tiny scraps of food; then fish it. Once you've caught the first one, you can also use fish guts for bait and chum.

It's important to be able to clean your own fish, as well as know how to cook them. I recommend finding an experienced person to teach you all this. I think there is nothing tastier than fresh fish cooked any number of ways over a campfire!

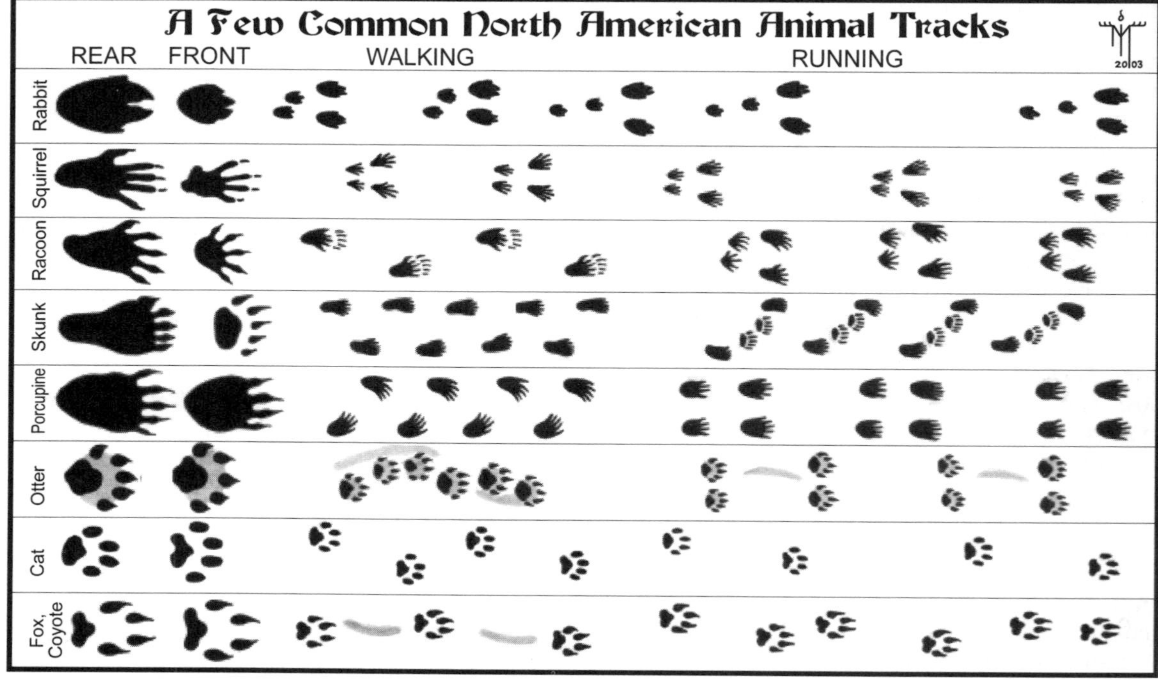

Class V: Adventures in Nature

"Adventures! Nasty disturbing uncomfortable things! Make you late for dinner! I can't think what anybody sees in them." –Bilbo Baggins, *The Hobbit* (p. 4)

1. Introduction: Nature is the Greatest Teacher

Regardless of Bilbo's opinion, I love to go on adventures (and even he eventually came to love adventuring). In my 60+ years, I have climbed to the tops of mountains and dived to the bottom of the sea. I have crawled through narrow passageways of prehistoric painted caves, and celebrated total eclipses of the Sun within ancient stone circles. I have hiked through the rain forest jungles of Peru, Australia, New Guinea, and Costa Rica, wandered amid the redwoods of Califia, and swum in clear pools at the base of high mist-shrouded waterfalls in Hawaii.

I have walked with unicorns at the Renaissance Faire and swum with mermaids in a South Pacific lagoon. I have ridden camels and elephants, petted tigers and dolphins, and hung out casually among herds of wild deer and kangaroos, scratching them behind their ears.

I have slept out in the high desert and scrambled down into the craters of extinct volcanoes. I have walked the Inca roads, and explored their ancient ruins under the full Moon. I have bathed in natural hot springs, and frozen my ass off on an Alaskan glacier. I have combed for shells on beach sands that were black, white, and glass. I have kayaked with 10-foot alligators in the Florida Everglades and snorkeled with 30-foot whale sharks in the Coral Sea. And I have trod the paths of the Dead, where bones and skulls were stacked like cordwood by the hundreds of thousands on either side.

All these things and more…I have always regarded Life as a continuing adventure story. And every adventure I have gone on has taught me Lessons. The most important Lesson of all, however, is this: Nature is the Greatest Teacher.

Lesson 2. Water

Water—Nature in your own home

—by Lady Pythia

Water can soften, shape, and polish even the hardest stones. When you need to learn to be flexible, adaptable, when life is giving you difficult lessons and making you tighten up with fear or pain, if your heart becomes hurt while learning lessons about loving and giving, and you are tempted to grow as hard as stone to protect yourself—stop for a moment, and choose the healing power of Water as teacher. Give yourself to Water, even if it's just soaking in the bathtub.

A bath of seawater can be effectively replicated by adding 1/2 cup of salt and a cup of cider vinegar to a tub of hot water. This creates a gentle cleansing soak that removes toxins from the body and feels like ocean water on the skin. If you like, seaweed can also be added. The water in which you immerse yourself will cleanse away any negative energy, fears, sorrow. Water can and will transmute you if you learn to offer your sharp corners for cleansing and polishing. It will absorb your weariness, and combined with salt, purifies away anything you need to let go of. Learning to let go is one of the greatest lessons of Water, thus may you more greatly understand what surrendering to the great primeval ocean of consciousness, like the ocean from which all life emerged, has to teach you in the silence of your own Inner Self, into which Water can bring you, even at home.

Should you ever find your temper getting the best of you, you will find a resource in gently falling rain as well. Go stand in the rain, and let your anger be changed by the raindrops, for as they gently cleanse the Earth and bring nourishment to growing plants and trees, so too can the same rain bring you growth and renewal, if you allow it. Allow the falling water to help you find your balance point, and return to your situation with a healthier, different perspective.

The River

For eleven years of my later life (the longest ever in one home), I lived with my family right on the Rushing River (or *Russian River,* as it was called by mundanes…). Our backyard was a private beach and swimming hole, with a rope swing dangling from a high tree. Salmon and otters played in the running waters, ospreys and kingfishers hunted in the pools, and friends hung out all the time. At the beginning of each Summer, I would go to a tire store and buy up a bunch of used but airtight truck inner tubes. Most weekends, we would gather up a bunch of folks and tubes, take everyone a few miles upstream in trucks, and float down the river back to our place—or sometimes much further.

Along the way, the experience itself offered so many lessons that I came to think of it as a magickal teaching all its own. There were rapids with white water, deep still pools, giant boulders forming nar-

row passages, tall rocks to jump from, sandy beaches, and gravel bars. Drifting along, arms and legs draped over the sides of the tube, embraced in the arms of the river nymphs and watching the world go by, has been the most perfect place I have ever known for meditation and reflection. By coming to know the river, I now *know* rivers, and I can tube, raft, canoe, or kayak along them with perfect ease. I have even done serious white-water rafting down world-class rivers in Costa Rica!

Here are some of the best lessons I've learned from the river:

1. The stream of consciousness flows like a river.

Spirit moves like water. It's always seeking to return to the Source, and it always finds its own level. Like water, Spirit can be bottled up, diverted, or dammed for a time. But eventually the container will break and Spirit, like water, will flow free and move to continue its passage downstream. Water or Spirit diverted will find a way around and cut new channels to rejoin its course. Dams will one day overflow and be swept away, and the flow will continue—always towards the ocean, from whence it came. As water flows ever downwards to merge with the vast ocean below, Spirit flows ever upwards to merge with the eternal cosmic ocean above.

2. Go with the flow.

Any time you come to a fork in the river, a big rock in the way, a log jam, an island, or rapids ahead—and you can't see ahead to know which passage to take—the trick is to look at the current. Wherever the current is strongest, there will be a "V" in the water. All you have to do is steer your tube down the center of the "V." Trusting to the flow, rather than fighting it, you become one with the current, which will carry you around and over all obstacles. Often, newbies will try and paddle desperately to avoid the fast water, and they find themselves getting swept into rocks, logs, and embankments—or just going round and round in a little side eddy and left behind by the rest of us. Just so in life; the trick is to learn to see the flow of the current, and then steer your course right into the middle of it. The heart of the flow may seem too fast and scary, but it is truly the safest course.

3. You *can* change the course of mighty rivers with your bare hands!

Every river begins with a tiny stream. If you go far enough back upstream towards the source, the course of that stream can be changed by moving only a few pebbles. Further down, it takes boulders, and far enough along, whole mountains would have to be moved. I've moved plenty of pebbles in my time—and even quite a few boulders, and I've diverted tiny streams that have become mighty raging torrents, which have carved great canyons and washed away mountains. Consciousness, like water, ultimately cannot be resisted, and through Dark Times (such as are going on as I write), I draw my hope and inspiration from this certainty.

Quest: Inner Tube Trip

Find a river or large stream somewhere you can get to easily, that is suitable for inner tubing in the Summer. You may have to ask around a bit. Not so small that the water doesn't flow, or it's too shallow to float in; and not so big or fast as to be dangerous. Ideal rivers for kayaking are often also good for tubing, as long as there's enough of a current to carry you along. Get some friends—and at least one experienced adult—who'd like to make a day of tubing. Get truck inner tubes, and over-inflate them into the shape of a fat donut. Wear sneakers or good rubber sandals that won't come off in the water. Practice maneuvering in a still pool before you venture into the moving water. If you should capsize, hold onto your tube! You'll need a big pick-up truck to carry yourselves and your tubes to the upstream drop-off place, and then drive down to the other end to pick you up. Start with a short easy trip—maybe a mile or so—and try longer ones as you get better at it. Go with the flow, and become one with the cosmic stream of consciousness....

The Ocean

We are the children of the great Mother Ocean, the womb of all Life, to which our pre-human ancestors once returned, and to which we still feel irresistibly drawn. The plasma of the very blood that courses through our veins is basically seawater, with the same chemical composition as that of the ancient seas from which we first internalized our circulatory systems, more than 500 million years ago.

Movements of human populations have traditionally followed water pathways. Whether along a coastline, or along rivers, early settlements are always found near water. It is not difficult to envision early *hominids* (proto-humans), and later true humans, walking, wading, and swimming along coastlines and rivers, thus populating the globe. If they were swimmers and divers, it would only serve to drive them on, in the search for food as populations rose and the climate changed (Phillip V. Tobias, "Water and Human Evolution").

Quest: Return to the Sea

If you live anywhere near the ocean, learn to experience its magick and mystery. Go beachcombing and tidepooling, and see what you can find for your collection (but *never* take anything alive from a tide pool!). Become a good sea swimmer, and learn bodysurfing (and even boogie boarding, if you're in the right place). Get yourself a good set of ocean fins, a mask, and snorkel, and explore the undersea world (*always* with a partner!). If the water is cold in your area, get a wet suit. And for the most complete experience of the ocean, take SCUBA lessons, get certified, and go diving with a group and a professional dive-master.

SCUBA diving is, to me, the ultimate experience, connecting us at once with our entire 500-million-year heritage as creatures of the sea, and also giving us a taste of the weightlessness of outer space, wherein lies our ultimate destiny. There is simply nothing in all the world comparable to the feeling of floating—indeed, flying—in perfectly balanced buoyancy far beneath the waves, the surging sea around us at one with the pulsing ocean within our bodies. I even suspect that our love of roller coaster rides, and our universal dreams of flying, reflect our deep memories of weightless life in the sea, and our intuitive reaching towards the heavens.

Lesson 3: Night

Cold-hearted orb that rules the night,
Removes the colors from our sight.
Red is black and yellow, white.
But we decide which one is right…
And which is an illusion.
—Moody Blues, *On the Threshold of a Dream*

For 150 million years, dragons ruled the Earth. During all those long aeons, while dinosaurs grew to as much as 100 feet long, weighing up to 100 tons, the biggest mammals were no larger than a house cat. If we think the reassembled skeletons of those prehistoric monsters seem huge to us now, imagine how much more gigantic they would have seemed to our tiny ancestors! Dragons completely dominated the lands, the seas, and the air. Sea dragons grew to the size of modern whales, and flying dragons were as big as small airplanes. They occupied every environmental niche—except three. No dinosaurs burrowed into the Earth; no dinosaurs climbed trees; and very, very few dinosaurs hunted at night.

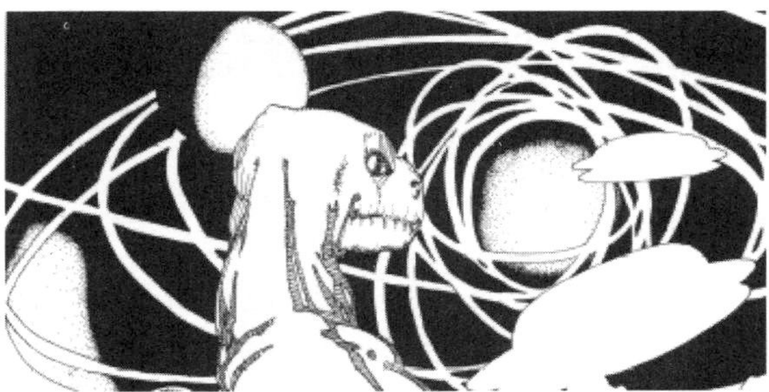

The dragons were not great, sluggish, stupid cold-blooded lizards, as people have assumed for so long. They were active, warm-blooded (and often feathered) members of a class all their own—*Archosauria*—of which birds are the only surviving members. And like modern birds, dragon eyes were primarily designed for day vision, with full-color receptors (called *cones*). Only towards the end of their reign, with the rise of the raptors, did some of them develop the huge eyes full of ultra-sensitive black-and-white receptors called *rods*, such as we find today in owls and nighthawks. Raptors—by far the most intelligent of all dragons—were the first and only ones to be able to hunt at night, like cats and owls do today. What did they hunt? Like owls and cats, they hunted nocturnal mammals.

The only way mammals had managed to survive at all during those 150 millions years of dragon dominion was by occupying those three tiny niches. Some burrowed in the ground, and others came to live in trees. The little rat-like burrowers came out only at night, when the dragons slept. In order to be able to see in the dark, those mammals gave up the cones in their eyes entirely and filled their retinas with nothing but rods. This is why nearly all modern mammals still don't see in color—even after the dinosaurs were exterminated—because almost all later mammals descended from those nocturnal burrowers.

But some mammals moved into the trees, where the predatory dragons couldn't reach them. Among these were the *primates* ("first ones"): tree shrews, which later evolved into lemurs, monkeys, apes—and us. Because we lived in trees, we didn't have to give up color vision for night vision, and we kept both cones and rods. Primates (and marsupials) remain the only mammals that can see in full-color; and both of us can still see better at night than nearly all birds.

When I was a boy, I would climb out of my bedroom window at night when there was a full Moon. While everyone else slept, I would explore this strange silver-lit world of blacks and greys. No other people would be abroad, and I was free to wander the yards, fields, and forests around my neighborhood alone. I thrilled to the night sounds of crickets, cicadas, coyotes, owls, and whippoorwills. I would come across other nocturnal creatures making their nightly rounds, and discovered they had no fear of me in the dark.

Many, many years later, my lifemate Morning Glory made a profound observation: *"True Witches (and Wizards) are not afraid of the Dark."*

Faces in the Moon

Our Moon is gravitationally locked so that the same side always faces the Earth. This side has very distinctive large dark areas of lava flows that look from here like oceans. Thus the ancients called them *maria* ("seas"). When we look up at the full Moon, these maria seem to resemble the features of a face. In different countries, these lunar patterns were seen as the Lady in the Moon, the Man in the Moon, or the Rabbit in the Moon (seen from Australia). Next time there's a full Moon, see if you can find them.

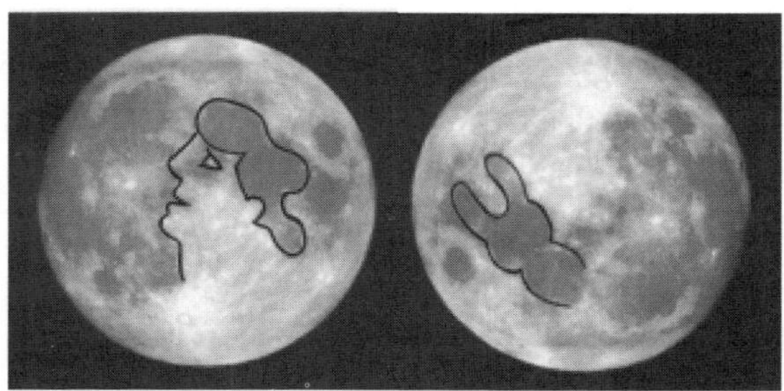

Lesson 4: Ley Lines

The verdant landscapes of the British Isles are crisscrossed with mysterious lines that run arrow-straight from horizon to horizon, like the once-imagined "canals" on Mars. These are called *ley lines,* and they have been the subject of much study and speculation—and a number of books. Hills, tall standing stones, and circular stone henges have been erected along their courses and intersections, and over millennia, many Christian churches have been built on those sites. The biggest mystery concerning them is: What is their basis? Some have thought that they trace the course of underground rivers, or geomagnetic currents, and call them "Dragon Paths." Others believe they are remnant roads of lost Atlantis—or aliens. I have walked along some of these lines and have seen from the Tor of Glastonbury the obelisk stones that mark where they pass over the horizon. And so I asked some magickal friends in London about these lines, and they told me a remarkable story:

During the last Ice Age, so much water was bound up in the mile-high glaciers that covered much of the land that the sea levels were 400 feet lower than they are now. The English Channel and the North Sea were all dry land, right up to Scandinavia, and Western Europe looked much like Tolkein's map of Middle Earth, with the Shire being in England. Across all that tundra country, vast herds of caribou traveled on their long annual migrations—just as they still do in parts of Canada, Alaska, Siberia, and Scandinavia. Then as now, they filed in straight and narrow lines, and over tens of thousands of years, these became clear trackways—especially as the ground became deeply fertilized from aeons of their *fewmets* (droppings)!

When the caribou had passed over, psychedelic *amanita muscaria* mushrooms sprang up in this rich manure. And the nomadic tribes who lived off the great deer and followed them (as they still do in places) ate those mushrooms, and were enlightened. And so they erected tall stone markers on the horizons and high hills along these trackways, so they could be easily followed even when the ground was covered in snow. Important crossings would be marked with circles of stones, which remained long after the ice had melted and the seas had risen, and the caribou were long-gone. Ages later, these became sacred ritual sites. So of course, when the Christian missionaries wanted to build their churches, where better than at these most sacred places?

Lesson 5: Sacred Places

(by Jesse Wolf Hardin)

All of the natural world is sacred...magickal and inspirited. It all has something to teach us, and every bit of it needs our protection and love. But at the same time, some places are more intensely charged than others, with heavier concentrations of energies and insights available to the seeking Wizard. The *genius loci* ("spirit of place") informs, excites, and inspires through specific sites, through landforms vibrating with that magickal force the early Greeks called the *plenum.* They're often edges and extremes, featuring symmetric shapes and mythic themes: caverns and caves, waterfalls and wellsprings, river canyons and high mountain peaks, enchanted deserts and ocean coves, circular clearings and oaken groves.

Sacred sites are sometimes charged not only by the intentions and spirits of the living Earth, but also by the ritual reverence and mindful maintenance, the ceremonies and spells of countless caring generations. Most everyone has some acquaintance with the better-known sites such as Colorado's Mesa Verde, Britain's Stonehenge, and ancient Petra—but every single region, every watershed has its own special spots where the vibe is most intense, where our visions seem clearest, our dreams most urgent and alive.

As a young man I basked in the emanations of Mt. Shasta, walked barefoot through a forest of whispering pines of the Black Hills in Sioux country, and snuck past the locked Park Service gates in order to spend a night in the underground kivas of Chaco. Each gifted me with new experiences and lessons, and I tried to serve them all equally well. Then, in 1980, I followed the most powerful revelation of my life to an exact bend of a particular New Mexico river, deep in the enchanted Gila wildlands of the American Southwest. Up until 900 years ago, our Sanctuary home served as the ceremonial center for those ancient Indians that archaeologists and mundanes call the "Mogollon," but who knew themselves as the Sweet Medicine People. These days when students and apprentices come to study with us here, they're each helping re-establish a sacred lineage of purpose and commitment, magick and love.

Whether sojourning to the wildest wilderness or to a treasured and hidden niche in an overgrown neighborhood park—one way we can measure a sacred site is by how deeply it affects us. It often starts with what seems like an invitation, either an omen or sensation. We may sense we're being observed or evaluated by the resident entities, provoking a moment's fear or dread. Yet with our minds quiet and hearts pure, we're soon not only accepted but initiated and instructed, emboldened and equipped! Sacred sites affirm our personal roles in Gaia's unfolding sacred purpose... and a place of power will ultimately be where we feel more powerful as well.

Canyons

(by Jesse Wolf Hardin)

Like most young boys, I was usually attracted to the tallest peak around, to those places where I could see in all directions at once, and feel some distance from the mundanes who muddled below. But once I got to puberty I began to find myself drawn down into the secretive hideouts in drywash gullies, and into the wetness of a river forever carving its direction

and intention in solid mountain rock. A canyon embodies the feminine, and we males seek balance as well as beauty in the embrace of her spirit and form. It is here that both aspects of our being, the yin and the yang, meet and combine. Womanly water strokes our legs and feet, while reflecting the manly cliffs lifting skyward like granite wings.

Even those who will never visit them know the names of some of the gorges of Africa, of Utah's Canyonlands and Mexico's *Canon de Cobre,* the serpentine twists of Idaho's Snake and the Black Canyon of the Gunnison. It's said that the average visitor spends only five minutes at park sites overlooking the majestic Grand Canyon, but of course the real experience of it begins in an exploration of its inner depths. A canyon, like a river, requires our complete immersion in order to do its magick on us. We don't walk so much as plummet forward—trembling with anticipation, totally buzzed from the thrill of the dive.

A canyon is an opening into the Earth, like a cave without a ceiling. It is a way into increased sensuality and self-knowledge—into deeper intimacy with self and other, place and Spirit. I remember the first time I saw what was to become my fateful mission and lifetime canyon home, 200 miles southeast of the Grand, in the Gila of New Mexico. Getting from the parking area on National Forest land to the center of the sanctuary requires a trip over seven jeep-sinking river crossings, each passage putting us closer in touch with our spirits and bodies as well as with the enchanted surroundings. As the canyon narrowed I felt myself approached, approved, and held, and I quickly fell in love. Here I found metaphor made real, a perfect marriage of male and female: the hard and the soft, inner and outer, celebration and manifestation.

For the practicing or aspiring Wizard, a journey into the flesh and mystery of a river canyon becomes a sacred quest: an exploration of meaning and place, an adventurous relationship with magickal self and animate spirit—a setting for pledges kept by—and promises given to—the ever-inspiring Earth.

Wells and Springs

Wishing wells were once believed to be guarded by faeries or other Nature spirits, who had to be appeased with a coin before the wish would be heard. These and other holy wells may have first gained their reputations because of healthful minerals in their water. Since early people would have drunk from them unaware of this reason, they regarded the curative powers with awe. Romans brought valuable gifts to please the well spirits before they drank, thus gaining their favor. It is said that water taken from three different wells, if poured half on the ground and then administered to the sick, will cure fever. —Patricia Telesco

I have soaked in natural hot springs deep in the redwood forest of Oregon, and out in the Mojave Desert, and in Colorado canyons. Some have been crystal clear, and others so thick with white clay you felt you were bathing in milk. In one called Hot Creek, there are these big circular holes in the shallow creek bed, where you can sit around the outside of them up to your neck and dangle your feet in the upwelling hot water from below. If you swim underwater across the holes, you can feel with your entire body the crashing of huge boulders being churned far beneath; it sounds just like the heartbeat of the Mother!

Waterfalls

Waterfalls are sites where both wonderful rituals and terrible accidents have occurred. The power of the rushing water has an almost hypnotic effect, and often draws people inwards. Some say the voices of the ancestors are echoed in the crashing waters, and can grant wisdom and insight as well as reverberate with warning.
—Patricia Telesco

I have been to Yosemite Valley in NorCalifia a couple of times, in the Spring, when its many waterfalls are swollen with the melting snows high above. There are trails that you can climb to take you above them and below them. The sound of the crashing water falling from hundreds of feet above is nearly deafening, and you get totally soaked by the spray, but the rush of excitement from the negative ions formed in the rainbow-filled mists will take your breath away!

Tidal Pools

—by Abby Willowroot

It is in the tide pools that we have a chance to experience sea life in microcosm. A tide pool can be as small as six inches square and only a few inches deep, yet it still may be filled with a wide variety of life forms, some familiar, and some you may never have seen before. Look deeply and remember what you see. With the next tide, many of the inhabitants will depart, and others come to live for a time in the tide pool, along with the barnacles and other long-term residents of these miraculous seaside kingdoms. The tide pool you see exists for only a few hours, and then it is gone forever, replaced by a new pool and new creatures. Every tide pool is a living reminder of life's truths of fragility, change, and impermanence.

Tide pools are places of infinite wonder. They are to be experienced and explored, but never ever plundered. Gifts of the sea wash up on the shore with each high tide. The treasures of the tide pools are all-important parts of these tiny living biospheres. To take from a tide pool is to intrude upon another realm, and the home of other creatures. There are many lessons to be learned by observing these small magical environments without interfering by our presence.

Caves

From the most ancient times, caves have been felt to be the womb of Mother Earth. As soon as we gained mastery of fire enough to allow us to venture into the twisting passages that had never known the light of day, we entered a world whose only other inhabitants were blind bugs, fish, and newts—and sonar-equipped bats. In the dawn of humanity, caverns became our first temples.

In 1986, I made a pilgrimage to Les Eyzies, in the Dordogne Valley of France. There, 20,000 years ago, Cro-Magnon peoples had made their homes in the fronts of the countless caves in the incredible cliffs that tower over and surround the valley. And in the deep hidden recesses they had painted magickal images of the animals that shared their world. Here are some notes from my journal:

86.3.7.8:00 PM — ♄ Today we joined a tour to la Grotte *(cave)* de Font-de-Gaume—*one of the few painted caves still open to the public. This is what I came to find. And I was amazed to discover something that the photos can never show. The "paint-*

Daniel Blair-Stewart

ings" are far more than that. Natural bulges and hollows *are painted to give both convex and* concave *3-D effects, wherein lights and shadows cast by moving hand-held shell oil lamps would bring the figures* to life! *Like those concave hollow bas-relief of faces that seem to move and follow you around the room, these figures have a life of their own.*

I lagged behind the group as we came back out, to better study the images. I saw that all these painted animals were streaming towards the cave entrance—to be born. As a somewhat dazed initiate made his way towards the opening along with the animals, he would emerge from the cliff-face at dawn to see those very animals grazing in great herds across the valley floor below. And he would know: We are all born of the Earth—all Children of the same Mother.

The Forest

Any forest that has never been logged is a world of its own, and connects us to an ancient and primordial Mystery, from before the Age of Men. Tropical rainforests are the Earth's oldest living ecosystems. Many of the fruits and vegetables we eat originated there. Rainforests now cover only 2% of the Earth's surface yet they are the home to over half the animal and plant species on our planet. Rainforest fruits and vegetables include; avocados, bananas, pepper, brazil nuts, cayenne pepper, cashews, cocoa, cinnamon, cloves, coconut, coffee, cola, corn, eggplant, figs, ginger, peppers, lemons, oranges, papaya, paprika, peanuts, pineapple, rice, winter squash, sweet pepper, sugar, tomato, turmeric, vanilla, and yams. The medicines of the future will come from rainforests.

When Morning Glory and I moved onto the land of Greenfield Ranch back in 1977, much of it was deeply forested with Douglas fir, oak, madrone—even some redwoods. However, the loggers had gone through about 50 years before, and had clear-cut some areas. These were a mess—old tree-stumps, gouged-up "cat-skinning" roads, and slash (trimmed-off branches) everywhere. One wide flat place above our main spring looked like Isengard after Saruman tore up all the trees! We called it "the Blasted Heath." Over the next few years, we started doing annual New Year's tree plantings all over the land, with seedlings we got free from the Department of Forestry. These were cedar, Coulter pine, and redwoods—intended for commercial timber. And we planted thousands of them—starting with the Blasted Heath.

We moved off the land in 1985 and just go back for rituals held there. At Beltaine a couple of years ago, the present caretakers said they wanted to show us something. They took us on a hike up the hill to where the Blasted Heath had been. Only now it was a deep, lush forest of 50-foot Coulter pines. Nesting birds sang in the branches, and rabbits scampered off through the undergrowth. There was a stillness and peace that radiated through the place—it felt like the Elven forest of Lothlorien. And all this was a magick we had created simply by planting for the future.

Clearings

Sometimes, in the middle of a thick forest, you will come upon a clearing—no trees—not even stumps, but just green grass. Such clearings feel like islands in the sea or oases in the desert. These are private and magickal places. When you find such a clearing, go into the center, and sit or lie down on the grass. Meditate and open yourself to the natural world around you. Close your eyes, and listen to the sounds of birds and insects, as they rise and fall, circle and spiral in the waves of a stereo symphony. Let yourself be carried by the waves into a realm where the language has no words, and the Song is in your blood.

Daniel Blair-Stewart

Faerie Rings

Some kinds of mushrooms will send up their toadstools at the outer edge of the underground organism, making a circle that can be 10, 20, 30 feet or more in diameter. These are called Faerie Rings because some kinds of Faeries are considered to be the spirits of the mushrooms, and the rings are then the places where they dance in a circle. Some of these Faerie Rings are formed of psychedelic mushrooms, and some even of poisonous varieties. You should never lie down (and especially, never go to sleep!) inside a Faerie Ring—you might wake up in another time and place altogether!

Class VI: Your Magickal Garden

1. Introduction: A Wizard's Garden

ARDENING IS A WONDERFUL MYStery. There are magickal lessons that can only be learned through the experience of planting, nurturing, and harvesting food and herbs for the sustenance of your body and spirit. I have been utterly fascinated watching those first tiny leaves unfurl, daily growing larger and stronger into plants which produce fragrant blossoms, get pollinated by bees and butterflies, and then create luscious food that grows fat and ripe for our table.

As I am writing, it is now early May, and I've just spent the day working in the garden. My muscles ache, but I feel great! I have found that growing a garden is a special kind of magick that is very important to a Wizardly life. There is nothing quite so miraculous in all the world as the emergence of new life—whether it's the birth of a human baby, or puppies, the hatching of an egg, or the sprouting of a seed. Over the coming months, I'll be taking breaks from this writing to be tilling, weeding, planting, irrigating, nurturing, and harvesting. Won't you join me?

If you have any space at all in your backyard that can be turned into a garden, I recommend you do so. If you don't have such a space, perhaps you have a friend with a garden you could work in together. Some city neighborhoods have community gardens that you can participate in. If you're not able to work in a garden at all, at least try and visit some of the beautiful public gardens that others have created.

There are several types of gardens—herb gardens, veggie gardens, flower gardens, even ornamental gardens. In this Class I would like to encourage you to grow veggies and herbs—with a few special flowers mixed in. The information I am setting out here should provide you a good foundation, but, depending on just where you live, it may have to be adapted considerably. Consult with your local nurseries when you buy plants and seeds. Get to know the people who work there, and ask them lots of questions! You might even go over some of the following material with them, and get their opinions…

Tools & Supplies

Only a few basic tools are needed for small-scale gardening. You should also have a place to keep them out of the weather when they are not being used.

Shovel and **spading fork:** Get a round-nosed shovel with a 47" handle for moving dirt. Also pick up a 4-tined garden fork.

Pickax: This will only be needed if you have very rocky soil; otherwise, don't bother.

Steel rake: Get the bow type rather than the kind with its handle attached directly to the head. A good size is about 15" wide with 14 teeth.

Hoe: Get one with a 7" blade and a 4'-5' handle.

Trowel: This is used in digging small holes for setting out starter plants.

Garden hose: You will need a long enough hose to reach from your outside faucet to all parts of your garden, along with a spray nozzle (or wand).

Gloves: Good sturdy garden gloves are a must!

Four Rules for Successful Gardening

There are many important factors in planting and caring for a garden. It is the act of being in balance with Nature that will produce a beautiful garden. Walk through your garden every day while thanking Mother Earth and the Nature Spirits, and thinking positive thoughts to your plants, and you will be greatly blessed for your care and attention.

1. **Use only natural fertilizers**—manure, lawn and garden clippings, kitchen scraps, compost.
2. **Mulch your plants** when they get about a foot tall, to conserve moisture and keep the ground cool.
3. **Use only natural pesticides**—make your own sprays from garlic, onions, peppers, etc. Encourage predatory insects and garden spiders. Attract birds with birdbaths and feeders. Interplant insect-repelling companion plants (see following).
4. And finally, **garden by the phases and signs of the Moon**.

Lesson 2. Laying Out Your Wizard's Garden

Designing and laying out your garden is a real art form, and many people make detailed maps showing just what is planted where. If you are making a large and complex garden, with many different kinds of herbs and vegetables, that could be quite a project. However, even a very modest amount of sunny space can be turned into a small garden. And if you don't have any yard space at all, perhaps you can plant a window box with a few strawberries or other plants.

Here's a simple concept for your first garden, with a few basic plants that will give you a good start. This is based on having four square or rectangular sections, each about 6–10 feet on a side, with plenty of sunlight. These can be grouped into a single large square or rectangle, or end-to-end in a line, or even separated in different parts of your yard. If they are together, you will need to keep clear pathways between them, so you can get at them from all sides without stepping on the plants. If you're not able to handle four plots, at least try one or two. You might find making an herb garden to be the easiest.

Plot One will be for corn, pumpkins, and morning glories.
Plot Two will be for tomatoes, chives, basil, and catnip.
Plot Three will be for zucchinis, squash, watermelons, sunflowers, and snow peas.
Plot Four will be your magickal herb garden.

Rotation

These recommended veggies are for a basic first-year starter garden. For future years, you might want to consider other crops—especially if you have plenty of space. So here are a few tips for maintaining a good garden year after year:

Avoid planting the same or related vegetables in the same place two years in a row. Shifting them around from year-to-year is called *rotation,* and it's necessary to prevent soil exhaustion and to starve out soil-borne disease organisms. The best way to do this is like rotating the tires on a car—move the main crops of each plot to the next space each year. The basic rules are:

1. Alternate corn with *legumes* (peas and beans) in the same space.
2. Alternate leafy vegetables (spinach, lettuce, cabbage...) with root crops (carrots, beets, onions...).

Lesson 3: Your Garden Altar

Every magickal garden should have a garden altar. Ours is a concrete bench, which we set up near the middle of our veggie garden, right by the path. As the seasons go by, I change the altar cloth and place different things on it, according to the Wheel of the Year (see 4.VI). A particularly appropriate place to set up your garden altar, however, is right in the middle of the pentagram of your herb garden, in plot four (see following). It can be a large flat stone, or anything else you like. The garden altar is a great place to do special magick outdoors, under the Moon and Sun. You should think of your whole garden as a sacred ritual space (see 4.II).

Garden Goddess: It's not a requirement, of course, but a garden Goddess is a great addition to any magickal garden! We've picked up a several very nice ones at flea markets—*Ceres* (the Roman grain goddess from whose name we get "cereal"), *Kwan-Yin,* and *Hygeia* (goddesses of healing—our word *hygiene* comes from Hygeia). You should look for concrete or even plastic rather than plaster, as plaster will crumble in the rain.

Kwan-Yin

Witch Ball: Perhaps you have seen those large mirrored glass gazing balls they sell in garden shops? These are giant versions of blown glass Christmas tree balls, and are traditionally called "Witch Balls." Their mirrored surfaces are to create a spell of protection around your garden. We keep ours on a stand in the center of our rose garden. However, a big one isn't really necessary—even a fairly large Christmas ornament will do, as long as it has that plain mirrored surface. It would make a perfect centerpiece for your garden altar.

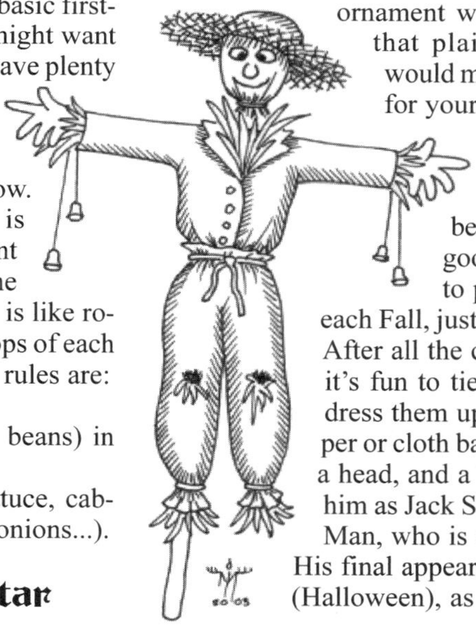

Scarecrow: Although the birds don't seem to be terribly frightened of my goofy scarecrows, I still like to put one up in the garden each Fall, just for the sake of tradition. After all the corn has been harvested, it's fun to tie the stalks together and dress them up with an old shirt, a paper or cloth bag stuffed with leaves for a head, and a big straw hat. I think of him as Jack Straw, ghost of the Green Man, who is cut down in the harvest. His final appearance will be at Samhain (Halloween), as Jack O'Lantern.

Bird Bath: A pretty bird bath near your garden will welcome birds to eat some of the nasty bug pests that will be trying to attack your plants—especially leaf-eating caterpiggles, like tomato hornworms. Make sure the bath is high enough (such as hanging from a nearby tree) to keep your cat from catching the birds it attracts, and always keep it full of water.

Lesson 4: Your Veggie Garden

First, make a diagram or map of your planned garden before you do any actual work. Keep your garden map in a safe place where you can refer to it throughout the year—you might tack it to the wall or inside door of the garage or tool shed. Each Winter, make up a new map with a new layout. I use ruled graph paper. Mark in the rows, spacing them the right distance apart to the map scale. Write in the names of the plants you intend to grow, and the dates you intend to plant them (see following). If your garden is on a slope, run the rows across the grade to prevent water erosion. Put your tallest crops—such as corn and sunflowers—in the North so they won't shade the smaller plants.

While I am giving you the information about ideal planting times according to the signs and phases of the Moon, the ideal is not always the practical reality. Most of the time, you work in your garden when you have a moment and the mood strikes you, when the Sun is shining and you feel like being outdoors. You also work the soil and plant when it's not raining, and when the soil isn't so soggy that it loses its structure when worked.

Also, in different climatic zones, the growing seasons vary, along with which plants are most suitable, and the best times to plant them. If you live in the tropics or the far North, you may not be able to grow the following plants successfully, but there will be others that will grow better where you are. So consult with your local nursery and make adjustments. A good Wizardly approach is to observe what grows well in your area and talk to other gardeners. Really good gardeners observe other people's gardens—great gardening is mostly watching what the plants are doing naturally and enhancing it.

Plot One

Corn: The best time to plant corn is between Beltaine and Litha, during the 2nd quarter of the Moon (◐-○). There are many different strains available, but *Golden Cross Bantam* is considered the best for the home garden, as it is hardy, tasty, and pest-resistant. Plant corn in square plots with plenty of sunlight for best pollination. If space permits, plant three varieties that will mature in 75, 85, and 95 days—or space your planting time over several lunar periods to extend your harvest. Plant your corn in 4" deep trenches, with 12" between plants and 30" between rows. If you plant from seeds, put three in each spot and cover them with 1" of soil. After the first shoot appears, pull out the others and discard them—but leave the small suckers alone. Pile up soil around the base as the stalks grow.

Pumpkins: Pumpkins grow over a very large area (around 16 square feet), so you need to plant only one hill, right in the center of your corn patch. This will yield plenty of pumpkins for Samhain! Plant them during the next 2nd quarter of the Moon (◐-○) following Beltaine. Dig a hole about 2' wide and 1' deep, and fill it with manure mixed with soil. Build it up into a crater-shaped mound and sow eight seeds in the crater, buried about 1 1/2" deep. Thin to 2–4 plants before they form vines, and guide the vines towards the corners of your corn patch. During the corn season, the pumpkin leaves will cover the ground and keep moisture in. Then, after all the corn is harvested and the bare stalks are bundled, the pumpkins will grow fat and orange among the corn-stalk teepees, watched over by your scarecrow.

Morning Glories: After your corn is in, and during the next 1st quarter of the Moon (●-◐), sow morning glory seeds in your corn patch. Soak the seeds overnight in warm water, and then plant just one seed near each corn seedling, covered with 1/2" of soil. They will twine around the corn stalks, produce beautiful flowers, and attract hummingbirds.

Plot Two

Tomatoes: Get your tomatoes into the ground as soon as frost danger is over. Plant them in a sunny spot during the 2nd quarter of the Moon (◐-○). Tomatoes should be transplanted from sets rather than trying to sprout them from seeds. Select starts 6"–8" high, and plant them 4' apart, deep enough to cover half the stem. Four tomato plants in your plot will be plenty, and you can even try one each of several varieties. You will need large tomato cages to hold up the growing plants. Check them every day, and keep the main branches inside the cages. Fertilize only at planting time, or you'll get nice leaves but few fruits!

Chives: Between Ostara and Beltane, during the 3rd quarter of the Moon (○-◑), plant a couple of clumps of chives on the outer edges of your tomato patch, away from the other plots. The best way is to get starts. Plant several bulbs together, about 3/4" deep. Then after the first year, you can divide your clumps and spread them elsewhere. Chives repel aphids, so to protect all our roses, we've now got clumps of chives and wild onions growing all around our yard.

Basil: Grow a few basil plants in the middle areas of your tomato patch. Sow the seeds in warm weather during the 2nd quarter of the Moon (◐-○). Thin the plants to one foot apart, fertilizing at that time.

Catnip *(Nepeta cataria):* Plant some catnip around your tomatoes during the 2nd quarter of the Moon (◐-○) to repel flea beetles. Keep it growing and spreading close to the ground by cutting back any vertical shoots, or it will grow up to 3' and crowd your basil and tomatoes.

Plot Three

The third plot is mainly for squashes and melons, which take up a lot of space but grow low along the ground. For your first garden, I recommend planting just three of these, about 6'–8' apart in a triangle: a zucchini, an acorn squash, and a watermelon (if you have abundant water for irrigation). The upper space of this plot is occupied with tall sunflowers and climbing peas or beans.

Zucchini: A single zucchini plant will produce so much food that you'll be trying to give it away to everyone who stops by! During the 2nd quarter of the Moon (◐-○), plant several seeds in a single manure-filled crater-shaped hill, exactly the same as for pumpkins, and thin to two plants.

Winter Squash: The main varieties of Winter squash are *Butternut, Hubbard,* and *Acorn.* I recommend acorn squash. During the 2nd quarter of the Moon (◐-○), plant half-a-dozen seeds in one crater-shaped hill, just as for zucchinis, and thin to two plants.

Watermelon: I recommend *Dixie Queen,* unless you live in a colder climate, in which case *New Hampshire Midget* will do best. During the 2nd quarter of the Moon (◐-○), plant 4–8 seed under 1" of soil in a manure-filled crater-shaped hill, as with zucchinis, but add some sand to the soil. When the seedlings develop, thin to one strong plant. Water regularly and well. Although watermelons are fun to grow and eat, they're not considered a good "starter crop." Consult with your local nursery. If it doesn't seem like watermelons are a good idea, try planting Summer squash here instead, following the same instructions as above for Winter squash.

Sunflowers: These can grow to 12' tall, producing enormous flowers with hundreds of tasty seeds for people and birds. Grow several of them in another triangle between the zucchini, squash, and watermelon. Plant during the 1st quarter of the Moon (●-◐) in early Spring, as soon as the frost is out of the ground, in soil that has been deeply dug, limed, and fertilized. Plant 2–3 seeds in each hole, and cover them with ½" of soil. When they sprout, thin for the strongest one. Tall varieties will need to be staked, and tied loosely with a strip of cloth. Water regularly and fertilize several times during Spring and Summer.

Pole beans: Plant pole beans at the base of each sunflower, so they will climb up the taller plants. There are several varieties to choose from. *Scarlet Runner Beans* have fiery red flowers that attract butterflies and purple pods of edible beans; but they don't have the best flavor. I think the tastiest pole beans are *Kentucky Blue Lake* or *Kentucky Wonder*—but consult with your local nursery and see what they advise. Plant early in the Spring, at the same time you plant your sunflowers. Sow 4–6 seed beans 2" deep, and thin to the best 2–3. As they grow, you may need to help them find the sunflower stalk. Fertilize them once or twice over the Summer.

Companion Planting

As you'll have noticed from the above, many garden plants grow well together and help each other in various ways. Certain plants will even repel nasty bug pests that attack your garden. Smart gardeners understand this, and plan gardens to maximize the effective use of "Companion Planting." Here are a few companion plants to consider for your Wizard's Garden. Some can be planted right in among your veggies, and others at the edges of your plots, or around your yard.

Calendula is a kind of **marigold** with orange or yellow flowers that repel pests. It is also an antiseptic when tinctured.
Catnip reduces flea beetle on tomatoes.
Chives repel aphids from roses. (Yellow roses in particular attract horrible Japanese beetles!)
Cosmos and **Coreopsis** repel insects.
Marigolds planted with beans repel most beetles. **French marigolds** attract nematodes, so plant them elsewhere as a "trap crop."
Mint and **mustard** repel cabbage pests.
Nasturtiums repel aphids, and the edible kind has more mustard oil than the mustard plant. They taste great in salads and stir-fry!
Painted daisies should definitely be included in your garden—not only for their beauty, but also for their insecticide abilities.
Onions repel cutworms.
Sage repels ants and cabbage pests.
Spearmint and **tansy** repel ants. Because they grow tall, plant them by the kitchen wall.

Lesson 5: Your Magickal Herb Garden

Many magickal people (especially Witches!) lay out their herb garden in the shape of a pentagram. Your fourth plot should be just about the right size. You can lay out the design with bricks, stones, or thin narrow boards woven and nailed together (ours is done in bricks). A pentagram gives you five well-spaced triangular spaces, allowing for a nice assort-

ment of herbs for magick, healing, and cooking. The center pentagon makes a perfect spot for your garden altar, and this is where I recommend you set it up.

All herbs should ideally be planted during the 1st quarter of the Moon (●-◐). Thin them ruthlessly. Select the hardiest seedlings, and give them room to mature. Keep the beds weeded, the soil moist, and cultivate the ground regularly to ensure good drainage. Above all, talk to your herbs, and let them know you love them. Harvest herbs when the blossoms appear and just before the flowers open. Magickal herbs are believed most potent if harvested on Midsummer's Day. When the morning dew is gone, cut the stalks and gently rinse the plants. Bind them in bunches and hang them in a dark, airy place. As they dry, the oil in stalk and stems drains into the leaves. After two weeks, strip off the leaves and flowers and store them in airtight jars with decorative labels.

Here's a selection of perennial herbs with a variety of uses; choose five—one for each section of your pentagram. I've included their Latin names and how tall they will grow, as well as some of their uses. These are best planted from starts, and you should consult with your nursery to determine which ones will work best for your garden, and in your climate.

Chamomile *(Anthemis)* (3'): Chamomile makes a popular tea for frayed nerves, helps you sleep, and is a good all-purpose incense. In the bath, it relaxes and soothes the skin. Carry chamomile in your mojo bag to positively influence others.

Hyssop *(Hyssopus officinalis)* (2'): Hyssop has protective properties, and repels evil. Hang a sprig at the window to ward off demons. The leaves and flowers soothe and refresh the body when added to bath water. Hyssop leaf tea excites passion.

Lemon Balm *(Melissa officinalis)* (2'): Called the "Honey Plant," for bees love it. It is often worn in a mojo bag as a love charm. The leaves make excellent tea. Crushed leaves in a muslin bag can be added to a soothing bath.

Mint *(Mentha)* (3'): Includes peppermint and spearmint. A good addition to teas and sweet things, mint dries and preserves very easily for later use in astringents and bath additives. Chewed fresh, it gives you the gift of beautiful speech.

Mugwort *(Artemisia vulgaris)* (3 1/2'): Mugwort is used in divination and prophetic dreams, for its aroma heightens awareness. It also promotes passion and friendship. Stuffing mugwort leaves into your shoes on a long hike prevents fatigue.

Rue *(Ruta graveolens)* (2 1/2'): Called the "Herb of Grace" for its protective qualities, burning the dried leaves of rue will dispel evil and ill will. Rue is good for vision, both physical and spiritual.

Sage *(Salvia)* (2'): The Latin name for sage means "to be saved" because the herb has so many uses. It's good in salads and to flavor turkey. Sage tea helps dry up moist coughs, lung congestion, tonsillitis, and sore throats. Sage also helps with bad breath, bleeding gums, and mouth sores. Crush the fresh leaves and apply to insect bites. And tied sage bundles make great smudge sticks!

Lesson 6: Nurturing Your Garden

Preparing the Soil

Start working on your garden long before you wish to actually begin planting; most experienced gardeners prepare the soil in the Fall and let it weather over the Winter. The first thing you will need to do (and by far the most work!) is to get rid of whatever's already growing there. If there are tall weeds, just go in with gloves and pull them out. Heap all the debris into a mulch pile to the side of your garden area. Then you can go over the area with a lawnmower, adding the grass clippings to the mulch.

As soon as the soil is dry, turn the sod with your shovel, and break it up even more with your spading fork, hoe, and rake. This is great exercise and much more fun if you can get some friends to help! As you work, walk backwards so as not to trample the dirt you've already loosened. If you've been composting your organic garbage (see following), spread the compost over the area and work it in as you go. Also spread animal manure (horse and turkey manure are excellent—and you can often find a stable or farm happy to sell it or even give it away free for the shoveling).

When you've gotten the whole area dug up and turned, our favorite technique is to cover it all with a large sheet of black plastic (available from any hardware store). The Sun will bake the soil under the plastic, and kill all the roots, weed seeds, and most of the bug pests. Check after a week or so to make sure there is nothing still green under the plastic. When the soil seems sufficiently cooked and you can see no remaining greenery, remove the plastic and finish breaking up the clumps of sod. Then rake it all smooth, clear your paths, and make trenches, rows, and craters for setting your seeds and starts.

Sprouting Seeds

In our garden these days, we plant almost everything from starts, which you can buy just about everywhere in the Spring. This is the easy way, and I highly recommend it for your first garden. However, several of the crops I've mentioned above can be planted successfully from seeds (particularly corn and squashes), and I would like to encourage you to give this a try, as it's particularly magickal to go through the entire process from seed to harvest.

The problem with planting seeds right in the ground is that birds love to eat them. One way to guarantee success from seeds is to sprout them yourself, and then transplant the seedlings into your garden. Some seeds need to be slightly sliced *(scarification)* before planting; some need to be in the freezer for a month *(stratification)* before germinating—read the package. Soak your seeds overnight in a bowl of water, and then lay them out on several layers of wet paper towel. Fold the layers over, and lay them on a tray. Keep the towels wet (but not soaking in a puddle) and check them every day. When you see little roots coming out of them, it's time for the next step.

All gardening supply stores have little peat pellets for sprouting, so pick up as many as you need (one for each seedling). Get a baking pan or Tupperware tray, and line it up with pellets. Then soak them with water until they soften and expand, keeping about ¼" of water in the bottom of the pan. Use a pointy object to doodle out a hole in the middle of each pellet, and carefully insert the sprouting seeds, with the roots sticking down. Gently cover them with loose peat, and place the tray in a window where it will get Sun. Keep the water replenished so the pellets don't dry out, and watch for the green shoots to come up. Re-use any pellets that don't sprout. When the sprouts get about 6" tall, you can transplant them into your garden. Very small seedlings are still vulnerable to snails, slugs, and bugs, so you might want to reserve some back-up replacements, and let them grow larger.

Mulching and Weeding

Once you have the starts well established in the ground, and they are about a foot tall, you should *mulch* around them to keep down the weeds and provide cover against moisture loss. This will make it a pleasant place for the plants as well as beneficial nematodes and earthworms. We've used straw and leaf mulch for this purpose, but the most effective mulch we've found is old newspaper. Save up a pile, and then lay them flat, several sheets thick, all around your little plants, covering up as much of the bare earth as you can. Then lay enough straw or leaf mulch over the papers to keep them from blowing away. Throughout the growing season, keep checking your garden for any weeds that have somehow managed to escape baking and mulching, and pull them out so they won't compete with your crops.

Irrigating

It is essential that you do keep your garden well watered—especially if you live in an area, like I do, where there's not much rain in the Summer. You want to get water to the soil and roots—not the leaves and flowers—especially with tomatoes, as the flowers will not produce fruit if they get wet. For a small garden, you can simply go from plant to plant with a hose every few days and soak the ground at the base of each one. This works especially well if you make a kind of crater around every plant, so it will hold a little pool of water. I've done this for many years, and it works just fine. It's a good way to make sure you get out into the garden regularly, for both watering and weeding. Or you can set up a drip irrigation system, with special drip and soaker hoses. But this is a lot of work, and fairly complicated (and costly for the hoses, timers, etc.), so if you want to go that route, you should probably get help.

> ***Important:*** *Never water your garden in the heat of the day; the beads of water act like tiny magnifying glasses to focus sunlight and burn the leaves!*

Composting

An important part of magickal living is recycling, and composting your organic garbage is where it starts. Keep a compost bucket with a lid in the kitchen, and throw all scraps into it except bones. Some of the best stuff to compost is coffee grounds and crushed eggshells. Store eggshells until dry and them pound them to a powder. Apply the powder to the earth around houseplants, garden plants, and roses. Or bury them whole in the soil around your plants. Eggshells have minerals to keep your garden healthy and strong.

Set aside a place right near your garden and mulch pile for a compost heap. Every few days, dig a hole in the center of the heap and empty the compost bucket into it, covering it all over with mulch and dirt. Turn the heap with your shovel as you do this, and you will create a rich source of nutrients for your garden next year. The more you turn it, the better it works (and the less it smells). You can also cover it with *clear* plastic to keep heat in. Spread the compost at the time you are preparing the soil for planting, and start building up the next heap for the following year. (Never put fresh compost on your garden; the escess nitrogen will burn the plants and kills them!)

Pests and Diseases

Unfortunately, we aren't the only ones who find fresh garden veggies tasty. Whole populations of "pests" descend upon our gardens each year trying to beat us to the harvest. Like thousands of generations of gardeners before you, you will have to battle these invaders. Here are a few tips:

Gophers can take out an entire big plant overnight by eating the roots out from under it. Gopher Spurge doesn't kill them, but if you grow it, when you find a hole you can break off the top of a plant and stick it sticky-stem side down into the hole. The gophers can't stand the smell or taste of the plant fluid. But of all the various ways I've tried to deal with them over the years, the most effective I've found are these battery-powered stakes you can drive into the ground that emit high-frequency whines every few minutes, which rodents cannot stand. The effective range of these is about 50 square feet, so one in the middle of your garden will cover you.

Moles are insectivores, and actually aerate the soil. *Voles,* on the other hand, are truly wicked and like to do such things as nipping off your pea plants about an inch from the ground, when they're tall and healthy and about to bloom. You can protect them with plastic bottles cut into cylinders placed around young plants.

As to bug pests, there are basically two kinds you have to worry about: *chewing insects* and *sucking bugs.* The chewers munch up the leaves, and these include grasshoppers, tomato worms, cabbageworms, and various beetles. Suckers feed like mosquitoes, sticking straw-like nozzles into the leaves and stems and sucking out the juices. These include leafhoppers, squash bugs, red spiders, and aphids. There are four ways to deal with these pesky bugs: barriers, bug-repelling plants, predators, and insecticides.

I mentioned bug-repelling plants earlier under "Companion Planting." Insectivorous predators include birds, predatory insects, and spiders, and I'll talk about them next. A birdbath will encourage the right kind of birds to catch bugs in your garden (don't put up a bird *feeder* near your garden, however, or you'll attract birds that will also want to eat your corn and sunflower seeds!). Barriers are useful against maggots, cutworms, and grubs. These can be as simple as toilet paper rolls for collars around seedlings.

As for insecticides, you can make your own from garlic, onions, peppers, or painted daisies, steeped in hot water like tea and used in a spray bottle. Be sure to spray the underside of the leaves as well as the tops. Ants HATE red pepper. Mix equal parts cayenne pepper and powdered Borax and spread it in a line along doorways, windows, or wherever the ants come into the house. If this still doesn't work, the best commercial treatments are *pyrethrum* and *rotenone.* Always wear rubber gloves to handle pesticides.

Slugs and snails can be eliminated by laying out small containers (like cat food cans) of beer. These slimy terrestrial mollusks love beer, but they really can't handle alcohol!

In addition to visible pests, there are also microscopic disease organisms that attack garden plants, such as fungi, bacteria, and viruses. Symptoms of these show up as discolored, spotted, wilted, curled, or distorted leaves. Once a plant is infected, there's not much you can do other than pull it up and burn it. Your best preventative is to plant disease-resistant plants, and treated seeds. There are several organic fungicides that can be can be sprayed on un-infected plants just as with insecticides. Some of these are *Zerlate, Zincate,* and *Karbam White.* Read the labels carefully, and follow the instructions.

Beneficial Bugs

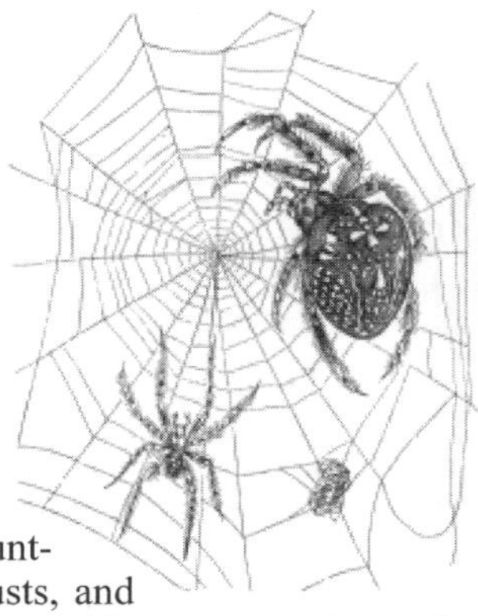

Some of your most effective allies against chewing and sucking bug pests are predatory insects and spiders. My favorites are praying mantises and the big tiger-striped orb-spinning garden spiders (*Argiopes*). Mantises are ferocious hunters of grasshoppers, locusts, and caterpiggles. You can buy mantis egg cases, but *only* if you can get them locally, because a different microclimate will kill them. They will hatch out about 100 hungry babies. Garden spiders just seem to show up in a flourishing garden, and capture many flying insects; you can encourage them by providing tall bamboo poles, spaced 2'-3'apart, for them to spin their webs between. Ladybug beetles come refrigerated in containers from feed and garden stores, and are great for aphids—release them in stages. The *larvae* eat about 10 times as many aphids as the prettier adults. Keep a bowl of water on your garden altar for your insect friends.

Bees and butterflies aren't predators, of course. Their benefit is in pollinating. Plant plenty of flowers and these enchanting little creatures will flock to your garden and bring it to life. Lemon balm will attract bees, and morning glories will draw hummingbirds. Earthworms burrow through the soil, helping to aerate and drain excess water. Their castings are rich with soil nutrients, which feed the plants. I recommend going to a bait store and buying a few cans of worms, and turning them loose in the freshly tilled earth before you plant. They love compost heaps and are especially crazy about coffee grounds.

Lesson 7: Gardening by the Moon

The Moon governs growth, and planting is most productive if the lunar influences are considered—not only the light or dark phases, but also the nature of the sign of the Zodiac the Moon is passing through.

Moon Gardening by Phase

Waxing Moon: ●●●●◐◐◐◐○○○○○○
Sow, transplant, bud, and graft. Fruit picked now will rot easily where bruised. Cutting grass now will stimulate its growth.

Waning Moon: ○○○○◑◑◑◑●●●●●●
Cultivate, weed, and reap. Bruised areas of fruit picked now will dry. Cut grass now to retard growth.

From New to First Quarter: ●●●●●◐◐
Plant aboveground crops with outside seeds, flowering annuals, herbs, leafy crops (lettuce, cabbage), celery, Brussels sprouts, grains, etc.

From First Quarter to Full: ◐◐◐○○○○
Plant aboveground crops with inside seeds (tomatoes, corn, beans, peppers, peas, squash, melons, pumpkins, etc.).

From Full to Last Quarter: ○○○○◑◑◑
Plant root crops, bulbs, biennials, perennials (onions, chives, potatoes, carrots, beets, radishes, etc.).

From Last Quarter to New: ◑◑●●●●●
Do not plant. Till and destroy weeds and pests; cultivate and harvest. Cut firewood now to season.

Lunar Gardening by Zodiac Sign

Consult a Moon sign calendar for phases of the Moon and its daily positions among the signs of the Zodiac. The Moon remains in each sign for about 2-1/3 days. The first day the Moon is in a sign is the best, followed by the 2nd and 3rd. The influence of each sign is greatly enhanced when the Sun and Moon are in the same sign. Water signs are the most fertile and best for planting. Earth signs are good for root crops. Fire and Air signs are mostly barren and good times to destroy weeds and pests. Reap when the Moon is in an Air or Fire Sign to assure best storage.

Fruitful Signs

♉ **Taurus** *(Earth)*: The best time to plant root crops is when the Moon is in Taurus—a moist and productive sign.

♋ **Cancer** *(Water)*: Most favorable time for all leafy crops bearing fruit above ground. Transplant and prune to encourage growth.

♎ **Libra** *(Air)*: Libra is the least beneficial of the Fruitful Signs, but is excellent for planting ornamental flowers and vines.

♏ **Scorpio** *(Water)*: A Scorpio Moon promises good germination and rapid growth. Prune for bud development.

♑ **Capricorn** *(Earth)*: Capricorn Moon promotes growth of rhizomes, bulbs, roots, tubers, and stalks. Prune to strengthen branches.

♓ **Pisces** *(Water)*: Planting under a Pisces Moon is especially effective for root growth.

Barren Signs

♈ **Aries** *(Fire)*: Cultivate, weed, and prune to reduce unwanted growth. Gather herbs and roots to store.

♊ **Gemini** *(Air)*: Harvest herbs and roots.

♌ **Leo** *(Fire)*: Foremost of the barren signs, a Leo Moon is the best time to destroy weeds and pests. Cultivate and till the soil.

♍ **Virgo** *(Earth)*: Plow, cultivate, and control weeds and pests under a Virgo Moon. Lay irrigation lines and tie pole plants.

♐ **Sagittarius** *(Fire)*: Plow and cultivate the soil, or harvest. Destroy weeds and pests. Prune to discourage growth.

♒ **Aquarius** *(Air)*: Perfect time for ground cultivation, reaping crops, gathering roots and herbs. Destroy weeds and pests.

Lesson 8: The Wheel of the Year in Your Garden

Ostara (March 21): The seasonal cycle we magickal folk call The Wheel of the Year begins at Spring Equinox. This is also a perfect time to begin your magickal garden by setting the first plants into the ground. Welcome the Nature spirits to your garden, and charge the seeds you'll soon be planting. Set up your garden altar with Easter decorations, like colored eggs, bunnies, baby animals, and flowers; use a light green altar cloth.

Beltaine (May 1): Decorate your garden altar with pretty Spring flowers, a May basket, wreaths, and colorful ribbons (ideally, cut from the Maypole!); use a dark green altar cloth.

Litha (Summer Solstice: June 21): Nurture your crops, and harvest magickal herbs from your garden. Decorate your garden altar with herbs, tomatoes, and Summer flowers; use a white altar cloth and candles, with a chalice full of water. We got a nice woven basket *Cornucopia* ("horn of plenty") at a junk store, and we keep it on the garden altar full of whatever fruits and veggies are in season.

Lughnasadh (Aug. 1): This is the first harvest. Decorate your garden altar with flowers (especially sunflowers!), blackberries, corn, tomatoes, squash, and other food that's ripe now; use a yellow altar cloth. Make corn dollies out of cornhusks, and place them on your altar.

Mabon (Fall Equinox: Sept. 21): Mabon is the second harvest, and a feast of thanksgiving. Decorate your garden altar with colorful Autumn leaves and small gourds, nuts, dried corn, seeds, acorns, and pine cones; use an orange and brown altar cloth. Tie up the empty corn stalks, and make some into a scarecrow. Any Thanksgiving items—like little turkeys—would go well on your altar.

Samhain (Nov. 1): Samhain (otherwise known as Halloween) is the third and last harvest festival, and is all about celebrating Death. Cover your garden altar with a black altar cloth, black feathers, etc. No leaves or flowers at this time, but fill a cornucopia or bowl with nuts, Indian corn, pomegranates, and colorful little gourds and squashes. Carve a Jack-O'Lantern out of one of the pumpkins you've grown. If you've collected any small animal skulls or bones, you might display them on your Samhain altar.

Lesson 9: Harvesting Your Herbs and Veggies

Basil: Pick the flowers of basil before they go to seed, and mash them into a paste made with pine nuts, garlic, olive oil, and salt...and presto! You've got *pesto.* Basil is used in Italian recipes such as spaghetti sauce. It can be added to egg and cheese dishes and to fresh salads. The scent of fresh basil promotes sympathy between people, making it perfect as an incense in forgiveness rituals. It is also used to promote faithfulness and fertility. Carry it in your mojo bag against hexes and bad luck.

Catnip: Pinch off leaves of catnip as needed. It can be used in a fertility charm and a tea made from its dried leaves eases the nerves. Catnip is said to make the most timid person fierce and powerful. It's sacred to Bast, the cat goddess—and your cats will love it!

Chives: Cut or pinch off the long green leaves of chives throughout the year. Chop bunches of them into little pieces with scissors for a tasty seasoning in potatoes, salads, veggie soups, stir-fry, etc.

Corn: Harvest corn when the silk turns brown and kernels are plump and "milky." Corn should be plucked right before eating, as the sugars turn to starch and corn rapidly loses flavor after picking. Set a pot of water on the stove to boil, then go out and pick enough ears for dinner. Shuck them on the spot, tossing the husks onto the mulch pile. Plop the ears into the boiling water. As soon as it gets back to a boil, turn off the heat and let it sit for 5 minutes before taking out the ears. Lay them on a towel to dry, then butter and salt. Yummy! Dried corn hung by the door or hearth insures the fertility of the household through the Winter.

Pumpkins: Harvest pumpkins in October, when the vines are nearly dead, but before the first frost. Leave the stems attached. Let them cure in the sun for about a week, then store in a cool place. When you hollow them out for a Jack-O-Lantern, save the seeds and bake them with a coating of tamari for a tasty treat!

Tomatoes: Let the fruits ripen fully (bright red all over) on the vine and eat right away after picking. Or slice and fry green tomatoes for a popular Southern treat. Never put whole tomatoes in the refrigerator! In late Fall, harvest all fruits regardless of their color, before the frost comes. Keep them indoors, out of the sunlight, at about 65° F and they will soon ripen. Wrap green tomatoes in newspaper; it really works!

Pole beans: Pick just before you plan to eat them, when the pods are full and ripe, showing small knobs. Don't pick in early morning when vines are wet with dew. Keep picking all the pods as they ripen, and the blooms will continue.

Sunflowers: Harvest when the seeds begin to come out easily. They can be eaten raw or baked. Or just leave them out for the birds.

Watermelon: You can tell a watermelon is ripe by bonking it with your knuckle. Ripe melons have a "plunky" sound. It takes a little practice, but once you get it, you can't miss. Pick it when the thump gets dull and heavy, and eat it within a day or so. Chill it in your refrigerator (or cold water) for an hour before eating for a real Summer treat!

Winter Squash: Harvest before the first hard freeze in the Fall, and burn the remaining plant. Leave a bit of the stem on the fruit. Allow the picked fruits to remain in the sun for a few days. Keep them in a dry place at about 70°F for two weeks, then store at about 45°F. To cook, slice them in half, hollow out the seeds, put a chunk of butter in the hollow, and bake until tender.

Zucchini: Harvest throughout the Summer, before the fruits get too humungous! Leave a bit of the stem on the fruit. Harvest anything left on the vine before first hard freeze in the Fall, and burn the remaining plant at end of season. Allow the picked fruits to remain in the sunlight for a few days, then store in a cool place where they won't freeze. One of the tastiest ways to cook zucchini is to cut them into coin or finger-shaped pieces, dredge them in egg and flour, and fry them in olive oil.

Course Three: Practice

Course Three: Practice

Class I: Ethics of Magick

"Listen to me now. Have you never thought how danger must surround power as shadow does light? This sorcery is not a game we play for pleasure or for praise. Think of this: that every word, every act of our Art is said and is done either for good, or for evil. Before you speak or do you must know the price that is to pay!"
—Ursula K. LeGuin (*A Wizard of Earthsea*, p. 23)

1. Introduction: Ethics & Morals

THICS ARE THE PRINCIPLES WE HOLD deep within ourselves that govern our choices in life, our actions, and our behavior towards others. Our ethics grow out of our most deeply held beliefs, our understanding of who and what we truly are, and our vision of our life's mission and Destiny. Ethics are very different from *morals,* which are rules that others impose upon us based on what *they* want us to do, and often not in our own best interest. And neither ethics nor morals are the same as *laws*, which are rules created by lawmakers, for the purpose of keeping everyone in line in a smoothly functioning and governable society.

Whether our behavior is based on ethics, morals, or laws does not in itself determine whether we are helpful or hurtful to others. Some people's ethics require that they treat others with integrity, honesty, and compassion; others hold ethical standards that justify persecuting and abusing others they deem "inferior" or "unworthy." Likewise, morals and laws may enhance people's lives in positive and liberating ways, or enslave them to a corrupt dictatorship.

No matter how we formulate our philosophy, the true test of our strength and principles lies in our *behavior*—our ability to embody the principles we hold dear, and apply them in our daily lives to the building of relationships and community, the integrity of our actions, and the strength of character that inspires others to grow and positively transform the world around them. To that end, there are a number of basic ethical principles that true Wizards hold to. As my Apprentice, I expect you to embrace these principles as well.

Lesson 2. "With Great Power Comes Great Responsibility"

—Stan Lee (*Spiderman,* 1962)

This is the Prime Directive of all those who wield power—whether superheroes, magicians, or Wizards. The power to control your life, and in turn affect the lives of others, is one of the greatest powers that exists. With this power comes the responsibility to use it properly. Whenever you are working Magick to affect your own life, you need to be as certain as possible that what you wish to accomplish is in your best interest. When your work will affect the lives of others, it is advisable to have the others' permission first. To understand what may be in someone else's best interest is much more difficult than knowing what is best for yourself. Many come to Magick in hopes of wielding power over others. Eventually, they fail or learn the truth: True power is power over yourself.

Personal power gives us great freedom in how we choose to live our lives. The necessary counterpart to this freedom is the willingness to be personally responsible for *all* of our actions, and for our effects upon the planet. Only through the practice of personal responsibility can we become responsible collectively and live a life of freedom and maturity. We must all take equal responsibility for making things happen, preventing harm, or cleaning up mistakes.

For the greatest principle of Power (indeed, the essence of Natural Law) is: **"Actions have consequences."** Whatever we choose to do—or choose not to do—will send its reverberations throughout the great Web of Life. The great 19th Century genius Robert G. Ingersoll once remarked: "In Nature there are no rewards or punishments; there are consequences." Therefore, I say: "How you treat me is up to you; how I treat you is up to me."

Power

Power is the ability to manifest one's Will in the physical plane. Power is thus equated with Magick. Those who are acclaimed as "great" in our histories and myths achieve such legendary status through the impact they have on our world, our society, and our lives. For a time, they hold Power. But they key question of Power is always: How will one use it—and to what ends? There is power to ***do***—to accomplish, to create, to build, to manifest, and thus to change the world. There is power to ***control***—to rule others, and force them to one's bidding against their own will and their own interests. There is power to ***prevent***—to keep things from happening that ones does not wish to happen, against the will of others who do.

Those who wield Power in the social and political arenas do so through the voluntary support and allegiance of their *constituencies,* who comprise their friends, gangs, minions, armies, and political parties. Such support may be gained through love (as is often the case with religious cult leaders), or through fear (as with bullies and dictators). And the choice that stands before anyone who holds such Power is the same: to rule or to serve.

It is a test that is offered to all our leaders, at every level. How would *you* choose?

Authority

> *"I'm the head wizard now. I've only got to give an order and a thousand wizards will... uh...disobey, come to think of it, or say 'What?', or start to argue. But they have to take notice."*
> —Terry Pratchett (*Lords & Ladies,* p. 162)

The word *authority* has two very different and often opposing meanings, confusion of which causes endless trouble. The first listed in *Webster,* and the one that most people seem automatically to presume, is based on *power over:* "1. The power or right to give commands, enforce obedience... 6. Persons, esp. in government, having the power or right to enforce orders, laws, etc." Power-based authority is called *authoritarian:* "Characterized by unquestioning obedience to authority, as that of a dictator, rather than individual freedom of judgement and action." Power-based authority is rooted in fear, as it is enforced by threat of punishment.

The second and oft-neglected definition is based on *expertise:* "8. Self-assurance and expertness that comes with experience. 7. A person with much knowledge or experience in some field, whose information or opinion is hence reliable; expert." Expertise-based authority is called *authoritative:* "2. Based on competent authority; reliable because coming from one who is an expert or properly qualified." This kind of authority is rooted in respect for attained wisdom.

Unfortunately, our language fails to distinguish these two concepts when we refer only to "authority," as in the popular slogan, "Question Authority." It is the automatic presumption that the term refers to the authoritarian definition that makes one of my favorite buttons so amusingly ironic: *"Question Authority. Ask me anything!"* This Grimoire of apprenticeship is designed to maximize your "knowledge, experience...information...competence" and expertise. Those who become adept in Wizardry gain no "authority" to order people around, but, hopefully, they do gain the authority of expertise wherein their opinions are considered worthy of respect.

Lesson 3: The Law of Thelema and the Wiccan Rede

The Law of Thelema

François Rabelais (1494–1553) was a French physician, author, and satirist who wrote almanacs, poetry, and social commentaries. A student at the University of Montpellier in 1530, he was also a classmate of Michael Nostradamus. In his 1532 novel, *Gargantua,* Rabelais used the phrase "do as you wish" when describing the motto of an ideal and utopian "Abbey of Theleme."

Pierre Louÿs (1870–1925) was perhaps the first to pair the ideas of "do no harm" with "do what thou will." In 1901 novel titled *Les Aventures du Roi Pausole* ("The Adventures of King Pausole"), Louÿs told a humorous and risqué story about a king with 1,000 wives who believed in sexual freedom for everyone. As part of the story, King Pausole reduced an ancestral "Book of Customs" to a more understandable phrase by issuing a two-part proclamation: "I. Do no wrong to thy neighbor. II. Observing this, do as thou pleasest."

In April 1904, the notorious magician Aleister Crowley (1875–1947) received a message from a discarnate astral entity named Aiwass. Channeled through Crowley's wife, Rose, this entity dictated an exquisite magickal treatise called *The Book of the Law.* It contains a rephrasing of Rabelais's Law of Thelema: "Do what thou wilt shall be the whole of the Law." Though some have interpreted this to mean doing just as one pleases, Crowley claimed it actually means that one must do as one *must,* and nothing else. He believed that if people fully understood their true Wills and followed them, they would attune themselves into harmony with the Universe; and therefore could do no wrong.

The Wiccan Rede

"The Rede of the Wiccae (Being knowne as the Counsel of the Wise Ones)" is a collection of 26 rhyming couplets of advice that were passed on to her heirs by Wiccan Priestess Adriana Porter, who was well into her 90s when she died in 1946. Gerald Gardner (1884–1964), the founder of most modern Wicca, claimed that this Rede was derived from Louÿs's fictional "Good King Pausol." Many people in the magickal community feel it is the only rule they need. The final verse of the Rede states simply:

> *Eight words the Wiccan Rede fulfill;*
> *An* it harm none, do what ye will.*
> —Lady Gwen ("Wiccan-Pagan Potpourri," *Green Egg,* VII, 69; Mar. 21, 1975; p. 10)
> **An* is archaic Middle English for "if."

The basic principle of "Harm no one" does seem to be a good prerequisite for behavior that is both ethical and moral. It is, in fact, the first rule of the Hippocratic Oath sworn by all doctors since it was originally written by the father of medicine, Hippocrates of Greece (460–377 BCE): "Never do harm to anyone." In his *Republic,* Book I, 335e, Plato wrote: "For it has become apparent to us that it is never just to harm anyone." And certainly we can all adopt the splendid motto of motto of Saint Peter Fourier: "To be of help to all and to harm no one."

Lesson 4: What Goes Around, Comes Around

Karma

Karma is the Hindu term for the cosmic principle of cause and effect, which holds that for every action in life, there is a reaction: Good is returned by good, and evil is returned by evil. I'm sure you have learned that if you treat others the way you wish to be treated, your life moves more smoothly.

> *The moral arc of the universe is long, but it bends toward Justice.* —Martin Luther King, Jr.

Threefold Return

However, with Magick this rule may be amplified. Some Witches maintain that there is a natural principle they call the Law of Threefold Return. By this, they mean that whatever energy we put out into the world, for good or for ill, shall return to us multiplied three times. This is a very powerful element of magnification, as long as you remember that Love is the highest law.

> *There's no Justice. There's just us....* —Death, from Terry Pratchett's *Discworld* books

Love is the Highest Law

Love for our fellow man, the Earth, and Her creatures is one of the elements that defines our humanity. "Love is the highest law" means to allow Love to be your guide in all of your actions. When your Magick is ruled by Love you will know that your intentions are in your best interest and the best interest of others.

The Greater the Circle, the More the Love Grows

If you share your cookies with your friends, you will eat fewer cookies. With Love, sharing causes the opposite to occur. As you share your love with others, the love that is given to you will increase. The more you love, the more you are loved. This is a great and wonderful truth.

Pay It Forward

The best way to make sure that good energy goes around in the world is to put it out there yourself. A wonderful way to do this, and to change the world by simple acts of kindness, was conceived by author Catherine Ryan Hyde in a wonderful book and movie called *Pay It Forward.* It's an action plan within a work of fiction. Since the book was released in January of 2000, a real-life social movement has emerged, not just in the U.S. but worldwide. What began as fiction has become much more.

Reuben St. Clair, the teacher and protagonist of the book *Pay It Forward,* starts a movement with this voluntary, extra-credit assignment: *Think of an idea for world change, and put it into action.* Trevor, the 12-year-old hero of *Pay It Forward,* thinks of quite an idea. He describes it to his mother and teacher this way: "You see, I do something real good for three people. And then when they ask how they can pay it back, I say they have to Pay It Forward. To three more people. Each. So nine people get helped. Then those people have to do 27." He turned on the calculator, punched in a few numbers. "Then it sort of spreads out, see. To 81. Then 243. Then 729. Then 2,187. See how big it gets?"

You can do this, too. If you'd like to learn more, check out the Pay It Forward Foundation at: *www.payitforwardfoundation.org/.*

> *In every revolution, there's one man with a vision.* —James T. Kirk, *Star Trek* ("Mirror, Mirror" by Jerome Bixby)

Lesson 5: Be Excellent to Each Other

> *We will get respect if we walk our talk, act with integrity, stand by our values, treat people with excellence, and truly care about each other and about the Earth.* —Kyril Oakwind

A Wizard sees the Divinity in all living things. Therefore we respect the free will of others. We prefer to lead, not by guilt or coercion, but by inspiration and example; not only to be excellent to each other, but to strive for excellence in all our endeavors, no matter how seemingly insignificant. Tribal values we hold include Loyalty, Generosity, Fairness, and Hospitality.

You are a spark of the great soul-fire of Nature, and you are filled with the essence of Divinity. To truly honor the Divinity within each other is to treat each other with respect, kindness, courtesy, and conscious consideration. This involves honest and responsible communication, including the avoidance of gossip and rumor-mongering, and the willingness to reach for understanding rather than judgment. Learn how to communicate with others in a positive, life-affirming way.

Be Excellent to Yourself!

Divinity resides within as well as outside us, so how you treat yourself is how you treat that Divinity. Self-abuse, whether through irresponsible use of substances, overwork, self-denial, self-deception, or simply undermining your self-esteem, are all insults to the Divinity within. Treat yourself kindly, with compassion rather than judgment, and it will be easier to treat others that way. Take care of your body, home, and possessions, as a piece of Gaia that has been entrusted to you. Be a conscious guardian to the Temple of the Divine Spirit within.

Honor Diversity!

In Nature, a diverse ecosystem has more stability. There are many styles of living and ways of living, each of which has something to offer to the overall puzzle of life. Be open-minded and receptive to new ideas because this usually manifests in growth of the spirit and the mind. Learn about differences rather than judge them. Sexism, racism, or rude remarks directed towards other's sexual preferences, body type, or personal habits (insofar as they do not harm others) have no place in the magickal community. All life is sacred.

Walk Your Talk! (And talk your walk!)

Talk is cheap. It is fine and well to proclaim a stand for Truth and Justice and to preach heady principles. But it is only through practice that words become Truth, and change becomes manifest. But do not be afraid to fail, for in order to grow, our reach must exceed our grasp, and it is through failing that we learn.

The Power of Compassion

Compassion, the ability to feel what others feel and to care about it, is an important part of a Wizard's power. This is not just because compassion is "nice" (a good enough reason to be compassionate), but because our power stems from being connected with other beings. Magick is the result of our consciousness at work, and for that action to affect anything other than yourself, you must form a connection and understanding with the target of your working. The more attuned you are to the feelings and desires in the Universe around you, the more powerful these connections will be, and the more powerful your magick. Remember, without sympathy, there can be no sympathetic magic (Ian Lurking Bear Anderson).

> *Never doubt that a small group of thoughtful, committed citizens can change the world. Indeed, it's the only thing that ever has.* —Margaret Mead (quote from origination of Earth Day in 1970)

Lesson 6: The Golden Rule

The most fundamental ethical precept is **"Do as you would be done by."** This principle is so universal that it is called The Golden Rule. All of the previous are just elaborations and commentary: This is the essence. As Confucius said, this is the only rule you need. Here are a few other ways this idea has been expressed in different religions through the ages:

> *"Do unto another what you would have him do unto you, and do not do unto another what you would not have him do unto you. Thou needest this law alone. It is the foundation of all the rest."*
> —*The Analects of Confucius* (Confucianism)
>
> *"Do nothing unto others which would cause you pain done unto you."*
> —*Upanishads* (Hindu 3,000 years ago)
>
> *"Hurt not others in ways that you yourself would find hurtful."* —*Udana-Varga* 5:18 (Buddhist)
>
> *"We should conduct ourselves toward others as we would have them act toward us."*
> —Aristotle (Ancient Greek)
>
> *"Do not do to others what you would not like others to do to you."* —Rabbi Hillel (Judaism)
>
> *"Whatever you wish that men would do to you, do so to them, for this is the law and the prophets."* —*The Bible,* Matthew 7:12 (Christian)

When it comes right down to it, this means: No ripping off; no screwing over; and be polite. After all, absolutely no one, not even the most psychopathic criminal, wants to be ripped off or screwed over!

Lesson 7: The Code of Chivalry

The Code of Chivalry was the Rule of the Knights of the Middle Ages, who were formally sworn to uphold it as the first true Champions of Justice. It was said to have been first established by King Arthur for the Knights of the Round Table. If that's so, then the Wizard Merlin would certainly have helped to design this code of conduct! Here are its ten most important commandments:

1. Be True to your Faith.
2. Stand up for your Beliefs.
3. Defend the Weak.

4. Love your Country.
5. Show Courage against Opposition.
6. Oppose Evil.
7. Do your Duty.
8. Speak Truth, and keep your Word.
9. Be Generous to all.
10. Be the Champion of the Right and the Good against Injustice and Evil.

Lesson 8: Tribal Values

Outside the boundaries of civilization and Empire, the people of the country have always lived in clans, tribes, and villages—as many traditional peoples still do today. Other tribal peoples, such as the gypsies and diasporic Jews, have been displaced from their homelands by conquerors and scattered among other nations where they have lived as "guest peoples." What has held all such tribes together have been shared *values* that cannot be stolen away or overthrown. These values are passed down in myths, legends, and fairy tales. They are not based on *beliefs,* as religions are, but upon *customs and traditions*, which promote social cohesion. There are several such values that appear to be universal among tribal peoples, which are well worth remembering and holding to. Some of these are:

Honor—keeping our word
Loyalty—faithfulness in defense and support of our own
Integrity—"walking our talk"
Honesty—not lying, cheating, or stealing
Respect—courtesy, consideration of others
Fairness—being just and impartial to all
Gratitude—thankful appreciation
Hospitality—courtesy to guests and hosts
Generosity—willingness to give and share
Reverence—honoring that which is sacred
Reciprocity—giving and receiving value for value
Responsibility—accepting the consequences of actions
Resourcefulness—ability to deal effectively with challenges
Interdependence—cooperation; we're all in this together!

Just as the Code of Chivalry was a set of rules for independent heroes and champions, mostly regarding how to treat strangers, tribal values are the expectations for people living together and dealing with each other on a daily basis. You may notice, however, that they are complimentary, and there is a good deal of overlap. These values are what your parents are supposed to teach you, and what you, in turn, will teach your children. And by living them, we live well.

Lesson 9: Good vs. Evil

All stories of heroes and Wizards involve the eternal conflict between "Good" and "Evil." This is, essentially, the choice of whether to help others, or to harm them; to serve others, or to attempt to rule them.

The Stupidity of Evil

Evil is ultimately stupid, and therefore ultimately doomed to fail. The reason for this is basic and obvious: No one really likes a bully. The only support that such people can command from others is rooted in fear—and that from minions, henchmen, thugs, and goons who are even more stupid than they are. There is no true loyalty in fear, and those who follow bullies can only be treacherous cowards who will betray and desert their master whenever they deem it to their advantage. Those who wish to harm or control others and rule the world (or the galaxy!) are blinded by their inability to imagine that everyone else doesn't hold the same desire, and that others are not also arrayed against them. In their own insatiable drive for revenge and dominion, they can only imagine that others they have wronged are similarly plotting retaliation; after all, that's what *they* would do. And the more people they wrong, the vaster become the imagined armies of their enemies. And so they are defeated by their own paranoia, as they see enemies everywhere, even among their own troops. Eventually they begin to turn against those closest to them, and inevitably their own fears destroy them.

"It is as hard for the good to suspect evil, as it is for the bad to suspect good." —Marcus Cicero, Roman statesman, orator, writer (106–43 BCE)

The Wisdom of Good

Good, however, has enormous power. Revolutions have overthrown tyranny and oppression throughout history. Heroes are those who win the loyalty of others by the sheer force of their own integrity and decency. They command loyalty because they give it to others. A person who stands strongly for Truth and Justice, and treats others with honor and compassion, will always find loyal companions to stand beside him (or her). And the wisest, bravest, and best will come forward to join them, until a tiny trickle of decency becomes a vast tidal wave washing over the land. Such people as Mohandas Gandhi, Martin Luther King, and Nelson Mandela won the devoted loyalty of millions who were willing to stand and march together to liberate their people and change the world.

Whatever you can do, or dream you can, begin it.
Boldness has genius, power, and magic in it.
—Goethe

Class II: Tools of Magick

"But they say that if you take his wooden staff from a sorcerer, he has no power left. Probably there are evil runes written on the staff." Thar shook her head again. "They carry a staff, indeed, but it is only a tool for the power they bear within them."
—Ursula K. LeGuin (*The Tombs of Atuan*, p. 50)

1. Introduction: Magickal Tools

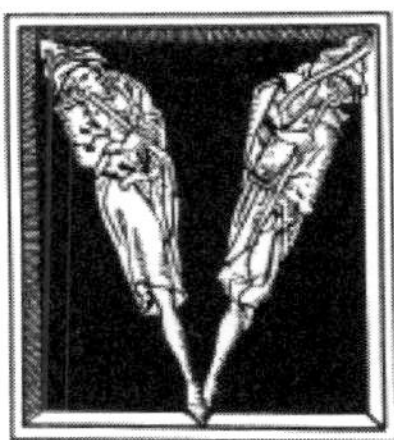

ARIOUS MAGICKAL TOOLS HAVE BEEN associated with Wizardry since time immemorial. We can scarcely imagine a Wizard without his magick wand, staff, or crystal ball! In some hands, these may be just psychological props; but properly made and consecrated, such tools can be reservoirs of magical energy that can be tapped into and used by the Wizard, much like batteries. Of course, the true power of the spell comes from the Wizard's mental concentration and emotional will to make it succeed. Raven Grimassi adds that magickal tools are also "independent bridges to the inner mechanism of Nature. While the Wizard's psychological element is clearly an important component, there is a pre-existing consciousness at work outside of the Wizard that likewise empowers the tool. Magic is a partnership with that inner mechanism and with the source that lies behind it. The legends surrounding such tools as the Holy Grail and the sword Excaliber speak to something greater in the tool than it be being simply a 'psychological prop' of its former owner. The psychological aspect is the meeting place where the source and the Wizard connect and make magic possible."

In the old days, it was traditional to make all of your own tools, except for those special ones that were handed down from Masters to Apprentices or given as Initiation gifts. Many tools can be purchased these days from excellent magickal craftspeople, but there is a very special satisfaction in making your own. Also, learning the skills necessary to make your own tools is an important part of your magickal training! When you master such skills in this way, you may even find that they support you as a craftsperson later on. In this Class, I will only be teaching you how to make and prepare these tools and implements. Their actual use will be described in other Classes…

When buying any magickal tools, it is traditional never to haggle about the price, but pay willingly whatever is asked. I recommend checking out garage sales, swap meets, flea markets, yard sales, and second-hand stores—I've always found the best magickal stuff that way, and at great prices, too!

> Nybor says: *"Over the years I have acquired four sets of tools; each is for specific reasons. I label them thusly, with examples:*
> ***FIRE****— Tools I have made myself: the chest I made for my magickal implements and my Tarot deck;*
> ***AIR****— Tools I have purchased: a handmade Book of Shadows and most of my candles and incense;*
> ***WATER****—Tools I have been gifted with by others (also includes initiation gifts): a beaded owl's wing fan and a statue of my titular deity;*
> ***EARTH****—Tools I have found (gifts of the Goddess as I call them): a red and white altar cloth and a wand.*
> *I would suggest that apprentice Wizards look at the tools they have in this light."*

The primary set of magickal tools are derived from the Elemental symbols seen in the tarot cards of **Wands, Cups, Discs,** and **Swords**—representing respectively the Elements of Air, Water, Earth, and Fire. Give serious attention to collecting or making your magickal tools, for in time these simple tools will become the representation of your own dynamic Will and potential Power. Remember to always treat your tools as the sacred objects that they are!

> ***NOTE:*** *In describing positions for objects to be placed on your altar, I use the directions East, South, West, and North. This seems to presume that your altar is placed at the North side of your temple area, in which case East would be to your right, and West to your left. But no matter where your altar is actually placed, you should still position things with the same right-left orientation, as if they were sitting on a map with the bottom (South) facing you. The orientation is to this map, not necessarily to the compass. For truly, your altar is actually a miniature stage representing the world in symbolic form. What you put on your altar represents what you include in your world.*

Lesson 2: The Magick Wand (Air)

The first and most important magickal tool you should make is the *wand,* which is especially associated with the powers of divination and prophecy. Different versions of the wand include the stage magician's wand, the batons of the symphony conductor and the drum major, the swagger sticks of the army general and the movie director, and the divining rod used for dowsing or water-witching. The wand is a *phallic* (penis) symbol, and has always been associated with divine wisdom. As an Elemental tool, it represents the Element of either Air or Fire. (Although I associate the wand with Air and the athamé with Fire, in Ceremonial Magick the wand is considered a tool of Fire, and the dagger is an Air tool.)

To a magician, his wand is an extension of himself—a measure of his ability, wisdom, and imagination. Personalized as to size, shape, and design, he values this tool above all others. In ritual, the wand serves to unite our body, mind, and soul with that of universal consciousness to bring into manifestation our magickal desires. The wand has remained such a classic symbol of the Wizard and his powers that fraternal societies of stage magicians often perform special wand-breaking ceremonies at the funerals of their members.

In some traditions, wands may be made of metal as well as wood. The snake priestesses of Minoan Crete used metal snake wands. Some Kurgan grave goods also contain items identified as metal wands. Most commonly these were made of bronze, but silver and gold were also used. The Druidic Priesthood included seven levels, and each priest carried a ceremonial wand of a metal specially designated to that level. Metal wands may be seen as a balance of all Elements, as all are necessary to their creation.

A number of excellent magickal craftspeople like Abby Willowroot and Don Waterhawk make beautiful wands of metal, with crystals and fancy filigree. Abby feels that their primary energy is Air and Fire. Because the actual function of a wand is to be a conductor of magickal energy, any conductive metal (such as silver or copper) will certainly serve. Wooden wands, however, are the most traditional in Wizardry, and this is what I'll be teaching you here. Later, you may acquire others as well, which you may use for various purposes....

The wand you will be making in this lesson is called a *baculum* (Latin for "stick;" also the term for penis bones in some mammals—bears, raccoons, whales...). It is used for finding things out, for directing your energies, and for sending your thought images out to work their magick in the world. Like many other magickal tools, your wand should be specially made by and for you alone, according to your own measurements. As this is your most basic tool of Magick, I'll be going into far more detail on its making than for any other tools.

Task: Cutting Your Wand

First, find a living fruit tree, such as a hazel or almond (willow will do if you can't find a fruit or nut tree), with a straight section of branch, free of twigs, at least as long as your arm from your elbow to the tip of your longest finger. The thickness is not as important as the length, as long as it feels right in your hand. If you live in the southeastern part of the U.S., you may be able to find branches that have been twisted into spiral shapes by vines growing around them. If you can't find a vine-twisted fruit or willow branch, you may be able to find one of dogwood. These make terrific wands!

Once you have found a tree from which you wish to cut your wand, wait until sunset on a Wednesday (the day of Mercury) when the Moon is waxing. Before you make any cuts, pour water on the roots of the tree and explain to it what you wish to do. Ask permission from the dryad of that tree, saying something like:

> *"Gracious Willow, I offer you water and I ask a boon. I request a branch from you that I may make a wand with which to practice magick in the service of all Life. I pledge to honor your sacrifice and use it wisely. Blessed be."*

Sit quietly for a few moments and listen carefully with your heart for the tree's answer. If the answer is no, bow to the tree and go elsewhere. If the answer is yes, bow to the tree, mark where you want to make the cuts, and use a sharp hacksaw to make smooth cuts at each end. Cut it a bit longer than you think you will need, then trim it up later. Be sure to put some mud on the tree's wound to help it heal, and thank the tree before you leave.

Trimming and Shaping Your Wand

You should trim your wand on the same evening as you cut it. Using a sharp paring or pocketknife (or *athamé* if you have one), carefully peel all the bark from the branch. Avoid as much as possible cutting or nicking the inner wood—or yourself! While you are doing this, you should chant to keep your magickal intention focused on your task: *"Blessed by thou rod of power; Blessed be thou rod of wisdom...."* When this is done, place the larger end of the branch on your arm inside your elbow (left or right; the hand you use to write with). Bend your elbow, hold your forearm straight up, and mark the branch right at the tip of your longest finger. Cut if off there. You now have the basic baculum.

Wrap it in linen or silk, and set it aside to dry for a month, until the next Wednesday of the waxing Moon. The wood will be good and dry, so unwrap your wand and sand it smooth with fine sandpaper, chanting as you work. Then get some linseed oil from your local hardware store and rub several coats of oil in with your hands until dry, chanting all the while: *"Blessed by thou rod of power; Blessed be thou wand of wisdom..."* This will deepen the color, accentuate the natural grain, seal the wood, and give a fine luster. Finally, polish it with beeswax for a silky finish.

There are two ways to finish off the small end of your baculum; either as a *thyrsus* (pronounced THIR-sus), or with a crystal. The *thyrsus* was the pinecone-tipped staff carried by Dionysos, Greek god of wine and revelry. If you wish to finish your wand as a thyrsus, carve the end into a knob with a sharp knife so it resembles a pinecone. Or you can attach an actual small unopened pinecone on the end, in the same way as I'll next describe for attaching a crystal.

If you prefer, find a crystal the same diameter as your wand. To create a powerful conductor of energy, magnetize a length of piano wire by stroking a magnet along it in one direction over and over until it will pick up paper clips. Cut a thin notch with a hacksaw into each end of the wand, and then anchor the magnetized wire into the notch at the tip end. Next, make a small wad of beige-colored epoxy putty (or melted pine resin if you want to be really traditional!) and press it onto the small end of your wand. Carefully set the crystal into place and smooth the putty so it blends seamlessly into both the wood and the crystal.

Use the wire to wrap the joined place to cover the putty, then continue in a wide open spiral all the way down the Wand to the base, where you may add another tight wrap before anchoring it into the other notch. Cap the base end with a *cabochon,* a smoothly rounded gemstone with a flat back. Or you could cap the end with a small round magnet, as medieval alchemists used to do (allowing for special "magical" effects). Be sure to remember to measure carefully, and cut off a bit of the base if necessary after the tip crystal is in place, so that your finished wand is still exactly the length of your forearm and hand.

After you have finished, wrap your Wand in linen or silk, declaring: *"So mote it be!"*

Engraving and Consecrating

On the next Wednesday of the waxing Moon, unwrap your wand and, chanting all the while, mark the following runes—first in pencil, then in ink, working from right to left, from tip to base:

These commonly used runes (and all those following) come from the *Greater Key of Solomon.* Bill Hedrick, head of the Ordo Templi Orientis magickal lodge, says that they are a degenerate crypto-Hebraic script, and they translate as "cut a green young branch." This is just the first step of instructions, rather than anything particularly mystical. But they have become traditional through centuries of use. As with any of these tools, you don't have to use these traditional runes. Instead you might just inscribe your own magickal name in Theban runes. Many Wizards give special names to their wands, staffs, knives, and swords. If you decide to do so, you might also inscribe that name into it.

If you have the skill, you may then carve out the runes with a small sharp knife (X-Acto makes some great V-shaped carving blades for just this kind of work—but be careful not to cut yourself!), engrave them with a Dremel (best), or burn them in with a wood-burning tool. You may even fill in the carved runes with paint of whatever color you choose.

To consecrate your wand for magickal use, burn some Mercurial incense, such as cinnamon. Pass your wand through the smoke, saying:

I consecrate thee, Rod of Skill
To focalize my Truest Will.
May my power flow through thee,
As I do Will, so mote it be!

When you are finished, wrap it again in linen or silk.

Using Your Wand

Your wand is made for channeling and focusing your personal energy. To use it, hold the base end in the palm of your hand, and point with the thyrsus or crystal end. Visualize your auric energy being gathered and focused through the glowing wand to beam forth as a laser, directing your magickal Will to whatever purpose you desire. You may use it in rituals to draw the Circle or salute the four Quarters. In divination, use your wand to point to the cards, or runes, or whatever you are using, to help focus your concentration and receive the correct message. When you work spells, use your wand to point towards whatever you want your energy to reach, such as healing an injured friend, or protecting an endangered forest. Treat your wand as a part of your own body—a very special and magickal part, but still yours, and no one else's. And always keep it wrapped whenever you are not using it! Lay it on the front of your altar, or at the East (right) side—the direction of Air.

Lesson 3: The Chalice (Water)

The magickal cup, or chalice, represents the ancient Cauldron of Goddess Cerridwen, which granted poetic inspiration, rebirth, and immortality. The Holy Grail of the legends of King Arthur is another version of the chalice. Containing the Mysteries of Life and Death, the cauldron, bowl, or cup symbolizes the womb of the Goddess, from which all life comes forth. The chalice, therefore, is seen as female in nature (as the wand is male), and the water that it contains is the sacred Elemental Water of Life. As the wand is the tool of the mind or intellect, the chalice is the tool of the emotions—especially Love.

To make your own magickal chalice, you must first buy a drinking goblet (a cup on a stem with a base). It may be any size and as fancy as you like. The chalice may be of ceramic, silver (or silver-plated), horn, or pewter (not glass)—though horn or silver is much preferred. A chalice should never be made of brass or copper, as it can then only be used for water—never wine or fruit juice—because these metals become poisonous in contact with the citric acids in juices or wine.

Consecrating Your Chalice

To consecrate your chalice, wait until the Moon is almost full. It is also best to do this on a Monday—the day of the Moon. Mix up some of the following herbs in a bowl of salt water: basil, fennel, hyssop, lavender, mint, rosemary, sage, valerian, and verbena. (These can come from the herb section of your local natural foods store.) For a lunar incense, sprinkle some lavender, jasmine, white rose, honeysuckle, and/or mugwort on a burning charcoal block. If you'd rather consecrate your chalice to Venus (for Love), do it on Friday and use an incense made of sandalwood, orris root, rose, and/or rosemary. You may use natural herbs, or buy a compounded lunar or Venus incense at an occult shop. Sprinkle your cup with the herb tea, then pass it through the smoking incense, visualizing a blue purifying light surrounding it, and chanting:

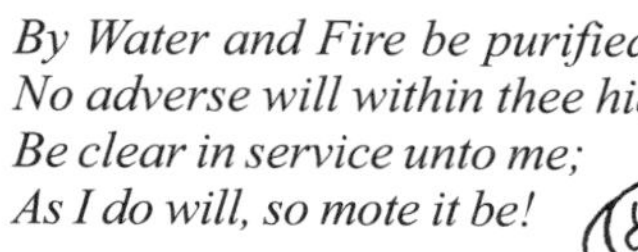

By Water and Fire be purified
No adverse will within thee hide.
Be clear in service unto me;
As I do will, so mote it be!

The Chalice Runes

Paint or engrave (with an engraving tool or Dremel) the appropriate runes around the bowl of the chalice. If painting, use a new fine brush and black or white enamel paint. As you inscribe each rune, chant: *"Blessed be thou cup of Water."* The traditional runes from the *Greater Key of Solomon* (which nobody seems to be able to translate anymore) are as follows:

If you are not comfortable with these, you might just use the Theban runes to write "Blessed be thou Cup of Art" around the bowl instead. Then, using the Theban runes, write your own magickal name around the base of the chalice, speaking each letter aloud. When you are finished, say, *"So mote it be!"*

Using Your Chalice

Your chalice should sit on your altar, on the West (left) side (the direction of the Element Water). It should always have fresh water in it. It's also okay to float a fresh rose in the water. In magickal rituals, the water in the chalice may be consecrated with the wand or athamé before sharing with the others in your Circle (saying *"May you never thirst!"*). Or a few drops may be used to anoint the different parts of the body in healing or blessing rituals (saying *"Blessed be thy mouth, that speaks the sacred names..."*). Or some may be sprinkled over images of the gods when making offering or prayers for Their blessings.

Lesson 4: The Panticle (Earth)

The *panticle paten* is a disc engraved with a five-pointed star, or *pentagram,* and may also include other symbols relating to the Earth, the natural forces, and protection. It is commonly misnamed *pentacle,* a synonym for *pentangle*, which means "five angles"; ***pan****ticle* means "***all*** angles." Sometimes called the *Pentacle of Solomon*, the pentagram design is the time-honored universal symbol of Magick, and it signifies the five properties of the Great Magickal Agent, the five Elements of Nature, the five senses, and the five outstretched extremities of the human body: head, arms, and legs. The panticle is used in Ceremonial Magick as an instrument of protection, or a tool to evoke spirits. Different versions with various symbols have been designed for each of the planets, and for many other uses. Panticles are also hung over doors and windows to act as protective devices, or used in rituals to draw money.

The panticle is essentially passive; it is the foundation from which we build, and is symbolic of the forces of Nature and physical manifestation. The pentagram on it represents the Element of Earth and forms a shield of protection to guard us from hostile forces. In ritual the panticle will provide you with the ability to ground and center your intentions. The panticle may be made of stone, clay, or metal (earthy material).

Task: Making Your Panticle

Although you can now buy beautiful panticles

of metal or ceramic at any occult store, you can also easily make your own. Go to an arts and crafts supply store and pick up a package of air-drying clay (Mexi-Clay is a kind I often use). Roll out a flat disk between two sheets of wax paper with a rolling pin, just as if you were making cookies. Don't make it too thin, or it'll get easily broken. A half-inch thick is good. Then use a large round can (like a coffee can) or Tupperware to cut out a circular piece.

Trace or copy a pentagram design onto paper (the right size for your piece), such as this one, and center it over your cut-out clay disk. Use a sharp skewer to poke holes through the paper into the clay at the five points. Then use a round-ended stick to inscribe a circle around the design (it helps if you can find a circular object like a tin can the right size to trace around), and use a ruler to draw straight lines with the same stick connecting the points. This is your basic panticle.

If you wish to inscribe other sigils and symbols into the design such as on this Panticle of Earth, do so now. The inner symbols are the traditional runes from the *Greater Key of Solomon*, while the outer ones spell out "E-A-R-T-H" in Theban runes. On the back side you should inscribe "Blessed be thou Panticle of Art" and your own magickal name in Theban runes. While you are making and inscribing your panticle, you should chant: *"Blessed be thou Panticle of Earth."*

Then let the whole thing dry hard, and sand the surface smooth. Now you have a perfect panticle of Earth. Of course, if you have access to a kiln, such as in your school art department, you can make such a Panticle of ceramic and fire it into a magickal artifact that will last forever! Consecrate it during the waxing Moon by sprinkling salted water over it and passing it through the smoke of burning incense compounded of rosemary, cedar, sandalwood, pine resin, and lavender oil.

An Earthly Star before me rests
A vessel strong to manifest.
All things that I would conjure here,
Or banish forth the things I fear.
So mote it be!

Using Your Panticle

When positioning your panticle on your altar, it should be placed in the North (back), the direction of Earth, or in the center. Use it as a receptacle upon which to place amulets, charms, crystals, or other objects to be ritually consecrated. Any ritual food, such as bread, cookies, or fruit slices, can be served on the Panticle as a plate. However, if it's made of Mexi-Clay, you should cover it with a circle of waxed paper so the clay won't get into the food.

Lesson 5: The Athamé (Fire)

The *athamé* (pronounced variously as a-THAH-may or AH-tha-may) or magickal dagger represents power, action, and domination. The first iron blades were made from meteoric nickel-iron—practically the same as stainless steel—and were considered (rightly so!) to be the thunderbolts of the gods. Thus, the athamé symbolizes the Element of Fire. Here is the quintessence of masculinity corresponding to the positive and creative forces of Nature. Such magickal blades have been used in every culture throughout the world over the past 3,500 years.

An early version of this name for a magickal dagger appears in the Grimoire called the *Clavicle of Solomon,* dated 1572, where it is written as *arthana.* You will use your athamé to cast the Magick Circle, consecrate water and salt, and banish unwanted entities. Traditionally, it should be seven to nine inches long, with a double-edged blade and black handle.

In recent years several knife companies have been producing spectacular blades with magickal and fantasy designs, and these have become quite popular among magickal people for athamés—as long as they have a double edge.

While the traditional athamé has a steel blade, certain workings (especially with faeries and Nature spirits) require no iron and some, no metal at all. For these purposes, some magickal craftspeople are now making beautiful athamés with blades of napped flint, copper, brass, crystal, wood, bone, antler, or polished stone. Once you have your basic athamé as described here, you might wish to acquire some of these others.... For your first basic athamé, I recommend shopping at flea markets, where you can usually find a nice selection of simple and inexpensive double-edged daggers in several styles. Try several of these: Hold them in your hand, and cut the air in twisting figure-8 patterns to get the feel of them. Be sure and get a matching belt sheath along with the knife! After you buy it, take it home and hone it to a sharp edge and point with a whetstone.

Some Wizards make their athamés completely from scratch, cutting a blade out of a sheet of metal and carving a handle of wood, bone, or antler. This is a more complex process than I think it necessary to go into here. For detailed instructions on making such a dagger, see Ray Buckland's *Complete Book of Witchcraft,* pp. 29-31.

Consecrating Your Athamé

On a Tuesday (the day of Mars) when the Moon is waning, compound an incense of Martial herbs, such as dragon's blood resin, powdered rue, ground peppercorns, ginger, and sulfur. Prick your finger or the heel of your hand with the point of your blade, and mix in a few drops of your own blood. Set half of this mixture aside, and burn the rest in your thurible (see following). Purify the blade by sprinkling it with distilled water from your chalice, and then pass it through the incense smoke.

Now take the remainder of your Martial herb compound and stir it into your chalice. Heat the blade of your athamé on the thurible coals until it gets as hot as possible. When it is good and hot, plunge it into the mixture in the chalice, chanting these words:

Blade of steel I conjure thee
To ban such things as named by me.
Cut cleanly through adversity,
As I do will, so mote it me!

Do this three times to temper the steel, and visualize the blade glowing with power after each immersion.

In ancient times, such blades were always magnetized, giving them a truly magickal power. To magnetize your athamé, stroke the blade repeatedly with a lodestone or bar magnet. Hold your athamé in your dominant hand, the magnet in your other, and beginning at the handle end, draw the magnet down the whole length of the blade to the very point. Do this over and over again for at least five minutes, always stroking in the same direction, while chanting these words:

Blade of steel I conjure thee
Attract such things as named by me.
Draw tight the circle 'round the tree,
As I do will, so mote it be!

After you have finished, wrap your athamé in linen or silk, declaring: *"So mote it be!"*

Engraving the Athamé Runes

On the next Tuesday of the waning Moon, unwrap your athamé and paint or engrave the appropriate runes along the handle or the blade. If painting, use a new fine brush and black enamel paint. A Dremel or engraving tool may also be used for this. As you inscribe each rune, chant: *"Blessed be thou Blade of Fire."* If you prefer, rather than the traditional runes just inscribe your magickal name in Theban runes. If you decide to give a special name to your athamé, you should also inscribe that name into the blade on the other side.

By far the most magickal way to inscribe runes on a steel blade is by acid etching. To do this, first draw the runes you've decided to use onto the blade or your athamé with a black felt-tip pen. Then melt a batch of beeswax or white candle ends in a disposable pot. Next, heat the blade enough so that the wax will stick to it, but not enough to damage its magnetic field. Then cover the blade with melted wax and let it harden. Do several layers to make sure the metal is completely sealed, but make sure you can still see the runes clearly through the wax.

Then use a sharp inscribing tool (a sharp nail will do) to trace the runes. Be sure to cut all the way through the wax to expose the metal beneath. Then carefully pour on sulfuric or hydrochloric (battery) acid, iodine, vinegar, or other etching agent. The acid will eat into the metal, etching it, where you have inscribed it, but the wax will protect the rest of the blade. After awhile, wash off the acid, clean off the wax, and you will have a beautifully etched athamé.

> ***TIP:*** *Practice this technique first on a cheap kitchen knife so you will know how long to leave the acid on before flushing it away. A simpler approach is to just purchase an etching kit or pen at your local hardware or crafts store. These look like ballpoint pens, but contain acid instead of ink. Be very careful in using acid, as it can burn!*

When not in use, your athamé should be laid at the South (front) of your altar. It may be sheathed or unsheathed. When in use, it should be hung in its sheath from your belt.

Lesson 6: Other Altar Implements

In addition to the four major tools listed above, you will also want to acquire several other magickal items for your altar and magickal workings. These are also associated with the Elements—and less symbolically!

Candlesticks (Fire)

Nothing sets the magickal scene like flickering candlelight in an otherwise darkened room, and no other Element has been so significant to the evolution of humanity as Fire. Fire represents the divine spark of creative Energy, provides light and warmth, and symbolically delivers us from darkness. There should be two candles on your altar: one on the right to represent the masculine/God powers, and one on the left to represent the feminine/Goddess. Candles of various colors are used for different kinds of spells, as explained elsewhere. Otherwise, you can burn candles according to the colors of the season (orange and black for Samhain, red and green for Yule…), or any colors you happen to like at the time. Many people burn a black and a white candle for normal use, or two white ones. Small votive candles in little glass jars are very popular, and I recommend them especially if your space is limited. Taper candles in fancy matching candleholders are also nice, and more traditional, if you have plenty of clearance for them. If you do get such candlesticks, here are the traditional magickal runes you can paint around their base. Or, if you prefer, you may just write your magickal name in Theban runes.

Thurible or Censer (Air)

The *thurible* (THUR-i-bull) or *censer* is a container in which incense is safely burned to represent the Element of Air. It can be anything from a simple incense burner or chafing dish to an ornate swinging brass censer on a chain. In magickal terminology, a thurible is an open dish, usually set upon three legs, while a censer has a cover with little holes in it to let the smoke out. Censers are often fitted out with chains, so they can be hung or swung, like those used in the Catholic Church. Such censers are almost always made of brass.

If you cannot find a suitable thurible, you can easily make one. Any small metal or ceramic bowl or deep dish will do. This should be large enough to also burn a small piece of paper in as an offering when required. It should have a wide opening at the top to allow circulation, made of fire resistant material, and also have a pleasing appearance. It is recommended to place some sand and /or ash in the bottom of the thurible. This will absorb the intense heat of the charcoal and protect the thurible and the surface it rests upon. Earth, salt, sand, or small rocks may also be used for this purpose. It is nice to use some kind of sacred earth such as sand from a favorite beach or desert location. After many uses the sand can be stirred to mix it with the ashes, keeping it clean and fragrant. The sand may also be carefully rinsed to clean the ash and debris from it. A *trivet* or heat resistant base is also recommended to be placed under the thurible so it will not scorch your altar or altar cloth.

When the Moon is waxing, consecrate your thurible by burning a little dragon's blood incense in it, saying *"Blessed be thou Censer of Air."* The traditional thurible runes from the *Greater Key of Solomon* are shown here. Paint them around the base, or, if you prefer, just inscribe your magickal name in Theban runes. Either way, finish off by saying *"So mote it be!"*

This is your completed thurible or censer. With it you are able to consecrate, bless and purify anything you pass through the smoke of burning incense.

> ***NOTE:*** *Incense used in magickal rituals is an art in itself, and special formulas are given for different spells. Stick or cone incense can be used, but most Wizards prefer the raw or granulated incense that is burned on self-igniting charcoal blocks, available in all metaphysical shops and many health food stores. To compound your own incenses, you will need a mortar and pestle (see next…).*

Mortar & Pestle

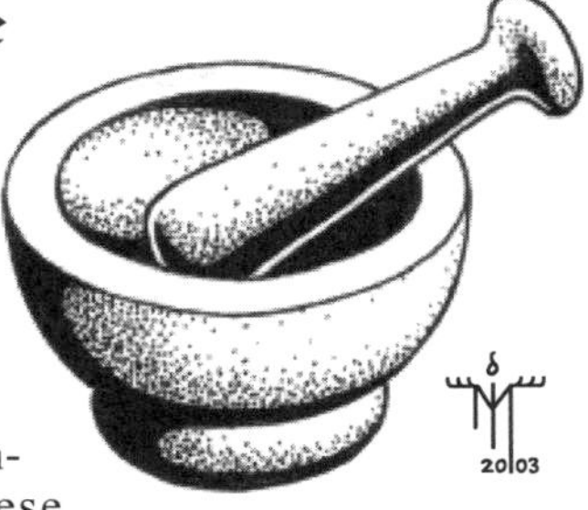

A small mortar and pestle can be purchased at any occult shop and many health food stores. These are essential for grinding up herbs, seeds, etc. in the compounding of incenses. However, these items need not necessarily be kept on your altar. I keep mine in a drawer of my magickal cabinet, along with containers of various herbs and incenses, spare candles, extra tools, and many other items I may not want to have out at that time.

Salt & Water bowls (Earth & Water)

Little cups containing salt and water are useful for all rituals for purification and consecration. A favorite salt cup among modern Wizards is a hollow geode, cut neatly in half to make a little crystal bowl. Likewise, sea snail shells—particularly those with a wide opening, like turbans, moons, or whelks—make lovely containers for water. Nice little matching cups can be readily found that were designed for, say, sweet & sour sauce for Chinese meals.

Bell

The bell is a ritual instrument of great antiquity. Ringing a bell unleashes vibrations that have powerful effects according to its volume, tone, and material of construction. Any type of bell may be used, including a Tibetan bell bowl, but the most favored design for magickal work is a brass or silver bell with a wooden handle, as shown here.

The bell is a feminine symbol and so is often used to invoke the Goddess in ritual. It is also rung to ward off evil spells and spirits, to halt storms, or to evoke good energies. Placed in cupboards or hung on the door, it guards the home. Bells are sometimes rung in ritual to mark various sections and to signal a spell's beginning or end. The only runes associated with the bell are astrological glyphs, as shown here, but if you like, you can inscribe "Blessed be thou Bell of Art" and your magickal name in Theban runes.

Lesson 7: Books of Magick

Right at the beginning of these lessons, I set you your first Task—to acquire a magickal journal and begin writing in it. I trust you have been doing so. When you fill the first one up, go out and get another. Eventually you will have a whole shelf full of your journals over the years! There are three other types of magickal books you should write yourself. Each one is your own personal record, and so should also be written in your own hand—or at least typed on your own keyboard! In the old days, we Wizards had to make our own paper and bind our books as well—usually with leather. Even pens and inks were handmade, of goose quills and chimney soot. Not too many of us go to that much trouble these days, although you can still buy such beautiful handmade books at Renaissance Faires and metaphysical stores—which are good places to buy lots of magickal stuff! (More about these places in Class V of this Course: "Entering the Magickal World.") Above all, keep your own hand-written magickal books to yourself and only share them with people you trust completely.

Every Wizard should keep a Book of Shadows and a Grimoire. Traditionally, such magickal workbooks had black covers, and were often referred to simply as "black books," but yours can be any color you feel is right. Most modern Wizards now use looseleaf notebooks or binders so we can insert or rearrange pages, and now many of us who have computers also keep a "Disk of Shadows." I have a whole shelf of such fat binders containing Grimoires and Books of Shadows from a number of different magickal traditions with which I've studied.

Your Book of Shadows (or BoS, as it is commonly abbreviated) is for writing down lesson notes from your teachers, rituals, songs, poems, chants, prayers, magickal lore, and all the other records and teachings of your particular magickal tradition. You will keep adding to your BoS throughout your life. If you study with a teacher, you will copy material from their BoS into your own. And if you someday become a teacher yourself, your students and apprentices will copy your BoS into theirs.

Your Grimoire is sort of like a cookbook containing spells, charms, recipes, herb lore, incense formulae, tables of correspondence, magickal alphabets, and other reference material. Like any other book of recipes, you will also keep adding to your personal Grimoire all your life. Many Grimoires—like this one—have been written by Wizards who have come before you, and some of these have been published and can be purchased at your local occult or metaphysical bookstore. But avoid the *Necronomicon*—the spells it contains are for conjuring up really nasty imaginary monsters and demons, which are a damned nuisance, as they're never properly housetrained, and they leave a terrible mess…

Finally, there is your dream diary, which you should keep right beside your bed, and in which you record, every morning upon awakening, as much as you can remember of the dreams you had the night before. (See 1:VI: "Perchance to Dream") This will serve a twofold purpose: first, to help you learn to be conscious in The Dreaming; and second, to provide a record of your own spiritual growth and evolution that you can look back upon over coming years. Perhaps you will discover that some of your dreams are psychic or prophetic, and have come true. If so, your dream diary will help you learn how to tell which ones are the true dreams.

Lesson 8: The Speculum, or Magick Mirror

—by Raven Grimassi

The *speculum,* or magick scrying mirror, is one of the oldest tools of divination. The classic speculum is a dark concave surface of reflective material. You can easily construct one for yourself by using the curved glass face of a clock and painting the *convex* (bulging) outer side with glossy black paint. Antique stores are a good source for old clocks with rounded glass faces. The traditional preparation of a speculum begins on the night of the full Moon—preferably when the Moon is in Pisces, Cancer, or Scorpio.

Once you have painted the glass and it has thoroughly dried, then bathe the mirror in an herbal brew of rosemary, fennel, rue, vervain, ivy, and walnut leaves or bark. While the glass is still bathing in the potion, hold both your hands out over it, palms down, and say:

Awake, all ye slumbering spirits of old,
Whose eyes reveal what in darkness is told,
Give to me visions within this dark well,
And make this a portal of magickal spell.

Visualize a silver mist forming around the mirror. Take a deep breath and then slowly exhale outward upon the potion. Mentally envision that your breath moves the silver mist into the mirror. Repeat this three times. Next, remove the mirror from the potion and dry it off thoroughly. You are now ready to attune the mirror to your aura. Hold the mirror out in front of you with its convex side resting on your right palm. Then place your left palm above it, about three inches away from the glass surface, and begin making a circular clockwise motion staying within the dimensions of the mirror. Avoid touching the inside of the mirrored surface, as you will leave fingerprints!

Once completed, take the mirror out beneath the full Moon so that its light falls upon the concave side. Slowly fill the glass to the brim with the herbal potion. Hold it up towards the Moon, almost level with your eyes. Don't worry about any spillage. While looking at the Moon allow your eyes to unfocus slightly. If you are doing this correctly, you will see three lines of light emanating from the Moon. Continue to squint until the vertical line coming from the bottom of the Moon seems to touch upon the mirror.

Once the moonbeam is touching the mirror, speak these words:

Three are the lights that now here are seen
But not to all the one in-between,
For now the Enchantress has come at last
To charge and empower this magick glass.

Quickly close your eyes so that you break eye contact. Open them again looking down towards the glass. Pour out the potion upon the Earth in libation, then rinse the mirror off with fresh clear water, and dry it thoroughly. Wrap it in a silk cloth to protect its lunar magnetism, and never allow sunlight to fall directly upon the mirror. Your speculum is now ready to be used for divination.

Crystal Ball

Crystal balls—also known as *scrying,* seeing, or show stones—have always been associated with Wizards. In the crystal ball, the Wizard could conjure scenes far distant in space or time—sort of like live video! To do this, you gaze deeply into the ball in the same way as I instructed you in reading auras (1.V: "Magickal Skills"), and images from your intuitive subconscious will be projected into the depths of the ball to reveal what you are seeking (more on this in a later Class...).

In the past, such spheres were always made of natural quartz, beryl, or calcite. They range from clear through smoky to opaque, and come in a variety of colors—including pink and black. These are still made today, and can be purchased at magickal marketplaces at prices ranging from $20 to thousands of dollars, depending on the size, material, and clarity. But the development of high-quality optical glass has provided less expensive alternatives for many modern Wizards, and many perfectly serviceable crystal balls are now available of glass, leaded glass, or even acrylic plastic. Various bases are also available, from simple wooden rings to fancy three-legged brass stands.

The sphere is a symbolic form of the Goddess, as are all circles and round things, and the icy coldness of genuine rock crystal is symbolic of the depths of the sea. The crystal ball is a magickal object touched with the Divine, and should be guarded carefully. When not in use, keep it wrapped in a black cloth of silk or velvet, to keep off dust and oils in the air. Exposure to the light of the full Moon will increase its potency, as will rubbing it with fresh mugwort leaves, or washing it in an infusion of mugwort.

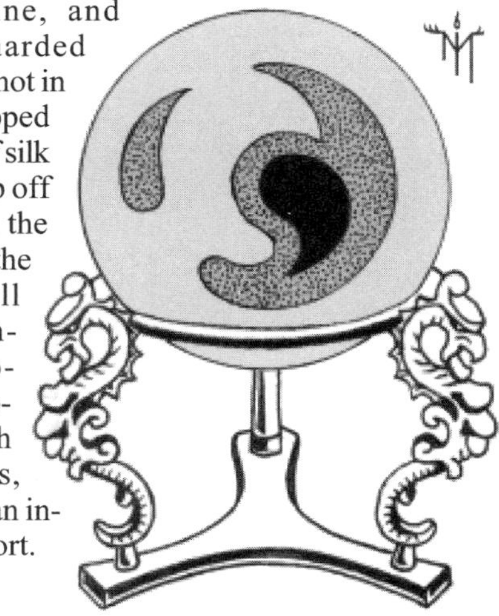

Class III: Wizardly Regalia

The old gentleman that the Wart saw was a singular spectacle. He was dressed in a flowing gown with fur tippets which had the signs of the zodiac embroidered all over it, together with various cabalistic signs, as of triangles with eyes in them, queer crosses, leaves of trees, bones of birds and animals and a planetarium whose stars shone like bits of looking-glass with the sun on them. He had a pointed hat like a dunce's cap, or like the headgear worn by ladies of that time...
—T.H. White, describing Merlin (*The Sword in the Stone,* p. 31)

1. Introduction: The Costume of a Wizard

HEN WE PUT ON ANY CLOTHES WE ARE creating a *persona* (character) to present ourselves to both others and ourselves within a context; all clothes are costumes designed to hide or reveal the real you. Your magickal *regalia* (splendid clothes; finery) are sufficiently different from everyday clothes to help remind you and others that you are now in the role of the Wizard, instead of the role of school student, athlete, or other mundane identity. Just as other roles have their traditional costumes and uniforms, so does Wizardry.

Each Wizard develops a unique individual style all his own, and no two Wizards appear quite alike. Wizards do not buy their magickal clothes off the rack at the department store, but rather design and sew their own, or acquire them from other skilled seamsters and seamstresses in the magickal community. Being able to design and sew your own clothes is a very important skill for a Wizard, and I strongly urge you to learn this. If you do not have a sewing machine, try to get one, and learn how to use it.

Merlin, by Daniel Beard

You might want to go to your neighborhood fabric store and check out the sewing patterns available. If you ask for help (tell the clerks you're making a costume for a party or for Halloween), you will find that there are many fine patterns for wizardly robes, cloaks, tunics, jerkins, and even Wizard's hats. I'll list a few such patterns here, although most of these designs are so simple that you probably won't even need a pattern other than the diagrams I have drawn here for you.

> ***IMPORTANT:*** *Use natural materials, such as cotton or linen. Avoid man-made fibers like polyester or nylon, as they are insulators against natural energies.*

Lesson 2. Tunics & Jerkins

The basic generic costumes worn by men and boys throughout all of European history until modern times have been simple tunics and jerkins. These are also the traditional costumes of the Apprentice Wizard, and so they are the first ones I will teach you to make. It's really easy! Jerkins and tunics look best when worn with leggings, tights, or baggy pants with elastic at the ankles.

First, look through all the different kinds of fabric in the store, and pick out something you really like. For a tunic or jerkin, it can be any color you want, but it should not have a printed pattern. Have them cut a length of this material about as long as you can hold each end in the grip of your outstretched hands. Since fabric measurements are in 6" increments, have it cut slightly shorter rather than slightly longer. Also, if you wish to work with a regular sewing pattern, Simplicity pattern #5840-C,D and #9887-C offer excellent (and somewhat different) tunic designs. #9887-C includes a short cape.

The Tunic

For a tunic, fold the material in half from end-to-end; and then again from side-to side, so it is in quarters. Lay it out neatly as shown here, with the open corners matching at the lower left, and the folded corner at the upper right. From the upper right corner, use a water-based felt marker to draw a cut line along

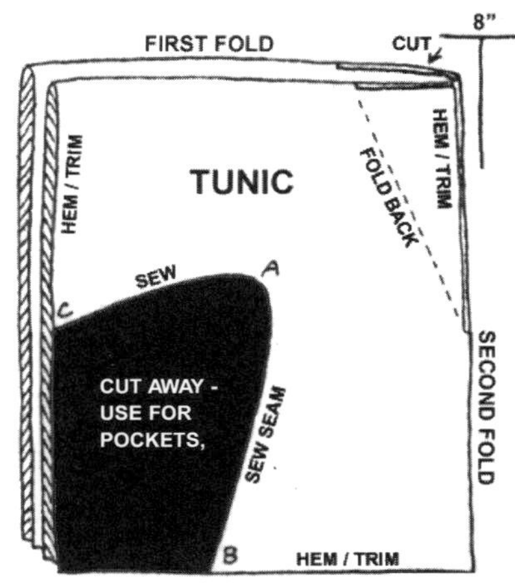

top edge for a neckhole. This should be no more than 4" to each side, for a total width of 8" (see diagram). Then mark another cut line straight down the right edge, about the same length (this can vary, depending on how deep you want the neckline). The final cut mark will be in the form of a "T."

For the sleeves and sides, first inhale deeply and measure your chest at its widest point. Divide that number by 4, and add 2". This is the minimum distance from the right centerfold to the underarm cut line, and you should make a little mark at that point, halfway between the top and bottom (A). Now mark out a line from the left and bottom, starting about halfway up the left side (C) and curving around as in the diagram to hit the bottom edge (B). Make sure that the furthest point of the right edge of this line comes just to the previous chest measurement mark (A). While keeping the material carefully folded, pin along the inside line of the underarm sections. Try it on now, just to make sure it fits. Then cut it out with sharp scissors through all four layers. Then unpin, and unfold the front fold so it lays out flat like a shirt. Pin each side again for sewing, and now cut out the neck "T." Sew up the sides, and you're done!

As a final touch, you should hem the bottom edge, sleeves, and neckline. You might also add trim, if you wish, at the bottom and sleeves. You can also use the leftover material to add a hood, outside panels, pockets, etc. A wide over-belt completes the effect. If your material is cotton, a "Ghost Dance" style tunic may be made by leaving a couple inches along your seams, turning the seams to the outside, and fraying the edges, like so:

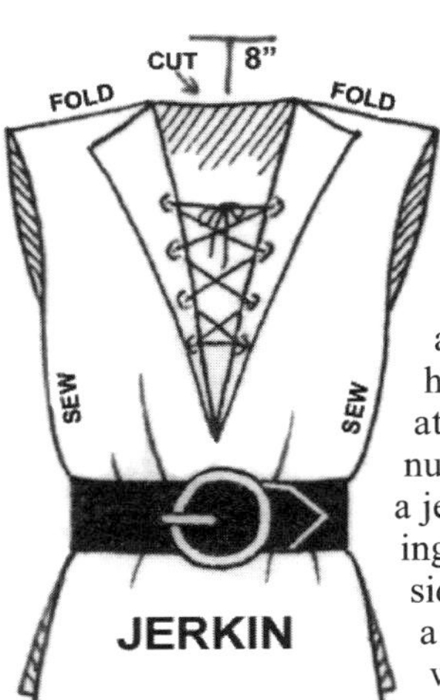

The Jerkin

Soft leather is a favored material for a jerkin, but you may, of course, use anything you like. The length is the same as for a tunic. To measure the width, inhale deeply and measure your chest at its widest point. Divide that number by 2, and add 4". Because a jerkin is sleeveless, there is nothing to cut away; just sew up the outside, leaving a slit at the bottom and a foot or so for an armhole. Just as with the tunic, the neckhole is a simple "T" cut 8" wide along the top fold, with the vertical cut in front. I like to make the front cut much deeper, then fold back the sides into triangular lapels. I then add grommets and lacing for a very cool look. A wide belt with an impressive large buckle completes the effect.

Lesson 3: Your Wizard's Robe

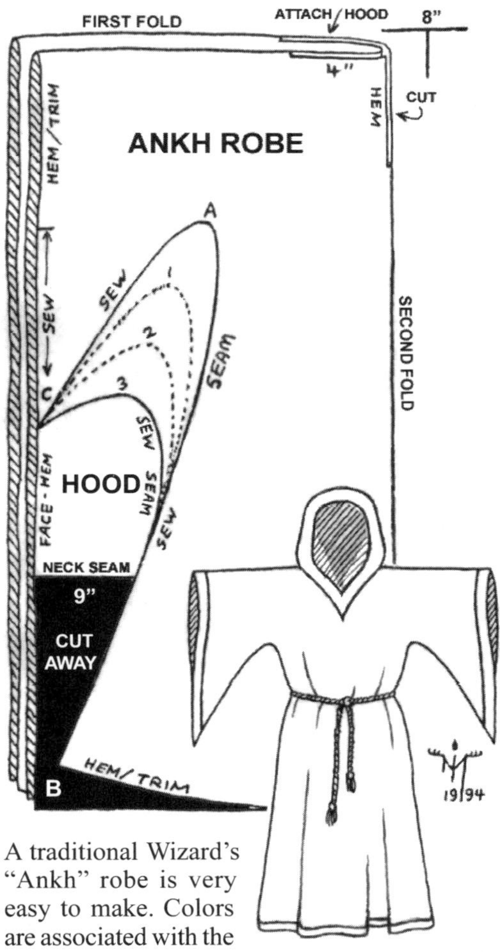

A traditional Wizard's "Ankh" robe is very easy to make. Colors are associated with the Wizard's Path (see "Color-Coded Wizardry" in 1.III, "Foundations of Magick"), and also with one's grade. Apprentices traditionally wear white robes; Journeymen wear robes of their path color; and Adepts wear pretty much anything they fancy, including robes with stars and astrological symbols. So you should make your first robe of white fabric. Then you can wear your colored tabard over it that you made earlier. Although I prefer the basic design I am describing here, Simplicity pattern #5840-A,B also has two somewhat different open-front robe designs, for male and female. And Simplicity 9887-A,B is quite spectacular!

The length should be twice the distance

from your shoulder to the ground. As with the tunic, fold the material in half from end to end, and then again from side to side so you will have a quarter up.

Mark an armpit point (A) about a foot down from the top fold, and far enough out from the centerfold to fit comfortably over your chest. (This is important! The main mistake people make on robes is failure to allow adequate chest space.) Inhale and measure your chest at its widest point, add 10% comfort room, and divide by 4 to give the distance out from the centerline to point (A). Then mark a line (A-B) from that point to the bottom outside corner (B) and another line (A-C) to the middle (C) of the outside edge. Then round off these lines and the armpit angle (A), and add at least an inch for the seam. If you are very large, the amount cut away here can be reduced proportionately; see lines 1-3 in diagram. Pin and cut out along the lines, and sew up the cut edges (I like to also sew halfway up the outside of the pointed "butterfly" sleeves for pockets).

As with the tunic, the neck-hole is a simple "T" cut along the top fold, with the vertical cut in front. The horizontal cut should total 8" across, but the vertical cut is up to you (how much of your chest do you want to expose?). You might make it short at first, as you can always cut it deeper after you try it on; but you can't make it shorter again!

The hood is made out of two of the leftover pieces cut out earlier. These are then cut square across the bottom at 9". The back can be rounded, as I show here, or pointed if you cut along line 4 (a very popular design). The crucial dimension is that the neck of the hood must match the horizontal cut of the neck-hole in the robe, to which it will be attached; so each piece must be 9" across the bottom.

After you sew the hood and robe together, fold back and hem all your edges (put it on, belt with a cord, and have someone pin up the bottom to ankle length). Arms outspread, the completed robe with hood will form an "Ankh." Trim may be attached at the ends of the sleeves, around the front of the hood, or around the bottom of the robe; and leftover materials may be used to add outside panels, pockets, etc.

Lesson 4: Your Cingulum

The *cingulum* (SING-gu-lum) is a special braided cord you tie around your waist, over your robe. A cingulum is always handmade by the one who will be wearing it. Like your athamé and wand, no one should ever use your cingulum except you. There are three traditional lengths: 9' for cord magick; 6' to be used in marking out the radius of a Magick Circle; or your exact height, which is called your *measure*.

The color of your cingulum is keyed to the color of your grade, exactly like belts in karate. Different traditions assign different colors to these cords. In my tradition of Wizardry, these colors are: green for Apprentices; red for Journeymen; and blue and purple for Adepts. It is, however, traditional to weave in one gold cord among the colors as a reminder of the Magick we all share, no matter what our grade.

To make your Apprentice's cingulum, go to your fabric store and purchase standard 3/8" twist cord. It comes on a roll, and you will need to buy 21' in green and gold. If you like, you can get three 7' lengths with different shades of green. On an evening when the Moon is waxing, purify these cords at your altar by sprinkling them with water and salt; then pass them over the candle flame and incense smoke. Chant the following spell as you do so:

Water and Earth, where you are cast
No ill or adverse purpose last.
Fire and Air, I conjure thee
To purify and blessed be!

Knot the three ends together as one with an overhand knot, leaving about 6" loose ends to be unraveled. Then start braiding them, binding in the magick moonlight with each twist, and chanting the following:

Made to measure, wrought to bind
Blessed be thou cord entwined!

As you braid, concentrate on putting your personal energies into it so it becomes part of you. When you have finished, tie another overhand knot to prevent the ends from unraveling. Now, starting from the first knot, tie a knot at 3 1/2', another at 4', another at 4 1/2', another at 5', and a final one at 5 1/2'. Leave another 6" loose ends to be unraveled, and cut off the rest.

You will now be able to use your cingulum as a compass cord with which to make different-size Magick Circles for different rites and numbers of people. Whenever you are doing Magick, or in a Magick Circle, you should wear your cingulum bound about the waist of your robe, under your tabard. But a cingulum is *not* worn with a tunic or jerkin!

Lesson 5: Your Wizard's Belt

Your cingulum, however, is not meant to hang things from, nor is it to be worn in public. For that you will need a belt. You can, of course, just use your regular belt, which many people do. But you might want to create a special Wizard's belt. You can go to a used clothing store and hunt through the racks for the longest 2" belt you can find, or you can make one yourself out of a long strap of 2" wide leather, which you can buy at any leatherworking supplies store. You will also need a leather punch to make buckle holes in the right places. Your Wizard's belt should be at least a foot longer than the diameter of your waist, so you can knot and hang the loose end. Wear it with your robe, tunic, or jerkin. You may have to search a while for the perfect belt buckle. Flea markets and county fairs are good places to look, as well as Renaissance Faires and magickal marketplaces. Your belt buckle is a very personal and unique item, and you will know the right one when you find it!

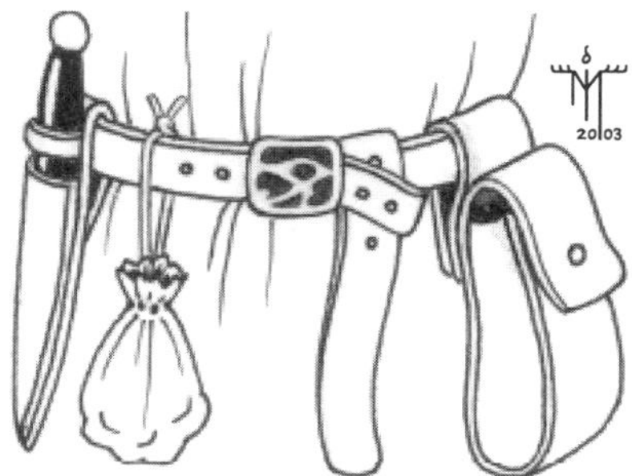

Pouches and Bags

You will need to have several pouches and bags to hang from your belt, to keep things in. These can be of different sizes and materials, and you can buy them or make them yourself. Simple drawstring bags are both easy to make and readily available, but they aren't very convenient for getting stuff into and out of. I always wear one or two larger leather pouches with closable flaps on my belt, in which I carry my wallet, glasses, and various other small items I like to keep with me. Simple belt pouch designs are available at the same leather supplies stores where you can also get the leather and tools with which to make them, so I won't bother with further instructions here.

Your Reticule

However, there is one very simple kind of drawstring pouch that I will show you how to make. This is called a *reticule* ("net"), and it is used particularly for holding *runestones.* To make a reticule, get a piece of *chamois* material from your local auto-supply store. Spread it out on the table and lay a big dinner plate face-down on top of it for a template. Trace the outline of the plate with a felt-tip marker, and cut out the circle of chamois with scissors. Now use a paper punch to punch evenly spaced holes every two inches all around the edge of the circle. The holes should be about 1" in from the edge, which is about the depth of the punch. Get about 3' of cord or leather thong (from a fabric or leather store), and thread it through the holes. Then tie the cord off with an overhand knot, and pull the thong to gather the reticule into a bag. When you spread it out flat, it becomes a round surface for casting your stones.

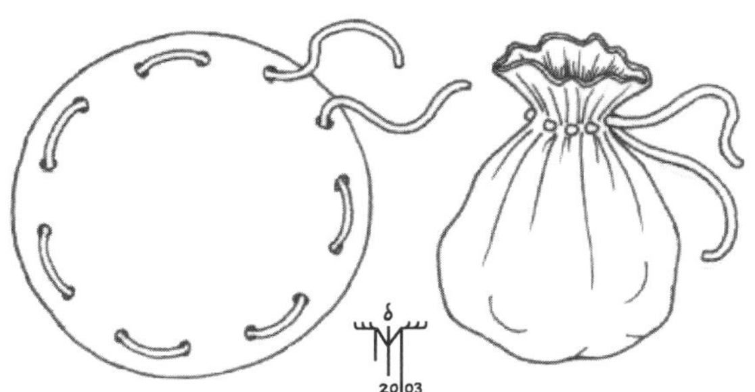

Belt Knife

A belt knife is a pretty essential item for a Wizard, but you may not be able to wear it in public (and certainly never at school!), as many places have laws against double-edged knives. However, you should have no problem wearing such a knife at Renaissance Faires, magickal gatherings, and other special events where the rest of your wizardly ensemble will also be suitable. Your athamé for this is perfect, provided you have a good sheath for it. The sheath should have a little snap-strap above the guard to keep your knife from accidentally falling out. If there isn't one already included, you can easily make it.

Drinking Horn

Anywhere you venture forth in your wizardly regalia, you will find it useful to carry a drinking horn slung from your belt. I have made several nice ones from simple cow horns, which I spent many hours sanding and polishing. After your horn is all cleaned up, polished, and beautiful, you should wash it out thoroughly with hot soapy water, dry it very well, and then fill it with melted beeswax that you must pour out immediately to coat the inside with a thin layer. To attach it to your belt but still have it removable, you can tie a leather strap anchored at both ends of the horn, and have a belt clip, like for car keys, with which you can clip it on and off. To keep the leather strap from sliding off the horn, use a bit of Super Glue.

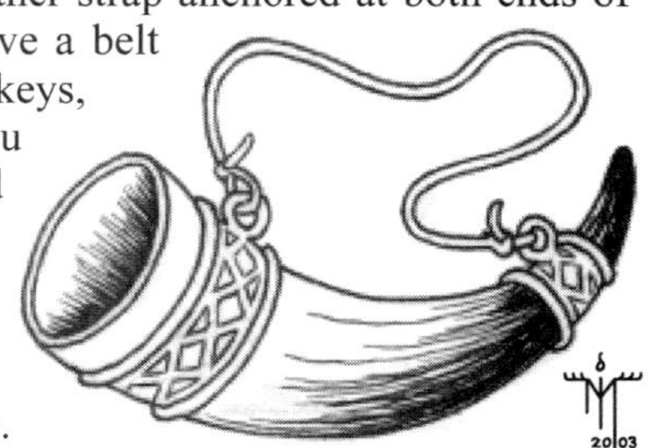

Lesson 6: Your Wizard's Cloak

When you go out into the magickal world, you will find that the most immediately recognizable item of clothing worn by just about everybody (especially in the evenings, or when the weather is cold!) is a long dark cloak. A Wizard's cloak forms a full semicircle when spread out, and you will come to really love yours! It will keep you warm sitting around a campfire; it can be wrapped around someone sitting

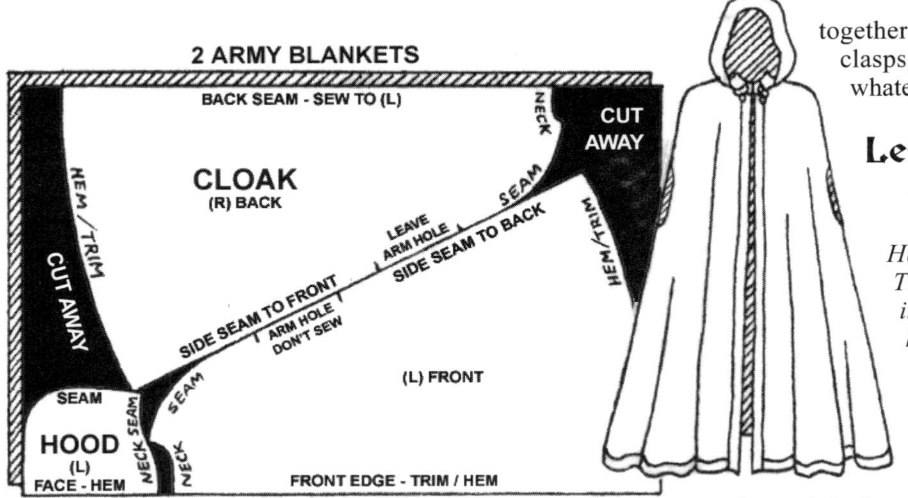

next to you; and you can even roll up in it as a sleeping blanket. I never go anywhere without my familiar grey cloak, which I've had for decades!

Go down to your local fabric store, and pick up either the Simplicity pattern #7016 or the McCall's pattern #6774 for cloaks. These are both excellent, and it will make your work easier to use one of them. Simplicity #9887-B,C,D also offers great cape and cloak designs, including a fine Wizard's hat (A). For cloak material, I recommend getting two U.S. military wool blankets, which are relatively inexpensive and come in several colors, depending on branch of service (the white Navy blankets can be died any color you like). The cloak design requires four right triangles, which just happen to be exactly the size and shape of diagonal cuts in two blankets. The curved section left over from the shoulder area is just right for a hood. You can buy such blankets at military surplus stores.

Of course, you can also use any other thick material you like of the right size. Many magickal people have cloaks of beautiful velvet, with fancy trim. And if you would like to make a real Cloak of Invisibility, get some of that thin "pearlescent sheer" material that changes colors in different lights and angles. This material comes in several shimmery colors, but the best for invisibility outdoors are those that include green. Keep the seams as narrow as possible, using an overhand stitch. Make it long enough to hide your feet, and make sure the hood is big enough to pull down completely over your face. For a Cloak of Invisibility, I recommend Simplicity pattern #9887-D.

To line your cloak, just use the same pattern for some other lining material—from cotton to satin, as you wish. Some people use camouflage material so they can become invisible by turning their cloak inside out! (But don't line a Cloak of Invisibility—you need to be able to see out through it!) Be sure to leave wide slits in the side seams for armholes, at the position of your elbows. Finally, your cloak can be held together by ties, frogs, buttons, clasps, or fancy cloak pins—whatever you like.

Lesson 7: The Wizard's Hat

Hats were important. They weren't just clothing. Hats defined the head. They defined who you were. No one had ever heard of a wizard without a pointy hat—at least, no wizard worth speaking of. And you certainly never heard of a witch without one.... It wasn't the wearing of the hats that counted so much as having one to wear. Every trade, every craft had its hat. That's why kings had hats. Take the crown off a king and all you had was someone good at having a weak chin and waving to people. Hats had power. Hats were important.

—Terry Pratchett
(*Witches Abroad,* pp. 223–24)

The tall pointy hats traditionally associated with Wizards and Witches have a long and illustrious history. Several striking conical hats made of beaten sheet gold have been excavated in Germany and France, dating back to the Bronze Age, between 1400 and 900 BCE. Their elaborate embossed decorations consist of symbols clearly representing the Sun, Moon, planets, and stars—just as we see in pictures of Wizards from the Middle Ages to modern times. Sabine Gerloff of Erlangen University says about these hats that: "They showed that the wearer was in contact with the gods, also symbolized by the cone pointing to heaven, and knew the secrets of celestial movements, possibly of the future."

Similar pointy hats are shown on small bronze statues, cylinder seals, and carvings from Turkey, Syria, Cyprus, and Greece, dating from 2500 BCE onward. Two of these have even been found in Sweden. Out in the Gobi Desert, West of China, some ancient Caucasian mummies have recently been discovered. One woman, dated at about 200 BCE, was still wearing a tall black conical hat looking exactly like those traditionally worn by Witches!

Witch and Wizard hats have become so popular for costumes that you can now pick up perfectly fine ones at any costume store—especially around Halloween. However, if you'd like to make your own Wizard's Hat, Simplicity pattern # 9887-A shows a fine Wizard's hat with a brim.

Lesson 8: A Wizard's Jewelry

Magickal jewelry is very important to a Wizard (or a Witch!). Each piece is chosen with great care, and such jewelry always has deep personal significance to the wearer. Pieces of magickal jewelry are usually inscribed with or cast in the form of pentagrams, hexagrams, ankhs, *udjats* ("Eye of Horus"), scarabs, caduceus, Thor's Hammer, Celtic knotwork, astrological symbols, God or Goddess symbols, dragons, and many other mystical designs. Once you learn some of these, you will always be able to spot other magickal people by their jewelry—even when we are otherwise cleverly disguised as mundanes! In fact, this is the main way we recognize each other.

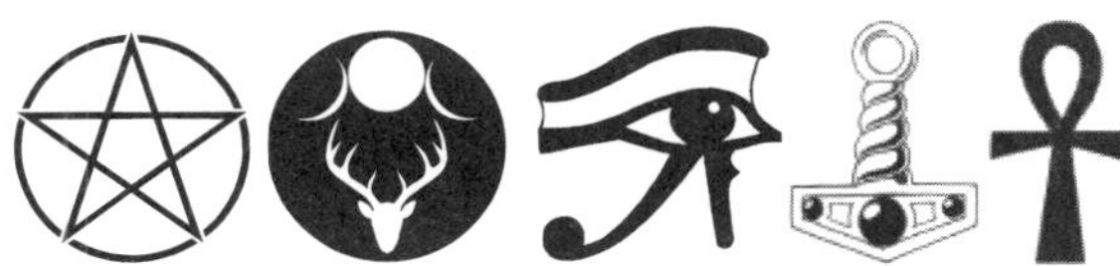

Many pieces of jewelry may also be charms, amulets, talismans, and other magickally charged items worn for protection, luck, or healing (see 3.VII.7: "Amulets & Talismans"). Keep in mind, however, that if you are going to wear magickal jewelry in public, you should be prepared to explain it at any time—because people will ask about it. You might want to consider keeping a pendant hidden inside your shirt, for instance, and only show it to those whom you know will understand.

Necklaces: Necklaces of all kinds are very popular among magickal folks—especially Witches. These may be strung with special magickal stones, such as turquoise or amber, or items such as acorns, beans, or wooden beads, or contain charms in the form of mystical symbols or *totem* animals. To mundanes, these may appear to be just ordinary necklaces, but if you look carefully, you'll the difference in the symbols represented. The most famous magickal necklace of legend was *Brisingamon,* worn by the Norse goddess Freya.

Torques: Torques are circlets of three thick metal wires or rods twisted tightly around each other into a spring-like spiral, with the ends open and capped, often with animal heads. They were worn by the Celts and Norse to signify leadership and a connection with the Gods.

Pendants: Pendants worn by magickal folk are often in the form of disks, pentacles, or amulets with special sigils to promote protection, luck, health, or other benefits. As such pendants may be of any size, the possibilities for designs are endless. The other most popular pendants are crystals of various sizes and types (most commonly quartz), often with a beautiful silver setting. Such crystal pendants may also serve as *pendulums* for divination (see 5.II: "Divination"). Other kinds of pendants may be figures of dragons, faeries, unicorns, God or Goddess images, Ankhs, Thor's Hammers, or anything else the wearer fancies. In fact, I have personally designed a number of such pendants, which are worn by many people. My own favorite, which I always wear with my Wizard's robe, is a large working *astrolabe* (shown here).

Rings: Magickal rings have been worn by Wizards throughout history. Some of these, such as King Solomon's famous ring, have become renowned in legend for the powers attributed to them. It would be very rare to find a magickal person without at least one ring, and some wear rings on every finger! Often at least one ring will have a pentagram design—the essential symbol of Magick. Others will contain special magickal stones (see 3.VII.7.8: "Magickal Minerals"), often in ornate settings. Signet rings, with the wearer's personal sigil, are another popular design; these can be used to make an impression in sealing wax as an identifying seal (see 3.VII.7.5: "Design your Personal Sigil").

Armbands: Though nowhere near as universal as pendants and rings, armbands, and wristbands are also worn by many magickal people. Often the designs for these are adapted from Celtic or Norse originals. Spiraling snakes are also popular, especially with women. Priestesses in some traditions wear a wide silver bracelet with certain inscriptions; priests wear a torque-like gold or brass bracelet with special symbols.

Earrings: Earrings are worn by practically all female Witches. Indeed, getting their ears pierced is an essential rite of passage for many girls. Pendant earrings with magickal designs—especially pentagrams and ankhs—are very popular among girls and women. This custom is also becoming more common among magickal menfolk, who tend to wear simpler designs, such as rings or posts.

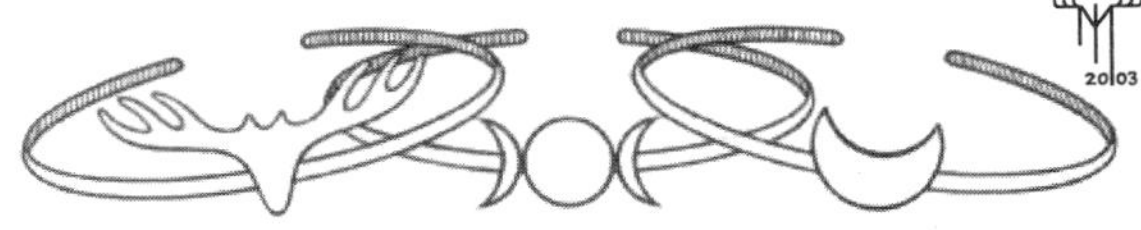

Headbands, tiaras, and circlets: Although you will seldom see them on the street, magickal people—especially women—often wear beautiful headbands, tiaras, circlets, and crowns when we are among our own kind, or in rituals. You will see many of these if you go to Renaissance Faires or magickal gatherings. Some may be very simple, such as a thin band with a pentagram, moon, or little horns on the front; these are often worn by priestesses and priests. Others may be of elaborate filigree or have large horns, antlers, or bird wings attached.

Lesson 9: The Wizard's Staff

A Wizard's staff is called a *verendum.* It is his most personal and important possession, and the one into which he puts the greatest part of his energy. It serves to contain, direct, and focus his personal *mojo;* it's practically a part of his body! Such a staff is traditionally of exactly the same height as the Wizard himself. Often it has a metal tip and is set atop with a large crystal. The crystal may be rigged to illuminate, as was Gandalf's. Mine is so designed. As with a magickal wand, athamé, or sword, a Wizard's staff is given a name of its own. Mine is called "Pathfinder," and it is known and recognized throughout the magickal community. Here is what it looks like:

Because a true Wizard's staff is invested with so much energy in its creation and its use, a Wizard will tend to have only one in his lifetime—unless something happens to it and he has to replace it. I have had my only staff since 1972. I even made a special shipping tube for it to go on airplanes, and I have carried it all over the world in my travels.

However, such a staff is no more suitable for an Apprentice Wizard than is a sword. There are several reasons for this. This first and most obvious is the matter of height. As long as you are still growing, any staff made to your exact height now will be outgrown in a few years and will have to be replaced. It is bad magick to put that kind of energy into a deeply personal magickal implement that will shortly become obsolete and have to be abandoned! Secondly, the degree of commitment and energy required to create a true Wizard's staff cannot be expected at the Apprentice stage of your training—any more than you can be expected to get married and have children at this stage in your life! Therefore, I will not be providing instructions in this Grimoire. However, if you wish to make and carry a simple walking staff, there is certainly nothing to stop you from doing so; just don't consider it to be a true Wizard's staff!

The Besom

Although much is made of Harry Potter's Nimbus 2000 magick broom, in reality, such enchanted brooms (called *besoms*) are not flown by Wizards, but only by Witches, who traditionally ride them in magickal flight and astral travel. The besom is basically the symbol for a female Witch, and it is her mystic vehicle for travelling in The Dreaming or between the dimensions.

As a phallic symbol, the besom is connected with a number of fertility rites. Jumping into the air while riding broomsticks used to be an old Magick ritual to encourage the crops to grow as tall as the broom riders could jump. The most popular use of the besom today is in the custom of "jumping the broomstick" at the conclusion of a handfasting (marriage) ceremony. Afterwards, the couple will hang the besom—decorated with ribbons and flowers—over their marriage bed or over the family altar. Such decorated besoms are favorite wedding gifts among magickal folk.

The best time to make or acquire a new broom is Ostara, or Spring Equinox (March 21). It is traditional for Witches to give their besom a name, just as Wizards do with their staffs. The besom should be ritually consecrated, and may be used to sweep clean a Magick Circle.

Here is some folklore concerning brooms: A broomstick laid across the threshold of a house, or set just inside the door, will keep bad luck or evil spirits from coming in. Placing a broom under the bed protects the sleepers in The Dreaming. Never sweep after sunset, or wandering spirits may be disturbed and happiness will be swept away. An old broom sweeps misfortune into a new home. Always sweep the inside of the house first, sweeping away from the door so that luck won't leave. Dust balls swept into the middle of a room will protect against bad luck. Wishes made while using a new broom for the first time will come true, as will wishes made if a broom is accidentally dropped while sweeping. But never use a new broom to sweep the outside of a house, or luck will be swept away with the dirt!

Class IV: Your Sanctum Sanctorum

Introduction: Your Magick Room

WIZARD'S PRIVATE STUDY IS called his *sanctum sanctorum,* which means "a place of utmost privacy and inviolability." If you are fortunate enough to have a room of your own in your house, you've probably already begun filling it with magickal things. If you continue to pursue these studies, you'll wind up with far more stuff than you can possibly display at any one time, so it's important at this early stage to develop some system. Perhaps there are also other rooms around your home that you can claim for certain purposes—like an attic, basement, garage, shed, or barn. But even if you live in a tiny apartment and share a bedroom with a kid brother, you can still imagine and plan for a future sanctum sanctorum.

Before you begin turning your room (or any other room in your home) into a wizardly sanctum sanctorum, you will need to get your parents' permission as to the space you use—and also get their ground rules about what can or cannot be done in that space. For instance, open flame (as in candles) or burning incense may be a no-no. And remember, no matter how "private" you may wish your sanctum to be, your mom *will* come in!

Lesson 2. Your Library of Arcana

The word *library* comes from the Latin *liber,* meaning "book." It has often been said that in a Wizard's home, every wall is covered with bookshelves. If there is one thing that Wizards are famed for, it is our love of knowledge. Hence every Wizard is at heart a librarian and a museum curator—and every Wizard's library is unique. As you acquire your own books, you should begin thinking of categories for them, and put them on different shelves, or separate them with other objects. My library began as a child when my parents acquired for me the *World Craft Encyclopedia* and *Child Craft Library.* Since then, my collection has grown to many thousands of books, and people come from all over to consult them. Here are some of the main categories in the Ravenheart Library:

1. **Magick**—lore and practice, comparative religions and traditions, systems of divination, Grimoires, Books of Shadows, spellbooks, etc.
2. **Science & Nature**—all the sciences, including geology, biology, zoology, ecology, physics, chemistry, astronomy, paleontology, etc.
3. **Weird Science**—UFOs, unexplained phenomena, anomalies, cryptozoology, Bigfoot, Loch Ness Monster, dragons, squid, bestiaries, etc.
4. **History**—archaeology, timelines, restorations, maps, travel, histories of every culture and civilization from the dawn of humanity.
5. **Myths & Legends**—stories from every people; Gods & Goddesses, epic adventures, creation myths, sagas, folk tales, Faerie lore, etc.
6. **Modern Fiction**—in my library, the vast majority of this is science fiction and fantasy!
7. **Art books**—all my favorite artists, plus books of photos, cartoons, graphic novels, comics, etc.
8. **References**—sets of encyclopedias, dictionaries, almanacs, Time/Life series, etc., both general and specific. I have LOTS of these!
9. **Videos, DVD's, tapes & CD's**—all my favorite movies and music, recordings of TV shows, series, and specials, etc.

At the back of this Grimoire, I'll list a few books to get you started on your own magickal library. As for the rest—you're on your own! Always check the used book sections of bookstores, junk shops, and flea markets, as many of the best books for your magickal library will be really old anyway. Another good source for old books is your public library, which periodically clears old books from their shelves to make way for new ones. Sometimes they'll put out a bin which people can go through and help themselves. You should get a library card in any case, and ask your librarian when they're doing their next giveaway.

Lesson 3. Your Temple

Your temple is the space where you will do nearly all of your magickal workings and rituals. This needn't be a large space, nor does it have to remain set up all the time. Your bedroom will do fine. The only permanent item in your temple is your altar, which you will hopefully have already set up clear back in 1.II: "Becoming a Wizard." This can be your own "Special Altar" to celebrate your life and the magic around you, and you can put on it anything you find particularly magickal.

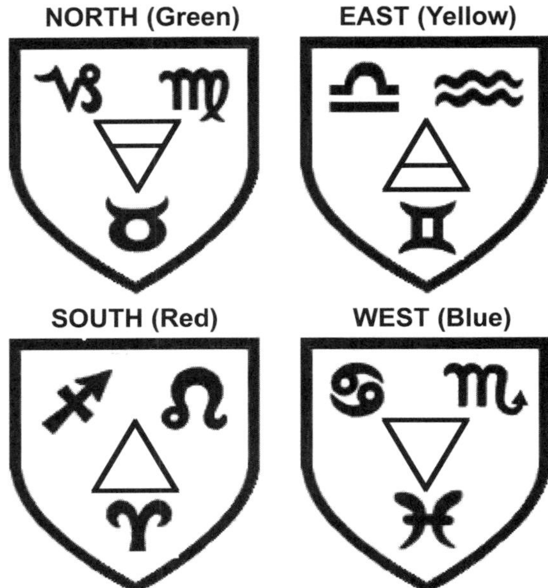

Your temple should have indicators of the four cardinal directions—East, South, West, and North. Determine which walls or corners of your room most nearly align to those directions, and then decorate them accordingly. Some people get very imaginative with this process, even hanging different colored banners of paper or cloth marked with appropriate sigils (see above). Others put up pictures that remind them of each of these Elemental directions, such as scenes of clouds (E), a fire or erupting volcano (S), the ocean (W), and mountains (N). And I have created a series of Elemental wall plaques to be used for this purpose.

Your temple should also have a space where you can lay out a Magick Circle. Traditionally, these were marked on the floor with a piece of chalk, then cleaned up afterwards with a damp cloth or sponge. If you have made your cingulum as I instructed in the last Class, you will have an easy way to measure and draw such a circle, by anchoring the first knot at the center, and holding the chalk at one of the other knots as you draw it around like a compass. You can also make a big circle of string.

Abby Willowroot has put together a beautiful online Goddess Temple and Green Man Grove that you might want to visit. It may be found at: *www.spiralgoddess.com.*

Lesson 4: Your Magickal Museum

Like T.H. White's Merlin, Wizards of old were famed for their "Cabinets of Curiosities." Such collections became the foundations of the world's great natural history museums. There are many natural (and unnatural) objects you can collect. Find a place in your room, like a table, desk, windowsill, or the top of a dresser, and make a special place for these magickal treasures you discover. Buying things is okay, but it's cooler to find treasures that others forget to notice.

For serious collecting, however, you might want to organize and display your collection. Small objects, no bigger than chicken eggs, can be organized in egg cartons. These work well for collections of rocks, minerals, and crystals, and may even be suitable for seashells if you stick with smaller ones. Larger objects will require larger display modules. You can usually find pigeonhole boxes of various sizes at stores that specialize in shelving and organizing materials. These can be of wood, plastic, or cardboard. Sometimes boxes from the grocery store that have held bottles will contain dividers, and these can be cut and adapted to make excellent collection organizers. A really nice collection also makes a great exhibit for school projects and science fairs. Whatever you are collecting, you should make a nice little identification card for each item. Then your life becomes one great scavenger hunt, as you search for items for your collection everywhere you go!

Collections

Seashells: These were one of the first things I collected as a boy, and I ended up displaying them on a large Masonite wallboard, running wires through the holes in the board to hold the shells in place.

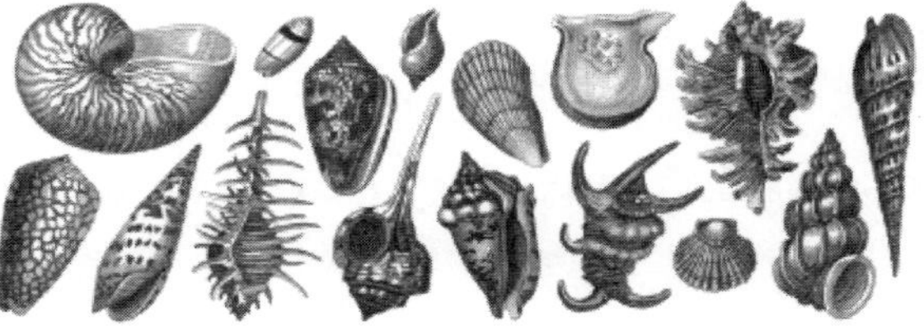

Leaves, Seeds, and Flowers: A great way to get to know your local Ents (as I mentioned in 2.IV: "Back to Nature") is to make a collection of dried leaves and seeds from all the trees you can find in your neighborhood. Or collect and press wildflowers, and see how many you can find! Pressed leaves and flowers don't take up much space, as they can be kept in a photo album. Don't forget to label them.

Rocks and Crystals: In collecting rocks, minerals and gems, you might keep in mind their magickal associations as well as their mineral qualities, and note these on the identifying cards. With nearly 2,000 different minerals on Earth, you can keep busy collecting samples for a long time! On the other hand, you might want to specialize, and just collect specific kinds of crystals.

Skulls: My favorite personal collection consists of dozens of different kinds of skulls of animals and birds that I have cleaned and prepared from road-kills since I was a boy. I find animal skulls to be absolutely fascinating, each with their unique architecture, dentition, and arrangements for the sense organs. When I find a fresh unsquashed road-kill, I carefully cut off the head; then I take it home and plop it into a pot of boiling water. Of course, I have to keep refilling the water, but after a few hours, all the flesh falls away from the bones, and I can carefully separate it out after a few rinses in a bowl of clear water.

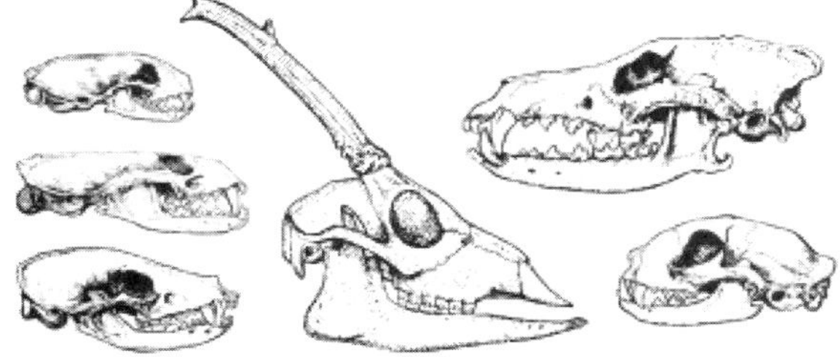

Be especially careful of the front teeth, as these will easily fall out and get lost once the flesh of the gums is gone. Good tools for cleaning skulls are dentists' probes (ask your dentist for used ones he would otherwise throw away), clay-working tools (from a crafts store), and an old toothbrush. I go over the teeth and skull joints carefully with white glue (wiping it down with a damp sponge), and then I glue the two halves of the jaws together (holding them with rubber bands). The final cleaned skull is a very beautiful thing.

Insects and Butterflies: When I was a boy at summer camp, my mentor, Captain Bennings, showed me how to make a net and collecting jar for butterflies, moths, and other interesting insects. I made display cases of shallow boxes with glass panes and developed quite a collection. The "Holy Grail" of butterfly collectors, however, is the elusive and ethereal Luna Moth, which is an unearthly pale green color like the *luciferin* in lightsticks. Finally, after many years of searching, I caught one. I killed it in the cyanide jar and proudly mounted it in my display case. And so I was absolutely devastated when its luminescent hue soon faded to a sickly straw-color. The Luna Moth, I learned, was a creature of Faerie, not meant to be killed and put on display for mortal eyes. And after that I never collected another butterfly.

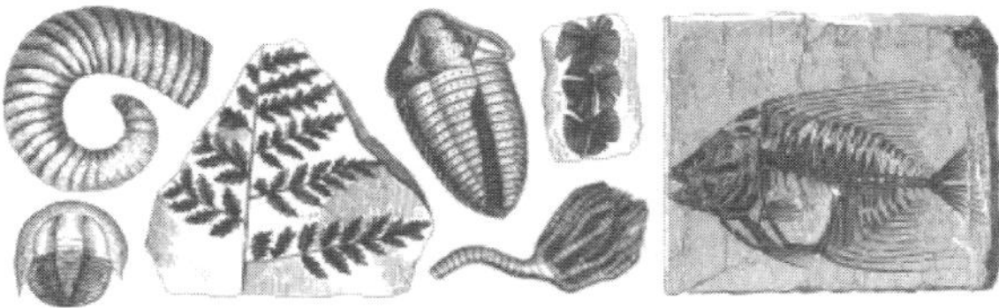

Fossils: Fossils are fun to collect, especially if you happen to live in some area where there are a lot of them. When I lived in the Midwest, I could often find fossils of *trilobites* and *brachiopods* along riverbanks. Egg cartons were perfect ways to display these. The *Golden Nature Guide to Fossils* is very helpful, with many specimens illustrated.

Indian Artifacts: There are no fossils in NorCalifia, where I live now, as these lands only formed fairly recently in geological time. But the ranch I lived on during many years was once a major camping area for the Pomo Indians, and many arrowheads, flints, scrapers, and other artifacts would turn up in the freshly turned earth of our gardens after rains. I never collected these, but other ranchers did, and this got them involved in native archeology and working with local tribes.

Curiosities: Really unusual "one of a kind" things are called *curiosities.* In this category, I have things like a meteorite *tektite* from the impact that killed the dinosaurs; a very realistic shrunken head made of goatskin; a human skull (from my days in medical school); and various little souvenirs and items of local handicraft I've picked up on my travels around the world.

Dioramas

Dioramas are little model scenes with miniature figures, landscaping, and painted backgrounds. I was always fascinated by these in museums when I was a lad, and so I made a number of my own. All you really need is a sturdy wooden box, which you lay on its side with the open top in front. Try and find a matching picture frame you can attach to the open front (junk stores and flea markets are great places to find such frames). You should install a little Christmas tree light in one of the upper front corners behind the frame to provide illumination. A background picture can be made from any painting or photo enlarged at a copy center. Glue it onto a sheet of cardboard, and wrap it around the inside back and side in a continuous curve, so there are no corners.

You can create a scene using action figures, railroad miniatures, D&D figurines, spaceships, animals, sea life, or (in my case) dinosaur models, as I've drawn for you here. The ground can be sculpted using "kitchen clay" with moss for grass and pebbles for boulders. Appropriate plants can be made using real twigs, ferns, etc.; or you can use plastic plants from aquarium supplies and miniature trees from railroad hobby stores. If you have a place to put them, you can have a lot of fun making such dioramas—and even enter them into science and hobby fairs

How to make kitchen clay: Mix 1 cup cornstarch with 2 cups bicarbonate of soda and 1 1/2 cups cold water. Add food coloring for color, and heat over medium burner, stirring constantly until you get a dough-like consistency. Cool, covered with a damp cloth, until you are ready to sculpt. A coat of shellac will seal and preserve the finished products.

Lesson 5. Models & Contraptions

Many Wizards have also been great inventors, such as Imhotep, Archimedes, and Leonardo da Vinci. They also tended to collect interesting and intricate gizmos and artifacts—especially timepieces and instruments for observing and plotting the motions of the heavenly bodies.

Globe & Maps: You should have at least one globe of the Earth, so you can familiarize yourself with your home planet. In addition to a modern globe, I have a small replica of a Renaissance globe with dragons and sea monsters. I found it at a junk store. I also have small globes of the Moon and Mars. All kinds of nifty maps from the National Geographic Society can also be found in junk stores, including star maps. If you have enough wall space, it's very wizardly to have a good map up; you can even change maps periodically, as I do (right now I have a map of Middle Earth up on my wall).

Sand Timers: Sundials, water clocks, astrolabes, hour candles, and sand timers (often generically called "hourglasses") were all invented ages before mechanical clocks. Of all these, sand timers are still widely available, and remain very useful. I keep several for different lengths of time, and we use them particularly for meetings, giving everyone the same amount of time in which to talk.

Leonardo's Ornithopter: Leonardo da Vinci (1452-1519) was the greatest Wizard of the Italian Renaissance. Of all his many achievements and inventions, however, he is most famed for his ingenious designs for a flying machine, which never actually flew. Unfortunately, Leonardo's studies of the flight of birds were based on small swallows. If he had studied large soaring birds like eagles, vultures, and albatrosses, he'd have realized that flapping wings were not the best plan for large flyers, and he'd have probably created a true hang glider. A flying machine with flapping wings is called an *ornithopter* (meaning "bird wings"), and various small versions that actually do fly are available in toy shops. I have several of these, and they are fun to display as well as fly.

27" wingspan working model of Leonardo da Vinci's Ornithopter by Coast Kites

Lesson 6. Menagerie

...six live grass snakes in a kind of aquarium, some nests of the solitary wasp nicely set up in a glass cylinder, an ordinary beehive whose inhabitants went in and out of the window unmolested, two young hedgehogs in cotton wool, a pair of badgers which immediately began to cry Yik-Yik-Yik-Yik in loud voices as soon as the magician appeared, twenty boxes which contained stick caterpillars and sixths of the puss-moth, and even an oleander that was worth two and six, all feeding on the appropriate leaves, ... an ants' nest

between two glass plates,...a nest of field mice all alive-o.... —T.H. White, *The Sword in the Stone,* pp. 33–34)

If you have room in your sanctum—or even elsewhere in your home—you might wish to create a little magickal menagerie of fascinating creatures. The most important thing about keeping any animals, of course, is knowing how to take proper care of them so they will thrive in your hands. Your local pet store will have little booklets on the care and keeping of various types of critters, and you should pick up copies of these for any animals you choose to keep.

Terraria (*terra,* "earth"): These are the easiest "starter kits" for small critters. All you need is a large aquarium with a secure screen lid. Measure the dimensions of the bottom, and then go out and cut a piece of natural sod to fit. Cut the sod about 3" thick, and leave room for a 3" deep water pan, at least 6" square, at one end. If you can get a square-sided pan of clear plastic or glass (like a baking pan), that would be ideal. Put it against the front of the aquarium so you can see underwater.

In such a terrarium you can keep frogs, toads, newts, turtles, lizards, small snakes, and large bugs—all of which you can find in the wild or buy in a pet shop. Of course, you should be aware that frogs, toads, turtles, and some snakes eat bugs and worms, and some snakes eat toads and frogs. So if you are particularly fond of any critters, don't put them in the same terrarium with their natural predators!

I recommend having a separate terrarium altogether for interesting bugs. There you can keep beetles, crickets, grasshoppers, spiders, centipedes, millipedes, grubs, worms, and caterpiggles (caterpillars, as some folks call them). Spiders, of course, eat smaller bugs, so you should gather a bunch of little insects just for spider food.

When I set up my first terrarium as a boy, I enjoyed going out into the fields and fens searching for little critters to take home and keep. In my insect terrarium, I collected caterpiggles and cocoons, and loved watching the new butterflies and moths break out and unfold their wings before I released them. One time I got hold of a praying mantis egg case (which can be ordered for pest control through garden stores). Each egg case hatches out about a hundred tiny mantids, and I had fun raising these up, feeding them first on fruit flies (easy to do; just leave an overripe banana in your terrarium with a small opening, and soon you'll have plenty!), and later on crickets. Mantids are notoriously cannibalistic, so long before they were grown there were only a few left. Eventually, of course, they escaped, and there were all these really weird 6"-long bugs all over the house.... I thought they were cool; my Mom was remarkably indulgent, as I look back....

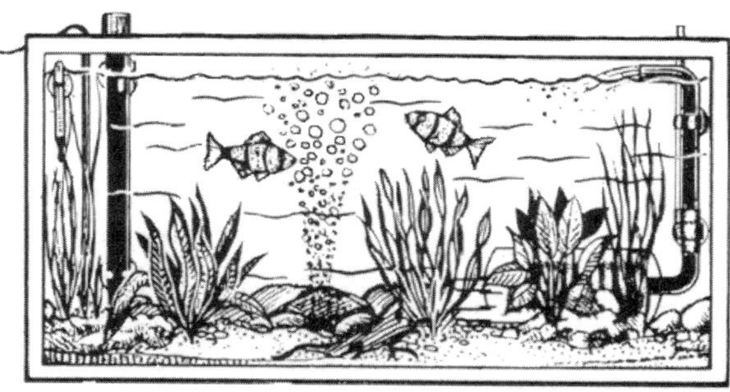

Aquaria (*aqua,* "water"): Of course, you can always go the fancy route, with store-bought tropical fish and cute little plastic castles, divers, and sunken ships. But my favorite aquariums were ones in which I planted natural water plants and filled with local pond life. I would go down to the marsh with a net and bucket, and catch crayfish, minnows, baby turtles, tadpoles, newts, snails, and water bugs. Some of these killed and ate each other, but I could always go and get replacements.

Aviaria (*avis,* "bird"): If you don't have a cat, and have room in your house, you can hang a birdcage and keep small birds, such as canaries, finches, and budgies. Make sure it's big enough for them! I have developed a great appreciation for birds since I learned that they are the last surviving dinosaurs!

Lesson 7: Resources

Supplies and equipment for your sanctum sanctorum can be obtained from various sources, some quite inexpensively. Stuff doesn't have to be new—in fact, the older the better! So the first place you should look is junk shops, used stuff stores, flea markets, yard sales, and so on. Just about everything I've mentioned above I have found in such places—quite cheap! Newer items may be found in magickal stores (look in your local Yellow Pages under "Metaphysical & Occult Supplies").

Here are a few on-line resources for magickal supplies:

My altar statues and Elemental wall plaques can be found at: *www.MythicImages.com.*

Abby Willowroot's metal wands, magickal jewelry, and altar items are at: *www.RealMagicWands.com.*

Don Waterhawk's incredible wizardly creations are at: *www.WaterhawkCreations.com.*

Katlyn Breen's incense, censers, books, mirrors, and oils are at: *www.HeartMagic.com.*

Beautiful cloaks, tapestries, drums, masks, and jewelry (including my designs) are at: *www.AncientCircles.com.*

Raven's Loft specializes in a wide variety of traditional occult supplies: *www.RavensLoft.biz.*

Class V: The Magickal World

1. Introduction: The Gathering

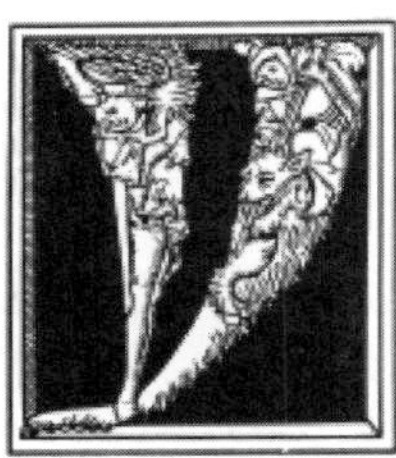

ES, THERE REALLY *IS* A WORLD OF magick beyond the boundaries of the mundane. Just over that hill, or inside that forest, or behind those doors, or down that country road, there are magickal people gathering. Everyone in long flowing robes and dark swirling capes and cloaks, faces mysterious behind paint or masks…Women wear lovely gowns of silk and velvet, corsets and bodices, or beautifully-batiked Balinese saris and sarongs, fantastic jewelry, armbands, necklaces, rings, anklets, and belly-dance belts, headdresses, tiaras, and pointy Witch's hats with wide brims…Men in kilts, khitons, leathers, breeches, togas, tunics, robes, and jerkins—helms and headbands with horns and antlers…and even more fantastic sights than can be described.

Come with me to the Gathering…

When you enter the gathering place, you are greeted with warm smiles and big hugs. Everyone tells you, *"Welcome Home!"* And you know they mean it, for you feel in your heart that, indeed, you *have* come Home. Music is playing everywhere, from madrigals to rock, from flutes to drums. Colorful banners flutter from walls, trees, tents, and pavilions. Hearty feasts are set, where crowds sit together at large tables, joking, laughing, and sharing stories in between bites. Children of various ages are running through it all in happy packs. Workshops teach mask-making, macramé, belly dance, chants, spells, drum-making, weaving, figure-sculpting, story-telling, cloak-making, drumming, healing, tarot-reading, crystal-gazing, fire-building, yoga, meditation, mead-making, and pretty much anything else imaginable that someone wishes to teach and others wish to learn. Circle after Circle comes together in the fields and groves, the rings of stones, the medicine wheels, and around great trees. Group after group conducts rituals enacting myths and Mysteries as old as Time and as new as Tomorrow. Circles range from silly to solemn, from loud and boisterous to totally silent.

If the gathering place is outdoors (as most are, when the weather is pleasant), there will be campfires in the evening, and candles and torches will light paths and shrines. As you walk into a circle of firelight, glowing faces turn to welcome you. Folks make room around the fire, and pull up a seat for you (it may be just a log…). Someone passes you a chalice or drinking horn, saying "Never thirst." Folks are singing songs, or telling jokes and stories. At the big central bonfire, there will definitely be drumming and dancing around the fire—and this could go on all night. At some gatherings, there will even be a midnight fireworks and laser show.

And wherever you go, you are welcomed.

Lesson 2. The Magickal Marketplace

The real-life magickal marketplace is more fantastic than any bazaar from the *Arabian Nights*. The finest craftspeople of the New Renaissance proudly display their best arts and handiworks—all in one place! There are wands, knives, swords, staves and chalices; robes, cloaks, gowns, hats, and capes; jewelry, headgear, horns, and chain mail; books, cards, paintings and posters; statues, figurines and dolls of goddesses, faeries, dragons, and unicorns; creatures, crystals, candles, and cauldrons; masks, music, and magick.

But you don't have to wait 'til you go to your first magickal gathering to shop in the magickal marketplace. There is hardly a major city in the English-speaking world today that doesn't have at least one magickal store, and some may be found even in small towns. In black and Hispanic neighborhoods, they are called *botanicas* ("herb shops"). You can look these up in your local *Yellow Pages* under "Metaphysical/Occult Stores." Or you can check them out on-line state-by-state at The Witch's Voice: *http://www.witchvox.com/links/net_books.html.* Though all these stores are independent, many are interconnected, and most of them carry my statues and jewelry. You can tell 'em Oberon sent you!

These metaphysical and occult stores are your best gateway into the magickal community. Get to know the folks who work there. They will usually have a bulletin board listing events, contacts, and local groups. Many of them offer classes on various magickal topics, and sometimes they will bring in speakers and presenters (I often make guest appearances at such stores). Don't be surprised, however, if some stores won't let you attend classes or buy materials without the permission of your parents, as they don't want to get into trouble with mundane parents.

Lesson 3: Faires, Festivals and Pagan Gatherings

If you happen to have been blessed by being born into a magickal family, you will surely have already attended such gatherings as I have described above—and could even add much to what I have said here! If you have magickal friends at school who come from mundane families, you can let them know that it's all true. If your parents are mundane, but you feel drawn to the magickal path and world (you must be, or you certainly would not be reading this Grimoire!), seek out other magikids at your school (look for those pentagrams!). Some of them will have magickal families, and perhaps they can introduce you to the magickal world.

Here are several events that occur annually in or near many large cities, and that are always attended by many real magickal folk. These are open to the public and widely advertised in local papers, so check the "Entertainment" sections. Once you learn to recognize us at these events by our dress and jewelry, you'll be able to make many magickal friends.

Renaissance Faires

"Ren Faires," as we call them, are the most public of these gatherings, being held every weekend over a couple of months and advertised everywhere. The Ren Faire is sort of like an outdoor theme park set in a fantasy version supposedly recreating the period of the English Renaissance in the late 1500s. The common language spoken at the Faire is *Elizabethan*—the English of Shakespeare. Sometimes there will be elements of historical accuracy, such as having Queen Elizabeth or Henry VIII as the reigning monarch. Unlike the real Middle Ages and Renaissance, however, there's no Black Plague or Witch-burnings here, and magickal people are quite public!

I started doing Ren Faires in 1980, the year our first unicorns were born. That was when I first began to appear in public with them as a Wizard, in my robe and cloak, and carrying Pathfinder, my then-10-year-old staff. My lifemate, Morning Glory, appeared as an Enchantress. Over the next few years, the fame of our unicorns spread so widely that we were invited to bring them to every Ren Faire in the United States and Canada. I've often wondered how many people realized that the Wizard was as real as the unicorn!

At the Faire, there will be jousting matches with

Houston Sun, *Sept. 29, 1982* *(Photo by Carol Shugart)*

armored knights battling on horseback with real lances. Bands of pirates will fence with wicked swords over looted booty—"Aaarr!"—and will teach you a bit of swordplay, if you wish. Gypsies will be camped in the woods, with gaudily painted wagons, and will tell your fortune by cards and crystal balls. You might meet Robin Hood, Maid Marian, and the green-clad Merry Men and Women of Sherwood Forest. Real Wizards and Witches will be afoot—cleverly disguised as Wizards and Witches of fantasy (but you'll know if you check out their rings…).

The marketplace at the Faire goes on and on—with all that I have described above, and more! This is where I got my astrolabe and pocket sundials. Beautiful costumes like those worn by regular Faire-goers can be purchased at specialty boutiques. Exotic foods can be bought at stalls—such as "Toad in the Hole," shepherd's pies, turkey legs, the Queen's buns, and the King's nuts. On stages small and large, performers will be acting out sidesplitting comedies—and may even bring you on stage to join them if you stand too close! Strolling minstrels, musicians, and magicians provide continuous entertainment, and bawdy wenches in overflowing bodices will turn your head and give you whiplash.

And here's a good hint for you: Don't go to the Ren Faire in mundane clothes, such as jeans and a T-shirt. Dress in your most magickal regalia, or even a simple tunic and leggings. Rent a Shakespeare movie, like *Romeo and Juliet*, *A Midsummer Night's Dream*, or *Shakespeare in Love*, and learn to speak in Elizabethan. The best way to enjoy the show is to become part of it! Try and talk your parents into taking you (get them to dress up too!), and bring your friends.

Pagan Festivals and Gatherings

Many (though not all) people in the magickal community are involved in the Pagan spiritual movement. Pagan festivals and gatherings, however, are not generally open to the public, and seldom advertised. The description I gave at the beginning of this Class depicts a typical outdoor Pagan festival—and there are hundreds of these going on every year, all over the world. Ones I've been to range in size from less than a hundred participants to over 1,500. While most are held outdoors, there are also several Pagan hotel conventions held in different cities each year—such as Pantheacon, held every February in San Jose, Califia. These are very much family events, and if your family is Pagan, you will have already been to some. However, minors are not admitted without legal guardians (or at least signed permission slips), so if your folks aren't Pagans, you'll have to wait to attend such a gathering.

Lesson 4. Working With Others

During your early apprenticeship, you will probably be doing much of your magickal studies and practices alone. Hopefully, though, you will soon be meeting other Magikids at school. When you do, you may want to form a "magicklub" or study group. There's a lot of stuff you can do as a group that you can't do all by yourself.

Forming a school study group: Most high schools have all sorts of special-interest study groups, and if you have some friends interested in Magick and Wizardry, you might want to form such a study group. You will need the sponsorship of a teacher. Find the coolest teacher you know—especially someone who really likes Harry Potter—and ask for help. You will have to arrange a meeting time and place. A study group is not a place to do actual magick, spells, or rituals, but you can talk about your magickal studies, share ideas, discuss magickal books you're reading, do divinations for each other, play games, and make things together, following the instructions I've given throughout this Grimoire. You might even do some of the exercises I've given you to develop your psychic powers. And, of course, you can play various magickal games (see the next Lesson).

Once you have a Wizardry or Magick study group meeting, you will have plenty of other kids wanting to join it, so you might consider giving them some assignment, such as reading a certain book that everyone else has read, before you can just let anybody in. I recommend that, once you have the first little group together, any new member should come in only by the agreement of all those members already in.

Forming your own magickal group: Once you have a group together, you might want to decide on a place to meet where you can set up a temple or circle and actually do some magick. You will want to pick a regular time to get together for this—once a month is the usual practice ("...and better it be when the Moon is full," said Aradia to the Witches). But if you're meeting indoors, you may have other considerations than the phase of the Moon. Each day of the week has its own magickal associations (see Tables of Correspondence in the next Class), and you might even want to try and meet on different days to do different kinds of magick.

And of course you will want to have a cool name. You might name your group after a mythical creature, a magickal symbol (like ankh, pentagram, caduceus, etc.), something from a favorite story, or anything else you want! One of the most famous magickal groups, for instance, was called the Order of the Golden Dawn, and the 5th book in the Harry Potter series is called *The Order of the Phoenix*.

Networking online: At the time of this writing, there don't seem to be any online websites or chat groups dedicated to Wizardry or Magick that are suitable for teens, and that aren't specifically *Pagan* or *Wiccan*-oriented. Paganism and Wicca are *religious* orientations, whereas Magick and Wizardry are *studies* and *practices* that are independent of any particular religion. And I'd like to keep it that way! So we have created a special online **Grey School of Wizardry** for you at *www.GreySchool.com* where you may further your studies and meet other students.

Finding a magickal group: There may already be a Magickal group in your area. Again, check with your local occult store. Sometimes semi-public groups will leave flyers or notices at such stores. They may host a monthly open house, or occasionally offer a class or introductory presentation through the store. If you find there is an open meeting that you can attend, bring along a couple of your magickal friends; if your parents are interested and sympathetic, you might want to bring them along too. Some groups do have special programs for teens, but you will have to have parental permission to participate. Still, you might at least get to meet some of the people.

However, I do *not* recommend that you go out and try to *join* any existing group at this stage. First, you should get to know the folks in a number of different groups, so you will have a basis of comparison. You are still an Apprentice, and the best way for you to learn the wizardly arts is to study these lessons, do these tasks and Quests, work with your closest friends, and build up your own little Circle of Magick. Learn everything you can from others, of course—read any books that interest you, attend workshops and classes, ask lots of questions (Question Authority!), and make friends of those you respect. There'll be plenty of time to join a group later on, if you want to—after you've developed your own sense of what's what and who's who.

Lesson 5: Wizard Games

These magickal games are designed to develop and hone your magickal skills and powers. They will challenge and stimulate your imagination, your quick thinking, your vocabulary, and your powers of observation. They're also fun and can be played anywhere. And the best thing is, you don't need to buy any special equipment, shoes, uniforms, books, playing pieces, trading cards, or CDs!

Elven Chess: A Game for All Seasons

(by Diane Darling [as taught by Eldri Littlewolf])

Elven Chess is a game of cooperative pattern-making, and a favorite in our community. Like many wonderful things, it has its roots in the beginningless past. I was taught it by my friend Eldri Littlewolf, but this game is not only for were-coyotes and naked apes. It is played by several kinds of birds as well as octopuses, at least one cat, sea worms, some kinds of crabs, and, of course, Elves. Elven Chess may even be the game we can play with extraterrestrials!

Elven Chess can be played by any number of people, but it becomes too slow with more than four or five. Children and adults can play together. Elven Chess answers the question, "What am I going to do with all my neat little stuff?" Elven Chess can be played anywhere, with or without special pieces. It requires cooperation and sharing. Everyone wins. It has only three rules, any of which may be broken if everyone agrees:

1. *In each turn you may move three pieces.*
2. *Turns go clockwise.*
3. *The game is over when everyone is done.*

That's all. Now let's see how to get set up.

First, you and the other players will each want to have your own Elven Chess sets. Take a basket around your room (or your house) and fill it with small special things—like shells, beach wrack, beads, buttons, crystals, little animal bones, polished rocks, jewelry, small odd-shaped pieces of driftwood or twigs, tiny gaming figurines—even glow-in-the-dark rubber cockroaches if you like! It is useful to have more than one of some things—such as four arrowheads, nine tiny shells, two chicken wishbones, a dozen small polished stones—though most pieces will be one-of-a-kind. Any amount of stuff from a handful to a small basketful will be enough, and your set will grow as time goes by. Now find a beautiful scarf or other piece of cloth. Round or square are best, and of a mostly solid color (though tie-dies can be pretty cool!). This is your Elven Chess board; keep it in the basket with the other stuff.

Now to play. In an out-of-the-way place, sit in a circle on the floor or around a table with the other players. Spread the cloth out smoothly in the center. Everyone dumps their Elven Chess pieces at the edge of the board in front of them. Arrange your set for easy sharing, and admire each other's little treasures. Decide in your own way who will move first. (Rolling dice works well.) This person may now place three pieces from his or anyone else's set upon the board. Then the next person may place three pieces. Moving a piece already on the board counts as a move, but wait one turn before changing someone else's move, or ask his permission.

There are no accidents in Elven Chess. A caterpillar crossing the board, a ferret stealing the rubber cockroach, all count as moves. Very beautiful moves may be appreciated softly *("Oooh...").* And so on, until no one wants to make another move, and everyone is satisfied with the design. Every game is different, but patterns such as circles, spirals, linked chains, snowflakes, and smiling faces will appear again and again. This is wonderful. Certain pieces will also be used for favorite moves in many games. After all players are finished, admire and talk about the pattern. Elven Chess games look very different from each player's place, so go around and look to see what each other player sees. At the end, take back your pieces. You may want to gift or trade with others at this time.

Elven Chess may be played every day if we are open to the idea of cooperative pattern-making. One game was played using only M&Ms as pieces. Altars, salads, shelves, your entire room, or your back yard may be used to play this ancient game. It can also be played at the beach with driftwood and sea wrack. The great stone circles of our ancestors, Zen gardens, your garden, Bowerbird nests, and octopuses' gardens in the shade are all examples of Elven Chess. The game can be as small as the reach of your hand, or as large as your whole life.

Observation

This can be played with 2–6 people. Each player needs a sketch pad and a good pencil with an eraser. Also needed are a bell, a watch or clock with a second hand, a serving tray, and a large enough opaque cloth to cover it. Each player takes a turn at being "Setter," until everyone has had the same number of turns. Here's how it's played:

The Setter takes the tray and cloth into a different room, away from the other players—preferably a room with lots of little things (like my study!). There he/she finds eight objects small enough to arrange on the tray, without any of them touching each other, and sets them up (hint: Don't include things than can roll around, like eggs or marbles!). Then the Setter covers them all with the cloth, and brings the tray back into the room with the players, setting it down in front of them. All players should close their eyes, take a few deep breaths, and center themselves. The Setter rings the bell, at the same time removing the cloth. The players all immediately open their eyes and look at the objects on the tray, committing each of them and their position to memory.

After 30 seconds, the Setter again rings the bell, and covers the tray. The players should each close their eyes again, and take a few more deep breaths, holding the image in their mind as a visualization. Then, when they are ready, each player opens their eyes and attempts to draw the objects and his positions on their sketch pad. As soon as he is done, he should lay the pencil down. When all are done, the cloth is removed, and scores are listed according to how many objects each player has indicated in their proper place. The drawings do not have to be good—even very crude sketches will do, as long as it's clear what they are of, and they are in approximately the right position in relation to the others.

Then the next person takes a turn at being Setter, in exactly the same way—using different objects, or some of the same ones, as they choose. When each player has taken a turn as Setter, the first round is completed. For the 2nd round, however, use 10 objects, and only allow 25 seconds for the players to look at them. For the 3rd round, use 12 objects and allow 20 seconds. For the 4th round, use 14 objects and allow 15 seconds. And the 5th and last round should use 16 objects and allow 10 seconds viewing.

Add up the scores for each person. The more you play this game, the better you'll get at being able to instantly take in visual information and hold it as a visualization in your mind. You'll find this skill to be immensely valuable in many ways.

Advanced version: Use a large pizza-baking pan for the tray, and cut a circle of paper to fit it. Use a compass to draw three concentric circles about the same distance apart. Then draw radiating lines out from the center to divide each ring, and mark them as follows: Inner circle—yin/yang. Next circle—divide in four, mark with glyphs for Elements. 3rd circle—divide in seven, mark with glyphs for Planets. Outer circle—divide in 12, mark with glyphs for Signs of the Zodiac. Then when placing objects, arrange them within various of these sections.

Using this game as a magickal exercise: Learn to fix the image of the objects on the tray as one single picture, and practice holding it so strongly and vividly that when you open your eyes, you can still see an image of the objects hanging in the air above them. Practice holding the image for longer times. Start with only one object, and work your way up to where you can do this with many.

The Never-Ending Story

This is an old favorite to play around the campfire with 6–12 friends. Story-telling is a very important Wizardly art, and through playing this game you'll get quite good at it. Stories like this always start out with some ritual phrase to let you know that a story is about to begin and to set it in the past, such as: *"Once upon a time..."* or *"Long, long ago in a galaxy far away..."* or *"When I was your age,"* or *"One time, at band camp...."*

So the way the Never-Ending Story goes is like this: You start the story by saying something like: *"Once, long ago, I set out to...and this is what happened...."* And you make up a silly, outrageous, funny, weird sequence of events that took "you" to a bizarre cliff-hanger situation—like on a TV series where they say, "To be continued...." Don't take too much time in your turn—I recommend getting a three-minute sand timer, and passing it around to each person in turn to time themselves. Wind up by saying something like: *"So there I was (hanging upside-down over the alligator pit), and then...."* And that's when you pass the timer—and the story—to the next person, who has to pick it up from there, with *"...and then..."*

Each person continues telling the story in the first person (*"I"*). The Never-Ending Story can go anywhere your imaginations can take it, as you'll have no idea where the adventure will be at when it comes your turn to pick it up. The most important thing to remember is, at the end of each turn, when the sand in the timer runs out, the story-teller must say, *"...and then..."* as he passes the ball to the next in line. There are no losers in this game—everybody wins!

Word Games

Hinky-Pinky: *Hinky-Pinky* is a traditional Wizard game—and a fun one to play in the car on a long trip! It can be played with as few as two people. It's about creating two-word expressions in which all the syllables of one word rhyme with all the syllables of another. Depending on how many syllables the words have, these are called "Hink Pinks" (one syllable), "Hinky Pinkys" (two syllables), and "Hinkety Pinketys" (three syllables). It's played like this: You think of a rhyme (the Hinky Pinky), and then come up with a definition that you offer as a riddle. Other players have to guess the Hinky Pinky that answers it. Here are some easy samples—you'll have to build up your own collection yourself:

"What's a Hink Pink for an obese feline?"
Answer: *"A fat cat!"*

"What's a Hinky Pinky for a magical snowstorm?"
Answer: *"A Wizard blizzard!"*

"What's a Hinkety Pinkety for magickal embroidery?"
Answer: *"Witchery stitchery!"*

The thing about Hinky Pinky is you can just spring one on anyone who knows the game, anytime you feel like it—even with other people around, like in the lunchroom. This is my favorite word game! So, what's a Hinky Pinky for the favorite beverage of a Celtic Priest?

Fictionary: *Fictionary* requires a dictionary—preferably one with really obscure words. There's one we like to use called *Mrs. Byrne's Dictionary of Unusual Words.* This game plays best with 5–10 people. Everyone needs to have a little notepad and an indelible pen. Each player in turn gets to be the Fictionaire and take the dictionary and search for some really odd word that no one playing would know. Then the Fictionaire writes down the word on a paper and writes under it three definitions, numbering them in random order. Two of these should be completely made up, but seem plausible; the third should be an actual definition from the dictionary (if there are more than one, pick any one you like!).

Then the Fictionaire reads the word aloud to everyone, and the definitions, numbers 1, 2, and 3. The players write it down and try to guess which is the real definition, and write that number down on their notepad. Anyone who gets it right scores a point. Then you pass the dictionary to the next person in turn.

The Wizard's Cat: This game is best with at least a dozen players, and can be done with many more. It's especially good around a campfire. Sitting in a circle, everyone chants together: *"The Wizard's cat is a _____ cat!"* Taking turns around the circle (*deosil,* of course), one at a time, each person has to fill in the blank with a one-word adjective describing the Wizard's cat. But the trick is, each person's word has to start with the next letter in the alphabet! An example might be:

1st player: *"The Wizard's cat is an Angry cat!"*
2nd player: *"The Wizard's cat is a **B**eautiful cat!"*
3rd player: *"The Wizard's cat is a **C**alico cat!"*
4th player: *"The Wizard's cat is a **D**irty cat!"*

...and so on through the alphabet, and around the circle. The chant has to move right along with no pause between each turn. To keep the rhythm steady, everyone claps on the main syllables: *"The **WIZ**ard's **CAT** is a **HAP**py **CAT**!"* If someone cannot think of a word when their turn comes, they have to drop out. You can make it tougher as it goes along by slowly increasing the tempo of the clapping. The game can go on as long as you want, or until you reach the end of the alphabet, or until there's only one survivor.

Wizards' Whispers: (Say it aloud several times rapidly!) This is a variation of "Telephone"; the more players, the better. Everyone sits in a circle. You start by writing down a magickal term and a short definition, just like in the Glossaries I've put here and there in this Grimoire (in fact, you can just use these glossaries for this game). An example might be: *"Magick is the art of probability enhancement."* Then, without letting anyone else see what you've written, whisper your sentence into the ear of the person on your left. That person, in turn, must whisper those same words to the next, and so on around the circle.

Each person should pass on exactly what they *think* they heard, whether or not it seems to make sense. When it gets back to you (or whomever started), speak it aloud to everyone, and then read aloud the original statement you'd written down. Invariably the original sentence will get so garbled as it is passed from person to person that the final version can be quite humorous! For the next round, the next person in the circle starts in the same way.

Psychic Games

Games to demonstrate psychic abilities are popular for small circle meetings of 5–7 people. Here are a few examples:

Levitation: One person sits in a chair and four people stand around the sitter. The people put their right index fingers under the armpits and knees of the person who is sitting and try to lift him or her. Generally, it can't be done. Then the standing people put their hands over the head of the sitter, raising and lowering their hands together to the count of five. They quickly place their index fingers as before and easily lift the sitting person into the air.

Rigor Mortis: One person lies down on the floor, on his/her back, arms at sides, eyes closed, and prepares to go into a trance, breathing deeply and steadily. The other people line up on either side and count slowly backwards from 10 to 0 while gently stroking the person from head to toes. At the count of *"zero,"* everyone says *"Rigor Mortis!"*—whereupon the person goes completely rigid, stiff as a board. Then everyone picks the person up and lays him/her like a bridge between two facing chairs, feet on one and head on the other. If you have done this successfully, you can sit on the belly of the "bridge" person and he/she won't collapse!

Free Fall: This one is often used in Initiations, and is a lot of fun. One person stands on a low stool, cinder block, or box—no more than a foot off the ground. Another person stands in front of him/her and says: *"Close your eyes and breathe deeply. Feel safe and secure, completely trusting that no harm shall come to you. Lock your knees so your legs won't bend, and prepare to fall backwards."* Meanwhile, everyone else gets behind the person on the stool and prepares to catch him/her. After giving the person a moment to prepare, the one in front touches a finger to the breastbone of the one on the stool, and gently pushes him/her backwards. And everyone else catches him/her, and lifts them high in the air, before setting him/her back on his/her feet.

Transmission: People pair up, sitting back to back. Each person has a notepad and pencil. Taking turns, one person (the Sender) thinks of an image and draws a picture of it, concentrating and focusing on transmitting it to the other person while drawing. The other person (the Receiver) tries to pick up the image his partner is sending and draw it on his own pad. Do three different images before switching Senders and Receivers. Then compare drawings and see how close you've come. After a set of six images (three in each turn), switch partners with someone else, until everyone has gotten a chance to pair up with everyone else.

Dowsing: One person hides a quarter somewhere in the room (or yard, if outside). Tape another quarter to the center of a Y-shaped forked "dowsing" stick. Holding the ends of the two branches in your hands, and using the main part of the stick as a pointer, try to locate the hidden coin. You can make up as many dowsing sticks as needed for everyone to search at the same time. Whoever finds it keeps the quarter!

Role-Playing Games

(by Jack Griffin)

Role-playing games are a great way to learn what it's like to see the world from another's eyes. In their way, all role-playing games can be considered a form of acting—a seemingly mundane skill with roots in true magickal shapeshifting. Though there are many different types of role-playing games, each has this in common: It offers the chance to be someone else, to experience what it might have been like to be a hero (or a villain), and to live inside of a story.

When playing a role-playing game, imagine what it would be like to *be* that character. Try to see yourself as that person inside the story, and listen to the images presented. Smell the winds. Hear the horses gallop. Experiment. See what happens. Perhaps the spirit of that character will teach you something. When interacting with the other players, try to think like that being would, in that instance. Why are they the way they are? What motivates them to be who they are?

In their way, role-playing games provide a beautiful framework for a shared dream, allowing us to express parts of ourselves that might be difficult to let out in mundane society. But be warned. Role-playing games are a powerful tool and can be seductive. The idea of living in the story of a hero, free from crisis and challenge, is compelling. It is a challenge to take the story's lessons to the beautiful world beyond it. Our ability to project ourselves into different worlds is no less important than our ability to pull ourselves back from them.

Class VI: Correspondences

Lesson 1: Systems of Classification

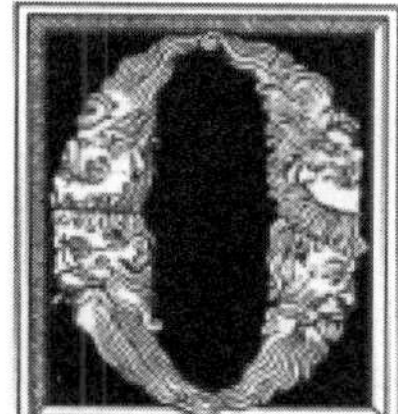

NE OF THE MOST IMPORTANT ASPECTS of magickal thinking is classifying the world in terms of associated *correspondences*. By sorting things into different categories, we gain a powerful understanding of them on a deep symbolic level. Thus we reduce the infinite diversity of Nature into something that our minds can grasp and make sense of.

All of the natural sciences began as systems of classification based on perceived commonalities. In biology, for example, Carl Linnaeus (1707–1778) developed a sorting system of only seven *taxonomic* ("arranged by law") categories into which every single living thing is ranked. Originally published in his *Systema Naturae* ("Systems of Nature"), in 1735, this is called the **K-P-C-O-F-G-S** system, for **K**ingdom, **P**hylum, **C**lass, **O**rder, **F**amily, **G**enus, and **S**pecies, with each being listed under the previous, as in an outline. Here's how the Linnaean classification works for you (and every other person):

I. Kingdom *Animalia* (animals—contains 10 *Phyla*)
- **1. Phylum** *Chordata* (having spinal chords—contains 10 *Classes*)
  - **A. Class** *Mammalia* (having milk glands—contains 20 *Orders*)
    - **a. Order** *Primates* (having opposable thumbs—contains 15 *Families*)
      - **(1) Family** *Hominidae* (apes—contains 5 *Genera*)
        - **(A) Genus** *Homo* (humans—now only 1 *Species*, though there used to be others)
          - **(a) Species** *Sapiens* ("thinking;" modern humans: us)

Tree of Evolution

Taxonomy is a classification system of *vertical hierarchy,* in which multiple members of each group are subsumed into the next higher *taxon.* At the top level of Kingdoms, there are only three: Plants, Animals, and Fungi. But at the lower levels, there are no set limits to the number of members of each taxon; more than 40,000 species of spiders have so far been identified! Vertical classification schemes can be diagrammed as a branching tree, just like the tree of evolution shown here.

Now think of the Sorting Hat at Hogwarts which grouped every incoming student into one of four Houses, according to their essential nature.

HOUSE	**GRYFFINDOR**	**RAVENCLAW**	**HUFFLEPUFF**	**SLYTHERIN**
FOUNDER	Godric Gryffindor	Rowena Ravenclaw	Helga Hufflepuff	Salazar Slytherin
HEAD	Minerva McGonagall	Professor Flitwick	Professor Sprout	Severus Snape
MASCOT	Lion	Raven	Badger	Snake
COLOR	Red	Blue	Yellow	Green
QUALITIES	Brave, daring	Intelligent, witty	Loyal, hardworking	Sly, power-hungry

This is a *lateral,* or horizontal system of classification, in which each of the categories are essentially equal. Lateral systems of correspondence are the basis of all magickal ordering. By understanding a thing's correspondences, a magician can influence that thing. The key to their use is simply the number of divisions, as in these Houses. Although one might imagine that such numbers could go to infinity, for most practical uses only about a dozen are actually needed. Here are some examples for each number:

1 Singularities: ("There can be only One!")
2 Dualities: Yin-Yang (Taoism)
3 Trinities, Triads, Triplicities
4 Directions, Seasons, Elements
5 Elements (Pythagorean)
6 Realms of Existence (Buddhism)
7 Days of Week, visible Planets
8 Sabbats in Wheel of Year (see 4.VI)
9 Psychic Centers in Body (Taoism)
10 Sephiroth on Tree of Life (Qabalah—see 5.V)
11 (There are no sets of 11 anything…)
12 Signs of the Zodiac, months of the year

> Dutch Grey Council member Luc Sala says: "Correspondences are the connections or links between the various worlds, kingdoms, traditions, worldviews, cultures, etc. If we see the whole of the Universe as having unseen dimensions, as we do in magick, then there are innumerable possible connections between those dimensions or worlds. However, some of those links are special, and they can be compared with the nerve connections in our body in that they take care of the information flow. They are the invisible but powerful links between the worlds and can be used to convey the magickal messages."

Lesson 2: The Magick Circle

> The four-quartered Circle of Magick is a central component in most rituals. It is called the portal between the worlds, a means of connecting with the deities, spirits, and Elemental powers of a realm beyond the material Universe. It is envisioned as a vortex within which we focus our innate psychic powers, called forth by ritual actions from the subliminal depths of the mind and soul. It is a sacred space, a sanctuary for communion with the Old Ones.
>
> Many levels of symbolism are intrinsic to the Circle: Images and truths of diverse colours and textures speak in a language as old as human history. Among these are metaphysical and mystical concepts that describe the greater reality within which our lives are experienced. The four "corners" of the Circle of Magick correspond with the compass directions and each is associated with an Element: Earth, Air, Fire, or Water. A fifth Element, Spirit, is often associated with the center of the Circle or with the Circle as a whole. The vertical axis (*axis mundi* or world axis) is an essential part, sometimes seen as a tree connecting the three worlds.
>
> The realm of wind, water, stone, and flesh is manifest Spirit; the realm of Earth, Moon, Sun, and stars is manifest Spirit. Time and space, energy and gravity, the realm of imagination, memory, emotion, and desire, all are Spirit manifest: that which can be named and known. Yet the aspect of Spirit that transcends naming and knowledge, incomprehensible in its mystery, is the Source of Heaven and Earth.
>
> —Bran th' Blessed

All of the various magickal systems of correspondences can be diagrammed on the Magick Circle, which is read like a clock face. This is done by overlaying a series of polygrams, with their points evenly spaced around the Circle, as at the numbers on the clock. Outer concentric circles are then divided into the appropriate number of segments, just like the hours and minutes on a clock face. And like the hands of a clock, time as well as magickal work moves through each of those segments *sequentially* (one after another) in a Dance of the Hours.

It is important to understand, however, that all these systems have just been made up. Their usefulness comes not from them being the actual *territory,* but from them being common *symbolic maps* that many magickal people share and understand. Most of these magickal systems were developed a long time ago and were based on the limited scientific knowledge of the people who created them (at that time, for instance, people thought the Sun revolved around the Earth…). These systems can still work for us today, but their limits have to be recognized, and they often have to be tweaked to adjust for the problems in their original design.

But you don't have to *believe* in everything that's in here in order to successfully become a Wizard. It's entirely possible to be an effective magician without believing in astrology, for example. This is particularly important to remember because you're going to have science teachers who will either react dismissively or outright mock you if you raise topics like astrology, chakras, and other magickal studies.

Back in 2.I.4, "The Circle of Life," I explained the difference between the mundane view of Time as *linear* (going in a straight line in one direction, from past to future), and the magickal view of Time as *cyclical* (looping around and around again in an endless circling spiral, like a spring). This same distinction applies to these two systems of classification. Just as the branching Tree is the key pattern for all linear systems of vertical classification, the Magick Circle is the key to the circular categories of all magickal systems. After counting off 12 hours, the hands of the clock come round again to the same point—but Time itself has now moved forward half a day on the spiraling cycle!

> *We shall not cease from exploration*
> *And the end of all our exploring*
> *Will be to arrive where we started*
> *And know the place for the first time.*
> —T.S. Eliot in the last of his *Four Quartets*

On the next page is a *mandala* diagram I have drawn of the Magick Circle. Correspondences of 2, 3, 4, 5, 6, 7, 8, 12, and 13 are shown. In addition, I have divided the outermost rings into 52 "minutes" for the weeks of the year, and 366 "seconds" for the days (one extra for leap year). Different versions of this design will be used throughout this class to illustrate various sets of correspondences. If you want to try something really cool, make a copy the same size as the face of your wall clock, and color it in with markers. Then open up the front of your clock and glue it into place.

Lesson 3: Monads, Dyads, and Triads

Monads and Unities

Monism ("oneness") is the philosophy that there is only one ultimate substance or principle, whether mind/spirit (*idealism*) or matter/energy (*materialism*). That is, all of reality is one organic whole, or unit. This is expressed perfectly in our concept of the *Universe* ("all together")—which is also called Creation, the Cosmos, and the World. In Taoism, this is known as the *Tao* ("way").

Anaximander of Miletus, a Greek philosopher of the 6th century BCE, proposed that reality had its foundation in an all-pervasive, unending substance that he called the *Infinite* or *Boundless*, the Divine Source of all things. The Boundless divided itself into two components by spinning about its center. Its hotter and lighter component was flung outward to form the Heavens while its colder and heavier component sank toward the center to form the Earth. Later the Earth separated further into the dry land and the wet oceans.

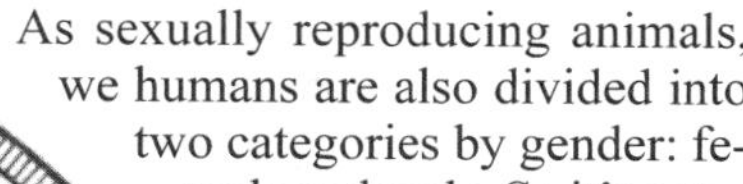

Various religions envision Divinity as the ultimate One. Hindus call it *Atman-Brahman,* who is universal Spirit as well as the actual physical cosmos. The Greeks expressed the same idea as *Pan* ("all"): "Pan is all, and all is Pan!" The three *monotheistic* ("one-god") religions of Judaism, Christianity, and Islam believe in one Supreme Being whom they usually call simply God. Moslems call this deity *Allah,* meaning "the One." This Supreme Being is said to possess the following universal qualities, being:

Eternal—Existing forever, beyond time;
Omnipresent—"All-present" everywhere;
Omnipotent—"All-powerful";
Omniscient—"All-knowing"; and
Omnibenevolent—"All-loving."

(All of this, of course, implies that the Supreme Being is responsible for everything that happens!)

Dyads and Dualities

Duality is a concept fundamental to humans. Because we are symmetrical creatures with two hands, two eyes, and two ears, we tend to see everything in terms of "either/or," "this or that," "on the one hand…but on the other hand." Duality thus becomes the first form of classification, as we sort everything into one category or the other. The most perfect symbol to express this concept is the familiar Taoist yin-yang.

As sexually reproducing animals, we humans are also divided into two categories by gender: female and male. So it's natural for us to tend to think of the world as being filled with two kinds of things that fall into these categories. Many languages, such as Latin, Spanish, French, Italian, and German, refer to various things not as "it," but as "he" or "she," the way we do in English with ships. As the ancients envisioned their deities to explain the world, naturally, they conceived both Gods and Goddesses, assigning gender values to various qualities and activities that are often still with us today (seeing testosterone-fueled aggression as "masculine," for example, or estrogen-fueled compassion as "feminine").

The Taoists saw Yin as the female principle and Yang as the male, and believed that everything was either mostly one or mostly the other, but still always contained elements of both (thus, the little dot of black inside the white area of the yin-yang, and vice-versa). This is called *polarity:* the idea that everything in the world exists somewhere along a spectrum between two poles (right and wrong, masculine and feminine, light and dark, cold and hot, etc.). This is a more helpful and accurate way of seeing the world than *duality,* which divides everything sharply into black and white ("It's either good or bad, and can't be somewhere in between.")

Many cosmologies include a dualistic notion of archetypal opposites in myths describing the first gods being born as twins. In the Assyrian story of creation, the first couple, *An* (Sky) and *Ki* (Earth), was born to *Tiamet* (Great Serpent-Mother of Chaos and the Primordial Waters). This duality was continued in the names of their grandchildren: *Anshar* ("Totality of the Upper Elements") and *Kishar* ("Totality of the Lower Elements"). The Hindu *Vedas* describe *Atman* and *Brahman*, the former being *immanent* (within), the latter *transcendent* (without).

Because one of the primal dualities is Good and Evil, it is all too easy to apply those corresponding values to whatever we list on opposite sides. This sort of thinking has caused untold grief in the world, as people inevitably list themselves on the side of Good, and therefore anything or anyone they think of as "other" automatically gets listed as Evil. The world really isn't a stark division of Good and Evil; there are infinite shades of grey in everything. This is an essential piece of knowledge for a Wizard: It allows you to view others with compassion and to understand that even those who claim to stand for something righteous will inevitably carry within them a bit of what they claim to be against. If everyone understood this, it would be impossible for zealots and demagogues ever to come to power. One important reason for developing the following categorizations of multiple correspondences is to enable us to see beyond dualism to diversity.

Keeping in mind that the Multiverse really can count higher than two, and that people are not really creatures of absolutes, but complex beings embodying infinite facets and qualities, the following tables of correspondence illustrate some of the traditional Dyads, Dualities, and Opposites.

Practice creating your own tables of magickal correspondences. Begin with two. Choose a concept that is an important aspect of your life (family, art, music, yourself…), and try to see a way that concept could be divided into two opposite or complimentary things. (For example, the concept of "Parents" includes "Mom" and "Dad.") Try associating those concepts with different colors ("Mom likes purple and Dad likes red…"). Ask, "If each of them were an animal, what kind of animal would it be?" And you can go on that way. As you study these various tables here, feel free to add to them, or even make up your own.

Triads and Trinities

Just as any concept of Unity may be divided into two opposing Dualities, two opposites may be reconciled into a new *synthesis* ("put together"). The Greek

Tables of Magickal Correspondences 2 and 3

Dyads/Dualities

Chinese Taoism

YIN	YANG
Earth	Heaven
Moon	Sun
Feminine	Masculine
Receptive	Creative
Negative	Positive
Passive	Active
Cold	Hot
Darkness	Light

Wiccan

GODDESS	GOD
Mother	Father
Habondia	Herne
Cerridwen	Cernunnos
Isis	Osiris
Artemis	Apollo
Psyche	Eros
Persephoné	Hadés
Moon	Sun
Chalice	Blade
Crescent	Horns
Spiral	Staff
Cat	Stag
Dog	Wolf
Horse	Bull
Rabbit	Snake
Bear	Boar
Owl	Eagle
Spider	Fish

Triads and Trinities

SEASON	Spring	Summer-Autumn	Winter
AGRICULTURAL	Planting	Harvest	Fallow
PLANT PART	Blossom	Fruit	Seed
TIME OF DAY	Morning	Afternoon	Evening-Night
PHASE OF LIFE	Childhood-Adolescence	Maturity-Parenthood	Seniority-Old Age
WIZARD'S JOURNEY	Apprentice	Journeyman	Adept
PASSAGES (male)	Puberty	Fatherhood	Sagehood
PASSAGES (female)	Menarche	Parturition	Menopause
TRIPLE GOD	Youth	Father / Man	Sage
TRIPLE GODDESS	Maiden	Mother / Woman	Crone
MOON PHASE	New-Waxing	Full	Waning-Dark
QUALITY	Innocent	Creative	Wise
ATTRIBUTE	Inspiring	Loving	Frightening
FUNCTION	Creation	Preservation	Destruction
STATE	Fresh	Ripe	Decaying
QUANTITY	Filling	Full	Empty
COLOR	White	Red or Green	Black

EGYPTIAN GODS	Osiris (father)	Isis (mother)	Horus (child)
CHRISTIAN	Yahveh (father)	Shekinah (holy spirit)	Kristos (son)
HOLY FUNCTION	Creation	Resurrection	Redemption
HINDU GODS	Brahma (creator)	Vishnu (preserver)	Shiva (destroyer)
NORSE WORLDS	Asgard (Heavens)	Midgard (Earth)	Hel (Underworld)
CHINESE REALMS	T'ien (Heaven)	Ti (Earth)	Jen (human)
NORSE NORNS	Urd (past)	Verdandi (present)	Skuld (future)
GREEK FATES	Clotho (spinner)	Lachesis (measurer)	Atropos (cutter)
TAOIST TREASURES	C'hi (vitality)	Shen (spirit)	Ching (essence)

ALCHEMICAL	Salt	Sulfur	Mercury
PRINCIPLE	Body	Mind	Spirit
KINGDOMS of LIFE	Mineral	Vegetable	Animal
GURDJIEFF	Affirming	Denying	Reconciling

philosopher Pythagoras called three the perfect number, because it includes "beginning, middle, and end." A triangle is the most stable structure in geometry, and a three-legged stool doesn't wobble. The symbol of Odin, Norse god of wisdom, is the triangular *Valknot,* shown here.

Many religious *theologies* ("word (or study) of god") claim that the Divine Unity manifests in a three-part *Trinity.* The three principle gods of Hinduism (Brahma the Creator, Vishnu the Preserver, and Shiva the Destroyer) are collectively referred to as the *Trimurti* ("three-formed"), because they represent the three aspects of Atman, the universal Spirit. Cylinder seals from ancient Crete depicted a Trinity of Mother, Daughter (*Koré*), and Son (*Kouros*). In Egypt, the divine Triad consisted of Isis (Mother), Osiris (Father), and Horus (Son). Buddhists embrace a doctrine of *Trikaya*—the three bodies of the Buddha (Law, Enjoyment, and Magickal Creation). Celtic and Wiccan tradition associates the Great Goddess with the three phases of the Moon, as Maiden (waxing), Mother (full), and Crone (waning). And the Christian Trinity affirms the three aspects of God as Father, Son, and Holy Spirit.

The Welsh Triads (*Trioedd Ynys Prydein)* are a collection of more than130 listings of legendary personages, events, or places as groups of three. They were probably designed to be easily memorized by the Bards. There are numerous versions with differences in names, meanings, and the order in which they are listed. Portions are included in all of the early manuscripts, such as the *White Book of Rhyderrch* from the early 1300s. Here's an example of one of these Triads: "Three Men Who Received The Might Of Adam: Hercules the Strong, and Hector the Strong, and Samson the Strong. They were, all three, as strong as Adam himself."

Lesson 4: Elements and Directions

There is probably no system of correspondences more widely used than that of the four Elements: **Earth, Water, Air,** and **Fire** (see 2.III). This concept can be mainly attributed to Pythagoras (580–500 BCE) and Aristotle (384–322 BCE), but the ideas behind it can be traced back through Greek, Hebrew, Egyptian, Persian, and Assyrian traditions. The four Elements model is so universal that it underlies virtually all other magickal systems. It is fundamental to alchemy, which grouped all substances into this model. These associations are also the foundation of the Enochian magickal system. The twelve signs of the Zodiac are assigned three each to these categories: Earth (*Capricorn, Taurus, Virgo*), Water (*Pisces, Cancer, Scorpio*), Air (*Aquarius, Gemini, Libra*), and Fire (*Aries, Leo, Sagittarius*). The 72 cards of the tarot are arranged in four Elemental suits: Discs, Cups, Swords, and Rods; and these are also reflected in standard playing cards as diamonds, hearts, spades, and clubs. The universal symbol for the Four Directions and Elements is the *Celtic Cross,* also known as the Native American Medicine Shield, and the astrological sigil of planet Earth.

Rituals of modern Wicca and Ceremonial Magick construct their Magick Circles by assigning the Elements to the four directions and seasons of the year. These associations are deeply imbedded in Nature Herself, and in our own personal experience of the natural cycles. The accompanying table of Elemental correspondences may be one of your most important magickal tools. Study it well, and learn these associations; they will serve you greatly throughout your magickal life.

***NOTE:** The diagrams and tables presented here are based on correspondences for the Northern Hemisphere. South of the equator the seasons and directions are reversed. Imagine the whole Magick Circle inside the Zodiac viewed in a mirror! So Fire is North and Earth is South; Air is West and Water, East. Spring Equinox is Sept 21, and Winter Solstice is June 21. Moreover, the hands on the clock face—and all ritual directions—move counter-clockwise in Australia!*

The Fifth Element

The Fifth Element, *Spirit,* acts to both unify and transcend the other four Elements in traditional Western magickal systems. Some consider Spirit as the quintessence of all manifested things. The other four Elements constitute the basis of the physical universe, and Spirit is the additional quality that imparts Life and Consciousness. On the Magick Circle mandala, Spirit is represented as the Center of the Circle, or the top point of the pentagram.

Table of Magickal Correspondences 4 — Elements

ELEMENT (state)	**AIR** (gas)	**FIRE** (plasma)	**WATER** (liquid)	**EARTH** (solid)
DIRECTION / WIND	**East** / Eurus	**South** / Notus	**West** / Zephyrus	**North** / Boreas
MAGICKAL MUDRA				
ALCHEMICAL GLYPH	🜁	🜂	🜄	🜃
ELEMENTALS	Sylphs	Salamanders	Undines	Gnomes
RULERSHIP	Tempest, storms, winds, mind, intellect, learning, wisdom	Flames, lightning, Sun, volcanoes, energy, spirit, will	Ocean, tides, lakes, rivers, springs, love, sorrow, emotions	Mountains, caverns, stones, vegetation, wealth, creativity, nature
COLOR / (Lakota)	Yellow / (Yellow)	Red / (White)	Blue / (Black)	Green / (Red)
MUNDANE ANIMAL	Eagle (L. Eagle)	Lion (L. Mouse)	Serpent (L. Bear)	Bull (L. Bison)
MYTHIC ANIMAL	Griffin	Phoenix	Dragon	Unicorn
ARCHANGEL	Raphael	Michael	Gabriel	Uriel
ALTAR TOOLS	Wand & Censer	Athamé & Candle	Chalice & Water	Pantacle & Salt
TAROT SUITS	Wands (Rods)	Swords	Cups	Pentacles (Discs)
COURT CARDS	Knights	Kings	Queens	Pages
PLAYING CARDS	Clubs	Spades	Hearts	Diamonds
CELTIC TREASURE	Spear of Lugh	Sword of Nuada	Cauldron of Dagdha	Stone of Destiny (Lia Fal)
SABBAT	Ostara	Litha	Mabon	Yule
SOLAR MIDPOINT	Spring Equinox	Summer Solstice	Autumn Equinox	Winter Solstice
ZODIACAL POINT	0° Aries	0° Cancer	0° Libra	0° Capricorn
SEASON and GLYPH	Spring	Summer 	Autumn 	Winter
TIME OF DAY	Dawn	Noon	Sunset/dusk	Midnight
WEATHER	Windy	Hot	Rainy	Cold
STAGE of LIFE	Birth	Growth	Death	Decay
HUMAN AGE	Infancy	Youth	Maturity	Old Age
BODY ANALOG	Breath	Spirit (aura)	Blood	Flesh & bones
BODY HUMOUR	Phlegm	Choler	Blood	Melancholy
ATTRIBUTE	Intellectual, joyful	Spiritual, potent	Emotional, fertile	Physical, safe
FUNCTION	Thinking	Feeling	Intuition	Sensation
SENSE	Smell	Sight	Taste	Touch
CARDINAL SIGN	Libra	Aries	Cancer	Capricorn
MUTABLE SIGN	Gemini	Sagittarius	Pisces	Virgo
FIXED SIGN	Aquarius	Leo	Scorpio	Taurus
ALCHEMY PROCESS	Evaporation	Combustion	Solution	Precipitation
METALS	Mercury or Aluminum	Iron or Gold	Silver	Lead
JEWELS	Topaz, Chalcedony	Fire Opal	Aquamarine, Beryl	Quartz, Rock Salt
INCENSE	Galbanum	Olibanum	Myrrh, Onycha	Storax
PLANTS	Pansy, violet, yarrow, primrose, vervain	Garlic, hibiscus, onion, pepper, nettle, mustard	Lotus, fern, melon, seaweed, water plants	Ivy, comfry, apples, grain: barley, oats, wheat, etc.
TREES	Aspen	Almond, in flower	Willow	Oak
GODDESSES	Aradia, Arianrhod, Aditi, Nuit, Ourania	Hestia, Pelé, Vesta, Brigit, Sekhmet	Aphrodite, Amphitrite, Mari, Tiamet, Yemaya	Ceres, Demeter, Gaea, Rhea, Mah, Nepthys
GODS	Enlil, Hermes, Shu, Thoth, Vayu, Zeus	Horus, Hephaestos, Vulcan, Loki, Agni	Poseidon, Llyr, Dylan, Neptune, Ea, Oceanus	Cernunnos, Dionysos, Adonis, Pan, Tammuz
POWER of MAGUS	To Know	To Will	To Dare	To Keep Silent

Lesson 5. Planets, Days and Chakras

Sun Day

Moon Day

Tiw's Day

(Teutonic god of war)

Woden's Day

(Teutonic god of wisdom)

Thor's Day

(Norse god of thunder)

Fria Day

(Teutonic goddess of love)

Saturn Day

(Roman god of the harvest)

Planets & Days

The word *planet* means "wanderer." Ancient peoples observing the heavens noticed that there were seven celestial objects that changed their positions, moving against the unchanging background of the fixed stars. These were the **Sun, Moon, Mars, Mercury, Jupiter, Venus,** and **Saturn.** And so they referred to them as the Wanderers, or *planetes* in Greek, even though we now consider our Sun a star, and our Moon a, well, moon—and with our telescopes we have since discovered three other planets beyond Saturn: Uranus, Neptune, and Pluto (of dubious planetary status). As they traveled through the heavenly realms, these seven visible planets were identified with seven gods and goddesses (or angels) in every culture. To the Egyptians these were, respectively, Ra, Sin, Set, Thoth, Isis, Hathor, and Nepthys. In Greece they were called Helios/Apollo, Artemis, Ares, Hermes, Zeus, Aphrodite, and Chronos. The Romans gave them the names we still use today: Sol, Luna, Mars, Mercury, Jupiter, Venus, and Saturn.

The Moon revolves around the Earth every 27.3 days, completing a cycle through all her phases in 29.5 days. These two cycles average out to 28.3 days, which we call a *lunation,* or *month* (from "moon"). Since at least the 3rd millennium BCE (in Sumer), every calendrical civilization has divided these 28-day periods into four weeks of seven days each. Initially, these were simply numbered, but eventually each day was assigned to a planet (or deity). Since the Sun and Moon are the brightest and most important planets, the first and second days of each week are always theirs. The attributions of the other days are also very similar across cultures: Tuesday belongs to the God of War; Wednesday to the God of Magick and Wisdom; Thursday to the God of Thunder; Friday to the Goddess of Love; and Saturday to the God of Time and Death. These seven Planets/Days have been assigned numerous Correspondences, some of which are indicated on the accompanying Table.

The system was introduced into Hellenistic (Greek) Egypt from Mesopotamia, where astrology had been practiced for millennia and where seven had always been a sacred number. It became the norm throughout the Middle East and was used informally in the Roman Empire by the 1st Century CE. In 321 CE, Emperor Constantine (ruled 312-337 CE) grafted this astrological system onto the Roman calendar, declaring the first day of the week—*dies solis* ("Day of the Sun")—a holy day of rest and worship for all. This new Roman system was adopted with modifications throughout Western Europe, and is the basis of our modern calendars.

The recent convention, becoming more common, to start calendar weeks on Monday, is a result of Christian influence. The Bible says: "Remember the 7th day and keep it holy." Since the time of Constantine, most Christians think of Sunday as their holy day, so they prefer to number it as the 7th day, rather than the 1st, which it is. Historically, however, Saturday has always been the 7th day, and also the *Sabbath* ("to rest"), as in Judaism—even for Moslems and Eastern Orthodox Christians. In Hebrew, this is *Shabbat;* in Arabic, *asSabt;* and in modern Greek, *Savvato.*

Chakras

Chakras ("wheels" or "lotuses") are energy centers of the astral body that are associated with parts of the physical body. The seven major ones are associated with areas along the spine and with the central nervous system. Hindu Yoga teaches that *prana* ("life force") flows through the body via a network of very fine channels called *nadis.* This is like an astral version of the network of nerves, or of blood vessels. The main nadi (*sushumna*) parallels the spinal cord, running from the base of your spine to the top of your head. Like the major plexuses of the nervous system, the Chakras are a series of resonance nodes or vortices along the sushumna. From bottom to top, these are: 1 Root, 2 Sex, 3 Solar Plexus, 4 Heart,

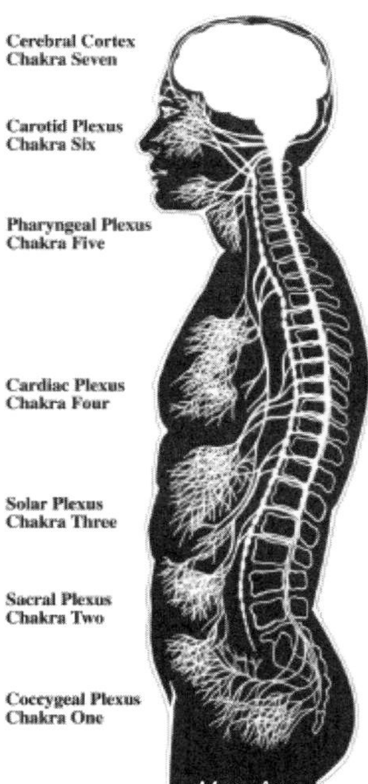

5. Throat, 6. Third Eye, and 7. Crown. We also have minor chakras throughout our bodies, such as in the palms of our hands and the soles of our feet.

The whole concept of the chakras is a vast field of study—far more than I can include in this introductory Grimoire. If you wish to learn more about this system, I recommend the book *Wheels of Life: A User's Guide to the Chakra System* (Llewellyn, 1987) by my dear friend Anodea Judith. However, because you will encounter many references to chakras in your

Table of Magickal Correspondences 7 - Planets/Days

PLANET	SUN	MOON	MARS	MERCURY	JUPITER	VENUS	SATURN
SYMBOL	☉	☽	♂	☿	♃	♀	♄
DAY	**Sunday**	**Monday**	**Tuesday**	**Wednesday**	**Thursday**	**Friday**	**Saturday**
GERMANIC	Sunna *(f.)*	Mani *(m.)*	Tiew	Woden/Odin	Thor/Donner	Freyja/Frey	Santur
CELTIC GOD	Belenos	Arianrhod	Tiw	Lugh	Taranis	Rhiannon	Arawn
ROMAN GOD	Sol	Luna/Diana	Mars	Mercurius	Jupiter/Jove	Venus	Saturnus
GREEK GOD	Helios	Selene/Artemis	Ares	Hermes	Zeus	Aphrodite	Kronos
EGYPTIAN	Ra, Aten	Khonsu	Set	Thoth	Isis	Hathor	Nepthys
HEBREW	Shemesh	Levanah	Madim	Tzedek	Nogah	Shabbathai	Shabbat
BABYLONIAN	Shamash	Sin	Nergal	Nabu	Marduk	Ishtar	Ninib
SUMERIAN	Utu	Nanna	Gugulanna	Enki	Enlil	Inanna	Ninurta
ORISHAS	Obatala	Yemaya	Ogun	Eshu	Chango	Erzulie	Samedi
ARCHANGEL	Raphael	Gabriel	Kamael	Michael	Tzadkiel	Haniel	Tzaphkiel
ANGEL	Michael	Gabriel	Zamael	Raphael	Sachiel	Anael	Cassiel
SEPHIRAH	Tiphareth	Yesod	Geburah	Hod	Chesed	Netzach	Binah/Daath
RULERSHIP	Leo	Cancer	Scorpio/Aries	Gemini/Virgo	Sagittarius	Taurus/Libra	Capricorn
ATTRIBUTES	Ego, fame, extroversion, individuality, conscious, left brain	Emotions, psychic, intuition, subconscious, right brain	Physical body, heat, actions, power, energy, aggression	Intellect, speed, messages, duality, youth, communication	Expansion, good fortune, money, material possessions, optimism	Love, beauty, harmony, luxury, sex, esthetics, friendship	Deprivation, constriction, pessimism, death, cold, discipline
CONCERNS	Hope, money, respect, fame, luck, success	Dreams, theft prevention, prophecy	Physical power, courage, war, victory, strength	Communication, memory, truth, business	Honor, wealth, health, peace, fame, power	Love, passion, friendship, joy, safety, fertility	Harvest, long life, protection, stability, safety
ELEMENTS	Fire/Air	Water	Fire	Water/Air	Air/Fire	Water/Earth	Earth/Water
COLOR	Gold/Orange	Silver/White	Red	Yellow	Purple	Green	Black
METAL	Gold	Silver	Iron	Mercury/Aluminum	Tin	Copper	Lead
GEMSTONES	Topaz, Yellow Diamond	Moonstone, Quartz	Bloodstone, Ruby, Garnet	Fire Opal, Agate	Amethyst, Sapphire	Emerald, Amber	Obsidian, Onyx, Black Pearl
TREES	Birch, Laurel	Willow	Holly, Thorn	Hazel, Ash	Oak	Apple, Rowen	Alder, Cypress
MUNDANE ANIMALS	Eagle, Lion, Cock, Scarab	Cat, Hare Deer, Wolf	Ram, Owl Scorpion	Jackal, Ape, Ibis, Serpent	Peacock Bull, Eagle	Dove, Swan, Dolphin, Fish	Crow, Raven, Crocodile
MYTH ANIMAL	Phoenix	Unicorn	Dragon	Hippogriff	Gryphon	Mermaid	Basilisk
PLANTS	Heliotrope, Goldenseal, Cinquefoil, Saffron, Ash, Sunflower, Dandelion, Marigold, Citrus, Yarrow	Lunaria, Seaweed, Aloes, Watercress, Lemon, Jasmine, Lotus, Mushroom, Cucumber, Poppy	Basil, Nettle, Chili Pepper, Rue, Gentia, Wolfsbane, Patchouli, Hellebore, Mustard, Garlic, Ginger	Wormwood, Valerian, Dill, Carraway, Vervain, Horehound, Fennel, Lavender, Mandrake	Anise, Mint, Solomon's Seal, Cedar, Balm, Olive, Oak, Clover, St John's Wort	Apple, Elder, Rosemary, Sandalwood, Rose, Orris, Geranium, Eryngo, Fig, Almond	Aconite, Yew, Cannabis, Hemlock, Thyme, Deadly Nightshade, Jimson Weed, Cypress
INCENSE COMPOUNDS	Frankincense, Laurel, Balm of Gilead, Bayberry oil, Olibanum, Flax seed	Jasmine, Poppy, Myrtle, Cucumber oil, Aloes, White Sandalwood, Gum Benzoin	Pine, Cypress, Tobacco, Rue, Strafe, Sulfur, Peppercorns, Iron filings, Dragon's Blood	Storax, Mace, Sandalwood, Gum Mastic, Cinnamon, Sassafras, Wormwood	Cedarwood oil, Nutmeg, Frankincense, Juniper berry, Hyssop, St John's Wort	Jasmine, Egg whites, Gum Benzoin, Rose petals, Lignum Aloes, Musk oil, Red Coral	Civet, Myrrh, Cinnamon, Rue, Mullein, Yew berries, Patchouli, Cypress leaves

magickal work, I have here provided a table of correspondences that will give you a basic foundation of the system.

Lesson 6: Months and Signs of the Zodiac

From the very dawn of time, when our most remote ancestors first looked up into the heavens in wonder at the diamond-dusted vastness of the night sky, we have sought meaning in the random patterns of the stars. The constellations that have become such familiar elements of our sky-maps were drawn up many thousands of years ago by "connecting the dots" of prominent stars and have changed little since. Taurus is depicted as a great bull in the 15,000-year-old cave paintings of Lascaux, complete with seven dots of the Pleiades star-cluster on its shoulder. The great Sphinx of Egypt is believed to have been originally carved more than 10,500 years ago in the form of a crouching lion, representing the constellation of Leo. Scorpio has always been seen as a scorpion. The Sumerians identified the constellations in their present arrangement as early as 2500 BCE, but it was the Hellenic Greeks who named the *Zodiac* ("circle of animals").

Taurus, Leo, and Scorpio are three of the twelve constellations we call the signs of the Zodiac. These fall across the path of the *ecliptic,* the band in the sky against which the Sun, Moon, and all the planets appear to travel (see 2.I.5: "Zodiacal Aeons" for a more

Table of Magickal Correspondences 7 — Chakras

CHAKRA	MULA-DHARA	SVADHISH-THANA	MANIPURA	ANAHATA	VISUDDHA	AJNA	SAHAS-RARA
SYMBOL							
PETALS	4	6	10	12	16	2	1,000
MEANING	Root	Private place	Lustrous gem	Unstruck beat	Purification	To perceive	Thousandfold
LOCATION	Tip of Spine	Sacrum	Solar Plexus	Heart	Throat	"Third Eye"	Crown of head
COLOR	Red	Orange	Yellow	Green	Bright Blue	Indigo	Violet
PLANET	Saturn	Moon	Mars/Sun	Venus	Mercury	Neptune	Uranus
ELEMENT	Earth	Water	Fire	Air	Sound	Light	Thought
ARCHETYPE	Mother	Lover	Magician	Healer	Messenger	Visionary	Wise One
GODDESS	Dakini	Rakini	Lakini	Kakini	Sakini	Hakini	
GOD	Brahma	Vishnu	Rudra	Isa	Sadasiva	Sambhu	Paramsiva
ANIMALS	Elephant	Fish, Sea monster	Ram, Lion	Antelope, Dove	White Elephant	Owl, Butterfly	Ox, Bull
GEMSTONES	Garnet, Hematite, Bloodstone	Coral, Carnelian	Topaz, Amber	Emerald, Rose Quartz	Turquoise	Lapis lazuli, some Quartz	Amethyst, Diamond
FOODS	Protein, meats	Liquids	Complex Carbohydrates	Vegetables	Fruit	Psychedelics	None (fasting)
ENDO. GLAND	Adrenals	Gonads	Pancreas	Thymus	Thyroid	Pineal	Pituitary
EMOTION	Security, fear	Passion, guilt	Confidence, shame	Love, grief	Inspiration, repression	Imagination, illusion	Understanding, attachment
SENSE ORGAN	Nose	Tongue	Eyes	Skin	Ears		
SENSE	Smell	Taste	Sight	Touch	Hearing		
MAIN ISSUE	Survival	Sexuality, emotions	Power, energy	Love, relationships	Communication	Insight, vision, imagination	Understanding, grokking
PRINCIPLE	Gravity	Attraction of opposites	Combustion	Equilibrium	Sympathetic vibration	Luminescence	Consciousness
PROPERTY	Contraction	Connection	Expansion	Balance	Resonance	Radiance	Awareness
RIGHT	To Have	To Feel	To Act	To Love	To Speak	To See	To Know
GOALS	Grounding, prosperity, stability, physical health	Fluidity of movement, pleasure, connection	Strength of will, vitality, purpose, effectiveness	Balance in relationships, compassion, self-acceptance	Harmony creativity, communication, resonance	Ability to perceive patterns, to "see," to grok	Expanded consciousness, cosmic awareness
BIO. FUNCTION	Elimination	Reproduction	Digestion	Respiration	Assimilation	Recognition	Comprehension
YOGA PATH	Hatha Yoga	Tantra Yoga	Karma Yoga	Bhakti Yoga	Mantra Yoga	Yantra Yoga	Jnana Yoga

detailed explanation of the ecliptic). The 360° Zodiac has been divided into twelve equal sections, or *signs,* of 30° each, and these are named for the constellations that most closely approximate them. That is, the signs are not the actual *constellations* of stars, but simply their equal portion of the Zodiac belt. These are the months of the Zodiac. In order of the Sun's passage through each of them during the course of the year, beginning with Spring Equinox, they are: Pisces (fish) ♓, Aries (ram) ♈, Taurus (bull) ♉, Gemini (twins) ♊, Cancer (crab) ♋, Leo (lion) ♌, Virgo (maiden) ♍, Libra (scales) ♎, Scorpio (scorpion) ♏, Sagittarius (archer) ♐, Capricorn (sea-goat) ♑, and Aquarius (water-bearer) ♒..

For the purposes of divination, astrologers since ancient Babylon have assigned symbolic meanings to these Signs. The accompanying table of correspondences shows some of these many attributes. In astrology, these correspondences are held to influence whatever planets (with *their* attributions) happen to be passing through the signs at any given time. Horoscopes are circular diagrams that show those positions at a chosen moment, such as one's time of birth.

The Magick Circle mandala is a perfect way to display the calendar of the Zodiac as a clock face against which the Sun and Moon can be seen as the "hour" and "minute" hands. The Sun completes a circuit once a year, while the Moon goes through all the signs in a month.

A note of interest: There are actually 13 constellations along the path of the Ecliptic. The 13th, *Ophiuchus* ("the Serpent-Bearer") falls between Scorpio and Sagittarius (the time I was born). But a calendar of 13 months does not divide up easily into four seasons, and 12 was the favored number for all ancient mathematical systems, as it is divisible by 2, 3, 4, and 6. So 13 was considered an unlucky number, and Ophiuchus was excluded from the Zodiac.

Full Moons

All the original ancient calendars were entirely lunar, rather than solar, as is our current one. Even today, the Jewish, Moslem, Hindu, and Chinese calendars are still lunar, and they have to be readjusted every few years to keep the months from becoming completely out of phase with the seasons. As the word "month" is, after all, derived from the cycles of the Moon, some peoples have chosen to name the months for "Moons," rather than constellations, gods (Janus, Februus, Mars, Maiesta, Juno), Roman Emperors (Julius Caesar, Augustus Caesar) or simply numbers (*Apero, Septembro, Octobro, Novembro,* and *Decembro* mean simply "2nd, 7th, 8th, 9th, 10th").

Full Moons draw attention to themselves by the way they dominate the sky from dusk to dawn, so that each one has acquired at least one special name. One enduring set of names for the full Moons was recorded in a 1508 English Edition of *The Shepherd's Calenda*. These names were carried over into the Americas by the early British colonists, where they merged with Native American associations. Here are some of the most popular of these names for the full Moons of each month:

January - Old Moon, Wolf Moon, Storm Moon
February - Snow Moon, Hunger Moon, Opening Buds Moon, Chaste Moon
March - Maple Sugar Moon, Sap Moon, Worm Moon, Crow Moon, Seed Moon
April - Grass Moon, Pink Moon, Frog Moon, Planter's Moon, Hare Moon
May - Milk Moon, Flower Moon, Budding Moon, Dyad Moon
June - Rose Moon, Strawberry Moon, Mead Moon
July - Thunder Moon, Buck Moon, Blood Moon, Wort (herb) Moon
August - Green Corn Moon, Corn Moon, Sturgeon Moon, Barley Moon
September - Fruit Moon, Harvest Moon, Blood Moon, Moon of Pairing Reindeer
October - Harvest Moon, Hunter's Moon, Moon of Falling Leaves, Snow Moon
November - Frost Moon, Beaver Moon, Oak Moon
December - Long Night Moon, Cold Moon, Wolf Moon

The French Revolutionary Calendar

And finally, Grey Council member Fred Lamond reminded me of the French Revolutionary Calendar, which was in use in France from 1792 to 1801 and was very Nature-based. The year started at the Fall Equinox and was divided into four quarters of 91-92 days, each in turn divided into three months of 30-31 days. Thus the months pretty much correspond to those of the Zodiac. The names of these months were:

Autumn *vendémiaire* = grape harvest month (Libra)
brumaire = misty month (Scorpio)
frimaire = frosty month (Sagittarius)
Winter *nivose* = snowy month (Capricorn)
pluviose = rainy month (Aquarius)
ventose = windy month (Pisces)
Spring *germinal* = sprouting seeds (Aries)
floréal = blossoming flowers (Taurus)
boréal = warm winds (Gemini)
Summer *messidor* = cereal harvest (Cancer)
thermidor = summer heat (Leo)
fructidor = ripening fruit (Virgo)

Table of Magickal Correspondences 12 — Signs of the Zodiac

SIGN	PISCES	ARIES	TAURUS	GEMINI	CANCER	LEO	VIRGO	LIBRA	SCORPIO	SAGITTARIUS	CAPRICORN	AQUARIUS
SYMBOL	♓	♈	♉	♊	♋	♌	♍	♎	♏	♐	♑	♒
IMAGE	Fishes	Ram	Bull	Twins	Crab	Lion	Maiden	Scales	Scorpion	Archer	Sea-Goat	Water-Bearer
CIVIL PERIOD	Feb. 20- Mar. 20	Mar. 21- April 20	April 21- May 21	May 22- June 21	June 22- July 23	July 24- Aug. 23	Aug. 24- Sept. 23	Sept. 24- Oct. 23	Oct. 24- Nov. 22	Nov. 23- Dec. 21	Dec. 22- Jan. 20	Jan. 21- Feb. 19
ELEMENT	Water	Fire	Earth	Air	Water	Fire	Earth	Air	Water	Fire	Earth	Air
RULER	Neptune	Mars	Venus	Mercury	Moon	Sun	Mercury	Venus	Pluto	Jupiter	Saturn	Uranus
NATURE	Mutable	Cardinal	Fixed	Mutable	Cardinal	Fixed	Mutable	Cardinal	Fixed	Mutable	Cardinal	Fixed
CYCLE	Distributes	Generates	Concentrates	Distributes	Generates	Concentrates	Distributes	Generates	Concentrates	Distributes	Generates	Concentrates
DIRECTION	South, Below	North- East	South- East	East, Above	East, Below	North, Above	North, Below	North- West	South- West	West, Above	West, Below	South, Above
COLORS	Soft Sea Green	Red	Pink, pale Blue	All (esp. Yellow)	Gray, Green	Golden Orange	Navy Blue, Dark Gray	Pale Blue, Pink	Dark Red, Maroon	Purple, dark Blue	Black Brown	Electric Blue
METAL	Tin	Copper	Copper	Mercury	Silver	Gold	Mercury	Copper	Iron	Tin	Lead	Uranium
GEM-STONE	Moonstone, Bloodstone	Diamond	Pale blue Sapphire	Agate	Pearl	Ruby	Sardonyx	Sapphire	Opal	Topaz	Turquoise	Amethyst, red Garnet
INCENSE	Ambergris	Dragon's Blood	Storax	Worm- wood	Onycha	Frankin- cense	Narcissus	Galbanum	Opoponax	Ligne Aloes	Musk, Civet	Galbanum
TREES	Willow, Water trees, Fig	Thorn Trees & Shrubs	Ash, Cypress, Apple	Nut trees	Trees rich in sap	Orange, Citrus, Bay, Palm	Nut trees	Ash	Blackthorn, bushy trees	Mulberry, Lime, Oak, Ash, Birch	Willow, Poplar, Pine, Elm	Mosses, Fruit trees
ANIMALS	Fish Dolphin	Ram, Owl	Bull, Ox, Buffalo	Magpie, Hybrids	Crab, Turtle	Lion	Virgin, Anchorite	Elephant, Tortoise	Scorpion, Wolf, Eagle	Centaur, Dog, Horse	Goat, Donkey	Peacock, Eagle, Man
BODILY SYSTEM	Lymphatic	Cerebral (brain)	Speech (throat)	Nervous, Pulmonary	Digestive	Cardiac (heart)	Alimentary	Renal (kidneys)	Repro- ductive	Hepatic (liver)	Skeletal	Circulatory (blood)
MOON	Seed	Hare	Dyad	Mead	Wort	Barley	Blood/Wine	Snow	Oak	Wolf	Storm	Chaste
DEITY	Neptune	Minerva	Venus	Apollo	Mercury	Jupiter	Ceres	Vulcan	Mars	Diana	Vesta	Juno
ARCHANGEL	Amnitziel	Malkidiel	Azmodel	Ambriel	Muriel	Verkiel	Hamaliel	Zuriel	Barkiel	Advakiel	Hanael	Kambirel
ANGEL	Vakabiel	Sharhiel	Araziel	Sarayel	Pakiel	Sharatiel	Shelathiel	Chedeqiel	Saitziel	Saritiel	Samequiel	Tzakmiqiel
HOUSE ANGEL	Pasiel	Ayel	Toel	Giel	Kael	Oel	Veyel	Yahel	Sosul	Soyasel	Kashenyayah	Ansuel
TRIBE	Simeon	Gad	Epharim	Manasseh	Issachar	Judah	Naphtali	Asshur	Dan	Benjamin	Zebulon	Reuben
HEBREW NAME	Dagim "Fishes"	Taleh "Lamb"	Shor "Bull, Ox"	Teomim "Twins"	Sarton "Crab"	Ari "Lion"	Betulah "Virgin"	Moznaim "Scales"	Akrab "Scorpion"	Qasshat "Bow"	Gedi "Kid"	Deli "Bucket"
BABY-LONIAN NAME	Shimmah "Great Swallow"	Luhunga "Hired laborer"	Gud-Annu "Bull of Heaven"	Mashtab- Bal-Gal-Gal "Twins"	Allu "Crab"	Urgula "Lion, Great Dog"	Abshim "Spike of Corn"	Zibanetum "Ravening Dog"	Girtab "Scorpion"	Pa-Bil-Sag "Overseer"	Sukhur- Mashu "Goat-fish"	Gula "Giant"

Class VII: Signs & Symbols

"Before there was writing, there were pictures. The desire to control the forces of nature led Paleolithic humans to create images of the world around them. If the gods made the world, then graphic imitation was a godlike act that carried with it the illusion of power." —Leonard Shlain (*The Alphabet versus the Goddess: The Conflict Between Word and Image,* p. 45)

1. Introduction: Magickal Symbolism

A *SYMBOL* IS SOMETHING THAT REPRESENTS something else by association, resemblance, or convention. The word is derived from the Greek *symbolon,* which was a token used for identification by comparison with a counterpart. In essence, a symbol is something that is given an authority by being paired or connected with another thing. The chief difference between a magickal symbol system and the mundane symbol systems we use everyday is that magickal symbols are arranged in layers of *correspondences* (see 3.6: "Correspondences"). Each association of a symbol is like a band of light in a spectrum, or a note in an octave. The different attributions of magickal symbols can be considered as expressions of the spirits of those symbols in different states of being. Every object, every thought, every emotion is but the symbol of an eternal principle. The *arcana* ("secret knowledge") of the Mysteries were never revealed to the uninitiated except through symbols. Temples of the ancient Mysteries each evolved their own sacred symbolism and languages, known only to their initiates and never spoken outside the sanctuary.

The magician constructs rituals so that every object in the range of the senses has a symbolic connection with the idea and intention of the ceremony. In a ritual context, the objects, symbols, and colors take on a magickal quality in and of themselves, holding or creating the energy necessary to accomplish the desired results.

Lesson 2. Ancient Writing

Cuneiform

The oldest known form of writing was developed in ancient Mesopotamia ("Land between the Rivers"), between the Tigris and Euphrates Rivers—in the country that is now Iraq. As some of the world's first cities arose here, this area is often referred as "the Cradle of Civilization." It's greatest capital was Babylon, established around 2000 BCE. The first Mesopotamians were known as Sumerians, and their principal cities were Ur and Uruk. Beginning in 3100 BCE, the first *cuneiform* ("wedge-shaped") symbols were made by gouging tiny wedge-shaped marks with sharp sticks into wet clay. By 2800 BCE, each symbol represented an object, action, idea, or concept. For centuries, Sumerian scribes only used this writing to record transactions of offerings to the temples. Only much later was cuneiform used to transcribe deeds of kings, religious rites, myths, poetry—and even later, divination, mathematics, medicine, and law.

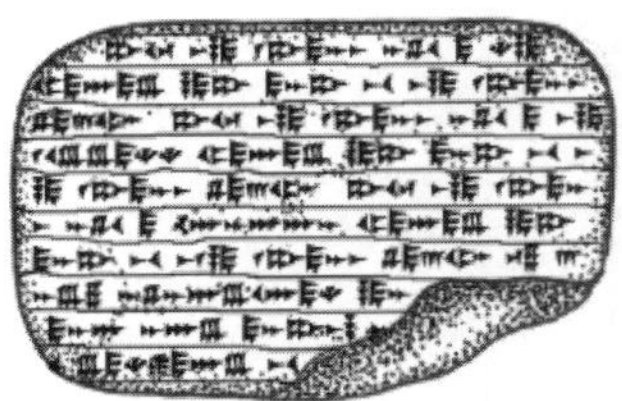

Egyptian: Hieroglyphics, Demotic & Hieratic

Around 3000 BCE, the ancient Egyptians developed a very complex form of pictorial writing we call *hieroglyphics* (HY-ro-GLIF-ix, "sacred carvings"). Each *glyph,* or image, served three functions: 1. representation of a thing or action; 2. standing for the sound of a syllable; 3. clarifying the meaning of adjoining glyphs. For concepts that could not be expressed in pictures, the scribes invented 25 special symbols to stand for each of their language's spoken consonants, allowing the reader to sound out the words. This is the principle of the alphabet, although the Egyptian scribes failed to realize its potential and used it but sparingly.

During Egypt's New Kingdom (1550-700 BCE), scribes resurrected an older alternative form called *Hieratic* (hy-RAT-ik) script, which began to replace hieroglyphics. They converted the glyphs representing the consonants into abstract letters. Unlike hieroglyphics, which could go in any direction, hieratic script was always written horizontally. Oddly, it seems not to have occurred to the scribes that they no longer needed the larger number of glyphs (6,000 of them!), which they still retained.

The inhabitants of the imperium of Meroe in Ethiopia selected just 23 out of the thousands of Egyptian hieroglyphics to create a simplified alphabet, known as *Demotic.* Many magickal orders, past and present, have drawn heavily from an ancient Egyptian background. For them, Egyptian hieroglyphs are an ideal magickal alphabet.

Hebrew (הברו)

The first true *alphabet*—that is, only a couple dozen signs used to represent all consonants—was the one in which Moses wrote the original "10 Commandments," in 1628 BCE. He claimed he had been given the words directly from *Yahweh*—the Hebrew God. This writing became known as *Hebrew* (from *Habiru,* meaning "dusty travelers"). An "alphabet" by definition is any form of writing that contains fewer than 30 letters, and Hebrew contains 27.

After receiving their first written Commandments, the Hebrews changed their name to the Israelites. A couple of generations later, they invaded and conquered the land of Canaan (modern Palestine), renaming it Israel. Coastal Canaanites around Syria (the Ugarits) adapted the Hebrew script, and spread it throughout the Eastern Mediterranean via the seafaring Phoenicians. Like former forms of symbolic writing, Hebrew contained no vowels, leading to endless arguments as to how various words were pronounced. Most significant of these is the name of their God, written in Hebrew as Yהvה or YHVH. Since it was forbidden to speak it aloud, Biblical scholars still debate whether that should be "Yahweh," "Yahveh," or "Jehovah."

Greek (Γρεεκ)

Influenced by the alphabetical writing of the Phoenicians, with whom they traded, around 800 BCE the Greeks developed the modern "alpha-bet"—from A *(alpha)* and B *(beta).* It became the first to include vowels as well as consonants. With it, literacy spread throughout the civilized world, especially during the expansion of the Macedonian Empire under Alexander the Great.

Beginning in 50 BCE, a succession of Roman Caesars conquered and absorbed the entire Greek world—along with nearly everyone else—creating what we call the Greco-Roman civilization. All literate Romans read and spoke Greek as well as their own language, Latin. But for writing in Latin, they modified many of the Greek letters into the Roman alphabet, which is pretty much what I'm writing in here. And we teach it to our kids as "The A-B-C's."

Runes (ᚱᚢᚾᛖᛊ)

Legend tells us that the *runes* were first brought to the world by Odin, Chief of the Norse Gods of Asgard. While hanging himself upon the great World-Tree, he had a vision of these symbols, which could be used to represent all sounds of spoken speech.

The word *rune* means "mystery" or "secret" in Early English and related languages. It is certainly heavily charged with overtones and for good reason. Runes were never a strictly mundane alphabet. From their earliest adaptation into Germanic usage they served for divinatory and ritual uses. There are three main types of runes: Germanic, Scandinavian, and Anglo-Saxon—each with numerous variations. *Futhark,* like "alpha-beta," takes its name from the first few letters—F, U, Th, A, R, K. This is the most popular and widespread runic alphabet in use among modern Wizards.

Ogham (ᚑᚌᚆᚐᚋ)

The early Celts and their priests, the Druids, developed their own form of alphabet. It was known as *Ogham* (OH-um) *Bethluisnon* (see 3.VI.7: "Calendar of the Trees"). As with others, it takes its name from the first few letters: B *(beth),* L *(luis),* N *(nion).* This was an extremely simple form and was used more for carving into wood and stone than for general writing. With a center line, it lent itself especially to carving along the edge of a stone or a piece of wood.

While the Bethluisnon correspondences with trees are well-known through Robert Graves' interpretation of the "Tree Calendar," Ogham letters were also assigned to the joints of the fingers, and messages could be passed in secret by indicating the parts of the fingers to spell out the words.

Pictish

The ancient Picts of the British Isles developed an elaborate "swirl" style of writing. The symbols are very similar, however, and you need to be careful in writing them to avoid confusion. Pictish lettering, artwork, and ornamental designs were later adopted and elaborated by the Celts, especially in Ireland.

Lesson 3: Magickal Alphabets

From the Middle Ages through the Renaissance, when thousands were being tortured and burned at the stake on the charge of Witchcraft, there were many (including priests, bishops, archbishops, and even popes of the Christian Church) who practiced magick quite openly and unrestrained. The reason they were able to work so freely lies in the word *practice*. Witchcraft was viewed as a *religion* and hence, a rival to Christianity. But magick, of the ceremonial or ritual variety, was only a *practice,* like medicine, and therefore no cause for concern by the Church. It was also a very expensive and learned practice, and consequently only available to the select few who not only had the education and time to devote to its pursuit, but also access to the necessary resources.

In those days, each magician worked alone and jealously guarded his methods of operation—not so much from the Church authorities, as from other magicians, among whom there was often great rivalry. To conceal their doctrines and tenets from the profane, many invented their own *cryptograms* ("secret alphabets"). Some of these scripts have been passed down through the centuries in Grimoires and the records of magickal societies, and continue to be used by magicians, Witches, and Wizards today.

Magicians use magickal scripts, glyphs, and sigils to *charge* (with power) everything they need. You have already done this if you have inscribed the runes on your wand, athamé, and other tools. Learning one or more of these traditional magickal alphabets, and writing certain spells, inscriptions, and messages in them, can put great power into your words and works. Writing in ordinary, everyday English script requires no special attention or energy. You are so used to writing this way that you can do it almost unconsciously. On the other hand, when you write in a strange alphabet that you do not know well, you really have to concentrate and focus your mind on what you are doing.

Hermetic Alphabets: Chaldean (); Malachim ()

Often called sacred or *hermetic* alphabets, these are used almost exclusively by Ceremonial Magicians, though occasionally you may find an individual Witch or Wizard using them on a talisman. The best-known scripts are: *Passing the River, Celestial,* and *Malachim.*

Celestial is also known as *Angelic* or *Enochian,* and it is still used in the higher degrees of Masonry. It came from Dr. John Dee's work with Edward Kelly, who in 1581 produced a set of 21 symbols which he claimed had been revealed to him as the true alphabet of the angels, used to compose the names of the heavenly hosts. These symbols became the foundation of Dee and Kelly's *Enochian* system, used to invoke angels and demons. The figures of *Malachim* are said to be derived from the constellations—though which ones, it is impossible to say. Malachim is sometimes confused with the "Writing of the Magi."

Theban

The *Theban* script is also called *Honorian* in honor of its creator, Honorius III (Pope 1216–1227). It has always been a very popular alphabet among Wizards, and it is also used extensively by modern Witches—so much so that it is often referred to as the Witches' alphabet. When I received my first training in Witchcraft, back in 1970, my teacher, Deborah Letter, insisted we learn to read and write fluently in Theban—not just for spells and magickal inscriptions, but also for communications among our fellow coveners. I remember showing up for a meeting one evening to find the following note pinned to the front door—see if you can translate it!

Roman numerals (I, II, III, IV, V, VI, VII, VIII, IX, X)

The Romans, who gave us our modern alphabet, also devised what is possibly the most stupidly useless numerical system in history. Roman numerals worked well enough for tallies and small numbers, as long as you were simply counting them off (they are still used for clock faces and outlines, like our Classes). But larger numbers became hopelessly complicated, and you would have to work out exactly what they meant. The year "1888," for instance, had to be written as "**MDCCCMLXXXVIII**." Moreover, there was no "zero." What all this meant was that it was impossible to do even the simplest arithmetic in Roman numerals. They could not even be added or subtracted, let alone multiplied or divided! No one relying on this system could keep financial records, calculate the dimensions of a space, figure percentages, or do any of the "countless" mathematical operations we use every day.

Ancient & Magickal Alphabets

Anglo-Roman	Cuneiform	Hieratic	Demotic	Hebrew	Greek	Futhark	Ogham	Pictish	Theban	Chaldean	Malachim	Magi	Celestial/Angelic	Passing the River	Masonic/Rosicrucian	Tengwar (Elf)	Angerthas (Dwarf)
Aa				א	Aα												
Bb				ב	Bβ												
Cc				ש	Xχ												
Dd				ד	Δδ												
Ee					Eε												
Ff				פ	Φϕ												
Gg				ג	Γγ												
Hh				ה	Hη												
Ii					Iι												
Jj				ח	ϑφ												
Kk				כ	Kκ												
Ll				ל	Λλ												
Mm				מ	Mμ												
Nn				נ	Nν												
Oo					Oo												
Pp				פ	Ππ												
Qq				ק													
Rr				ר	Pρ												
Ss				ס	Σσ												
Tt				ת	Tτ												
Uu					Yυ												
Vv				ו	ςϖ												
Ww				וו	Ωω												
Xx				צ	Ξξ												
Yy				י	Ψψ												
Zz				ז	Zζ												
Th					Θθ												
Ng																	
Eo																	

And from the time of the Roman Empire until the Renaissance—1,500 years—Roman numerals were the only kind of numbers used among all the Latin-speaking literate people of Europe. Latin was also the only written language—tightly controlled by the Church of Rome, which kept all known books under lock and key in their monastery libraries. But the Jews, who had spread throughout Europe in the great *Diaspora* (dee-AS-por-ah, "scattering") after Rome destroyed Jerusalem in 70 CE, didn't use Roman numerals. Highly literate (at least the men, as all boys were required to learn to read Hebrew—though girls were generally not permitted to learn reading at all), the Jews used *Arabic* numerals, which they picked up from the Babylonians—the same ones we use today. They could do calculations, accounting, equations, bookkeeping, etc. Therefore the Jews came to be the merchants, bankers, mathematicians—as well as magicians, alchemists, Wizards, and scientists. This is why so many of the old Grimoires (like *The Key of Solomon*) are based on Jewish magickal systems, such as the *Qabalah* (ka-BALL-ah)—and why so many sigils and talismans are traditionally inscribed with Hebrew writing.

Lesson 5. Glyphs & Sigils

Long before any form of writing had been invented, people represented things and ideas with simplified drawings or carvings. We use the Greek word for such carvings: *glyphs.* From the earliest cave drawings we find simple stick figures representing people and animals, arrangements of dots, circles, and lines, and geometric symbols like squares and triangles (downward-pointing = female; upward-pointing = male).

Sigils (from L. *sigillum,* "seal") are glyphs specifically representing the symbolic identities of individual deities, spirits, or people—or even organizations (such as company logos). Sigils may be based on geometrical shapes, astrological signs, runes, alchemical symbols, or just doodles someone liked. Sigils may represent complex concepts or even contain the entire essence of a spell. An individual may design a personal sigil to sign artwork, or inscribe on magickal tools. Sigils may be used in spells or engraved on talismans.

Egyptian

The Egyptians developed the most extensive use of pictographic writing, which the Greeks called *hieroglyphs* ("sacred carvings"). Words and entire concepts were represented by these symbols, and many of them have been adopted for magickal use in by Wizards throughout the ages. Here are a couple of the more currently popular Egyptian hieroglyphs:

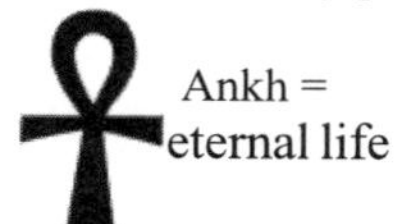

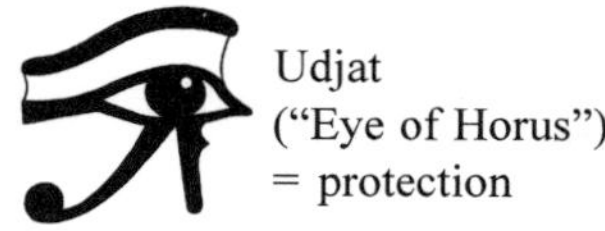

Pythagorean

The Pythagorean Mysteries (see 5.VI: "Mathemagicks") linked all their teachings to geometrical symbols, especially *polygrams* ("many-pointed writing"). Most important was the *pentagram*, or Solomon's Seal, symbol of light, health, and vitality. It also symbolizes the Fifth Element (Spirit). A *hexagram,* formed by the union of two triangles (male—point up and female—point down), is the symbol of marriage. It is also called the Star of David. A *heptagram,* or 7-pointed star made with one continuous line (*unicursive*), is also called an elfstar by modern magickal folks. Another important symbol of the Pythagorean Mysteries was the *golden spiral,* as shown in the shell of the chambered nautilus.

Pentagram

The *pentagram,* or five-pointed star drawn with one unbroken line, is a favorite sign of magicians, Wizards, and Witches. Inscribed within a circle it is the most popular symbol for modern Witchcraft. It was used in ancient Babylon, over 4,000 years ago (one is inscribed on a pot from Tell Asmar dated to 2750 BCE!), where it represented the Star of Ishtar, the planet (and goddess) we call Venus. Enclosed in a circle or drawn on a disk, the pentagram becomes a

Sunday	Monday	Tuesday	Wednesday	Thursday	Friday	Saturday
Michael	*Gabriel*	*Camael*	*Raphael*	*Sachiel*	*Anael*	*Cassiel*
☉ ♌	☽ ♋	♂ ♈ ♏	☿ ♊ ♍	♃ ♐ ♓	♀ ♉ ♎	♄ ♑ ♒

Names and Sigils of the Angels governing the days of the week (after Reginald Scot, 1584)

pentacle, which is used in tarot cards and on magickal altars to represent the Element Earth, or the material plane. Placed in windows or worn as a pendant, it is a charm to repel evil. The five points of the pentagram stand for the four Elements (Earth, Air, Fire, and Water) plus Spirit, which is at the top, over all. They also stand for the five senses by which we know the world.

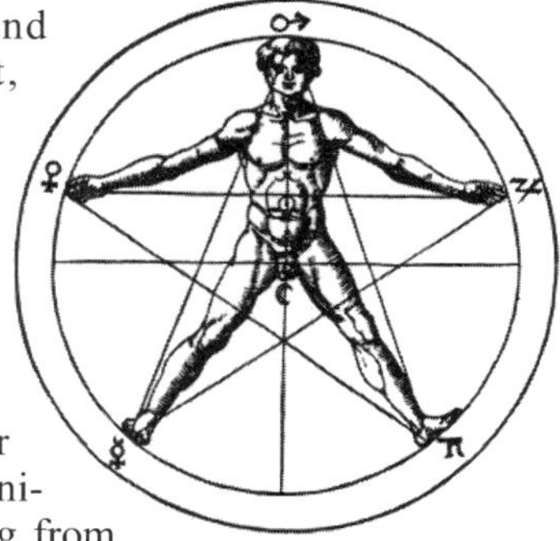

The pentagram represents the human *microcosm*, or tiny model of the Universe. In this drawing from Agrippa's *Occult Philosophy,* it is seen as a person standing with feet set wide and arms outspread. In this the pentagram is also a way of representing the Goddess. In the inverted or upside-down position, the pentagram resembles the head of a goat, with two horns up, two ears out, and his beard hanging down. Some Witches use it in this way to represent Pan, the Horned God. But it is also used in this position by Satanists to represent the face of the Christian Devil.

Astrological

Astrological glyphs are familiar to most people. Here are the ones representing all the planets:

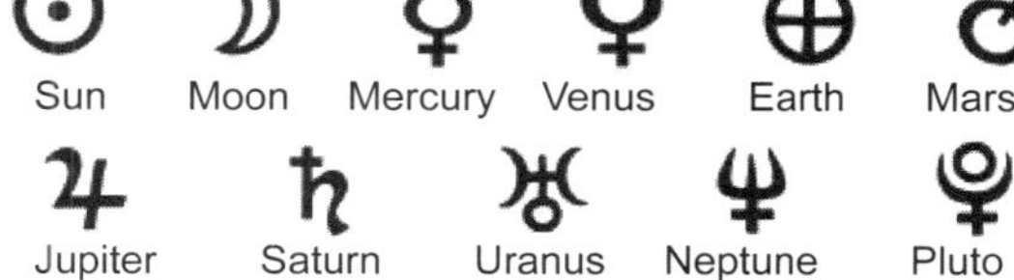

And here are the twelve signs of the Zodiac:

Task: Design Your Personal Sigil

Many Wizards—as well as many artists and writers—create personal glyphs or sigils with which they sign their works, and by which they come to be known. They may even have these made into signet rings or personal jewelry. My own glyph, which I have used for more than 40 years, looks like this. Whenever you see that mark on a piece of artwork, for instance, you'll know that I made it.

I recommend you to design your own sigil. One way is to make a design out of your initials, the way J.R.R. Tolkien did *(right)*. This is called a *monogram.* But you don't have to just use the English alphabet; you can use Theban, or any other alphabet, historical or magickal. Letters can be modified, stretched, or even reversed. The Futhark Runes in particular lend themselves to clever glyphs and sigils, as they can be combined by *superimposition* (putting one on top of another). This way, you can convert your entire name into a single runic figure. Here is an example, using my name:

OBERON = ᛟᛒᛖᚱᛟᚾ =

The first ᛟ is repeated, so only one is needed. ᛒ contains ᚱ. Fitting them all inside the ᛖ makes the design shown here, with the little crosspiece of the ᚾ coming off the side. This is called a *bindrune.* Also, any runes can be reversed (as in a mirror image)—and always are when doubled (as in HELLO, written in Runes as: ᚺᛖᛚᛚᛟ).

Try working with your own name and initials, and play around with different versions till you come up with something you like. The aim here is to make your monogram as simple as possible, yet incorporate all the letters. When you finally have your own personal glyph, sigil, or bindrune, you can use it to sign everything from letters to artwork.

Lesson 6: Glossary of Magickal Symbols and Objects

Sigil: A design, symbol, or cryptic device used to represent someone or something. Also called a *glyph* ("carving"), as in *hieroglyph* ("sacred carving").

Cryptograms: Literally, "secret writing." Any of various magickal alphabets created and used by magicians, alchemists, and Wizards.

Runes: Any of various ancient Germanic alphabets, each letter of which contains an *esoteric* ("secret") meaning as well as representing ordinary sounds.

Runestones: Stones marked with letters of a runic alphabet and used for divination by "casting the runes."

Charge: To imbue something with magickal energy and intent.

Talisman: A magickally charged object or drawing that one makes or acquires, then carries on one's person in order to bring good luck, or as a tool to accomplish a specific purpose. Usually engraved with appropriate symbols, talismans may be made or bought, and any object may be turned into a talisman by magickally charging it.

Amulet: An object charged with power for protection, or to turn aside bad luck, and carried on one's person. Amulets are usually made from found natural objects, such as holy stones, fossils, crystals, shells, meteorites, acorns, bones, etc. However, amulets can also be made or drawn.

Charm: Spoken or written magickal words. Also, objects carried on one's person for their magickal powers or properties.

Cantrip: A written spell or charm that reads the same forwards or backwards.

Object link: Any object, such as a lock of hair, which by association becomes a link between the magician and the person for or against whom the magick is being worked.

Ligature: A magickal binding of a person.

Measure: A length of cord used to measure a person's height—often made as a part of an Initiation rite.

Pact: A binding written oath, or agreement between two entities.

Fetish: Any object believed to have magickal power.

Icon: A sacred image or representation of a deity or spirit, such as a picture or statue.

Poppet: A doll or figurine made in the image of an actual person or animal that acts as a focus for magick. Also called *fith fath.*

Witch bottle: A container filled with reflective or sharp objects and buried near the home to deflect away negative energy.

Lesson 7: Amulets and Talismans

Amulets

An *amulet* (from L. *amuletum,* "means of defense") is an object charged with magickal power for protection, or to turn aside bad luck, illness, or evil, and carried on one's person. Traditionally, amulets are usually made from found natural objects—especially ones whose unusual shape or color caught one's eye—such as holy stones, fossils, crystals, shells, meteorites, acorns, bones, etc. These would be drilled with a hole and strung on a cord to be worn around the neck, or else kept in a little *gris-gris* (GREE-gree) bag worn around the neck. The magickal properties of such objects were felt to be *intrinsic* ("within").

No single amulet is all-purpose (other than for general "good luck"), but they are not usually as specific as talismans. The Roman naturalist, Pliny the Elder (23–79 CE), described three basic types of amulets, based on their purpose: protection against misfortune, healing and protection against ill health, and medicinal.

Here are a few traditional amulets: A necklace of *chicken bones* worn around your neck protects against psychic attacks. A *black holey stone* is a powerful jinx-breaker and keeps away evil. *Garlic* worn around the neck keeps away vampires (and everyone else also!). A *mandrake root* cures ill health and protects against evil. *Turquoise* protects against the "evil eye." The most popular good luck amulets are *four-leaf clovers* and *rabbit's feet* (but first, ask the rabbit!). To attract good fortune, wear an amulet of *sarsaparilla root* around your neck, light a green candle, and chant three times: *"Bad luck decline; good luck be mine!"*

In addition to simple found natural objects, ancient Egyptians, Assyrians, Babylonians, Arabs, Hebrews, Greeks, and Romans created countless sculpted amulets based on symbolic images. For instance, frogs promoted fertility; *ankhs* were for long life; the *udjat,* or "Eye of Horus," was for good health and protection against evil; the *scarab* beetle protected against evil magick, and guaranteed resurrection in the Afterlife. To the Assyrians and Babylonians, rams stood for *virility* (male sexual potency), and bulls for virility and strength. Eyes and phallic symbols are nearly universal protections against evil spirits and the "evil eye."

Religious symbols are also popular amulets. Pagans wear images or symbols of their gods (such as the Hammer of Thor, the Caduceus of Hermes, or the Eye of Horus). Jews wear the 6-pointed *Mogen David* ("Star of David"). Christians wear crosses, fish, and medals of saints. Witches wear pentacles.

Talismans

A *talisman* is a specially made object charged and endowed with magickal powers, as a tool to accomplish a specific purpose. There are talismans for making fortunes, winning in gambling, preventing sudden death, improving memory, and even making good speeches. Like amulets, talismans are usually carried on one's person. The most powerful talismans are ones actually made by the person who will be using them. A talisman made for you by someone else can never be as strong as one you make yourself.

A talisman can be of any shape or material, but traditionally, some substances are more appropriate than others, and their use will imbue the talisman with more power. The most commonly used materials for talismans are based on the planetary correspondences for the days of the week (see 3.VI.5: "Table of Correspondences Planets"). Look at the chart, and see that each day is associated with a planet, and each planet is associated with a concern. Because each planet also has an associated color and metal, talismans reflecting those concerns should be made of those metals—or at least painted in those colors. (Because metallic Mercury is a liquid, tin or aluminum are considered appropriate for Mercury talismans.)

Most talismans are made in the form of metal discs, with appropriate sigils and symbols engraved on each side. Then they may be worn on a chain as a pendant. Suitably engraved talisman disks can, of course, be purchased at most occult shops. But if you are really serious about your intention, you should make your own. Some metals can be bought in hardware stores. Lead fishing weights can be beaten flat for Saturn. Iron, however, can't be easily beaten flat without making it molten in a forge. Disks of gold, silver, and copper can be made by taking coins and beating them flat with a hammer and anvil. A solid gold coin for the Sun may be a bit expensive, but a gold-plated or gold-alloy one will serve. You can engrave them using the same techniques I described for engraving the runes on your athamé (see 3.II.5).

Talisman for Success in Gaming. (Le Petit Albert, *1722)*

Talisman for Discovering Treasures. (Grimoire du Honorius, *1629)*

A talisman should be engraved on the appropriate day—even the right times of day have been calculated (see 4.V.2: "Dance of the Hours"). See 5.VII.3: "Talismans of the Planetary Powers" for traditional talismanic sigils for the seven planets. The center sigil is the astrological glyph; the upper represents the character; the lower left represents the governing Spirit; and the lower right represents the governing Intelligence.

On the other side of the talisman, engrave your name, personal sigil, and the specific intention or purpose in your favorite magickal alphabet.

Lesson 8: Magick Minerals

During the Middle Ages, crystals and other stones were used as amulets and set into talismans for every magickal purpose, from protection, sleep, and pleasant dreams, to fortune-telling and healing. Pigments and shapes were considered significant in determining these magickal uses, and such crystals were believed to have a life-essence of their own. These are most commonly worn in jewelry, such as rings and pendants, but loose stones may also be carried in a pouch or mojo bag. Below are some of the magickal associations of various gems and minerals.

Magickal Gems and Minerals for Talismanic Jewelry

MINERAL	ATTRIBUTES
Agate	Eloquence, intelligence, truthfulness. (Black) Love, victory, strength, courage, self-confidence, prosperity. (Red) Protection against lightning.
Amber	All-purpose spell strengthener. Protection, heals illness, brings money.
Amethyst	Spiritual ideals and virtues. Peace of mind. Transform negativity. Shrewd business decisions, protection for soldiers, prevents drunkenness.
Aquamarine	Health, youth, hope, happiness.
Beryl	Harmony in relationships, mental agility, physical energy, hope. Cures laziness.
Bloodstone	Grants wishes, eloquence, victory, protection, health, admiration. Guards against deception.
Carnelian	Friendship, cure for depression. Luck, protection, hope, eloquence and bold speech.
Cat's Eye	Long life and protection against evil.
Chrysolite	Prudence, discretion and wisdom.
Chrysophase	Joy and gaiety.
Corundum	Helps mental stability.
Emerald	Foreknowledge, faith, truth, mental agility, resourcefulness, insight, fidelity.
Garnet	Loyalty, faithfulness, sincerity, devotion, energy, health, charity. Guards against nightmares.
Hematite	Attraction, charm, alertness, spiritual well-being. Improves destiny.
Jacinth	Worn in a shoe, provides hospitality and protection for travelers against injury or sickness.
Jade	(White) Believed to be the melodious essence of concentrated love. (Black) Strength and power.
Jasper	Joy, happiness, relief from pain. (Red) Night protection. (Green) Healing. (Brown) Grounding.
Lapis Lazuli	Capacity, ability, success. Increases psychic and magickal energy.
Lodestone	*(Magnetite)* Personal attraction, charisma, honesty, integrity, virility. Attracts true love. Protection against baneful magick.
Malachite	Enhances visions. On a cradle, protects infant.
Moonstone	Inspires passion, aides foreknowledge. Promotes love, compassion and sympathy.
Obsidian	Dedicated to Hecate, used for magick mirrors.
Olivine	Happiness, pleasure, modesty and simplicity.
Opal	Memory, cognitive abilities. Spirituality, fidelity and assurance.
Pyrite	*(Fool's Gold)* Protection against tempers and falsehoods.
Quartz	Purity, infinity, Vision, divination. Protects wearer from unpleasant dreams & evil influences. Holds energies like a battery.
Ruby	King of gemstones. Mental & physical health, heals wounds. Peacekeeping, love and passion.
Sapphire	Magician's aid for understanding omens, antidote for many poisons. Most potent of all, **Star Sapphire** is "Stone of Destiny," bringing luck, victory, faithfulness. Protects against fraud & treachery.
Sardonyx	Vivacity, brightness, good humor, fame.
Topaz	Love, affection, sweet disposition and nature.
Turquoise	Averts accidents, improves second sight. Power and protection against psychic attack. Enhances verbal communication.

Course Four: Rites

Course Four: Rites

Class I: Practical Magick

1. Introduction: Believing in Magick

S A WELL-KNOWN PUBLIC WIZARD, I travel all over the world doing workshops and personal appearances. I've been interviewed for books, magazines, newspapers, radio and TV shows. And one of the questions I get asked the most is: "Do you really believe in magick?" This always amazes me. I mean, you don't talk about *believing in* things that are part of your everyday reality. No one asks if you *believe in* cars, television, or trees; they're just *there.* Well, this is the way it is for me and magick. I *live* magick. Every day, every moment, with every action I take, I am coming from a place of magick, and magick is moving through me. My thoughts are magick; my dreams are magick; the creation of a piece of sacred sculpture is pure magick. Organizing my thoughts and knowledge of magick into the creation of this Grimoire for you is itself a great act of magick. And right now, I am writing these very words by magick. As the search engine of my mind draws forth the appropriate words out of the vast library of experience and information in my memory banks, my fingers automatically tap the right keys on my keyboard, and the words of my thoughts magically appear on the screen before my very eyes.

So I usually answer something along the lines of: "Do you believe in Love?" But then, again, there are people out there who don't even believe in Love. They can hardly be expected to believe in Magick.

Lesson 2. Why Study Magick?

— by Sheila Attig (from *HOME Cooking,* 1997)

The path of Wizardry is not for everyone. It requires extraordinary honesty, dedication, persistence, and a deep commitment to change. Real magick requires a fundamentally balanced personality willing to take on the challenges of accelerated growth. The decision to embark on the magickal path should never be taken lightly, for once begun there is no turning back. It is a decision to trust your individual experience, and to take responsibility in all areas of your life.

To call in *(invoke)* is to call forth *(evoke),* and each person who contemplates beginning this path has chosen to accelerate the development and resolution of all the things in your life experience to clear the way for concentration on the magickal path. From the beginning, the student will perceive that the lessons you most need to learn are delivered with astonishing clarity. Along the way, you will be presented with many tests and difficulties unique to the Magickal path. The ability to learn from these experiences and thrive is the true measure of Initiation.

Unlike most forms of religion, Magick has no central written codex of laws and offers no easy escape routes. The laws under which it operates are uniform, but are discovered only through direct experience. To truly begin, then, is to commit yourself to a lifetime of discovery and sacrifice offered without reservation. For those few with the honesty and courage to choose this path there is no turning back. Once begun, you can cease to practice, but the lessons will still be delivered on schedule in your life.Opening yourself to the Innerworld opens the way to change at the deepest inner levels. Without the courage to confront and change all the aspects of this Innerworld that will be presented, the risk of confusion and self-deception is great. To undertake such study without the foundation of a balanced personality, and clear knowledge of the best and worst aspects of the self could be gambling with your sanity. Until you know firmly who you are, why take such a risk? Magick has a way of calling in old business that must be cleared before serious work can begin, and many who approach it decide to stop when they first experience their share. Not everyone will find that dire consequences immediately ensue when they choose the Magickal Path. For those who choose it rightly, the speed at which things clear in your life will be experienced with a distinct sense of relief.

Magick is powerful, but it is foolish to undertake it as a part of a quest for increased personal power. If you desire to be a master, rather than a servant, Magick is not for you. Before beginning, ask yourself, "What do I intend to *do* with my Magick?" Make no mistake, the only true answer for real Wizards is: "I desire to *serve*—Spirit and humankind—and I am willing to take the risks to complete that service."

3. Glossary of Magickal Acts

Oral tradition: Information passed on through memorization and recital, rather than in writing.

Incantation: A hypnotic and sometimes rhyming chant or formula used in spell casting.

Litany: A repetitive, hypnotic prayer.

Asperge: To sprinkle with holy or magickally-charged water for purification and to disperse negative energy.

Smudge: To purify by wafting the smoke of burning incense over and around whatever or whomever is being smudged.

Deosil: "Sunwise." The natural direction of the Sun. This is clockwise in the Northern hemisphere and counter-clockwise in the Southern hemisphere. Usually considered the best direction to move when working positive magick.

Widdershins: "Against the direction." Opposite of *deosil*. Contrary to the apparent course of the Sun. Counter-clockwise in the Northern hemisphere and clockwise in the Southern hemisphere.

Incubation: Going into a temple or other sacred place alone for a period of time to receive divine inspiration, visions or dreams.

Mudra: Physical gestures used primarily as magickal associational devices by linking parts of the bioenergetic system.

Mantra: Words or sounds that trigger parts of the bioenergetic system, energize parts of the astral plane, or trigger powerful energies for magickal, mystical, or health purposes. They are also used as magickal associational devices.

Mandala: A visual image used primarily as a magickal associational device, particularly when drawn in a circular design.

Object link: Any object, such as a lock of hair, that by association becomes a link between the magician and the person for or against whom the magick is being worked. Also called *relics*.

Poppet: A doll or figurine made in the image of an actual person or animal, which acts as a focus for magick.

Charm: Spoken or written magickal words. Also, objects carried on one's person for their magickal powers or properties.

Incantation: The words of a spell that are chanted or sung, often in a repetitive and rhyming form.

Cantrip: A written spell or charm that reads the same forwards or backwards.

Spell: An organized act to alter probabilities in the direction desired; simply, to make something more or less likely to occur. A spell may include *mudras, mantras,* and *mandalas*.

Ritual: Specific actions and/or words designed to produce specific results, and often repeated for the same purpose.

Working: Any magickal act.

Banish: To send away or demand the departure of entities whose presence is no longer wanted.

Exorcism: A formal ritual of magickal banishment invoking the authority of a higher power.

Conjure/Conjuration: Summoning up non-physical entities or spirits.

Invoke/Invocation: "To speak from within." Inviting a deity or spirit to enter into us, so that we speak with its voice and/or manifest its attributes in our own person. *Invoke* also means "to petition or call for help or aid."

Evoke/Evocation: "To speak from without." Summoning a deity or spirit into visible manifestation outside of ourselves—usually within a triangle of art, crystal, or image—or into another person. Evoke means "to summon and cause to appear;" or "to produce through artistry a vivid impression."

Grounding: A shutting down of psychic awareness and returning to normal conscious thought patterns.

Charge: To imbue something with magickal energy and intent.

Consecrate/Consecration: To sanctify or bless. The act of setting apart the sacred from the mundane.

Blessing: The use of magick to benefit yourself or others.

Blighting: The use of magick to harm others.

Binding: Magically restraining someone or something.

Curse: A magickal spell intended to harm another or wish misfortune upon them.

Dharma: "Work." A religious precept, or sacred tasks.

Karma: "Action." The concept that one's deeds can be counted either for or against spiritual advancement, in this life or over several lifetimes.

Enlightenment: A state of deep and total awareness, experiencing constant connectedness with all and everything.

Lucidity: A state of enhanced awareness, with an exceptional understanding of the "is-ness" of things, people and events and their connectedness.

Lesson 4: Doing Magick

Ritual

The power of magickal rituals comes from their ability to arouse the *emotions* necessary for spell-casting, from the correspondences between the rituals and the desired results, and from the correspondences between the rituals and the Universe, including our own minds and memories. This includes memories of former incarnations and memories that predate our existence as civilized beings—or even as human creatures. Emotional control and release are necessary in the practice of magick. Control enables you to concentrate, visualizing the effect you want to produce. Emotional release allows the visualized desire, with its accompanying strong emotion, to surge up and be propelled forward toward the subject of your spell. Your emotions are the basis of your ability to do magick. No matter the magickal system, personal power must be infused with the need and intention, and then released. The energies of magick are those of Life itself.

This is why just any old ritual will not work. You must be completely convinced—emotionally and subconsciously as well as consciously—that it *will* work. To be that convincing, the ritual must reach below the level of the conscious mind and arouse those psychic powers and abilities little understood (or even acknowledged) by modern science. When you are able to do this successfully, you will create a "suspension of disbelief" similar to the state you place your mind into when you are deeply engrossed in a gripping novel, or a good movie. You're just "there"—immersed in the scenario—and you leave your critical faculties aside for the moment. This means you are experiencing the ritual through your right hemisphere rather than your left—as if you were dreaming, hallucinating, or under hypnosis. And in this state, anything becomes possible.

In doing rituals, some overlap and repetition is intended. Rituals gain power through repetition; the more you do them, the stronger they get. This is much like with Gods—the more people believe in them, and the more they are invoked and prayed to, the more powerful they become.

Theurgy: Prayer and Petition

As living beings, we are filled with the life force, or Spirit, that sustains our existence. We fuel ourselves with Elemental energies from the Sun (Fire), food (Earth), drink (Water), and breath (Air). We release these energies as we move, work, dance, play, exercise—and do magick. And as conscious beings, we are each reservoirs of great magickal power—most importantly, the power to *choose.*

The individual cells in our bodies are organized into *organs,* and organs are parts of the several *systems* that make up our bodies. In the same way, we are all individual members of humanity, and humanity is a part of the greater Kingdom of Life on Earth. Thus we are cells in the vast body of Gaea—Mother Earth Herself. At each level of organization, there is a *synergic* ("combined") *awareness* or *consciousness.*

Each cell is a tiny creature, following its own little agenda and making its own decisions. So are the organs and systems. And so are we. But this synergic process of ever-increasing manifestations of consciousness doesn't stop with us, as we also are parts of larger systems, and at each level, new synergic consciousnesses come into being. Also, of course, many other beings—some with physical bodies and some without—all have their own agendas and consciousnesses. We refer to these entities as Gods, Goddesses, angels, demons, djinn, saints, ghosts, devas, Elementals, totems, faeries—or just spirits.

Prayer is based on contacting and communicating with these other consciousnesses, just as we would with other people. And in the same way we might ask for help from our parents, teachers, or others who may have greater authority or power in a certain area than we have, so we might *petition* ("seek, ask") wiser or more powerful Spirit beings for help or guidance. This is called *theurgy,* or religious magick—and it is probably the most universal and common practice of magick, done by members of virtually every religion in the world.

The most common form of petition Magick is done by writing a request on a piece of special paper—such as parchment, rice paper, or flash paper (my favorite!). Then the paper is ceremonially burned in your thurible, firepot, or with the Fire candle on your altar—thus sending your request into the Astral Realm.

Lesson 5: Thaumaturgy: Sympathetic Magick

Under the **Law of Sympathy,** a Wizard is able to affect people and events through sympathetic magick—the magickal manipulation of some object that is similar to or has *sympathy* ("affinity") with the subject. This principle states that *"things that have an affinity with each other influence and interact with each other over a distance."*

Sympathetic magick is also called *thaumaturgy* ("wonder-working"). This is the use of magick to effect changes in the reality of the outer world—what we call practical magick. Thaumaturgy is also often referred to as "low magick" or sorcery—especially when it is provided in the service of others. All forms of *folk magick*—which served the villages and common people—became known as low magick. This is the magick practiced on an everyday basis to affect matters of daily life, such as ensuring that one's cows give milk, that one's illness is cured, or that one's home is protected from natural or supernatural disasters.

Imitative and Contagious Magick

To create an effective spell, the ritual should in some way imitate the result you want to achieve. For instance, if you want it to rain, sprinkle water on the ground, or spray it into the air. This is called *imitative* or *homeopathic* magick. It is based on the **Law of Similarity,** which states that *"like produces like and an effect resembles its cause."*

One of the most striking examples of imitative magick is *envoutement*—a Voodoo term that refers to the use of waxen images or poppets (proxy dolls) to curse an enemy. The poppet is identified with the subject of the spell, and so named. As the Voodoo doll is punished, so will the victim, represented by the doll, be hurt. Of course, the same principle works for helping or healing someone by proxy.

There is more to it than that, however. An *object-*

link and *incantation* are commonly used to make the poppet the magickal representative of the subject, and link the living subject of the spell with your Magick ritual. An object-link may be established by the use of a *relic,* which is anything formerly connected with the subject. This is called *contagious* magick, based on the **Law of Contact,** which says that *"things once in contact continue to affect each other."* The strongest relics by far are parts of the subject's body—such as hair, nail clippings, blood, a tooth, and the like—containing the person's DNA. These would then be incorporated into the making of the poppet.

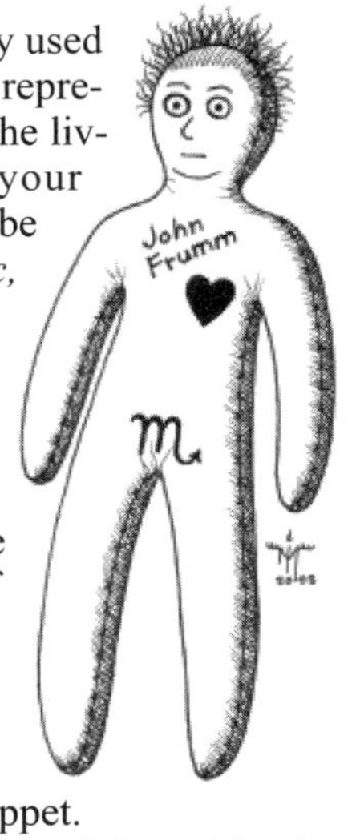

Other suitable relics are items of the subject's clothing in which the poppet would be dressed or personal jewelry belonging to the subject. Samples of handwriting (especially signatures) also work well as object links, and photographs are now commonly used, especially for long-distance healings.

Tasks: Sympathetic Magick

Here are a few types of sympathetic magick that you can try yourself. Once you've done a few of these, you'll have a sense of how sympathetic magick works, and you can begin to create your own.

Candle Magick

Candles have been used in sympathetic magick for millennia to represent people as well as things and concepts: love, money, luck, success, health, harmony, strength, fertility, and all manner of things. The candles can be of any size or shape; it's the *color* that's important. See the listings of color correspondences in 1.III.8: "The Colors of Magick." Also consult the Tables of Correspondence in 3.VI for the colors associated with the Elements, days of the week, and signs of the Zodiac. Briefly, here is a spectrum of some of the most popular color associations for candle magick:

White—Purity, truth, sincerity; blessing, or anything you want!
Pink—Honor, love, morality.
Red—Physical work, as in healing of people and animals; strength, health, passion, and sex.
Orange—Pride and courage; heroism and attraction.
Yellow—Mental work, meditation, divination.
Green—Vegetation, as in gardening; fertility and prosperity; luck.
Light blue—Emotional work, love, etc.; peace and protection.
Dark blue—Impulsion, depression, changeability.
Purple—Power, wealth, good fortune, ambition.
Black—Evil, loss, discord, confusion; blighting or binding.

Candle magick should be done on your personal altar—just make sure there is nothing anywhere near or above it which could catch fire, and *never* leave candles burning unattended!

If you are burning a candle for yourself or some other person, you should first choose a candle of a color that expresses your intention or purpose. Botanicas and occult shops sell candles of various colors in the shape of men and women, which are very excellent for this kind of candle magick, but these are not required. Ordinary tapers or votive candles will do, as long as they're the right color.

Next, inscribe the subject's name into the candle with a sharp instrument—ideally, the point of your athamé. As you do, visualize the subject (you might want to have a photo to look at, or a mirror if it's you), and name the candle accordingly, saying something like:

This waxen candle I do name
As (subject's full name); may its flame
As (subject's first name)'s spirit now burn bright
Empower my spell with magick might!

Then you should "dress" the candle by anointing it all over with the appropriate oil. You can buy essential oils of almost any herb in health food stores, botanicas, occult shops, and even some drug stores (see Tables of Correspondence in 3.VI). To dress the candle, put a few drops of oil on it, and rub them in with your hands from the center outwards, while concentrating your thoughts on the person and purpose.

Now, light the Fire candle on your altar, then turn out all the lights in the room. Begin the ritual by drawing a Circle around yourself and the altar with your wand or athamé, calling the Directions and invoking whatever Spirits you wish to join you (consult Tables of Correspondence). See 4.IV: "Conducting a Ritual" for more information on this. Now meditate for a moment on your intention, visualizing what you want to happen as a result of this working.

Then light the candle representing the subject of this spell, saying something like:

Candle burning in the night,
With your flame enchanted;
By the power of your light
May my wish be granted.

Sit for a while, staring into the flame in a meditative state, and visualize the desired outcome of your spell. When you feel it is complete, thank the Spirits and the Elements you had invited, and release the Circle. Finally, say something like the following, and blow the candle out:

Though these flames of the material world
be darkened,
They shall ever burn in the worlds beyond.
The rite is ended. Blessed be.

Repeat this ritual every day until the candle is burned down to a mere lump. This is a typical candleburning spell, using sympathetic magick. There are as many possible variations as your needs and imagination can conceive. Good references for magickal candle-burning spells and rituals are: Ray Buckland's *Practical Candleburning Rituals* and *Advanced Candle Magick* and Gerina Dunwich's *Candlelight Spells* and *The Magick of Candle Burning*.

Cord & Knot Magick

Any simple emotion, objective, or Elemental force can be tied and controlled by the simple means of binding it in a knot. Love, magickal power, winds, clouds, rain, illness—all can be tied into a cord to create a kind of "storage battery" to hold the power of the spell. A Rite of Knots may be performed for any purpose desired, and the knotted cord either carried or worked into some part of one's clothing, or used in other ways. The knots might be untied later to release the spell, or (to banish negativity) the cord may be ceremonially burned or buried. Any small ritual may be created for the tying of the knots, and a number of them are recorded.

Olaus Magnus, Historia de Gentibus Septentrionalibus *1555*

In the woodcut above, a Wizard is selling a knotted Wind Cord to some sailors. Winds are tied in the cord, so that if the sailor needs wind for his sail, he just unties a cord—one knot for a light breeze, two for a strong wind, and three for a gale!

To cure a cold or other minor illness, a Witch or Wizard may "buy" it from the subject for some small sum of money and immediately knot a string to "tie in the sickness." The string should then be hung on a bush or buried in some remote place where it will molder away. To cure warts, take a piece of string and tie a knot in it for each wart, and touch the knot to the wart. Hang the string under the eaves of your house and the rainwater running down the string will wash the warts away. After the next rain, bury it in the Earth.

In the Spell of Nine Knots, a series of nine knots are loosely (so they can be untied later) tied in a special 13" scarlet cord used just for this purpose. As each knot is tied, the intent of the spell is visualized ever more strongly, directing the focus and power into the knot. The knots are tied in the following order and pattern, with these (or similar) words:

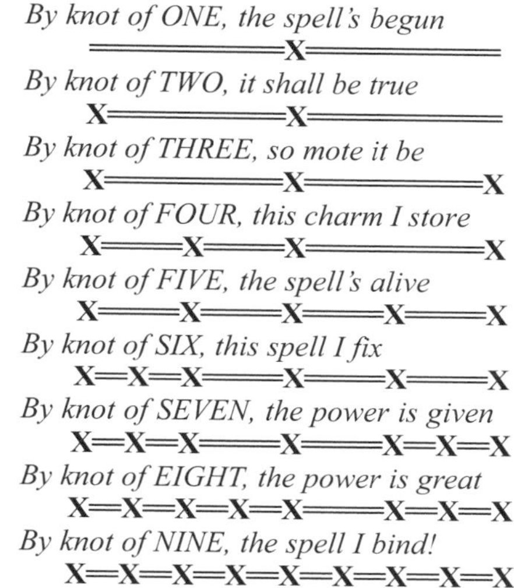

At the tying of the last knot, all the energy is directed into the cord and knots, with a final visualization of the intent. The power raised is now stored in these knots, where it can be kept until the proper moment for its release. Although the knots were tied in one ritual, they must be released one at a time over nine consecutive days. Release them in the same order they were tied—NOT the reverse order! Start with the first one in the middle, and finish with the last one next to it. Each day, before you untie the knot, once again concentrate on what is to happen, and repeat the same words of the tying spell as you untie that knot.

Weather Working

> *The weatherworker's and seamaster's calling upon wind and water were crafts already known to his pupils, but it was he who showed them why the true Wizard uses such spells only at need, since to summon up such earthly forces is to change the earth of which they are a part... "Rain in Roke may be drought in Osskil," he said, "and a calm in the East Reach may be storm and ruin in the West, unless you know what you are about."*
>
> —Ursula K. LeGuin
> (*A Wizard of Earthsea*, pp. 53-54)

Many forms of sympathetic magick have been applied to weather working. As I explained in 1.5.4: "Auras: Cloud Busting," large-scale weather working should not be done casually, as there can be unforeseen consequences. If you have a large group working together, you can use the techniques of "Auric Cloud-Busting" from 1.5.4 to clear the sky, or to push a weather front away from your area. Or, conversely, to pull one toward you, if you know it's out there somewhere.

The most famous weather spell is: *"Rain, rain, go away; come again some other day."* I've used this one very effectively with several thousand people all linking hands and chanting together with serious intent. But if the rain *does* then go away, eventually there will come that other day, and it might not be one you choose! So to balance the equation, you should pick a day you *want* it to rain, and say the counter-spell: *"Rain, rain, come today; wait no more another day."* Sympathetic magick for weather work simply consists of trying to reproduce on a small scale what you want to happen on a larger scale. One effective technique is to lay out a large map of the area you wish to affect. If you want rain in a place, sprinkle water over it. If you want sunshine, use a mirror to reflect a spot of sunlight there.

In serious weather working, the most important thing is to know the prevailing weather patterns for the area, and what factors might be affecting them at the moment. Shifting of the jet stream, El Ninos, a high-pressure build-up over the Pacific Ocean, a hurricane forming in the North Atlantic, a cold front moving down from the North Pole—all these elements need to be taken into consideration. Fortunately, with weather satellites and the Weather Channel on television, this is much easier for us now than it was for our predecessors! In Medieval times, it was believed that a Witch could raise or calm the winds by throwing a rock over one shoulder, tossing sand in the air, burning sage leaves, whistling, or speaking appropriate incantations. Of these, whistling up the wind remains a common technique. My own favorite tune to whistle a wind is "They Call the Wind Mariah," from the 1969 movie *Paint Your Wagon,* with Clint Eastwood.

Olaus Magnus, Historia de Gentibus Septentrionalibus *1555*

Traditional American rainmakers during the 1930s used fireworks (simulating lightning, and making smoky clouds) and sprinklings of water, such as you can do with a lawn sprinkler or a garden hose set on "spray." A smoky fire (using green leaves) will simulate clouds, and a dry, non-smoky fire will simulate a hot, sunny day. Rain sticks (a long hollow tube with many nails driven all the way into it, with some gravel inside and capped at both ends) are popular for rain-calling, as are rain dances with lots of loud drumming, simulating thunder.

Here's an old sympathetic magick rainmaking spell: Boil water in an iron cauldron or kettle over an outdoor fire. When the steam is rising to the sky, stir the water with a stout wooden rod, then wave the rod through the steam, and strike it three times hard on the outside of the pot, loudly calling each time to the sky:

Hither, cloud, and loose thy flood!
Whither, drought, let rain come out!

When he was a kid, my son Bryan was an excellent young Wizard. He developed his own system of Magick using stones, which he would collect based on their appearances. To use one, he would simply place it on his altar and say a little spell of intention. Among these was one he called a "snow-stone" because it had white snowflake patterns all over it. One snowy December, when Bryan was around 11, he stuck a snowball in the freezer. The following April, on a sunny day, he came home from school and informed us that he had decided to make it snow, as there hadn't been any snow since Yule, and he wanted to play in the snow. Moreover, he had told his friends he was going to do this! He got out the snowball and placed it in a bowl on the altar to melt, with his snow-stone on top of it. The next day there was a blizzard—in mid-April!—and they had to close the schools.

Sympathetic Magick for Schoolwork

Try this yourself: Choose which subject in school seems to be the most challenging for you at this time. Find the appropriate color, stone, tool, and other items, and make a small altar dedicated to this subject. Focus on how you wish to succeed: getting an A on a test or an essay, etc. Quiet your mind and charge the stone as you visualize your success. Keep the stone in your pocket to focus you on your success while taking the test, writing the essay...

Lesson 6. The Laws of Magick

Magick can either be seen as a purely internal process, or it can include influences and connections with outside entities, ghosts, gods, or Spirits. Either way, magick operates along its own internal systems of rules and logic, just like physics and mathematics. Once these rules are understood, they can be used by the magician just as a chemist uses the laws of chemistry.

Eliphas Levi, in his *Dogma and Ritual of High Magic* (1856), described three fundamental Laws of Magick:

1. **The Law of the Human Will.** The success of magick depends upon the will summoned and directed by the magician.
2. **The Law of Astral Light** and the intermediary ethereal principle: an energy permeating the Universe, which the magician can access and use to effect changes at a distance.
3. **The Law of Connectedness,** linking inside and outside, the material and the ideal, assuming there is no difference between the microcosmos and the macrocosmos.

To these, another law was later added by the Order of the Golden Dawn:

4. **The Law of Imagination or Visualization,** calling upon powers within and without.

The terminology and Laws of *Sympathetic, Imitative,* and *Contagious* Magick were coined by Scottish anthropologist Sir James Frazer (1854–1941) in his comparative study of myth and magick, *The Golden Bough* (1890). Other writers have categorized the laws differently, and there are many traditions, all of which can work. The Laws of Magick are not legislative laws like traffic laws, but, like those of physics or of musical harmony, are practical observations that have accumulated over thousands of years, with remarkable similarity in almost every known human culture.

The Law of Resonance

Some believe that all the Laws of Magick can be summed up in a single Great Law or Principle. Dutch Grey Council member Luc Sala calls this:

The Law of Resonance: The fundamental principle of magick is *Resonance* ("echo"), in and between the material world, the world of ideas, and the Spirit World. Resonance in time, form, content, frequency, and *is-ness* (the deeper essential quality of material and immaterial things) is what makes a connection meaningful. Acts of magick consciously (willfully) use these resonances, but the *efficacy* (result) often depends on greater resonances, and therefore defies the laws of normal *causality* (cause and effect).

This refers to the correspondences listed in chapter 3.VI, and includes Sympathetic, Contagious, Theurgic, and other forms of magick. It also includes the notion that resonance in Time is a magickal tool and that the past and the future are mirrors, both accessible from the present. Love is the Great Resonator and connector and therefore essential for magick.

The three factors of magickal work—and in fact of all spiritual development—can be summed up as: **Love is the key, Truth is the goal, One is the prize** (as the connectedness we sometimes experience can be seen as the prize, the result of the work).

Another development is that in modern physics the "normal" causal reality is slowly giving way to insight and laws like *Quantum Dynamics,* the *Uncertainty Principle,* and the *Non-Locality Paradox,* whereby the role of the observer and even consciousness plays a role. These effects are only noticeable at the extremes of our cosmos, at the very small and the very large dimensions, like inside the atom and at the stellar levels. But at a more normal level, the quantum effects are sometimes noticeable, as in "quantum tunneling," when particles manifest across a mechanical barrier they could not normally pass.

Quantum effects—where the wave and particle characteristics of elementary building blocks at the atomic level are subject to probabilities and are in a sense unpredictable—resemble magickal acts, which are similarly unpredictable in the sense that 1+1 is not always 2, but sometimes 0 or 1. Science and magick are re-converging in the notion that all and everything is connected. According to Luc Sala, the Laws of Nature as we know in science are therefore only a subset of the Laws of Magick, and normal reality is likewise a subset of the wider and Ultimate Reality. However, according to Dragon Singing, the Laws of Nature are a SUPERset of the Laws of Magick, as magick is only a small part of what happens in the infinite Multiverse!

> *"There is no matter as such! All matter originates and exists only by virtue of a force... We must assume behind this force the existence of a conscious and intelligent Mind. This Mind is the matrix of all matter."* —Max Planck,
> Nobel Prize–winning father of Quantum Theory

Lesson 7: The Magickal Process

> *"Whatever you can do, or dream you can, begin it. Boldness has genius, power, and magic in it."*
> —Goethe
>
> *"The only difference between the Possible and Impossible is just that the Impossible takes a little longer to pull off."* —Marc Bolan

It is often said that any great work is 1% inspiration and 99% perspiration. This is certainly true. And there is a step-by-step process in working magick that is just like creating any other kind of manifestation in our life. These steps can be listed as: **Inspiration,**

The Laws of Magick

The most complete description of these laws that has been made to date is by Isaac Bonewits, noted magician, ArchDruid, and author of *Real Magic, Authentic Thaumaturgy,* and *Witchcraft: A Concise Guide*. Isaac is also an Advisor to the Grey Council. The following Laws of Magick are adapted from the 2nd Edition of *Authentic Thaumaturgy,* Isaac's handbook on real magick for fantasy role-playing gamers.

1. **Law of Knowledge**: Understanding brings control; the more you know about a subject, the easier it is to control it. "Knowledge is power."
2. **Law of Self-Knowledge**: The most important magical knowledge is about oneself; familiarity with one's own strengths and weaknesses is vital to a magician. "Know thyself."
3. **Law of Cause & Effect**: If exactly the same actions are done under exactly the same conditions, they will produce exactly the same results; similar strings of events produce similar outcomes. "Control every variable and you control every change—lotsa luck!"
4. **Law of Synchronicity**: Two or more events happening at the same time are likely to have more associations in common than the merely temporal; events rarely happen in isolation from nearby events. "There's no such thing as a *mere* coincidence."
5. **Law of Association**: If any two or more patterns have elements in common, the patterns interact through those common elements, and control of one pattern facilitates control over the other(s); the greater the commonality, the greater the influence. "Commonality controls."
6. **Law of Sympathy**: Things that have an affinity with each other influence and interact with each other over a distance. "Everything is connected to everything else."
7. **Law of Similarity**: Like produces like and an effect resembles its cause; having an accurate image of something facilitates control over it. "Look-alikes *are* alike."
8. **Law of Contagion**: Objects or beings once in contact with each other continue to interact after separation. "Magick is contagious."
9. **Law of Positive Attraction**: Like attracts like; to create a particular reality you must put out energy of a similar sort. "That which is sent, returns."
10. **Law of Negative Attraction**: Like attracts unlike; energy and actions often attract their complimentary "opposites." "Opposites attract."
11. **Law of Names**: Knowing the name, you know that which is named; knowing the complete and true name of an object, being or process gives one complete control over it. "What's in a name?—Everything!"
12. **Law of Words of Power**: Certain words are able to alter the internal and external realities of those uttering them, and their power may rest in the very sounds as much as in their meanings. "A word to the wise is sufficient."
13. **Law of Personification:** Any phenomenon may be considered to be alive and to have a personality, that is, to "be" an entity or being, and may be effectively dealt with thusly. "Anything can be a person."
14. **Law of Invocation:** It is possible to establish internal communication with entities from either inside or outside of oneself, said entities seeming to be inside of oneself during the communication process. "Beings within…"
15. **Law of Evocation:** It is possible to establish external communication with entities from either inside or outside of oneself, said entities seeming to be outside of oneself during the communication process. "…Beings without."
16. **Law of Identification:** It is possible through maximum association between the elements of oneself and those of another being to actually *become* that being to the point of sharing its knowledge and wielding its power. "You can become another."
17. **Law of Infinite Data:** The number of phenomena to be known is infinite; we will never run out of things to learn! "There's always something new."
18. **Law of Finite Senses:** Every sense mechanism of every entity is limited by both range and type of data perceived. "Just because you can't see it doesn't mean it's not there."
19. **Law of Personal Universes:** Everyone lives in and quite possibly creates a unique universe which can never be 100% identical to that lived in by another; so-called "reality" is in fact a matter of consensus opinions. "You live in your cosmos and I'll live in mine."
20. **Law of Infinite Universes:** The total number of universes into which all possible combinations of existing phenomena could be organized is infinite. "All things are possible, though some are more probable than others."
21. **Law of Pragmatism:** If a pattern of belief or behavior enables you to survive and to accomplish chosen goals, than that belief or behavior is "true" or "real" or "sensible" on whatever levels of reality are involved. "If it works, it's true."
22. **Law of True Falsehoods:** A concept or act may seem nonsensical and yet still be "true," provided that it "works" in a specific context. "If it's a paradox it's probably true."
23. **Law of Polarity:** Any pattern of data can be split into at least two patterns with "opposing" characteristics, and each will contain the essence of the other within itself. "Everything contains its opposite."
24. **Law of Synthesis:** The synthesis of two or more "opposing" patterns of data will produce a new pattern that will be "truer" than either of the first ones were; that is, it will be applicable to more realities. "Synthesis reconciles."
25. **Law of Dynamic Balance**: To survive and become powerful, one must keep every aspect of one's universe(s) in a state of dynamic balance with every other one; extremism is dangerous on all levels of reality. "Dance to the music."
26. **Law of Perversity**: Also known as "Murphy's Law:" If anything can go wrong, it will—and in the most annoying manner possible. "If anything *can* go wrong, it will."
27. **Law of Unity:** Every phenomenon in existence is linked directly or indirectly to every other one, past, present or future; perceived separations between phenomena are based on incomplete sensing and/or thinking. "All is One."
28. **Law of Unintended Consequences**: (from Robert Jordan) Whether or not what you do has the effect you want, it will have at least three you never expected, and one of those usually unpleasant. "There's always something else."

Synchronicities, Perspiration, and **Manifestation.**

An example is this Grimoire I am writing at this moment. It began with an inspired Vision, which I had when I went to see the first Harry Potter movie in December 2001, with a bunch of kids like you. My Witchy wife, Morning Glory, and I had been invited to come and talk to a Jewish *schul* ("school") about real Witchcraft and Wizardry. After the talk, we all went to see *Harry Potter and the Sorcerer's Stone.* Morning Glory and I were in our full magickal regalia, of course, but many of the kids were also wearing capes and cloaks. The theater was packed, and we sat way in the back. As I looked over that huge audience of all those kids, I had several flashes of insight.

1. Inspiration

The first thing that came to me was that many of the kids in this audience (and in similar audiences all over the world over the next few years, as new books and movies keep coming out) are going to be inspired to become Witches and Wizards themselves. And I thought, how can I, as a practicing Wizard, offer something to help? So my next thought was that the first thing they will need to do is establish a personal altar. And I make altar statues. So I decided to create a pair of special God and Goddess altar statues just for kids.

My third thought was that you will need a handbook of real Wizardry. So at the same time I was working on the statues, I started making an outline of what such a book should contain. I wrote the opening "Wizardly Soliloquy," which I read at our Bardic ritual for Imbolg, in honor of Brigit, Irish goddess of creative inspiration. Over the next few months, I kept coming back to it and adding more stuff, rearranging the order, and putting in notes.

2. Synchronicities

The new statues arrived from our factory at the beginning of June, 2002, and I set up a little altar with them, and did a ritual for success in reaching the teen market. Then over Summer Solstice, I went to the International New Age Trade Show in Denver, Colorado, for the first time to show off my line of statuary to prospective stores. While there, I ran into a Wiccan friend, Trish Telesco, who has written about 40 books on Witchcraft and magick. She chided me over not having yet written any books of my own and offered to introduce me to her publisher, New Page Books, who happened to have a booth there also. So I sat down to talk with these fine folks, and of course they wanted to know what kind of a book I had in mind to write. I explained my idea for this Grimoire, and promised to send them a proposal and chapter outline.

A few weeks later, I was attending a large magickal festival as a speaker, and I ran into a friend who had modeled for one of my statues. And she told me that she was now working as a publicist for New Page! By this time the Synchronicity Wave was getting far too big to ignore. When I got home, I received a huge bouquet of flowers, with a card saying: "From your friends at New Page."

3. Perspiration

Over the next few months we were in constant communication, working out the details of what this book would look like—contents, size, cover design, everything. Over the Internet, I contacted other Sages, Mages, Wizards, and Wise Ones I knew throughout the magickal community and set up the Grey Council. Everyone was very enthusiastic about this project.

I re-read all my favorite fantasy books featuring Wizards, and I dragged dozens of my magickal books off my shelves and started looking things up, spreading books open all over my desk and floor. I also began avidly watching all the TV shows featuring "magickal" kids in high school: *Sabrina, Buffy, Roswell,* and *Smallville.* I wanted to completely saturate myself in this milieu.

And writing—every day I am putting in at least a good 8–10 hours at my console. I am thinking about this book constantly—even in my dreams! I am meeting regularly with several new Apprentices, showing them each Class as I write it, and using this as our actual study material. And all this energy will be released for me in December when I send off the finished copy to be printed.

4. Manifestation

And now, finally, you are holding this Grimoire in your hands, and reading these words. It came into being through magick, starting with an inspired Vision. And all the rest has been a process of turning that Vision into a concrete Manifestation. This is the way true magick works, and you can do it too. All you have to do is wrap as many things in your life as possible around the thing you are trying to accomplish, to the point where it becomes the focus of all your thought and attentions. And thus, you shift the probabilities so that, as suffragette Susan B. Anthony said, "Failure is impossible."

> *"To accomplish great things we must not only act, but also dream; not only plan, but also believe."*
> —Anatole France

Class II: Ritual Spaces

1. Introduction: Ritual Spaces

RITUALS MAY BE HELD IN MANY KINDS of spaces, some temporary and others permanent. Temporary Circles may be set up in your home or in public places, such as parks or rented meeting halls. Depending upon circumstances, a ritual area may be set up quite elaborately, with a Gate, Quarter Altars, statues, banners, Maypole, bonfire circle, and other items. Or it may consist of no more than clearing a little space in your room and placing a simple altar in the middle of it. The important thing is, form should follow function. So here are a few notes on designing appropriate rituals areas for your Circle:

Lesson 2. Indoor Temples

Any suitable indoor space may be made into a temple, as long as it has room enough for the people who want to use it to gather together in a Circle. If you are working solitary, you won't need much space, and the description of creating your temple in your sanctum sanctorum (3.IV.3: "Your Temple") should be entirely adequate. However, if you expect to be doing rituals with three or more people, you will want to create a larger ritual space. Circles should be odd-numbered feet in diameter. The traditional Witches' Circle, for instance, has a diameter of 9 or even 13 feet, to provide room for a full coven of 13 Witches. But smaller groups can certainly get by with smaller Circles, such as 7' or 5'.

Some people actually paint a ritual Circle on the floor of their temples, often inscribing a pentagram within it, and marking areas and points in different colors. This can be as simple as a plain circle with the four directions indicated; or as elaborate as the Magick Circle Mandala I drew in 3.VI.2: "The Magick Circle." Such a painted Circle may be covered with a rug when not in use.

A way to make a permanent Magick Circle for your temple without painting on the floor is to use a large piece of cloth (black is recommended, so it will seem as if you are standing in outer space). A top sheet for a California King-size bed should be just about the right size (8' square). Find the exact center of the sheet by folding it carefully into quarters diagonally from corner to corner, and iron it. Put a dot of white chalk at the center, and then spread the whole sheet out on a flat wooden deck or floor that it won't matter to stick thumbtacks or nails into (this may be a bit of a Quest!).

Tack down the four corners of the sheet with just enough tension to get rid of the wrinkles. Then insert a thin finishing nail through the knot at the end of your cingulum. Hammer this into the center of the sheet, but not so far that you can't easily pull it out again. Then hold a piece of chalk at the first knot, and draw the circle round. This will be 7' in diameter. Then draw over the chalk lines with a white fabric marker. Where the ironed creases extend beyond the circle to the corners of the sheet, use the fabric marker to draw symbols of the four Quarters.

When setting up an indoor ritual area, be sure to check on the alignment of the cardinal directions! (I think every Wizard should consider a compass to be a basic magickal tool.) Symbols of the Elements should be placed at the four Quarters. These may be as simple as colored jar candles (E = yellow, S = red, W = blue, N = green), or as fancy as full-scale semi-permanent Quarter altars. Determine which walls or corners of your temple most nearly align to those directions, and then decorate them accordingly. Some people hang different colored banners marked with appropriate sigils. Others put up pictures that remind them of each of these Elemental directions, such as clouds, birds, or a sunrise for East; an erupting volcano, lightning, or Sun for South; a seascape or underwater scene for West; and mountains, crystals, or a snowy Winter landscape for North. I have even designed a set of directional wall plaques just for this purpose, and many people use these: a bird goddess for East; a Sun god for South; a sea goddess for West; and a Green Man for North. Here they are:

Green Man (North)

Bird Goddess (East)

Sun God (South)

Sea Goddess (West)

Lesson 3. Outdoor Circles

Nature magick is meant to be performed in the open air, in forests and meadows, under starry skies, and around an open fire. When magickal rituals are regularly performed in a wooded place, especially one remote from "civilization," it will come alive in both obvious and subtle ways. Growing things will prosper; wild animals will find the area pleasing and appear in greater numbers. Those who are psychically sensitive will soon observe that there is a definite *charge* or aura about the place, and often Faeries, wood-sprites, and other Nature spirits will be seen—first at night, and later even by day.

My own magickal practice and tradition (HOME) evolved out in the country, during the eight years when our core people were living together in a homesteading community in the Mendonesian Mountains of NorCalifia. There were a bunch of us, and we didn't have any large indoor space to hold rituals—our biggest homes were 20'-diameter round *yurts.* So we held almost all of our group rituals outdoors, even in the middle of Winter. We started with the primary Circle—just a fire pit, with space to sit around it. This is the original and most ancient form of ritual Circle, and this is where our ancestors first became human. Gathering around the magick fire, keeping our bodies warm through the cold nights, seeing each other's faces illuminated by the dancing flames, telling our stories, singing our songs, beating our drums, dancing our celebrations, enacting our adventures—ritual, drama, music, poetry, myth—all evolved from our prehistoric tribal campfires.

Over the years, our simple campfire Circles acquired more accoutrements. At Annwfn, we refined the fire pits with rocks, cleared the grass, leveled the areas, and made benches to sit on. Later we planted flowering hedges around the perimeters, and built stone and wood altars at the four Quarters. Gates were made at the entrances to the Faerie Circle and the Maypole Circle, of branches woven into archways (when in use, these are festooned with ribbons, bells and flowers). At the Western Gate of the Faerie Circle, a rocking bridge was built over which to cross into the Underworld at Samhain (the rest of the year, it is kept roped off and covered with a fishing net). Although we kept the fire pit at the center of the Moon Circle and the Sun Circle on Pwyll's Meadow, the one in the Faerie Circle was eventually replaced with a great stone altar. And, of course, the Maypole Circle has the pole itself as its centerpiece.

Lesson 4: Ritual Altars

Altars are the primary stages for the microcosm of a magickal ritual. An altar is a miniature symbolic model of the Universe, containing representations of whatever Elements are to be addressed. Various magickal traditions have specific customs regarding the placement and decoration of their altars. For instance, Hindus, Moslems, Jews, and Christians place their altars in the East, whereas several traditions of Witchcraft and Ceremonial Magick put altars in the North. I feel these arrangements can be flexible, depending on the theme, season, and purpose of the ritual itself. Here are some of the altars we use in our rituals:

Central Altar

In my tradition, we almost always have a central altar, right in the middle of the Circle. Pretty much the only exceptions are when we have a fire or a Maypole there instead. This altar is the main focus area, around which the entire rite revolves. We prefer it to be round, like the Earth Herself. Around 18" tall and about 2–3' in diameter is a good size. Perfectly fine low round lamp or coffee tables of appropriate dimensions may be found readily (and inexpensively) at used furniture stores, or you may make your own altar by cutting a circle out of plywood and affixing it to a base.

A central altar is traditionally set up to be viewed from the South, just as if it was a map. It should be covered with an altar cloth of color and material appropriate to the occasion. Square silk scarves are very popular as altar cloths, but other materials may serve as well, as long as they complement the theme of the ritual (I don't recommend paisley prints, checkerboards, or pictures of Mickey Mouse…). Block-printed, tie-dyed, or batik cloths are often available through the magickal marketplace, or you may make your own, painting anything from a simple pentacle to a full "Magick Circle Mandala." As many rituals have seasonal themes, seasonally appropriate colors are always a good idea: red and green for Yule, red for Brigit, gold for Harvest, orange and black for Samhain, green for almost anything else (see 4.VI: "Wheel of the Year").

In the middle of our central altar we usually place figurines of the God and Goddess we wish to invite into the Circle for this ritual (I have created an entire line of these over the years). Sometimes we may use a mirror instead, if we wish to reflect and call forth the deity within each participant. We usually place two taper candles to either side of these statues, the colors depending on the season and/or purpose of the rite. In the absence of figures, these candles alone may represent the God and Goddess. In fact, candles in the form of male and female figures are even available in most occult shops. Candleholders may be made of metal, glass, or pottery in symbolic shapes.

Other items on the altar would be those to be used in the ritual itself. These might include anointing oils, incense or herbs, a copy of the ritual script (perhaps done up as a scroll…), divinatory implements (a tarot deck, crystal ball, Runestones, black mirror…), necessary materials for spell casting, photos of people needing healing (or of the beloved dead in a Samhain rite); totem animal figures representing people or pets, etc. We also often weave seasonal paraphernalia among the altar implements, such as wreaths of holly and ivy at Yule, flowers in Spring, berries and fruit in Summer and Fall, bones at Samhain, and so on. Again, use your imagination!

Quarter Altars

Our community is really into altars, and we have lots of them. For our ritual areas, whether indoors or out, we often have Quarter altars at the points of the cardinal directions outside the actual Circle. These may range from simple shelves on wall brackets, as in the Temple of Annwfn, to the big stone-and-wood structures at Annwfn's Faerie, Moon, and Sun Circles. These altars can be quite imaginative, as their purpose is to honor the Elemental spirits. An advantage is that if you have Quarter altars outside the Circle, you don't have to have all that Elemental stuff on the central altar! For large rituals, especially all-nighters held outdoors, many of our tools are kept on the appropriate Quarter altars when not in use. All the incense is kept by the Eastern altar, along with the temple sword; space candles are stashed in the South; extra water, juice, coffee, and other beverages are kept at the West; and the Northern altar serves as a place to keep the ritual bread, fruit, and other food.

East

So an Eastern altar may be made of branches festooned with yellow ribbons, bells, feathers, little faeries, and wind chimes. A Southern altar may be a section of fire-blackened tree with lava stones, red draping, a dragon, and a firepot. A Western altar may be made of driftwood and covered with assorted seashells, with a mermaid sculpture and a large chalice of water. Also in the West, as the Gateway to the Underworld, we may have a special altar to our Beloved Dead. There we might place a black candle or a skull, as well as photos and other mementos of our discorporate loved ones. A Northern altar is always made of stone—a large, flat stone is ideal. It may be decorated with crystals and potted plants, especially ferns and moss.

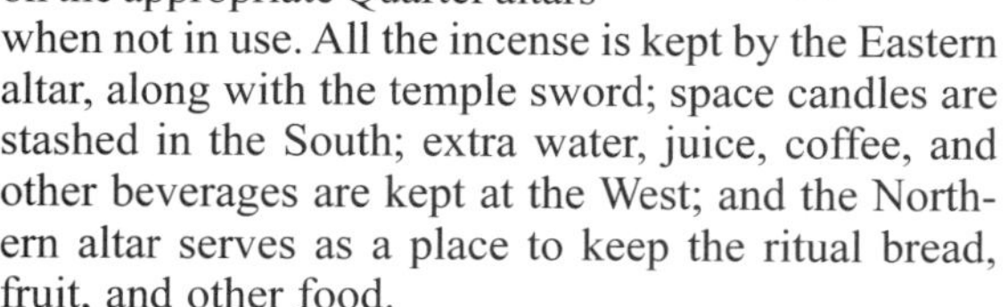

West

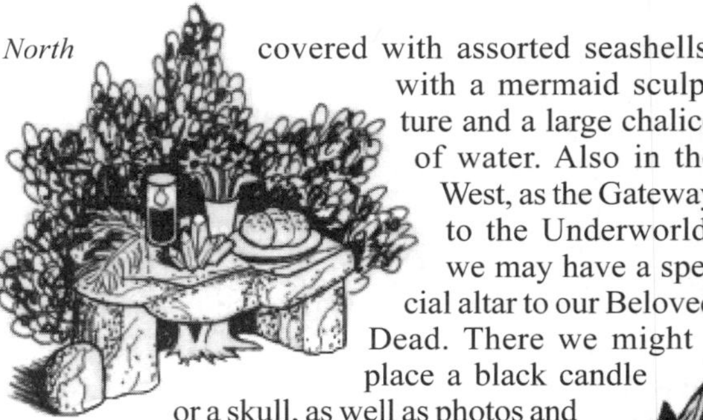

North

South

Household Altars

It's hard to imagine a magickal home without at least one household altar. Around our place, such altars tend to multiply like tribbles, until every horizontal space has been made into an altar, and every vertical space has been converted into a bookcase! Altars become established for the various Gods and Goddesses to whom we personally relate. So our main Ravenheart Family Altar is on the mantle over our parlor fireplace, and it is primarily dedicated to Mother Gaea and Brigit (patron of our creative work). But we also have a healing altar dedicated to Kwan-Yin, an altar to Aphrodite and Eros in the bedroom, an altar to Ti'en Hou for our business, and various others around the house and in our rooms.

Household altars may be fairly easily incorporated into bookcases, but they may also be established on the tops of bureaus, dressers, or cabinets. An altar can be kept in a small corner of the bedroom, a niche in a sewing rooms, or a convenient closet. Household altars are not usually the focus of group rituals, but rather of personal and family observances, prayers, and devotions. The most important thing is to keep them clean and fresh—don't let them get covered with dust and cobwebs!

Your Personal Altar

I've already covered this subject in 1.II: "Create Your Personal Altar," so I won't say any more here.

Lesson 5: Shrines

Shrines are similar in concept to altars, but are usually more focused and permanent. There are countless variations—a shrine can be almost anything from an elaborate structure with chambers and doors that open on various scenes, to a simple box containing sacred objects and relics; or just a marker, monument or memorial to someone.

Devotional

Devotional shrines are often in the form of miniature temples for particular Gods or Goddesses—sort of like a little dollhouse. A common form is a kind of cabinet or shadow box that may be decorated both inside and out. Frequently these have doors that may be closed or opened, often with scenes painted on the inside. The main item in such a shrine is an image of the God, Goddess, Saint, or even teacher, such as the shrines devotees of Indian gurus create for their teacher. This can be in the form of a statue, photo, or other representation (including something purely symbolic, such as the Chinese Taoist shrines that are simple red posts and lintels).

Many churches and temples have niches set into their walls, with statues of saints and deities. Hindus, Buddhists, ancient Greeks, Romans, Egyptians, and others all established such shrines throughout their lands. In Catholic countries, shrines to the Virgin Mary are everywhere. Statues in such shrines may range in size from tiny plastic images to huge and imposing figures many times life size. One of the main things you notice about such shines are the offerings left by pilgrims. Candles, incense, flowers, and personal items may be piled at the foot of the shrine. Healing shrines may be piled high with abandoned crutches. I saw a shrine to the Virgin Mary high in the mountains of Peru that had thousands of football-sized river rocks stacked up all around it. Apparently, part of the pilgrimage involved carrying such rocks from the river far below all the way up the mountain.

When you are out in Nature, you will sometimes find yourself in a special place. You feel that there is some special energy there. It could be the abundance of bio-diversity, many kinds of trees, birds or animals, special rock formations, or just a beauteous spot. You may feel the inspiration to honor that place with a prayer or small ritual. You can do this all in your mind, visualizing a Circle or altar, but you could also create a little devotional shrine. Don't disturb the beauty, but placing some stones, flowers, and the like at the Quarters is usually not a problem; and why not use that special rock, tree, or creek as the center of your altar or Circle?

Commemorative

Commemorative shrines are called memorials. Some may be in the form of small temples, such as the Lincoln Memorial, with a statue of the person being commemorated. Others may be more symbolic, such as the Washington Monument, which is a tall Egyptian-style *obelisk,* otherwise known as "Cleopatra's Needle." Graveyards are common places to find commemorative shrines to the Beloved Dead. Often the gravestone itself becomes such a shrine, as grieving friends and relatives place photos and flowers on it. The graves of famous people can become shrines for pilgrimages—I once visited the grave of Jim Morrison (poet and lead singer for The Doors) in Paris, France, and the whole area was covered with flowers, poetry, and offerings from his many fans, decades after his death. War memorials are often regarded as shrines—particularly the Vietnam Memorial in Washington, D.C.

Other commemorative shrines are the ones you sometimes see at the side of a highway where someone has been killed in an accident. A little cross may be erected with the person's name and maybe even a photo. Sometimes there will be flowers, cards, prayer ribbons, and other offerings, just as in a graveyard. After the destruction of the Twin Trade Towers in New York, the walls and fences of the neighborhood were covered with photos and mementos of the dead. Visiting such a memorial can be a very emotional experience, with much shedding of tears.

Lesson 6: Medicine Wheels

Medicine Wheels are large circles marked out with rings of stones on the ground, with a central *cairn* (pile) of rocks and radiating spokes of pebbles. There are usually big rocks or cairns where the spokes join the outer circle. The whole structure looks like a huge wagon wheel laid out on the ground, so the term *Medicine Wheel* was first applied to the Big Horn Medicine Wheel in Wyoming, the most southern one known. The "medicine" part of the name implies that it was of religious significance to Native peoples.

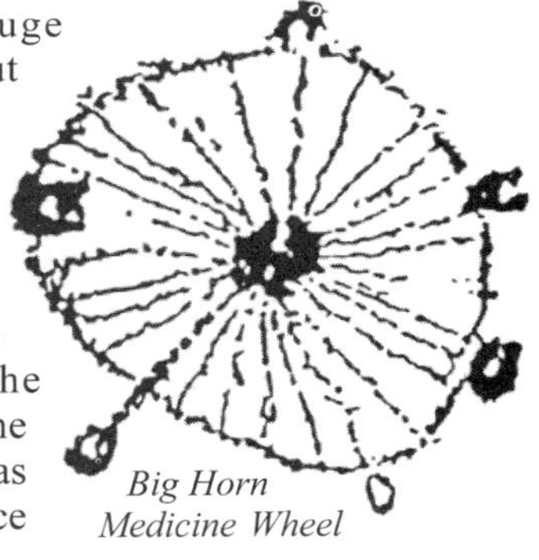

Big Horn Medicine Wheel

Dozens of these Wheels, many more than 40' diameter, were made in remote areas of the Western U.S. and Canada by Native Americans. Two-thirds of the 70 known are in Alberta. One, Majorville Medicine Wheel, contains an enormous central cairn 30' in diameter, surrounded by a stone circle 90' across. Twenty-eight spokes link the central cairn with the outer circle. Several dating techniques reveal that the central cairn was constructed some 4,500 years ago! Apparently, it served as a ceremonial center for several thousand years. Hunting magick or buffalo fertility might have played a part in the rituals, but the deeper meaning of the site is lost in time.

One of the most interesting theories is that there are significant stellar alignments present at the Medicine Wheels. Astronomer John Eddy suggested that a line drawn between the central cairn and an outlying cairn at the Bighorn Medicine Wheel pointed to the rising point of the Sun at the Summer Solstice. Other alignments, both to the Summer Solstice sunrise and to certain bright stars such as Aldebaran, Rigel, or Sirius, have been proposed for a number of Medicine Wheels. The Wheels may thus have functioned as a calendar to mark the longest day of the year. Presumably, such a calendar would be used for the timing of important rituals.

You can make your own Medicine Wheels almost as a game of Elven Chess, using stones that happen to be lying around. Sometimes such circles are created on lawns or in gardens, and people will bring in special rocks to mark the central cairn and the places where the spokes join the outer circle. These may be assembled in a rocky area, such as a park or wilderness, and left standing for other visitors to come upon.

Lesson 7: Henges and Stone Circles

If you have space to set it up, it can be really cool to build a stone circle around your ritual space! Such circles are often referred to as "henges" because of the famous Stonehenge in England, but technically, that is not correct. Typical *henges* ("hanging things") are simply circular enclosures bounded by a bank on the outside and a ditch on the inside. One or more entrances lead to the center. The oldest henges were built beginning about 3300 BCE, and the largest enclose up to five acres. The bank is outside the ditch, so they would not have been defensive enclosures, but were more likely a form of religious and ceremonial gathering place. Some henges have stone circles within them, while others once contained circular arrangements of wooden posts.

Stone circles are much more common than henges. At least 900 of them still exist, though many more must have been destroyed in the march of "progress." The most famous is Stonehenge in Wiltshire, with an extremely complex history spanning well more than a millennium. Most of what is visible today represents the last phase of construction of standing stone arrangements inside the bank and ditch and was probably completed about 1700 BCE. And no, Stonehenge was *not* built by the Druids; they missed out on all the hard work by more than a thousand years!

Many outrageous claims have been made for the purpose of these circles, from UFO landing pads to astronomical observatories. Most evolved from the earlier henges, functioning as multipurpose tribal gathering places for ritual observances having to do with the seasons and the fertility of the Earth. As with Medicine Wheels, certain stones aligned with particular bright stars and the rising of the Sun at Solstices, thus serving as annual calendars the same way a sundial marks the hours.

Stonehenge

When the late Professor Alexander Thom surveyed more than 1,000 *megalithic* ("great stone") structures in the British Isles and Western France, he was amazed to find that they had all been built using the same unit of measurement. Thom called this unit a *megalithic yard* (MY) because it was very close in size to a British Imperial Yard, being exactly 32.64 inches.

Lesson 8: Labyrinths

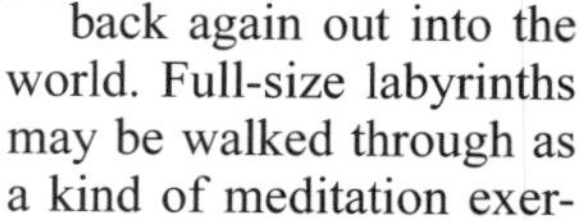

Labrys

The word *labyrinth* means "house of the labrys," and a *labrys* is the ritual double-bladed axe of ancient Crete. Legend tells how Theseus slew the Minotaur at the center of the Labyrinth of Knossos in Crete, escaping with the aid of a ball of string given him by the princess Ariadne. Labyrinths can be done as simple drawings or incised into a surface of wood or clay so that you can follow their path with your eye or finger.

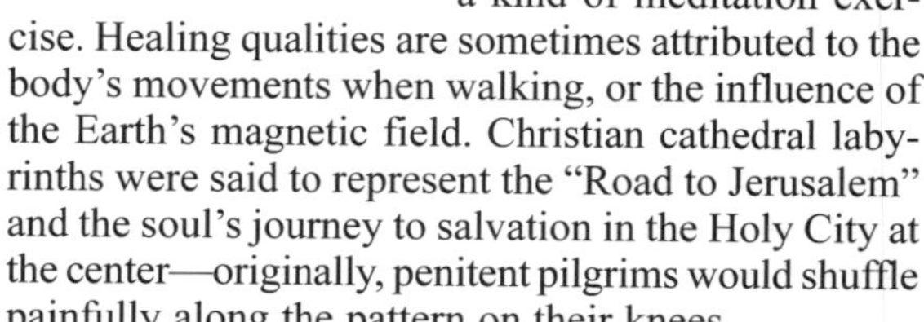

From Montfaucon's Antiquities, *16th century*

A labyrinth combines the imagery of the circle and the spiral into a meandering but purposeful path. The labyrinth represents a journey to our own center and back again out into the world. Full-size labyrinths may be walked through as a kind of meditation exercise. Healing qualities are sometimes attributed to the body's movements when walking, or the influence of the Earth's magnetic field. Christian cathedral labyrinths were said to represent the "Road to Jerusalem" and the soul's journey to salvation in the Holy City at the center—originally, penitent pilgrims would shuffle painfully along the pattern on their knees.

Labyrinths and mazes have often been confused. When most people hear of a labyrinth, they think of a maze. A maze is like a puzzle to be solved. It has forks and blind alleys. But a labyrinth is *unicursal,* with only one circuitous path. There are no forks or blind alleys. The single path leads you into the center (and perhaps back out again).

The oldest design is the classical seven-ring labyrinth found on ancient Cretan coins and in many places throughout the world—from Spain to Scandinavia, and from Arizona to Afghanistan. One example has been found in a 4,000-year-old Neolithic grave in Sardinia. This one is the easiest to lay out without sophisticated measuring equipment. I have created several on-the spot on sandy beaches, and also mowed them into long grass in fields.

The archetypal seven-ring labyrinth design prevailed throughout the world for millennia. Its immediate successor, the Roman mosaic labyrinth, has survived into modern times as a wide border framing a central picture, usually of Theseus slaying the Minotaur. The nine-ring path of the square Roman design methodically fills one quarter before progressing to the next, where the pattern is repeated.

Roman Labyrinth

A great breakthrough came in the development of the Medieval labyrinth design. This had eleven rings and the paths ranged freely through the quadrants. In contrast to the square Roman pattern, these were typically round or octagonal. The earliest surviving full-sized example dates from 1235 CE and is set in mosaic into the floor of Chartres Cathedral in France. I have visited this and walked it. This Chartres design has become very popular, especially among New Age Christians, and it has been reproduced many places (including churches) in recent years. Indeed, there are now entire "Labyrinth Projects" going to help establish these all over.

Chartres Labyrinth

A few years ago, I created a unique new labyrinth design. The path (in this case, the solid line) winds around interlaced images of the Goddess and the Hornéd God. I call it the *Dearinth,* which means "House of the Gods," or temple.

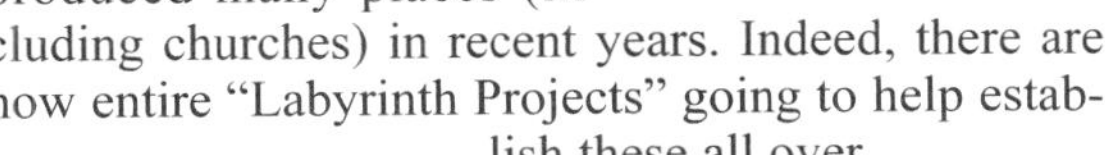

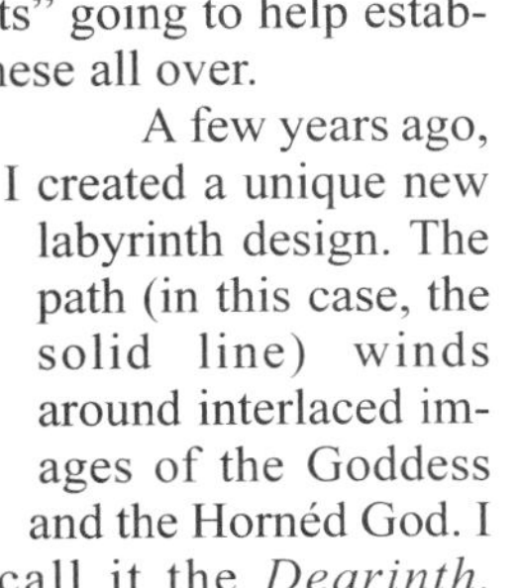

Dearinth

You can create your own Labyrinth from materials available anywhere. I recommend a variation on the classic Cretan design that provides for a direct path out from the center, so several people can walk it at once without bumping into each other on the way out. Such a design is called a *processional labyrinth.*

This pattern can be laid out on the ground with lime, stones, bricks, or even a long chain or rope. It can be grooved into the sand at the beach, mowed into long grass with a lawnmower, or cut out of turned sod and planted with flowers for a more permanent installation. It can even be marked on a floor with masking tape or painted onto a large piece of canvas. All you need to do to mark it out is start in the middle, and use a compass cord to inscribe a series of seven concentric circle paths, each wide enough to walk through (also allow room for the barrier, of course). Then connect the rings with arcs in the pattern shown, to make one continuous looping path.

Processional labyrinth

"Build it, and they will come." I guarantee you'll not only have fun yourself, but folks will come from all over just to walk your labyrinth!

Resources

My own statues of Gods and Goddesses and Elemental wall plaques (including a Dearinth mini-altar) are available from: *www.MythicImages.com.*

Large tapestries printed with Labyrinths and Celtic designs can be obtained from Ancient Circles: *www.AncientCircles.com/textiles.*

All kinds of Labyrinth designs and products—as well as detailed instructions for laying out your own Labyrinth pattern—are available from Labyrinth Enterprises at: *www.labyrinthproject.com.*

Class III: About Rituals

1. Introduction to Rituals

—abstracted from "Creating Rituals,"
by Hallie Inglehart (*HOME Cooking,* 1997)

ITUALS ARE A WAY TO FOCUS AND acknowledge our energy and awareness. We all perform rituals throughout the day—some more conscious than others—that influence and support our attitudes and behavior. We get dressed in the morning, we celebrate our birthdays, we meet with others, we mark major events in our lives. The quality that makes "ordinary" life a ritual is very subtle. Lighting a candle and burning incense do not alone make a ritual, but the state of mind and awareness accompanying or resulting from an action does. Ritual is a metaphor for all of conscious living.

Mythology, archaeology, linguistics, art, and history tell us of the magickal rituals that our ancestors performed. Caves as wombs of the Earth Mother were natural sites for birth and rebirth rituals, and the carved and painted animals and plants, and markings of the cycles of the moon and seasons still preserved in some of these caves are vivid reminders of ancient rituals. In the past, ritual was a comprehensive celebration and expression of human creativity and cyclic regeneration. Many of our arts—theater, poetry, and song—originally evolved as parts of one ritual-making process. As people became more alienated from Nature and their inner selves, the arts became isolated from each other and fragmented from their original unifying spiritual source. We can still feel the spiritual power of ritual in the best of art, however. The energy of performance is very similar to that of ritual: the intense focus, the channeling of energy, the exchange of energy between performers and audience.

Lesson 2. The HOME Tradition

I have learned my Wizardry from many teachers and have been initiated into a number of groups. However, the magickal tradition with which I am most closely aligned is the Holy Order of Mother Earth, or HOME. The roots of HOME were planted in the Fall of 1976, when Morning Glory and I arrived in Eugene, Oregon and met Anna Korn. She had been trained in a British Tradition of Dianic Witchcraft (focused on Diana, the Moon Goddess) by Mark Roberts and Morgan McFarland in Texas. Morning Glory had pieced together her own path of "Shamanic Wicca" out of personal experiences and published materials. I had founded the Church of All Worlds, and been trained in Italian *Strega* and Ceremonial Magick by Deborah Letter in St. Louis, as well as Ozark "Druidism," Greek and Egyptian myth and ritual. The three of us integrated our respective training into a coherent system, and formed the Coven of *Ithil Duath* ("Moon Shadow") to practice it. That Winter and the following Spring, Morning Glory and I refined all these materials and practices into an organized magickal study course, which we taught at Lane Community College as "Celtic Shamanism."

In July of 1977, Morning Glory and I moved to *Coeden Brith* ("Speckled Forest"), a 220-acre parcel on the 5,600-acre NorCalifia homesteading community called Greenfield Ranch. Coeden Brith was owned by Alison Harlow. The 55-acre parcel next door had recently been acquired by Gwydion Pendderwen, a Welsh Bard and co-founder of the Faerie Tradition. Together we founded the Holy Order of Mother Earth as a magickal order of land stewardship and ritual.

Other magickal residents of the Ranch included people with backgrounds in Faerie Tradition, Dianic Wicca, the New Reformed Order of the Golden Dawn (NROOGD), Hindu, and Native American practices. We began meeting and working magick together, and over the next eight years, through Moon cycles, rites of passage, seasonal celebrations and daily practice, we wove all those strands together into a unique tradition that was actually rooted in our own daily and seasonal lives on the magick land, thus giving rise to a new magickal path: the HOME Tradition. The course materials Morning Glory and I had developed for our classes in Eugene provided a foundation for our developing *Grimoire of Lights and Shadows.*

Other members of the Greenfield ranch community came to join our HOME Circles, and the tradition grew. We planted trees and gardens, raised pet deer and unicorns, sang our songs and told our stories around the campfire. Babies were born on the land, blessed in ritual, and raised up in the Circle, assimilating our customs and traditions into a new generation. In our growing magickal community we actually lived the legendary lives of our ancient tribal forebears. In 1983, Anodea Judith founded Lifeways School, creating a "Magick 101" training program based on the rituals and materials we had all developed over the years in HOME. Many people took these classes and were trained in the HOME magickal tradition. Meanwhile, we all moved off the land to other places. In 1997, I wrote and edited the first of what was intended to be three volumes of material called *HOME Cooking*. But after that, my life and work took me elsewhere as I started sculpting statuary of Gods and Goddesses for the Mythic Images Collection, and I never completed the other volumes.

When Gwydion was killed in a car wreck at Samhain of 1992, our community was plunged into deep grief as for the first time we dealt with death in our own family. Our rituals developed a new and darker aspect as we created funerary rites and wakes, exploring the Underworld through the mythic Mysteries of Samhain, Walpurgisnacht, and the Eleusinia.

Lesson 3: Planning a Ritual

(by Anodea Judith [from *HOME Cooking,* 1997])

Anodea and I have worked together for more than 25 years on many major rituals, training programs, and other projects. She is the author of *Wheels of Life: A User's Guide to the Chakras* (which I illustrated), along with several other books synchronizing Eastern and Western magickal systems. Here are some questions she feels are important to ask in planning a ritual:

1. **What is the purpose of the ritual?** Why are you doing this, what do you wish to accomplish, what is the problem you wish to solve? Answers can be anything from the removal of nuclear weapons to simply having a good time. This dictates the theme.
2. **What time is it?** What time of year, season, Moon cycle, day or night, time in your life, time in a group's life (such as initiation, closing, etc.), or what time in a succession of rituals, such as planetary, or chakra rituals, which may go in a certain order.
3. **Who is it for and who will take part?** This encompasses number of people, level of experience, age, physical capabilities, children, all women, all men, mixed, closed intimate circle, large public ritual, or anything in between.
4. **Whom do you wish to influence?** This is slightly different from #1, and may also be skipped, as in a purpose of simply having a good time. If your purpose is to remove nuclear weapons, you may wish to influence politicians in the White House, or you may wish to influence families in the neighborhood to inspire them to write letters to congressman. A word of warming must always be added on this one, that what you're doing doesn't become manipulation, which is both exhausting and of questionable ethics.
5. **Where will it be held?** Indoors, outdoors, in a home, temple, classroom, etc.
6. **How long should it last?** This relates to #2 and #5, for outdoor, nighttime rituals may need to be shorter than others are. It also must take into consideration who will be there. For example, children cannot sit through long rituals. Planning the length of time is important and subroutines of the ritual should also be planned (such as casting the Circle: 5 min.; Invocations: 10 min.; etc.).
7. **What do you have to work with?** If it's outdoors on a Full Moon, you have the time and the place to work with, and whatever elements they invoke. A mountaintop gives you one thing, the ocean another. What tools do you have, what invocations, skills, people, robes, dances, chants? Sort through what you have from your Grimoire and Book of Shadows and lay out all the things that are appropriate. You may not use them all, but you can sort and order them later when the skeleton comes into play.
8. **What will be the main techniques for working?** Meditation, dancing, chanting, healing, walking, drumming—which is most appropriate to the purpose and theme?
9. **How do you symbolize on a microcosm what you wish to work?** If you wish to cross the Abyss, how can you set that up in the ritual? If you wish to open people's hearts, how can that be symbolized in a direct, subliminal way?
10. **What should be on the Altar?** This comes out of the symbolism of #9. If you are working with Air, then you would have feathers and incense; if you are working with Earth, you might have crystals. In different seasons you might have seasonal items.

By the time these questions have been asked and answered, a general thread should start to appear. Be creative. Look for lines of flow and how one part can flow into another naturally and gracefully, all feeding the central theme and purpose that was chosen. Once the theme becomes clear and you know what you have to work with, these answers can be fed into the ritual structure outline (see 4.IV.2: "Ritual Structure") to create the actual ceremony. Allow for a certain amount of overlap and repetition, like the chorus of a song. It is far more important that the ritual actually *work* on a gut level, than having every little thing in place. Give yourself full rein for experimentation, and know that there is *no* "one true right and only way."

Lesson 4: Ethics of Magic and Ritual

(by Anodea Judith [from *HOME Cooking,* 1997])

Everything is connected to everything else. All elements of life—the trees, the weather, the emotions we feel, the words we speak, the time of day, and the way we move—all are intimately connected, inextricably interwoven within a greater field that surrounds us. What affects one element, affects all, expressed by the maxim: "As above, so below." What occurs without occurs within and vice versa. The various planes are but mirrors for each other, and mirrors for our very souls. In this way, magick is but a microcosm of the larger forces—a microcosm small enough to influence, but one which in turn influences larger forces that might otherwise seem beyond us.

Magick does not manipulate this field as much as it follows the natural lines of force as Life flows into the stream of Time. In this stream, nothing is stationary or stagnant; everything is constantly moving and changing. It is this fluid movement that allows magick to occur, for in the midst of change we can reach in and create new realities as the forces of Life journey from chaos to manifestation.

As everything in the magickal world is interconnected, it makes for an interesting question of ethics. We, ourselves, are not separate from this field, nor can our actions be separate, nor their results. Thus magick has built within it its own sacred immune system. All that we do within the magick realm, we do to the field around us and hence, to our very selves. Magick can, in fact, be one of the quickest karmic feedback systems we experience!

This is summed up in the *Wiccan Rede:* "An it harm none, do as ye will." This means that the sovereignty of one's personal will is highly respected as long as it does not cause harm or interfere with the rights of another. To do so would be to harm the basic underlying fabric that connects all things, and reflect back negatively upon the practitioner. Yet to act upon one's own will is also to be responsible for it—to follow up on actions, to avoid blaming others, to live responsibly and consciously.

Ritual within a Magick Circle is basically an amplifier for energy, amping the effects of one's actions. Therefore, whatever we initiate magickally expands, sometimes exponentially, into the outer world. If our intentions are unclear, if we do not act with respect and affinity for all that may be affected, then the results of these actions, as they run through the connective web of all life, eventually return to us in magnified measure. Thus the magician must take full responsibility for any actions initiated within the Circle—and indeed, throughout one's life. This even includes unintentional mistakes, which can happen to anyone. We are still required to be fully responsible for those mistakes, and doing so always provides valuable lessons in magickal and spiritual growth.

Wizards have an essential responsibility to treat the Earth with respect, to reuse and recycle, to treat each other excellently, to empower their word by speaking truth at all times, and to be as conscious of their behavior as possible. The wise know that there is no stern "father in Heaven" to sit in judgement of us, damning us to some eternal hell. There is merely the state of the world we wish to live in, which we can make into a heaven *or* a hell, depending on our own actions. Magickal ethics, therefore, are based more on cause and effect than an arbitrary sense of right and wrong. They are intrinsically woven, inseparable from all action. Opinions of right and wrong may differ, but results are the definitive experience for each individual practitioner.

Lesson 5: Circle Lore and Etiquette

Someday you will very likely want to attend rituals put on by other people and groups. Here is a little guideline for how to behave, along with some useful information to help you feel comfortable. This was written by Eldri Littlewolf and Wendy Hunter, and published in *HOME Cooking*.

The Circle is a manifestation of cyclic energy in the form of a vortex. This sacred time and space is separate from the world and contiguous with all other Circles. The Circle is an animate universe between the worlds that we empower by our agreement. Therefore:

1. **A ritual is not a spectator sport.** If you don't wish to participate, please stay far enough away that your conversations won't interfere in the rite.
2. **Leave your mundane self and earthly business outside the Circle,** and enter with your magickal self. Enter the Circle in Perfect Love and Perfect Trust, having worked through personal difficulties beforehand.
3. **Meet everyone's magickal self in the Circle as if for the first time,** remembering that we have been partners since life began. Treat everybody and everything in the Circle with respect, tact, courtesy, and love.
4. **A ritual is like a religious service,** one in which considerable power may be raised, so please behave reverently and carefully in Circle.
5. **Keep solemn silence** except when Truth wishes to speak through you. Speak only Truth in Circle, and your magickal affirmations will have the force of that Truth.
6. **A ritual need not be solemn,** yet it should be serious in that humor should be used with purpose. Gratuitous remarks can disrupt the Circle's energy and focus, so please refrain from making them.
7. **The best rituals are those that seem spontaneous,** yet they've often been planned carefully. So look to those leading the rite for clues on when to join in with chanting, drumming, etc.
8. **When moving about in the Circle, always move in the direction of casting** (usually deosil/clockwise). Walk around the Circle if necessary, but don't walk across or against the flow.

9. **Ritual objects and tools are invested with power** and should be treated with respect. A person's tools and musical instruments are private and should not be touched without permission—especially anything wrapped, sheathed, or boxed.
10. **Once the Circle is cast, enter or exit only at great need.** If you must enter or exit the Circle, please cut yourself a door or have one of the ritual officers do so.

One of the priestess's or priest's jobs may be to channel the Goddess and/or God in the Circle. Help them:

- Watch them, listen to them, follow them.
- Empower them and the ritual by your participation. Feed your energy and visualizations through them into the Circle.
- Put objections aside and save criticism until later. If you cannot go along with something, leave the Circle.

We are all sisters and brothers in the Circle, but we may work in different ways. Be sensitive to different needs and styles during a ritual. Respect the differences between all magickal selves and include them, for they are all needed to complete the Circle.

Lesson 6: Types of Rituals

The Working is the core, heart, and purpose of a magick ritual. There are many types of workings that may be done—indeed, this phase of the ritual may be as varied as your own purposes and imagination may conceive. Here is a brief explanation of a few basic types of ritual workings.

Worship/Celebration

Worship and celebration are perfectly good purposes for a ritual. This basically means throwing a party and inviting the Gods to attend! Such a rite should include lots of drumming, singing, dancing, music, feasting, and general merrymaking. Most of the great Seasonal Sabbats are of this nature (see 4.VI: "The Wheel of the Year"). Remember, when you invite the Gods to attend your Circle, Their first response is going to be: "This had better be good!"

One of our favorite such rites is a Convocation of the Gods, wherein everyone comes prepared to *aspect* (take on the persona of) their favorite Divinity, with appropriate costumes, masks, and associated accoutrements. It is important to remember, however, that if you invite the gods to attend a really good party, They will most likely show up! Be prepared!

Anodea says: "When you take on a deity role in a ritual, it's of the utmost importance that you *know/become* that deity. You must have ample resources and time available to immerse yourself in that energy. I suggest you build and dedicate an altar to the deity and that every day you devote some time getting to know that persona."

Shielding/Protection

Shielding and protection may be done for an individual, a group, or a place. Such rites involve throwing up a protective field around the target that will repel unwanted energies. Shielding is done by taking the basic barrier of the Circle itself and strengthening it into an impenetrable shell, reflectively mirrored on the outside. Use visualization as well as actual handheld round mirrors as you circle around the person or place to be protected, holding your hands up as if against an invisible wall.

Healing/Transformation

Healing may be done for someone actually present in the Circle, or for someone far away who is known to one or more of the participants, who can link with him or her and relay the energy. A common method is for the person(s) to be healed (or their surrogates) to sit or lie in the center of the Circle while everyone else directs healing energy into them through their hands, which may be laid on the person's body, particularly over any specific areas that may need healing. Then everyone breathes together, deeper and faster, making sounds with each breath, until finally reaching a crescendo, simultaneously pumping out the combined chi of the group into the center person(s) with the release of the last total exhalation.

Another method involves the person to be healed remaining linked in the Circle, with everyone holding hands and facing to their right. A current is created and built by each person in a wave snapping their head around to catch the eyes of the person on their left and blowing out with a "whoosh!" while simultaneously squeezing the hand of that person. At the same time, that person inhales the breath, and then repeats these actions towards their left. After a few times around the Circle, this wave can gather tremendous power. When the one to be healed feels it is strong enough, all they have to do is break their link with the next person on their left, thereby collecting the full force of the energy wave without passing it on.

Transformation rituals can use these same techniques imbedded in a more complex psychodrama.

Web Weaving

Web Weaving is a particularly delightful type of magickal working, the purpose of which is to create magickal links among previously dissociated elements of the physical or spiritual world. Here's a typical example of such rituals as I have participated in:

A ball of twine is passed around the Circle, and each person takes his own "measure" by stretching a length of twine from middle fingertip to middle fingertip of his outstretched hands, then cutting off that piece. Then, while everyone holds one end of their measure, the free ends are gathered together and tied into a knot in the center, along with the end of the remaining ball of twine. When the knot is tied, everyone pulls their ends of twine taut, raising the entire array high enough above the ground so that someone can sit comfortable beneath it. While everyone sings a Web Weaving chant (usually: *"We are the flow and we are the ebb; We are the weavers, we are the Web..."*), one person sits under the web and ties the string from the ball into an expanding spiral, one strand at a time outward along the measures. As the knots are tied in each person's measure, that person may call out the name of something they wish to link into the Web.

Once made, such a Web may continue to be used in subsequent rituals. I now have several that I helped weave: one from Australia, one from Peru, and another from Texas. Each time such a web is deployed, everyone holding an end may tie another knot into it to link whatever they wish into the collected energy field. Also, other items, such as crystals, ribbons, talismans, and so on may be tied into the web as people wish to make their personal connections.

Initiations/Mysteries

Throughout the 1940s and 50s, Wiccan rituals, as well as those of the Masons, Rosicrucians, and other secret societies (all of which were similarly structured) consisted mostly of Initiations. First entry into the Circle, as well as passage into each successive grade or degree, was/is conducted in the form of an Initiation, in which the initiate is blindfolded, often stripped and bound, brought to the gate, and challenged ominously. Passwords are required, and an ordeal must be endured and passed. Initiations may include welcoming of new members to the community, dedications to a path or course of study, or ordination as a priest or priestess of an order or tradition. Often such Initiations are elaborated in the form of dramatic Mysteries, of which no more will be said here, as these cannot be described, but only experienced.

Fire-Rituals

> *Fire-rituals are very basic. Most traditions honor and venerate fire, often in connection with the Sun. The first hymn of the Hindu Rig-Veda is devoted to Agni, the Divine Fire. There are the old Persian Mithras-cult, the comprehensive Vedic Agni rituals, Buddhist Goma/Homa fire rituals, Egyptian Earth/Star fire worship, Irish Bridgid, the Slavic Kupalo Solstice and the Aztec and Mayan New Fire ceremony every 52 years, the Phoenix and Promethean myths, the volcanic Pele worship of Hawaii, the Celtic Beltaine and Samhain, the middle column of the Qabalah as the pathway of fire, but even today bonfires are very common.* —Luc Sala, "The Fire-Ritual"

Some of the most popular fire rituals are just drumming and dancing around a blazing bonfire. Frequently, these go on all night at magickal festivals, where the fire may be built as big as a house! Other fire-rituals may even involve walking barefoot on hot coals or demonstrations of fire-spinning.

Bardics

A Bardic is a wonderful experience that can easily be done by anyone in a small group. This is a ritual of sharing during which each person in the Circle gets a turn to offer something to the rest of the group—usually a song, poem, or story. The typical way a Bardic is conducted is by having a large chalice of fruit juice, wine, or mead ("Bard Oil") passed around the Circle. As it comes to each person, that one may take a drink and offer his piece, taking another drink before passing it on. If he does not wish to contribute anything at this time, he may just take a drink and pass the chalice.

Lesson 7: Rites of Passage

Rituals of transition and life changes, called Rites of Passage, mark significant periods in life, movement between life-stages, and personal transformations. These are rituals of honoring and empowerment. They are a public acknowledgment and recognition of growth. Just as the seasons pass in order, so do the stages of life. The inner and outer worlds mirror each other, so Rites of Passage provide a further link with the Earth and the Cosmos. Rites of Passage include coming of age, marriage or handfasting, pregnancy and birth, elderhood, handpartings, death, and rebirth. The following general explanations come mostly from Paul Moonoak, a priest of the Church of All Worlds.

Birth

When a child is born it is a remarkable event; when a child who is loved by many and nurtured by a whole community is born, it is a miracle. When we gather to name and honor a new baby, we honor life itself. Another term for this rite is *seining,* or baby blessing. At this time those who will nurture the child are identified: Goddessmothers, Godfathers, parents, siblings, and other loved ones who may have a part in the baby's life are recognized before all. We pass the new baby around the Circle, with magickal gifts and blessings for long life, health, and happiness.

Coming of Age

Centuries ago, this phrase originally meant "of age to marry," but in these days we no longer expect people to marry so young! Normally held between the ages of 11 and 13, the Coming of Age ceremony celebrates the onset of puberty in one's body and mind. From this point begins the exploration of our new and changing bodies. You must learn your own boundaries, likes and dislikes, and about your right to say yes or no when it comes to *your* body. Usually this rite is performed by adult members of the child's own sex, and may involve an initiatory ordeal and the giving of a magickal use-name.

Adulthood

This rite can occur anytime between the ages of 16 and 21, depending on the individual and local laws concerning legal maturity. This ceremony heralds the beginning of the journey into adulthood, adding adult attitudes, abilities, responsibilities, and maturity to our best youthful attributes. The rite usually involves a sacred/special place, a Vision Quest, and a rebirth into the community of adult men and women. Some symbol is gifted to the new adult and s/he is honored before all—often with a new magickal name.

Handfasting (Marriage)

Choosing to live with a mate or partner is a commitment to that person, a joining of two independent beings because they are *more* together than they are apart. Handfastings are made "for as long as love shall last" because even though a couple may stay together for the rest of their lives, they also may not, and both choices are honorable. This rite sends them off on a joint adventure, with as much joy and passion as possible! And if they should someday decide to part, a ceremony of *handparting* will allow them to do so with honor and goodwill.

Parenthood

Although birth rites are centered on the baby, parenthood is marked by a ceremony for the new parents. It is a time for honoring the mother and father whose life journey has brought them to this place. We bless the new parents with a baby shower and a circle of love and support. This is a celebration, a party, a time for giving gifts, and of saying "We're here if you need us—you don't have to raise this kid alone!"

Elderhood (Crones & Sages)

Elders, like children, are priceless treasures of our community. After the age of 50 or so, we acknowledge and honor our elderfolk for their wisdom, knowledge, skills, or whatever they have gained from their years on Earth. Often it's they who settle disputes, bless babies, and speak with greatest authority in councils. At this rite, another symbol may be gifted to them in recognition of their value.

Death/Rebirth

Near or at the time of death, we give comfort and compassion in a Rite of Passing. Beloveds gather to say goodbye, and to send the spirit out through the Circle. We ask that they be blessed with peace, a time of rest, and then a new journey, a new birth. After death, we remember them with a gathering called a *wake***.** This is a farewell party where we share treasured memories and stories. A funeral may follow, in which a few chosen speakers may deliver a *eulogy* ("good words")—speaking of the impact of the departed person's life on theirs, and on the world.

A time of death is a sad time, but also one filled with hope and joy, for Death is part of Life, and just as the seasons turn, so we also will be reborn and continue. It is a time to let go and move on. Perhaps we may even have inherited a guardian angel in our lives. The Great Cycle, the Spiral leading ever forward, continues, one within the other: the moments of a day, the seasons of our lives, our lives themselves, generations, planets, stars, galaxies, and universes, all turn in the great Circle of Life—one of which we are proud to be a part, because fun, adventure, and growth are among the greatest of treasures!

Lesson 8: Sacraments

(Liza Gabriel and I wrote this lesson together.)

A *sacrament* is something regarded as holy, or sacred. Ordinary acts or substances may be elevated to the status of Sacraments in a ritual context, thereby becoming gateways into a greater awareness of the beauty and power of the Cosmos and our part in it. Sacraments may be grouped under two categories: **actions** and **substances.** *No one should ever be compelled or coerced into partaking of any sacrament without their full knowledge and consent.*

Actions

Magick—We like to define Magick as "the art of probability enhancement." The study, practice, and mastery of such arts is a lifelong quest, involving the ability to formulate, embrace, and shift the very paradigms that constitute our consensual "reality."

Environmental action—As we are all children of the Living Earth, we should regard Her maintenance and protection as our most sacred duty. This includes all forms of non-violent environmental activism, including highway and park clean-up campaigns, tree plantings, and demonstrations against despoilers of Nature.

Sacred sexuality—The appropriate expression of sexuality at each season of life is essential to a life fully lived. Sex is a source of power, creative as well as procreative. The giving and receiving of sexual pleasure is an endlessly varied art. We are born out of this act of pleasure. This miracle has been a source of awe and a method of magick from the dawn of time. We all have in us somewhere the primordial belief that if sex can create *us,* sex can create *anything.* Out of such simple belief some of the most powerful and effective magick can be woven. Our bodies are the particular piece of the Great Mother especially entrusted to us. In the experience of that sacred trust, sex becomes an act of worship, engaging and awakening the God and Goddess in our partners. *"For behold; all acts of Love and Pleasure are My rituals"* (Doreen Valiente, "The Charge of the Goddess").

Substances

The four Elements, Earth, Water, Air, and Fire, are actually the four states of matter: solid, liquid, gas, and plasma, going from lesser to greater energy. These comprise the Body, Blood, Breath, and Energy of Gaea. All of material existence is composed of these Elements in varying combination, and so we honor them in our rituals. Many also add Spirit as a fifth Element. Within these broad categories may be grouped all the Sacred Substances:

Earth

Bread, Fruit, and other foods are considered to be the body of the God and/or Goddess. The most common phrases to accompany the passing of food are: "May you never hunger," or "May you always have sufficiency."

Chocolate is jokingly referred to in many magickal Circles as the "Fifth Element." Celebrants are known as "Chocolytes," though those who over-indulge are known as "Chocoholics." Chocolate beverages were considered a drink for the Gods during the time of the Aztec Empire. Chocolate has a divine taste as it melts in your mouth. The chemical *theobromine* (literally, "food of the gods") in chocolate causes a euphoric state that satisfies the deepest of desires and most compelling of cravings.

Water

Water is the essential foundation of all life, comprising 80% of our body mass. Water is the very blood of Mother Earth; the chemical constituency of the blood in our veins is the same as that of the ancient seawater of 540 million years ago, which we assimilated into our bodies as we developed in Her oceanic womb. We are all One—sharing the same blood! Blood, sweat, and tears are the waters of our lives. The physical properties of water, manifesting as solid, liquid, and gas at biologically compatible temperatures, and water's unique property of having a solid form (ice) that floats in the liquid, allow the possibility of life on Earth—and throughout the Universe. The sharing of Water is a sacred act of communion in which we say, "Water shared is Life shared."

Of course, other liquids, such as **wine** or **fruit juice,** may be shared sacramentally as well; they all partake of the "essence" of Water.

Air

Breath—Breath is a rhythm that accompanies every moment. Unlike our heartbeats, we can consciously control breath by holding it, speeding it up, slowing it down, making it shallow or deep, raspy or smooth. Yet when we are asleep or unconscious, our breath continues. Because breath can be controlled both by the conscious and unconscious minds, it is used as a bridge between the two.

In many languages the word for "spirit" and the word for "breath" are the same: *ruach* in Hebrew and *esprit* in French. In other traditions the word for "breath" and "life energy" are the same: *prana* in Sanskrit and *pneuma* in Greek. Breath has been used since prehistory not only as a bridge between the conscious and unconscious, but as a bridge between body and spirit. Breath is used in ritual to raise and focus energy and to bring an experience of full aliveness, embodying the spirit and inspiring the body.

Music—Music plays a central role in almost every religious tradition. Diverse groups of people can grow very close very fast through an experience of music or singing. Music fills the air around us, embracing everyone present and echoing in our souls. The magickal community is blessed with many inspired musicians and Bards, and these folk contribute to every large ritual and occasion, often inviting everyone to join in. The two most ancient and widespread sacred instruments are voice and drum. Both are intimately connected to the rhythms of the body—the voice to breath and the drum to heartbeat.

Fire

Campfires—The most ancient and distinctively human experience is that of sitting around a campfire, sharing songs and stories with your clan. A campfire automatically forms the focus of a primal circle, and *scrying* into the flames may reveal many things....

Firewalking also has been learned and practiced by some of us as an initiatory and transformative experience.

Burning candles of selected colors may be used in spellwork (see 4.7: "Spells").

Spirit

Dance—One of the most primal and prevalent scenes at magickal festivals is a fire circle with drummers and dancers. Expressing the joy, sorrow, and beauty of our lives through our bodies and through dance affirms our identity as part of the natural world and prevents our rites from becoming mere head-trips.

Humor—Magickal people seem to have an inordinate fondness for humor and jokes, both clever and dumb. Puns especially are virtually a trademark of our sense of humor, and the references from which these are drawn are an affirmation of our common group heritage.

Class IV: Conducting a Ritual

1. Introduction: "HOME Cooking: The Magick Circle"

—by Anodea Judith (*HOME Cooking*, 1997)

HE FIRST AND MOST BASIC ELEMENT of conducting magickal ritual is the creation of sacred space. Ritual is something made special, set apart from everyday, requiring a focused attention. The setting up of sacred space marks this time as different from that time; these words as more significant than idle chitchat; these movements have significant meaning. It allows us to alter our consciousness, to redirect our attention.

The Circle is the sacred center in which all ritual takes place. Like a cauldron in which we mix and stir a magick elixir, the Circle forms the psychic boundaries that keep unwanted energy out, while at the same time allowing the magickal energy within to be contained until transformation is complete. As such the Circle is seen as a place between the worlds—a place outside the ordinary stream of time and space, yet a place which inevitably influences this stream. Therefore, the Magick Circle is extremely important, as it is the essential foundation of all ritual. This means that the space in which the Circle is held is purified and consecrated for the rite in question, that care is taken to be as conscious as possible of all words and actions within the Circle, and that there are certain codes of behavior for protecting the sanctity of the Circle.

One of these codes is the law of Perfect Love and Perfect Trust. This means that we only enter into a Circle with the feeling and intention that we can behave toward all members and toward the rite in general with this attitude. It means we agree to open our hearts and minds to each person in an aura of trust, and to not betray the trust of anyone in the Circle. If we cannot enter a Circle in this manner—for instance, if we have a major quarrel with someone in the Circle—then we should not enter the Circle at all.

Since in my tradition, the Holy Order of Mother Earth, we often refer to our magickal practices as "HOME Cooking," I like to use the analogy of baking a cake to represent the various aspects of creating a magickal Circle. Before baking the cake, it is necessary to clean off the counter. We do not want to prepare food on a counter cluttered with yesterday's dirty dishes. This corresponds to purifying the space we are going to use, and may involve magickally banishing unwanted energies, or it may be simply sweeping the floor and unplugging the phone. This clears the field in which we wish to work and makes the work proceed more smoothly. Then it is time to put up the Circle. This is like getting out a large bowl in which to hold the ingredients so they can be mixed together. In this way, the Circle becomes a cauldron to contain the energies we invoke until they can adequately transform. This container is formed by casting the Circle. This marks the physical area, clearly defined as sacred space. It may even be marked on the ground or floor by drawing with chalk or cornmeal. Often it is drawn in the air with a magickal tool, such as a wand or athamé. Yet it can also be created only in the realm of your imagination.

Once we have a clean bowl and a clean space to work, we bring in our ingredients, according to the recipe chosen. For a cake, it's eggs, flour, milk, and sugar. For a Circle, this includes the four Elements and directions, the deities and spirits, and whatever else is appropriate for the purpose of the ritual. These ingredients are invoked into the Circle and "stirred" together. The deities who are called into the Circle are the special magick that makes for a good cake. It is not enough to merely follow a cookbook; a talented cook adds those special spices that make it unique. The deities are the archetypal principles that we wish to connect with in ourselves and remember as influences in our working. This divine essence cannot be controlled, but it can be *invited* by invocation.

Then comes the working. This is where we stir the ingredients together. Do we beat them like meringue, or gently fold them together, like marble cake? Do we mix some separately before adding? This is the most creative part of a ritual, and it is the real essence of the magick. Then we need to raise energy for transformation of the ingredients into something new. In baking a cake, this is the part where we stick it in the oven and turn up the heat. In a Circle, it may be drumming and dancing, chanting, meditating, or focusing energy on symbolic objects. When this energy is applied, as in the case of heat from the oven, a transformation does indeed take place. Afterwards, a cooling-off period is needed. The cake holds better if it is allowed to sit for a bit, and a Circle often spends this time sharing food, drink, and discussion that is in some way backing off from the previous intensity of raising energy.

Once cooling has taken place, the cake can be taken out of the pan. It will hold its new shape and can be shared outside the kitchen. In the Circle, it means the magick has taken place in whatever fashion it was intended, and the Circle can be removed to allow that magick to pass on to wherever it is intended. The pans are cleaned, the ingredients put away, and the ritual is ended.

Lesson 2. Ritual Structure

Here is an outline of a basic generic ritual structure commonly used in many circle rites throughout much of the American, European, British, and Australian magickal community. If you learn this form, you will be at home in just about any Circle anywhere, in all of their infinite variations. There are entire books, tapes, and CDs full of variations on this basic form, with countless different chants, invocations, and blessings—many of which are in the forms of songs and poetry. What I offer here are only samples. One of the best things about magickal rituals is that they offer so much room for creativity!

I. BANISHING/CLEANSING *(optional; not used in all rituals)*
A. Smudging
or: B. Asperging *(with salt water)*

II. GROUNDING *(optional; not used in all rituals)*
A. Guided meditation ("Tree of Life")
or: B. Physical movement

III. CASTING THE CIRCLE (*Deosil*/clockwise for "doing;" *widdershins*/counterclockwise for "undoing." All movements within the ritual should follow direction of casting.)
A. Walk circumference with blade or wand.
or: B. All dance circumference
C. Chanting/singing
D. Visualization

IV. CALLING THE QUARTERS
A. East (Air)
B. South (Fire)
C. West (Water)
D. North (Earth)
Optional: E. The Great Above (or Spirit)
F. The Great Below (or Abyss)
G. The Center (or Faerie)

V. INVOKING DEITIES & SPIRITS
A. The Goddess
B. The God
Optional: C. Ancestors
D. Animal Totems
E. Higher Self

VI. STATEMENT OF PURPOSE
Clarifying the intention of the ritual.

VII. WORKING
Elements of the ritual are symbolized and/or represented. Dynamics between chosen elements are dramatized, healed, transformed, or energized (this is the most creative part).

VIII. POWER RAISING & RELEASING
A. Chanting and/or Drumming
B. Dancing

IX. COMMUNION
A. Charging/Blessing and Sharing:
1. Food (cakes, bread, fruit, etc.)
2. Drink (water, juice, wine, etc.)

X. HIATUS
A. Meditation
or: B. Discussion ("Sacred Bullshit")
C. Silence

XI. THANKS & RELEASING OF ELEMENTS & SPIRITS
A. Deities/Spirits *(in reverse order of invocation)*
B. Directions/Elements *(in reverse order of invocation)*

XII. OPENING THE CIRCLE *(in reverse direction of casting)*
Usually done in same manner as it was cast, i.e. by song, dance, blade, wand, etc.

> ***NOTE:*** *There is usually personal ritual preparation before the rite begins. This can include silent meditation, a purifying bath, fasting, dancing, stretching, and so on. Circles are usually cast deosil, starting in the East, but at Samhain, Walpurgisnacht, and for Greek rituals, the Circle and Quarters are cast and called widdershins, beginning in the West. In the Southern Hemisphere, the directions, movements, and seasons are reversed from those here indicated.*

Lesson 3. Preparations

For millennia, Wizards, Witches, and Magicians have used the Circle to define our area of magickal workings. There are many reasons for this: The Circle leads back into itself and is consequently a symbol of unity, the absolute, and perfection. It therefore represents the Heavens in contrast to the Earth, or the spiritual in contrast to the material. There is a close connection between the Circle and the wheel. As an endless line, it symbolizes time and infinity.

When the Circle is inscribed with a magickal implement it forms a protective barrier against external negativity, and a lens within which to focus the energy of the individual or group. It is a good idea in the beginning to mark the Circle with tape or string on the floor, or inscribe it in the dirt with your athamé if outdoors. We have even drawn Circles of lime for outdoor rituals in grassy parks. This will serve as a visual aid to focus your attention on the proper boundary line. Mark out a circle using your cingulum as a compass, with the knots measuring the radius (see 3.III.4: "Your Cingulum").

The dimensions of the Magick Circle will largely depend upon the number of people who will be using it. For solitary work, a 3- or 5-foot circle will do nicely; for small groups, 9–13 feet may serve. There should be enough room for a small altar in the middle and for those in attendance to move around it comfortably.

Purifying the Temple

If the room or area where you will be working is normally used for mundane activities (such as a living room), you may want to cleanse your temple of any negative thoughts and vibrations before beginning the ritual. Put some water into a small bowl and add a scoop of salt from the blade of your athamé, stirring it into the water. Beginning in the East, use a sprig of herb (rosemary, basil, lilac, or pine) to sprinkle the salt water around the room in a deosil direction, saying:

Water and Salt, where you are cast,
No spell or adverse purpose last
That is not in accord with me.
As I will, so mote it be!

Then light a bundle of sage or cedar and, starting in the East, carry it around the room deosil (we hold it in an abalone shell), fanning it into all the corners with a feather fan or bird's wing, while chanting:

Fire and Air, this charge I lay:
No phantom in your presence stay
That is not in accord with me.
As I do will, so mote it be!

As you do this, visualize with your mind's eye all of the negative thoughts and vibrations leave, and only the pure white light of Spirit permeate the area. Your temple is now ready for whatever ritual or work of magick you wish to perform.

Lesson 4: Smudging and Grounding

As people enter the ritual area, or after everyone has assembled into a Circle, we will often have a *smudging* in which smoking incense (usually sage or cedar) is carried around the Circle in an abalone shell, and the smoke is fanned over each person with a feather fan or bird's wing. This helps to cleanse our personal auras of any energies we do not want to bring into the Circle.

Grounding is done to harmonize the energies of everyone in the Circle and tune us all into the vibrational field of the Earth. In my tradition, we use a grounding we call "The Tree of Life." We stand in a circle, close our eyes, and visualize as if we are trees in the forest. The person who is leading the grounding will say something like this:

"Imagine that you are a tree. Plant your feet firmly on the ground. Now send your roots deep into the Earth. Feel the layers of cold soil and rock beneath your feet. Feel the roots of other plants and trees, as you reach down through the bones of your ancestors, through the pages of the Ages, down, down, to the molten heart of Mother Earth. Now draw that heat up through your roots, up into your trunk. Feel Her life force flow upwards through your body, filling you with Mama's magick. Now stretch your branches up, way up, reaching your leaves towards the Sun, towards a million billion suns, and draw the cosmic radiance from the Universe down into your body, where it meets the hot energy you drew up from the center of the Earth. Feel yourself filled with light and life, with the blended energies of Heaven and Earth. Take a deep breath, let it out, and be here now!"

Everyone opens their eyes and the Rite begins.

Lesson 5: Casting the Circle

The Magick Circle is a space between the worlds of Mundane and Faerie. A boundary is created around this space by "Casting the Circle." This is done by walking deosil around the edge of the Circle, starting in the East, while chanting something like this:

Magick, magick, everywhere
In the Earth and in the Air!
Magick seals our Circle round
Between the worlds it shall be bound!
Three times around, three times about
A world within, a world without!

The person doing the Circle casting holds a wand or athamé and uses it to draw a surrounding ring of astral

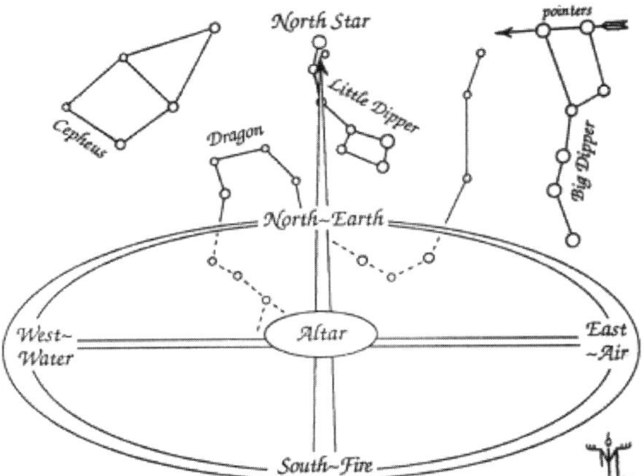

light (which everyone should visualize together as ultraviolet flames or lightning). This ring will contain the energies raised in the Circle, until it is time for them to be released. The wand or athamé should be touched to the ground at the Eastern point in the beginning, then raised to shoulder level and pointed straight out to the edge of the Circle, which will be inscribed in air with its tip. When the person casting has come full circle and returns to the East, they once again touch the ground with the tip of the wand or athamé, thus grounding the Circle.

Once the Circle is cast, it must not be entered or exited without cutting a gate. This is done with a wand or athamé, starting at the ground and drawing a line up, over the top, and down the other side to make a doorway you can then walk through. Or you may draw a line straight up from the ground to above your head, and just zip it open and step through. Don't forget to close your door behind you!

Lesson 6: Calling the Quarters

The Magick Circle, like a clock face, is also a map of Time and Space. As such, it has four points of the compass: North, South, East, and West. Each of these points has special associations, or *correspondences,* which we call upon to remind us of where and when we are (see 3.VI.4: "Directions & Elements"). Each of the Directions is associated with one of the four Elements: East=Air, South=Fire, West=Water, and North=Earth. The words of the callings (which may be in the form of chants and songs) are based on these correspondences, so familiarize yourself with them.

It is customary to have an object representing each of the Elements on your altar. Many people just use their magickal tools, which have their Elemental associations. But you may also use a feather, bell, or incense for Air; a candle for Fire; a cup of water or seashell for Water; and a crystal, stone, geode, or bowl of salt for Earth. In my tradition, we often set up small altars at the outer edge of the Circle area, at each of the four Quarters, which are then decorated with appropriate symbols and colors. At nighttime rituals these usually include votive candles in colored glass holders—yellow for Air, red for Fire, blue for Water, and green for Earth.

If there are enough people in the Circle, we ask a different person to call each Quarter, but if the Circle is very small (or solitary) one person can call all four. Again, we always begin in the East, where the Sun rises, and go deosil—except at Samhain and Walpurgisnacht (May Eve), when we begin in the West and go widdershins. We have special gestures, or *mudras,* in which we hold our arms at each Quarter to identify with the essence of each Element. For small Circles, the person doing the calling stands in that direction and faces outward. But for very large Circles, the caller will stand opposite the direction, facing across the Circle, so everyone can see and hear him.

East: The person doing the calling faces the East, arms raised and held out like wings, palms up and fingers spread. Everyone else also faces East with the same gesture. The one calling will say something like:

O soaring Eagle of the East, rider of the Winds of Change, come to us from beyond the sunrise and bring us inspiration! Hail and be welcome!

And everyone else echoes, *"Hail and be welcome!"* At this time, incense and/or the yellow East candle may be lit, and a bell may be rung.

South: Then everyone turns to the South, holding hands above our heads, fingertips and thumbtips together in a peak, making a triangle like a flame. The South caller says something like:

O golden Lion of the burning South, ruler of the flames and lightning, come to our Circle and bring us enlightenment! Hail and be welcome!

The red South candle may be lit. If you are outdoors and have a fire-pot or central campfire, you may also light it now.

West: Now we turn to the West, still holding our hands in a triangle with finger and thumbtips together, bringing them down below our waist like a cup. The caller says something like:

O great Whale of the Western Sea, come to us from your watery depths and teach us the lesson of flowing! Hail and be welcome!

A cup or shell of water may be splashed on the ground, and the blue West candle may be lit.

North: Finally we turn to the North. Hands are held low and out from the body, palms down, reaching like roots for the Earth. The caller says something like:

O mighty Bull of the frozen North, come to us from your land of ice and mountains and teach us the lesson of stability! Hail and be welcome!

Salt may be sprinkled on the ground, and the green North candle may be lit.

Lesson 7: Invocations

Now, into this Magick Circle where we are gathered, we invite the deities to join us, for our magickal workings are done in Their honor, and with Their blessings. As ritual is basically a spiritual experience, the invocation of spiritual energies is common. Spirit beings may be invoked in whatever form is appropriate—calling on Hermes, for instance, to aid in our magick; or Brigit for creative inspiration (see lists of deities and their correspondences in 7.II: "Gods of All the Nations"). Angels, spirits of the ancestors, animal totems, the faerie folk, or anyone else we may desire would be called in at this time. In HOME, we often have people costume themselves as deities for ritual; the drawings here are of some of our folks as various gods and goddesses.

Some magickal practitioners regard these Spirit beings merely as symbols representing differing aspects of human consciousness. However, it is my experience that the Deities, Angels, Totems, and other Spirit beings of the various cultural *pantheons* (families of deities) are very real personalities, just as we are. They each have Their own stories, histories, attributes, and most importantly, Their own *agendas* (plans)—which may not be the same as ours! The main difference between Them and the rest of us is that They are *trans-corporeal*—independent of bodies—and hence immortal. They are *not,* however, *omniscient* (all knowing) or *omnipotent* (all-powerful), though They do know things and have influences that we mortals do not. Just as in dealing with anyone else, we must treat and respect Them as real beings if we are to develop a real relationship with Them.

It is entirely up to you to decide whom you want to invite into your Circle, and there is no one true right and only way to do it. Whatever works and feels right *is* right. Many rituals will invoke both a Goddess and a God, just as you might invite both your Mom and your Dad to a play, concert or soccer game you're in. There are, of course, many different Gods, Goddesses, and other Spirit beings to choose from. Every culture that has existed throughout history has had its own pantheon, and I recommend you study some of these and become familiar with Them.

Of course, beings of Spirit are all around us all the time, just like radio waves and TV transmissions. What we are really doing is making *ourselves* receptive to *communion,* or contact with Them at this particular time and place. This is much like turning on your TV and choosing the channel you want to watch. This is done by invocation, similar to our Quarter callings, where we address the Deity or Spirit as we would a friend or relative, saying something like:

Oh, most (gracious, wise, beautiful, powerful, beloved, etc.) (name), (Lord, Lady) *of*

(attributes…) *we invite you to enter this Circle and join with us in our magick work. Bring us your* (wisdom, strength, inspiration, courage, etc.) *and your blessings. Hail and be welcome!*

And of course, everyone else echoes, *"Hail and be welcome!"* As They are called, candles may be lit for Them on the central altar.

Lesson 8: The Working

Now we have reached the heart of the ritual: working the magick! Magick is "the art of probability enhancement." We work our magick by focusing our individual or group energies all in the same direction, like a laser beam, to shift the patterns of possibilities so that the things we want to happen are more likely to come about. The power of magick comes from our *will.* When we do magick, we never say, "I *hope* such-and-so will happen," or "I *wish* such-and-so would happen." We say, "It *will* be so!" The ritual words for this are *So be it!* or *So mote it be!*—which everyone else in the Circle repeats.

There are several steps in doing a magick working in the Circle. First is the *declaration of intent*, where the purpose of the working is explained and agreed upon by everyone. Then comes *raising the cone of power*, where everyone's energy is combined and built into a powerful force. Next is *releasing the power* and sending it out to do its work. Finally come *centering* and *meditation*, as we recover some of the energy we have just put out.

Declaration of Intent

The purpose of using magick is to change things for the better. Most of our workings are for healing—healing ourselves, healing each other, and healing the planet. Other purposes might be protection, peace, or justice. Finding love, a good job, a home, or an answer to some problem may also be a goal of a magick working. At this point in the ritual it is important to decide exactly what the energy you are raising will be used for, and to state this plainly. This is your *declaration of intent.* Often, the declaration of intent is determined and written down before the ritual even starts.

Sometimes the declaration of intent may be stated by one person (especially if you are doing a solitary ritual!). A good way to do this is to write down the Intent in the form of a brief spell—especially in the form of a little rhyming couplet that will be easy to hold in mind during the power raising. (A simple example could be something like: *"Bring the one I love to me; As I will so mote it be!"*) At other times everyone in the Circle may be given a turn to state what it is they want to accomplish. It works best, however, if everyone focuses on the same basic goal, to keep the group's energy together. If some folks really want to work for different things, these workings should be done in different rituals.

After everyone agrees and the intent is clearly stated out loud, say, *"As I/we do will, so mote it be!"* and everyone should repeat, *"So mote it be!"*

Raising and Releasing the Power

If you are working a solitary ritual, one of the best ways to raise and release energy is through the Breath of Fire. You sit in a meditative position, and breathe rapidly and deeply in and out as fast as you can. Repeat over and over the words of your intent or spell in your mind, while visualizing the thing you want. Start out slowly and go faster and faster until you feel like you're about to explode. Finally, when you can stand it no more, exhale with a last great rush while shouting out: *"So mote it be!"* Fling your thought and visualization out into the Universe as if you were throwing a spear. Then just collapse and lay down until you have the energy to sit up again.

A favorite way to raise energy in a group is the Circle Dance. While everyone holds the intent in their mind, hold hands and dance faster and faster deosil around in the Circle, weaving your steps in and out in a "Grapevine" step, like this:

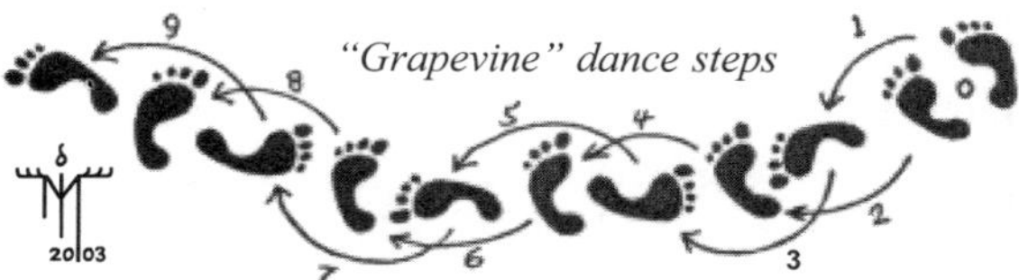

"Grapevine" dance steps

Slowly bring your hands up as you dance, until at the most exciting point they are high above your heads. At the same time, visualize a cone of bright shining energy forming around everyone in the Circle, raising higher and higher, like an upside-down tornado. Or, if the working is to create a spell of protection, imagine your combined energies spreading out into a great dome—an umbrella-shaped shield, with an outside surface like a mirror that will reflect away all negativity.

For the energy-raising Circle dance, a good drumbeat is great (or you can put on a CD with a good heavy beat!), and a Circle dance song will help create the right juice. Here's one of my favorites, which I have found to be very effective:

Circle 'round the fire
To raise the cone of power
To win what we desire
So mote it be!

Repeat louder and faster until you can't dance and sing any faster, then on the final "So mote it be," scream that *"beeeee!"* as loud as you can, breaking loose of each other's hands as you fling your hands to the sky, releasing all that energy to go and work your will. Visualize the top of the cone erupting like a volcano, sending a beam of power where you want it to go. Then everybody collapses to the Earth, grounding yourselves and letting the Mother's strength and love flow back into your bodies.

If the magick working is a healing for someone in the Circle, the energy raised will not be sent out, but inward to the person to be healed. This can be very powerfully done by everyone laying hands on the person and pushing healing energy into them, or pulling pain and illness out. Visualize a warm red light glowing in you and spreading out through your hands, just like you've seen in movies. Use deep, fast breathing to pump up your *auric* energy before you send it into the person. Then be sure to shake your hands off and ground them into the Earth so that you don't catch their problem yourself!

Centering and Meditation

After raising and releasing so much energy, it is important to bring your own energy back to your center with a simple meditation. Sit in a meditation position and gaze into the flame of the center candle on the altar, or the fire if you are doing this outdoors and have a bonfire. Let your mind cut loose of all thoughts, especially of the working you've just done, and just become one with the flame. After a few moments of this, when you feel completely calm and relaxed, you might softly begin to hum *"Omm,"* letting your voice merge with everyone else's into a harmonic chant: *"Auu-ommmmm..."* fading away when it has completed its work.

Lesson 9: Communion

In magick, as in life, the balance between gravity (the heavy stuff) and levity (the light stuff) is very important. After raising and releasing all that energy, we now move to the light and more joyous part of the ritual: *Communion* ("sharing") and *Sacred Bullshit.* On the altar you should have a plate (or use your Panticle) with an uncut round of bread.

Communion usually begins with the Consecration of the Sacraments. *Consecrating* means "blessing for our use." This is much like saying a blessing before meals, except that because the Spirit beings are already with us in the Circle, we don't need to ask Them again for Their blessings. They are blessing us and all we do by Their very presence. Instead, we *charge* our food and drink with Spirit, remembering that our nourishment and refreshment not only come *from* Them, but actually *are part of* Them, which we are about to make part of ourselves.

Consecration

Consecrating the sacraments is done with the athamé and the chalice, which is filled with water, fruit juice, or wine (all are equally appropriate in any ritual, depending on your preference). This part represents the joining of the male and female forces, which gives rise to all life. If you are doing this solitary, you should hold the chalice in your left hand and the athamé in your right hand, and speak these lines yourself. If you have a girl in the Circle, she should hold up the chalice with both hands while you hold the athamé above it. Lower it point down into the chalice, while saying: *"As the athamé is to the male..."*

She continues: *"So the chalice is to the female."*

You reply: *"Together they become Whole."*

And in unison, you both say: *"There is no greater Power in all the world than the Union of Love. Blessed Be!"*

Now, with your athamé, cut the bread, saying something like the following:

The seed of life itself is roused
By the heat of the Sun's desire.
Thus are we fed and nourished.
May you never hunger!

Take some and pass it around, everyone saying to the next person: *"May you never hunger."*

Then bless the chalice of drink with something like:

From water does all life come;
Unto water we shall return.
Water shared is life shared.
May you never thirst!

Drink, and pass it around, everyone repeating to each other: *"May you never thirst."*

Communion

While the bread and drink are being passed around, you might softly sing or chant something like: *"Lord of the Sun, Lady of the Earth, We are one with the energies of the Universe!"* (If you are doing this solitary, simply eat and drink in thoughtful silence.)

This Communion Feast of Fellowship is as old as time, a sacred part of nearly every culture in the world. Sharing food and drink in the Circle is a reminder that we share our lives and our purpose. Also, because everything on Earth is part of the body of Mother Earth Herself, this Communion reminds us

everything we eat and drink is sacred, as it really is Her flesh and blood we are taking into our bodies to become our flesh and blood. We also honor the Lord as the Sun God and the Green Man, by remembering that His solar rays provide the energy to ripen all plants, and He is cut down in the Fall to yield the grain for the bread that nourishes us. That is why we call the food and drink that we share in Circle *sacraments.* They have been consecrated and so they are *sacred,* or holy, filled with the Divine Spark. We are also reminded that *our* bodies are sacred too; our lives also filled with the same Divine Spark.

Sacred Bullshit

After the bread and drink have gone around once, they can continue being passed, for now comes the time called Sacred Bullshit, first called that by the New Reformed Order of the Golden Dawn. This is the time for announcements and messages (but not stuff like school, TV shows, or other mundane bullshit!). Time and place of the next meeting may be decided, chants and lore may be shared, and other magickal things talked about. This part may even become a Bardic, where each person in turn around the Circle may sing a song, recite a poem, or tell a story or joke (see 4.III.4: "Types of Rituals: Bardics").

Lesson 10. Ending the Ritual

Thanking the Deities

This enchanted evening we have been blessed by the presence of beloved Spirits. They have been our special guests, and we must now thank Them for coming, and say goodnight. If different people invoked Them, the same ones should now bid Them farewell, and in reverse of the order in which they were first called.

A farewell to the Three-Fold God, for example, might go something like this:

Blessed Lord of Light and Laughter,
Thank you for your blessings here.
We are yours forever after—
One with oak and sun and deer!
Blessed Be!
(All repeat, *"Blessed Be!"*)

And then to the Triple Moon Goddess we might say:

Lady of the Silv'ry Wheel,
Maiden, Mother, ancient Crone,
We bear within your mystic seal—
We thank you, for we are your own!
Blessed Be!

If candles have been lit for Them on the central altar, they should be put out now—either with your fingers or a candle snuffer, rather than blowing them out.

Releasing the Elements

Thanking and releasing the Elements is also done in reverse order, starting in the North, and then to West, South, and finally East. These releases (often called *dismissals*) should also be done by the same people who called them before. Then, one at a time, the Quarter candles are put out. Here is a very common model for releasing the Elements:

O Guardians of the frozen North,
(wat'ry West; fiery South; windy East),
We thank you for attending our rites.
Go if you must; stay if you will.
And ere you depart to your fair and lovely realms,
We bid you hail and farewell!
(all repeat, *"Hail and farewell!"*)

Opening the Circle

When we cast the Magick Circle at the beginning of this ritual, we closed off a little bubble of sacred space between the worlds. The last thing we do now is burst that bubble and return this space to the mundane world. We call this "releasing" or "opening" the Circle rather than "closing" it, because we are now opening the door to leave.

Whomever cast the Circle in the first place now goes back to the East, where it began. Pointing your wand or athamé at the ground, walk widdershins around the outside of the Circle, saying something like:

Circle of magick, circle of art—
The rite is ended; now we part.
This Circle drawn between the worlds
Begone! as Time and Space unfurls...

Returning once more to the East, fling your arms wide to the outside, saying, *"The rite is ended. Blessed Be!"* And all repeat, *"Blessed Be!"* It is customary in many traditions for everyone to add, *"Merry meet and merry part, and merry meet again!"* And now everybody helps pick up and put away all the stuff so the ritual area is clean. Group hugs all around, and we bid our farewells to each other before heading home to our own beds and magickal dreams.

Class V: Magickal Times

To every thing there is a season, and a time to every purpose under heaven:
A time to be born, and a time to die; a time to plant, and a time to harvest what was planted...
—Ecclesiastes 3:1-8 (*King James Bible*)

1. Introduction: Timing is Everything

S WITH ANYTHING ELSE IN LIFE, THERE are favorable and unfavorable times for working various spells and rituals, and the more favorable times you can line up together, the more powerful will be your magick. This doesn't mean that you cannot work a spell or do a ritual unless those vibrations are correct. It merely means that these are the ideal conditions under which to do your work. During these times you are taking advantage of the natural tides and currents of the Universe rather than working against them. If, however, you have something of great importance and urgency to do, you can plan it fairly well just with the aid of the table of planetary hours I've given below in Lesson 6.

Lesson 2. Moon Phases, Times & Seasons

The two greatest divisions for magickal workings are the waxing or waning phases of the Moon. The Moon is both your clock and your calendar for working magick. Work of a beneficial and *con*structive nature, as well as charging an amulet or talisman with power, is usually done when the Moon is waxing to full. The greatest power is between the first and second quarters, when the Moon is rapidly growing full. When the Moon is waning to darkness, the times are perfect for *de*structive magick and rituals of a more earthly nature. *Necromancy* (communicating with the dead), spells of binding and blighting, and all works of trouble and deceit, are done during a waning Moon. The dark of the Moon, the most ominous time of all, is reserved for works of definite destruction and death.

*Con*structive magick is done for increase and building up, such as health, wealth, success, and advancement. *De*structive magick is concerned with the ending and tearing down of things, such as a love affair, a bad habit, or a way of life.

The very fact of whether a ritual or spell is done during the day or at night plays a major role in its aspects. Generally, rituals for positive and beneficial purposes (such as healing) are done during the day—preferably before noon so that you have some hours of daylight left to increase the power generated. Spells done during the dark hours are usually for enchantments, or for promoting your desires and advantages over others (as in winning a contest or a competition). These are also frequently planned so that there will be some hours of darkness following to enable the currents that have been set into motion to continue.

When at all possible, the seasons of the Earth and Sun should be taken into consideration. This, of course, may not be possible for every ritual, and is usually reserved for special occasions, such as the eight great *Sabbats*. In this manner, spells that would be of the type done during a waxing moon would be done between Winter Solstice and Summer Solstice. Rituals that might normally be appropriate during the waning Moon would be done between Summer Solstice and Winter Solstice. As you can see, the power of the Sun is on the increase from Winter to Summer, and on the decrease from Summer to Winter. Thus the degree and amount of power the Sun bestows on the Earth is regarded in the same way as the phases of the Moon.

The four large seasonal cycles marked by the Solstices and Equinoxes are called the *Elemental Tides*, and each has its own special type of magick. From Spring Equinox to Summer Solstice is the *Tide of Planting* (or beginnings). Summer Solstice to Autumn Equinox is the *Tide of Harvest* (or culmination). Fall Equinox to Winter Solstice is the *Tide of Planning* (or calculation). And Winter Solstice to the Vernal Equinox is the *Tide of Destruction* (or replacement).

SIGN		PERIOD	PURPOSE
♈	Aries	3/21-4/19	Curing illness and disease; gaining eloquence of speech; acceptance and honor
♉	Taurus	4/20-5/20	Curing fevers; becoming gracious, devout, and religious.
♊	Gemini	5/21-6/20	Gaining good health, friendship, and happiness; preventing boredom.
♋	Cancer	6/21-7/21	Ridding of poisons; attaining wisdom.
♌	Leo	7/22-8/21	Curing colds; gaining an eloquent and ingenious nature.
♍	Virgo	8/22-9/21	Curing fevers; gaining acceptance and eloquence.
♎	Libra	9/22-10/21	Fighting disease; gaining friendship and happiness.
♏	Scorpio	10/22-11/21	Provoking passion and lust.
♐	Sagittarius	11/21-12/21	Curing illness; gaining acceptance and honor.
♑	Capricorn	12/22-1/20	Keeping people and places safe and secure.
♒	Aquarius	1/21-2/19	Gaining health and happiness.
♓	Pisces	2/20-3/20	Protecting against fevers and evil.

Lesson 3. Signs of the Zodiac

The signs of the Zodiac play an important role in the workings of various rituals and spells. Of course, a working can be done at any time; it is just that certain times are more effective than others are. Above are the types of workings best suited to each Sign, starting with Spring Equinox

Lesson 4. Planetary Aspects

Each of the seven visible "Planets" (including the Sun and Moon) has certain associated qualities that contribute to rituals and spellwork. These qualities are numerous and complex (see 3.VI.5: Table of Correspondences: Planets), but briefly they are as follows:

☉ **Sun** *(Sunday)* The Sun brings you honor, acceptability, and elevation. Your work will go well, making you a master of whatever you try. You will achieve success, but it won't go to your head. The Sun brings money and the support of powerful people, as well as aiding you in finding lost treasures. The days and hours of the Sun are also good for divination and dissolving bad qualities. The hours of the Sun, in general, are good for works of love and kindness, bringing about happiness and friendship.

☽ **Moon** *(Monday)* The Moon can make you pleasant, friendly, happy, honored, and cheerful. It aids in removing all malice or evil thoughts you may have. Security for travelers, monetary gain, long-lasting health, and elimination of enemies are among the fortunate aspects of the Moon. The hours of the Moon are good for preventing theft and recovering stolen goods, obtaining prophetic visions, and anything related to water (including travel by sea or river). Also for winning love and mending quarrels, invisibility, seeing visions, and raising spirits.

In magick, the Moon is the most important heavenly body. In relation to this, use the following code when planning lunar workings:

For invocations of spirits, recovery of stolen goods, and calling of the dead, the Moon should be in an **Earth** sign (*Taurus, Virgo, Capricorn*).

For love, honors, and invisibility, the Moon should be in a **Fire** sign (*Aries, Leo, Sagittarius*).

For all manner of destruction, hatred, or anger, the Moon should be in a **Water** sign (*Cancer, Scorpio, Pisces*).

All other workings that cannot be classified under the above should be done when the Moon is in an **Air** sign (*Gemini, Libra, Aquarius*).

♂ **Mars** *(Tuesday)* Mars is about power—brute physical power. It aids works of hatred or discord, destruction, and military ventures. Often used to destroy, or arouse anger, hatred, or jealousy in another, Mars is also used in necromancy when contacting the dead who have died by violence. The basic idea of Mars is one of total disruption; it brings barrenness and troubles. But you can use it in its fortunate aspect to bring enduring power and a will to fight. Honors and victory in physical competition, courage, and the ability to defeat your enemies are also of the beneficial aspect of Mars.

☿ **Mercury** *(Wednesday)* Mercury can help make you grateful, accepting, and understanding, as well as aiding you to do what you please. It keeps away poverty, both material and mental. Mercury can help improve your memory and your abilities in communication and divination, encouraging you to seek higher knowledge and great truths. The hours of Mercury are good for divining the future, seeing spirits, prophetic dreams, gaining knowledge, and discovering the truth. Mercury aids anything concerning merchandise and commerce and brings success in business, contests, games of skill, sports, etc.

Jupiter *(Thursday)* Jupiter is used to gain wealth, health, love, favors from others, friendship, peace, and fame. It brings you honor and helps to protect you from enchantments. Spells done in the day and hour of Jupiter bring business success, political power, and any other personal wishes.

Venus *(Friday)* Venus brings love and friendship, personal pleasure, and lusty passion. It aids in ending quarrelling and strife, and brings about generosity, peace, and happiness. Venus brings fertility to humans and animals, and safety to travelers. Venus also releases enchantments that others may have put on you.

Saturn *(Saturday)* Saturn is important in works of injury, destruction or death, as well as causing anger, discord, or jealousy in others. It also brings long life, safety, and power, and helps in obtaining knowledge (especially about others). Saturn aids you in building things, enhancing anything concerning man-made structures. It is good for protection, works of stability, and lasting spells. It can be used to bring success or failure to business, harvest, possessions, and so on. In the hour of Saturn, you can summon spirits with ease, but they must only be those who have died naturally.

Lesson 5: Dance of the Hours

The truest measure of the passage of time is found in the apparent movements of the stars and planets. When accurate clocks replaced sundials and hourglasses in the Renaissance, 60-minute intervals became significant in ritual magick. Each hour was assigned the rulership of a different planet. These were called the *planetary hours*, and rituals were performed accordingly. The following system is attributed to Peter of Abano, in his Grimoire *Heptameron,* or *Magical Elements.* It is anchored at noon (*meridian*—the highest point of the Sun) and midnight, and is therefore independent of time zones or daylight savings.

You can greatly enhance the power of any magick spell or ritual by doing your working not only on the

PLANETARY HOURS of the DAY (Noon to Midnight)

		SUNDAY	MONDAY	TUESDAY	WEDNESDAY	THURSDAY	FRIDAY	SATURDAY		
Noon										Noon
Afternoon	1PM	**Sun**	**Moon**	**Mars**	**Mercury**	**Jupiter**	**Venus**	**Saturn**	1PM	Afternoon
	2	Venus	Saturn	Sun	Moon	Mars	Mercury	Jupiter	2	
	3	Mercury	Jupiter	Venus	Saturn	Sun	Moon	Mars	3	
	4	Moon	Mars	Mercury	Jupiter	Venus	Saturn	Sun	4	
	5	Saturn	Sun	Moon	Mars	Mercury	Jupiter	Venus	5	
	6	Jupiter	Venus	Saturn	Sun	Moon	Mars	Mercury	6	
Evening	7	Mars	Mercury	Jupiter	Venus	Saturn	Sun	Moon	7	Evening
	8	**Sun**	**Moon**	**Mars**	**Mercury**	**Jupiter**	**Venus**	**Saturn**	8	
	9	Venus	Saturn	Sun	Moon	Mars	Mercury	Jupiter	9	
	10	Mercury	Jupiter	Venus	Saturn	Sun	Moon	Mars	10	
	11	Moon	Mars	Mercury	Jupiter	Venus	Saturn	Sun	11	
	12	Saturn	Sun	Moon	Mars	Mercury	Jupiter	Venus	12	
Midnight										Midnight

PLANETARY HOURS of the NIGHT (Midnight to Noon)

		SUNDAY	MONDAY	TUESDAY	WEDNESDAY	THURSDAY	FRIDAY	SATURDAY		
Midnight										Midnight
Graveyard	1AM	Jupiter	Venus	Saturn	Sun	Moon	Mars	Mercury	1AM	Graveyard
	2	Mars	Mercury	Jupiter	Venus	Saturn	Sun	Moon	2	
	3	**Sun**	**Moon**	**Mars**	**Mercury**	**Jupiter**	**Venus**	**Saturn**	3	
	4	Venus	Saturn	Sun	Moon	Mars	Mercury	Jupiter	4	
	5	Mercury	Jupiter	Venus	Saturn	Sun	Moon	Mars	5	
	6	Moon	Mars	Mercury	Jupiter	Venus	Saturn	Sun	6	
Morning	7	Saturn	Sun	Moon	Mars	Mercury	Jupiter	Venus	7	Morning
	8	Jupiter	Venus	Saturn	Sun	Moon	Mars	Mercury	8	
	9	Mars	Mercury	Jupiter	Venus	Saturn	Sun	Moon	9	
	10	**Sun**	**Moon**	**Mars**	**Mercury**	**Jupiter**	**Venus**	**Saturn**	10	
	11	Venus	Saturn	Sun	Moon	Mars	Mercury	Jupiter	11	
	12	Mercury	Jupiter	Venus	Saturn	Sun	Moon	Mars	12	
Noon										Noon

day associated with the appropriate planetary attributes, but also on the hour as well. The most powerful magickal alignments, therefore, would be created by matching up the hour, day, and sign of the Zodiac—all with the same purposes.

On the previous page is Abano's basic "Table of the Planetary Hours." To use it, first check an almanac to find the exact times of sunrise and sunset for the day. Midway between them is either midnight or noon, and these are the actual times you should go by. Note that these times seldom fall at exactly 12:00 noon or 12:00 midnight by the clock. From this, you will be able to see what planet rules which hour.

The Planetary Hours (German woodcut, 1490)

Lesson 6. Clock of the Flowers

The great Swedish naturalist Carolus Linnaeus (1707-1778) once planted a timekeeping flower bed which he called "Flora's Clocks." Arranged in a clock-face design, these became very popular in the ornamental gardens of 19th Century Europe.

But flower clocks are rare today because of the difficulty in finding and cultivating flowers that will keep time in various seasons and localities.

Here are examples of common flowers found in England and the US whose times of opening and closing are regular enough to keep time within ½ hour on a sunny day. The exact times may vary somewhat in different locations, but will still occur hourly.

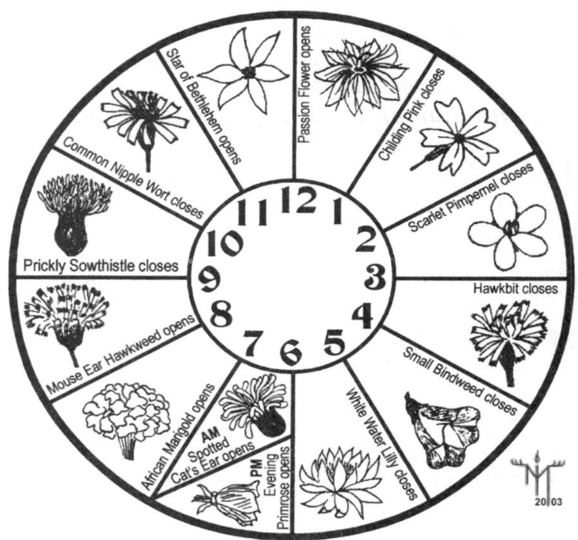

Lesson 7. Moon Signs

And then the Moon, always punctual,
To mark the months and make division of time:
The Moon it is that signals the feast,
A luminary that wanes after her full.
The month derives its name from hers,
She waxes wonderfully in her phases,
Banner of the hosts on high,
Shining in the vault of heaven.
—Ecclesiasticus 43:6-9 (*Jerusalem Bible*)

As the Moon moves across the sky from night to night in its 28-day cycle, it advances by 12.86° on each successive evening, taking it through each of the 12 signs of the Zodiac. Thus it spends 2.3 days in each sign. The Moon rises an average of 50 minutes later each night, but close to the Equinoxes, it rises just 25 to 30 minutes later across the US, and only 10 to 20 minutes later for much of Canada and Europe.

When the Moon is in a certain sign, the lunar attributes will be influenced by the characteristics of that sign, and different sorts of magick may be worked. Because the actual constellations vary greatly in size, while the signs are assigned 30° each, the Moon may sometimes appear in a constellation different from its official sign. Here, starting with Aries, are the 28 colorful names and magickal workings traditionally associated with each position of the Moon among the stars. Names in parentheses are those of the nearest constellations or named stars.

1. ***Horns of Aries***— Destruction and discord.
2. ***Belly of Aries***— Finding treasures; reconciliation.
3. ***Showering*** (Pleiades)— Good fortune to hunters, sailors, and scientists.
4. ***Eye of Taurus*** (Aldebaran)— Discord, revenge, separation; destruction of man-made things.

5. **(Alchatay)**—Safe return from a journey; aid to scholars; health and good will; winning favor of teachers, rulers, and bosses.
6. ***Little Star of Great Light***—Good hunting; revenge; enchanting one into love.
7. ***Arm of Gemini*** (Pollux)—Friendship and love; manifesting good desires.
8. ***Misty*** (Cancer)—Love, friendship, companionship; victories.
9. ***Eye of the Lion***—Discord, illness; troubles to travelers.
10. ***Neck of Leo*** (Regulus)—Strengthening man-made things; bringing love, happiness, protection against enemies; curing illness.
11. ***Hair of the Lion***—Good for journeys, material gains, childbearing.
12. ***Tail of Leo***—Good harvests; trouble at sea; separation of lovers.
13. ***Dog Stars*** (Virgo)—Benevolence and agreement in all things.
14. ***Flying Spike*** (Spica)—Love in marriage; good for all to do with sea but not of land; curing many illnesses.
15. ***Covered Flying*** (Libra)—Finding treasures in the Earth; bringing destruction and discord.
16. ***Claws of Scorpio***—Bringing troubles to journeys, marriages, harvests.
17. ***Crown of Scorpio*** (Antares)—Strengthening and improving love, workers.
18. ***Heart of Scorpio***—Discord, conspiracy, and revenge.
19. ***Tail of Scorpio*** (Cat's Eyes)—Driving away others, destruction.
20. ***Arrow*** (Sagittarius)—Aid in hunting; destroying wealth of others; making another go where you say.
21. ***The Desert*** (no stars)—Good for gain, traveling, harvests.
22. ***Head of Capricorn***— Escaping bondage; curing disease.
23. ***Swallowing*** (Aquarius)—Liberty, divorce, and health.
24. ***Star of Fortune*** (Aquarius)—Benevolence and victory.
25. ***Butterfly***—Revenge against others.
26. ***First Drawing*** (Pisces)—Health, union and love.
27. ***Second Drawing*** (Pisces)—Gains and health; mischief to others.
28. ***Pisces***—Increasing business; safe journeys; happy marriages.

Lesson 8: Lunar Lore

Full Moon Names

It's fun to devise our own Moon calendar in much the same way as the ancients. For example, the full moon of May will be Barefoot Moon for me (when we start being able to wear no shoes!). June will be Barbecue Moon since by then my mini fire festival is in full swing, and so on. Think about the natural cycles in your own life and region, and then honor those by giving names to the full Moons. — Patricia Telesco

The tradition of naming the year's full Moons began during the era of Roman occupation in England. A few reflect Roman influences, but most relate to farming activities. These correspond to the zodiacal months, rather than our modern civil calendar, and begin at Spring Equinox.

Seed *(Aries)* Sowing season and symbol of the new year.

Hare *(Taurus)* In Roman lore, rabbits were associated with springtime and fertility.

Dyad *(Gemini)* The Latin word for "pair" refers to the twin stars of Gemini: Castor and Pollux.

Mead *(Cancer)* During late June and most of July, the meadows (*meads*) were mowed for hay.

Wort *(Leo)* Now the *worts* (from Anglo-Saxon *wyrt,* "plant") were gathered to be dried and stored.

Barley *(Virgo)* Persephone, maiden goddess of rebirth, carries a sheaf of barley as symbol of the harvest.

Blood *(Libra)* At this season, domestic animals were sacrificed for Winter meat. (Libra's full Moon became the **Wine Moon** if a good grape harvest was expected to produce a superior vintage.)

Snow *(Scorpio)* Scorpio heralds the dark season when the first snow falls.

Oak *(Sagittarius)* The sacred tree of the Druids and the Roman god Jupiter is most noble as it withstands Winter's blasts.

Wolf *(Capricorn)* The fearsome wolf represents the dark of the year.

Storm *(Aquarius)* A storm is said to rage most fiercely just before it ends, and so does the year.

Chaste *(Pisces)* This archaic word for pure reflects the custom of greeting the new year with a clean slate.

Native American Names for Moons

The *Old Farmer's Almanac* gives the North American Indian names for the full Moons:

Wolf Moon: Amid the cold and deep snows of midwinter, the wolf packs howled hungrily outside Native American villages. Thus, the name for January's full Moon. Sometimes it was also referred to as the Old Moon or the Moon After Yule. Some called it the Snow Moon, but most tribes applied that name to the next Moon.

Snow Moon: Because the heaviest snow usually falls during this month, native tribes of the north and east most often called February's full Moon the Snow Moon. Some tribes also referred to this Moon as the Hunger Moon, because harsh weather conditions in their areas made hunting very difficult.

Worm Moon: As the temperature begins to warm and the ground begins to thaw, earthworm casts appear, heralding the return of the robins. The more northern tribes knew this as the Crow Moon, when the cawing of crows signaled the end of Winter; or the Crust Moon, because the snow cover becomes crusted from thawing by day and freezing at night. Sap Moon, marking the time of tapping maple trees, is another variation.

Pink Moon: This name came from the herb moss pink, or wild ground phlox, which is one of the earliest widespread flowers of the spring. Other names include Sprouting Grass Moon, Egg Moon, and among coastal tribes, Fish Moon, because this was the time that the shad swam upstream to spawn.

Flower Moon: In most areas, flowers are abundant everywhere during this time. Other names include the Full Corn Planting Moon, or the Milk Moon.

Strawberry Moon: This name was universal to every Algonquin tribe. Because the relatively short season for harvesting strawberries comes each year during the month of June, the full Moon that occurs during that month was named for the strawberry.

Buck Moon: July is normally the month when the new antlers of buck deer push out of their foreheads in coatings of velvety fur. It was also often called the Hay Moon or Thunder Moon, because thunderstorms are most frequent during this time.

Sturgeon Moon: The fishing tribes are given credit for the naming of this Moon, because sturgeon, a large fish of the Great Lakes and other major bodies of water, were most readily caught during this month. A few tribes knew it as the Red Moon because, as the Moon rises, it appears reddish through any sultry haze. It was also called the Green Corn Moon or Grain Moon.

Fruit or **Barley Moon:** The names Fruit and Barley were reserved only for those years when the Harvest Moon is very late in September,

Harvest Moon: This is the full Moon that occurs closest to the Autumn Equinox. In two years out of three, the Harvest Moon comes in September, but in some years it occurs in October. At the peak of harvest, farmers can work late into the night by the light of this Moon. The chief Native American staples corn, pumpkins, squash, beans, and wild rice are now ready for gathering.

Hunter's Moon: With the leaves falling and the deer fattened, it is time to hunt. Because the fields have been reaped, hunters can easily see fox and the animals that have come out to glean.

Beaver Moon: This was the time to set beaver traps before the swamps froze, to ensure a supply of warm furs. It is sometimes also referred to as the Frosty Moon.

Cold Moon; or **Long Night Moon:** Long Night Moon is a doubly appropriate name because the midwinter night is indeed long, and because the Moon is above the horizon for a long time. The midwinter full Moon rides high across the sky because it is opposite a low Sun.

Lesson 9: Calendar of the Trees

According to poet Robert Graves (*The White Goddess,* 1948) the Celtic Druids designed the world's most perfect calendar. They divided the year into not twelve, but thirteen months of exactly 28 days each. These added up to a total of 364 days, and one *intercalary* ("called between") day was added each year right after Winter Solstice to reset the calendar. This day was considered to be outside of time, between the worlds. Whatever one did on that day didn't count in the "real world." Every four years, a second intercalary day was inserted after Summer Solstice, for Leap Year. This meant that the dates of the days of the week never changed from month-to-month or year-to-year, and a single month page was all you needed forever.

Each month was named for a consonant of the Druidic *Ogham* alphabet, with some of them doing double-duty. Because the first three consonants in order of months were *Beth* (B), *Luis* (L) and *Nion* (N), this is also sometimes called the *Beth-Luis-Nion* calendar, just as we refer to the *alphabet* (from the first two letters in Greek: *Alpha* and *Beta*). Each of these 13 months was assigned a tree (two trees in a couple of cases, plus vines and reeds)—often based on the seasons when that tree (or vine, or reed) first puts out leaves, flowers, or fruit. The five vowels were also assigned trees but were not included as months of the calendar. Rather, they were designated as fingers on the hand. These were **AILM (A) Silver Fir** or **Elm, ONN (O) Furze** or **Broom, UR (U) Heather, EADHA (E) White Poplar,** and **IDHE (I) Yew.**

Graves's version of the Tree Calendar is his own invention, used by many magickal folk today. There is a Celtic Tree alphabet, and he basically took that alphabet and turned it into a calendar. Here is a listing of his Tree months, along with the ogham letters and drawings of the leaves of each. (See their positions on the Magick Circle Mandala on page 131.)

Calendar of the Trees by Robert Graves

1. ᚁ BETH (B) Birch
(Dec. 24-Jan. 20)

One of the earliest trees to put out new leaves each year, *birch* is a symbol of fertility and new beginnings. Birch brings luck when planted near the home. Bundles of birch twigs are used both for the exorcism of evil spirits and for the brush of the *besom,* or Witch's broom.

2. ᚂ LUIS (L) Rowan
(Jan. 21-Feb. 17)

Rowan rules the festival of *Imbolg* (Feb. 2), representing the revitalization of the year. It is excellent for protection and magick. Rowan is used for magick wands and for the shaft of the besom. The leaves and berries may be carried to increase psychic powers or can be added to divination incense.

3. ᚅ NION (N) Ash
(Feb. 18-March 17)

Sacred to Poseidon, God of the Sea, *ash* is connected with sea power, prosperity, knowledge, and protection. *Yggdrasil,* the Norse World-Tree, was an ash. Ash leaves under a pillow bring prophetic dreams. Ash burnt at Yule brings prosperity. Ash is excellent for besom shafts, healing wands, and Wizard's staffs.

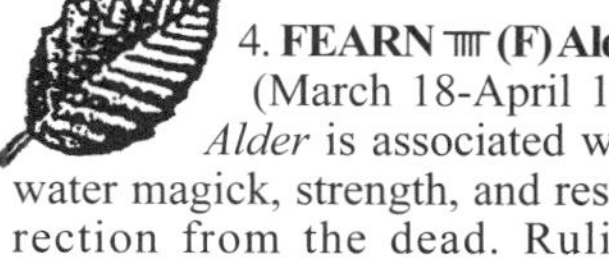

4. FEARN ᚃ (F) Alder
(March 18-April 14)

Alder is associated with water magick, strength, and resurrection from the dead. Ruling *Ostara* (Spring Equinox), the spiral pattern of the alder bud reflects the spiral of rebirth. Alder is also used to diagnose disease by divination.

5. ᚄ SAILLE (S) Willow + ᚎ ZTRAIF (Z) Maple
(April 15-May 12)

Sacred to Hecate, goddess of the crossroads, and ruled by the Moon, *willow* is the tree of Death. When carried, willow bark provides protection from nightmares and from affliction, unfaithful love, and betrayal. Willow is used for magick wands and in binding the brush twigs to the besom.

Offering sweet syrup, *maple* is associated with love and money. Maple wood is excellent for making magickal jewelry boxes, hope chests, treasure chests, cabinets, and altars.

6. ᚆ HUATH (H) Thorn
(May 13-June 9)

Hawthorne is the tree of purification and chastity. Flowering hawthorne is gathered on *Beltaine* (May 1) to decorate front doors. It is unlucky to cut down hawthorne bushes, as they are sacred to the faeries. Faeries may be seen wherever oak, ash, and thorne grow together.

7. ᚇ DUIR (D) Oak
(June 10-July 7)

Associated with most thunder gods, *oak* symbolizes the name principle. It is the tree of endurance and triumph, and it makes an extremely powerful healing amulet. Oaks were so sacred to the Druids that it was considered an act of sacrilege to mutilate them. Oak was often used for sacred fires, such as Yule and Midsummer bonfires.

8. ᚈ TINN (T) Holly
(July 8-Aug. 4)

Flowering in July, *holly* is the tree that rules the waning half of the year. A masculine tree, holly is associated with luck in money as well as protection against lightning, poison, and evil spirits. Holly leaves are sometimes used for divination: The number of berries indicates the severity of the Winter to come.

9. ᚉ COLL (C) Hazel + ᚊ QUIRT (Q) Apple
(Aug. 5-Sept. 1)

Sacred to Hermes (Mercury), *hazel* is the tree of Wisdom. Strings of hazelnuts bring luck and protection of the faeries to a home. Forked hazel rods are used for *dowsing* (divining) for hidden water, buried treasure, and criminals. Irish heralds carried white hazel wands, symbolic of their office. Hazel also makes an excellent magick wand.

Cultivated in Europe since Roman times, *apple* is a particularly sacred tree in mythology. It represents immortality, eternal youth, and happiness in the Afterlife. Cutting one down was considered so unlucky that the *Triads of Ireland* call for a living sacrifice in payment.

10. ᚋ MUIN (M) Vine
(Sept. 2-Sept. 29)

Associated with poetic inspiration, ecstasy, and prophecy, the *grapevine* is sacred to Dionysos (Bacchus). Sometimes, however, its wine brings on divine madness, and the grape is then associated with anger (as in "the grapes of wrath"). Magickally, the grapevine is used for fertility and money spells.

11. ᚌ GORT (G) Ivy
(Sept. 30-Oct. 27)

Also sacred to Dionysos, *ivy* is said to prevent drunkenness and rules over the boar-hunting month. Because it doesn't change throughout the seasons, ivy is associated with constancy in relationships. Considered female, ivy sometimes represents fertility. Unlucky inside a house, ivy is very lucky outside and presages financial problems if it dies or falls away.

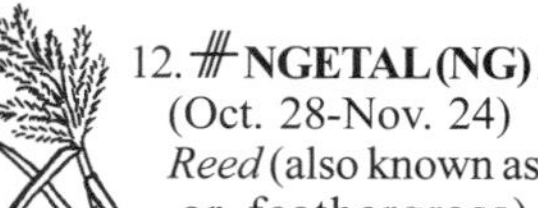

12. ᚍ NGETAL (NG) Reed
(Oct. 28-Nov. 24)

Reed (also known as cane or feathergrass) is a single worldwide species. It becomes ready for cutting in early November and so rules the month of the Autumn storms, particularly those that pound the shore. Reed was an ancient symbol of royalty in the Middle East. In Ireland, reeds were used to thatch houses; a home was not considered established until the roof was on.

13. ᚏ RUIS (R) Elder
(Nov. 25-Dec. 22)

Ruling the 13th month and the Winter Solstice, *elder* has long been associated with both Death and Magick. Irish Witches rode elder rods as magick steeds. If hung over doors and windows, elder keeps evil out; but if burned, it invites evil spirits to come in.

ᚚ **PEITH (P)** Intercalary; no tree
(Dec. 23) "Time outside of Time"

Class VI: The Wheel of the Year

Come all ye gentle Pagans,
Come all ye of good will;
The feasting table's laden,
The drinking vessels filled.
Come gather with rejoicing—
A holy day is here!
With carols gladly voicing
At turning of the year.
—Leigh Ann Hussey

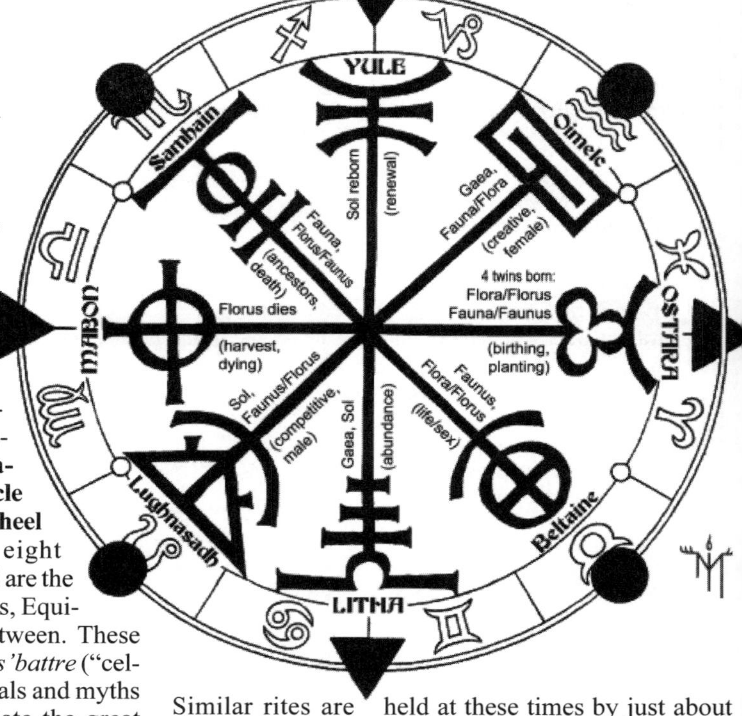

1. Introduction: The Wheel of the Year

HE ANNUAL CYCLE OF the seasonal celebrations is variously referred to as the **Sacred Round,** the **Cycle of Sabbats,** or the **Wheel of the Year.** The eight spokes of this Wheel are the Great Festivals that occur at the Solstices, Equinoxes, and Cross-Quarters midway between. These are also called *Sabbats*, from the French *s'battre* ("celebrate"). As the year progresses, the rituals and myths associated with each Sabbat recapitulate the great Cycle of Life, from Birth to Death to Rebirth. Some version of most of these festivals are celebrated by nearly all peoples of the temperate zones, and they have even been assimilated into the Christian calendar, as Saints' days and Masses. A bonfire in the evening is the most common feature. Often, people stay up all night around the fire, singing songs and telling stories.

In my community and tradition, we have for many years been evolving a complex cycle of celebrations that have incorporated numerous elements of custom and folklore from our ancient heritage. We have drawn mainly from Western Europe and the British Isles, but as Greek mythology has always been a strong component of our collective Western lore, we also bring the Eleusinian ritual cycle into our seasonal observances. Often, the ritual will include a dramatic performance or Mystery Play related to the mythos. The main characters in our seasonal dramas are Mother Earth (*Gaea*), Father Sun (*Sol*), and their children: the leafy Green Man (*Florus*) and flowery Maid (*Flora/Kore*), and the hornéd Red Man (*Faunus/Pan*) and furry Maid (*Fauna*). For more about these characters and personae, see 2.II: "The Soul of Nature."

I'll tell you a bit about how we celebrate these Sabbats in my community, where we meet on our 55-acre sacred land of *Annwfn* (AHN-uh-vun). We also celebrate with our family at our home—Raven Haven. Similar rites are held at these times by just about every magickal group in the entire worldwide magickal community. The only difference is between the Northern and Southern Hemisphere. South of the equator, the seasons are reversed, and so the calendar dates on the Wheel for these Sabbats are opposite. For those of you who are not involved with a larger group to meet with, I'll give you some ideas for your own celebrations at home—by yourself, or with your family. For each Sabbat you should redo your altar with appropriately colored altar cloths, candles, and seasonal decorations.

As the Wheel of the Year forms a circle, any starting point is arbitrary, and several of these Sabbats are regarded as New Year in various traditions. For the purpose of this writing, we will begin, as if casting a Circle, with the East and the Festival of Spring:

Lesson 2. Eostara

With day and night in measure,
The hornéd Ram is king
Who sows with reckless pleasure
The seed that sparks the Spring.
Safe is the Rowan's keeping—
All ill it has fast-bound.
The Spring-fire wakes from sleeping
The green things underground.
—Leigh Ann Hussey

Eostara (yoh-STAR-ah), also called *Spring's Height,* is the Sabbat of the *Vernal* (Spring) *Equi-nox*, occurring about March 21. Day and night are of equal length. Eostara is named for Eostre ("Eastern Star," i.e. the planet Venus), Saxon goddess of dawn and fertility, who is elsewhere called Ishtar, Astarte, Ashera, Aphro-dite, Inanna, and Venus. The female *estrous cycle* of fertility and sexuality takes its name from Her. Eostara has been Christianized as *Easter,* another variant of the Goddess' name. Eggs, bunnies, and ducklings are, of course, all symbols of fertility, and are universally associated with this festival.

This is the New Year on the Zodiacal calendar, and the name of each 2,167-year astrological age is based on the sign in which the Vernal Equinox falls in its continuing precession (see 2.II.6: "The Cycles of Time"). Eostara is a festival celebrating fertility and birth, when Mother Earth bears two sets of Holy Twins: the Green Man and Maiden, and the Red Man and Maiden, representing the plants and animals. Hot cross buns *(paska)* are a traditional treat, representing the balanced Sun. In the Eleusinian cycle, Persephone returns from Her six months in the Underworld, reborn as Kore, the Flower Maiden.

At Annwfn & Raven Haven

At Annwfn and Raven Haven, the children dye Eostara eggs, and each egg has the name of a Goddess written on it. These "oracular eggs" are then chosen blindly from a basket, and each person must learn the lessons of their chosen Goddess in the coming year. We also go out into the beautiful Annwfn garden where everyone plants the first flowers, herbs, and vegetables.

At Your House

Eostara is a time of new beginnings and planting spells for future harvest. Celebrate the first day of Spring by breaking the dead bonds of Winter. During the week before, you should take stock of any outstanding bad feelings or arguments you may have with your family and friends. Write these down on a piece of paper, and seek to settle these with apologies, recompense, or whatever you need to do to restore the balance. At Eostara, having balanced your karma, you should burn the paper to wipe clean your karmic slate.

Eostara is the time we celebrate the awakening of the Earth. You can dye your own Eostara eggs, and have someone hide them to be found. (You never grow too old to decorate eggs; *I* still do, and we all enjoy seeing how artistic we can make them!) This is also a particularly appropriate time to begin your magickal garden by setting the first plants into the ground. Welcome the Nature spirits to your garden, and charge the seeds you'll soon be planting. Set up a garden altar with colored eggs, bunnies, baby animals, and flowers; use a light green altar cloth and candles. And for a yummy treat, bake some hot cross buns!

Lesson 3. Beltaine

With ribbons spiral winding
We dance the Beltaine pole.
The Fey are loosed of binding,
Divided worlds made whole.
The Hawthorne brings, in whiteness,
The blessing of the May;
On high, the balefire's brightness
Ill-fortune drives away.
—Leigh Ann Hussey

Beltaine (BEL-tayne) or *May Day* (traditionally the first of May, but astrologically falling several days later, at 15° Taurus), is the great celebration of sexuality. The Sacred Marriage of the Red Man (Robin, Fauna) and Green Maid (Marion, Flora, Blodeuwedd, Maia) is celebrated in the Maypole Rite. (May marriages among mortals are considered ill-fated, however, as they are linked to the doom of the May King.) Leaping the balefire made of nine sacred woods is said to secure protection from evil, bring good luck, and increase one's fertility. Floral wreaths are worn and May Baskets left on doorsteps for loved ones. The Green Maid dances with the Red Man, and men may dress as women. It is traditional to wear green, the color of the Faeries. The ancient Celtic peoples drove their herds near the Beltaine fires, praying for the health and protection of the cattle. Also called *Flora Day, Hare Day,* and *Summer's Beginning,* Beltaine was Christianized as *Roodmas.*

The night before (May Eve) is called *Walpurgisnacht* (supposedly named for St. Walpurgis, an English woman missionary to Germany who died there in 780 CE; but *Walburg* is an old Teutonic name for the Earth Mother). This evening celebrates the begetting of Spring by Wodan and Freya, and the bonfire must be lit using spark from flint and steel. In ancient times, great fires were lit upon hilltops to signify the coming of Spring and to pray for an abundant Summer. Walpurgisnacht is traditionally regarded as a night of madness, when the veil between the worlds is particularly thin; it is the opposite hinge of the year from Samhain, and the beginning of the Summer half of the year. In classical times May Eve was the Festival of Hades, Lord of the Underworld.

At Annwfn

At Annwfn we hold an all-night ritual and Bardic on Walpurgisnacht, generally with a theme involving a journey into the mythic realm, or Faerie. We hold bawdy May games to select the Queen and King of the May, who are crowned as Hornéd Man (Robin) and Flower Maid (Marion), and who represent the men and women of our community during their reign (until Samhain for the King; a full year for the Queen). Children's May Games are also held to select a May Princess and Prince, and the new Royal Court will convene at festivals throughout the Summer season. During the year, they visit the homes of the people, bringing blessings into each.

The maypole dance is, of course, the centerpiece of Beltaine, and the women prepare the Maypole crown, the Circle, the Gate, and the hole, decorating them with ribbons and flowers, while the men go off to bring in the huge 20' maypole. The pole is carried in procession on the shoulders of the men, led by the King. It is brought through the Gate with great merriment, crowned, placed in the hole, and raised (it's anchored with rocks). Everyone grabs an end of the many long ribbons hanging from the crown, and we dance the weaving dance to wrap the pole and the King while pipers and drummers play a lively beat. The Maypole Rite is the Sacred Marriage of the new Queen and King, and he is bound to the pole while she dances around him.

At Your House

Beltaine is a time of courtship, and if there is someone you especially like (including your mother), this is a perfect occasion to give him or her a May basket full of fresh-picked flowers. Decorate your altar with Spring flowers and colorful ribbons; use a dark green altar cloth and candles. Make and wear floral wreaths. This is the festival of regeneration of the Earth. Express love and care to those close to you; feed each other in a special ritual meal. You might even crown a May Queen and King.

If you have room in your backyard, you can put up a maypole—at least 10' tall! Ribbons should be about 1 1/2 times as long as the pole and fastened to the top before the pole goes up. There must be an even number, and it's best to have them in just two colors: red and green (or red and white). There has to be one dancer for each ribbon, so if you only have four people, just use four ribbons. People alternate ribbon colors, facing opposite ways: Red turns to the left, moving *deosil* (clockwise), and green to the right, moving *widdershins* (counter-clockwise).

You dance the circle by alternately moving outside and then inside of the people coming towards you, weaving the ribbons over and then under theirs in turn. Finally, when the woven ribbons get too low on the pole to keep dancing, all the dancers run deosil to wrap the remainder around and tie them off as a spell for prosperity and growth in the coming year. Afterwards, when you take down the pole, you will find that the woven tube of ribbons can be slipped off the pole like a stocking, and saved as a special charm for lovers. It makes a great wedding gift!

Lesson 4. Litha

When day is at its longest,
Folk, fields and flocks all thrive;
The sunlight at its strongest
Feeds everything alive.
The stately Birch, most splendid,
Brings all good things within.
The Summer fire is tended
To be the bright sun's twin.
—Leigh Ann Hussey

Litha (LITH-ah), also called *Midsummer*, is the *Summer Solstice,* about June 21. Litha is the name of a Saxon grain goddess, cognate with Demeter or Ceres, and Her festival is one of joy, abundance, and play. It was Christianized as St. John's Day. On this longest day of the year, picnicking, swimming, and water play are customary, as are bonfires and fireworks in the evening.

Throughout Europe, lovers clasp hands or toss flowers to each other across the bonfire, or leap through it together before disappearing into the woods and fields to sleep together under the stars. This celebration is specifically in honor of the Great Earth Mother, who nourishes us with Her bounty from Her ever-flowing cauldron, but we may also honor the Sun Father at this time. Litha is a festival for families, marriage partners, and children. It is the best time for marriages, and also a time for future visions and faerie favors.

At Annwfn & Raven Haven

Annwfn is part of a much larger 5,600-acre homesteading community known as Greenfield Ranch. From the community's founding in 1972, Summer Solstice has always been the biggest party of the year, with swimming, potluck feasting, live bands, and entertainment. We have lots of water games in the big ranch pond: watermelon races, water ballet, rope swinging, jumping into the water from high in the overhanging trees. A great Circle is held to spread a magickal umbrella of invisibility and protection over the entire land. Fireworks light up the night, with drumming and dancing around the great bonfire. We may even have a dramatic performance, such as Shakespeare's *A Midsummer Night's Dream*, with all the kids taking parts.

For eleven years, I lived with my family beside the Rushing River, and we often held Litha at our beach there. Some of our favorite things to do were inner-tubing down the river (see 2.V.2: "The River") and wallowing in a "Primal Ooze Pit." This was made by positioning an inflatable kids' swimming pool over a shallow pit dug in the sand, with a thin slick "ooze" made with water and powdered white porcelain slip we bought at a ceramics supply store. We'd also make up bowls of colored ooze from powdered tempera paints, and decorate each other. We'd let the ooze dry on our skin, and then wash it off in the river.

At Your House

Litha is a classic time for magick of all kinds. Celebrate Nature's sacrifice and renewal, and make changes in your own life. Make a protective solar talisman to put up on your door. Nurture your crops, and harvest magickal herbs from your garden. Decorate your altars with Summer flowers; use a white altar cloth and candles, and fill your chalice with water. Litha is also a special time for honoring and blessing animals, so bring your pets and familiars into your Circle. Give them special treats and attention, letting them know how much you love them.

Since Litha is just before the US Independence Day on the 4th of July, you can often buy fireworks at this time (unless you live in a very dry area with high fire danger in the Summer). My favorites are fountains, which can be safely set off at a beach, around a campfire, or on the driveway. These have the colored sparkles and special effects of the high-exploding skyrockets, without the dangers of shooting them into the air. Each firework can be set off as a spell, naming the purpose before you light it. Be sure to keep a water hose handy just in case any sparks get away!

Lesson 5. Lughnasadh

For Lughnasadh is given
The first fruits of the grain,
John Barleycorn is riven
But rises up again.
The Oak is door to wonders;
The Golden Bough it bears.
The fire of Lammas sunders
All sorrows and all cares.
—Leigh Ann Hussey

Lughnasadh (LOO-na-sahd, meaning "Games of Lugh"), traditionally August 1st but astrologically falling several days later (at 15° Leo) is named for Lugh, an Irish solar god. It was traditional to hold faires at this time. Marking the beginning of "Earth's sorrowing Autumn," as Emer said to her husband Cuchulain, this Blessing of the First Fruits is also called *Bron Trogain,* or "Harvest's Beginning." As the *Feast of Bread,* it is commemorated by baking the first loaves of bread from the first grains to be harvested; the bread represents the body of the fallen God.

Once a month-long festival held in Ireland at Teltown on the River Boyne (named for the cow goddess Boann, "She of the White Track," i.e. the Milky Way), Lughnasadh is traditionally celebrated with competitive games among men and boys. The winners are declared champions and heroes and held responsible for the defense of the village. This is a festival dedicated to male energy, and priests serve as the Green Man and Red Man, presiding over opposing teams. The Irish Tailteann Games were origi-

LAMMAS • LUGHNASADH

nally held in honor of Tailtiu, mother of Lugh; but other competitive masculine games of strength and skill have traditionally been held at this time as well, including the Olympics, the Panathe-niac Games, the Highlands Games, and modern football season. It is also a time for male initiations. This festival has been Christianized as *Lammas,* or "Loaf-mass."

At Annwfn

We hold Games of Lugh at Lughnasadh and give special fun awards to the winners in various categories. The traditional five games (*Pentathlon*) are: running (50- or 100-yard speed race); long jumping (from a running start, over a sand pit); wrestling (gripping only above the waist; whomever can get the other's shoulder to touch the ground wins); boulder heaving (a bowling ball is about the right size and weight; the winner is the greatest distance); and taber tossing (a long pole, like a flagpole, thrown at a haybale target; the winner is the one who comes closest to the target).

At Your House

As Summer passes, we remember its warmth and bounty in the food we eat. Every meal is an attunement with Nature, and we are reminded that everything changes. Lughnasadh is the first of the three Harvests and Thanksgivings. Bake a loaf of special ritual bread (cornbread is good), including some berries you have picked yourself. Share it with your friends and family, with thanks and blessings. Go camping if you can; or at least spend the day outdoors, maybe at the park, taking a picnic lunch and playing active physical games, such as Tag and Frisbee, with your friends. It's especially fun and traditional to play Hide & Seek in the evening, as it gets dark. Lughnasadh is a good time to make and bless magickal tools. Decorate your altar with Summer flowers and food from the fields (especially grains, like corn and grass seeds); use a yellow altar cloth and candles.

Lesson 6. Mabon

We praise the Earth who feeds us,
And raise the Harvest Home.
The stag with light step leads us
To dance the season come.
Ash links the worlds, entwining
Our realms with Gods and Elves.
The bonfire blesses, shining,
Our food, our drink, ourselves.
—Leigh Ann Hussey

Mabon (MAA-bon), or *Autumn Equinox,* is named for the Welsh god of the harvest, the Sacred Son of *Modron* ("The Great Mother"). He is the Green Man whose blood is intoxicating beverage: Dionysos (wine), Osiris (beer), and John Barleycorn (whiskey). The bay tree is sacred to Mabon, as its magickal action is preservation, a time-honored harvest occupation. Also known as *Harvest Home, Kirn Feast, Mell Day, Ingathering,* and *Harvest's Height,* this festival commemorates the ritual sacrifice of the Green God and His descent into the Underworld, and the brewers' art that produces the sacrament of this season. In Nor-Califia, where I live, it is the Festival of the Grape Harvest.

MABON • AUTUMN EQUINOX

In Latvia this harvest festival is called *Vela Laiks,* the "Time of the Dead." Just as at Eostara, the day and night are of equal length. Harvest Home is the traditional name for this feast of thanksgiving in England, but the Plymouth pilgrims had a late harvest, so Amer-ica's Thanks-giving is celebrated much later. The most universal tradition throughout Europe was the "Corn Dolly" made from the last sheaf of grain to be harvested. It was believed that the spirit of the grain resided in this doll and it must be treated accordingly, presiding over the Harvest Feast.

At Annwfn

The full Moon closest to the Autumn Equinox is the time of the Eleusinian Mysteries, and since 1990 folks in my tradition have been enacting an annual recreation of this ancient Greek festival, in which Persephone, the Flower Maid, is abducted by Hades, Lord of the Underworld, to reign as His Queen for the next six months, until She returns at the Vernal Equinox. Those who are chosen to take the roles of Hades and Persephone for this rite become our Underworld Royalty for the Winter half of the year, holding court at Samhain, and offering counsel in matters dealing with personal Underworld issues.

At Your House

Mabon is a good time to cut new wands and staves of willow. Make a little corn dolly for your garden altar from an ear of corn by twisting and binding the shucks into a body, legs, and arms (you can make the head by breaking off part of the cob, leaving a short piece attached to the rest). Decorate your altars with colorful Autumn leaves and small gourds, nuts, dried corn, seeds, acorns, and pine cones; use an orange and brown altar cloth and candles.

Throw a "going away party" for the Green Man, and charge seeds for next year's crop. Prepare a meal for your loved ones—or at least make some special food to share. Give thanks for all that you have harvested in this time. Remember, "An attitude of gratitude is the guidance of the Gaia-dance!" Write down on a piece of paper the things you have planted in your life this year, which you are now harvesting. Read your list aloud, saying, "For all these things, I give thanks." Then, burn the paper.

Lesson 7. Samhain

The Blessed Dead are hallowed
The darkness holds no fear
When fields at last lie fallow
At twilight of the year.
The Yew and Hazel showing
Rebirth and vision true.
The lights of need-fires glowing
Shall mark the passage through.
—Leigh Ann Hussey

Samhain (SOW-ahn, meaning "Summer's End") is the Celtic Feast of the Dead, when the veil between the worlds is thinnest and departed spirits may return to commune with the living. Bonfires were lit and blazing straw from the fire was carried through the villages and over the fields. Traditionally celebrated on Oct. 31, Samhain falls astrologically several days later, at 15° Scorpio. It is the opposite hinge of the year from Beltaine, and is the Celtic New Year, marking the beginning of the Winter half of the year. Also called *Third Harvest* or *Winter's Beginning,* this festival has been thinly Christianized as *All Saints Day,* with the night before being called *All-Hallows, Hallowmas,* or *Hallowe'en;* long a favorite holiday for magickal folks of all ages and an occasion for masquerades, pumpkin-carving, and trick-or-treating. In Mexico it is called *Dia de los Muertos,* the "Day of the Dead."

In many lands, candles are lit in every room and food and drink put out for the souls. This is a time to honor our ancestors, remember our dead, and hail our descendants, and the most important element of Samhain Eve is the Rite of the Dumb Supper, a meal of Underworld foods (mushrooms, nuts, black olives, pork, beans, chocolate, etc.) shared in total silence, wherein the spirits of the beloved dead are invited to join the feast and be remembered in honor and love.

At Annwfn & Raven Haven

At Annwfn, the King and Queen of the Underworld hold court, presiding over the Dumb Supper and the laying down of the May King's crown (an alternative to his ritual sacrifice!). One of our ritual dramas has the Red Maid seeking Her lost love, the Green Man, who descended into the Underworld at Mabon, and now reigns there as King. *Scrying* may be done at this time with a crystal ball or concave, black magick mirror. The Sam-hain Circle is considered to be held in the Underworld, and the energies move widdershins.

SAMHAIN·ALLHALLOWS

At Raven Haven, we go all out in this season to completely redecorate our entire Victorian house with spider webs, plastic skeletons, masks, black draperies, purple string lights, and black lights. In the garden, the cornstalks are bundled to gether, and we carve some really strange pumpkins. In our back yard we have created a special "family graveyard" to honor our beloved dead. I've made a number of styrofoam tombstones with names, dates, and epitaphs for people we've known who have died. In mid-October we throw an annual "Addams Family Reunion" party, inviting all our friends to dress up in their best Goth gear and Victorian ensembles.

At Your House

There are so many things you can do for Samhain! Spook up your home with Halloween decorations, carve weird pumpkins, hang "ghosts" (balloons covered with cheesecloth) from trees, and throw a costume party for your friends. One very special thing you could do at this time is to make your altar up to honor your ancestors. Get small photos of departed grandparents or anyone you love and admire who is no longer living. Frame them nicely, each with a little label, and arrange them on your altar. Use a black altar cloth and candles, black feathers, a small sand timer, a pomegranate, and other items that symbolize death. If you've collected any small animal skulls or bones, you might display them here. It's fun to make and decorate traditional Mexican Day of the Dead sugar skulls, and these can also be part of your ancestor altar. Samhain is an especially good time to do divinations and necromancy, connecting with the Spirit World.

Lesson 8. Yule

The Yule comes in with gladness
Though weather be unkind,
And banishes all sadness
From every heart and mind.
The Spruce and Pine and Holly
Are proof that life will last;
The Yule log burning brawly
Defies the icy blast.
—Leigh Ann Hussey

Yule (meaning "Wheel" in Norse) is the Festival of *Winter Solstice,* around December 21, and the longest night of the year. This is one of the most universally celebrated festivals, and in Northern countries, the most important, commemorating the birth of the infant Sun God from the womb of Night. Yule is also known as the Festival of Lights, for all the candles burned this night. In ancient Rome it was called *Natalis Solis Invicti*—"Birthday of the Unconquered Sun"—and it took place during the longer festival of the *Saturnalia,* the greatest festival of the year, from which we get our New Year's image of old Father Time (Saturn) with his scythe. Yule is opposite to Litha, and while the emphasis now is on the newborn Sun God, Mother Earth is still honored as the *Madonna* (mother with child on her lap).

Yule was the first Pagan festival to be Christianized, in 354 CE, when the birthday of Jesus (originally in late September) was officially moved to the Winter Solstice and called *Christmas.* The many customs associated with Yuletide (candles, decorated trees, Yule log, wreaths, pine bough decorations, gift-giving, *wassail,* and caroling, costumed mummers' plays, mistletoe, "decking the halls with boughs of holly," etc.) are all Pagan, and provide a rich store of material for our contemporary celebrations. There is no record of Christians decorating their homes with evergreens, holly, ivy, and the "Christmas" tree before 1605. This symbolized to the ancients the eternal life of Nature, as these plants were the only remaining greenery during Winter. These Pagan customs were forbidden to Christians, but in 1644, they had become so widespread that they were outlawed in England by an act of Parliament.

At Raven Haven

We hold our Yule celebration in a Great Hall, with a large fireplace (for many years now, it's been at Raven Haven). We set up a big Yule Tree and hang it with special decorations we've been collecting and making for decades. Often I have climbed up into an oak tree and cut down a big mistletoe ball, decorating it with foil ribbons and hanging it from the rafters.

A ritual drama may enact the story of the first Yule, when the Sun went away and the children had to go and bring it back. Some of the characters in our Yule ritual may include the Wintery Queen, the Queen of Night, Father Winter, Father Time, Lucia (a maiden with a crown of candles), and always, of course, the young Sun God. We bring in the Yule log amid singing and toasting. We have a big potluck feast, drink *athelbros* (traditional Scotts wassail), exchange gifts, and share songs and stories around the fire, holding vigil until the dawn. We maintain that *somebody* has to stay up all night to make sure the Sun comes up in the morning...

At Your House

Since Yule is the original version of Christmas, practically anything you might do for Christmas is appropriate for Yule as well. Make a wreath for your front door, and decorate your house with string lights. "Deck the halls with boughs of holly," pine, ivy, and mistletoe. Set up a Yule tree, and decorate it with special magickal symbols, amulets, and hand-made talismans (blown-out eggshells are great to paint and decorate). Citrus fruits to represent the Sun are also traditional to hang on your tree. If you have a fireplace, you can decorate and burn a special Yule log. As you light it, make pledges for new projects you wish to give birth to.

Fix up your altar with a Santa Claus figure, reindeer, and little decorations in the shapes of animals, trees, presents, snowflakes, icicles, and all the rest. Use a red and green altar cloth, or put a sheet of cotton down for an altar cloth that looks like snow. Burn lots of green and red candles. And most important, make special gifts for your loved ones. These can be artwork, crafts, projects, or collages. Give Yule presents to the birds and faeries by hanging ornaments of fruits, nuts, seeds, and berries on the branches of outdoor trees. Strings of popcorn and cranberries are fun to make, and the wild creatures will love them! You can make them for your own inside tree first, then take them outside later.

Lesson 9. Oimelc, Imbolc, Brigantia

CANDLEMASS·BRIGANTIA

With candles all aglowing
There comes the Imbolc maid.
With milk and honey flowing
Our Winter's hunger's laid.
The Apple in sweet flower
Shows mystery five-fold.
The fire of Brigid's power
Will break the Winter's hold.
—Leigh Ann Hussey

Oimelc and **Imbolc** are variants of the name for the Cross-Quarter Sabbat traditionally celebrated on February 2, but falling astrologically several days later, at 15° Aquarius. *Oimelc* (EE-melk) means "ewe's milk" and *Imbolc* means "in the belly," referring to this as a festival of pregnancy, birth, and lactation ("Got milk?"). It is the celebration of the bursting of the locks of frost, and the bursting of waters as the sacred sets of Twins lower in the womb of the Earth Mother. This is a festival of light and fertility, once marked with huge blazes, torches, candles, and fire in every form.

The Celtic Festival of Waxing Light, it is also called *Brigantia* and dedicated to Brigid, Irish goddess of fire, the forge, inspiration, herbal healing, poetry, and midwifery. Customs of this festival include making a Brigit's Bed and Brigit Doll to sleep in it. Her festival marks the beginning of both the lambing and plowing season. Opposite the men's festival of Lughnasadh, Oimelc is celebrated with women's mysteries, and rites of passage into womanhood. It is a time of Dianic initiation and celebration of sisterhood. Called *Lady Day* in some Wiccan traditions, Oimelc has been Christianized as *Candlemas* or *Candelaria*, and popularized as *Ground Hog's Day.*

At Annwfn & Raven Haven

Brigit fires up the forge and leads us to each craft talismans in token of our pledges to complete some creative project during the year. The goddesses reign, and two priestesses may take the parts of the Red and Green Maids. At the Brigit Bardic in front of the cozy hearthfire we pass around a horn of mead and share poetry, songs, and stories attributed to Her inspiration, and dedicated to Her. In honor of Brigit's healing arts, we give each other massages and foot rubs, and drink good herbal teas.

At Your House

The fires of Brigit represent our own illumination and inspiration as much as light and warmth. The primary magickal tool of this Sabbat is the candle. Invite your friends and family to a Bardic Circle in honor of Brigit. Ask them each to bring poetry, songs, short stories, and even jokes to tell—best, of course, if they have written these themselves! If you have a fireplace in your house, you should light the fire and some red candles, and turn out all other lights. Fill a drinking horn or chalice with apple juice, and pass it around the Circle deosil. As the juice comes to each person and they drink, they must share something they've written, or at least tell a joke.

Fix up your altar to Brigit; use a red and white altar cloth and candles. Fill your chalice or a bowl with milk. A besom and cauldron would be suitable to display. A very traditional Brigit doll can be made with nothing more than a simple old-fashioned clothespin wrapped in red cloth for a gown. A traditional Brigit Bed is just a small box lid with a little pillow, mattress, and blanket made from scraps of cloth. You can make little "feet" for the bed with pushpins. If there is snow outside, fill your chalice with it, set it on your altar, and let it melt to hasten the end of Winter and the beginning of Spring. Sweep out your temple with the besom: "sweeping out the old" so there'll be room for the new.

Class VII: Spellcraft

1. Introduction to Spell-Casting

UCH OF THE WORKING OF MAGICK INvolves the casting of spells. A spell is an organized act designed and performed to alter probabilities in the direction desired; simply, to make something more or less likely to occur. There are many techniques used in spell casting. The general idea is to pull as many correspondences together in one place to increase the level of synchronicities. In doing so, you shift the probabilities along a continuum from impossibility → improbability → possibility → probability → inevitability → manifestation.

Your surroundings when working spells and rituals are extremely important. All the various correspondences (candles, colors, incense, etc.) are intended to create a unified and harmonious space to put your mind into complete accord with the intention of your spell. Therefore, the most important thing is that it all *feels right to you.* If you are doing a spell which recipe calls for a particular combination of roots and herbs, but you feel that one should be left out or substituted—do so. Always go with your hunches! Each spell you cast and working you do is another practice exercise, further attuning your own psychic senses and intuitions, and developing your own personal magick. So do what feels right to *you*, and if it doesn't make sense to you, don't do it! A basic principle in dealing with magick is called "Diddy-wa-diddy." This means, if you don't know what it is, don't mess with it!

And each time you do a spell, make sure to record it in your Book of Shadows (see 3.II.7: "Books of Magick"). Note the date, day of the week and hour, using the astrological and planetary glyphs. Record the candle colors, incense, chants, and other elements. And later on, go back and note the results.

Lesson 2. Magic Squares & Sigils

A magick square (*kamea* in Hebrew) is an arrangement of numbers in a square so that each row and column adds up to the same sum. In most magick squares, the sum of either diagonal also equals that same number. Each number from one through the number of divisions in the square is used. Hence, magick squares that are attributed to the seven planets have 9, 16, 25, 36, 49, 64 or 81 divisions. Each of these planetary kamea is also associated with a planetary *sephirah* ("sphere") on the Qabalistic Tree of Life (see 6.IV.3: "The Tree of Life").

The number of rows or columns is determined by the number of the appropriate sephirah in order (there are 10 total, but only 7 are associated with the planets). You can't make a magick square with only one or two rows and columns, so we start with number 3. The kamea of Venus, for example, has 7 rows and columns because Venus is attributed to Netzach, the 7th sephirah. 7x7=49, so there are 49 divisions within the square of Venus. Here are the numbers and sephiroth for each of the planets:

Number	Sephirah	Planet	Divisions	Sum
3	*Binah*	**Saturn**	9	15
4	*Chesed*	**Jupiter**	16	34
5	*Geburah*	**Mars**	25	65
6	*Tiphareth*	**Sun**	36	111
7	*Netzach*	**Venus**	49	175
8	*Hod*	**Mercury**	64	260
9	*Yesod*	**Moon**	81	369

Magick squares are used in the production of sigils in talismanic magick. Each kamea has a *seal,* which is a design that touches all the numbers of the square. The seal represents the epitome or synthesis of the kamea, and serves as a witness or governor for it. Each planetary kamea is also assigned a "Spirit" and an "Intelligence." The Intelligence is seen as an guiding and inspiring entity, while the Spirit is considered more of a neutral force. Each Intelligence and Spirit has a sigil that represents its associated name, number, powers, etc. A sigil is just another way of representing a name, and magickally, they are in every way equivalent. These sigils are created by first converting the letters in the name of the Spirit or Intelligence into numbers, then tracing a line from number to number on the appropriate square.

The same system can be used to create a sigil for any word or name, including your magickal name—tracing it out on a planetary kamea to reflect the influence of that planet. This is done by assigning numbers to each of the letters of the alphabet, in repeating order, like this:

Number:	**1**	**2**	**3**	**4**	**5**	**6**	**7**	**8**	**9**
Letters:	**A**	**B**	**C**	**D**	**E**	**F**	**G**	**H**	**I**
	J	**K**	**L**	**M**	**N**	**O**	**P**	**Q**	**R**
	S	**T**	**U**	**V**	**W**	**X**	**Y**	**Z**	

Using this chart, you just replace the letters of a word or name with the equivalent numbers. For instance, my first name, Oberon, is written in numbers as: **625965.** To create a sigil for myself under the influence of the Sun, I use the Square of Sol, which is:

6	32	3	34	35	1
7	11	27	28	8	30
19	14	16	15	23	24
18	20	22	21	17	13
25	29	10	9	26	12
36	5	33	4	2	31

Square of Sol

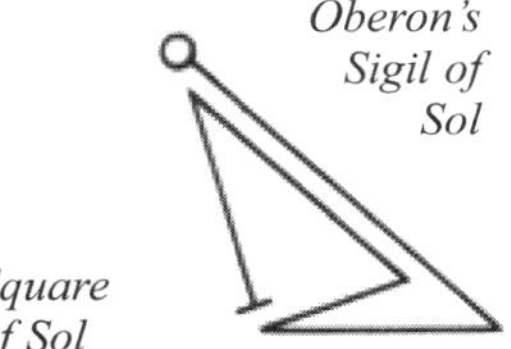

Oberon's Sigil of Sol

First, I lay a piece of tracing paper over the appropriate kamea. I draw a tiny circle over the first letter/number of my name: "6." Then, using a ruler, I draw a straight line down to the middle of the next letter/number: "2." Then a straight line over to "5," another to "9," back up to "6" (alongside the previous line), and finally back to "5," indicating the end by either another little circle, or a bar. My final sigil, then, looks like the above right.

It means "Oberon under the influence of the solar attributes." Now try this with your own name! When you make a planetary talisman, draw your own appropriate sigil on the backside to tune the talisman to yourself. This is why such talismans should be made by the person whom they are intended to serve.

Lesson 3: Talismans of the Planetary Powers

Spells can be done for just about any purpose you can imagine, but most of them can be grouped under the influences and correspondences of the seven planetary powers. Study the tables of correspondence (3.VI) and 4.V.4: "Planetary Aspects" to see what types of spells are suitable for each planet, and then gather all the associated materials (colors, candles, herbs, incenses, animals, metals, etc.). Do your spells on the planetary day and hour, and fine-tune the focus with the appropriate tools.

Here is a more detailed description of these planetary aspects as they relate specifically to spellwork, with their squares and sigils for pentacle talismans. Although such talismans are ideally supposed to be engraved on disks of the appropriate metal, they can also be simply drawn on colored paper, parchment, or cloth for use in spells and charms. I list them here in the order of their kamea:

 Saturn (3)

Pentacle of Saturn:

Positive color – indigo
Negative color – black

4	9	2
3	5	7
8	1	6

Square of Saturn = 15

Governs: Long life, building, protection, stability, security, harvest, destruction. Older people, old plans, debts and their repayment, agriculture, real estate, death, wills, stability, inertia.

♃ Jupiter (4)

Pentacle of Jupiter:

Positive color – blue
Negative color – purple

4	14	15	1
9	7	6	12
5	11	10	8
16	2	3	13

Square of Jupiter = 34

Governs: Wealth, health, honor, friendship, peace, fame, success, political power. Abundance, plenty, growth, expansion, generosity, spirituality, long journeys, bankers, creditors, debtors, gambling.

 Mars (5)

Pentacle of Mars:

Positive and negative color – bright red

11	24	7	20	3
4	12	25	8	16
17	5	13	21	9
10	18	1	14	22
23	6	19	2	15

Square of Mars = 65

Governs: Physical power, strength, courage, victory in war, overcoming enemies. Energy, haste, anger, construction or destruction, danger, surgery, vitality, magnetism, will-power.

 Sun (6)

Pentacle of Sol:

Positive color – orange
Negative color – yellow

6	32	3	34	35	1
7	11	27	28	8	30
19	14	16	15	23	24
18	20	22	21	17	13
25	29	10	9	26	12
36	5	33	4	2	31

Square of Sol = 111

Governs: Hope, riches, honor, respect, success, good fortune, finding treasure. Superiors, employers, executives, officials, life, illumination, imagination, mental power, health, growth of all kinds.

♀ Venus (7)

Pentacle of Venus:

Positive & negative color – emerald green

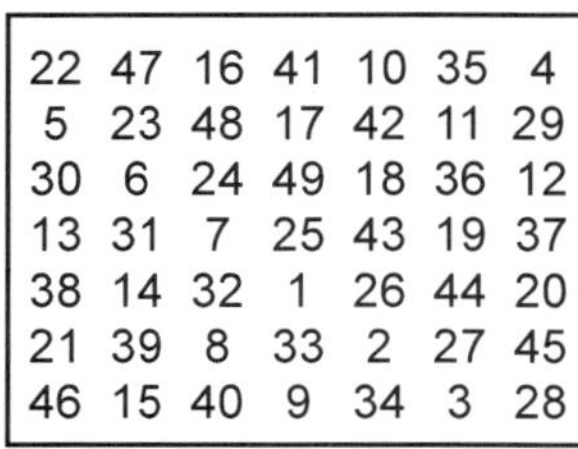

22	47	16	41	10	35	4
5	23	48	17	42	11	29
30	6	24	49	18	36	12
13	31	7	25	43	19	37
38	14	32	1	26	44	20
21	39	8	33	2	27	45
46	15	40	9	34	3	28

Square of Venus = 175

Governs: Love, friendship, pleasure, passion, sex, peace, happiness, fertility, safety. Social affairs, affections & emotions, women, younger people, all pleasures, the arts, music, beauty, extravagance, luxury, self-indulgence.

Mercury (8)

Pentacle of Mercury:

Positive color – yellow
Negative color – orange

8	58	59	5	4	62	63	1
49	15	14	52	53	11	10	56
41	23	22	44	48	19	18	45
32	34	38	29	25	35	39	28
40	26	27	37	36	30	31	33
17	47	43	20	21	46	42	24
9	55	34	12	13	51	50	16
64	2	3	61	60	6	7	57

Square of Mercury = 260

Governs: Communication, magick, memory, divination, truth, judgement. Business matters, buying & selling, bargaining, literary capabilities, writing, books, papers, contracts, short travels, neighbors, giving & obtaining information, intellectual friends.

Moon (9)

Pentacle of Luna:

Positive color – violet
Negative color – blue

37	78	29	70	21	62	13	54	5
6	38	79	30	71	22	63	14	46
47	7	39	80	31	72	23	55	15
16	48	8	40	81	32	64	24	56
57	17	49	9	41	73	33	65	25
26	58	18	50	1	42	74	34	66
67	27	59	10	51	2	43	75	35
36	68	19	60	11	52	3	44	76
77	28	69	20	61	12	53	4	45

Square of Luna = 369

Governs: Dreams, prophetic visions, security, preventing theft, mending quarrels. Women, general public, personality, changes and fluctuations, short journeys and removals, sense-reactions.

Lesson 4. Elemental Powers

As with the planetary aspects, another consideration in spellwork is the Elemental associations. See 2.III: "The Elements," and also 3.VI: "Tables of Correspondence." Here are some of the main concerns associated with the various Elements:

🜁 **AIR:** Wisdom, thought, communication, logic, intelligence, math, memory, education, music, literature, poetry.

🜂 **FIRE:** Passion, sex, success, career, ambition, goals, courage, energy, swift movement.

🜄 **WATER:** Emotions, drink, psychic pursuits, psychology, dreams, imagination.

🜃 **EARTH:** Physical health, food, material wealth, manifestation, protection, binding.

🜁🜂 **AIR/FIRE:** Beauty, art, luck, gambling, spirituality, reincarnation.

🜂🜄 **FIRE/WATER:** Romantic love, relationships, partnerships, soulmates, marriage.

🜄🜃 **WATER/EARTH:** Fertility, gardening, cooking, household, joy.

🜃🜁 **EARTH/AIR:** Business, travel, adventure.

🜁🜄 **AIR/WATER:** Harmony, dance, parties, social matters, gatherings.

🜃🜂 **EARTH/FIRE:** Politics, sports, competition.

Lesson 5. Spellcraft

When doing spells, there are two types of chants—those handed down through Grimoires and spell books, and those you make up yourself. Both have their advantages. Ones that have been used for some time by many others have built up a certain magickal charge around them, and when you use them, you are also tapping into all that *morphic resonance.* On the other hand, the ones that you create are the work of your own vision, imagination, and magickal Will, which will become a powerful force the more you exercise it. The powers of the subconscious mind are most easily tapped by creating visualizations in your head, and by the types of chants and incantations that employ both rhyme and rhythm. This is because these elements operate in the right hemisphere of your brain, connecting you directly to the greater magickal realms.

Burning candles of selected colors are commonly used in spellwork (see 4.I.5: "Candle Magick). Use candles with any spell to enhance or fine-tune the influence of planetary, Elemental, or other correspondences. Many magick-users speak of distinctions between "white," "grey," and "black" magick, shading from benevolent to malevolent. This is not about the nature of the actual magick itself (see 1.III.7: "The Colors of Magick"), but rather the *intentions* and purposes for which it is used. These intentions are determined by the ethics of the practitioner, and should be considered before doing any spell.

White Magick: Magick that affects only you, and doesn't involve the will of others. For example, attracting love, increasing wealth/prosperity, or protecting your home. There is no harm in these uses, and no ethical problem.

Grey Magick: Magick affecting the will of someone else, to a degree. It may alter their choices, livelihood, or community, but not drastically or permanently. For example, a spell to cause someone to fall in love with you, a healing, a binding spell on someone's malicious acts, or a spell to encourage harmony with someone who dislikes you. These purposes can be ethically questionable.

Black Magick: Magick that asserts your will over someone else in a strong, binding, and/or permanent way, or that is meant to cause damage, harm, or death. For example, a spell to cause pain, damage property, or exert control/power over someone. These are the kinds of spells that sorcerers do. These purposes are highly unethical, and should be avoided by Wizards.

The number of possible charms and spells is really limitless. There are whole books dedicated just to spellcraft, and volumes of folklore in which these have been collected. In addition to the above-mentioned, Grey Council member Patricia Telesco's *The Magick of Folk Wisdom* is a great reference, as are Ann Gramarie's *Witches Workbook*, Gillian Kemp's *Good Spell Book,* and Valerie Worth's *Crone's Book of Words*. Here are a few of my favorites from those and other sources, as well as some that Morning Glory and I have crafted and use. Once you get the hang of this, you might even begin to create some spells of your own!

Daniel Blair Stewart

Good Luck and Success ☉ ♃

MOJO BAG

Make a little mojo bag in which to keep small amulets and talismans, etc. These are also called medicine bags, spirit bags, conjure bags or *gris-gris* (GREE-gree) bags. Cut a 6" diameter circular piece of cloth, flannel, or chamois. Red is always a good color for a mojo bag, or you may pick a suitable color from the list in 1.III.6: "The Colors of Magick." Punch a series of holes around the outer edge, and thread a 30" red cord through them, tying the ends together. As you do, say:

I sew this bag for luck and wealth
With string of red for love and health
That it may keep by night and day
Woe and sickness far away!
(—Gerina Dunwich)

FOR SUCCESS IN YOUR WORK

On a piece of parchment, inscribe a Sun talisman sigil on one side, and a Jupiter talisman sigil on the other. Say,

My iron Will, my patient skill,
Within this Talisman instill
That I may fare successfully.
As I will, so mote it be!

Then attach it to an object associated with your work, and keep them both on your altar together (or at your place of work).

COINS

A silver coin buried under the doorstep of your home brings prosperity and good fortune. If you live in an apartment, try placing it under a decorative planter or taped securely under your doormat instead.
(—Patricia Telesco)

RED CORD

Take a red cord or yarn about 12" long and tie four knots in it, saying as you do:

One knot for luck,
Two knots for wealth
Three knots for love
Four knots for health.
(—Gerina Dunwich)

Keep the knotted cord in your mojo bag and wear the bag around your neck.

Health and Healing ♃ ♂

WART CURE

Tape a copper penny over the wart with a Band-Aid. Leave it on for three days, then bury the penny beneath a tree at midnight. Say as you do:

Wart begone away from me;
Grow instead inside this tree.
My skin be smooth for all to see,
And all my body Blessed Be!

ABRACADABRA

A very ancient and popular spell for curing fever or illness is the diminishing word "Abracadabra." Write it eleven times on a piece of rice paper, dropping one letter each line to form an inverted triangle:

A B R A C A D A B R A
A B R A C A D A B R
A B R A C A D A B
A B R A C A D A
A B R A C A D
A B R A C A
A B R A C
A B R A
A B R
A B
A

Roll the paper into a tight tube and tie it around the afflicted's neck. Wear it for nine days and nights, and then throw it over the left shoulder into a stream.

TO BANISH SICKNESS

Write the subject's name on a piece of parchment, and put it in a mojo bag with the following healing herbs: angelica, bay leaves, cinnamon, fennel seeds, horehound, rose petals, rosemary, thyme, vervain, and Violet flowers. Say:

Witches' herbs and magick flowers,
Fill this bag with healing powers.
Let the wearer of this charm
Be free of sickness, pain, and harm.
(—Gerina Dunwich)

HONEY ELIXIR

At noon on a Sunday, hold up honey to the Sun that their double gold may run shining together, mixed as one. Swallow three spoonfuls, then say this:

Sun charge me,
Gold serve me,
Alchemy change me,
Honey preserve me.
(—Valerie Worth)

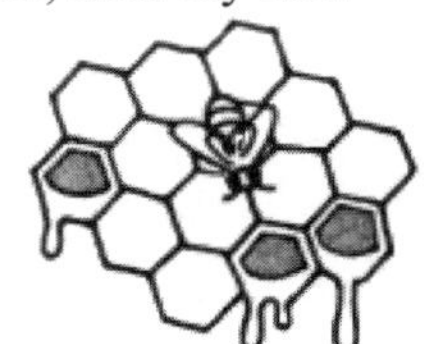

Protection ♄ ☽

WHEN PASSING A CEMETERY

Cross your fingers, hold your breath, and say aloud this verse for Death:

Keeper of bones, I know thy face,
But I shall yet outstrip thy pace.
(—Valerie Worth)

ELEMENTAL PROTECTION CHARM

On a piece of parchment, write the following words:

Air cannot freeze me.
Fire cannot burn me.
Water cannot drown me.
Earth cannot bury me.

Roll it into a tight tube, tie with a red cord or yarn, and carry it in your mojo bag.

LEMON PROTECTION CHARM

This Italian Strega spell for a friend or loved one is best performed at midnight of a full Moon. You'll need a fresh lemon, three white candles, and a box of colored pins. At the stroke of midnight, light the candles and stick the lemon full of pins, repeating as you do:

Queen of Moon and starry sea,
Diana, I present to thee,
With each pin I cast a charm,
Keep (name) from all harm!

Give it to your friend as a present. It will bring good luck and keep evil away from you and your loved one both.

CHARM WANDS

Get a test tube with a stopper, or use any small clear cylindrical container, such as a spice jar. Fill it with fennel seeds (a protective herb). Tie it with a ribbon, bless it, and hang it by your door. Any evil spirit that tries to enter will be compelled to count all the seeds, leaving no time to create mischief!

WITCH BOTTLE

These were very popular in England in the 17th and 18th centuries. Take a glass jar with a screw-on lid, and fill it with sharp objects: pins, nails, tacks, broken glass (*especially* shards of a broken mirror!), thorns, urine, salt, etc. Add herbs of rosemary, basil, and bay leaves. Screw the lid tight, and seal it with melted wax from a black candle, saying:

Witches' Bottle, herbs and charms,
Banish evil, ward off harm.
Protect me from all enemies
As my will, so mote it be!
(—Gerina Dunwich)

Hide the bottle in the back of the cupboard under the kitchen sink, or bury it at the farthest corner of your property when the Moon is waning. A Witch bottle protects its owner from harm, and makes a great housewarming gift!

IRON and GARLIC

Similar in concept to the Witch bottle is the ancient custom of driving iron spikes (very large nails will do as well, and it's most effective if they're magnetized) into the ground right before each entry into your house. Due to its magnetic qualities, iron creates a field that disrupts the coherence of non-corporeal entities, and is thus *anathema* ("curse") to all evil spirits.

Similarly, powerfully acidic spices, such as garlic bulbs and chili peppers, hung over your windows will keep evil spirits (especially vampires and dream demons) from entering.

TO KEEP OUT SORROW

Write these words on a piece of paper:

TREE
ROAD
EAVE
EDEN

Read from West to East and North to South, then speak aloud:

TREE of Knowledge,
ROAD of Pain,
EAVE of Home
EDEN again.

If you solve this riddle, burn the paper on your hearth. It will keep your house from sorrow, all year long.
(—Valerie Worth)

Travel and Communication ☿

CIRCLES OF LIGHT

Morning Glory and I use this one all the time as we travel: When you are walking in a dangerous place, riding in a car, or flying in a plane, you can set up a little portable Circle of protection around yourself and others with you. Close your eyes briefly, and make circles in the air in front of you with the index finger of your writing hand. Visualize these circles of light spiraling outward to completely surround you, as you repeat:

Wrapped am I in Circles of Light
No harm or ill may come to me.
In the darkness of the night,
I move safely; Blessed Be!

BEFORE AN AIRPLANE FLIGHT

You who would dare to journey by air must first be freed from folly and pride. In sunlight stand and pass your hand near to the gleam of a candle's flame. Kindle a feather within its fire, and when it is black, smother the wick. Gather soft wax and fill the cracks under your nails. Then say:

Too near to the Sun I may not fly,
Scorched I should run from his mocking eye.
Yet far from his scorn, below his sway,
Let me be borne and spared this day!
(—Valerie Worth)

FOR AN IMPORTANT LETTER

When your letter has been sealed and stamped, lay it on a black cloth and pour a circle of salt around it. As you do, say:

Words that run before my pace,
And carry me beyond this place,
Please the eyes that greet thee next
And work my Will within thy text.

Fold the cloth over it, and kiss the folds; then mail it immediately. (—Valerie Worth)

TO GET AGREEMENT

Light a pink candle for love and a blue candle for healing on a Wednesday or Friday evening. Say:

Please (name), do think again.
May the consequence heal my pain.
Grant my request and you will see,
The good in your heart set me free.
Bless you!
(—Gillian Kemp)

Exorcism and Banishment ♄

If a house or a person has become haunted or possessed by malevolent spirits, a ritual of exorcism or banishment should be performed. Light white candles in every room, or place five around the person. Draw a pentagram of salt on the floor of each room or around the victim, and sprinkle water into all corners, using a spring of fennel or rosemary. As you do, say:

Water, Salt, where you are cast,
No ill or adverse purpose last.
Evil spirits all must flee;
As I do will, so mote it be!

Then smudge with sage, going throughout the house or around the person deosil, and wafting the smoke into every corner and closet. Chant:

Through Smoke of Fire I purify
No evil shall remain nearby.
Cleansed of harm and ill are ye,
As my will, so mote it be!

Finally, take your besom and sweep out the entire house, sweeping the salt up with the dust, chanting:

Tout, tout, throughout and about,
Let peace remain, and strife go out!

Manifestation ☽ ☿

TO MAKE A WISH COME TRUE

Draw the sign of the waxing Moon with a thorn onto a short, fat beeswax candle (a white votive candle is perfect). Light the candle, gaze into the flame, and concentrate on your wish as you chant:

Gracious Lady Moon,
Ever in my sight,
Kindly grant the boon
I ask of thee tonight.

Blow out the flame but hold its light in your mind for as long as you can. An answer will be revealed to you.

GENERAL INCANTATION OF MANIFESTATION

For any spell you do, after you have completed the rest of the working, finish off with this:

By all the powers of Earth and Sea,
By all the might of Moon and Sun,
As I do will, so mote it be!
Chant the spell and be it done!

Love ♀

TO ATTRACT A LOVER

Crumble dried laurel leaves and scatter them over the burning charcoal in your thurible. Smell the smoke, and chant:

Laurel leaves, burn in fire,
Bring to me my heart's desire.

HEARTSTONE SPELL

Start with a small heart-shaped stone of amethyst, fluorite, moonstone, or agate. During the waxing Moon, burn a solid red candle. Mix a little vervain into the soft melted wax, and shape it around the stone into a red heart, saying:

Wax to heart thou art transformed.
Two be one, and love be warmed!

Hold it in your hand until it cools, and say:

Ishtar, Venus, Aphrodite,
Let a new love come to me,
By thy power, Wizard's Stone,
I'll no longer be alone.

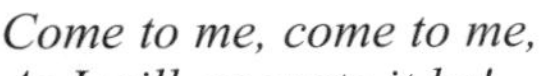

Come to me, come to me,
As I will, so mote it be!

Keep the waxen heart on your altar, or in your mojo bag. (—Ann Grammary)

TO MAKE LOVE GROW

Plant a flowering bulb, such as a tulip, daffodil, or narcissus, in a new clay pot. As you cover it with earth, repeat the name of the one you love. Then each morning and evening, say over it:

As this root now deeply grows
And its blossom gently blows,
Thus my true love's heart shall be
Gently turnéd unto me.

Wealth and Prosperity ☉ ♃ ☽

TO ACQUIRE WEALTH

Lay five gold coins in a circle around a little coin purse. Light five gold (or green) birthday candles, placing a drop of wax on a coin and then setting the candle upright in the wax. As you do this, repeat each time:

Bona Fortuna, hear my verse;
Gold and silver fill my purse.

Visualize images of money filling and overflowing your purse. Keep this up until all the candles are burned out. Then put the coins, covered in wax, into the purse and keep it on your altar.

MOONLIGHT SILVER

Take a shallow bowl of water, and sit down on the grass in a place where the full Moon shines. Set the bowl down in front of you, and catch the reflection of the Moon in the water, saying three times:

Aradia, Aradia, I implore thee,
Please to grant my wish for me.
By the powers of Moon and sea,
As my will, so mote it me!

Then gently skim your hand over the surface of the water, capturing the moonsilver in your hand. Before the water settles, empty the bowl onto the Earth, and return home. Do not look back at the moon after you've caught the moonsilver, or you'll break the spell!

TO FIND TREASURE OR LOST THINGS

On the first night of the full Moon, kiss the palm of your hand and hold it up to the Moon with the first three fingers folded down, and thumb and little finger outstretched. Recite the following:

Pray to the Moon when she is round,
Luck with you shall then abound.
What you seek for shall be found,
On land or sea or underground.

TO CALL A LOST PET

Place some favorite food in your pet's familiar bowl. Light a blue candle next to it and say:

My fair beauty gone astray
Please come back to me today.
With my yearning heart and wonder
Please come back to me from yonder.

Leave the candle to burn down, or snuff it out when your pet returns. (—Gillian Kemp)

Lesson 6. The Old Speech

You may have noticed by now that a lot of the unusual words that turn up in the *magicae artes* ("magickal arts") come from Latin (Roman) or Greek roots. This is because all these ideas and concepts have a long history, and the original names given to things in one language are often carried over into the language of the next dominant culture. This is particularly true in the field of Wizardry and of science, which grew out of it. In biology, for instance, all living species of animals and plants have a Latin "scientific name;" and extinct species (like dinosaurs) are given Greek names: *deinosauros* means "terrible lizard" in Greek. The original languages of the first Wizards were many—Egyptian, Hebrew, Sumerian, Assyrian, Babylonian, Persian, Arabic, Greek, Sanskrit, Chinese, and others. But over several thousand years, a succession of large empires arose, consolidating many cultures under one rule and imposing on all the language of the rulers, which everyone needed to learn in order to be able to communicate throughout the Empire. The older languages became the *arcane* ("secret") languages known only to the scholars who read the old books in which they were written.

Starting in Greece, by 325 BCE, Alexander the Great had conquered the entire civilized world from Italy and Egypt to India, and established the Mace-donian Empire. Greek became the universal language throughout the Western world, and Egyptian, Hebrew, Persian, and the others became the arcane languages of scholars and Wizards. Then in 50 BCE, Julius Caesar re-conquered Alexander's old territory, plus all of Europe clear into Britain, forming the Roman Empire. Latin became the new universal language, and Greek became arcane.

Rome ruled the Western world for 500 years, until it was sacked by the Vandals in 445 CE. The Roman Catholic Church took over, forming the Holy Roman Empire in the West (in the Eastern part of the old Empire, the Eastern Orthodox Church prevailed after the Great Schism of 1054). The Church ruled the world for the next 1,000 years, until the Reformation and Renaissance in the 14th-15th Centuries. During all that time, Latin was the only "official" written language, and Greek and Hebrew remained arcane.

The British Empire was born during the long reign of Elizabeth I (1533-1603), and soon expanded into a worldwide Empire, including North America, Australia, and India. English became the new universal language, and Latin became arcane. But early in this new era, in the 1660s, *science* ("knowledge") made an official split from *Wizardry* ("wisdom"). And that's how Latin became the arcane language of Catholicism, Wizardry, *and* science.

Unfortunately, Latin is a very complicated language to use properly, as each word must be spelled with different endings to indicate its usage, tense, case, etc. Also, as with all the languages spun off of it (*Romance* languages, from *Rome*—which include French, Spanish, Portuguese, and Italian), nouns for inanimate objects are arbitrarily assigned *gender* (male, female, or neuter), which must be taken into account as well. And the *syntax* (order) of words in a sentence is different from English as well: in Latin, verbs come before nouns, and adjectives and adverbs follow the words they are modifying—sort of the way Yoda talks.

Nonetheless, many ancient spells and words of power are in Latin, and it can be very useful for a Wizard to know what these mean and be able to use them in creating new spells. For, as Ursula LeGuin said, *"magic consists in this, the true naming of a thing."* So I am including here a few useful Latin words and phrases. And these will also help you when you are reading any books in which magick spells are in Latin. In order to use and pronounce them properly, however, you will need to take a course in Latin, which is beyond the scope of what I can offer you here. Some high schools do offer Latin (Morning Glory and I both took it)—if yours does, check it out!

Here are some famous Latin phrases and mottos:

"Love conquers all." – *Amor omnes vincent.*
"Knowledge is power." – *scientia potestas est.*
"As above, so below." – *Tam supra, quam subter.*
"All is in the magick." – *Omnia in arte magica est.*
"Everything is alive, everything is interconnected." – *Omnia vivunt, omnia inter se conexa.*
"With great power comes great responsibility." – *Cum potestate magna rationem reddere convenit.*
"Living well is the best revenge." – *Vivere bene est vindicata optima.* (the Ravenheart family motto)

And here's a basic Charm of Manifestation that can be used at the end of any spell or ritual. If you learn nothing else in Latin, this one will carry you far:

By all the powers of Earth and Sea,
Per omnes vires terrae et maris,
By all the might of Moon and Sun,
Per omnes potentias lunae et solis,
As I do will, so mote it be;
Velut volo, ut liceat esse;
Chant the spell and be it done!
Carmen canta et fiat!
Blessed be!
Beata sint!

A Basic English-Latin Dictionary for Spells

Nouns

arrow	sagitta *f.*
art	ars *m.*
blessing	benedicto *f.*
circle	orbis *m.*
conjurer	praestigiator *m.*
council	concilium *n.*
curse	maledicto *f.*
death	mortus *m.*
doorway	ostium *n.*
faith	fides *f.*
fate	fatum *n.*
fear	timor *m.*
fellowship	societas *f.*
food	cibus *m.*
fool	stultus, ineptus *m.*
fortune	fortuna *f.*
garden	hortus *m.*
gate	porta *f.*
illness	morbus *m.*
healer	medicus *m.*
house	domus *f.*
king	rex *m.*
life	vita *f.*
love	amor *m.*
magick	magicus *m.*
might	vis *f.*
mystery	arcanum *n.*
peace	pax *f.*
power	potestas *f.*
protection	tutela *f.*
queen	regina *f.*
sorcerer	venificus *m.*
sorcery	venificium *n.*
spell	carmen *n.*
spirit	anima *f.*
truth	veritas *f.*
will	voluntas *f.*
window	fenestra *f.*
witch	striga, saga *f.*
wisdom	sapientia *f.*
wizard	magus *m.*
wizardry	magicae artes *f.pl.*
word	verbum *m.*
work	labor *m.*
voice	vox *f.*

English	Latin
animal	**animal *n.***
ant	formica *f.*
bear	ursus *m.*/ursa *f.*
beast	bestia *f.*
beaver	castor *m.*
bat	vespertilio *m.*
bee	apis *f.*
bird	avis *f.*
bull	taurus *m.*
cat	feles *f.*
chicken	pullus *m*
cow	vaca *f.*
crow/raven	cornix *f.*
deer	cervus *m.*/cerva *f*
dog	canis *m.*
dragon	draco *m.*
frog	rana *f.*
horse	equus *m.*
kine/cattle	boves *m.*
lizard	lacerta *f.*
owl	bubo *m.*
phoenix	phoenix *m.*
spider	aranea *f.*
snake	serpens *f.*
toad	bufo *m.*
wolf	lupus *m.*

English	Latin
body	**corpus *n.***
arm	bracchium *n.*
back	dorsum *n.*
belly	abdomen *n.*
chest	pectus *n.*
ear	auris *f.*
eye	oculus *m.*
face	facies *m.*
feather	penna *f.*
finger	digitus *m.*
foot	pedus *m.*
a hair	pilus *m.*
head hair	capillus *m.*
hand	manus *m.*
heart	cor *n.*
head	cephalus *m.*
horn	kernus *m.*
leg	crus *n.*
mouth	os *n.*
neck	collum *n.*
nose	nasus *m.*
tail	caudus *m.*
wing	ala *f.*

English	Latin
family	**gens *f.***
boy	puer *m.*
brother	frater *m.*
daughter	filia *f.*
father	pater *m.*
girl	puella *f.*
kin	cognati *m*
man	homo *m.*
mother	mater *f.*
sister	soror *f.*
son	filius *m.*
woman	femina *f.*

English	Latin
nature	**natura *f.***
air/breath	pneuma *f.*
earth planet	tellus *f.*
earth element	solum *n.*
earth/land	terra *f.*
east	oriens *m.*
fire	ignis *m.*
flower	flos *m.*
leaf	folium *n.*
moon	luna *f.*
mountain	mons *m.*
north	septentriones *m.*
river	flumen *n.*
sky	caelum *n.*
space	spatium *n.*
star	stella *f.*, astrum *n.*
sea	mare *n.*
south	meridies *f.*
sun	sol *m.*
tree	arbor *f*
water	aqua *f.*
west	occidens *m.*
wind	ventus *m.*
east wind	eurus *m.*
north wind	aquilo *m.*
south wind	auster *m.*
west wind	favonius *m.*
world	mundus *m.*

English	Latin
metal	**metallum *n.***
gold	aurum *n.*
silver	argentum *n.*
iron	ferrum *n.*
quicksilver	mercurium *n.*
tin	stannum *n.*
copper	cuprum *n.*
lead	plumbum *n.*

English	Latin
time	**tempus *m.***
dawn	aurora *f.*
day	dies *m.*
evening	vesper *m.*
morning	mane *n.*
night	nox *f.*
winter	hiems *f.*
summer	aestas *f.*
spring	ver *n.*
fall	autumnus *m.*

Verbs ("to-")

English	Latin
awaken	exsuscitare
banish	pellere
begin	incipere
bind	ligare
bless	beare
call	vokare
cast	iacere
chant/sing	cantare
close	claudere
conjure	elicere
conquer	vincere
decrease	decrescere
flee	fugere
fly	volare
go	ire
heal	sanare
increase	increscere
make	facere
open	aperire
praise	laudere
protect	defendere
sleep	dormire
stop	finire
transform	transmutere
work	laborare

Pronouns

English	Latin
you	te
me	me
myself	ipse
he	ille, hic, is
it	ipse, hoc, id
she	illa, haec, ea
our	noster
ourselves	ipsi
they	illi hi, ii
themselves	ipsi

Articles

English	Latin
and	et
be	esse
by	per
from	ad
in	in
is	est
out	ex
this	hic
therefore	ergo
so, thus	sic
to	ab

Adjectives, Adverbs

English	Latin
after	post
all	omnis
always	semper
bad	malus
beautiful	pulcher
before	ante
behold	ecce
best	bonum
big	magnus
brave	fortis, acer
bright	clarus
good, well	bene
dark	tenebrus
down	deorsum
faithful	fidelis
far	longinquus
fast, quick	celer
long	longus
many	multi
mythical	fabulosus
never	nunquam
up	sursum
sacred	sacer, sanctus
slow	tardus
short	brevis
small	minimus
strong	fortis

English	Latin
black	niger
blue	caeruleus
green	viridis
grey	ravus
purple	purpureus
red	ruber
white	albus
yellow	flavus

Course Five: Spectrum, Part 1

Course Five: Spectrum, Part 1

Class I. Meditation (Aqua)

1. Introduction: Levels of Mind

EDITATION AND VISUALIZATION ARE the foundational skills of all magickal practice, which is why this Class occupies first place in the 12-color Spectrum of Magicks. We are beings of Spirit as well as physical Matter. Meditation techniques and practices are designed to bring all these aspects of our beings into harmony and attunement.

The Four Levels

Our minds are layered like an onion (or a parfait). But unlike these metaphors, the deeper we go into the depths of our minds, the bigger the territory becomes, until the very deepest place is One with Universal Spirit. Think of this like waves in the sea: Each of our own individual conscious minds is like the tip of a wave. But the base widens out the deeper you go, until the bottom of the wave is the entire ocean. Or consider a house, with the rooms we live in, and the ones where we store stuff, but seldom enter.

So the topmost layer of waking consciousness is the ***conscious mind.*** This is the part of your mind that is active, alert, concerned with your everyday life and your physical well-being. Your conscious mind is the rooms of your house that you actually live in—and whatever is up on your monitor!

The next level down is your ***subconscious mind.*** This is like your basement or attic, where all sorts of stuff is stored that you've forgotten about—or would just as soon forget about! Your subconscious contains your memory banks and files—including things you thought you had relegated to the trash.

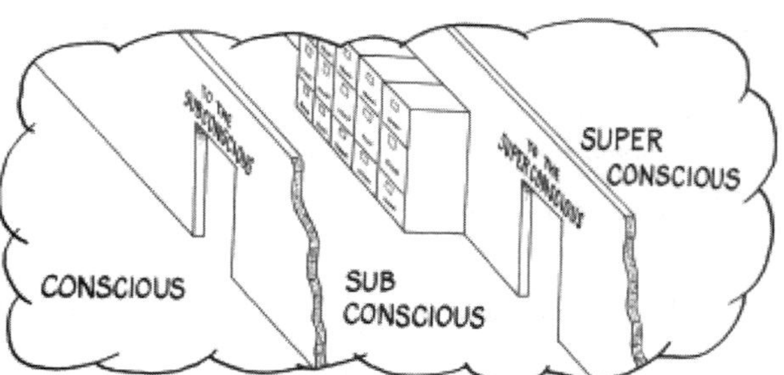

However, your subconscious is also the gateway to the next level…Your ***super-conscious mind,*** often called your "Higher Self." This is concerned with your spiritual well being, and contains your universal memory, past-life experiences, and lessons over the whole evolutionary history of your soul. In many ways, this is the foundation of your house, and it can also be seen as your programs and operating system.

And then, below all these levels of individual consciousness, accessible only in deep sleep, is the realm we call ***The Dreaming.*** This is the place we share with everyone else—the ground under the foundations of your house. The Dreaming is the World Wide Web of planetary consciousness.

And, of course, it doesn't stop there. Below the level of planetary consciousness is cosmic consciousness and universal consciousness…

Brain Waves

The vibrational frequencies of our brain waves in cycles per second are designated as follows:

Freq.	Cycles/Sec.	State of Consciousness	Brain Waves	Connection
Beta	14-30 cps	Fully awake, alert, excited		Conscious
Alpha	8-13 cps	Deeply relaxed, composed		Subconscious
Theta	4-7 cps	Drowsy, tranquil, unconscious		Superconscious
Delta	.5-3.5 cps	Deep unconsciousness, sleep		The Dreaming

In a meditational trance, your brain frequencies range from low alpha to high theta, averaging about 7.5 cps. The vibrational frequency of the Earth's magnetic field is also about 7.5 cps. When you are meditating, therefore, you enter into a resonant state with Gaea. This harmonic resonance between our field and the field of the entire planet gives a tremendous boost to your psychic energies, allowing you to transmit telepathy and healing over great distances through Gaea's field. Grounding and centering is really a matter of getting in synch with Gaea.

Chakras

Our spiritual and physical bodies are connected at seven vital centers, called *chakras* (see 5.2.3: "Chakra Healing"). Chakras are a way of visualizing human energy, but they are only one system or language—the other major ones are *meridians* in Chinese and *auras* in Western occult lore. In chakra meditation, these are opened and awakened in successive order, from the bottom upwards. Meditation, however, does not inherently open chakras; it can, and various techniques increase the chances. As in the basic "Tree of Life Grounding" in 4.IV.4, a powerful energy wave is sent coursing upwards through your body from root to crown. However, opening chakras in and of itself is not necessarily a good thing, any more than opening your front door is always a good thing.

Lesson 2: Basic Technique

> *Meditation allows you to learn to control the restless, materially-oriented conscious mind and reprogram the subordinate subconsciousness, in order that you may function from your spiritually-oriented higher consciousness. It opens up the channel to your Higher Self.*
> —Raymond Buckland

Various techniques for meditation are taught by different schools, and you may run into some of these later on. None of these are wrong; anything is right that works for you. Here is a good basic technique that I have found to be very effective. Once you become comfortable with this one, you may experiment with others as you encounter them. (And if uncomfortable feelings or thoughts come up during meditation, you should consult a reliable and knowledgeable adult.)

Find a quiet place where no one will disturb you for 20 minutes or so, and shut the door to keep out noise. Make sure there are no ticking clocks or dripping faucets. Set the temperature at a comfortable level, and wear loose clothing, such as a robe. Place a cushion on the floor against a wall (or use a yoga backjack). Place a small table or other stand about three feet in front of the cushion, and place a lighted candle (in a candleholder that will catch any melting wax) on the stand. Don't use a candle in a jar for this, as you need to be able to see the naked flame. Then turn out all the other lights, and sit down cross-legged on the cushion, with your back against the wall or backjack. Fold your hands together in your lap, and sit up straight. (Some people like to lie down flat on their backs to meditate, but I don't recommend this, as it is too easy to fall asleep!)

Relax your body, stare into the candle flame, and just let your thoughts fade away until your mind becomes clear and void. One way to do this is to count slowly backwards in your head, starting with 100 (and add "one thousand" with each number for timing). Let your eyes become unfocused, but keep them open for as long as possible, blinking very rarely (you don't want to go to sleep!). Breathe deeply, inhaling and exhaling as you slowly count each number: (inhale) "ninety-nine..." (exhale) "...one thousand." (inhale) "ninety-eight..." (exhale) "...one thousand."

Allow your mind to become still. Eventually, all thoughts will disappear (including the counting), as will all objects in the room, until there is only the flame and your breath.... You will be in a state of *trance.* But don't worry if you don't succeed right away; this can take a while to learn, and no one gets it right at first. Just keep practicing—even a few minutes every day can make a difference—and it will come to you. After a while, you won't even need the candle, and it won't matter if you close your eyes. Your awareness and perceptions will awaken to new degrees of clarity in which everything you know falls into place, and your path lies clear before you.

Third Eye

After you have gotten comfortable at candle meditation, a more advanced technique that I find very effective is to focus on your third eye. This is a spot right in the center of your forehead, between and slightly above your eyebrows. This is your 6th chakra, and corresponds to your pineal gland inside your skull.

When you are looking at a candle flame or other focus of meditation, you are usually looking downwards or straight ahead. The position of your eyes affects the orientation of your thoughts and mind as well, so that downward-looking tends to connect to the subconscious, with all its buried issues. Looking straight ahead reflects your normal conscious state and your relations with others—as we look at each other eyeball-to-eyeball when we communicate. But focusing your eyes inward and upward towards your third eye connects you to your Higher Self and the realms of Spirit. Do this exactly the same way as with the candle, except now close your eyes and visualize that flame glowing right above the center of your eyebrows. You may need to strain your eye muscles a bit to focus your eyes inside your head—like going cross-eyed—but that's part of the exercise.

Other Approaches

Once you have learned the technique I have given you, I would encourage you to experiment with different ways. As time goes on, and you get really good at this, you might try meditating in special places and "power spots." One of my favorite places to meditate is deep in a quiet woods, sitting with my back against the trunk of a large tree (I live in Northern California, among the giant Redwoods). But it can be wonderful to meditate by a waterfall, or at the seashore, on top of an enormous rock, or in a cave....

What I have described here is one method of meditation, given as an example. But please realize that this is not the only way to meditate—some meditations are done with eyes open, some with eyes shut; some with counting, some with a *mantra* (chant); and some in silence. Some accept whatever thoughts come to mind; others attempt to block them out. Some teachers advocate absolute stillness, and some encourage movement. Most Asian mediation techniques were originally designed to be practiced by initiates under the guidance of a teacher, who "seeded" the mediations by his presence, so the initiates were digesting that energy.

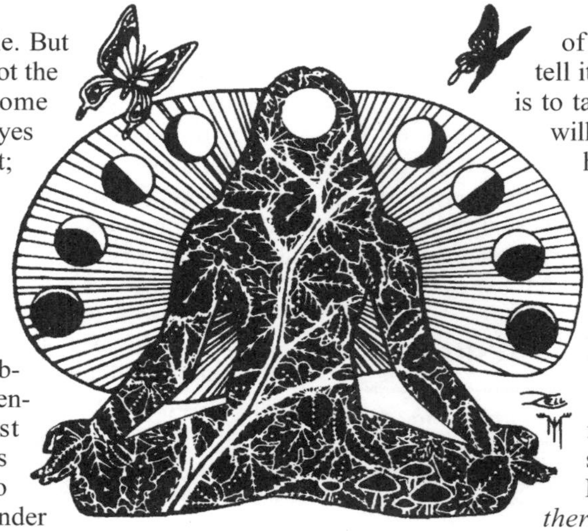

Stillness does not suit everyone; some people mediate better in flowing movement. If you are a person who says, "I just can't seem to get into meditation" or can't stay focused on your meditation, a working meditation might be able to get you started. Find a task to do that is repetitive and does not involve active thinking. Raking leaves, kneading bread dough, washing a wall with repetitive strokes, and pulling weeds are all activities that can help you move your mind into a meditative state. The act of keeping your body engaged while releasing your mind is often a good starting place. Soon, you will be more easily able to practice a seated meditation. There are many wonderful tapes and CDs available to aid in meditation, and once you have done a few sessions and are getting the hang of meditation, I recommend that you check out specialty bookstores and Websites and places like *Amazon.com* to find them.

Lesson 3: Autosuggestion

The subconscious is most accessible in the minutes just before you drop of to sleep or upon waking. For this reason, try to be in as relaxed and peaceful state as possible when you go to bed. Set your worries and concerns aside—and especially, never go to bed angry! Take a few minutes at bedtime to center yourself and enter into meditation—and then just let yourself drift naturally into sleep and The Dreaming.

Autosuggestion is a technique by which you can reprogram your subconscious. It's really just about creating a *statement of intention* and repeating it over and over to yourself in a meditation state. And the best time to do this is as you go to sleep. Here are a few tips:

1. When you program the subconscious with an intention to break some bad habit, leave out all mention of time and space. If you try and tell it when and where the change is to take place, your subconscious will fight back and look for a loophole. My late friend Leo Louis Martello, who was a Sicilian *Strega* ("Witch"), used to say: "When you are doing magick, never say 'I *wish*' or 'I *hope*' I might do something. Say 'I *will* do this.' Your words have power—use them that way." This is why magickal charms and chants so often conclude with "So It Is" or "So Mote It Be!" Now *there's* power! Always express your intention not as a request, but a command: "That's an order, soldier! Make it so!"

2. Prepare a knotted scarlet cord (see 4.I.5: "Cord and Knot Magick"), with 27 or 36 knots in all. Or, even better, make up your own Wizard's rosary by using colored beads of wood or glass, tying a knot between each bead (for a rosary, add a pentagram, ankh, or other amulet, and tie the whole thing into a circle). Just before you go to sleep, take your cord or your rosary and repeat once for each knot or bead the phrase of your magickal intention, such as: "I am confident and capable, and growing more so every day"—until you reach the end of the chain. Repeat this if you get up at night, and again the first thing upon awakening in the morning.

Lesson 4: Visualization

Once you have learned basic meditation and can clear your mind fairly well, the next step is *visualization*. Practically every kind of magickal working and spell will include the instruction to visualize something. So here's how:

Place yourself in a meditative trance, close your eyes, and clear your mind. Now imagine a golden triangle floating in the darkness. When you can see it clearly, imagine it becoming three-dimensional and turning into a golden pyramid. When the pyramid seems solid enough that you could reach out and touch it, allow it to expand in your field of vision until you can see that it's made of individual blocks of stone. Then, in your imagination, back away from the pyramid until you can see that it's resting on the desert sands. See shifting dunes and date palms. See other pyramids on either side. Visualize a camel walking by, and then a whole caravan. See the starry sky above, with Orion's belt above the pyramids…

When you can see all this in your mind's eye, you will have completed this exercise. In future medita-

Pagan Kids Activity Book
by Amber K

tions, visualize other things and scenes. Try visualizing a rose, and then a whole rosebush, and then a garden of many flowers, with butterflies and hummingbirds. Visualize the faces of those closest to you, until you can see them as clearly as a photograph. Visualize fantastic creatures, such as Dragons. Learn to visualize anything you can imagine....

> ***NOTE:*** *Becoming skilled at meditation and visualization requires patience and long attention spans. If you are having trouble maintaining your focus, you might try watching less TV and stop playing video games for awhile! But it is also true that some people are just not visually oriented. You may be better able to imagine hearing or feeling things than seeing them. If you simply cannot visualize no matter how much you work at it, don't despair—there will be plenty of other magickal things you can do!*

Lesson 5: Creating Your Astral Sanctum

A *sanctum* is a study or private room where one is not to be disturbed. As I said before, a sanctum sanctorum is a place of utmost privacy and inviolability. Your astral sanctum will be your own special "headquarters" in The Dreaming, where you can go to rest, study, learn things—and where you will always be safe from harm. Many magickal disciplines instruct their students early on to create an astral sanctum. Here's how:

In your meditational trance, visualize standing before a closed door. On that door is written your own magickal name. When you can see it clearly, open the door and walk into the room beyond. The light is very dim at first, but it slowly brightens, revealing the size and contents of the room—your sanctum. The first thing you notice is a large chair—almost a throne. It is the most perfect chair you can imagine, a chair suitable for a Wizard. Visualize it clearly, from every angle. And then sit in it. As you do so, it shapes itself to the contours of your body. It is your chair.

Now, as you sit in your chair, visualize a large screen across the wall in front of you. On the screen, you can see a three-dimensional projection of your bedroom. When you can see it all clearly, try manipulating the controls on the armrests. You will be able to bring up any scene you wish, zoom in or out, change angles, move forward or backward in time—all you have to do is visualize it. Now swivel your chair slowly around and let the rest of the room come into view. A bit at a time, visualize everything you could want in the room. This is your sanctum, and what you have in it is entirely up to you.

Opposite the door you came in is another door, and there are also two doors at right angles to those, completing the four Quarters. The door you came in is yellow, at the East. To the right, the South door is red. The West door is blue, and the final door, at the North, is green. Through these doors you can step into other rooms, containing anything you wish. And each of those rooms will also have doors that lead elsewhere.

But do not concern yourself for now with what lies beyond the doors in your sanctum; you may fill those rooms in time. For now, your task is to solidify your visualization of your sanctum itself. Study it all carefully, and memorize every detail. You can add or change anything later, but for now, the important thing is to make this become a real place in The Dreaming. In your meditations and directed dreaming, continue to return to your astral sanctum. Each time, remember all the details you have created in your visualizations. The more you do this, the more "solid" it will become, and the more real for you.

Lesson 6: Automatic Writing

You might wish to cultivate the talent of automatic writing, as it can be useful to yourself and others. A good way to start is to lay a pad of paper on the table before you, and hold a pen in your hand. Place your mind in a receptive condition and simply begin writing whatever happens to come, without helping or hindering or even particularly thinking about it. Try holding the pen in the hand you don't normally use to write with, to allow your normally dormant hemisphere to express itself. After some practice, your talent will grow rapidly.

There are three types of automatic writing:

1. Automatic or **mechanical:** The hand writes absolutely automatically, without your knowing what will be written. This method can also give you drawings, paintings, messages in other languages, etc.

2. **Inspirational:** It's as if you were "thinking aloud" inside or outside your own personality. The messages may come from the depths of your soul or from outside. You *know* what you will write.
3. **Intuitive:** You have the *feeling* that you did it yourself.

Lesson 7: Astral Projection

Astral projection is the practice of separating your astral body from your physical one and sending it out on a journey. This most often happens when you are sleeping, and such experiences may seem very similar to regular dreams. But the more you get into the practice of Magick and train yourself in techniques of meditation, visualization, and lucid dreaming (see 1.VI.5), the more you will find that "regular dreams" are seldom that! One way to tell the difference between dreams and astral projection is in your point of view. In a dream, as in waking life, you "see" only what is in front of you. But in astral projection, you can see in all directions, all around you. Often the first thing you see, in fact, is your own body lying in bed as your astral self separates from it.

In astral projection, the astral body is connected to the physical body by a "silver cord" that only severs at the time of death. This cord is infinitely elastic and will retain its connection no matter how far you journey. And like Ariadne's thread that Theseus followed back out of the Cretan Labyrinth, you can always return to your body along the length of the cord, so you don't have to worry about getting lost—unless, of course, you go *borrowing* (that is, transferring your consciousness into the mind of another living creature). We'll deal with borrowing in the Class on "Beast Mastery" (6.I).

By now, if you have been keeping your dream journal for some time, you will have developed your ability to remember your dreams quite well. If you have, in the evenings just before going to sleep, fix your mind on some place you would like to visit, or some person you would like to see. Then, in your dreams, *will* yourself to be wearing different clothes, or *will* yourself to suddenly be in some other place. Practice this very frequently.

How to Astral Project

Here is a technique to get into your astral body:

First, you must learn to visualize and develop your astral body until it is just as real to you as your physical body. Practice by standing naked in front of a full-length mirror and memorizing every detail of your body. Then close your eyes and visualize seeing yourself clearly. Hold that image for a few minutes, then open your eyes slowly, mor-phing your internal vision with the image in the mirror.

Do this over and over until you can see yourself just as clearly inside your mind as in the mirror. Then practice moving your arms and legs, matching those movements with those in your astral body as if by remote control. Finally, make the arms and legs of your astral body move without moving your physical body.

When you are able to do all this, the next thing to do is to move your astral body outside of your own. Try to transfer your consciousness to your astral body, looking back at your physical body from the other side. Your own body has its eyes shut. Use the eyes of your astral body to see and describe objects in the room behind you. When you can do this, try and rotate your astral body to look all around the room, and finally back to see your own physical body still in its place. By this time, it might be better to sit down in a chair.

Practice this for many sessions, until you can do it easily. Over time, try lying down on your back, and visualize your astral body rising up from your physical one, taking your consciousness with it. As you come to feel more at home in your astral body, let it rise higher into the air. Keep on feeling the sense of rising; keep looking about you as you rise until you see landscapes and beings of the Astral Plane or of the physical world. As you get better and better at this, you may venture further afield—to anyplace, in fact, that you may wish to go.

Take short journeys at first, and extend them into longer periods as you become more experienced. When you are ready to return to your physical body, you don't have to retrace your steps. All you have to do is visualize your physical body lying where you left it, and make your astral body coincide in space with your physical one, until they are merged completely together in a unity of consciousness. Then open your physical eyes and look around you; you're back, safe and sound!

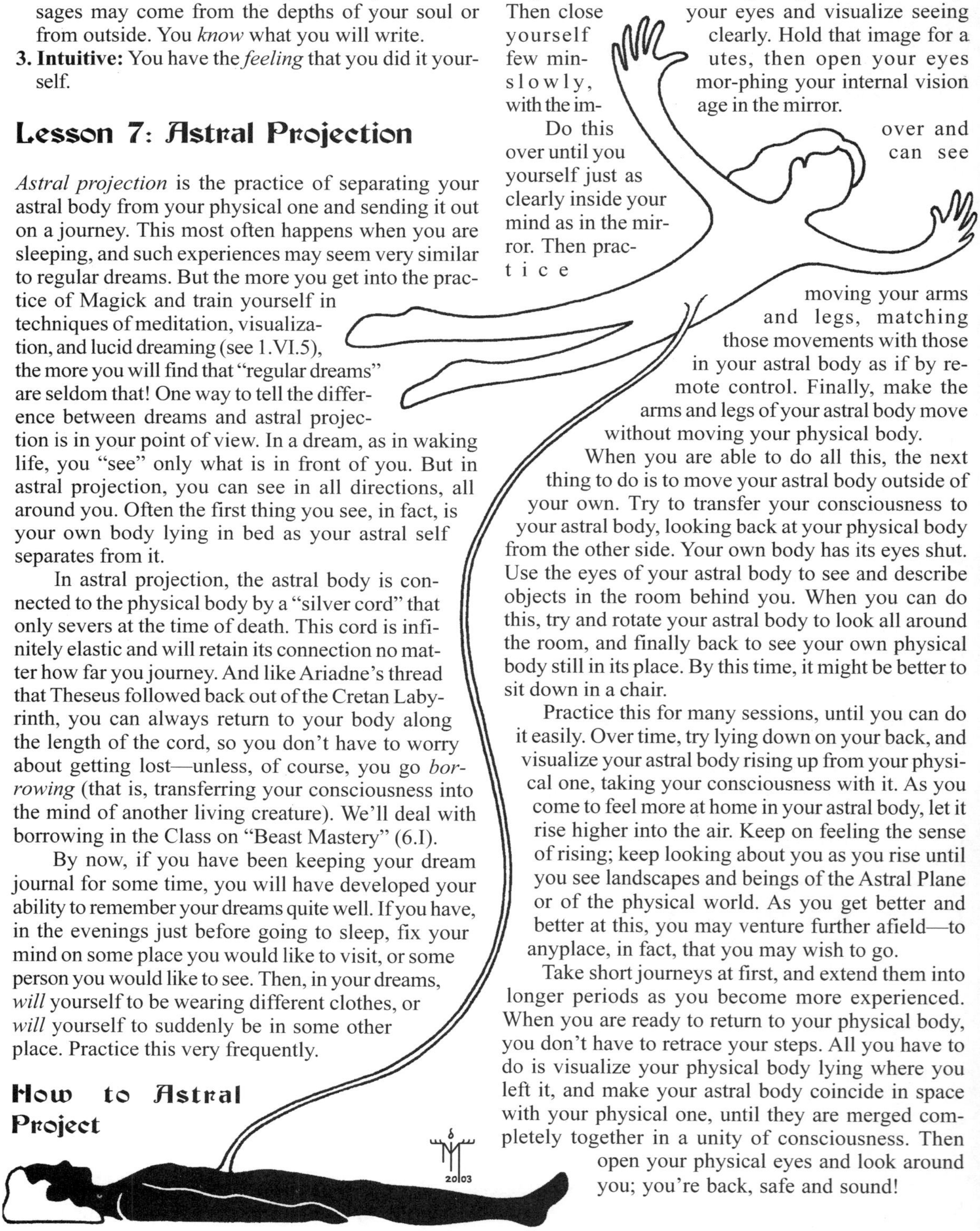

Class II: Healing (Blue)

1. Introduction: The Healing Arts

EALING REFERS TO ALL FORMS OF magickal arts and practices devoted to curing diseases, relieving aches and pains, promoting tissue regeneration, restoring vitality and fertility, and so on. Throughout history, healers have been the folk doctors, nurses, and midwives—especially in rural and "primitive" communities without access to officially licensed physicians and pharmacists.

Some types of magickal healing I will be explaining in this Class are:

Chakra healing—Aligning and balancing the seven primary energy centers in the body.

Auric healing—Changing the condition of a person by visualizing a specific color of light surrounding them.

Pranic healing—Sending energy (*prana*) from the healer's body to the afflicted parts of the patient to stimulate and restore normal functioning. This type of healing usually involves the laying-on of hands. *Reiki* is an Oriental version of this practice.

Color healing or ***chromatotherapy***—Bathing a suffering person in colored light of certain prescribed spectral frequencies.

Absent healing—Sending healing energy to a person who is not physically present, usually in the form of "white light."

Gem therapy—Using different types of gemstones of various properties and colors, which are worn on the body to attune vibrations.

Herbal healing—Utilizing the medicinal properties of plants for natural remedies.

Lesson 2. Principles of Psychic Healing

In magickal or *psychic healing,* the healer makes vital force flow from his or her own body into that of the sick person. Generally, this energy is transferred through the hands. To do psychic healing, you must above all be healthy and sound physically, and possess surplus vital force. You must also have excellent character, for you will transfer your own personal vibrations into your patients.

Generally, in psychic healing, you draw the vital force from the Universe and "stream" it consciously into the one who is sick. Always concentrate that the patient will be better and better hour by hour and day by day. In order to become an effective healer, it will also be important for you to study anatomy and the causes and symptoms of various diseases. Infectious diseases or those requiring operations should by all means be left to conventional medicine! Modern medical science is extremely effective and should never be ignored or dismissed. But psychic healing can aid in recovery from operations and for maladies that don't respond to medicine. It can even effect relief or cures from some "incurable" illnesses. Migraines, allergies, stomach troubles, and illnesses that may have a *psychosomatic* ("mind-body") origin respond very well to psychic healing.

Guidelines of Psychic Healing:

1. First, ask the person's permission for you to do a healing for them. Even better is to ask them, *"Can you visualize yourself as healed in body, mind, and spirit?"* This activates their own self-healing powers and promotes responsibility on their part for their own healing.

2. Before approaching the sick person, draw at least seven breaths of vital force from the Universe into your body. Remember that healing energy comes *through* you, not *from* you.

3. Let this vital force shine out through you like a sun, until the radiant energy of your aura extends far enough out to encompass the patient.

4. When you feel that you are glowing with life force, your very nearness to a sick person will feel as a healing presence.

5. Transfer this energy through your hands into the patient—whether into injured or affected portion of their body, their chakra, or their aura. Visualize the healing force as a bright blue light flowing out of you and into them.

6. With all your Will, direct this compressed radiant energy to stream into your patient through his/her pores, and *WILL* that it heal!

Basic Principles of Psychic Healing:

1. You must be convinced that your patient is feeling better hourly and daily. *Will* the radiant energy not to leave until they are fully recovered. Load the subject with so much blue light that it extends three feet from his/her body. Repeat the loading after awhile to increase the tension even more. In this way you can treat many people without depleting your own strength or ruining your nerves.

2. Increase your radiant energy so far out that as you near your patient, he/she will actually be "swimming" in your blue light. Your patient must be firmly convinced that he/she is inhaling your radiant energy with each breath and that he/she is strengthening. He/she must believe that the healing power will remain within him/her, and that they will be getting better and better. If your patient cannot concentrate, or if he/she is a young child, imagine yourself that the energy is being absorbed into their blood, healing continually.
3. Press the vital power *directly* into your patient's body or into the sick organ or area through his/her pores. *Will* the vital force to renew itself constantly from the Universe until complete recovery. This method is only practiced with patients whose nervous systems possess some strength. It is the most popular method of healing.
4. An alternate healing method is to make direct contact with the person's mind, and then treat by the above means. This can be done while the patient is sleeping, especially if you become skilled in dreamwalking. Still other methods involve healing with the Elements or with electrical or magnetic fields.
5. Increase the power and focus of your healing field by creating a Magick Circle around and over your patient (see 4.IV.5: "Casting the Circle"). Visualize a mirrored surface on the inside of the domed circle, reflecting your blue light back into the center. This will contain your working, and reinforce the outer edge of your aura so that your energies will not dissipate and become depleted.
6. Have some nice soothing music to play in the background while you are working with a patient. Check out the "New Age" section of your music store, and ask the clerk what they would recommend. There are many, many tapes and CDs made just for this purpose.

Lesson 3: Chakra Healing

(by Anodea Judith)

The *chakra* system is an ancient means for expanding consciousness and balancing your energy system. It originates from the yoga philosophies of India, most specifically during the Tantric period of yoga, during the middle of the first millennium. *Tantra* literally means "loom," and Tantric philosophies were a weaving of many different beliefs, but most specifically they featured a weaving of mind and body, male and female, and honored all levels of experience.

The word *chakra* is Sanskrit for "wheel" and describes a swirling vortex of energy that emanates from the core of the energy body. There are seven major chakras that are based on the central nerve bundles branching out from the spinal column, so this is a magickal system that maps directly onto the body. That means we feel our chakras within our body and can gain access to them by paying attention to the body.

Chakras are organizational centers for the reception, assimilation, and expression of life force energy. You can think of them as chambers in the temple of the body. Like the various rooms in your home, each chamber is designed to handle a different type of energy, such as Earth, Water, Fire, Air, sound, light, or thought. These chambers generate the patterns of our lives through core programming that we receive as we are growing up about how to behave and create life around us. Because of this, chakras are often out of balance and can generate negative patterns that we would rather not have! By aligning and balancing the chakras, we can become more conscious about the patterns we create. By understanding the chakras, we can use them as a magickal system for aligning our inner energies with the sacred architecture of the world around us.

The chakras have many associations based on their different locations within the body. They rule over mental and emotional states, as well as physical states. They have a seven-element system with a wide association of deities, colors, sounds, and symbols. The table of correspondences in 3.VI.5 shows you their various associations. You can use these correspondences to better understand the meaning and function of each chakra, or to access the chakra's energy in your magickal practice. Below is a brief description of each center to give you an overview of the system.

Chakra One is associated with the Element Earth and the indrawing force of gravity. It forms the foundation of the entire chakra system and represents survival instincts. Use this chakra to develop your grounding and create stability and prosperity in your life. Its name, *Muladhara,* means "root support." Allowing structure in your life will give you support for other things you want to do. If you resist structure, you are resisting the grounding and solidity that the first chakra can provide.

Chakra Two is associated with the Element Water and the rise into duality. This center relates to the emotional and sensate aspects of consciousness, and the urge to bridge duality through erotic union with another. Its name, *Svadhisthana,* means "one's own place." Because water is fluid and moving, this chakra helps us move forward in life, following our desires. Desire is an important fuel for the will, but if excessive, it can keep us bound at this level, unable to rise to the other chakras. Like all things, it must be held in balance.

Chakra Three is associated with the Element Fire and represents vitality and power. Here we develop our will, directing the raw energy of the body according to the intentions set by consciousness. Its name, *Manipura,* means "lustrous gem." This chakra develops when we strengthen our will by sticking to a course of action and focusing our energies. It is supported by having a solid ground (first chakra) and being able to speak up for ourselves (fifth chakra), as well as having vision and knowledge to guide our will (sixth and seventh chakras).

Chakra Four is associated with the Element Air and relates to the heart and its aspects of love, compassion, and relationship. The heart chakra lies in the middle of the chakra system and integrates mind and body, spirit and matter, inner and outer in perfect balance. Within this balance lie the seeds of deep peace. Its name, *Anahata,* means "unstruck" or "unhurt." We open the heart chakra by opening our heart to others, through kindness and consideration, through trust and compassion. We can also access this chakra by working with the breath as the Element Air. By expanding our breath we expand our chest capacity and feel an expansion in the heart.

Chakra Five is associated with the Element Sound (*Ether* in ancient texts). It is the chakra of communication and creative self-expression. It relates to the truth we hold within us and the great truths that we all share. It opens through use of the voice and through deep inner listening. Its name, *Vissudha*, means "purification." We access this chakra by toning and chanting, playing or listening to music, speaking our truth, and listening deeply to the communication of others. When this chakra is open, our creativity increases as a vital form of self-expression.

Chakra Six is associated with the Element Light and relates to the psychic faculty of deep inner seeing or insight. It opens us to the beauty of the inner world, the symbolic realm of archetypes and dreams, and the awakening of a guiding vision. Its name, *Ajna,* means "to perceive" and "to command." We access this chakra through paying attention to our dreams, developing our psychic abilities, paying attention to the patterns that we see, and learning about the archetypes through mythology. This chakra is strongly supported by meditation, especially the kind in which visualizations are used.

Chakra Seven is the thousand-petaled lotus associated with pure Consciousness. It is the seat of enlightenment or realization, the abode of the god Shiva, the abstract realm of conception and ideas, and the mind of the cosmos. Its name, *Sahasrara,* means "thousand-fold." This means that its realm is infinite, as the realm of consciousness is infinite. This chakra opens us to divine wisdom, cosmic consciousness, intelligence, and understanding. It is accessed by learning and study in which you challenge and utilize your mind. However, its deepest jewels are gained through a regular practice of meditation. For yogis, it was the entrance into the supreme world of absolute bliss.

All seven chakras need to be open and functioning to have a healthy balance in our lives. In this way the chakras are a template for transformation and a profound formula for wholeness. This system can be a lifelong guide to keep you centered and on track in all that you intend to do. Healing the chakras requires understanding the meaning and function of each one and determining if the chakra is over or underactive (excessive or deficient). In short, excessive chakras need to let go, relax, or discharge energy, whereas deficient chakras need to bring energy in, get charged up, or hold on. In either case, massaging or moving the part of the body (as through yoga postures or dance, for example) can help to balance the chakra by relaxing the energy. When something that has been held tightly can open and relax, it will fill with energy. When something overactive relaxes, it releases energy.

In both cases, healing the imbalances requires bringing your attention to the affected area and working with visualization, breath, and movement. See the chakra filling or emptying, expanding or contracting according to what is needed. Move your body and breath in ways that support what you are trying to accomplish, focusing on the exhalation for decreasing energy and on the inhalation for increasing. Imagine that your hands can bring energy in toward the body or move energy out from the body by working in the auric field. Because everyone is different in how they react to various techniques, be creative, have fun, and experiment to see what brings the best results for you. For more information on chakras go to *www.sacredcenters.com.*

Lesson 4: Auric Healing

The *aura* is the bioelectrical field that emanates from all living things—and even, to a lesser extent, inanimate objects. For all things are, at their most basic sub-atomic level, composed of vibrations, and vibrations radiate energy, creating a field. As we discussed earlier, the aura around the entire human body is called the *aureole,* and the part just around the head is called the *nimbus.* In Christian religious art, the nimbus is often shown as a glowing golden *halo* (or *gloria*) around the heads of saints and holy figures. In Moslem art, the nimbus is shown as a ring of flames around the heads of the prophets. Crowns of kings and headdresses of priests also symbolize the nimbus.

Work on the exercises described in 1.V.4: "Seeing Auras." With practice, you may become able to see colors, which can indicate a person's emotional or physical condition. Any state of the individual's being causes reactions in the aura. Emotional states will primarily affect its color. Physical conditions not only affect the color, but also cause peculiarities in the patterns of the aura, such as ragged edges or holes over injuries or sore spots.

Auric healing involves visualizing a specific color of light, and infusing these healthy colors into the damaged areas of your patient's aura. The colors are chosen according to the patient's problem (see below). Here are a few examples:

For *headaches* and *soothing the nerves,* use violet and lavender.
For *mental inspiration,* use yellow and orange.
For *stomachaches,* and to *invigorate the organs,* use grass green.
To *stimulate the blood,* use bright red.
For *bleeding,* use dark blue.
For *fever,* use cool blue.
For *chill,* use hot red.

Keep up these visualizations for as long as you can, seeing the patient completely bathed in the appropriate healing colors.

Lesson 5: Chromatotherapy

Aura healing also works very well in conjunction with *chromatotherapy*, or "color healing," which is based on using light. Light is radiant energy traveling in the form of waves, like the waves that lap upon the seashore. The colors of light come from the *frequency,* or rate of vibration, of those waves, from the short waves at the blue end of the rainbow spectrum to the long waves at the red end. Sunlight contains frequencies ranging from ultraviolet to infrared (and way beyond as well, into radio waves, X-rays, and other invisible frequencies). Living creatures (including us) select from sunlight whatever frequencies, or colors, are needed for health and balance, absorbing those vibrations into our bodies in the same way that plants use sunlight for photosynthesis. After all, there is only one atom of difference between a molecule of green chlorophyll (in plants) and one of red hemoglobin (in our blood).

The principle of chromatotherapy is simply to give the ailing body an extra dose of any colors that may be insufficient. For this, you can install light bulbs of appropriate colors and bathe the patient in their light. Or you can tape colored plastic over sunny windows to concentrate a particular color of sunlight—however, it is most important that the colored light actually falls on the patient, particularly on the ailing areas of the body. Basically, the red end of the spectrum stimulates, and the blue end calms. Here are the healing properties of the seven colors of the spectrum:

RED: Warming and invigorating. Excellent for blood diseases, anemia, and liver infections.
ORANGE: Similar to red, but not as intense. Good for the respiratory system, asthma, and bronchitis. Also a tonic and laxative.
YELLOW: Excellent for the bowels and intestines. A mild sedative, helping to remove fears and giving a mental uplift. Also good for indigestion, heartburn, and constipation. Also good for menstrual problems in women.
GREEN: The Great Healer, green is a general tonic and revitalizer. Excellent for heart troubles, ulcers, colds, headaches, and boils.
BLUE: An antiseptic and cooling agent. Excellent for all inflammations, including internal organs. Good on cuts and burns; also for rheumatism.
INDIGO: Good for emotional disorders, indigo will allay fears—especially of the dark. Excellent for the eyes; also for deafness.
VIOLET: Good for the nervous system and mental disorders; also for blindness and female complaints.

Lesson 6: Pranic Healing

Healing by laying-on of hands, or *pranic healing,* is one of the most widespread and effective practices. The principle involves sending *prana* ("vital force") from your body into the diseased or affected parts, stimulating the cells and tissues to normal activity and allowing the waste material to leave the system. Prana is the vital spirit essence (the 5th Element) that underlies all physical action of the body. It causes circulation of the blood, movement of the cells, and all motions upon which life depends. You receive prana from the food you eat, the water you drink, the air you breathe, and the warmth of the Sun or fire—the other Four Elements. And you can send it forth through your aura into another person in directed healing.

Before you attempt to do any healing, increase the force of your prana by deep breathing. *Pranic breathing* balances the negative and positive bioelectrical currents throughout your body. It calms your nerves and regulates your heartbeat, reducing blood pressure and stimulating your digestion. As you breathe in, visualize energy and strength flowing into all parts of your body. Feel it traveling along your arms and down your legs. Draw Prana from Gaea, and from the living Cosmos, and fill yourself with it to overflowing!

Here is the basic exercise for pranic breathing:

1. (a) Slowly breathe in through your nose to a count of eight.
(b) Slowly exhale through your nose to a count of eight.

2. (c) Slowly breathe in through your nose to a count of eight.
(d) Hold your breath for a count of three, visualizing all the love, energy, and strength you have inhaled circulating throughout your body.
(e) Slowly exhale through your mouth to a count of eight, breathing out any negativity within you.

Do "1" once, then do "2" three times. Now you are fully charged and ready to heal. Have your patient lie on his/her back, ideally with head towards the East. His legs should be together with arms at the sides. He should close his eyes and concentrate on seeing himself surrounded in a ball of pale blue light. You kneel or sit on his left if you're right-handed, or on his right if you're left-handed. Reach out your arms and hold your hands with palms inwards above the top of his head, about an inch away from actual physical contact.

Take a deep breath. Then, holding it, bring your hands smoothly down the length of his body on both sides, not quite touching the skin the whole way. Visualize prana radiating from your hands, penetrating deep into your patient, and drawing out the pain and negativity like drawing a comb through hair. As you come away from his feet, exhale and shake out your hands as if you were shaking water off them. You are actually shaking away all the negativity that you have drawn from them. Repeat this process seven times.

Then sit back and relax for a moment, visualizing your patient surrounded in pale blue healing light. Repeat the above exercise for pranic breathing. Now you are ready for physical contact—laying-on of hands. Lay your palms against the sides of your patient's head, thumbs on their temples. Close your eyes and concentrate on sending healing prana flowing from your hands into them. Then once again sit back and relax, visualizing the healing light. Take another series of pranic breaths, and repeat the same hands-on working, this time over their heart. Finally, after another rest and series of breaths, lay your hands on the specific area of complaint, and again direct your prana into healing the afflicted area. Visualize and concentrate with all your might.

Complete the process with a final period of rest. Close your eyes and visualize your patient healthy and radiant, surrounded in blue light. You will probably feel drained and exhausted, so when you are all done, pour yourself a tall glass of cold fruit juice!

Lesson 7: Healing Over Distance

It is possible to conduct psychic healing for someone even without them being physically present. The trick is to be able to visualize your patient as if he/she were right in front of you. A great help for this is to have a photograph of him that you can put up on your healing altar. Make sure, however, that there is no one else in the photo! Color healing with only a photograph is called *graphochromopathy.* Ideally, the afflicted area should be visible in the picture. Place the photo (best if it is framed) under the appropriately colored light, or cover it with a sheet of colored plastic or acetate and set it in a sunny window.

Light a candle of the appropriate color as indicated above, and go into a meditative state as in 5.1.2: "Basic Technique." Visualize the person, and see the area of his/her affliction in your mind as a dark blot in her aura. Then, just as in the techniques described above for auric healing, visualize appropriately colored light flowing into the ill place and healing it until it glows brightly, along with the entire person. To increase the power of your healing over distance, begin with pranic breathing as above.

Lesson 8: Gem Therapy

Minerals are imbued with prana just as are living creatures and plants. Stones are the bones of Gaea. Crystals in particular grow almost like living things, and some (such as quartz) can even generate peizo-electric charges. From the most ancient times, people have treasured various minerals—especially crystalline gems. These have been used to ornament clothing and bodies, altars and sacred objects, magickal tools and instruments. They are valued for their spiritual, magickal, and healing properties, and considered as aids in meditation and psychic development.

The prana of gemstones and other minerals can be absorbed into the human body and used in healing. *Gem therapy* is similar in concept to color healing. The most important thing is to go by the *color* of the stone, using the same correspondences as above. The most popular stones for such use are polished lumps of various types of quartz, which are available cheaply in baskets at any rock shop. Choose ones of a size and shape that fit comfortably into your closed hand, like a bird's egg. Before using them, your gems should be cleansed, consecrated, and empowered. First, hold them in a stream, in the ocean, or even under a running faucet. Then let them soak overnight in the moonlight in a glass of spring water or seawater.

The stone should be placed directly on the afflicted area (it can even be held in place with a garter, belt, tape, or bandage and left there for at least an hour each day. For the rest of the time, it should be kept as close to the body as possible, such as in the patient's pocket, or worn around his/her neck in a mojo bag. If he/she has a pendant, headband, or other jewelry with appropriately colored stones, these should be worn as much as possible.

For a list of many gems and their associated magickal properties, see the Chart of "Magickal Minerals" in 3.VII.8. Here is a sampling, arranged according to color. Note that some gems come in multiple colors:

PINK: Fluorite, moonstone, rhodochrosite, rose quartz.
RED: Aventurine, carnelian, red coral, chrysolite, bloodstone, garnet, jasper, opal, ruby, sardonyx, topaz.
ORANGE: Amber, carnelian, opal, sunstone, tiger eye.
YELLOW: Amber, beryl, chrysolite, jasper, opal, topaz.
GREEN: Aventurine, beryl, bloodstone, chrysolite, emerald, fluorite, jade, jasper, lapis, opal, topaz, turquoise.
BLUE: Aventurine, beryl, fluorite, lapis, moonstone, sapphire, topaz, turquoise.
INDIGO: Lapis, malachite, opal, sapphire, sodalite.
VIOLET: Amethyst, fluorite, lapis, sapphire.

Lesson 9: Herbal Healing

(by Ellen Evert Hopman, Master Herbalist; and Morning Glory Zell, Hedge Witch)

The wise Wizard should never be at a loss when it comes to healing themselves, their friends and family, or even a pet. Sometimes the simplest remedy will do wonders—for example, taking a hot bath will often ease the symptoms of a cold, especially if a little salt and some lavender flowers (about a cup of each) are added to the water. In the past, all children were taught basic herbal remedies so they could doctor themselves and their friends. By using natural remedies you will be helping to preserve an ancient art. In this Lesson you will find an assortment of natural remedies using easily available ingredients from the kitchen shelf. After you have mastered the use of these "home remedies," you may wish to progress to further study using medicinal plants from Nature or a local health food store (suggestions for further reading are given at the end of this chapter).

Some basic guidelines for kitchen herbal recipes:

1. Never cook with aluminum utensils; the aluminum flakes off and can lead to health problems. Use cast iron, steel, copper, or ceramic cookware only.
2. Be sure you simmer ingredients in a pot with a tight lid so the volatile oils won't evaporate into the air. (Do not boil herbs, or they will lose their virtue).
3. Herbal teas can be kept in the refrigerator for up to a week in a glass jar with a tight lid. They can also be frozen into ice cubes and stored in a bag in the freezer for later use.
4. Whenever possible use organic ingredients so you avoid pesticides. Fruits and vegetables must be cleaned with hot soapy water and rinsed thoroughly to remove pesticide residues, which are often oil-based to make them stick to the skins of fruits and vegetables.
5. Dried herbs and seeds should come from commercial organic growers. It is irresponsible to purchase wild-crafted organic herbs and spices, as in many cases these are becoming endangered species in their natural habitats.
6. Flowers and leaves are steeped in freshly boiled water that has been removed from the stove. Roots, barks, and berries are simmered—never boiled.
7. Honey is not suitable for babies as it may harbor bacteria.
8. If any herbal preparation does not agree with you or makes you feel bad, then DON'T USE IT. "An ounce of caution is worth a pound of cure."

9. Sleep, exercise, and healthy foods are the true keys to a long, happy life.

> *NOTE: Be sure to work under the guidance of a parent or teacher whenever you prepare herbal remedies!* **IN THE EVENT OF A SERIOUS MEDICAL CONDITION PLEASE CONSULT A HEALTH PROFESSIONAL BEFORE USING HOME REMEDIES.** *If any of these remedies cause an unpleasant side effect (itching, burning, rash, cramps, etc.) discontinue the treatment immediately!*

ACNE, RASHES and SKIN PROBLEMS

Cranberry juice helps pimples, acne, and bad skin. A poultice of mashed cranberries can be applied to boils and other skin eruptions and infections. Mash the fresh berries (or frozen ones that have been thawed out), spread them on a clean cloth, and apply. Leave the poultice on for an hour and then discard. Repeat daily until the skin is healed. For pimples and acne, try washing the face with *lemon* juice. Allow the juice to dry on the face; it will help dry the blemishes. Do this morning and evening. Or you can slice the lemon into very thin pieces and lay them on the skin as a face masque. Allow it to remain for a half hour. These juices work like a glycolic peal and should be discontinued if any irritation develops.

Lemon juice also makes an excellent hair rinse. For dandruff, try massaging into the scalp lemon juice mixed with equal parts of water, allowing it to dry before shampooing. If you are lucky enough to live in a climate where lemons grow outdoors, you can apply freshly squeezed lemon juice to your hair daily and keep it in while you go out in the sun. Over time it will bleach your hair. Apply lemon juice frequently to a wart to make it disappear.

Adding *honey* to hand lotion helps to heal very chapped, irritated, or dry skin. Grate fresh *ginger* root, boil it in water, and make a poultice and apply to boils to get them to come to a head. *Olive* oil is a wonderful skin healer. It even stops the itch of chicken pox. Apply it to stings and burns, bruises, itching, and sprains.

BEE STINGS and POISON IVY

First, remove the stinger by scraping with the blade of a knife; never pluck it out. Then make a paste of baking soda and your own saliva and apply it to the site of the sting. Or else apply fresh *lemon* juice or a slice of raw *onion* to the sting of a wasp or a bee (never use baking soda and lemon juice together; they cancel each other out). Crush fresh *sage* leaves and apply them to insect bites.

Crush a few cloves of *garlic* and apply to poison ivy. Leave it on for about 30 minutes.

BRUISES and INFLAMMATIONS

First, any sprain or bruise should be treated with an immediate ice compress. Make a hot poultice of *arnica* flower tea and apply it to a bruise or strain. Grated raw *potato* can be applied to sprains, bruises, and *synovitis* (a type of joint inflammation). A cooked *potato* poultice can be placed over any organ that is ailing; for example, the lungs when someone has bronchitis. The poultice will help pull heat and fever out of the system.

BURNS

Aloe is cooling and soothing and loaded with skin healing vitamins. Whenever someone gets a burn, either from cooking or from the Sun, split open one of the fleshy leaves and apply the moist inner gel to the burn. A little *butter* is a quick remedy for a slight burn (not for a serious burn) or for dry skin. You can also rub the juice of *cucumbers* directly onto the skin to help heal burns, inflammations, and other skin irritations. *Honey* makes a great dressing for a burn. Honey contains propolis, a substance made by bees that heals burns. Mash fresh *strawberries* and apply them to the face as a masque or to treat sunburn. Leave on for half an hour and then wash the face with water; do not use soap.

COLDS, COUGHS, and SORE THROATS

In ancient times when poor people had no access to doctors, *garlic* was one of the most important cure-alls. Added to soups it can help cure colds, fevers, and flu. Garlic kills viruses and bacteria. Please don't use dried garlic capsules or genetically engineered or de-scented garlic. Old-fashioned stinky garlic is best when it comes to fighting infections. For colds, try chopping a peeled clove of garlic into pill-sized portions and swallowing them with water into which fresh lemon juice has been squeezed. You can also dry roast the cloves by placing them unpeeled in a frying pan. Do not add oil or water. Roast slowly over low heat until the garlic cloves are soft. Remove from the stove and peel. (The garlic should be like a warm paste inside the peel.) Eat freely. Yummy!

Ginger root is a very warming spice. According to the Chinese it "causes internal secretions to flow," meaning that it loosens phlegm and other internal liquids. Ginger is good for a cold or the flu. Be careful not to overdo it, however. Too much ginger tea can actually irritate the lungs. Take no more than two cups of the tea a day.

A mixture of two cups V-8 juice, juice of ½ fresh *lemon,* a few cloves of *garlic,* one teaspoon grated *horseradish,* and a pinch of *cayenne pepper,* blended well, will help cure a cough or cold. (Hint: The horseradish helps open blocked sinuses. Add more if you can tolerate the taste.) Half a teaspoon of grated horseradish, flavored with lemon juice, can be taken twice a day for sinus conditions. Horseradish has loads of vitamin C and also helps clear mucus out of the human body.

Steep two teaspoons of *sage* leaves in a cup of freshly boiled water for half an hour to make sage tea. Take a quarter cup, four times a day, to dry up moist coughs and lung congestion. The best tea of all for coughs is made from dried coltsfoot leaves (from a health food store). Steep two teaspoons dried leaves in cup of hot water, strain, and mix with a little honey to taste.

CONSTIPATION and DIARRHEA

Cinnamon tea is very helpful for diarrhea and to stop vomiting, but you can't just use the powdered kitchen spice. Simmer a quarter teaspoon of the ground bark or a small piece (about 1/4 inch) of cinnamon stick in a cup of water for ten minutes, strain, and drink. Saltine crackers and firm cheeses can also stop "the trots." *Cucumber* salad helps chronic constipation. *Lettuce* and salads in general help keep you healthy and regular. *Oatmeal*, prunes, and prune juice are also laxative foods.

CUTS and WOUNDS

If you accidentally give yourself a small cut in the kitchen, you can pour powdered *cayenne pepper* directly on the wound to make it stop bleeding (this is gonna sting!). *DON'T GET CAYENNE PEPPER INTO YOUR EYES!* It won't harm your eyes but it will sting like crazy. If you do get it into your eyes, flush them immediately with a strong continuous spray of cold water. Alum, used for pickling, will stop bleeding from small cuts immediately. Any bad cut should be taken to a doctor for stitches.

Honey makes a great wound dressing. After carefully cleaning a wound, put honey over it, and then bandage it. The honey absorbs water, and germs cannot live without water. Mashed, fresh garlic can be applied to a wound, covered with honey (to keep out air), and then bandaged. If infection should occur, resort to antibiotic creams or other antiseptic treatments.

FEVER

Suck on ice chips to reduce fever and help stop vomiting and stomach upset from flu. *Lemon* juice mixed with honey and water helps lower a fever. *Pomegranate* juice is a refrigerant, meaning it can actually lower body temperature. Clean and scrape the bark off *willow* twigs to make a tea that lowers fever; you can add honey to help with the bitter taste.

Mild fevers are quite natural and a way for the immune system to develop, but if fever does not lower, or goes above 103°F, call a doctor. *Oatmeal* or *cream of rice* is very digestible and should be given to those who are weak from illness and fever. It can be flavored with raisins, a little grated lemon, cinnamon, honey, and a little rice milk.

HEADACHE

For headaches, dip a cloth into a strong batch of *basil* tea and apply it to the forehead as a warm compress (it works even better if you add 2 tablespoons of *witch hazel* extract). Use 1 teaspoon of basil for each cup of water. Bring the water to a boil, remove from the stove, and add the basil. Allow the basil to steep for 10 minutes in a non-aluminum pot with a tight lid. For a quick remedy, cut a *lime* in half and rub it on your forehead. It feels very good to make a cool compress by boiling water and lavender flowers (breathing the steam is good for you too); refrigerate the mixture, then soak a cloth in the cold mixture and put it on your forehead. The throbbing will go away.

MOUTH PROBLEMS

People with *halitosis* (bad breath) should make a habit of eating *parsley* as a condiment (and have a dentist check their teeth and gums!). Take vitamin C for bleeding gums. Steep 2 teaspoons of *sage* leaves in a cup of freshly boiled water for half an hour to make sage tea. You can use the tea as a gargle for tonsillitis, laryngitis, and sore throats. Sage also helps with bad breath, bleeding gums, and mouth sores. Eating raw *raspberries*, *blackberries,* and *strawberries* in the summer helps dissolve tartar on the teeth, and helps build the immune system. To whiten teeth, allow the fruit to remain on them for five minutes and then brush the teeth with a mixture of water and bicarbonate of soda. Sore gums, teeth, or throat can be helped temporarily by gargling a cupful of hot water with 4 teaspoons of dissolved sea salt.

STOMACH PROBLEMS, INDIGESTION, and GAS

To make an antacid that helps upset stomachs, colic, and gas: Take one half teaspoon each of *caraway* seeds, *fennel* seeds, *peppermint* leaf, and *spearmint* leaf. Place in a cup and pour boiling hot water over the herbs. Cover the cup with a plate and allow to steep for 10 minutes. Stir well, strain, and take one cup four times a day, not with meals. Hint: If you have a mortar and pestle, you can place the seeds into it and pound them. They will release more of their medicinal virtues this way.

Cinnamon water helps with chronic indigestion and gas. Put one quarter teaspoon of the ground bark into a cup of freshly boiled water, stir, cover, and allow to steep for 15 minutes; strain and drink. *Oregano* tea is great for indigestion, nausea, and colic. It also helps relieve gas, lowers a fever, and is soothing to the nerves. *Peppermint* helps with flatulence (farting) and upset digestion and is also cooling for a fever, so they are an ideal combination. *Ginger* tea helps with mild nausea and motion sickness.

Class III: Wortcunning (Green)

1. Introduction: About Wortcunning

ERBALISM IS THE LORE AND ART OF knowing and using the magickal, medicinal, and other properties of plants—especially herbs or (in Old English) *worts*. The old word used for the knowledge of the secret properties of herbs is *wortcunning* (herbal wisdom), and this has always been a particular study of Witches. Wortcunning has two aspects. The first deals with the chemical and medicinal properties of herbs; the second is concerned with their occult and magickal properties. Ancient doctors, traditional herbalists, Wizards, and Witches have always considered both these aspects, but modern physicians and pharmacologists only concern themselves with the first. Ethnobotanists and psycho-pharmacologists study the cultural and psychological aspects of certain "medicine plants"—plants particularly known for their consciousness-altering effects.

Vast amounts of herbal lore, remedies, and recipes have been compiled into books called *herbals*. The earliest known herbal was written by the Greek physician Pedanius Dioscorides (40-90 CE). His famous text on botany and pharmacology was called *De Materia Medica* ("On Medical Matters") and it was the primary herbal source book for European Witches and Wizards throughout the Middle Ages. Many of today's medicines have come from these ancient herbal recipes, though most modern doctors dismiss them as mere superstitious "folk remedies."

I think that the most important thing about wortcunning is learning to grow and harvest the herbs yourself. My own greatest pleasure in wortcunning comes from gathering herbs in the wild—learning to recognize each one in its season and habitat. I recommend you get a good book on wild herbs, such as *Stalking the Wild Asparagras* by Euell Gibbons, and try going out into the fields and woods to see what you can find. Take a basket, a sharp little knife, and a pair scissors.

The home of an herbalist is a real joy to experience, with herbs growing in the garden, all around the house, and in window boxes, planters, and pots. Bundles of dried herbs hang from hooks in the kitchen and above the fireplace. The combined aromas are just wonderful! Hanging in the kitchen you will usually see a little doll of an old Witch riding a broom; this is the "Kitchen Witch," and she blesses the kitchen of any herbalist.

Lesson 2. Kitchen Witchery

—by Ellen Evert Hopman, Master Herbalist

In the previous Class on healing, I introduced a number of herbal remedies for common ailments. Here I will offer some additional herbal lore, the arts of which are referred to as "Kitchen Witchery."

ALLSPICE: This spice comes from the unripe fruits of an evergreen tree (*Eugenia pimenta*—commonly known as pimentos) that grows in South America and the West Indies. It tastes and smells a bit like clove and is used to season meats, curries, and pies. To make a remedy for stomach upset and gas, simmer ½ to ¾ teaspoon of the spice in a cup of hot water for ten minutes. The dose is 1 ounce for a child, 2 ounces for an adult.

ALOE VERA: *Aloe* can grow in the garden in warm climates and indoors in a sunny spot in colder areas. This is a plant that you will want to have somewhere near the kitchen for healing burns. Split open one of the fleshy leaves and apply the moist inner gel to the burn. Aloe is cooling and soothing and loaded with skin-healing vitamins.

ANISE SEEDS: *Anise* is a spice that was used by the ancient Egyptians, Greeks, and Romans. Anise seeds are used to flavor pies, cookies, and stews. The tea is a sedative and a great remedy for colic, gas, and indigestion. Steep two teaspoonfuls in a pint of freshly boiled water for ten minutes. Strain and take a tablespoonful as needed. Sweeten with honey if desired.

APPLE: "An apple a day keeps the doctor away" is a wise saying. People who eat two *apples* a day have fewer headaches and emotional upsets, as well as clearer skin. Eating raw apples increases saliva, stimulates the gums, and cleans the teeth—leading to better dental health. In Norse mythology, when the gods feel they are beginning to grow old they eat apples to restore their strength and youth. Do not eat the seeds as they contain strychnine, which is a poison.

ASPARAGUS: *Asparagus* spears should be simmered quickly or steamed for no more than 5 minutes. In this way they retain their vitamins (A and C) and minerals (calcium, phosphorus, sodium, chlorine, sulfur, and potassium). This food is *diuretic* (makes you pee) and cleans the kidneys and joints, which is helpful in arthritis.

BANANA: *Bananas* are best eaten when they show a few brown spots. They are loaded with vitamins A, B, G, and riboflavin, and the minerals potassium, magnesium, sodium, and chlorine. The minerals found in bananas replace the ones lost in diarrhea. Children with diarrhea will be able to keep up their weight and energy levels if they eat bananas. In Sri Lanka a cup of banana tree sap is given to a person who has been bitten by a venomous snake.

BASIL: *Basil* is used in Italian recipes, such as spaghetti sauce. It can be added to egg and cheese dishes and to fresh salads. It is easily grown in the garden. Basil tea is delicious when combined with a little fresh or dried mint or catnip leaf and honey. Basil tea is good for cold, flu, cramps, and bladder.

BEANS: The pods of *beans* (kidney beans, pinto beans, navy beans, green beans, snap beans, wax beans, etc.) have a lot of silica, which means they help strengthen internal organs. The pods are slightly diuretic, and they also help lower blood sugar levels.

BEETS: Did you know that you could eat *beets* raw? Grated raw beets and carrots can be served with a little lemon juice, olive oil, and sea salt. The green leaves can be steamed or lightly sautéed. Beets are loaded with vitamins A, B, C, and G along with plenty of blood building minerals.

CABBAGE: *Cabbage* is full of vitamins A, B, C, and U as well as calcium, iodine, potassium, chlorine, and sulfur. Cabbage is best eaten raw or as juice, not cooked. The outer leaves, which people often throw away, have the greatest concentrations of vitamins and calcium.

CARROT: *Carrots* are full of vitamin A, which is beneficial to the eyes, the lungs, and the skin. They also help build the immune system, which helps prevent diseases such as cancer. Everyone should eat raw carrots and carrot juice on a regular basis.

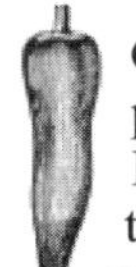

CAYENNE: *Cayenne pepper* is a very hot red powder that is often found on the kitchen shelf. It is used to make chili and curries and is added to Mexican dishes. It stops both internal and external bleeding.

CELERY: *Celery* has magnesium and iron, which strengthen blood cells. It also has elements of the B complex vitamins that help the nerves. Use it in juices mixed with carrot for flavor to help the nerves.

CHERRY: *Cherries* should be eaten raw, not canned. As with all pigmented foods, cherries help build the immune system. Cherries and all other berries should be eaten freely in summer when they are easily available.

CHIVES: *Chives* are a type of onion grass that is grown in the garden and used as a spice. They can be harvested, cut up with scissors, and stored in a plastic baggie in the freezer. One clump of chives can be harvested several times over the summer. They have vitamins C, A, B, and G and blood-building minerals such as sulfur and iron. Romanian Gypsies hang a bunch of chives, with their bulbs still attached, in the sick room to protect against "evil eye" and other catastrophes.

CINNAMON: *Cinnamon* is the fragrant inner bark of a tree that grows in Sri Lanka and other tropical areas. Ground cinnamon with milk is a good balancer after a heavy meal and aids digestion.

CITRUS FRUITS: Save the skins of carefully washed organic *grapefruits, lemons,* or *oranges* and cut them up. Add a teaspoon to a cup of freshly boiled water, steeping for 20 minutes. The tea will help with a cold. Try adding a little sage and mint to grapefruit rind tea to help break up a cold. *(IMPORTANT: Do not use commercially grown non-organic fruits for this purpose because the peels will be laden with pesticides.)*

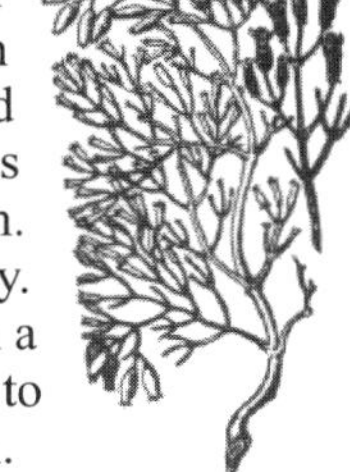

CLOVE: *Cloves* are actually the dried flower buds of a plant that grows in tropical areas. Cloves aid digestion and they are often stuck into foods, such as cooked apples and peaches and ham. Cloves can be used for aromatherapy. Place a few cloves in a vaporizer or in a dish of hot water placed on a radiator to fragrance the room.

CORIANDER: The ancient Egyptians and Greeks used *coriander* seeds for food and medicine. The ancient Romans brought them to Britain. The Chinese say the herb confers immortality. You can make coriander water to help with gas. Steep 2 teaspoonfuls in a cup of freshly boiled water for 10 minutes. Take ¼ cup four times a day.

CORN SILK: Did you know that the silky hairs found at the tip of a fresh ear of corn are actually good to eat? (Be sure to only use organic corn as standard commercial corn has been sprayed with pesticides.) Fresh corn silk can be eaten in salads and is very strengthening to the bladder and kidneys.

CRANBERRIES: *Cranberries* grow in bogs in New England. Being highly pigmented, they help build the immune system. Pigmented foods like red apples, red grapes, berries, red peppers, and tomatoes have the most bio-flavinoids.

CUMIN: *Cumin* is very healthy for pigeons and cures a pigeon disease known as "scabby back and breast." Take equal parts caraway, cumin, dill, and fennel seeds mixed with just enough flour and a little water so you can make little cakes. Bake the cakes in the oven until firm and feed them to the birds.

DATES: When camel caravans crossed the deserts in ancient times they often took only *dates,* almonds (which provide protein), and water with them for food. These things kept them going for months. Dates have calcium, which builds bone and muscle and strengthens the teeth and the nerves. They also have vitamins A, B, D, G, and minerals such as iron, chlorine, copper, magnesium, phosphorus, potassium, sulfur, and sodium.

DILL: *Dill* weed (the green leaves) and seeds are added to pickles, egg dishes, salmon, beans, cauliflower, cabbage, and peas. The seeds are the most potent part, medicinally. Take equal portions of dill seeds, anise seeds, and fennel seeds and use ½ teaspoon of seeds per cup of freshly boiled water; allow to steep for 20 minutes. This tea will help nausea, upset stomach, and gas.

FENNEL: According to Pliny, an ancient Roman herbalist and naturalist, snakes rub themselves against *fennel* stalks as they rub off their old skins. Hanging a bunch of fennel over the door on Midsummer Eve will repel evil (the herb St John's Wort will do the same thing; you can hang them together or alone). Add some fennel seeds to your bird's food. Fennel tea helps expel mucus.

FIG: Dried *figs,* dates, and other dried fruits should be eaten instead of candy. But be sure to brush your teeth afterwards because the sticky fruits will cling to your teeth, causing bacteria and cavities to grow. Fresh figs are slightly laxative. Do not eat too many or you can get diarrhea.

GARLIC: In ancient times when poor people had no access to doctors, *garlic* was one of the most important cure-alls. Garlic kills viruses and bacteria, heals infections, and removes parasites. Garlic has vitamins C, A, B, G, sulfur, iron, and calcium. It also has *allicin,* a chemical that kills germs such as *staphylococci.* (It can even kill some germs that penicillin can't, such as *bacillus paratyphoid.*) Of course, garlic also repels vampires and werewolves. Hang bunches around the house, windows, and doors.

GINGER: *Ginger* is a very warming spice. Add freshly grated ginger root to fish and chicken to remove toxins when you cook them. According to the Chinese, ginger "causes internal secretions to flow," meaning that it loosens phlegm and other internal liquids. Drink ginger tea with lemon and honey for a cold or the flu. Be careful not to overdo it, however. More than a cup a day can actually irritate the lungs. On a very cold day, eating some pieces of candied ginger will actually help keep you warm.

GRAPEFRUIT: *Grapefruit* is loaded with vitamin C, a vitamin that is not stored by the body and needs to be replenished daily. Did you know that the most vitamin C is actually in the white rind of the skin? The same is true of lemons and oranges.

LEMON: *Lemons* have vitamins C, B, F, P, and riboflavin as well as the minerals calcium, phosphorus, magnesium, potassium, and sulfur. Lemons are very important to prevent scurvy, a disease that sailors used to get because they were out at sea for along periods with no access to fresh fruits. In England there was once a law that every ship had to carry enough lemon or lime juice so that each sailor could drink one ounce a day after being at sea for ten days—which is why sailors were sometimes called "limeys."

LETTUCE: *Lettuce* leaves have vitamins C and A. The darker the lettuce, the more vitamins and minerals it will contain. Everyone should eat at least one salad a day.

MUSTARD: Did you know you could use powdered *mustard* to remove smells from old bottles and jars? Mix up a little dry mustard and water and fill the bottle or jar. Allow the liquid to sit in the bottle or jar for several hours, then rinse with very hot water.

OLIVE OIL: *Olive* oil is probably the healthiest oil for internal use; it benefits the heart by keeping cholesterol down. Use it in cooking and as a substitute for butter. In many countries people dip their bread into olive oil. You can also add a little chopped parsley, garlic, rosemary, or cilantro to flavor the oil.

ONION: *Onions* are antiseptic and loaded with vitamin C. For coughs, hoarseness, asthma, and colds, chop up a small, fresh onion and place in the blender with honey to make syrup. Take the syrup once every hour, in teaspoon doses. When there is sickness in the house, cut an onion in half and leave it in the sick room, replacing it daily. The onions used in this fashion should be burned or buried and never eaten, as they have become a magnet for germs.

ORANGE: As with grapefruits and lemons, *oranges* are loaded with vitamin C, but most of it is in the white rind just under the skin. Don't throw away your orange seeds! Plant them in a flowerpot, and when the trees are about three inches high you can snip the leaves and add them to salads.

PAPAYA: The Seminole Indians of Florida used fresh *papaya* leaves as a wound dressing. The leaves were also used to wrap meat to tenderize it. Modern meat tenderizers that you find in the supermarket are often made from dried papaya fruit and leaf. Papaya fruits are full of vitamins A, C, E, D, K, and also calcium, phosphorus, and iron. They also contain protein, citric, malic, and tartaric acids as well as sodium, potassium, and phosphoric acid, plus an abundance of natural sugar but no starch. They have enzymes that help the stomach to digest other foods. If eaten regularly on an empty stomach as a fruit or liquefied and then drunk, papaya helps rebuild the entire digestive tract. Try it if you have a hard time digesting things like onions, garlic, milk, or cheese.

PARSLEY: *Parsley* is sacred to the goddess Persephone and was used by the ancient Greeks in their funeral rites. They decorated tombs with wreaths of parsley and also used it to crown the winners in athletic contests. It was such a sacred plant that it was considered disrespectful to bring it to the table! Parsley leaves have large amounts of beta-carotene (water-soluble vitamin A) and vitamins C and B. They also contain trace minerals such as calcium, phosphorus, potassium, copper, iron, manganese, magnesium, sulfur, and iodine.

PARSNIP: *Parsnips* are root vegetables that look like white carrots. They are usually boiled with a little salt or placed in the pan when you roast a chicken. Cut up the roots along with carrots and arrange them along the sides of a roasting pan into which a chicken has been placed. Be sure to add a few inches of water. Parsnips have chlorine, iron, magnesium, phosphorus, potassium, sulfur, and silica. Parsnips help calm the nerves and strengthen the hair and nails.

PEPPER: In ancient times *black pepper* was very highly prized. For example, when Attila the Hun attacked Rome he demanded 3,000 pounds of it as a ransom to liberate the city! Black pepper taken internally is slightly laxative and aids digestion. It helps with nausea, gas, and diarrhea.

POMEGRANATE: *Pomegranate* juice is great to drink during the heat of Summer, and it can also be used to lower fevers. According to the prophet Mohamed, eating pomegranates purges anger and jealousy out of the system.

POTATO: When you eat *potatoes* always include the skin, as that is where the vitamins are. However, if the skin has turned green cut that section off or discard the potato, as it will then contain alkaloids, a type of poison. Did you know that potatoes are in the same family as deadly nightshade? If you mix potatoes and corn together it makes a complete protein. Potatoes have citric acid, which builds the immune system and repairs tissue, and the skins have vitamin K, which aids in blood clotting.

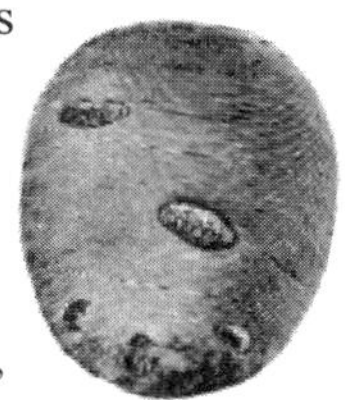

PUMPKIN SEEDS: Eating *pumpkin* seeds will help get worms out of your system. (Did you know that at any given time 80% of the human population has worms? We get them from walking around barefoot and from frequent contact with dogs, cats, and other animals.) You will need to fast from other foods while eating the seeds. Start on an empty stomach and eat a handful of seeds every hour for three hours. Chew the seeds thoroughly. You can also drink "pumpkin milk" at the same time, made by placing the seeds in the blender with cold water. Follow with a dose of castor oil to drive out the worms. Repeat the whole process if necessary. If you have a tapeworm be sure the whole thing comes out!

PRUNES: *Prunes* are actually dried plums. They are slightly laxative and should be eaten stewed by those who need help maintaining healthy bowel movements. (We all do from time to time!)

VINEGAR: *Vinegar* is an ancient and respected folk remedy for many conditions. Apple cider vinegar is an amazing aid to health. Many claim vinegar has magickal healing properties. As a daily tonic and cleanser, drink a glass of water with a teaspoon of honey and 3 tablespoons to ¼ cup of apple cider vinegar. Vinegar is also a great rinse for your hair (the smell goes away in a minute or two). To keep your cauldron clean, use vinegar to dissolve any crusty residue that may build up from use in burning. Vinegar is great for cleaning any metal ritual objects; rinse with clear water and wipe dry.

WATERCRESS: *Watercress* grows in streams. It is a valuable source of trace minerals and also helps clean the liver. By eating watercress and parsley often, you will get just about all the minerals available from land vegetables. Only seaweeds have more blood-building and tissue-nourishing trace elements. Watercress is used as a garnish and added to salads and egg dishes. Its leaves contain phosphorus, potassium, iron, manganese, fluorine, copper, sulfur, iodine, and zinc.

Lesson 3: Magickal Uses of Herbs

In addition to the above medicinal uses of herbs in healing and kitchen witchery, wortcunning includes the magickal uses of herbs for spells, amulets, talismans, and so on. Just as with gems and minerals, plants also have their own *prana,* or life force. Indeed, because they are living things, they each have a spirit unique to their species. Many feel, in fact, that Faeries are really plant spirits (sometimes called *devas*), who may be perceived in quasi-human forms as our minds interpret them.

For millennia, certain roots and herbs have been used in spells for the magickal qualities attributed to them. Many herbs and roots are used not only for their properties, but also because of their appearance. Mandrake root is used to gain power over others, but is most powerful if it is in the shape of a person. Mullein promotes gentleness partly because of its soft, fuzzy appearance. Magicians through the ages have concentrated on these various plant powers and have thus built up particular morphogenic fields around them. By working with the appropriate plants, you can tap into these fields and use them effectively for your own purposes.

Most of the roots and herbs listed below are activated by being carried on your person in a mojo bag. Sometimes, however, when they are meant to influence others (as in healing), you must put them onto the other person—or at least as near to them as you can. Most of them can also be ground into powder and burned as incense in a ritual (see below under "Incenses"). Always keep a strong intention in your mind when making up an herbal spell or charm. In making a charm for another, explain to them what each element is for. This will help them to understand and concentrate on the intent. You must also tell each herb or root exactly what you want it to do—creating a combined force of your own will with the spirit of the plant.

Many of these herbs and roots you will find only in botanicas or magickal herb stores. When using them,

Magickal Roots & Herbs

*** * * * !! CAUTION !! * * * ***

PLEASE NOTE THAT NONE OF THE HERBS OR HERB SPELLS MENTIONED IN THIS TABLE ARE MEANT FOR INTERNAL USE! DO NOT PUT THEM IN YOUR MOUTH!

AMARANTH (Cockscomb): To repair a broken heart.
ASAFOETIDA: For protection from disease.
BASIL, SACRED: To protect body and family.
BASIL, SWEET: To get rid of bad luck and attract love.
BAY: For wisdom, protection, and psychic powers.
BETHEL NUTS: To increase mental and spiritual powers.
BLOODROOT: To avert evil spells.
CATNIP: To make the most timid person fierce and powerful.
CEDAR: For purification and healing.
CHAMOMILE: To make others more susceptible to your thoughts and ideas and more willing to please you.
CINNAMON: For spirituality, healing, and cleansing.
CLOVE: For cleansing, protection, and money.
CLOVER: For money, love, and good luck (*especially* a 4-leaf clover!).
FIVE FINGER GRASS: To ward off evil by hand; protection from physical harm and violence.
GARLIC: For healing and protection (especially against vampires!).
GINSENG ROOT (Sang Root): Carried by Chinese as the strongest protection from all kinds of evil.
GINGER: For money, power, and success.
GREEN HELLEBORE: Purges the premises of evil influences.
HELPING HANDS: To help you with your plans and give you the help you need in any situation.
HIGH JOHN THE CONQUEROR: To keep away confusing thoughts and for success in business and love; attracts money.
JEZEBEL: To make your wishes come true.
LIFE EVERLASTING: For a long, happy, peaceful life.
LOVING HERBS: Bathe in a tea from the herbs and be met only with pleasantness wherever you go for the day.
LOW JOHN THE CONQUEROR: For good luck and success in all personal matters.
MANDRAKE ROOT: To gain power over others.
MARJORAM: To keep away evil influences; for protection, love, and healing.
MOJO BEANS: For good luck.
MUGWORT: Place inside your pillow to reveal your future in your dreams. Make dream pillows with mugwort, balsam, marjoram, rosemary, and lavender.
MULLEIN: To bring about gentleness in others.
MUSTARD SEEDS: For faith.
NIGHTSHADE: To see ghosts.
ORRIS ROOT: Powdered orris root brings love between two people if sprinkled on the clothes by one who desires the love. Also called *Queen Elizabeth root* and *fortune-teller root*, it was the original psychic pendulum. Tie a 13" long piece of white thread to the root and then ask "yes" or "no" questions while holding the end of the thread. The root will swing back and forth or circle for "yes;" for "no" it will remain motionless.
ROSEMARY: To improve your memory.
RUE: To keep from being deceived in love.
SAGE: For protection and wisdom.
SANDALWOOD: To enable you to see the true light in all things and not be deceived by others.
SMALLAGE ROOT: Rub it on a person who has been a bad influence for you to end all their power over you.
SOLOMON SEAL ROOT: To gain wisdom.
STAR ANISE: Carry as a special good luck charm.
ST. JOHN'S ROOT: Good for dieting; chew to keep from being hungry (it tastes like chocolate). Hang the plant over your bed to dream of your future mate.
THYME: For healing and to enhance psychic powers.
WILLOW: For love and divination.
WISHING BEANS: To make your wishes come true.

combine various ones according to your desires, but never put herbs with conflicting attributes in the same charm! Collect small jars and bottles for herbs at flea markets and yard sales. Make your own interesting labels for them, either hand-drawn or created on your computer. Eventually, you will assemble your own little collection of favorites.

Take another look at the tables of correspondence in 3.VI, and you will note that there are herbal correspondences listed for each Element, planet, sign, etc. These are the appropriate herbs to be used in incenses, oils, tinctures, sachets, and mojo bags for creating charms and spells relating to those purposes. Above is a chart showing the magickal correspondences of the herbs themselves.

Lesson 4. Potions & Philtres

"I don't expect you will really understand the beauty of the softly simmering cauldron with its shimmering fumes, the delicate power of liquids that creep through human veins, bewitching the mind, ensnaring the senses…I can teach you how to bottle fame, brew glory, even stopper death…"
(—Professor Snape in *Harry Potter & the Sorcerer's Stone,* by J.K. Rowlings, p. 137)

Potions are any kind of specially-prepared liquid brew intended to be drunk by the person they are meant to affect. All orally-administered medicines, for

Mandrake

example, are potions. So are teas, hot chocolate, and even poisons. A *bezoar* is an antidote to a poisonous potion. *Philtres* are "love potions" meant to cause one person to fall in love with another. These were very popular in the Middle Ages but are not much used in modern times, as they are highly unethical in cases where the person affected isn't told. However, there is a demand for such philtres (called *aphrodisiacs*) among couples whose passion has diminished and who wish to rekindle it. A philtre generally consists of wine or water infused with special herbs or other elements.

The most common philtre ingredient throughout history has been *mandragore,* the root of the mandrake, or "love apple." In America, the equivalent plant is the May apple. Vervain is also a popular herb for philtres, as is fennel, briony, damiana, fern seed, hemp, ginseng, or "dragon's blood" gum. Orange or ambergris may be added for flavor and aroma. Other traditional elements have included animal reproductive organs or fluids, musk, or a tincture made by steeping some hair of the intended object of affection. ***(Don't do this!)***

Tonics and Elixers are meant to cure ills or promote good health and longevity. They are generally prepared by *brewing* (simmering), or *steeping* (soaking). Use one large handful of herbs to one pint of water or wine (if you are soaking an herb in alcohol it is called a *tincture*). Leaves and flowers are steeped, never boiled; boiling drives off the volatile oils which carry many of the curative powers. For an *infusion* (steeping), bring the liquid to a boil, remove from heat, then add the herbs. Cover and allow to stand for 20 minutes. Strain and drink while still hot. Roots, barks and berries are simmered (*decocted*) on low heat for 20 minutes, then cooled and strained. You can store herbal infusions and decoctions for up to a week in the refrigerator, provided that after careful straining you put the tea into a glass jar with a tight lid and keep it away from light. See the instructions in Ellen Evert Hopman's Class on kitchen witchery.

Here are some traditional tonics:

Aquae Vitae ("water of life")

1 pint Wine (elderflower, elderberry, or plum)
1 sprig Rosemary *(Rosemarinus officinalis)*
1 spring Spearmint *(Mentha viridis)*
1 Bay leaf *(Laurus nobilis)*
1 tablespoon Honey
1 cup Milk

Heat wine to boiling, remove from heat, add herbs, cover and steep for 20 minutes. Strain and add honey and milk. Refrigerate 'til needed.

Aurum Potabile

("drinkable gold")

Basil *(Ocium basilicum)*
Balm *(Melissa officinalis)*
Heather honey to sweeten
Marigold *(Calendula officialis)*
Honeysuckle *(Lonicera periclymenum)*

Brew in 1 pint of spring water.

Lesson 5. Oils & Incenses

Pure Essences & Essential Oils

Oils and *essences* play an important role in various rituals and ceremonies. Sometimes mixed with roots, herbs, and resins to make incenses or dropped directly onto lit charcoal, oils and essences lend their fragrances to the rites. To bring about the proper vibrations in many tools, candles, talismans, and charms, magi often *anoint* (rub) them with appropriate oils and essences. Indeed, practitioners often anoint themselves as well. Used as a perfume, bath oil, or dressing, oils and essences can play a major role in all phases of your magickal work. Oils can also be used to draw invisible runes and sigils onto doors and other items for blessing and protection. Draw them with your fingertip and let them dry. Many crystal gazers feel they obtain best results if they keep their crystal ball or scrying mirror wrapped in a cloth that has been scented with various oils and essences.

Although both are pure and full strength, there is a definite difference between *oils* and *essences. Oils* are the pure extracts of various flowers or plants with an oil base, obtained by pressing or squeezing the flower or plant and then filtering the oil to clarity. *Essences* are made by first crushing or grinding the plant into powder or mush, and then placing the results in either ethyl alcohol or water, depending on which of those liquids will best extract the plant's fragrance and virtues. The small bits of plant remain in the liquid.

When making a magical oil, pack herbs or flowers tightly into a ½-pint bottle that is ¾ filled with virgin olive oil. The bottle is then tightly capped or stoppered and shaken daily. A fortified oil can be prepared by straining off the oil every fourth day and adding fresh herbs. The entire process takes about 2-3 weeks. At the end of that time, filter the oil with a cotton cloth, wringing out all the oil from the cloth, and put it up in a clean bottle with a nice label. Any remnants of the

Flowers Used in Oils and Essences

Almond—Hope.
Apple Blossom—Preference.
Balm of Gilead—Healing, help.
Bayberry—Cleansing.
Coriander—Hidden merit.
Gardenia—Ecstasy.
Heliotrope—Devotion.
Honeysuckle—Bond of love.
Hyssop—Purity, cleansing.
Jasmine—Grace, elegance.
Lemon—Discretion.
Lilac—Youth, new love.
Lily—Purity, modesty.
Lily of the Valley—Return of happiness.
Magnolia—Peerless, proud.
Mandrake—Power over others.
Mimosa—Sensitivity.
Mint—Virtue.
Myrrh—Purification, cleansing.
Myrtle—Love.
Olive—Peace.
Orange blossom—Generosity.
Passionflower—Susceptibility.
Patchouli—Attraction.
Pine—Eternity.
Rose—Beauty.
Rosemary—Revival of dreams.
Strawberry—Excellence, perfection.
Verbena—Sensibility.
Violet—Love, modesty, worth.

plants are discarded. To make a salve or ointment, the finely crushed herbs are blended into a fatty base, such as cold cream. The combination is usually 1 tablespoon of herbs to 3 ounces of cream.

In addition to the roots and herbs mentioned above, many kinds of flowers are used in making essential oils and essences, each with their own particular significance. I will list a few of these below.

Combinations

Once prepared, pure oils and essences may be combined for particular purposes, such as in making a potion for Love, Luck, Success, Protection, Prosperity, Purification, and all the rest. You can buy many such combined formulations at botanicas and magickal shops, and you can also make your own according to the correspondences listed here. In addition, *musk* and *civet* (from special glands of male deer and weasels) are common ingredients in these formulations, as in perfumes; they attract love. When consecrating or anointing, use a combination that either expresses your specific intentions, or is sacred to a specific force planet, deity, Element, sign, etc.

Here are a couple of examples of simple combination formulas:

Ritual Anointing Oil

1 part mint
1 part vervain

Ritual Consecrating Oil

1 part frankincense
1 part myrrh

To See Things Honestly

1 part hyssop
2 parts lily
2 parts myrrh

Incenses

To make incenses for various rituals, grind all the appropriate herbs and roots into a powder (a mortar and pestle is an essential tool for any herbalist!). Add just enough essential oil (or olive oil) to make the mixture stick together into a paste. Also a bit of gum resin may be added to help hold it together, and aid in burning. For planetary incenses, powder or filings of the associated metals may be added to the incense as well. A bit of saltpeter (an ingredient in charcoal blocks) will also aid in burning, adding little sparkles—good for Mars. There are also various *resins* (mostly tree saps) that are commonly used in incenses, and even added to combination formulas of oils:

Amber—Protection, healing, wealth.
Ambergris—Drawing, controlling others.
Dragon's blood—To activate a spell.
Frankincense—To consecrate an area, person, substance, or object.

Incenses for Psychic Work

(by Katlyn Breen)

The best incense to use when working with any scrying device is lunar or psychic in nature. These types of blends may be purchased or created by yourself and must be burned on self-igniting charcoal disks. Here are some excellent recipes for fine quality magickal incense to be used for psychic work:

Lunar Incense

A base of white sandalwood powder, orris root, and myrrh (in equal parts)
Oil of jasmine and jasmine flowers
Oil of lotus and ambergris (synthetic)
A small pinch of refined camphor
Poppy and cucumber seeds

Scrying Incense

A base of mastic gum, myrrh, sandalwood powder, and frankincense
Mugwort and wormwood herbs
Rose petals, lavender buds
Green cardamom pods and star Anise
Bay laurel leaves
Oil of mimosa and lotus

Class IV. Divination (Yellow)

The Wizard's power has come first of all from observation. Much magical lore is built on the fundamental belief that, if we can understand the flow of the energies of the Earth and how these energies work in harmony, we can gain enormous insight and power. Observing, among other things, the patterns of the weather, the migration patterns of birds and the behavior of people around him, has gained the Wizard—in the eyes of those focused only on the reality of day-to-day survival—the uncanny "magical" ability of being able to see into the future. In fact, the Wizard has often been doing little more than paying very close attention to the present.
—Anton & Mina Adams (*The World of Wizards*, p. 6)

1. Introduction: Seeing the Future

VERYTHING YOU DO IS DIVINELY Ordained.

Yes, this is true, a Great Truth. You are part of the Universal Mind, and everything you do is part of its workings. It is also true that everything you do is according to your independent will. It is important to balance these truths. To believe everything you do is the Divine Will without questioning or thinking for yourself is to go down a very dangerous road. Our planet is littered with ruins left behind by those who were sure the Divine Power was on their side no matter what they did, no matter how cruel or deranged. Any spiritual path can be twisted beyond recognition by fanatics, so be careful about becoming one.

The healthy Wizard always questions and double checks what is truly in accordance with both the Divine and the individual will. You will always need to be on the lookout for your own mistakes, ready to turn out to be wrong about something. Consult with trusted people and do divination, even when you are sure of your course and think you know all you need to. You can be sure the Elders contributing to this Grimoire continue to question their actions and beliefs, even after they have become accomplished Adepts.

Divination, or "far-seeing," is the art of foretelling or predicting the future or discovering things that are lost, hidden, or secret. Although not all seers were Wizards, all Wizards are expected to be seers. Many ancient peoples were completely obsessed with divination and would hardly make a move without consulting diviners, seers, oracles, or prophets. Unusual occurrences, such as disturbing dreams and *omens,* were also given divinatory meanings—this is where we get our word *ominous.* Over the ages, seers have devised many techniques of divination—the mantic arts (from *mantis,* meaning "diviner").

Lesson 2. The Mantic Arts

Hundreds of different divination systems have been invented over the ages—and even given Latin names. Most systems begin with a random distribution of elements, and then attempt to make some magickal sense out of them by finding patterns or matching them against a key. Here are brief descriptions of some of the more popular ones:

Aleuromancy (ah-LURE-oh-MAN-see) *(bread)*—Divination by selecting pieces of bread into which previously-written statements have been baked, as in fortune cookies.

Arithmancy (AIR-ith-MAN-see) *(numerology)*—Divination by numbers, in which words and numbers are reduced to a single digit with an assigned mystic meaning.

Bibliomancy (BIB-lee-oh-MAN-see) *(book)*—Divination by opening a sacred book at random and reading what's on the page.

Cartomancy (KAR-toe-MAN-see) *(card reading)*—Divination by cards, particularly the Tarot. But there are other decks of divination cards as well, and even standard playing cards can be used.

Catoptromancy (ka-TOP-troe-MAN-see) *(mirror gazing)*—Divination by moonlight reflected in a mirror or water to see images and visions.

Chiromancy (KY-roe-MAN-see) *(palmistry)*— Divining a person's fortune by examining their hands and the lines on the palms.

Cleromancy (KLARE-oh-MAN-see) *(rune casting)*—Divination by tossing markers, upon which symbolic letters have been inscribed.

Geomancy (JEE-oh-MAN-see) *(Earth)*—Divination by tossing sticks or bones on the ground and interpreting the patterns formed.

Horoscopy (HORE-oh-SCAH-pee) *(astrology)*—Divination by the stars and planets, commonly done by casting a *horoscope* ("observation of the hour").

I Ching (EE-JING) *(Book of Changes)*—A Chinese system of divination by casting sticks or coins to obtain any of 64 *Trigrams* (3-line figures), each with assigned meanings recorded in the book.

Oneiromancy (o-NY-roe-MAN-see) *(dreams)*—Divination by noting the elements of a dream and comparing them to an index.

Pyromancy (PY-roe-MAN-see) *(fire reading)*—Divination by the appearances of flames after throwing in certain powders.

Rhabdomancy (RAB-doe-MAN-see) *(dowsing)*—Divination with sticks or wands called divining rods, commonly Y-shaped.

Scrying (SKRY-ing) *(gazing)*—Divination by looking into water, a mirror, a crystal ball, etc. Crystal ball gazing has always been a favorite technique among Wizards.

Taseomancy (TAY-zee-oh-MAN-see) *(tea reading)*—Divination by examining the suggestive patterns of tea leaves left in the bottom of a cup and matching them with assigned meanings.

In addition, there are numerous techniques that are not, strictly speaking, divination, but rather intended to determine a person's character. Casting a natal horoscope can be used for this purpose, as well as palm reading. Some other approaches are:

Graphology (gra-FOL-oh-gee, *handwriting analysis)*—Determining a person's character by analyzing their handwriting.

Phrenology (fre-NOL-oh-gee, *head)*—Interpreting a person's character by analyzing the shape and lumpiness of their skull.

Physiognomy (FIZ-ee-AH-no-mee, *appearance)*—Interpreting a person's character by analyzing their facial and bodily features.

Lesson 3: Augury (Reading Omens)

Rather than doing something and then interpreting or "reading" the results, as in most of the above-listed mantic arts, *augury* involves interpreting spontaneous occurrences and events in Nature, such as the shapes of clouds or the flight of birds. These are called *omens* ("signs"), and to say that something seems *ominous* is to say "the signs look bad."

Birds in particular have captured the attention and imagination of people throughout history, for their miraculous power of flight. The word *auspice,* another word for omen, derives from a Latin word meaning "observer of birds." In *ornithomancy* (or-NITH-o-man-see, "bird divination") the type of bird, how high it flies, the direction of flight, and whether or not it sings in the air are all considered. Some species are "naturally propitious," others are invariably "of ill omen," and the significance of certain birds depends upon circumstances and the person by whom they are seen.

Flight is especially important. A bird flying high with outstretched wings is a favorable sign; one that flies low with irregular wing-beats is unfavorable. If a bird appears to the right (East) of someone facing North, that is a good sign; and the contrary if it appears to the West (left—*sinister* originally simply meant "left"). A bird's song is judged according to its volume and frequency. Even the feathers of birds that may be dropped and found have significance. All birds—particularly birds of prey—are capable of providing portents, and eventually the very word for bird (*ornis*) came to mean "portent." Four species above all are esteemed for their prophetic significance: the eagle and vulture of Zeus, Apollo's raven, and Hera's crow.

A Few Forms of Augury

Aeromancy (AIR-oh-MAN-see) *(air)*—Interpreting events in the air and sky, such as clouds, fog, rainbows, etc.

Apanthomancy (ah-PAN-tho-MAN-see) *(animals)*—Interpreting random encounters with animals, as a black cat meaning bad luck.

Austromancy (AW-stro-MAN-see) *(wind)*—Interpreting the force and directions of wind.

Capnomancy (KAP-no-MAN-see) *(smoke)*—Interpreting patterns of smoke rising from a fire.

Ceraunoscopy (seh-RON-oh-SCO-pee) *(thunder)* —Interpreting thunder and lightning.

Hydromancy (HY-dro-MAN-see) *(water)*—Interpreting water, including movement, color, tides, and ripples.

Meteoromancy (ME-tee-OR-oh-MAN-see) *(meteors)*—Interpreting meteors by their direction, brightness, and the constellations in which they appear.

Ornithomancy (or-NITH-oh-MAN-see) *(birds)* —Interpreting the flight, calls, etc. of birds.

Xylomancy (ZY-low-MAN-see) *(wood)*—Interpreting found pieces of wood by shape, size, and flammability.

Traditional Augury Lore

Aeromancy *(air and sky):*

(The critical times for observation are sunrise and sunset.)

"Red sky at morning, sailors take warning; red sky at night, sailor's delight."

A hazy sun in the morning is the forerunner of a damp afternoon.

High fluffy clouds over the sky with a West wind portend fair weather.

Gray-yellow clouds, or murky vaporous ones that

thicken, portend a storm, especially with an East wind or a hazy Sun.

Clouds with harsh, defined edges mean gusty days.

High clouds crossing in a different direction from low ones indicates a change in bearing for the wind.

Heavy dew indicates dry weather to come.

If mist rises off the dew in the early morning, it means a fine day is to come.

If there is heavy dew at the end of a Spring day, the next day will be clear.

If there is fog in the morning, the afternoon will be warm and clear.

A rainbow around the Moon is a sign of very harsh weather soon to come.

If smoke from a chimney rises straight up into the air, the day will be clear.

Austromancy *(wind):*

The best time for fishing is when the wind is coming from the West or South.

The North wind brings cool, dry weather; the South wind, warm and damp.

From the East comes the veering wind, blowing in the same direction as the sun's course. A veering wind is purifying.

The West wind is called the backing wind because it moves against the course of the sun. This wind is supportive, erasing negativity and renewing confidence. *"May the wind be always at your back!"* (Irish blessing)

West winds are connected with Water and intuition.

North winds are associated with Earth and blessing or support.

South winds bring Fire and energy.

East winds are symbolic of creativity.

Here is a little verse about the four seasonal winds:

Heed the North wind's mighty gale;
Lock the door and drop the sail.
When the wind comes from the South,
Love will kiss thee on the mouth.
When the wind blows from the East,
Expect the new and set the feast.
When the West wind blows o'er thee,
Departed spirits restless be.

Ornithomancy *(birds):*

Seeing a bluebird in Spring foretells joy.

Seeing a red bird means that company will soon arrive.

A robin pecking on a window means a baby is about to be conceived by someone inside.

If you hear an owl hoot three times, or see one flying near you, it is time to check your behavior and motivation.

Hissing geese, loud hens, crying peacocks, doves cooing late in the evening, swallows flying low on the water, and birds weaving "baskets" in the air are all signs of coming rain.

Meeting a raven before a battle foretells victory.

A crow's call from the West means a great wind is soon to come.

A crow's call from the Southwest is a sign of unexpected profit.
A crow's call from the Southeast means an enemy is coming.
The following English verse applies to magpies seen together:

One is for sorrow, Two is for mirth;
Three for a wedding and Four for a birth;
Five is for silver, Six is for gold;
Seven's a secret to never be told.

And here's a similar one for crows, from Morning Glory's Mississippi grandmother:

One is for sorrow and Two is for joy,
Three's for a letter and Four for a boy.
Five is for sunshine and Six is for rain,
Seven is loss and Eight is a gain.
Nine is for friendship and Ten's for a home,
Eleven's for dreaming and Twelve is to roam.
And 13's the death bird who's always alone.

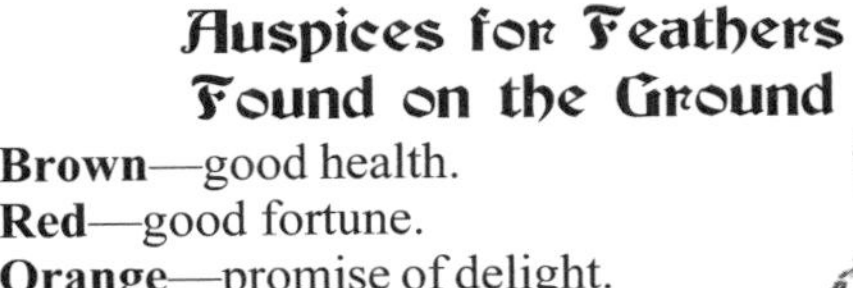

Brown—good health.
Red—good fortune.
Orange—promise of delight.
Yellow—be wary of false friends.
Green—adventure.
Blue—love.
Purple—an exciting trip.
Black—death or bad news.
Gray—peace.
Brown & White—joy.
Black & White—trouble averted.
Black & Green—fame and fortune.
Black & Blue or White—new love.
Gray & White—a wish coming true.

The Earth Oracle

—by Katlyn

Think of a question to which you most need an answer. Try to formulate it carefully. The wording of the question can be very important. Write it down once you have decided what to ask. There is a reason for everything in this meditation.

Take your question to the Oracle of Earth. Walk in the surrounding woods alone and be aware of every sign. There your answer lies. Each breeze or flight of a bird can speak to you. Each cloud may contain a vision, each stone a lesson. Walk with inner guidance, turning at will. Feel things pull you that need to become your oracle. Everything has meaning if there are ears and eyes to sense and a heart to receive it. Write down all you experience in your journal; there may be things that will become clear at a later time. If you find a token, then that will be a symbol of your answer.

Lesson 4. Horoscopy (Astrology)

Astrology is the art of interpreting and predicting the influences of the heavens—the real and apparent movements of the stars and planets. It has been practiced at least since the times of the ancient Sumerians (2900-1800 BCE) and is found throughout the world. Astrology assumes that the vast energies of the cosmos are projected upon the Earth, influencing all things. Events occurring in the heavens are mirrored by events on Earth, as in the prime hermetic axiom, "As above, so below."

The Sumerians, creators of the earliest human civilization, needed to measure yearly time to keep track of religious festivals and seasons for planting and harvest. To do this, they invented the calendar, which they divided into twelve months based on the cycles of the Moon. This led them to develop a complicated knowledge of astronomy and the invention of the Zodiac. I have explained the Zodiac in more detail in 3.VI.6: "Months & Signs of the Zodiac," especially in the table of correspondences for the Zodiac.

Horoscopy is the branch of astrology specifically related to casting and interpreting circular charts, or *horoscopes* ("view of the hour") based on the positions of the Planets (including the Sun and Moon) among the Signs of the Zodiac at particular times—such as the moment of one's birth. In any horoscope, the subject occupies the position in the center of the circle.

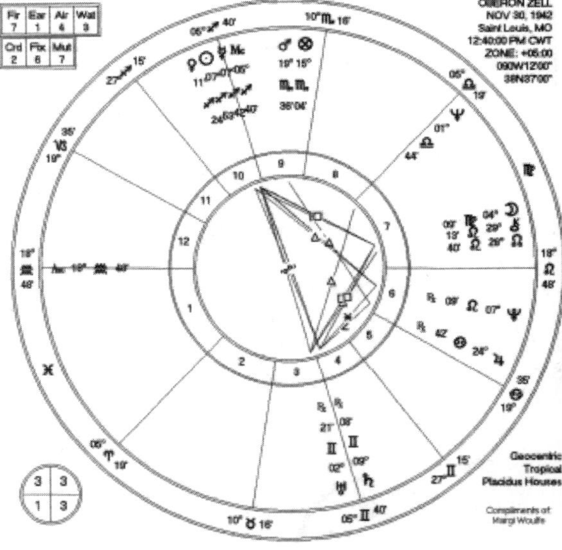

There are tables called *ephemerides* that list the precise positions of the stars and planets for any given date and time, and these are used by astrologers for calculating everything in a horoscope. But how to cast a horoscope is far too complicated for me to try to explain here. Moreover, you can get computer programs that will do it for you with no fuss or calculations! What I offer here is a little introduction of what a horoscope is, and how to understand it.

Each sign of the Zodiac has certain associated *attributes* (assigned qualities), which influence the planets appearing in those signs at a given time. The planets themselves have attributes, as do the times of day, and the combination of all these factors in a horoscope gives the reading for a person or event at the designated time. A horoscope is arranged just like a clock face, but starting at 9:00 and going counter-clockwise, and each of the 12 hours is called a *house.* These represent the areas of your life and concerns. The positions and attributes of the 12 **Houses** are as follows:

First (Ascendant) (9-8:00)—Appearance, identity, personality, physical body, health.
Second (8-7:00)—Money, material possessions, tools.
Third (7-6:00)—Sibling relationships, education, communication.
Fourth (6-5:00)—Parental home, family, heredity, domesticity, security.
Fifth (5-4:00)—Romance, creativity, sexuality, children, pleasure, risks.
Sixth (4-3:00)—Daily routine, service, career, health.
Seventh (3-2:00)—Community, partnerships, marriage, open enemies.
Eighth (2-1:00)—Accidents, death, cycles, inheritances, passion, soul.
Ninth (1-12:00)—Spirituality, philosophy, religion, education, travels.
Tenth (12-11:00)—Vocation, profession, fame, achievement, ambitions.
Eleventh (11-10:00)—Wishes, hopes, goals, friendships, social life.
Twelfth (10-9:00)—Sacrifice, solitude, privacy, unconscious, secret enemies.

The 12 signs are matched up with the 12 houses according to which sign is rising on the eastern celestial horizon at the designated time of day. This is called the *ascendant,* and it is noted at the "9:00-10:00" position on the horoscope—the 1st house. Then all the other signs follow clockwise around the circle, one per house. Here are some of the attributes of the various **signs,** as applied to personal qualities:

♈ **Aries**: Courage, impulsiveness, energy. Pioneer, leader, competitor.
♉ **Taurus**: Patience, persistence, obstinacy. Earthy, stable, practical.
♊ **Gemini**: Progressiveness, cleverness, instability. Dual, lively, versatile.
♋ **Cancer**: Inspiration, sensitivity, evasiveness. Protective, traditional.
♌ **Leo**: Dignity, power, vanity. Dramatic, flamboyant, broad-minded, warm.
♍ **Virgo**: Reason, logic, exactitude. Conscientious, analytical, meticulous.
♎ **Libra**: Harmony, evaluation, trivialities. Refined, fair, just, sociable.
♏ **Scorpio**: Profundity, insistence, roughness. Intense, secretive, ambitious.
♐ **Sagittarius**: Justice, propriety, sophistry (cleverness). Friendly, expansive.
♑ **Capricorn**: Independence, abstraction, stubbornness. Cautious, materialistic.
♒ **Aquarius**: Spirituality, conviction, illusion. Inquisitive, unpredictable.
♓ **Pisces**: Compassion, tolerance, imagination, laziness. Responsive, dependent.

There are 30° in each sign, and the positions of the planets within each sign at the moment the horoscope is drawn for are indicated by degrees. So, you might say that someone has their *natal* (birth) Mars at 12.4° Aquarius, in the 7th house.

The attributes of all the **Planets** are as follows:

☉ **Sun** *(Birth Sign):* Physical body, psychic energy, ego, identity, the male principle.
☽ **Moon:** Soul, emotions, memories, personality, change and fluctuation, female principle.
☿ **Mercury:** Intelligence, reason, skills, movement, connections, communication.
♀ **Venus:** Love, physical attraction, pleasures, the arts, sentimentality.
♂ **Mars:** Action, energy, impulsion, aggressiveness, challenges, sports.
♃ **Jupiter:** Expansion, wealth (material or spiritual), health, humor, happiness.
♄ **Saturn:** Limitation, concentration, inhibition, separation, maturity, responsibility, death.
♅ **Uranus:** Suddenness, originality, creativity, progress, science, magick, transmutation.
♆ **Neptune:** Susceptibility, fantasy, dreams, inspiration, illusions, mysticism, deception.
♇ **Pluto:** Power, dictatorship, politics, rebirth, renewal, resources.

Lines drawn between any 2 or more planets in a horoscope are considered significant if they form certain angles. These angular relationships are called *aspects. Conjunctions* (0°) and *oppositions* (180°) can be either good or bad, according to the planets concerned. Conjunctions increase the mutual influence of the planets, and oppositions cancel them out. If the angle between two planets is 90° *(square)* or 45° *(semi-square),* it is considered to be an unfortunate or difficult aspect. Angles of 120° *(trine)* and 60° *(sextile)* are considered fortunate aspects.

In a horoscope, then, all the above attributions and aspects are taken into consideration together. The first and most important thing is usually your *Sun sign* (that is, the Sign your Sun is in). The *rising sign* (the Sign in the ascendant position) is next in importance. Then your Moon, and the rest of the planets in the above order. So I would say, for instance, that my Sun is in Sagittarius, my rising sign is Aquarius, my Moon is in Virgo, my Mercury and Venus are in Sagittarius, etc. And the interpretation of my horoscope would be based on the attributions of those planets, in those signs, in those houses—plus their aspects.

There are a number of other factors that increase the complexity of horoscopes, but I won't try and go into them here. For more information, check out a book on astrology.

Lesson 5. The Tarot

The *Tarot* is a set of 78 special playing cards with particular symbolic images, used in divination. Although many believe the Tarot to be of ancient origin, there is no record of these cards before the 14th century, when they first appeared in Italy. Ever since, a knowledge of the Tarot has been considered essential for any Wizard. There are many, many different Tarot decks available. You should visit a store that sells them, and spend some time looking through various decks until you find one you especially like. The basic meanings are fairly universal, but some will have their own variations. Each deck comes with its own little booklet, explaining the symbolic meanings of all the cards in the deck. Study these until you can recognize them readily, and practice doing readings for yourself before you begin doing them for others.

The "Great Pack" of the Tarot consists of two sets of cards: the *Major Arcana* (22 cards) and the *Minor Arcana* (56 cards). The Minor Arcana is almost identical to a regular poker deck of playing cards which is derived from it, consisting of four Elemental *suits* (*swords, wands/rods, cups, pentacles/disks*—corresponding with spades, clubs, hearts, and diamonds). Each suit has ten numbered cards, plus four *court cards* (*Page, Knight, Queen,* and *King.* A poker deck has only three court cards: Jack, Queen, and King.)

The **suits** are associated with those aspects of human life that fall into the Elemental categories. They are:

♠ **Swords** *(Fire):* Political concerns, will, power, dominance, struggle.
♣ **Wands** *(Air):* Spiritual concerns, intellect, learning, career, honor.
♥ **Cups** *(Water):* Emotional concerns, love, relationships, friends, family, home.
♦ **Pentacles** *(Earth):* Material concerns, wealth, health, property, security.

The numbered and Court cards of each Suit also have their own significance, which are paralleled but unique according to the suit. Within each suit, these are:

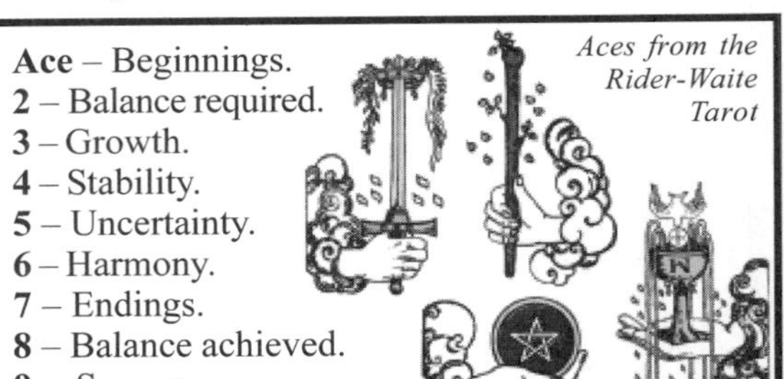
Aces from the Rider-Waite Tarot

Ace – Beginnings.
2 – Balance required.
3 – Growth.
4 – Stability.
5 – Uncertainty.
6 – Harmony.
7 – Endings.
8 – Balance achieved.
9 – Success.
10 – Completion.
Page – A youth affecting you, or a bringer of news.
Knight – Ambitious person, or bringer of change.
Queen – An important woman supporting your ambitions.
King – A dominant man affecting your pursuits.

The Major Arcana are also called the *Trumps.* These contain the symbolic pictures most commonly identified with tarot cards. These are numbered in a specific order, with established names and meanings, and are by far the most powerful cards in a reading. They also have astrological correspondences with signs and planets, letters of the Hebrew alphabet, sephiroth, and many other symbols. Here are the **Major Arcana**, with a very brief indication of their meanings:

0. The Fool Starting out on a new venture.

1. The Magician ☿ Gaining positive guidance & mentorship.

2. The High Priestess ♍ Gaining esoteric knowledge.

3. Empress ♎ Experiencing growth, fertility, increased creativity.

4. Emperor ♏ Needing to take responsibility & exercise discipline.

5. The High Priest ♃ Gaining spiritual wisdom.

6. The Lovers ♀
Experiencing choice & love.

7. The Chariot ♐
Finding your direction in life.

8. Justice ♑
Needing to consider a decision carefully.

9. The Hermit ♒
Needing to withdraw to solve a problem.

10. Wheel of Fortune ♅
Allowing things to take their course.

11. Strength ♆
Needing determination & persistence.

12. Hanged Man ♓
Needing self-sacrifice before change can occur.

13. Death ♈
Experiencing transition & change.

14. Temperance ♉
Needing harmony & time for healing.

15. The Devil ♄
Experiencing the effects of pride & arrogance.

16. The Tower ♂
Experiencing a major upheaval in your life.

17. The Star ♊
Experiencing hope & optimism.

18. The Moon ♋
Relying on intuition rather than reason.

19. The Sun ♌
Finding fulfillment.

20. Judgement ☽
Experiencing a rebirth in ideas or development.

21. The World ☉
Finding ultimate success.

(Cards shown are from the French Tarot of Marseilles)

Going through the Major Arcana in order can be seen as the Journey towards Enlightenment, as in the classical "Hero's Journey." The hero, of course, is The Fool (identical to the Joker in a poker deck) and, like the Joker, his number is outside of the rest of the sequence, and he can appear at either end, as either the first Trump, or the 22nd. Major Arcana are considered far more significant than Minor Arcana, and the number of Major Arcana in a reading is an indication of how powerful the reading is.

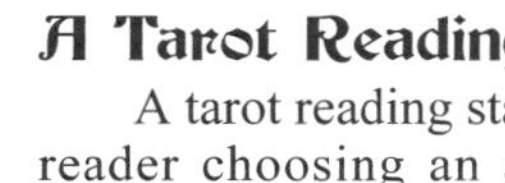

A Tarot Reading

A tarot reading starts with the reader choosing an appropriate court card to represent the *querant* (the person for whom the reading is being done) and laying it face up on the table. This is called the *significator.* The querant then shuffles the remaining cards while concentrating on their question. Then they *cut* the deck (take off a top portion and place the lower batch on top). The reader deals out one card at a time, laying them face up on the table in a particular arrangement, or *spread.* Like the houses of a horoscope, each position imparts its own significance to the card placed in it. Each card is then interpreted not only by its own meaning, but also by its position in the reading. When you do a reading for someone, you lay down a card, saying, "This is the card of the Future; this is what lies before you…, etc." There are a number of spreads used, depending on the preference of the reader, but the most common is called the *Celtic Cross.*

Here is the layout for the **Celtic Cross,** with each position listed in the order in which a card is placed in it.

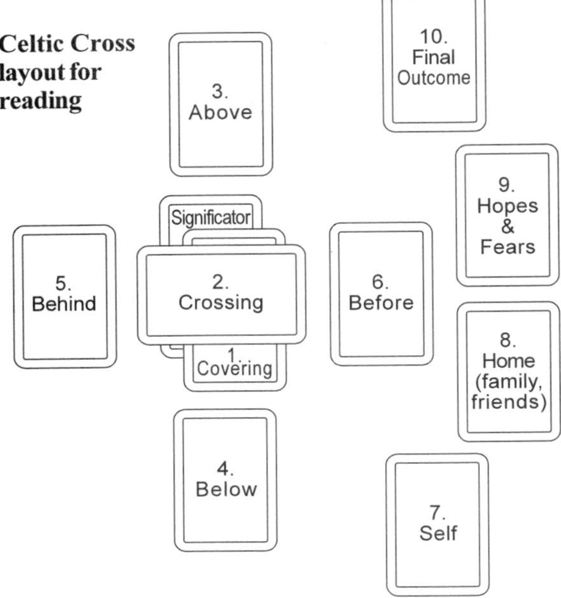

Celtic Cross layout for reading

0. **Significator:** the querant ("you").
1. **Covering:** what the reading is about.
2. **Crossing:** what crosses (or opposes) you.
3. **Above:** what crowns you (conscious).
4. **Below:** what is beneath you (unconscious).
5. **Behind:** what lies behind you (past).
6. **Before:** what lies before you (future).
7. **Self:** yourself in this context.
8. **Home:** your family & friends.
9. **Hopes & Fears:** what you either hope or fear.
10. **Final Outcome:** Conclusion and summation.

Lesson 6. Runestones & Oracle Stones

Oracle Stones

Oracle Stones are one of the simplest forms of divination, and require the least effort. When you are out and about—especially at the seashore or along riverbanks—keep your eyes open for small, pretty stones. To collect a set of oracle stones, you will need one white, one black, and one red stone—all gathered in the same area on the same day. All three should fit comfortably together in one hand. They should be smooth and polished, not rough or sharp. I have found such stones on beaches of America's East and West coasts, in Australia, Europe, and along riverbanks from the Colorado to the Mississippi, so I know they're out there. But if you happen to live someplace where there are no natural stones (such as Florida or the Great Plains), you can always buy them in a rock shop.

Here's how they work: Hold them in your non-writing hand and shake them up together while asking a question. The question must be one that can be answered by either "yes" or "no." Then toss the stones down together. The white one stands for "yes" and the black one for "no." The red one is the indicator—whichever one it lands closest to gives you the answer. The closer the red stone is to the other, the stronger the answer. You can also use these stones for the kind of choices you might otherwise toss a coin for—just choose "black or white" instead of "heads or tails."

Runestones

Cleromancy is divination by tossing markers upon which symbolic letters have been inscribed. The most popular system uses the *Runes* ("mysteries"), an ancient alphabet of the Teutonic peoples of Northern Europe—Scandinavians, Continental Germans and Anglo-Saxons. Although many of the rune-forms may have been inspired by early Mediterranean alphabets, others seem to come from early pictographs representing forces and things of Nature. Legend says that they were originally revealed to the Norse god Odin as he hung on the great World-Tree *Yggdrasil.*

There are several different sets of Runes—all very similar—but the most common is the *Elder FUThARK,* which takes its name from its first six letters: ᚠᚢᚦᚨᚱᚲ. This system was most widely used between 200 BCE and 900 CE. It contains 24 runestaves, divided into three groups of eight. Here is the old Germanic version of the FUThARK, with divinatory meanings:

FREYA'S ÆTT

F ᚠ *Fehu* (cattle)—Wealth, fertility, love, abundance. Hope, success, and happiness.

U ᚢ *Uruz* (aurochs/wild ox)—Energy, health, courage, strength. Opportunity for advancement.

Th ᚦ ***Thurisaz*** (thorn, giant)—Force, attack or defense. Conflict, destruction, change.

A ᚨ *Ansuz* (Odin, mouth)—Communication, insight, intelligence. A revealing message or gift.

R ᚱ *Raidho* (wagon, chariot)—Travel, journey. A vacation or relocation. Making the right move.

K ᚲ *Kenaz* (torch, beacon)—Creative energy, purifying force. Power to create your own reality.

G ᚷ *Gebo* (gift)—A gift, exchange of energy. Sacrifice and generosity. Contracts, partnerships.

W ᚹ *Wunjo* (joy)—Happiness, comfort, fellowship, blessedness. Prosperity, success, reward.

HAGALL'S ÆTT

H ᚺ *Hagalaz* (hail)—Disruption, change for good or ill. Wrath of Nature. Testing, trial.

N ᚾ *Naudhiz* (need)—Distress, necessity, fate. Endurance, survival, determination. Be patient.

I ᛁ *Isa* (ice)—Cold, stasis, stillness. Challenge, frustration. Cool off, turn inward, seek clarity.

J ᛃ *Jera* (year, good harvest)—Completion, cycles, growth, balance. Promise of earned success.

Ei ᛇ *Eihwaz* (yew tree)—Strength, endurance, protection. Acquisition as sense of purpose.

P ᛈ *Perthro* (dice cup, vagina) —Occult secrets, initiation, divination, fate, feminine mysteries.
Z ᛉ *Algiz* (elk) —Protection, shield, shelter, guardian. Warding off evil. Follow your instincts.
S ᛊ *Sowilo* (sun) —Success, honor, victory, health. Cleansing fire. Power for positive changes.

TIR'S ÆTT

T ᛏ *Tiwaz* (Tyr, war god) —Honor, justice, authority. Victory in competition or legal matters.
B ᛒ *Berkano* (birch tree) —Birth, mothering, fertility. Regeneration and personal growth.
E ᛖ *Ehwaz* (horse) —Transportation and progress by any means. Partnership, trust, loyalty.
M ᛗ *Mannaz* (humanity) —Social relationships, human potential. Receive aid and cooperation.
L ᛚ *Laguz* (water, leak) —Dreams, imagination, psychic matters. Healing power of renewal.
NG ᛜ *Ingwaz* (Earth god Ing) —Male fertility, common sense, simple strengths, family, home.
D ᛞ *Dagaz* (day, dawn) —Awakening, transformation, clarity. Time to begin something new.
O ᛟ *Othala* (ancestral property) —Heritage, home, possessions, safety, fundamental values.

Runestones are made by engraving or painting the runes on identical small, flat stones—such as those used in the game of *Go.* (Note that there is a 25th stone that is blank, representing Fate.) These stones are then kept in a little bag or pouch. You can make your own or buy a set in any magick store and many bookstores; they will come with a booklet of explanations and interpretations. When you have a question for them, simply reach into the bag and draw forth one, three, or five stones.

A one-stone reading is good to do each morning, asking "What will today be like?"

A three-stone reading is the most popular: read the stones in order as 1. the **problem,** 2. what **course** to take, and 3. the **outcome** (if you follow that course).

For a five-stone reading, select 1. **past,** 2. **present,** 3. **future,** 4. **help** that's coming, and 5. what **aspects** of the problem cannot be changed and must be accepted.

A more complicated method is to shake up the bag, and them dump the stones out onto a cloth. The ones that land rightside-up give the reading, according to how they are arranged and grouped.

Lesson 7. Chiromancy (Palmistry)

Chiromancers, or palm readers, study the lines in the palms of people's hands to divine their health, character, future, and fortune. Chiromancy was known in ancient India, China, Tibet, Persia, Mesopotamia, and Egypt. The art reached Greece around 500 BCE and was practiced by Anaxagoras (500-428 BCE). Aristotle (384-322 BCE) taught it to Alexander the Great and Hippocrates (the "Father of Medicine"). Banned in the Middle Ages by the Catholic Church, palmistry continued to be practiced by Gypsies. Its popular revival in modern times was a result of Sir Francis Galton's 1885 discovery that each person's fingerprints are unique.

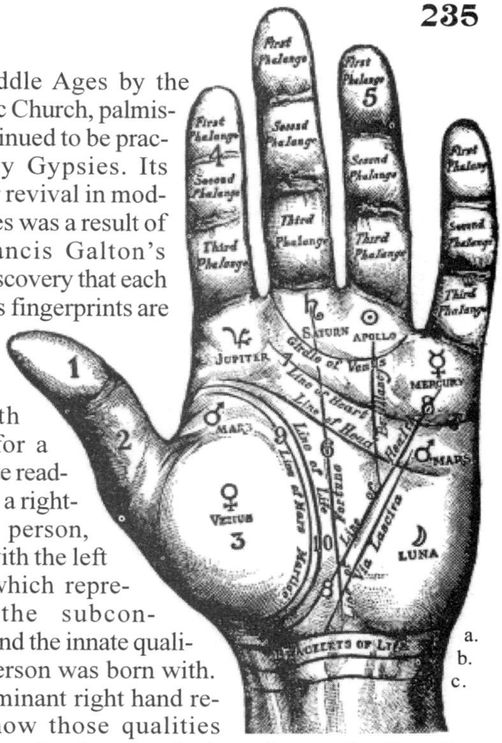

Examine both hands for a complete reading. For a right-handed person, begin with the left hand, which represents the subconscious and the innate qualities a person was born with. The dominant right hand reveals how those qualities have been developed and where they are leading. For a left-handed person, this is reversed.

In a standard palm reading, the *mounts* (fleshy mounds) of the palm are examined first, followed by the three major lines, in order: *life line, head line,* and *heart line* (see illustration). After that, compare the other lines, features, and patterns according to the keys in any book on palmistry. Lines are read starting at the finger end, and going towards the wrist. Squeeze the hand together a bit to accentuate the creases, and trace the lines with your fingertip. Generally, the longer and more distinct the line, the stronger its attributes. Broken lines and branchings influence the meanings, and lines touching or crossing each other are also affected.

Each of the mounts is identified with a planet, in the following clockwise order from the base of the thumb. Their relative prominence indicates those planetary influences. If a principal line originates in a mount, it carries that influence. Here are the **Mounts:**

Venus ♀: Love, instincts, vitality, sensuality, fecundity, bounty. One who appreciates and loves life.
Jupiter ♃: Religion, philosophy, ambition, leadership.
Saturn ♄: Stolidity, resignation, skepticism.
Apollo (Sun) ☉: Artistry, exhibitionism, success, fantasy. Love and appreciation of art and beauty.
Mercury ☿: Communication, teaching, writing.
Mars ♂: Aggression, courage, fidelity, strength.
Luna (Moon) ☽: Imagination, instability, clairvoyance.

And here are the **Principal Lines:**

1. **Life Line:** General constitution, vitality, lifespan, destiny. If broken, may indicate drastic changes.

2. **Head Line:** Intellectual capacities.
3. **Heart Line:** Sentiments, feelings, emotions, love, and romantic relationships.
4. **Fate** or **Destiny Line:** Pattern of life—compare with life line. Splits may indicate career changes.
5. **Apollo** or **Sun Line:** Artistic ability, chances of success. If visible, it typically bodes good fortune.
6. **Intuition Line:** Insight, intuition, psychic ability.

The **Secondary Lines** are:

7. **Girdle of Venus:** Passions, emotional sensitivity.
8. **Ring of Solomon:** Leadership, power to govern.
9. **Lines of Union:** Marriage, children.
10. **Martian Lines:** Personal triumph, glory in battle.
11. **Travel Lines:** Journeys, discoveries.
12. **Mercury** or **Health Lines:** Bodily, mental, and spiritual well-being. If broken, indicates ill health.
13. **Three Bracelets:** a. Health, b. Wealth, c. Happiness.

This is only a brief introduction to chiromancy. As with all these systems of divination, there is far more involved than I can explain here. If you are interested in studying and practicing palmistry, the classic books are Cheiro's *Language of the Hand* and Fred Gettings' *The Book of the Hand.*

Lesson 8. Scrying

Scrying ("seeing") is the art of gazing into a transparent medium with a reflective surface and seeing ("descrying") visions: *"Things that were, and things that are, and things that yet may be…"* (Galadriel, from *The Fellowship of the Ring*). Scrying with water (as in Galadriel's Mirror) is properly called *hydromancy;* mirror scrying is *catoptromancy.* And crystal gazing is called *crystallomancy.* Polished quartz crystals have been used for scrying all over the world since ancient times. Such crystals were found in the 8,000-year-old ruins of the Temple of Hathor in Egypt. In Roman Europe, small crystal balls were used by the Franks and Saxons. However, mirrors and water were the common mediums for scrying during the Middle Ages.

Crystal balls came into widespread use among Wizards from the time of John Dee (1527-1608), court Wizard to Queen Elizabeth I, who used an egg-sized "shew-stone." By the 19th century, crystallomancy had become firmly established as one of the most popular forms of fortune-telling, ranking alongside astrology, palmistry, tarot, and taseomancy. The largest pure quartz crystal ball known was displayed at the 1904 World's Fair. It was 18" in diameter!

In 3.II.8: "The Speculum, or Magick Mirror," I gave you instructions for creating a magick scrying mirror. Now, here are the instructions for how to use it:

The Black Scrying Mirror

—by Katlyn Breene

The *black scrying mirror,* or magick mirror (also called *speculum*) is a powerful psychic tool. History shows its use in many of the traditional Mystery schools and oracular temples. Today the serious student of magickal arts can rediscover the ancient rites of the magick mirror for these positive techniques are again coming to light.

Scrying can be defined as the mantic art of gazing into or upon a crystal or dark mirror, allowing the physical eyes to relax, thus letting the inner psychic eyes begin to open and receive desired visions or information. The use of the black mirror is felt to be one of the best methods of achieving the state of mind required for entering scrying work. It not only acts as a focal point for visualization but can become a "doorway" or window into the Astral plane. It allows communication with higher realms and spirit teachers, the subconscious, and access to Akashic records. The traditional crystal ball is also a wonderful tool, but it is more difficult to scry with and is extremely expensive. The mirror is a more efficient way to begin to learn to scry and journey in other realms. These techniques may be used with a Crystal Ball as well as the Black Scrying Mirror.

Consider the reality of the Akashic records, in which all ideas, actions, influences, and vibrations are stored. The practiced scryer has the ability to "read" these records and focus on this vast source of timeless knowledge with the aid of the mirror and a strongly directed imagination. Guides from the World of Spirit often lead the scryer in astral travel and mental journeying through the black mirror or crystal sphere. Scrying develops one's clairvoyant abilities and is especially helpful in strengthening the third eye.

Sit before your mirror and begin to imagine objects on its surface, one after another. You should try to see these images clearly in the mirror with your eyes open, just as if they were there in reality. Try simple shapes or colors first. Hold on to the image of each shape, object, or color one minute before dissolving it and going on to the next. For example, use a red triangle, a yellow square, a blue circle, and silver crescent. See them appear in the mirror using your firm imagination. For best results, do this exercise everyday for fifteen minutes until it is mastered. This exercise is well worth the effort. It gives magickal discipline and strengthens the inner eye, so visions can come with clarity and ease.

Class V: Conjury (Orange)

"The magician lives in a world that is not perceptible for the 'muggle.' But one of his functions is to re-enchant the world. To do so, he must suspend your rational mind, and the best way to do it is the use of trickery. Creating a suspension of disbelief, he makes you able to perceive the beauty and enchantment of the world. If he can create a state of mind—or better, a state of soul—and provoke an emotion of such quality that the only name you can give to that emotion is 'magic,' he has the right to be called a magician. This is the poetic aspect of magic, one of the superior forms of the art. We travel in far places all over the world, and magic, as a poetic language, has always been considered as a common language between us and the people we meet."

—Christian Chelman

1. Introduction: The Magic of Illusions

LSO CALLED STAGE MAGIC AND PERformance magic, conjuring or illusion magic deals with "miraculous" illusions and special effects. Designed to amaze and mystify onlookers, the conjuring arts originated with the first Shamans. Magic performance and theatre have always been linked to the magician (Shaman, Prophet, Wizard). *Theatre* means "see the gods." Various types of performance, such as magic acts, acrobatics, juggling, puppetry, and fire-eating all originated in such rituals.

Recall the transformation of Aaron's and the Egyptian magicians' staffs into snakes in the presence of Pharaoh. Aaron's snake eats those of the Egyptian magi, indicating that the Hebrews will gain their freedom. Magic was used to concretize the Prophecy. The magic of illusions and conjurations opens a door out of mundane reality into a magickal realm that reveals deeper truths.

Donald Michael Kraig says: *"Illusion magic is generally divided into three main categories: stage, parlor, and close-up. The difference is the location of the performance and how close the audience is to the performer. There is also another set of categories that has to do not with the setting, but rather with the presentation. Thus, comedy magic can be done on a stage, in a parlor, or close up. The same is true of mentalism, sleight-of-hand (most frequently described as manipulative magic), bizarre magik, etc. Of course, the 'Grand Illusions' of Copperfield or Siegfried & Roy involving vanishing assistants or big cats are often limited to the stage, although some smaller ones can be presented in the parlor setting."*

Lesson 2. Magical Special Effects for Theatrical Ritual

—by Jeff "Magnus" McBride

Today we watch as stage magicians cut beautiful women in half on television and then restore them to their smiling original form or Las Vegas showmen transform themselves into white tigers. "This isn't real magic," we might say... or is it? Are they telling a story? Could they really be shapeshifters? Could these often-unappealing exoteric dramas point beyond themselves to the greater esoteric themes of mythology and ritual?

The Shaman and the showman have much in common in the retelling of the great mystery dramas of life, death, and rebirth, and they still have much to learn from each other! Most performance magicians we see on stage or on television are not aware of the shamanistic origins of their artform. Until recently, many modern day ritualists had all but forgotten the traditional shamans' bag of tricks. Over the past 11 years I have been involved with creating ritual theater experiences for the magickal community. As a stage magician and a ritual theater director, I have gathered together a collection of magical goodies to add to your spell kit. Let us take another look at the techniques that have been handed down to us by our magical ancestors.

Many popular entertainments may be traced back to a single source—the rituals of Shamanism, which were functional rituals of similar pattern that operated within a variety of metaphysical systems. Authentic magical ritual often precedes popular magic. Very different types of performance, such as magic acts, acrobatics, puppetry, and fire-eating can be shown to have derived from, or at least been preceded by, the phenomena of such rituals, and thus provide the general framework for a general theory of origins.[1]

Magic and special effects have been used in enhancing the theater of ritual since the first fire was ignited. The wonder and awe generated by the early shaman lifted the participants in the ritual to a higher plane of consciousness. In ritual theater, we seek to move our participants into these trance states sometimes referred to as altered states of consciousness or shamanic states of consciousness.[2] The ritualized magic effects of the Hindu Basket, the East Indian Rope Trick, or the Greek Chorus are allegorical journeys to "otherworlds" where the performer undergoes a symbolic death and rebirth; themes that are ever-present in world mythologies. The ritual theater participants not only hear the storyteller weave the tale, but also witness the drama as it is acted out upon the stage that is the field of the ritual working.[3]

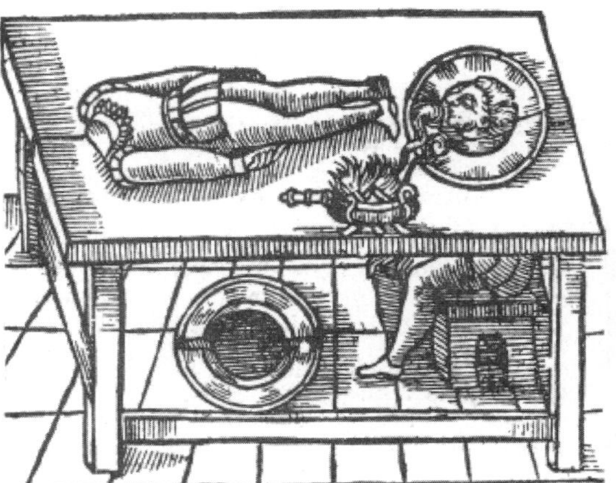

"To cut off ones head, and to laie it in a platter, which the jugglers call the decollation of John Baptist."
—Reginald Scot, The Discoverie of Witchcraft *(1584)*

Is it real Magic or Illusion...or both?

A Shaman summons his spirit allies and "escapes" his bonds during a healing seance. A statue of a goddess "speaks" to a priestess during an oracular divination ritual. A priest runs a sword through his body, "proving" he is immortal and also the most powerful magician of the tribe. These tricks of the trade are among the most common achievements of the Shaman's art.[4]

As a performance magician who is also involved with creating ritual theater experiences, I am often asked if I believe that what is happening at these reported events is "real" magic. Are these "real" powers or trickery? To debate this can be exhausting and is to miss the point. History is full of accounts of the miraculous. To the believer no answer is necessary; to the skeptic, none is acceptable. The magical displays of power all work to some degree, regardless if the Shaman or healer is using trickery or not. Theatrically, these magical skills are used as a way to enhance the energy raised for the ritual intention.

In ancient Greece, the doors of the Oracle's temple opened automatically as the altar fire blazed up, by means of secret hydraulics.

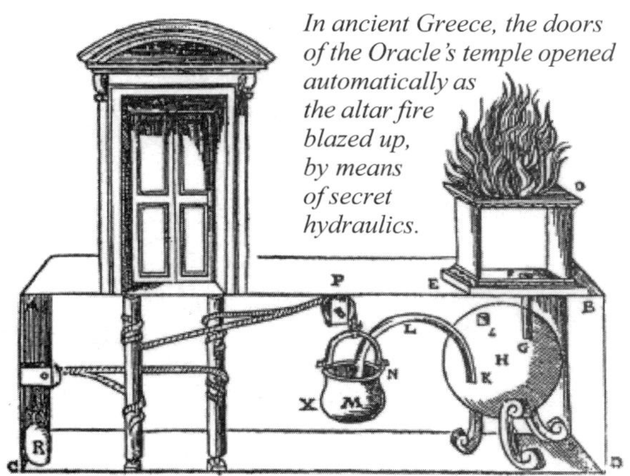

(From a manuscript by Hero of Alexandria)

> *"Shamanistic illusionism, with its ventriloquism and escape acts, seeks to break the surface of reality, as it were, to cause the appearance of a super-reality that is 'more real' than the ordinary. The principle of the 'more real' as the virtual ground of reality links spectacular and fraudulent trickery with demonstrations of the body's 'supernatural' physical abilities in the trance state."*[5]

As ritualists we seek to create a magickal space between the worlds, far from the mundane world—to use Kirby's phrase, "more real than real," to create a heightened sense of magickal possibility in our ritual and our lives. Often true transcendence is far too subtle to be easily perceived by a large group. It can be said that these created illusions are a *translation* of what is actually happening. In constructing effective ritual theater experiences, even knowledge of elementary magic effects and sleight of hand skills can bring about wondrous results.

(1) Kirby, E.T., "The Shamanistic Origins of Popular Entertainments," *The Drama Review,* Vol. 18, No. 1 (March 1974)
(2) Eliade, M., *Shamanism: Archaic Techniques of Ecstasy*, Bolligen Series, Princton U.P. 1964
(3) Taylor, R., *The Death and Resurrection Show,* Blonde 1985
(4) Boragas,W., "The Chuckchee," *American Museum of Natural History Memoirs*, XI, JE VII 1904, p.446)
(5) Kirby, E.T., *op cit.*

Lesson 3. Magical Powders & Potions

Faerie Lights and Glowing Water (Magnus)

Effect: Magical glowing light is emitted from the ritual tools of the magic workers. Wondrous glowing colors fill the ritual circle.

Arcanum: Hidden l.e.d. (light-emitting diode) lights

can be placed upon, within, or behind altar objects and tools to make them glow with magical light. A blue battery-operated l.e.d. placed in the bottom of an empty chalice shines forth a beautiful glow, creating an otherworldly effect.

Water into Magical Sweet Drinks (Oberon)

Effect: This one is great for kids. The Wizard lines up a row of empty wineglasses. Taking a clear pitcher of clear water, he pours some out into each glass. As he does so, the water in each glass turns a different color. The glasses can be passed out and drunk, and each will taste differently-flavored and sweet.

Arcanum: Buy a package of plastic picnic wine glasses with attachable stems from the grocery store. Also buy an assortment of small bottles of liquid food coloring and flavoring, and place a few drops of a different color into the bottom of each glass, along with a single drop of flavoring that matches the color. Let the coloring and flavoring dry completely and it will become practically invisible. Then, when you pour clear water into it, the dried coloring and flavoring will dissolve and color the water. Add sugar and ice to the water in the pitcher, and tell your audience that these are magickal sweet drinks!

Relighting Candle (Oberon)

Effect: A burning candle is blown out. A match is lit and held above the candle. A flame from the burning match jumps down through empty air and relights the candle. This can be repeated over and over.

Arcanum: This requires nothing more than a perfectly ordinary candle and matches. Light the candle and let it burn for a minute or so before blowing it out. Then light a match and place its flame directly in the column of smoke rising from the candle, about an inch above the wick. Experiment to determine exactly how far above the candle you should hold the match.

Flash Spells (Magnus)

Effect: During a simple burning ceremony, ritualists are given small sheets of paper to write their intentions for casting into the fire. The paper burns instantly in a bright flash, creating a heightened charge, and creating a "more real than real" moment.

Arcanum: High-grade chemical-impregnated "flash paper" is available at all magic shops

Colored Flames (Magnus)

Effect: Strangely colored flames dance as the Wizard makes his oracular divination from the voice and images leaping from the fire.

Arcanum: Various chemical blends can be added to fires to change the colors of the flames. This can create an otherworldly effect when utilized in a fire-gazing meditation. These compounds can be inexpensively obtained from stores that sell fireplace supplies.

Sparkles from Your Fingertips (Magnus)

Effect: When invoking deities into the ritual Circle, the magi pass their hands over the fire and twinkling sparks dance in the flames, rising as an offering towards the heavens.

Arcanum: Take a replacement flint for a Zippo lighter and grind it into powder in your mortar. Sprinkle carefully over flames. As with all fire effects, practice makes perfect!

Dragon's Breath (Magnus)

Effect: Witches dance in a circle chanting the names of power that will charge their intention. They spin faster and faster around the fire until the fire spirits shoot forth a sudden volcanic blast of fire to the heavens ...so mote it be!

Arcanum 1: A handful of *lycopodium* powder, safely tossed into the ritual fire at the height of a power raising, not only gives an added theatrical impact to the climax of the ritual but serves as a visual/auditory signal for the participants to target the energy raised towards the ritual intention. Be careful and practice to get the right dosage of powder, and keep it away from flowing ritual garb! Lycopodium is sold under the name of "Dragon's Breath" at magic shops.

Arcanum 2: (Oberon) While not quite as spectacular as lycopodium powder, Cremora (powdered coffee creamer) also creates an impressive fireball when you sprinkle a handful into the flames of a ritual fire. A few practice attempts may be necessary for you to learn the best way to get the most dramatic effect. Cremora works because it has a high fat content. Other powdered coffee creamers will work, but only if they have that high fat content.

> ***CAUTION:*** *Be* very *careful with chemicals and fire! Even if the chemicals you use are safe as described here, they may not also be safe if used with other chemicals, or with the potent drugs taken for asthma or other medical problems. Even something as simple as causing a flare-up in a bonfire by tossing in Cremora could be a problem for someone who has asthma and who gets a face full of dust, or if a person is standing too close to the fire. So be careful around fire, and make sure to provide yourself with proper fire prevention and emergency supplies: fire extinguishers, sand, water, and baking soda. And if you want to* experiment *with chemicals, do it in alchemistry class, with teacher supervision, not around a campfire or in your living room!*

Lesson 4. Performance & Showmanship

Many rituals are most successful if they follow a dramatic form, as in a play, where there is a build-up of intent, direction, and energy, followed by a climax—the release of the energy—and the final *dénouement.* Compose your ritual or performance as you would a play. Use it to tell a story, with one scene leading into the next, until the point has been made and the purpose fulfilled. The following are just a few of the many tips and tricks of the showman's trade that can be applied to the craft of theatrical ritual. By studying the stagecraft of performance magicians and actors, we can be inspired to move our rituals higher into the realms of "real magick."

Plan your ritual as a performance, and your performance as a ritual.

Patter & Pacing: *Patter* is what conjurers call the stuff they say while they are performing their illusions. This can be just a simple description of what you are doing as you go along (or, at least, what you want the audience to *think* you are doing!). A comedy routine can be a lot of fun, especially if you can work the illusions in as punch lines. *Bizarre magik* (see below) uses special effects to illustrate a story, just as in the movies. This is the magick used by Wizards from time immemorial—so learn to tell a good story to go with your performance!

An oft-repeated axiom in theatre (especially comedy) is that "timing is everything!" Pace your performance. Don't rush your patter; speak your lines clearly and distinctly—projecting them loudly enough so that everyone can hear every word. Pause between sentences and paragraphs, to give them a chance to sink in—especially if other people are expected to respond in any way (such as by laughing). Take deep breaths, and lower the pitch of your voice the way radio announcers do to give a greater resonance and power.

Motions: When you are learning to perform illusions, you should practice and rehearse them over and over in front of a mirror until you can do them smoothly, without dropping anything or stumbling over what comes next. First get the movements down perfectly, and then add your patter or spoken lines. Don't show an illusion to anyone else until you have perfected it to your own satisfaction in a mirror!

Staging: Some illusions are best performed with a table in front of you—such as at a dinner table. Many of these require a tablecloth. Others are better performed standing about 10' in front of your audience. These should always be done with a dark background, such as dark draperies—especially those requiring the use of invisible threads. Lighting should not be overly bright for thread illusions; several candles make an ideal light source and also contribute to a mysteriously "magical" atmosphere.

Costuming: The theatrical aspect of performance magic and illusion helps transport not only the practitioner but also the observer into other realms—a simple mask and cloak transforms "good ol' Joe" into the very image of a magickal and powerful being! Various illusionists have created many distinctive costumes for themselves, from traditional Wizard's robes and tabards to tuxedos and top hats. A costume with lots of pockets and loose pieces (long sleeves, cape, tabard, jacket, hat, etc.) can provide places to hide various props and gimmicks. Grey Council member Jeff "Magnus" McBride, who contributed much of the material for this Class, is a world-famous illusionist who is particularly known for his wonderful use of masks (shown here). So when you are putting together a performance routine of illusions and conjuring, consider your costuming along with all the rest, and come up with something appropriately magical and mysterious.

Props: *"Bizarre magik is often presented as if it is 'real.' A good example might be to imagine all of the magic that appears in the Harry Potter novels is real. The props often look the part. This means that a prop presented as an ancient grimoire looks like an ancient grimoire, and not like something purchased at the local stationery store."* (—Dave Birtwell)

If you're using handkerchiefs, get something with an arcane design on it. If using a bottle, prepare a mysterious label for it. For boxes or books, add raised designs made of epoxy putty and painted—you can even add fake eyes and other trim from an arts & crafts store. Be imaginative, and get creative!

Rays: Two performers do the same trick. They seemingly have the same skills, yet one baffles the audience while the other amazes no one. Why is this? One possible reason could be what the famous teacher of actors, Konstantine Stanislovski, called *rays.* By this he meant that the performer had to really believe in what he or she was doing. When performers do this they project "rays," which causes the audience to believe in what is being done. Of course, as a magician, you know you aren't really making that coin disappear. But if you really imagine what it would be like if you *could* make that coin disappear, you can project those rays and the audience *will* believe.

Magic Store: If you live in or near a large city, I would recommend a trip to a magic supply store. Check out what they have to offer, and talk to the folks there. Have an idea in mind of the kind of rituals you want to do before you go in, and don't even think of getting anything that doesn't advance your purposes. You are not simply trying to perform tricks, but to create special effects that will enhance your rituals and workings. Later, if just entertaining with tricks seems interesting, you can come back for those.

5. Glossary of Conjuring Terms

Magic: Anything that appears impossible or miraculous to the observer, especially the simulation of the miraculous or paranormal by secretive yet physically normal means.

Conjuring: The art of creating magical effects and illusions. (The same word is also used for invoking or summoning spirits, which is quite different!)

Bizarre magik: A magical performance with the emphasis on storytelling and entertaining rather than just fooling the audience. Theatrical elements are added to make the entire journey a magical experience.

Legerdemain (LEJ-er-di-MANE, "light of hand"): Performance magic, or conjuration.

Prestidigitation (PRES-te-dij-i-TAY-shun, "quick fingers"): Sleight-of-hand, involving manual dexterity, often without apparatus or gimmicks.

Mentalism: The imitation of psychic, ESP, and paranormal phenomena through normal but secretive methods.

Patter: The speech used by a conjurer to accompany his performance.

Routine: A set series of moves or effects done as a unit.

Work: Doing the actual physical actions that result in the magical effect. This could be anything from pushing a button on a box to a particular sleight.

Effect: What the audience sees.

Illusion: An effect in which appearances are contrary to the reality. This term is usually applied to large stage tricks, or "Grand Illusions," such as vanishings and appearances of people or large animals.

Levitations: Illusions that apparently defy gravity, in which a person or object appears suspended in midair with no visible support.

Production: Making things appear seemingly out of nowhere.

Production box: A seemingly empty box with a secret compartment from which *loads* can be produced.

Arcanum (ar-KAY-num): The Secret.

Surreptitiously (SUR-ep-TISH-us-lee): Secretly; in a way that goes completely unnoticed by your audience.

Secrete (si-KREET): Hide; conceal; put in a secret place.

Palm: To hold a small object in your hand in such a way that, combined with misdirection, your audience doesn't realize it's there. There are various types of palming, including front palming, back palming, finger palming, etc.

Switch: A secret substitution, in which one object is surreptitiously replaced with another.

Sleight: A secretive hand movement used to accomplish an effect.

Load: *(Verb)* To introduce something secretly into a container before or during a trick in which it is magically produced. *(Noun)* Item(s) that are so produced.

Steal: To get possession of an item secretly.

Misdirection: Directing the audience's attention away from where the "work" behind the effect is being done. On stages this may be done with sound, light flashes, people moving, or just looking in a different direction. For small audiences this may include words, looks, or other forms of body language.

Prop: Any object used in a performance that is not part of the conjurer's costume.

Wand: A standard conjurer's wand is 12"-15" long and about ¾" in diameter. Some are gimmicked. It is the symbol and essence of the Wizard's power.

Apparatus: Specially rigged props for tricks, as opposed to ordinary articles.

Gimmick: A small secret device that makes the trick work.

Servanté (ser-VAN-tay): A hidden shelf or suspended pocket concealed behind a table or chair to receive items discarded or exchanged.

Lesson 6. Conjurations

When starting out in conjuring, don't try to overdo the number of illusions you present at any one performance. Two, three, or four at most will be plenty. You will soon learn how many you can do before people begin to lose interest. Some of the world's most famous stage magicians have entertained audiences over long careers with fewer than half-a-dozen tricks. The following effects and illusions require the advance preparation of special trick props and gimmicks. Remember—practice to perfection before showing off!

Magick Envelope

Illusion: You can produce things from an empty envelope, or change things into something else.

Arcanum: Take a standard #10 white envelope. Cut a piece of white paper (card stock) to the exact same size as the envelope, so it fits perfectly inside. This makes a double envelope with two sections *(Fig. 1)*. To make things (silk scarves, flowers, notes, leaves, feathers, etc.) appear out of an empty envelope, first hide them in the back pocket, then hold that pocket shut with your thumb while you show the front pocket to be empty. Then close the envelope flap, and when you open it again, this time stick your thumb into the back pocket to hold it open while you dump out its contents into someone's hands. As you empty the back pocket, show your audience only the side of the envelope that doesn't have the opening, or they will detect the double pocket.

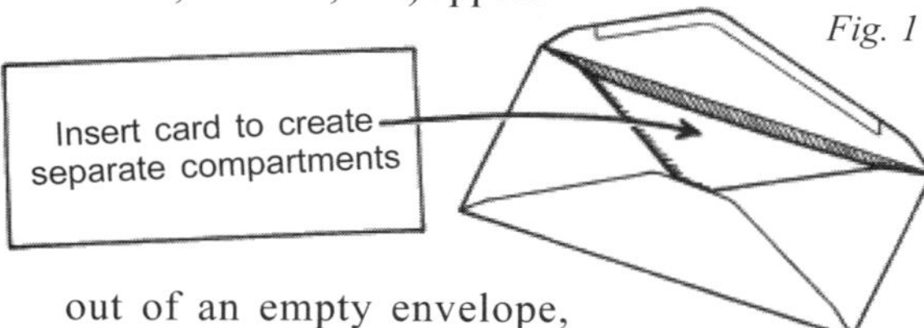

Fig. 1

You can use the same trick to make things turn into something else. You can turn a leaf into a feather, petals into a flower, or torn-up pieces of a leaf into a whole one.

Genie Bottle

Effect: You stick one end of an ordinary rope into the mouth of a bottle, and the bottle will just dangle in midair as you hold up the other end of the rope. You can even swing it around, and it won't fall off. You can then easily remove the rope and pass both rope and bottle around for inspection.

Arcanum: The secret is a small rubber ball (like for the game of jacks), just small enough to fit easily through the neck of the bottle. The bottle itself must be opaque, with a neck. Various juice drink bottles are excellent for this. The rope should be about ¼" thick. Keep the rubber ball in your pocket until you're ready to insert the rope, and you can even pass the bottle around beforehand. Palm the ball in the hand holding the rope *(Fig. 2)*, and drop it into the bottle as you insert the rope. Then turn the bottle upside-down to lower the ball, wedging the rope and ball into the neck of the bottle as you pull out slightly on the rope *(Fig. 3)*. When you're done dangling and swinging the bottle, pull the rope out gently along with the ball, and carefully palm the ball as it emerges. Pocket the ball surreptitiously as you offer the rope and bottle to your audience to inspect once again.

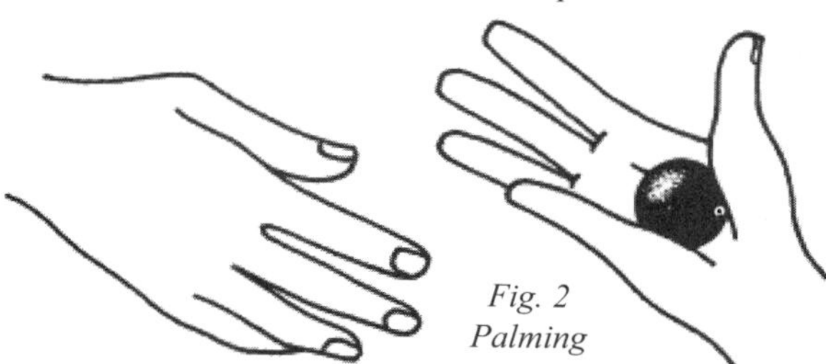
Fig. 2
Palming

Fig. 3

Rising Card

Effect: You, and only you, can make a card rise up from a glass on your command. You set an empty drinking glass on the table, and a deck of cards. Ask a volunteer to pick any card from the deck and hand it to you. Push the card down into the glass and challenge them to try and talk it into rising. Nothing happens. Try the same thing with someone else. When it's your turn, take your card and do something "mystical" (rub it on your sleeve, say a magic word, tap it with your wand…). Insert it into the glass and say: "Rise!" This time, the card slowly rises up on your command.

Arcanum: This requires a glass with tapered sides, narrower at the bottom, with the opening no wider than the width of a card. You have previously prepared the glass by rubbing a piece of dry soap along the inside, on opposite sides, leaving two strips about ½" wide *(Fig. 4)*. When you insert your volunteers' cards, push them down along the unsoaped sides. Then in your turn, push your card down along the soapy sides and it will slowly slide back up on the film of soap.

Fig. 4
(Soap film)

Invisible Thread Tricks

For the following effects, fine black thread or fine monofilament fishline is required. Also, you must wear dark clothes. These illusions must be performed in somewhat dim lighting, or far enough away from the audience that they cannot see the thread. The finer the thread, the closer audiences can be. Stretch out a length of thread across your set and test the lighting and distance yourself beforehand. If you can see the thread, so will your audience!

Rising Wand

Illusion: A stick dropped into a bottle held in your hand mysteriously rises out of the bottle and into the air, where you catch it in your other hand.

Arcanum: Tie one end of a 2' length of invisible thread

to your left front belt loop. Get an empty soda bottle, and cut a stick a little shorter than the bottle. The stick should be narrow enough to fit loosely through the neck of the bottle. Now, make a small slit in the bottom of the stick with a sharp knife, and slip the end of the thread through the crack *(Fig. 5)*. Loop the thread over your left thumb as you hold the stick—threaded and down. Pick up the bottle with your right hand and hold it under the stick. Drop the stick into the bottle as you transfer the bottle to your left hand, leaving the thread still over your thumb. Then move the bottle slowly away from your body as you make "mystic passes" over it with your right hand. As the thread pulls it, the stick will rise *(Fig. 6)*. When it is almost out of the bottle, catch it in your right hand, and pull it away, at the same time pulling the thread out of the crack to fall to your side. You can then let people examine both the stick and the bottle.

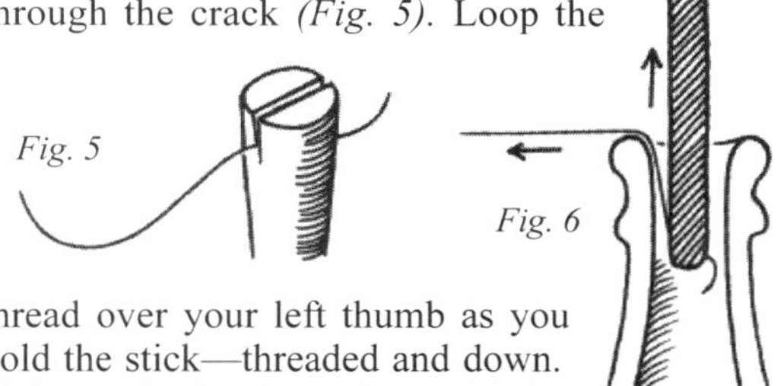
Fig. 5

Fig. 6

Ball on a Tightrope

Illusion: You hold up a length of rope outstretched between your hands and roll a Ping-Pong ball back and forth along it, balancing the ball impossibly upon the rope.

Arcanum: Use a rope and a piece of invisible thread, each about two feet long. Tie one end of the thread to each end of the rope. Hold the Ping-Pong ball in your right hand, and insert your index fingers between the thread and rope, with the thread facing you. Turn both hands palm up, and stretch the rope (and thread) out tight between them, creating a ½"-wide track for the ball to roll along *(Fig. 7)*. Carefully release the ball onto the track and roll it back and forth by alternately raising and lowering each end of the rope to change direction.

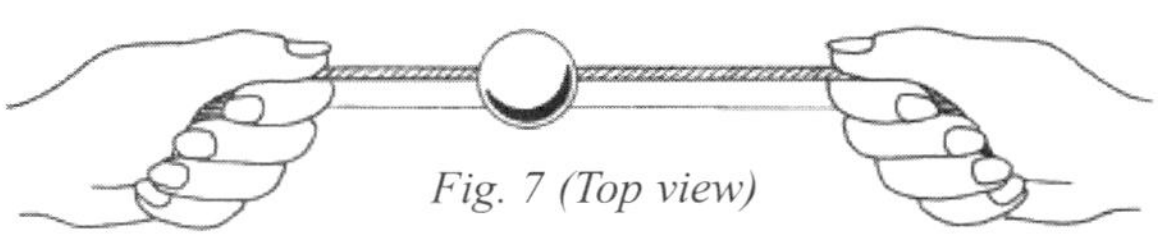
Fig. 7 (Top view)

When you have amazed your friends and family with some of these conjuring illusions, I can guarantee that they will ask you to "Do it again!" And everyone will want you to tell them how you did it. But the special charm of conjuring magic for an audience is in their *not* knowing how it is done. Once the secret of the illusion is out, it loses its mystery. Without that sense of wonder and amazement, no one will be interested in your illusions. So here are six basic tips from Grey Council member Todd Karr's book, *Backyard Magic:*

1. **Practice in front of a mirror,** including what you will say (your patter).
2. **Believe you're performing REAL magic.**
3. **Always have your audience in front of you** when you perform, not behind you.
4. **Put your props away** after your performance to avoid exposure (keep them in a box or knapsack).
5. **If your friends ask the secrets, tell them "It's magic!"** or just smile.
6. **Never do the same magic effect twice** for the same audience.

Lesson 7. Conjury Resources

Books:

Gilbert, George & Wendy Rydell. *Great Tricks of the Master Magicians* (Golden Press, 1976). This is my favorite book on conjury, with 150 tricks explained and illustrated in a large format.

Hay, Henry, *The Amateur Magician's Handbook* (Signet, 1950; 1972). This was one of the first magic books I ever purchased. My 1972 paperback version cost just $1.95!

Karr, Todd, *Backyard Magic* (Scholastic Inc., 1996). This is a perfect "starter book" of conjury for the young Apprentice Wizard. 15 really neat and easy tricks beautifully illustrated in full color cartoons.

Nelms, Henning, *Magic and Showmanship: A Handbook for Conjurers* (Dover, 1969). This book is recommended by most magic teachers. Jeff McBride even recommends it in his Master Classes.

Severn, Bill, *Magic in Your Pockets,* Young Readers Press, 1964. Easy-to-learn conjury for kids all ages.

Tarr, Bill, *Now You See It, Now You Don't* (Vintage Books, 1976). When it comes to describing and illustrating basic sleights, including palming, this book is the best. Ideal for teens and pre-teens.

Other Resources:

Here's a performance magic video dealing with "Pottermania." Andrew Mayne video: http://www.wizard-school.com/

DragonSkull is a great website devoted to Bizarre Magik, including arcane effects and supplies: http://www.dragonskull.co.uk/

Here's a link to Jeff McBride's Magical Wisdom site: http://www.magicalwisdom.com/

And here's the Miracle Factory: http://www.miraclefactory.org

http://www.yourmagic.com is a good source for magic books and supplies. They feature a great deal on Jeff McBride, David Parr, and Eugene Burger—one of Jeff's mentors. Eugene's books, tapes and effects are extremely useful.

Class VI: Alchemy (Red)

This art must ever secret be, The cause whereof is this, as ye may see:
If one evil man had thereof all his will, All Christian peace he might easily spill,
And with his pride he might pull down Rightful kings and princes of renown.
—"Ordinal of Alchemy," by Thomas Norton of Bristol (15th century)

1. Introduction and History

LCHEMY IS THE MAGICKAL ART AND science of transformation and transmutation. The name comes from Arabic *al-kimia.* Alchemy was the forerunner of modern chemistry, originating in Alexandria, Egypt, during the 1st century CE, when Egyptian metallurgy was fused with Greek philosophy and Middle Eastern mysticism. Some of the essential doctrines, however, were formulated before 400 BCE. A Greek papyrus from c.300 CE describes a method of changing the color of a metal to look like gold or silver, saying that the new metal would fool expert goldsmiths.

Alchemy has always been surrounded by a cloud of mystery, its origins ascribed to supernatural intervention. Legend has it that Hermes Trismegistus, later identified with the Egyptian god Thoth, was the founder of alchemy. This is why alchemy is known as the *Hermetic Art.* Mary the Jewess (4th century CE), one of the most influential early practitioners of this art, taught that alchemy is indeed *donum dei* (a gift of God); but this gift was not for alchemists in general, but only for Jews. A true understanding of alchemy required years of study and prayers to God for guidance, followed by more years of practical experiments.

Hermes Trismegistus, by Jean Jacques Boissard
(De Divinatione et Magicis, 1597)

Lesson 2. Goals & Practices of Alchemy

> *This, therefore, was the general aim of the Alchemists—to carry out in the laboratory, as far as possible, the processes which Nature carried out in the interior of the Earth.*
> —James C. Brown (*History of Chemistry*)

The main objectives of medieval alchemists were the *transmutation* of "base metals" (particularly lead) into gold and silver, and the discovery of the *Elixer of Life* that would heal all ills and bestow immortality.

The key to both the transmutation and the Elixer lay in the discovery of the *Philosopher's Stone,* a mysterious substance variously said to be either a stone, powder, or liquid that was recognizable only by the initiated. The Philosopher's Stone was believed to be a universal *catalyst* that could effect such transmutations.

A third goal was the creation of the *homunculus,* a miniature artificial man. In essence, this meant the creation of life itself—a goal still pursued by modern biologists without success. Several prominent alchemists left written instructions on how to create a homunculus, but I don't believe them!

Lesser goals of alchemy were the discovery of the *Alcahest,* or Universal Solvent; *palingenesis,* or the restoration of a plant from its ashes; the preparation of *spiritus mundi,* a mystic substance that could dissolve gold; the extraction of the *Quintessence,* or active principle, of all substances; and the preparation of *aurum potable,* or liquid gold, which could be drunk as a universal remedy.

Principles of Alchemy

As above so below,
and as below so above,
for the accomplishment of
the Miracle of The One Thing.
—The Emerald Tablet of Hermes Trismegistus

Alchemy accepted the division of all matter into four *Elements*—Earth, Water, Air, and Fire (what modern scientists call the four *states* of matter—solid, liquid, gas, and plasma). To this, they added four natural "qualities"—dry, wet, hot, cold—any two of which defined that Element. If these qualities are changed, then the Element itself can be changed. Water is cold and wet. Make it hot and wet, and it becomes Air (vapor). Fire is hot and dry. When it loses its heat and dies, it becomes Earth (ashes)—cold and dry.

Alchemists believed that everything that exists was formed from one original substance called "first matter." By eliminating its non-essential qualities (color, size, weight, shape) they believed that they could reduce any substance to that fundamental first matter, and then rebuild it into something else by adding the desired attributes.

Alchemy taught that everything in Nature was alive and contained a Divine spark or vital force (called *pneuma*—"breath") within it. The soul of all Nature was called *Anima Mundi* ("Spirit of the Earth"). The pneuma was the same as the soul of any living creature. If a piece of wood was burned, for example, the ash was considered the corpse (or *nigredo*), and the smoke was the "soul" being released to Heaven.

Metals were also "alive" with a desire to evolve to their highest state. Alchemists saw the planetary correspondences as a chain of evolution, leading from **lead** (Saturn) up through **tin** (Jupiter), **iron** (Mars), **copper** (Venus), **quicksilver** (Mercury), to **silver** (Moon) and finally, **gold** (Sun). In their laboratories, they tried to help base metals "ripen" from one stage to the next until they reached the highest, purest stage of gold.

The three primary substances of alchemy were sulfur, mercury, and salt—called the *Tria Prima,* or Three Principles. These represented Soul, Spirit, and Body. The various physical and metaphysical processes of alchemy focused on identifying and purifying these substances, in both senses. The key solvent used in the purification of the Tria Prima was dew, considered to be the precipitation of the Cosmic Fire and the distilled essence of Heaven above and Earth below.

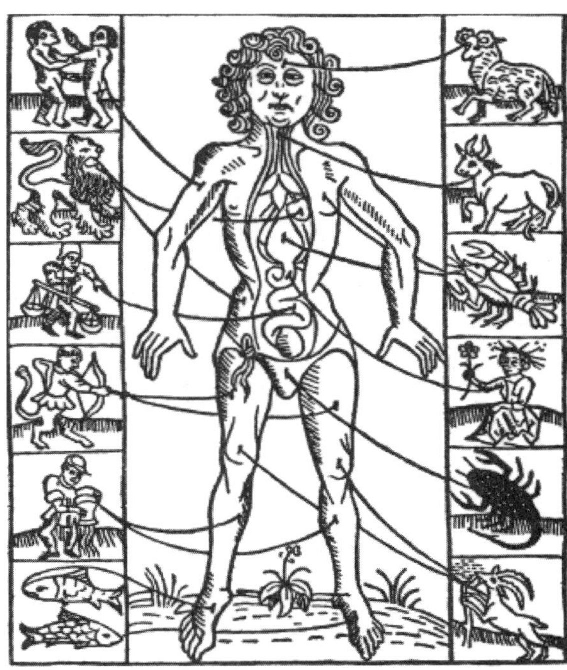

*Correspondences of human body to signs of the Zodiac (*Martyrologium der Heiligen nach dem Kalender, *1484)*

Alchemical Tree of Life (from Gloria Mundi*)*

The *esoteric* (secret) purpose of alchemy was mystical and concerned the spiritual regeneration and evolution of man—the refinement and perfection of the human spirit and achieving union with the Divine. Therefore, all the actual laboratory processes were also symbolic of the processes the alchemist himself underwent in his own personal inner work. So the alchemist would strive to strip and reduce himself to "first matter," and then restore and evolve his soul upwards through various stages of refinement to become purest gold.

From Alchemy to Chemistry

A favorite maxim of alchemy was *Solve et coagula* ("dissolve and coagulate"). In other words, break it down and then build it up. The esoteric significance of that phrase implied "dissolve the body and coagulate the spirit." Most of the processes of alchemy involved treating various substances in every conceivable manner: dissolving, mixing, distilling, burning, melting, filtering, refining, condensing, and precipitating. Through centuries of such experiments, Alchemists made a number of important discoveries that advanced the science of chemistry. Here are a few:

Caustic Potash—developed by Albertus Magnus (1206-1280), who also described the chemical composition of cinnabar, ceruse, and minium.

Bicarbonate of Potassium—prepared by Raymund Lully (1235-1315).

Zinc—described by Paracelsus (1493-1541), who was the first to prepare and use chemical compounds.

Benzoic Acid—discovered by Blaise Vigener (1523-1596).

Tin Oxide—discovered by Giambattista della Porta (1541-1615)

Sodium Sulfate (Glauber salt)—discovered by Johann Rudolf Glauber (1604-1668), and thought by many to be the long-sought Philosopher's Stone.

Phosphorus—discovered by Hennig Brand in 1669).

Porcelain—first produced in Europe by Johann Boetticher (1682-1719).

Although most modern scientists dismiss alchemy as a discredited "pseudo-science," the search for a method to change the atomic structure of base metals into gold or other elements continues today in chemistry laboratories, particle accelerators, and nuclear reactors. The principle of "first matter" is reflected in modern atomic theory, in which all atomic elements are composed of primary subatomic particles that are built up into increasingly heavy elements, from hydrogen, with only one proton and one electron, up to the "trans-uranium" elements, with hundreds of protons, neutrons and electrons. Biologists are still trying to create life in a test tube and have recently succeeded in cloning, at least. The search for the Elixer of Life continues in genetic research and the multibillion-dollar "Life Extension" industry. And many modern alchemists still experiment in the creation of chemicals to effect personal transformation and enlightenment.

Synthesis of the Alchemical Work (note 7 correspondences)
—Basil Valentin, L'Azoth des Philosophes

3. Glossary of Alchemical Terms

Acid: Any substance that reacts with a base to form a salt. Acid produces free hydrogen ions and turns litmus paper red.

Actinic: Producing *rays,* such as light rays, X-rays, gamma rays, etc.

Alchemy: The art and science of transformation and transmutation; forerunner of modern chemistry.

Alembic: A teardrop-shaped container used for mixing and heating substances in the process of distillation.

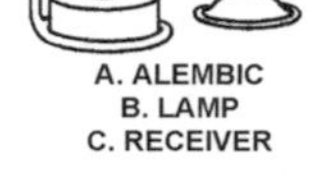

Alloy: A metal that is a fusion of several different metallic elements (bronze, brass, steel).

Aludel: A glass or ceramic vessel with spherical chambers for condensing vapors.

ALUDEL

Anima Mundi: "The Spirit of the World." Mother Earth; Mother Nature.

Athanor: A furnace like a kiln with a sealed upper compartment that can hold materials being heated under pressure.

Base: Any substance that reacts with acid to form a salt. Bases remove hydrogen ions from acid and turn litmus paper blue.

Base (i.e. "worthless") **Metals:** Common metals that readily react and oxidize, such as lead, copper, tin, and iron.

Catalyst: A substance that causes changes in other substances without being changed itself.

Coagulation: Turning a liquid substance into a solid.

Combustion: Bursting into flames.

Compound: A material made of several different chemically combined atomic elements.

Condensation: Turning a gaseous substance into liquid by cooling it down.

Crucible: A bowl-shaped heat-resistant container in which solid substances are heated to melting.

CRUCIBLE

Dissolution: Dissolving a solid material in a liquid medium.

Distillation: The process of evaporating the liquid out of a solution and then condensing it back into a pure fluid.

Elements: 1. The four states of matter (solid, liquid, gas, and plasma—called Earth, Water, Air, and Fire). 2. The 105+ known Atomic Elements of the Periodic Table.

Elixer: A magickal drink or potion, consisting of drugs in a solution of alcohol.

Elixer of Life: A hypothetical substance that, when imbibed, would heal all ills and confer immortality.

Evaporation: Turning a liquid substance into its gaseous form by heating it up.

Filtration: The process of separating solid particles and impurities from a liquid or gas by passing it through a porous membrane (the filter).

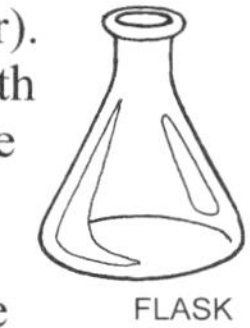

Flask: A small, bottle-shaped container with a narrow neck. Cone-shaped ones are called *Erlenmeyer flasks.*

Homunculus: A miniature artificial man.

Liquefaction: Turning a solid substance into a liquid.

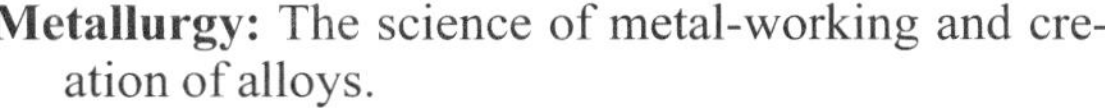

Metallurgy: The science of metal-working and creation of alloys.

Nigredo ("black stuff"): The stage in the alchemical process when the material has been broken down into a black residue, called "first matter." The *nigredo* was considered to be the "corpse" of the original material.

Noble Gases: Rare elemental gases that do not react with other elements, such as helium, neon, and radon.

Noble Metals: Rare metals which do not react with others, or oxidize, such as silver, gold, and platinum.

Oxidation: Uniting with oxygen, as in burning or rusting.

Periodic Table: A chart of all of the atomic elements, organized in order of their atomic weights and other properties.

Philosopher's Egg (also called *Aludel*): A spherical glass or ceramic bottle used to create the Philosopher's Stone.

Philosopher's Stone: A substance that has the catalytic power to effect transmutation of other substances.

PHILOSOPHER'S EGG

Precipitation: Allowing the solids in a suspension to settle on the bottom of the container.

Reduction: Bringing a substance into the metallic state by removing all non-metallic elements—particularly oxygen.

Residue: The solid matter remaining at the completion of a process, such as evaporation, combustion, filtration, etc.

Retort: A spherical container with a long tube, used in distilling.

RETORT

Solution: A liquid into which other liquid, gaseous, or solid materials have been evenly dissolved.

Still: A distilling apparatus with containers, coils, and tubes for boiling and evaporating liquid, then condensing the pure fluid.

COLD WATER
IN
BOILING IMPURE LIQUID
DISTILLED LIQUID
OUT
STILL

Suspension: A liquid into which fine particles of solid materials are mixed but not dissolved.

Transmutation: Changing one substance into another—especially pure elements.

Alchemist at his Athenor

Lesson 4: Your Alchemical Laboratory

Alchemy was the major occupation (and obsession!) of most Wizards throughout the Middle Ages and Renaissance times, and many of the old books and writings of Wizardry came out of those studies. Alchemy gave rise to modern chemistry, and those arcane magickal laboratories were the ancestors of all the modern chemistry and pharmaceutical labs. You probably don't have room for a full-scale alchemical laboratory in your home, but it can be worthwhile to have some basic equipment you can set up when you feel like doing some experiments.

Chemistry set—There are several excellent chemistry sets available, from very simple to extremely elaborate. These are sold at science and education stores and over the Internet. Check some out and get a sense of what you'd like, and put one on your list for your next birthday or Christmas! Your set should contain all the chemicals you will need for the alchemistry magick below. Extra test tubes and glassware are readily available from the same stores, or at chemical supply houses. If you can't get hold of a real chemistry set, you can still do a lot of cool alchemical experiments in chemistry classes at school—as well as get guidance and instruction—and you might even be able to get some basic equipment through the class.

Microscope—Most chemistry sets include a microscope, but if the one you get doesn't have one, you will want to pick one up. Sometimes you can even find perfectly good ones at places like Goodwill and flea markets. The best are those with a built-in light, and several lenses that can rotate into place. You will probably need to buy a batch of slides separately, but these are available at science and education stores. And even if you can't get hold of a microscope, a good magnifying glass can still reveal many wonders of the invisible world all around you!

Distiller—Perhaps the most important component of medieval alchemy labs was the steam distilling apparatus. A distiller evaporates all the liquid out of a mix, turning it into vapor, and then condenses it back into pure water, alcohol, or oil, leaving all solids and impurities behind.

Lesson 5: Wise Wizards and Safety

(by Abby Willowroot)

> *"Alchemy has never interested me. It's altogether too…too…"*
>
> *"Dangerous," said the Archchancellor firmly. "Lot of damn mixin' things up and saying, hey, what'll happen if we add a drop of the yellow stuff, and then goin' around without yer eyebrows for a fortnight."*
>
> —Terry Pratchett (*Moving Pictures, p.* 10)

CAUTION: Always be alert and careful. Even something as simple as causing a flare-up in a campfire by tossing in chemicals could be a problem for someone standing too close to the flames. Mixing fire and chemicals can equal Danger if you do not take proper precautions. Fire is not a toy—it is a living, breathing power that can quickly spring out of control if proper care is not taken. Firemen consider fire a living beast. So be careful around fire. **Keep a pail of water, sand, and a fire extinguisher handy if you are working with any type of fire.** Always be ready to tame the beast!

CONSIDER: Your health and the health of those around you can be adversely impacted by fire, smoke, or chemicals. Those with asthma or other health conditions (and their medications) can be negatively affected by substances that may be harmless to others. Wizardly awareness is an important skill to develop.

CHEMICALS can be harmful when mixed with other chemicals. Do not experiment on your own; stick to tried and tested formulas. Even if the chemicals you use are safe, as described here, they may not be safe if used with other chemicals. If you want to experiment with chemicals, do it in a chemistry class with teacher supervision, not around a campfire or in your living room. **Always be sure to have baking soda handy to dilute and neutralize acidic chemicals.**

CARE: The Wizard's ways are the ways of awareness, wisdom, and mastery. Taking proper precautions to ensure safety is an important early lesson that all Wizards must master before they can grow in their power. Wizards that are prepared for any eventuality and have taken proper safety precautions are more relaxed and confident. They have given due respect to the powers of elements and potions. If you want to shine, polish up your safety awareness.

Lesson 6: Alchemistry Magick

> ***NOTE:*** *Some of the chemicals required for these effects can be obtained from your pharmacy, but you will have to get others from a chemistry set, your school chemistry lab, or a chemical supply house. Check your* Yellow Pages. *If you feel drawn to study and practice Red Magick, then take chemistry classes in school!*

Salt Sculptures

Place a small piece of metal junk in a shallow bowl of salt water, add a bit of food coloring, and let it dry out in the sun. The evaporation process will deposit the salt on the object to create an interesting art piece.

Invisible Inks

Writing done with certain juices is invisible until it is developed by warming or treating it with a chemical *reagent.* Such "invisible inks" have frequently been used by spies, as well as conjurers. Lemon juice, grapefruit juice, vinegar, onion juice, milk—all of these can be used in the same way. You will have to use an old-fashioned nib pen to write with them. Write your message and then let the "ink" dry to invisibility. To make it reappear, heat the paper with a hair dryer.

Elastic Bones and Rubber Eggs

Save a few chicken bones, clean them thoroughly, and soak them in strong vinegar for 24 hours. At the end of that time, they will be so elastic that you can tie knots in them without breaking them.

You can do the same thing with a shelled egg, making the shell like rubber. But be careful not to break it!

Magic Handkerchief

Moisten a small white handkerchief with *cobalt chloride* solution. Dry it with a hair dryer, and you will find that it is blue when dry and warm. Cool it a bit by blowing on it or sticking it in the refrigerator, however, and it will turn white.

Pour Ink and Milk from the Same Pitcher

Get two plastic wineglasses. In one, put 1/4 tsp. of *tannic acid*, and put ½ tsp. of *strontium chloride* in the other. Add about a tsp. of water to each and stir until the chemicals are dissolved. Now, take a large glass of water, and dissolve 1¼ tsp. of *ferric ammonium sulfate* in it. Pour the water from the large glass, half into each wineglass—the liquid in the first will become black like ink, and the other will turn milky white. ***NOTE: Do not drink!***

Chemical Light

Here's how to make *luciferin,* the same glowing liquid you find in glowsticks. As you know, glowsticks glow as the result of mixing two chemical solutions, A+B. So mix up both of these batches of solutions separately, and only combine as much as you need at any one time, in equal amounts of each.

Solution A:
4 grams sodium carbonate
0.5 grams ammonium carbonate
0.4 grams cupric sulfate
1 liter of distilled water
and the magic ingredient—0.2 grams luminol
Mix together.

Solution B:
50 ml. distilled hydrogen peroxide
another liter of distilled water.
Once again, mix together.

Pour ½ cup of Solution A into a plastic wineglass, and then add ½ cup of Solution B. When you swirl them together, the mixture will glow eerily.

Pyrotechnics

The following salts, if finely powdered and sprinkled on a campfire, will impart their colors to the flames. You can also buy prepackaged colored flame chemicals at any place that sells fireplace supplies.

Red: Strontium nitrate
Orange: Calcium chloride
Yellow: Potassium nitrate or sodium chlorate
Apple Green: Barium nitrate
Emerald Green: Copper nitrate
Green: Borax
Blue: Copper sulfate
Purple: Lithium chloride
Violet: Potassium chlorate
White: Antimony sulfide

Colored Quarter Flames

These are great for Quarters in a Magick Circle! Get four little iron cauldrons (or other small fireproof containers). Mix the following non-toxic chemicals with methyl (wood) alcohol to make the flames burn in different colors. ***NOTE: Use no more than a tablespoon of the alcohol mix in each cauldron!***

Blue: All this requires is pure methyl alcohol, but make sure your cauldron is completely clean, as anything else will color the flame differently.
Green: Add one tsp. of boric acid—no more!—to a pint of methyl alcohol. Keep it sealed until ready to use.
Yellow: Put a tsp. of ordinary table salt (sodium chloride) into the alcohol in the cauldron, and add a tuft of new steel wool for a wick. Soak the wool with the mixture before lighting.
Red: Make sure your cauldron is completely clean, both before and after this mixture is used. Use new steel wool for a wick, as above. Add ½ tsp. of lithium chloride to a pint of alcohol, soak the wool in it, and light it.

Colored Smoke

Heat a spoonful of *ammonium chloride* over a flame, and it will give off thick clouds of white smoke. If you sprinkle some of the following powders onto a fire, they will create a dense colored smoke. (Use these only out-of-doors!)

Red: Paranitraniline red
Yellow: Magnesium powder, bismuth tetroxide, or potassium bichromate
Red to Green: Iodine
Blue: Indigo dye
White: Zinc dust

Transmutation of Metals

Now, after all this, I'll bet you're wondering if any of those old alchemists actually did manage to turn base metals into gold! Well, I've studied their reports and reviewed their experiments, and I have found two ways they were able to manage this trick. The first and most obvious is by *electroplating,* which deposits a metallic coating onto an object by putting a negative electrical charge on it, and then immersing it into a solution containing a salt of the metal to be deposited. The positive ions of the salt are attracted to the object.

Changing Lead into Gold

Suppose we have a metal object that we want to plate with gold. We attach a wire to the object, running from the negative pole of a battery. To a wire from the positive pole of the battery we connect a piece of gold. Keeping them separated, both the object to be plated and the gold piece are then immersed in a glass jar containing a solution of gold salt, and the electric current deposits a layer of gold atoms onto the surface of the object. You can't plate a metal *out* of a solution until you can dissolve that metal *into* the solution, but dissolving gold for plating requires a *very* strong acid, so it can't be done safely in your home lab.

But the most ingenious and convincing way to demonstrate transmutation into gold was by heating a small amount of mercury in a crucible, along with a pinch of red powder claimed to be the fabled Philosopher's Stone. The alchemist would stir the mixture with a long metal rod, and slowly it would change color, from silver to gold. Removed from the heat, it cooled into a solid nugget of genuine gold. The secret was that the metal rod was actually a hollow tube filled with gold dust and stoppered with a wax plug that would melt in the hot mercury, allowing the gold dust to trickle into the mixture. As the heat increased, the mercury gradually boiled away, leaving behind only the molten gold.

Unfortunately, there was a really nasty side effect to this trick. Mercury fumes are highly toxic, destroying brain cells and causing insanity—which might explain some of the stranger alchemical art and writings! *(Don't try this yourself!)*

Changing Silver into Copper

You can do your own little transmutation of metals by chemically plating silver with copper. Now, I'll admit there's not much of a demand for that, but it's still fun to do. Dissolve ½ tsp. of *azurite* and 1¼ tsp. of *sodium bisulfate* in 1 Tbls. of water. Place a silver dime or other silver coin into the solution, along with a small iron nail. In a few minutes the coin will be covered with a coating of copper, and will look just like a penny.

A Table of Chymicall & Philosophicall Characters wth their significations as they are usually found in Chymicall Authors both printed & manuscript

Lesson 7. Alchemical Symbols

To keep their secrets out of the hands of the incompetent and unworthy, alchemists hid their instructions and lab notes within a tangled code of symbols. Some of these were allegorical names representing materials and processes: *black crow, dragon, grey wolf, king, king's son, leper, lion, peacock, phoenix, tree, unicorn,* etc. Others symbols were glyphs, such as this table from Basile Valentin's *The Last Will & Testament* (1413).

As already noted , the seven primary metals were identified with the seven planets, and symbolized by their glyphs:

Gold ☉	Silver ☽
Iron ♂	Mercury ☿
Tin ♃	Copper ♀
Lead ♄	

The processes of Alchemy were symbolized by glyphs of the signs of the Zodiac:

Calcination ♈	Congelation ♉
Fixation ♊	Dissolution ♋
Digestion ♌	Distillation ♍
Sublimation ♎	Separation ♏
Incineration ♐	Fermentation ♑
Multiplication ♒	Projection ♓

8. Alchemy Resources

A number of different Chemistry sets are listed at Discover This: *http://www.discoverthis.com/chemistry.html*

An excellent distiller by Gary Stadler is at: *http://www.HeartMagic.com/EssentialDistiller.html*

Course Six: Spectrum, Part 2

Course Six: Spectrum, Part 2

Class I. Beast Mastery (Brown Magick)

1. Introduction: Living with Animals

BEAST MASTERY CONCERNS EVERYTHING TO do with animals of all kinds—especially animal communication. Beast masters include "horse whisperers," good animal trainers, pet psychics, and all people who seem to have an uncanny ability to communicate and work with animals. Such people often work in pet stores, animal hospitals, shelters, or zoos, or become park rangers or wildlife rescuers. And always they are surrounded by critters—whether pets, farm animals, wild creatures, or other animal companions. Animals that are particularly bonded to Witches and Wizards are called their *familiars.*

Beast mastery includes knowledge of zoology and the lore of *totems*. Beast masters seek to know the names of all animals, as well as how they evolved, what they eat, their behaviors, lifestyles, mating rituals, and languages. Medieval *bestiaries* were compiled to contain the same kinds of animal lore and attributions as herbals did for plants. These include not only natural animals, but legendary and mythical creatures as well. Indeed, the study of *cryptozo-ology* ("word of hidden animals") explores mysterious creatures—such as Bigfoot and the Loch Ness Monster—whose very existence still remains elusive.

Just like T.H. White's Merlyn, I have always had quite an assortment of wild animals living with me. I have shared my home with wild piglets, possums, ferrets, bunnies, budgies, owls, snakes (both small and huge!), iguanas, *caymans* (South American alligators), newts, frogs, dogs, toads, turtles, *tegus* (big lizards), tarantulas, praying mantises, fish, finches, herons, bats, rats, cats, Guinea pigs, goats, deer, and unicorns. I have also kept both fresh- and salt-water aquariums. For many years, Morning Glory and I were members of a local wildlife rescue and rehabilitation agency called Critter Care. When animals were injured in car accidents, or baby birds fell out of their nests, they were brought to us to care for, rehabilitate, and eventually release. Did you guess that my first color of Wizardry was brown?

Lesson 2. Totems

Totems are animal species that you strongly identify with. That is, if you were an animal yourself, what kind would you be? Many tribal peoples consider that their own family and clan is directly related to a particular species of animal—often claimed to be their ancestor. So they may be of the Clan of the Wolf, the Bear, the Coyote, or the Eagle. That animal is the totem of the clan. But an individual may have their own personal totem as well. As you explore the path of Brown Magick, perhaps you too will discover a particular identification with some species of animal. Perhaps it may be strong enough that you will adopt that creature's name for your own, such as Wolf or Bear. And if your friends take to calling you by that name also, you will know that you have a totem!

Some people, in fact, find that they acquire more than one totem. Sometimes in different periods of their life (My totems have been Serpent, Otter, Owl, and Raven successively over the years), and sometimes simultaneously, depending on circumstances (Morning Glory is both Possum and Tiger together—in fact, her truest totem is *Thylacine,* the marsupial "Tasmanian Tiger"). Totem animals bring you strength, healing, and protection on the spiritual level and can help you deal with a difficult world.

When you are faced with problems in your life, reach down into your deeper levels and call up the power of your totem to fill you and manifest through you. If your totem is Coyote, for instance, think, "What would Coyote do?" Sometimes, just visualizing your totem dealing with the situation can give you enough of a chuckle to pull you through. I have a friend whose totem is Lizard, but sometimes it manifests as Godzilla!

If you were living in a tribal society, your totem would come to you during a Vision Quest, where you would go out into the wilderness alone for a few days to fast and meditate on your Life Path and Mission, and find your true magickal name. You might meet your totem in the Dreaming, or an actual living animal might show up and hang out with you. In tribal societies, such Vision Quests are a rite of passage from childhood to adolescence that everyone goes through at the onset of puberty. Your totem then becomes your special spiritual mentor during those formative years, guiding you into adulthood.

If you are not able to do a Vision Quest, however, you can still open yourself to finding your totem through guided meditation and directed dreaming. Take an astral journey through the Dreaming, perhaps beginning, like Alice, by going down a rabbit-hole. Once you have a totem, you should always carry with you something representing that animal. A bit of fur, a feather, snakeskin, horn, tooth, claw, or bone is, of course, a direct object link. But a tiny carving or figurine will do, or even a picture. You can wear it as jewelry or keep it in your mojo bag (or "medicine pouch," as it is also called).

When you have a totem, seek to learn all you can about that species of animal—both its physical characteristics and habits, and its magickal correspondences and myths. Find out about its needs in the world of Nature. Is its habitat threatened? Perhaps you can volunteer or help raise money for an environmental group that is working to save your totem animal. The lore of totems may be found in the several sets of animal oracle cards available: *Medicine Cards* and the *Druid Animal Oracle* are both excellent and can be found in many bookstores.

Lesson 3: Familiars

A *familiar* is an individual living animal with whom you are deeply connected and psychically bonded. Your familiar should be attached to you specifically, and not just a family pet. Usually quiet animals are the best, as these tend to be most receptive to your thoughts. When choosing an animal for a familiar, keep in mind that you may perform meditations, healings, and magickal rituals that last for some time, so a familiar who will remain still for that time is ideal.

To create a familiar bond, you should be the primary human being with which your familiar has close contact. Ideally, you should raise them from infancy and become their *surrogate* (substitute) mommy—even if you are a boy! You should do all their feeding, cleaning, bathing, medicating, changing their litter box, etc. Perhaps you can even sleep together. More than a pet, or even a companion, your familiar is your best friend—and you are its.

I recommend choosing a familiar with a long life span, as you don't want to be starting all over in building such a deep bond with a new animal every few years. Dogs and cats live 10–20 years, and horses can reach 30. Frogs can live 10–15 years, and toads to 40. Female tarantulas can reach 25. Owls and parrots can live to 50–60, cockatoos over 100. Boas and pythons live to 40–50; and some turtles can live up to 200 years! But sadly, rodents, ferrets, and possums all have very short lives. American possums only live 1–3 years, hamsters 2–3, rats 3–4, and ferrets 4–5. Bunnies come in next at 6–8.

The most important clue to sentience in any animal is whether it looks you right in the eyes when communicating. Several times a day, you should hold your familiar and gaze deeply into its eyes, building a deep *rapport* (harmony) of love and trust between you. Meditate together. Soon you will begin to communicate by sensing each other's thoughts.

Cats and Dogs

The most popular familiars, of course, are cats and dogs. There are now 60 million dogs living in American homes, and 70 million cats. Dogs were the very first animals to be domesticated, more than 12,000 years ago, and cats were the last, about 4,000 years ago (in Egypt, where they were worshipped). They

have been living with people so long that they have become completely integrated into our human lives. They can be incredibly intelligent, sensitive, and psychic, and can bond as deeply as you are willing to with them. Clearly, these are very special furry people. One of the most satisfying ways to get a familiar is to go to an animal shelter and rescue a kitten or puppy and give it a home. You will be its hero for life!

I have had several remarkable feline familiars in my life. Octobriana, our tortoise-shell Siamese, was the most amazing. She would look right into my eyes and carry on a conversation, and we understood each other perfectly (cats have more than 100 vocal sounds; dogs only have about 10). We got her as a kitten from the animal shelter the day we moved to Greenfield Ranch in 1977, and she was with us through the next 16 years and many adventures. Then, one Summer day, she went over and had a conversation with a feral (wild) mama cat next door. Afterwards Octobriana laid down as if to sleep, and died. The next morning, one of the mama cat's wild kittens showed up at our door, insisting on being adopted. He claimed he'd been sent, and was reporting for duty! (Sadly, not only had his mother not been spayed, she also hadn't been vaccinated, and he was already infected with feline leukemia and died soon thereafter.)

So if you get a dog or cat, the most important thing is to have it spayed or neutered, and vaccinated! There are around 40–50 *million* homeless cats roaming the U.S., and probably half as many dogs. Animal shelters and humane societies kill more than 15 million unwanted dogs and cats *every year.* Only 30% of impounded pets are reclaimed, adopted, or rescued. The remaining 70% are destroyed. Many more die from disease, starvation, animal attacks, and cars. Not neutering an animal is just plain irresponsible.

Ferrets

A 2001 census of U.S. pet ownership listed one million ferrets in American homes. These "wascally weasels" are so adorable, curious, and fun-loving that most owners have two or more. "Wuzzies" can be litter-box trained, but not as reliably as cats, and they eat cat food. Ferrets have been domesticated for 5,000 years or so, originally for hunting rabbits. They have become enormously popular in the U.S. in recent years, even appearing in movies (such as *The Fellowship of the Ring*). However, as familiars, ferrets are awfully scatter-brained, excitable, and hyperactive—and they have very short lifespans. I once had a wuzzie named Lilly, and I was heartbroken when she grew old and died within just a few years.

Rats

Harry Potter's friend Ron has a rat named Scabbers as his familiar. Rats make excellent "starting" familiars, as they are smart, clever, curious, and sociable. They also have their own language in their complex colonies, so they are naturally receptive to human communication. However, once again there is the problem of a very short lifespan. The best food for rats is Purina Rat Chow or dry dog chow, but they are omnivorous and enjoy many other treats.

Rats now come in a variety of colors and patterns—a great improvement from my youth, when you could only get them in white. One white rat I had—named Hoopoo—joined our household at the same time our Siamese cat, Mai-Su, had her litter. He nursed right along with the kittens, and seemed to think they were his family. When the kittens were old enough, their mama taught them all how to use the litter box—including Hoopoo! And in his turn, he taught the kittens how to sit on their haunches politely around the cat food bowl and eat daintily with their paws. (And no, the mother cat did *not* teach Hoopoo to catch mice!)

Bunnies

Morning Glory has a gray rex bunny named Smoke. She says that bunnies make excellent familiars for girls in particular, as they are sacred to the Moon Goddess. But "Br'er Rabbit" is a popular and extremely masculine folk hero in the American South, especially among African-Americans. Bunnies are quite smart for prey animals and are social enough to get along well in a household, even with other animals. Unless you are breeding them, you should only have one. It can be kept either in an outside cage, or hutch, or live indoors like a cat or ferret. Your bunny can learn to use a litter-box, but it will chew the bindings off books on low shelves. They eat mostly alfalfa pellets, but they also enjoy treats and table scraps of garden veggies such as carrots and broccoli. Your bunny should not be turned loose in your yard, unless it is completely enclosed with a fence that is buried at least a foot into the ground. Bunnies are great tunnelers! However, you can make a temporary corral with a bit of wire fencing and move this around the yard over patches of clover. If you have a bunny familiar, you might keep it in your room at night and dream together at the full Moon.

Horses

Morning Glory says horses are not just for girls! They have been domesticated for 5,000 years, and for

millennia they were our best friends, as well as our only means of transportation. Horses have a large brain and are very social and intelligent beings. They are capable of profound depths of love and loyalty (stories like *The Black Stallion* and *My Friend Flicka* are drawn from real-life experiences). Horses have a great sense of humor, and older horses can be patient teachers and companions for children and teenagers. If you live in the country or near a stable, then you may decide to make the effort to get a horse. They require the biggest commitment and hardest work of all animals, even if you board your horse at a stable. But the magickal union of a horse and rider moving effortlessly together as one heart and mind is one of the greatest familiar experiences you can ever have.

If you are seriously interested in pursuing this path, the best books in the world to begin with are written by the real-life "horse whisperer," Monty Roberts.

Possums

I think possums make the best pets of all wild animals. Only one kind lives in North America—the original model that has remained unchanged since the days of the dinosaurs. However, many other kinds of possums live in South America, Australia, and New Zealand. I can only talk about the North American possum, as it's the only one I have experience with. These are in no way an endangered species, and they are not protected by law, so if you should come across a baby possum, you might want to give it a good home. Because the mother carries the babies around in her pouch or on her back, by the time you find one apart from its mama, it's old enough to be on its own. Baby possums are adorable little white fuzzballs with whiffly pink noses and ears like flower petals.

Get a little pouch to hang around your neck, or carry the baby possum around in your pocket. Possums don't eat very much, and they sleep most of the time. They eat almost anything (cat food is a good staple), but each one has its favorites. They are easily litter-box trained and very little trouble. We have had several over the years and have given them silly names (Pogo, Participle, Raspberry, and Able). They have slept with us under the covers, clung to my back when I rode around on my bicycle, and been great pets. A possum is sort of like a retarded cat—not too bright, but very sweet. Having a possum is one step above having a stuffed animal! However, they have too short a short life span to be a good long-term familiar.

Bats and Owls: "The Children of the Night"

Owls and bats teach us to not be afraid of the dark. When I was a boy, I had a little brown bat and a screech owl living in my bedroom. I found them both in an old barn I was exploring. They were wonderful and fun pets—very friendly and easy to care for (insect-eating bats thrive on liver sausage with a little boiled egg blended together with a few bugs, and owls eat whole mice or rats—one or two a day). My mother still tells of how her bridge club was thrown into chaos one day when someone left my bedroom door open and Boris, my "flittermouse," came flying out into the living room! Bats, however, are not suitable as familiars. Just encourage them to live around your house and eat flying insects. Moreover, these days some bats carry rabies, so they should be left alone. (But if I lived in Australia, I would definitely want to have a fruit bat!)

Owls have long been associated with wisdom and Wizards. Athena, Greek Goddess of Wisdom, has an owl named Bubo. Harry Potter, of course, has his beautiful snowy owl, Hedwig. Owls are also my very favorite birds. I have had several over my life—including a charming great horned owl with a broken wing who lived with Morning Glory and me for eight years when we worked with Critter Care. I named him Archimedes, after Merlyn's owl. Archimedes was a polite, sensible, dignified bird with a keen sense of humor. He and Octobriana used to play tricks on each other, and he would always pull his stunts with a satisfied "Gotcha!" chuckle. He was an excellent familiar for me, but keeping him also entailed having to raise rats to feed him one every night. I do *not* recommend this to you!

In the U.S., owls are now protected birds, and you can't keep them as pets anymore. However, if you volunteer with a local Wildlife Rescue center, you might get to help heal an injured owl and have the thrill of setting it free back into the wild. Maybe it will fly back to you in your dreams.

Birds

Birds will bond very closely with a person—especially if you "imprint" them as hatchlings—and many make excellent familiars. Cockatiels and lorikeets are really smart and can learn to speak human words. And they can live a *very* long time! I do not recommend, however, getting a parrot or macaw, as these are intensely social birds, and they require constant physical interaction and verbal stimulation to maintain their marginal sanity. Crows and ravens can also be taught to speak a few words, and ravens are now believed to be as smart as dogs. I have never had a crow or raven myself, but I've met some that other magickal people have, and they clearly have a deep bond and familiar connection with their person. Some states, however, now have laws against keeping any kind of wild bird. Again, Wildlife Rescue can be a wonderful resource.

If you live in the country, some barnyard fowl can make excellent familiars. I once had a goose named Gus, whom I raised from a hatchling. Geese are very smart and can live to 50 years. But they are *always* outdoor animals, because they crap constantly all over the place! Gus was utterly devoted to me, and followed me everywhere. Sadly, he froze to death one bitterly cold Winter night because he wouldn't go into the goose house with the other geese and insisted on staying outside by the back door.

Although most pets and familiars regard their human as a "mommy," birds will treat their human as a mate. They can be very possessive and jealous of your friends.

Reptiles

My lifelong fascination with dinosaurs turned my attention towards reptiles at an early age, and I have kept quite a few of them. A wide assortment of reptiles can be purchased at any pet store. That 2001 pet census listed three million snakes, turtles, and lizards in American homes. Box turtles are excellent house and yard pets, and no trouble whatsoever. They can live well over 100 years, and they eat most anything, from veggies to bugs (they *love* earthworms!). However, turtles are not particularly bright or sensitive, and I wouldn't recommend them as familiars. Iguanas are also pretty cool, especially as they like to hang out along the tops of curtains and drapes, and they grow to be quite large (5–6 feet). They are primarily vegetarians, but they also like bugs, mealworms, and raw hamburger.

Snakes make *great* familiars—especially boas and pythons. These giant serpents can grow to 10–30 feet long and are the most primitive of snakes, with little spurs on the males where they once had hind legs. Pythons lay eggs, but boas give birth to litters of live babies. All snakes evolved from a kind of eyeless, earless, legless, worm-like burrowing lizard. They had to reinvent eyes entirely, as well as other senses unique to them, such as infrared heat receptors. But they never reinvented ears, and they have no sense of hearing whatsoever. What they have instead is amazingly acute psychic sensitivity. All snakes are predators, and they must have whole animals to eat. Start with mice, and graduate to rats. When they're small, feeding once a week is enough, and once a month when they get big.

If you feel drawn to have a serpent familiar, I recommend a boa constrictor. Boas have been captive-bred for generations, so the best thing to do is find a pet shop that has some babies. Put your hand down into the tank, think loving thoughts, and wait to see if one of the little guys will come to you and crawl up your arm. If one does and then looks you right in the eyes, you've got yourself a familiar! But keeping a tropical snake like a boa or python is a big commitment, and you need to have the right setup to keep them safe and warm (85–95°F). If they escape from their well-heated *serpentarium* into the outdoors, they can die of exposure. Instead, you might want to start with a nice local gopher snake that you get from a pet store.

My very best familiar ever was a Columbian red-tailed boa that I named Histah. We were so deeply bonded that I could dreamwalk with her in my sleep ("borrowing") as she crawled around at night. After five years, she got mortally wounded in a tragic accident and could not be healed. One day, while I was away at my job, I felt her presence in my mind, as she was "borrowing" me. And then I felt her let go of her body, and settle into mine. I called home immediately and said, "Histah just died."

My wife said, "No, I just saw her in the bathroom."

I said, "Check again."

After a minute she came back to the phone. "You're right. She's dead. How did you know?"

I replied, "Because she's in me now."

And ever since, like Harry Potter, I have been a "parseltongue," with the ability to "talk" to snakes.

Amphibians

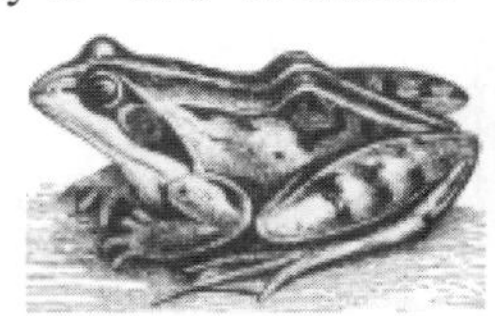

Amphibians include frogs, toads, newts, and salamanders. Their name means "dweller in two worlds," because they start out in life as water-breathing tadpoles and *metamorphose* (change) into four-legged air breathers. It can be a fascinating experience to keep some tadpoles in an aquarium and watch them go through their changes. Unfortunately, these days many kinds of amphibians are becoming endangered, so it is not wise to take adults from their natural habitats. However, some kinds can be purchased in pet shops, and these are alright. Even though Neville Longbottom has a toad familiar named Trevor, amphibians aren't very smart. Maybe this is why the kids at Hogwarts preferred other familiars. However, toads *do* live a long time—Trevor could get to be 40. Did you know that toads and frogs can only see things that are moving?

Tarantulas

These large hairy spiders were among the first creatures to live on dry land, more than 300 million years ago. Back in those days, they were the size of bulldogs! (Aragog and Shelob must be their descendants...) The females, which are bigger and fatter than the males, can live up to 25 years. Spiders don't even have a head, much less a brain, and yet they act with an uncanny and deliberate intelligence. To feed, they impale their hollow fangs into the body of their prey and inject stomach acids. Then, when the prey's insides are all digested the spider sucks out the juices through its own straws. Pet tarantulas are usually fed crickets or pinkie mice.

We have had several tarantulas; my favorite was a Mexican Red-Legged named Kallisti. She learned to recognize me and would crawl onto my hand when I reached into her terrarium. She would climb up and sit on my shoulder, tucked under my hair, and watch everything with intense interest and curiosity, holding her front legs up to listen (spiders have their ears in their armpits). She had a definite presence that impressed everyone who met her. So I think that tarantulas can make good familiars. A pet tarantula won't bite you unless very frightened, and in any case, its venom is pretty harmless to humans—about like a bee sting.

Lesson 4. Shapeshifting & Borrowing

We are not so far removed from the other animals as some people might like to think. Indeed, with all my years of experience and knowledge of animals, I find it easiest to relate to people in the same way as I relate to animals. Each has their own unique qualities and ways of being, and none of them are wrong. You can understand most of the important things about any animal just by knowing what it eats, how it gets its food, whether it's *nocturnal* (active at night) or *diurnal* (active in daylight), and its other lifestyle habits. The same is true of people. Looking at humans as though you are studying animals can be the most useful means of learning patience, tolerance, and insight!

Shapeshifting

Many of Merlyn's lessons for young Arthur involved *shapeshifting,* teaching him to take the forms of various animals to learn their ways and wisdom. When I was a boy, I too used to spend a day or so taking the form of a different creature—moving like the animal, making its sounds, trying to get into its mind and experience the world through its senses. I hopped around like a kangaroo, holding my hands up before my chest. I crawled around with my arms and legs akimbo like a lizard, and slithered under things on my belly like a snake with my hands at my sides. I learned to swim up and down like a dolphin, and wriggled through the water like an otter (I still swim like this). I stomped around like a T-Rex, my back level to the ground, arms tight against my body except for two fingers, snarling and snapping as I turned my head. I lumbered like a bear on all fours, walked on my knuckles like a gorilla, and imitated an elephant by extending my arm with my face against my shoulder. I made a wire headset so I could crawl around the house like an ant with my eyes closed and find my way by touching things with my antennae. I even got a pair of multi-faceted eyeglasses and wore them around to see how the world looks to an insect!

In recent years, Morning Glory has led whole groups of people in doing these kinds of exercises, each being a different animal, crawling around, interacting with each other. I recommend you try it, too—especially with a few friends! See if you can tell what kind of animal each other is.

If you add masks and costumes, you can carry shapeshifting to whole new levels. Accounts of "were-creatures" (*wer* is Old English for "man") come from all parts of the world throughout history: werewolves, were-leopards, were-bears, and *silkies* (were-seals). Many of these were people who deliberately costumed themselves as beasts and imitated their behavior as closely as possible. This would include special rituals to suppress their human side and bring out their animal nature—to *become* that animal. Plains Indians used to dress in buffalo robes to hunt bison, and such animal costumes have been important elements in Mystery rites from the Greek *Brauaria* (bear ritual) and Roman *Lupercalia* (wolf festival) to Medieval mummer's plays.

When we were living on Greenfield Ranch, Morning Glory and I raised up a few baby fawns that I found in my walks through the woods. We fed them on goat's milk and slept with them in our bed. When they grew up, they would spend their days out grazing with the other deer, but when we called their names, they would come trotting over for scritches and snackies. Now, I have a full deerskin robe, complete with hooves and antlers, just as in the pictures on ancient cave walls. One Fall, during the deer mating season, I sat in the meadow under a tree with Kira, who had become a lovely lady deer. A couple of handsome young bucks were trying to court her and were duking it out between them. Finally, the winner swaggered over to Kira, then stopped as he noticed me behind her.

He lowered his head and pawed the ground in challenge, so I did exactly the same back. We shook our antlers at each other, and made a few feints; he totally considered me to be another stag! But when I stood up, that was too much for him, and he ran off. Later, he and Kira did mate and had their own little fawn, which she brought home to us, to meet its "grandparents."

Borrowing

> *She Borrowed... You could ride the minds of animals and birds,...steering them gently, seeing through their eyes. Granny Weatherwax had many times flicked through the channels of consciousness around her. It was, to her, part of the heart of witchcraft. To see through other eyes...*
>
> *...through the eyes of gnats, seeing the slow patterns of time in the fast pattern of one day, their minds traveling rapidly as lightning...*
>
> *...to listen with the body of a beetle, so that the world is a three-dimensional pattern of vibrations...*
>
> *...to see with the nose of a dog, all smells now colors...*
>
> *But there was a price. No one asked you to pay it, but the very* absence *of demand was a moral obligation. You tended not to swat. You dug lightly. You fed the dog. You paid. You* cared; *not because it was kind or good, but because it was right. You left nothing but memories, you took nothing but experience.*
>
> —Terry Pratchett (*Lords and Ladies,* p. 52)

Borrowing is the art of dreamwalking into the mind of an animal, so you can feel what it feels and look out through its eyes. This is the most powerful kind of shapeshifting—a skill acquired only by a few, and only with much practice. When you are borrowing, you go into a deep meditative trance, leaving your body completely unconscious, allowing yourself to awaken within your chosen host. Borrowing is the ultimate experience you can have with a deeply bonded familiar, riding in the back of their mind as they go out on their forays. But there can be a danger in borrowing too long and too often—you may forget how to return to your human self! Never go deeply into this kind of trance without magically guarding your physical body—even arranging with someone for a "wake-up" call.

Calling

Before attempting borrowing, you should learn *calling*—bringing an animal to you. An easy way to start, of course, is with your own pets and familiars. Learn to call them not just by your names for them, but also by the kinds of sounds they make. The basic calling sounds for most animals are those that mothers and babies make to each other when they are separated. Learn to imitate these so well that your animals will respond back with the same sound. If you watch enough animal documentaries on TV or spend enough time out in the woods, you will hear such calls. You can also check out animal sound recordings from your library. And there are special calling devices available for some birds, such as ducks, geese, and turkeys.

When calling animals, however, it is not enough just to make the right sound. For many creatures, body language is more important than sounds. This is the secret of "horse whispering." Animals with any psychic sensitivity also respond to projected mental images and emotions. Envision their favorite food, or others of their own kind—such as mates, babies, herds, flocks, etc. Call butterflies, for instance, by envisioning flowers. And always think warm, loving, welcoming, comforting thoughts to all animals.

Lesson 5: The Natural Bestiary

The medieval bestiaries treated all animals as *allegories,* or moral lessons to be learned. Here I would like to offer a modern bestiary of a few natural animals (mythical beastes will be covered in 7.4).

Bear

Bear wants nothing more from others than to be left alone. When Winter brings cold snow to cover the ground, Bear hibernates, her fat built up through the Summer, so she needn't eat for four months. In the womb of her cave, Bear dwells in the Dreaming, while her babies are born and nurse as she sleeps. In the Spring, she is reborn, bringing new life out into the world with her awakening. Bear is the best mother and protector, teaching us strength and courage. Native Americans considered Bear to be like a human in a fur coat.

Coyote

Coyote is the great Trickster. His greatest pleasure is in outsmarting others, laughing at them as he pulls it off. But he tricks himself as often as others and continually falls into his own traps, never learning the lesson—unlike any of us! Coyote is one of the few wild animals who, in spite of trapping, is increasing his range.

Flutterby (Butterfly)

Because Flutterby *metamorphoses* (transforms) from caterpiggle through pupa into an exquisite petalwinged flying flower, people throughout the world have associated her with the Soul, which springs forth from the cocoon-like mummy or shrouded corpse. Indeed, the Greek word *psyche,* meaning "soul," is also their word for Butterfly, and the name of a goddess who was beloved of Eros, the god of Love. In China the Butterfly is the emblem of a happy marriage, and everywhere she represents transformation. Flutterbies and Moths are among the very few creatures that can see ultraviolet (black light), and a number of flowers have developed ultraviolet fluorescence to attract them.

Hummingbird

Tiny Hummingbird can fly fast as lightning in any direction—up, down, backwards, and forwards. He can even stop instantly and hover motionless. I once asked a Quechua Indian Shaman in Peru why there were so many images of Hummingbirds carved in the rocks and woven into tapestries. He told me: "The giant Condor soars at the top of the sky. He thinks, 'I am the lord of creation; all the world and all creatures are beneath me.' Then, suddenly there is this tiny little thing going zip! zip!—so fast he can hardly see it—flying circles around him. 'What is that?' he wonders. It's Hummingbird. We, the people of the land, are like Hummingbird. The great Inca lords and Spanish rulers don't even notice us. But we are everywhere."

Lizard

Many Lizards have long and beautiful tails that are only loosely attached to their bodies, designed to break off easily. If a predator catches such a Lizard, he finds himself holding nothing but a wriggling tail, while Lizard himself escapes under a rock. Over time, Lizard will grow himself a new tail. A wise Wizard will always have a "lizard tail"—something magnificent he is very proud of, but which he can abandon with no harm in an emergency. Because he likes to bask for house on a sunny rock, Lizard is considered to be a great dreamer, and his magick can help you enter the Dreaming.

Peacock

Peacock is certainly the most spectacularly *ostentatious* (showy, flashy, gaudy) creature on the planet! Who can possibly rival his display of a 6-foot diameter fan of brilliant iridescent eyes? But he pays a heavy price for his magnificence, as his glorious tail weighs him down when he flies, and the beautiful Peacock is easily spotted and caught by predators. But in his sacrifice, he ensures the survival of his wife and kids, who go unnoticed in their drab camouflage.

In Greek legend, Peacock was the bird of Hera, jealous Queen of the Olympian Gods, who used him to watch everywhere. The all-seeing eyes in his tail came from Argus, the hundred-eyed Titan. In the East, Peacock represents royalty, dignity, and authority. The Roman poet Ovid said he carries the stars in his tail, symbolizing immortality. His harsh, eerie cry is said to foretell rain.

Possum

Morning Glory says: Possum is a very creative *anachronism* (ancient survivor). She has been waddling this Earth since the days of the dinosaurs. Possums have seen many mighty creatures go extinct while they are still quietly living their short little lives. When you are a Possum, everyone is against you…even your own kind. Possum is a solitary animal, not part of a social group. Only the mother and babies have a link, which disappears when they are old enough to be on their own.

How can such a defenseless creature survive this long in the harsh world? The answer is Possum Magick. Possum has three tricks: 1. She is a very good mother and fights for her babies; 2. She will eat *anything;* and 3. She will faint when a predator attacks her, appearing to be dead. For this last reason, Possum is considered to be a trickster. Possum teaches us the power of surrender. She lives lightly on the Earth and doesn't need pride, courage, or intelligence to have both wisdom and evolutionary success.

Raven

Raven is the most intelligent of all birds. Many remarkable accounts testify to his cleverness. Raven is the Messenger and the Magician, and he represents all things magickal. Raven is a wise trickster in Native American lore who carries our magick to its target and our prayers to the Gods. Odin, one-eyed chief of the *Aesir* (the Norse Gods) and master of magick, has two Ravens, named *Huginn* ("thought") and *Muninn* ("memory"). They travel throughout the world and report back to him all they see and learn. Raven offers wise counsel to those who can understand him. Because of their natural tendency to fly home to roost in the evening, Ravens guided seafarers to port. But if all Ravens suddenly leave an area, it is a sign that drought or famine is soon to follow.

Serpent

Other than her sinuous shape, the thing that has most impressed people about Serpent is her ability to renew herself by shedding her entire skin—apparently achieving immortality. Some Serpents do live a long time and get very big—30 feet or more in the case of Python and Anaconda. And remains have been found of a huge Cretaceous Serpent *(Madtsoia)* that could take a dinosaur!

For all the power in her mighty muscled body, Serpent's head is actually quite delicate and vulnerable; her jawbones have multiple hinges to swallow prey much larger than herself. To avoid injury, therefore, Serpent immobilizes her prey and kills without a battle, either by relentless constriction or by rapid injection of deadly poison. Her unblinking lidless gaze appears to hypnotize her prey into immobility. Serpent moves forward either in sinuous waves or in a steady rippling of her stomach scales, like the tread of a tank. But she cannot back up.

Because she crawls through holes down into the Underworld, Serpent is the Messenger between the realms of the Living and the Dead. Because of her shedding, she represents healing, renewal, and rebirth—and also arcane knowledge and sexuality. In ancient Crete, Egypt, Greece, and Rome, snakes were kept in temples and under homes to control disease-bearing mice and rats.

Spider

Right after they hatch, tiny baby Spiders climb to a high place and spin long streamers of thread out into the wind, like kite strings with no kites. They let go their grip and are carried by the wind over the land, finally to settle like gentle parachutes in new homes. Wherever they go, they continue to spin out their webbing. Spider silk is the strongest material in the world—stronger even than steel cable. I look at satellite dishes on the rooftops, and then at Spider webs in the grass and garden, and I wonder, what signals are they picking up? Are Spiders spinning a worldwide web for Gaia?

In Greek legend, Arachné (from whom we get the scientific name for spiders—*arachnids*) was a weaver whose skill incurred the jealousy of the goddess Athena, who turned Arachné into a Spider. Other peoples say that Spider wove the world, the universe, the first alphabet, and the webs of Fate. She teaches us the creative magick of weaving and networking in our lives and destinies.

Chinese say, "A house without spiders is cursed by the gods." Your friendly little house Spider works hard to keep nasty bugs out of your home—including other, more dangerous Spiders. When her cobwebs become so dusty that you can see them, however, they must be cleaned out, because they cannot catch flies like that. Use a Webster to wind up the old webs, being careful not to hurt the Spider. She will then happily spin invisible new webs. *Never* intentionally kill a Spider, unless it is a Black Widow or a Brown Recluse (in the U.S.); learn to recognize them and avoid them. Of course, if you live in Australia, all bets are off—practically *every* Spider there is deadly!

Turtle

Some creation myths tell that the world is actually the shell of a giant Turtle. Our favorite author, Terry Pratchett, has written dozens of books about *Discworld,* a pancake-shaped world supported by four enormous elephants riding on the back of the great space-turtle A'Tuin.

Turtle is completely safe and secure inside his shell. Nothing can get at him to hurt him, as long as he doesn't come out. Without taking any risks, he can live for centuries…or exist, at least. Like Turtle, you too can erect a shield to protect you from the pains and injustices of a cruel world. And if, like Turtle, you're very careful, play it safe, and never stick your neck out, then nothing bad or good will ever happen to you. Still, Turtle's patient progress through life, like the race of the Tortoise and the Hare, can give us the lesson: "Slow and steady wins the race."

Wolf

In the Wolf pack, only the *alpha* (first) couple mates and has pups, and that couple mates for life. They are the pack leaders. Wolf exhibits profound loyalty to his mate and his family pack, which are all related by blood or marriage. However, just as there is an alpha couple, a pack will also have an *omega* (last), who is at the bottom of the social order and gets picked on and beat up by everyone else. Wolf is the essence of untamed wildness, as his descendant, Dog, is the very symbol of domestication. Wolf teaches us both loyalty and self-reliance.

Lesson 6: Mottoes of Animals

(by Morning Glory Zell-Ravenheart)

Each kind of animal has its own particular lesson to teach us, if we can truly understand them. Here are a few more lessons from the natural bestiary, in the form of "mottoes" by which they each live and survive. Consider these if you choose (or are chosen by) any of these animals as your totem. And then go and learn everything you can about that animal to find out *why* this is its motto!

Bee: "Bee-come so much a part of a community that you will gain from its strength and wisdom, bee-coming more than the sum of its parts."

Chameleon: "Blend into your surroundings so well that you never need to be fast or strong to survive."

Dolphin: "Grace, joy, and playfulness bring oneness with one's environment."

Eagle and Hawk: "See far and make your plan; then height and swiftness will not be your undoing."

Hermit Crab: "Adapt to whatever is around you by learning to use it to your own advantage."

House Cat: "Cut the deal on your own terms."

Lion: "Beauty and strength with cooperation is the key."

Monkey: "If you're clever enough and cute enough, others will put up with you when you are annoying."

Octopus: "Flexibility is the best protection and greatest advantage."

Skunk: "Sometimes it's not the worst thing to be unpopular."

Squirrel: "Make your work into play and life will be sweet every day."

Stag: "Listen to the wind with your whole body, and most of all with your heart, and you will learn to run with silken swiftness."

Class II: Cosmology (Violet Magick)

1. Introduction: The Celestial Arts

OUR FASCINATION WITH THE HEAVENS certainly goes back even further than our mastery of fire. Even animals are affected by the Solar cycles and the Lunar phases. Wolves were howling at the full Moon long before our ancestors walked upright. The great bowl of the night sky—the *Celestial Sphere*—that surrounds our tiny world has always been a subject of magickal and Wizardly studies. "Connecting the dots" of the stars to form constellations elevated our myths and legends into the heavens. The fixed position of the Pole Star in the rotating sky gave us a firm bearing in all seasons. The movements of the Sun, Moon and planets through the signs of the Zodiac gave us our Calendars, our first way of keeping time, and one of our earliest forms of Divination.

Celestial ("heavenly") events like: meteor showers, comets, eclipses of the Sun and Moon, the Aurora Borealis capture our imagination. Sometimes, as "Thunderbolts of the Gods," meteorites would plunge to Earth, bringing unexpected gifts. These were often made of a strange metal, unlike anything known on Earth: rustproof nickle-iron—the basis of our first iron weapons. This material could even be magnetized (as *lodestones)* gaining strange magickal properties different than any Earthly material.

Astronomy ("star classifying") is our oldest science. Babylonian, Egyptian, Chinese and European courts had professional astronomers long before there were professional zoologists, geologists or botanists. Ancient Sumerian tablets and carvings show that the movements of the planets were being carefully observed and recorded before 3,000 BCE. The three greatest Pyramids of Egypt were precisely aligned to match the three stars on Orion's belt, with the Nile River as the Milky Way. Stonehenge and Indian Medicine Wheels were positioned to mark the seasonal rising of the Sun and certain bright stars.

The first astronomical telescope was built in 1608 by Galileo Galilei (1564-1642). Gazing into the heavens, a year later he discovered the four largest moons orbiting Jupiter, and named them Io, Europa, Ganymede, and Callisto. Seeing these as a model for the Solar System, Galileo then proposed that the Earth likewise revolves around the Sun. For such a radical notion, he was tried and convicted of heresy by the Church.

Ever since Galileo, telescopes have been prized instruments of Wizards. Even a fairly inexpensive one will enable you to see the Galilean moons, Saturn's rings, Lunar craters, the Ring Nebula of Beta Lyrae, and the Andromeda Galaxy. If you can't get a telescope, however, a good set of binoculars will still show you many celestial wonders.

Through the ages, several Big Questions have been the focus of attention for all who study the heavens. The Truth is still out there...awaiting our future explorations and discoveries.

- What is the origin of the Universe? Did it have a beginning, or has it been here for eternity?
- How common are planetary systems around other stars—especially terrestrial planets like ours?
- Is there life elsewhere in the Solar System? If not, why is Earth special?
- Is there life beyond the Solar System—especially intelligent life? Is anyone else out there, or are we all alone in the dark?

2. Glossary of Astronomical Terms

Aphelion: The point in the orbit of a planet, comet, etc. which is furthest from the sun.

Corona: The very hot outer layer of the Sun's atmosphere, composed of highly diffused, superheated, ionized gases, and extending into interplanetary space. The hot gasses in the solar corona create the *solar wind.*

Fission: The splitting of heavier atomic nuclei into lighter ones. In the case of heavy atoms (e.g., uranium, plutonium), this will release energy. Fission is how nuclear power plants produce energy.

Fusion: The combining of lighter elements into heavier ones. For lighter elements (e.g., hydrogen, helium) this processes releases energy. Fusion is how stars produce energy, and is being researched as a way to produce power on Earth.

Heliosphere: The vast region starting at the Sun's surface and extending to the limits of the solar system, well beyond the orbits of the most distant planets.

Ion: An atom which has lost or gained one or more electrons so that it has a net electrical charge.

Light Year: A measure of distance, not time, based on how far a particle of light will travel in one year. Since light travels at 186,282 miles per second, a light year is about six trillion miles.

Orbit: The path of an object (such as the Earth) revolving around another object (such as the Sun).

Perihelion: The point in the orbit of a planet, comet, etc. which is closest to the sun.

Revolution: The motion of an object around another larger body, such as the Earth's yearly course around the Sun.

Rotation: The spinning of a body about its own axis, like a top.

Lesson 3: The Sun

The Sun (*Sol*) is the *nucleus* (center) of our Solar System. It is a great flaming ball of gas and plasma, which we orbit at a distance of 93 million miles. Our Sun is a pretty average-sized star, about 880,000 miles in diameter. If it were hollow, over a million Earths would easily fit inside. Its density is just under 1½ times that of water.

Like other stars, the Sun "pulses," creating an 11-year cycle of *Sunspots*—fringed dark holes in the outer layers that penetrate deep into the cooler interior. From 1645 to 1715, however, no sunspots were recorded. This period is called the *Maunder Minimum,* a time of exceptionally cold weather across the northern hemisphere of Earth. Its cause remains unknown.

The visible surface of the Sun is called the *Photosphere.* The next layers outward are the *Chromosphere,* then the *Corona.* Each layer is much hotter than the one below it. The very hot gasses in the corona generate the *solar wind*, blowing outward past the planets in great spiraling waves. Periodically, gigantic *Solar flares* erupt from the photosphere around cooler sunspot regions. Some flares extend upward more than 60,000 miles. Though flares last for only a few minutes to a few hours, they are among the most powerful events in the solar system.

The interior of the Sun is believed to be a gigantic nuclear furnace, transforming *hydrogen* ("water-born") into *helium* ("Sun-stuff," named for *Helios,* the Greek Sun-God) at a temperature of millions of degrees. Four million tons of matter are converted into energy every second. However, such nuclear reactions should produce vast quantities of subatomic particles called *neutrinos*—yet none have ever been detected coming from our Sun. In addition, the interior of the Sun is thousands of degrees cooler than the outer layers, with the corona being the hottest. To explain these anomalies, some scientists are considering alternative theories of solar mechanics. The most promising of these proposes electrical discharges through the plasma of the Solar corona, as if the Sun is a gigantic plasma ball.

An electrical *plasma* is a cloud of ions and electrons that can sometimes light up and behave in unusual ways. Familiar examples or electrical plasmas are in neon signs, lightning, and electric arc welders. Plasma permeates the space that contains our solar system. The solar wind is a plasma. Our entire Milky Way galaxy consists mainly of plasma. In fact 99% of the entire universe is plasma!

The Sun generates a vast magnetic bubble called the *heliosphere*, containing the Solar System, the solar wind, and the entire solar magnetic field. At the outermost edge of the heliosphere, called the *heliopause,* the solar wind meets the interstellar sea of plasma that permeates our galaxy. This is the true boundary of the Solar System.

Lesson 4: Eclipses

In ancient times, an eclipse—especially of the Sun—was viewed with great fear as an ill omen. In addition to reading the stars to predict the changing of the seasons—and the times for planting, floods, droughts, and religious festivals—one of the most important duties of professional star-gazers was to predict eclipses. Legend says that two Chinese astronomers who failed to predict an eclipse in 2136 BCE were put to death as frauds.

Although the enormous Sun is 93 million miles from Earth, our tiny Moon (about the size of the United States or Australia) is only 238,000 miles away. It is an amazing cosmic coincidence that the visual diameters of the Sun and Moon as seen from Earth are exactly the same size. Therefore, when the Moon passes directly between the Earth and the Sun, it perfectly covers the face of the Sun, giving us a total *Solar Eclipse.* In the same way, when the Moon is directly behind us, it passes through the shadow of the Earth, and we see a *Lunar Eclipse.*

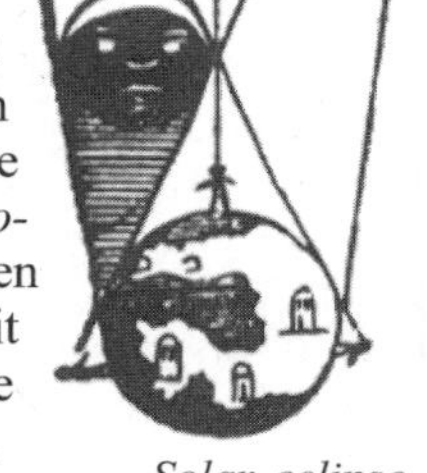

Solar eclipse (16th century)

An eclipse is a great cosmic light show. As the Earth's shadow passes across the face of the Moon, the light passing through dust in our atmosphere that gives us brilliant sunsets can turn the Moon a blood-red. But the most awesome spectacle of all is a total Solar Eclipse. In this case, it is the shadow of the Moon which is passing across the face of the Earth along a narrow path. If you can be at the center of that path—as I have been—you will see rippling waves of shadows rushing towards you across the land, as if you were underwater. The black Lunar disk makes an ever-narrowing ring of the Sun, until, at the last moment, the remaining sunlight blazes forth like a diamond (in fact, this is called the "diamond ring" effect).

Then comes the moment of totality, when the Moon completely covers the Solar disk, and you are standing in its shadow. Suddenly, the sky goes completely black, and the stars shine forth. Birds cry out and dive for night cover. Cows moo and lie down on the spot. A golden light shines all around the distant horizon, which is out of the Lunar shadow. Around the darkened Sun, the Solar corona blazes out into the sky in an aura of unearthly ultraviolet flames. It looks exactly like the iris of a great Cosmic Eye, with a black pupil at its center. The impression you get is that you are looking directly into the Eye of God. This image has been represented from time immemorial, and is depicted on the back of the US $1 bill. If you would like to see some incredible eclipse photos, go to www.mreclipse.com/MrEclipse.html

The next total eclipse of the Sun to be seen in North America will be on **August 21, 2017.** It will cross the entire continental US along a diagonal line from Portland, OR, through St. Louis, MO, Nashville, TN, and Charleston, NC. Don't miss it! The next ones for North America will be April 8, 2024; Aug. 23, 2044; and Aug. 12, 2046. Be sure to wear special mylar "eclipse glasses" so you will be able to look directly at the Sun; *DO NOT attempt to look at the Sun without such glasses!*

Lesson 5. Telling Time by the Sun & Stars

From years to seasons to months to days to hours, minutes and seconds, all our notions of time are based on the apparent movements of the heavens. Of course, most of those motions are of the Earth itself rotating on its axis and revolving around the Sun. But the Moon revolves around the Earth on a regular monthly cycle, and the visible planets also move across the stars. Sundials tell the time using a shadow cast by a stick or line (the *gnomen*) as the Sun traverses the sky. As the shadow reaches various marks on the dial, the hours are indicated.

You can tell how long the Sun will take to set by holding your hand out in front of you with your fingers at a right angle, like this: Each finger marks about 7½ minutes, and all four mark ½ hour. Line up your hand so the bottom edge is at the horizon, and you can estimate pretty accurately how many minutes 'til sunset by how many fingers the Sun is high. I use this trick all the time.

Sun
1/2 hr.
Horizon

But the whole night sky can be used as a great clock face, if you know how. The North Star is the center point, and the "hour hand" is the Little Dipper. The whole sky turns in 24 hours, so you have to imagine twice as many numbers, as if a regular clock was marked with a number every ½ hour. The Star-Clock turns counter-clockwise. To read it, make a little drawing of a clock face marked with 24 hours, like this:

Then draw the position of the Little Dipper as soon as you can see it, and note what time it is (it will advance about 1° each night, so you have to make a new diagram each time you want to do this). From then on, all you have to do through the night is look at the stars, and compare their positions with your clock face drawing. When the Little Dipper has gone ¼ turn, you will know that six hours have passed!

Many marvelous instruments have been developed by astronomers to model the motions of the stars for timekeeping: *sundials, astrolabes, planispheres, orrereys* and *armillaries.* No Wizard's study would be complete without one or more of these! Here are some of the nifty celestial contraptions I have in my study:

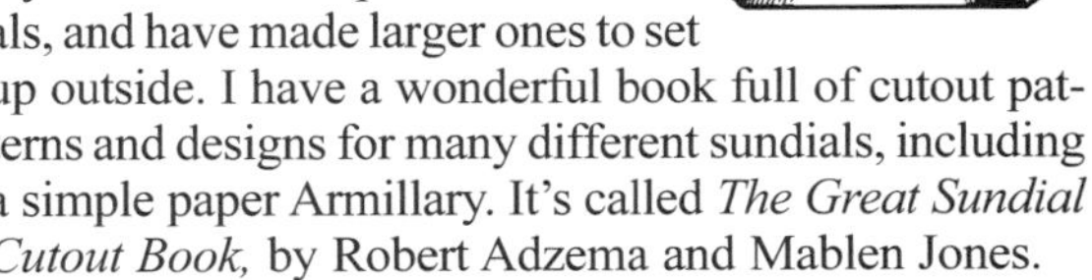

Sundials—there are many more possible designs for sundials than this popular garden variety. I have several pocket sundials, and have made larger ones to set up outside. I have a wonderful book full of cutout patterns and designs for many different sundials, including a simple paper Armillary. It's called *The Great Sundial Cutout Book,* by Robert Adzema and Mablen Jones.

Celestial Armillary—this is a clever model of the position of the Earth at various seasons in relation to the constellations of the Zodiac. You see these in many old pictures of Wizards. The Earth is represented as a little ball in the center of a spherical cage with rings representing the equator, tropics of Cancer/Capricorn, and the Arctic/Antarctic circles. An arrow running through the middle points to the North Star. A band marked with the signs of the Zodiac encircles the cage in the position of the plane of the ecliptic, and the whole thing can be rotated within a stationary frame marked with the dates of the year. Hogwarts Headmaster Albus Dumbledore has dozens of these all around his office. You can make one yourself from the pattern in *The Great Sundial Cutout Book.*

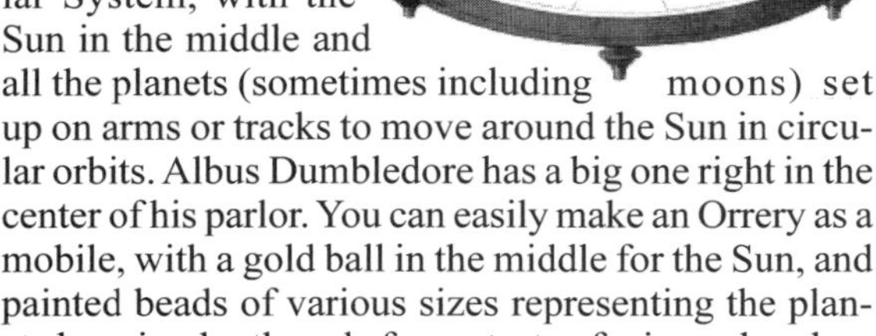

Orrery—this is a small model of the Solar System, with the Sun in the middle and all the planets (sometimes including moons) set up on arms or tracks to move around the Sun in circular orbits. Albus Dumbledore has a big one right in the center of his parlor. You can easily make an Orrery as a mobile, with a gold ball in the middle for the Sun, and painted beads of various sizes representing the planets hanging by threads from struts of wire or bamboo skewers. I made one of these for a science project in school, and it hung from my ceiling for years.

Lesson 6. The Planets, etc.

Just remember that you're standing on a planet that's evolving,
And revolving at nine hundred miles an hour...
That's orbiting at ninety miles a second, so it's reckoned,
A sun that is the source of all our power.
—Monty Python, *The Meaning of Life*

Nine known planets circle our Sun, with over 100 satellite moons orbiting them. In order outward, these are: **Mercury, Venus, Earth, Mars, Jupiter, Saturn, Uranus, Neptune** and **Pluto.** The first four plus Pluto are rocky planets, like the Earth, and are called *terrestrial* ("Earth-like") worlds. Venus and Mars also have atmospheres, mountains, and other surface features. The outer planets (except Pluto) are huge *gas giants,* with no clear surface, just layers and layers of clouds, many thousands of miles deep, getting ever denser, and eventually becoming liquid, and finally solid.

In addition to the planets and moons, hundreds of icy comets plunge in and out through the Solar system on elongated orbits. And there are vast numbers of smaller objects, from tiny meteorites to asteroids the size of Texas. An estimated 100 billion of these form outer "shells" of rocks, ice and debris surrounding our Solar System, and are the source of all comets. These are known as the *Kuiper Belt* and the *Oort Cloud* (named for Dutch astronomers Gerard Kuiper and Jan Oort), and their outer edge is two light years away! All these planets and objects are held within the gravitational field of the mighty Sun in the center.

The Titius-Bode Rule

In the 18th century, two astronomers, Johann Titius and Johann Bode, discovered a numerical formula for the sizes of the planetary orbits. By using the distance from the Sun to the Earth as a standard, called an *Astronomical Unit,* or AU, astronomers can calculate distances of the other planets in proportion to it. Titius and Bode noticed the following pattern—they started with 0, then took 3 and began doubling—0, 3, 6, 12, 24, 48, 96, 192, 384, 768. Then they added 4 to each number and divided by 10, and the result approximated the actual planetary orbits in AU's (see below).

In Titius' and Bode's time, the asteroid belt, Uranus, Neptune and Pluto were as yet undiscovered. However, the Titius-Bode Rule predicted a planet between Mars and Jupiter, which turned out to be right where the asteroid belt is. Some astronomers believe the asteroids were once a planet which exploded, and have named it *Krypton,* after Superman's mythical homeworld. The Titius-Bode Rule also predicted another planet out from Saturn, which turned out to be Uranus, but Neptune falls a bit short of the pattern, and Pluto doesn't fit at all.

To get an idea of the scale of distances in the Solar System, get a thin strip of wood (such as lath) at least 40" long. Stick a big yellow thumbtack at one end. Then, using the AU distances as inches, stick colored pins into the lath at those distances. The Earth will be a little blue pin 1" from the Sun-tack, and Pluto

Planetary Statistics

Planet	Mercury	Venus	Earth	Mars	Aster.	Jupiter	Saturn	Uranus	Neptune	Pluto
Distance from Sun	36 mm	67 mm	93 mm	142 mm	258 mm	484 mm	887 mm	1,784	2,796	3,676
Distance in AU	0.387	0.723	1.0	1.524	2.77 av.	5.203	9.539	19.18	30.06	39.44
Titius-Bode AU	0.4	0.7	1.0	1.6	2.8	5.2	10.0	19.6	38.8	77.2
Diameter (miles)	3,023	7,509	7,913	4,210		88,626	74,857	31,731	30,702	1,424
Mass : Earth	0.055	0.814	1.0	0.107		318	95.2	14.5	17.1	0.002
Gravity : Earth	0.25	0.85	1.0	0.36		264	117	0.92	112	0.059
Volume : Earth	0.06	0.92	1.0	0.15		1,318	736	64	60	0.178
Year : Earth	0.241	0.615	1.0	1.88		11.86	29.46	84	164.8	247.7
Year in days	87.66	224.6	365.25	694		4,383	10,592	30,681	60,266	90,582
Day in hours	1,416	5,832	24	24.6		9.8	10.2	15.5	15.8	153.6
Number of Moons	0	0	1	2		40	30	21	11	1
100 lbs. Earth=	25 lbs.	85	100	36		264	117	92	112	6

will be 39.44" away!

Here is a chart of some basic statistics for the nine Planets, plus the Asteroid Belt. Average Distances from Sun are in millions of miles; AU is Astronomical Units; Diameters at Equator are in miles; Mass, Volumes, Length of Year (revolution) are compared to Earth's; Length of Day (rotation) is in hours. The number of moons listed is how many we know as of Jan. 2003. And the last entry indicates how much a person weighing 100 lbs. on Earth would weigh on those worlds.

Pluto has an irregular orbit—it comes in closer than Neptune at one point—and is askew from the plane of the Ecliptic on which the other orbits lie. Most astronomers now think that Pluto is not a proper planet at all, but merely a stray body from the Kuiper Belt that has been captured by the Sun into a closer orbit. Some believe there may be a true 9th "Planet X" still to be found at around 77 AU. Although it hasn't yet been discovered, it's been dubbed *Persephone* (the Greek Queen of the Underworld, wife of Pluto/Hades).

Our Moon

Astronomers believe that our Moon was formed when a Mars-sized body smashed into the Earth, ejecting matter into orbit and lengthening our day to its present value of 24 hours. This happened 4.5 billion years ago, when the Earth was still in a molten state. Therefore Luna is truly the "daughter" of Terra.

Comets and Meteors

When comets come hurtling through our inner Solar System, the frozen gasses that bind them together boil off, creating the characteristic cometary "tail," which may be millions of miles long. The Great Comet of 1843 had a tail that would have reached from the Sun past the orbit of Mars, nearly 200 million miles! Released from the melting ice, great quantities of rocks, pebbles, and debris that had been held frozen together fall off and are strewn in a wake along the comet's orbit. When the Earth passes through one of these cometary wakes, we experience *meteor showers*. The rocks strike the Earth's atmosphere on the forward side (mostly after midnite) and burn up in bright fiery streaks. I think of these as "bugs on the windshield." Here are the peak dates, names, and centers of the best annual showers:

PEAK	SHOWER	CENTER LOCATION IN SKY
Jan. 3	***Quadrantids****	E—Between Bootes & head of Draco.
Apr. 22	***Lyrids***	NE—Between Vega & Hercules.
May 5	***E-Aquarids****	E—SW of Square of Pegasus.
July 28	***D-Aquarids***	SE—Aquarius
Aug. 12	***Perseids****	NE—Perseus.
Oct. 8	***Draconids***	E—Draco. Only storm every 6½ yrs.
Oct. 21	***Orionids***	E—Between Orion & Gemini.
Nov. 17	***Leonids*****	E—Leo. Sometimes BIG storm!
Dec. 14	***Geminids****	E—Near Castor in Gemini.

Best Prospects for Life

In addition to Earth, several other worlds in our Solar System also have possible conditions for life. Of course, we won't know for sure until we can send life-detecting probes to these planets and moons. Meanwhile, here are our best prospects, and the reasons why life might exist there:

Mars: Most Earth-like; much more so in the past. Much water ice in soil underground.

Jupiter: Warm, plenty of water and many complex organic chemicals.

Europa (a moon of Jupiter): Covered with ice, liquid water beneath.

Enceladus (a moon of Saturn): Icy surface, maybe liquid water beneath.

Ganymede (a moon of Jupiter): Maybe liquid water beneath icy surface.

Callisto (a moon of Jupiter): May have liquid water beneath icy surface.

Titan (a moon of Saturn): Complex chemistry and surface liquids likely.

Io (a moon of Jupiter): Complex chemistry, warmer than most moons.

Lesson 7: Stars and Galaxies

The sun and you and me, and all the stars that we can see,
Are moving at a million miles a day.
In an outer spiral-arm at forty thousand miles an hour
Of the galaxy we call the Milky Way.
Our galaxy itself contains a hundred billion stars,
It's a hundred thousand light years side to side.
It bulges in the middle, sixteen thousand light years thick,
But out by us it's just three thousand light years wide.
We're 30 thousand light years from galactic central point,
We go 'round every two-fifty million years.
And our galaxy is only one of millions of billions,
In this amazing and expanding universe!

—Monty Python, *The Meaning of Life*

Our own Milky Way galaxy is about 100,000 light years in diameter and contains around 100 billion star systems. Our Solar System is located in the Orion Spur of the Sagittarius Arm, about 27,000 light years out from the galactic center—which is located in the constellation of Sagittarius. At our speed of 135 miles per second, it takes us 250 million years to make a complete revolution around the galaxy.

To get an idea of just how really BIG the galaxy and the universe are, I recommend an amazing little Website called "Quarks to Quasars: Powers of Ten" at *www.wordwizz.com/pwrsof10.htm.*

Galaxies are formed, driven, and stabilized by dynamic electromagnetic effects. At the center of every galaxy lies a super-massive *black hole*. About a third of all galaxies (including ours) have a flattened main

main disk in the shape of a spiral with two or more arms and a large central bulge. Others are barred, elliptical, egg-shaped and even irregular, but all are believed to represent an evolutionary continuum leading from a huge quasar to a spiral form. Galaxies are gravitationally bound into clusters containing hundreds or thousands of members. Our own Milky Way is a member of the Virgo Cluster.

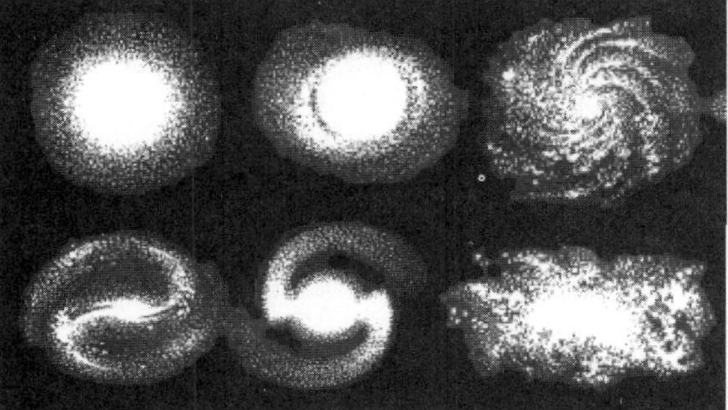

> *The size of individual galaxies with respect to the distance between them makes galaxies relatively much closer together than are the stars within them. It is therefore common for galaxies to collide without the stars within them colliding. One of the observed effects of galactic collisions is to increase the production of new stars within both galaxies due to the interaction of huge clouds of interstellar gas and dust. Slowly moving and rotating galaxies collide over periods of millions of years.* —Bruce Bryson, "Quarks to Quasars: Powers of Ten"

Star systems are formed within galaxies as whirlpools of cosmic dust and debris coalesce, gathering more mass together until the nucleus ignites. Smaller eddies of spinning vortices within these accretion disks eventually become planets. If they are big enough, they may even form into multiple stars, rather than just one. Our Sun is just an average-sized star. Tiny white dwarfs may be no larger than the Earth, while *Antares* (the red giant in the heart of Scorpio) is bigger than the orbit of Mars.

Stars go through multiple generations, forming initially out of pure hydrogen, which they convert to helium. When this process is completed, they explode in a supernova, which creates far heavier elements which are then scattered out into space. Out of those heavier elements, the next generation of stars form, this time with planets.

But all the stars, planets, dust and other matter in the universe accounts for only 4.4% of its mass! According to astronomers, 23% is bizarre "dark matter," and 73% is some unknown "dark energy."

Lesson 8. The Constellations

On a clear moonless night, we can see about 2,000 stars. The Roman astronomer Claudius Ptolemy of Alexandria (85-165 CE) grouped 1,022 of these stars into 48 pictures called *constellations* ("stars together"). Although Ptolemy's *Almagest*, completed in 129 CE, does not, of course, include those stars which can only be seen from the southern hemisphere, it forms the basis for the 88 constellations now officially listed by the International Astronomical Union.

These figures are purely a human invention as seen from Earth; the stars in them are not actually associated with each other in any way, and are really many lights years apart. From another star system they would look totally different. To see these star-pictures yourself, all you need to do is learn how to "connect the dots." However, the diagrams shown in most books don't make any sense. The ones I am adapting here were mostly worked out by H.A. Rey, in a wonderful book called *Find the Constellations* (1954).

The Circumpolar Constellations

The six Constellations that circle *Polaris,* the North Star, are called the *North Circumpolar Constellations,* and they are visible from the northern hemisphere at all times of the year. These are *Ursa Minor* (Little Bear), *Ursa Major* (Great Bear), *Draco* (Dragon), *Cepheus* (King) and *Cassiopeia* (Queen), and *Cameleopardus* (Giraffe). If you are star-gazing in the northern hemisphere, the first thing to do is to locate the Big Dipper in the constellation of Ursa Major. To find Polaris, and thus true Celestial North, trace a line through the two "pointer stars" at the end of the Dipper's bowl. Once you've found the Big Dipper, you can use it as a key to locate a number of other bright stars and their Constellations. Here is a diagram. Compare this with the night sky, and memorize these key figures:

(This view is in Spring)

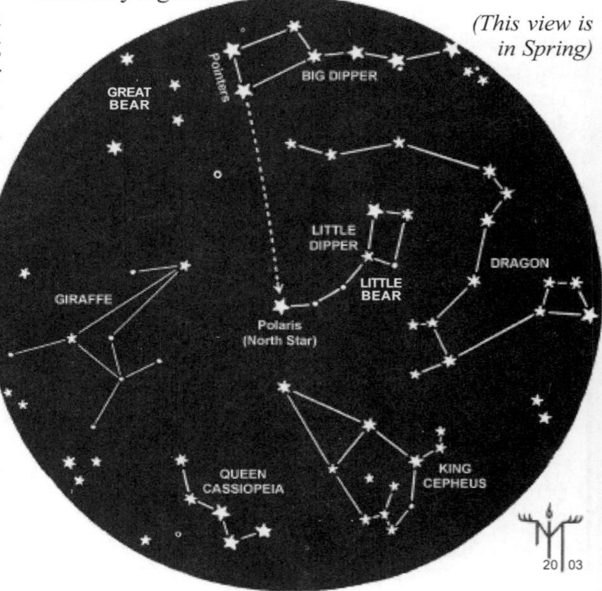

In the Southern Hemisphere, there is no South Pole Star like Polaris. The closest thing is the Southern Cross, which is depicted on the flag of Australia. As Earth's Southern Hemisphere faces away from the main disk of the galaxy, there are not very many bright stars or constellations visible, and I don't know of any ancient stories attached to them. The Inca people of Peru based their celestial mythology not on the stars, but on dark patches in the Milky Way itself, which is far more prominent in the southern sky. The *Magellanic Clouds* (two small companion galaxies of the Milky Way) are also visible near the South Celestial Pole. However, the equatorial Zodiac is visible from the South as well as the North.

The Brightest Stars

Stars are graded by *orders of magnitude,* the brightest being 1st magnitude, and the very faintest 5th magnitude. The brighter stars have all been given names in Latin, Greek, or Arabic. There are 16 1st magnitude stars visible in the Northern Hemisphere, and you should learn to identify all of them, as these have been used as celestial reference points through all of human history. In order of brightness, they are:

STAR	CONSTELLATION	COLOR	DISTANCE
Sirius	*Canis Major* (big dog)	Bluish	8.5 light-years
Canopus	*Argo* (Jason's ship)	Yellowish	650 light-years
Arcturus	*Bootes* (herdsman)	Orange	32 light-years
Vega	*Lyra* (lyre or harp)	Blue-white	23 light-years
Capella	*Auriga* (charioteer)	Yellowish	42 light-years
Rigel	*Orion* (hunter)	Blue-white	545 light-years
Procyon	*Canis Minor* (little dog)	Yellowish	10 light-years
Betelgeuse	*Orion* (hunter)	Reddish	300 light-years
Altair	*Aquilla* (eagle)	Yellowish	18 light-years
Aldebaran	*Taurus* (bull)	Reddish	54 light-years
Antares	*Scorpio* (scorpion)	Red	170 light-years
Spica	*Virgo* (maiden)	Bluish	190 light-years
Pollux	*Gemini* (twins)	Yellowish	31 light-years
Fomalhaut	*Pisces Austrinus* (s. fish)	White	27 light-years
Deneb	*Cygnus* (swan)	White	465 light-years
Regulus	*Leo* (lion)	Blue-white	70 light-years

Stories of the Constellations

Although we use their Latin names, the myths behind the constellations date back to ancient Greece. At first, most of the constellations were not associated with any particular story, but were known simply as the objects or animals which they represented. By the 5th century BCE, however, most of the constellations had come to be associated with myths, and the *Catasterismi* of Eratosthenes (276–194 BCE) completed the mythologization of the stars. Here are some of the best stories:

Perseus

No other story is so well-illustrated in the heavens as that of *Perseus* and *Andromeda,* which is told in the movie *Clash of the Titans.* King *Cepheus* and Queen *Cassiopeia* of Ethiopia had a lovely daughter named Andromeda. The vain queen foolishly bragged that she was more beautiful than the Nereids (sea nymphs), or even Hera, queen of the gods. The goddesses were insulted, and complained to Poseidon, god of the sea. Poseidon sent a monster *(Cetus)* to ravage the coast, demanding the sacrifice of Andromeda to call it off. The princess was chained to a rock by the sea to await her doom. But just as Cetus appeared, so did Perseus, son of Zeus, flying through the air with the winged sandals of Hermes on his return from a perilous mission. In a sack he carried the head of the Gorgon Medusa, a hideous snake-haired monster whose gaze petrified all who beheld her. When Perseus had beheaded her (using his polished shield as a mirror so as not to look into her eyes), *Pegasus,* the winged horse, sprang from her bloody neck. Perseus showed Medusa's head to Cetus, who was instantly turned to stone. Perseus and Andromeda were married and lived happily ever after. In commemoration, the gods placed all the main characters in the sky as constellations.

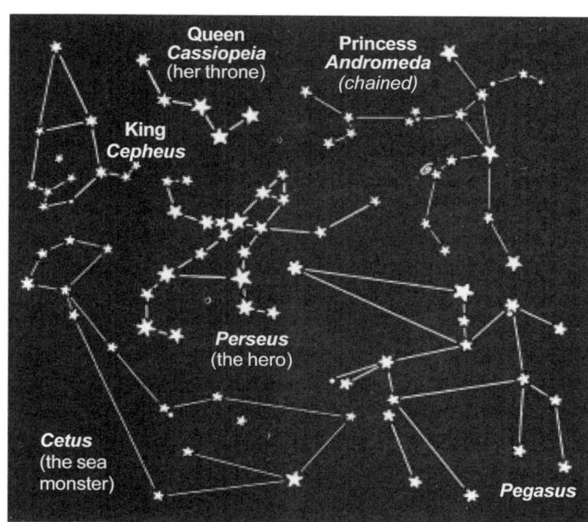

Orion

Orion's father was the sea-god Poseidon, and his mother was the great huntress Queen Euryale of the Amazons. Inheriting her skills, Orion became the greatest hunter in the world. Unfortunately, with his immense strength came an immense ego, and he boasted that no animal on earth could overcome him. Offended by Orion's vanity, Hera sent a little scorpion *(Scorpio)* which stung Orion in the heel, killing him. With his magickal serpent, Aesculapius the physician restored Orion to life. But Hades, Lord of the Dead, complained to his brother Zeus: What would become of his kingdom if the dead could be resurrected by doctors? So Zeus blasted both Orion and Aesculapius with his thunderbolts. He then placed Orion in the sky, along

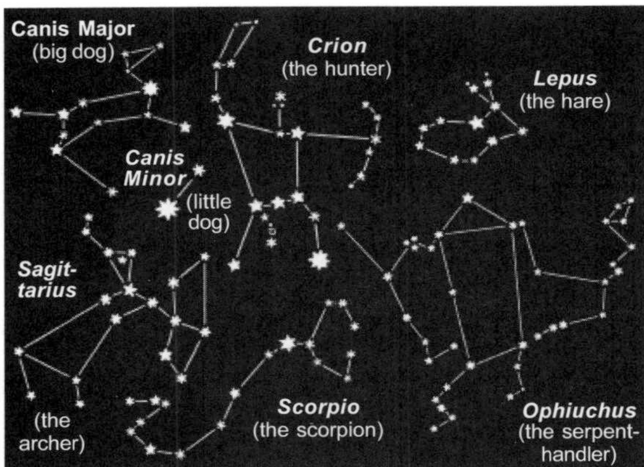

with his two hunting dogs (*Canis Major* and *Canis Minor)* and the rabbit they were chasing *(Lepus).* The Scorpion was also put in the sky, but on the opposite side, along with *Sagittarius,* the archer Centaur, Chiron, whose arrow killed it. Aesculapius (*Ophiucus,* the "serpent handler") was placed right above the Scorpion.

Castor & Pollux

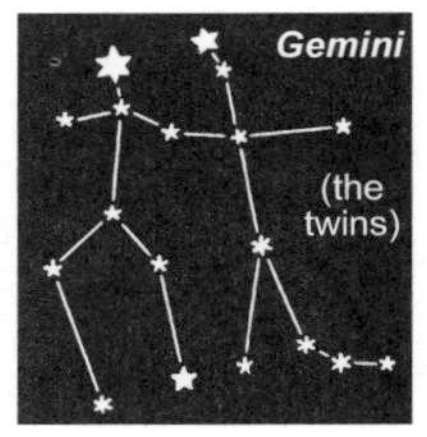

Castor and *Pollux* are the names of the two bright stars in the constellation *Gemini.* They were twin brothers of Helen of Troy but they had different fathers: In one night, their mother Leda was made pregnant both by Zeus in the form of a swan and by her husband, King Tyndarus of Sparta. Pollux, as the son of a god, was immortal and renowned for his strength, while his mortal brother Castor was famed for his skill with horses. Both brothers sailed with Jason and the Argonauts in search of the Golden Fleece and fought in the Trojan War. They loved each other dearly, so when Castor was killed in battle, Pollux, grief-sticken, asked to join him. Zeus placed them both in the sky together.

Europa & the Bull

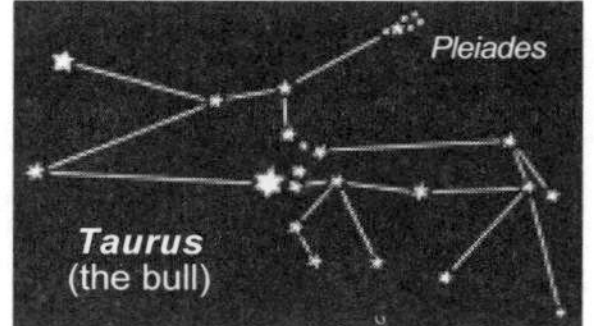

Zeus, king of the gods, appeared to princess Europa in the form of a magnificent white bull. She was impressed by his beauty and gentleness, and the two played together on the beach. Eventually, Europa climbed onto the bull's back, and he swam out to sea with her to Crete, where he revealed his true identity. There Zeus seduced her, and their children became the Europeans. The constellation *Taurus* shows only the head of the great bull, with the star cluster called the Pleiades on his shoulder. Although only six of its many stars are now visible, they are called "the seven sisters." Perhaps one of the others has dimmed since ancient times.

Ariadne's Crown

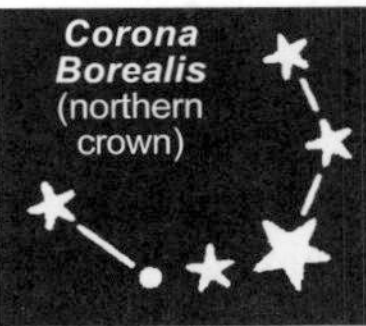

Princess Ariadne was the daughter of King Minos of Crete. His queen, Pasiphae, had borne a monster, the Minotaur—half man and half bull—which Minos had imprisoned in an underground maze called the Labyrinth. It was fed on Athenian prisoners. On the third feeding, one of those chosen as a sacrifice was Theseus. Ariadne fell in love with him, and offered help if he would take her away with him. He agreed, and she gave him a thread to unwind behind him to mark his passage. Theseus killed the Minotaur, followed the thread back out of the labyrinth, and sailed from Crete with Ariadne. But he abandoned her on the island of Naxos. Dionysos, god of the grapevine, found her there heartbroken, and made her his bride and priestess of his temple. When she died, he flung her crown into the heavens, where it remains as the constellation *Corona Borealis* ("northern crown").

Lesson 9. Cosmology & Cosmogony

Cosmology ("word of the universe") is the science, knowledge and lore of the Heavens. It concerns itself with the great Mysteries of Time and Space. Modern cosmologists and astrophysicists are focusing in particular on *cosmogenesis,* or *cosmogony:* the birth of the universe. There are two main competing views as to how the universe began, and in one version or another, each of these have waxed or waned in popularity over the millennia:

The Big Bang (a finite beginning)

The oldest, and by far most popular, is the creationist theory of **The Big Bang,** which proposes that the entire universe began around 14.1 billion years ago with a vast explosion, somehow suddenly coming into existence out of nothing. This is expressed eloquently in the Bible's Book of *Genesis,* where the Hebrew Creator God simply declares: "Let there be light!" The Big Bang has become an article of religious faith for many scientists; in 1951 it even received the blessing of Pope Pius XII!

There are several problems with this theory. The first and most obvious is that, if there really *was* such a big explosion somewhere 14.1 billion years ago, then there would be a vast area of space at "ground zero" that would be completely empty, from which all the galaxies are still rushing away. There is no such empty area. In all directions we look, the distribution of galaxies is fairly uniform, forming a kind of "froth" of bubbles of empty space surrounded by shells of galaxies. It appears, in fact, as if there have been countless "little bangs" rather than one big one.

Another problem is that when we turn our telescopes to the furthest and oldest regions of the universe, 14 billion years old and 14 billion light-years away, what we see is innumerable *quasars* ("quasi-stellar radio sources") —not concentrated in one small area of "beginning," but equally in *all* directions. Each of these blazes forth with the light of a hundred galaxies—a billion years before any galaxies are supposed to have existed. What are these, and where do they come from?

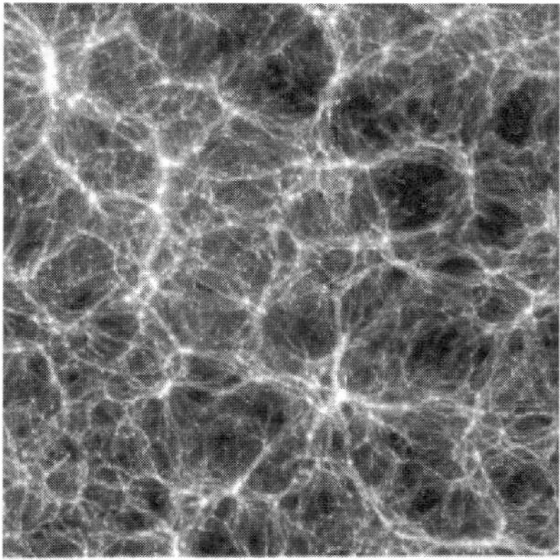
Computer simulation of cosmic structure, by Lars Hernquist & Volker Springel.

The universe does appear to be expanding, with galaxies moving farther apart through time. All calculations based on the premise of an original Big Bang predicted that the rate of expansion would eventually slow down—perhaps even come to a halt and begin to contract. But, in fact, we have now discovered that the expansion rate is *accelerating*! How can this be?

Continuous Creation (infinite & eternal; no beginning)

The opposing view to the Big Bang is the **Steady State,** or **Continuous Creation** hypothesis, which maintains that the universe has always been here, and that new matter is being somehow created continuously out of nothing. It's that "out of nothing" part that provides the greatest difficulty with any theory of cosmogenesis. Because, of course, the most obvious questions then become, "Where did it come *from? What was before?"* And neither of these theories answers these key questions. Just saying "God (or the Gods) did it," only begs the question: Then where did God (or the Gods) come from? You just can't have *something* coming from *nothing!*

Astronomers Paul Davies and John Gribbin write: "the Big Bang was the abrupt creation of the Universe from literally nothing: no space, no time, no matter. This is a quite extraordinary conclusion to arrive at—a picture of the entire physical Universe simply popping into existence from nothing." (*The Matter Myth*, p. 122) If there was no space, matter, or energy before the hypothetical "Big Bang," then there was obviously nothing to appear and nowhere for it to happen!

Cosmic Loopholes

Any good Wizard worth his salt seeks to answer cosmic questions in his own manner. I have have been working on an alternative theory of cosmogenesis that addresses some of these questions, as well as the mystery of the accelerating expansion of the universe. Every galaxy, of whatever size or shape, has a supermassive *black hole* in its center with a mass about 1% of its entire galaxy. Just like a vortex of water spiraling down the drain of your sink, that black hole is continually sucking down the rest of the galaxy, giving it its spiral shape. So where does all that stuff go?

Many astrophysicists believe that a black hole is a kind of "Star-gate"—the opening of a wormhole to somewhere else. But, according to theory, a wormhole is not just a tunnel through *space;* it's also a *time* tunnel. Stuff entering a small black hole of maybe 10 solar masses might come out in a "white hole," say, 100 light-years away, and thus also 100 years back in the past. Well, the black hole at the center of our Milky Way galaxy has a mass *three million* times that of our sun! If this is the opening of a huge wormhole, then the other end could easily be billions of light years away—and therefore billions of years in the past. What if all those distant quasars are the other ends of the black holes at the centers of all the galaxies, cycling through time and space in an endless series of cosmic loops?

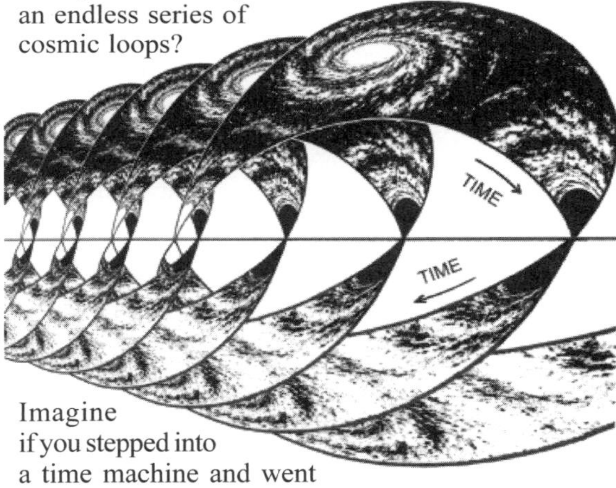

Imagine if you stepped into a time machine and went back to yesterday. There would then be two of you. And every other trip into the past where you already existed would add another one of you. Could all the galaxies be part of a single vast infinite series of loopings around and around through time and space—like the spring on a spiral notebook—adding one more with each cycle, and therefore continually expanding the past and pushing the present faster and faster into the future?

The universe itself keeps on expanding and expanding,
In all of the directions it can whiz.
As fast as it can go, at the speed of light you know;
Twelve million miles a minute,
And that's the fastest speed there is.
So remember when you're feeling very small and insecure,
How amazingly unlikely is your birth,
And pray that there's intelligent life somewhere up in space,
'Cause there's bugger-all down here on earth!

—Monty Python, *The Meaning of Life*
(written by Eric Idle)

Class III: Mathemagicks (Clear Magick)

1. Introduction: The Mysteries of Pythagoras

The natural world is an amazingly well-organized place. As I mentioned before, a major part of Wizardly seeing is in perceiving the forms and patterns in the world. This is also a part of scientific thinking, which grew out of Wizardry. From atoms to galaxies, and everywhere in between, there are forms and patterns, great and small. Many of these fall into numbers, and some of the earliest Wizardly Mysteries—those of Pythagoras (pi-THAH-go-rus) (580-500 BCE) in ancient Greece—laid the foundation for all mathematics; particularly arithmetic, geometry and music. The Pythagorean motto was: "All is Number."

According to Pythagoras, everything in the universe is based upon the same fundamental "blueprints" created by geometric patterns that repeat over and over in an endless dance of sound, light and color. These patterns form a matrix of grid energy derived from a central source. They create the entire natural world, and allow us to experience duality, emotions, linear time, and all the reality we perceive.

Sacred Geometry is based on these patterns, which were once understood and taught by the ancient Mystery Schools. But with the destruction of the great Library of Alexandria and the collapse of the Roman Empire, they became lost for centuries—only to be rediscovered as we evolve into higher consciousness awareness.

Mathemagicians work with a few very simple formulae and ratios—particularly the ones called *"Pi"* and *"Phi"*—to understand the common patterns and principles underlying and governing all things.

Lesson 2: Pythagorean Numbers

There are many aspects of the Pythagorean (pi-THAH-go-REE-an) Mysteries, but here we will just look at how they thought of Numbers:

Pythagoras, from Historia Deorum Fatidicorum

1. Called ***Monad*** (one), this is "the noble number, Sire of Gods and men." It represents that which is whole and complete—such as the Universe. It also represents things which cannot be divided—such as atoms were thought to be. A monad is the sum of any combination of parts, and it is also likened to the seed of a tree, which, when grown, has many branches (numbers). Pythagoreans thought of Mind/Consciousness/Divinity as the ultimate Monad, containing all things, infinite and eternal, with neither beginning nor end. The Monad is the symbol of the Great Father. In geometry, One can only be represented by a point—a position in space with no dimensions: •

2. ***Dyad*** (two) presents the first division. When there are two, each is the opposite of the other: good/evil, light/dark, truth/falsehood, positive/negative, active/passive, life/death, above/below—all dualities. While the Monad is the symbol of wisdom, the Dyad is the symbol of illusion, for in it exists the false sense of separateness. The Dyad is the symbol of the Great Mother. A Dyad can be represented by two points—and a line connecting them gives the first dimension: •——•

3. ***Triad*** (three) is the first balanced number, and considered particularly magickal in many cultures. Pythagoreans, Druids, and Brahmins made up long lists of sacred Triads. A tripod is a stable structure, as is a triangle; they cannot wobble or be distorted. Made up of both the Monad and the Dyad, the Triad is the number of knowledge. It represents the Holy Family—Father, Mother and Child—or the Trinity in Christianity: Father, Son and Holy Ghost. Three connected by lines make up a triangle, enclosing a space in two dimensions: △

4. ***Tetrad*** (four) is the root of all things, the fountain of Nature, and the first square (2x2). The Tetrad connects all Directions (East, South, West and North), Elements (Air, Fire, Water and Earth), and Seasons (Spring, Summer, Fall and Winter). Four points make a cross, and a cross within a circle is a Medicine Wheel—and the symbol of Earth. Four equidistant points in a flat plane can be connected by lines to make a Square, and six squares make up a Cube. Or four points in space can create a *Tetrahedron*—the first three-dimensional solid object, made up of four triangles:

5. The ***Pentad*** (five) is the union of an odd and even number (2 and 3). It is also called equilibrium, because it divides the "perfect number" 10 into two equal parts. The *Pentagram* is the symbol of light, health and vitality—as well as Witchcraft. It also symbolizes the Fifth Element (Spirit). The Pentad is symbolic of Nature, for when it is multiplied by itself the product contains itself—just as plants start from seeds and ultimately produce more seeds. A Pentagram contains within its center a *Pentagon,* and twelve pentagrams makes up a three-dimensional *duodecahedron.*

6. The ***Hexad*** (six) is the perfection of all the parts, representing the creation of the world. It is called the form of forms, the articulation of the universe, and the maker of the soul. A *Hexagram,* formed by the union of two triangles (male—point up; and female—point down), is the symbol of marriage. Called the "The Star of David," it is also the symbol of Judaism.

7. The ***Heptad*** (seven) was called "worthy of veneration." Seven is a sacred number among many ancient cultures. There are seven visible planets, and seven *Chakras* (energy centers in the body) in Hindu teaching. A *Heptagram* (or *Septagram*) is also called an Elfstar.

8. The ***Ogdoad,*** or ***Octad*** (eight), is sacred because it is the number of the first cube, with eight corners. Its keywords are love, counsel, prudence, law, and convenience. The shape of the number 8 is derived from the interwoven serpents on the *caduceus* (wand) of Hermes.

9. The ***Ennead*** (nine) is the first square of an odd number (3x3). It was associated with failure and shortcoming, because it fell short by one of the perfect number 10. It is called "the number of man" because of the nine months of gestation before birth. Nine is the limitless number because there is nothing beyond it but the infinite 10. Its keywords are ocean and horizon, because these are boundless.

10. The ***Decad*** (ten) is the greatest of numbers, containing all others and returning to the beginning of the Monad. As the perfect number, ten relates to age, power, faith, necessity, and memory. Roman numerals and the 10-based *decimal/metric* system come from counting on the fingers—the easiest way to reckon without written numerals or calculators.

Lesson 3: Numerology

Any complex number, no matter how large, can be reduced by simply adding together each of the digits it contains, as often as necessary, until there is only a single digit left. For instance, 365—the number of days in a year—would be reduced first by adding together the digits 3+6+5=14; then adding the 4+1 to get 5. Thus 5 is the "Magick Number" for a year. This year in which I am writing—2003—also becomes 5, because 2+0+0+3=5. As explained above 5 is the *Pentad,* and it represents light, health and vitality—as well as Witchcraft. It also symbolizes the Fifth Element (Spirit). The Pentad is symbolic of Nature, for when it is multiplied by itself the product contains itself—just as plants start from seeds and ultimately produce more seeds. So this is a very good year in which to be creating this particular ***Grimoire***—as it is my intention for it to plant seeds of Magick and Spirit!

Words and names can also be reduced to numbers in the same way. This is done by assigning numbers to each of the letters of the alphabet, in repeating order, like this: *(**NOTE:** Originally, the 27-letter Hebrew alphabet was used for this, but you should use the same alphabet in which you write your name!)*

Number:	**1**	**2**	**3**	**4**	**5**	**6**	**7**	**8**	**9**
Letters:	**A**	**B**	**C**	**D**	**E**	**F**	**G**	**H**	**I**
	J	**K**	**L**	**M**	**N**	**O**	**P**	**Q**	**R**
	S	**T**	**U**	**V**	**W**	**X**	**Y**	**Z**	

Then, using this little chart, you just replace the letters of a word or name with the equivalent numbers. For instance, my first name, *Oberon,* would be written in numbers as: 625965. Then, to get the Magick Number of my name, I would add all those digits together and reduce them to one, like so: 6+2+5+9+6+5 =33. 3+3=6, so 6 is the Magick Number of my first name. According to Lesson 1, 6 is the *Hexad*—the perfection of all the parts, representing the creation of the world. It is "the form of forms, the articulation of the universe, and the maker of the soul." Not bad!

For dates, you simply write out the date in numbers—month, day, and year—just as has become customary. The important thing to remember, however, is to write out the whole number for the year, not just the last two digits: "2003," not just "03."

This system is called *Numerology.* With it, according to numerologists, you can find out many things. You can apply this system to any word, name, number, or date. You can use it as a divination system to help determine a good day to do something, a place to go, what to name your Familiar, or make any choice between one thing and another. Just work out the magick number, and look up its significance!

Quest: Your Lucky Number

There are two personal Magick Numbers that everyone has: your *Birth Number* and your *Name Number.* First, work out your Birth Number by reducing all the numbers in the date. Then you can do the same with your name. Numerologists say that ideally, these two numbers should match. The reason is that your Birth Number—like your astrological sign—never changes. You might change your address or even your name, but your date of birth remains the same.

If your Name Number is different from your Birth Number, you might want to take that into account in choosing a new nickname, use-name, or Magickal Name. Some given names have many variations. For instance, a boy named "Alexander" might go by Al, Alex, Xander or Zander. A girl named "Elizabeth" might go by Liz, Lizzie, Eliza, Liza, Lisa, Beth, or Betty. Each of these versions will have a distinct number, which you should take into account when you decide how you want to be called.

In choosing a Magickal Name, you should check every name you consider for its number. Or you can create a name based on such numbers, just like making a word out of a telephone number. After all, each number (except 9) has three letters! If you get a set of numbered letters that make up a name you like, and add up to your Birth Number, you can even rearrange them into a different order without changing their number. Such rearranged word are called *anagrams* ("reversed letters"), and anagrams are often used as codes in magickal writings and spells. Scrabble games are useful for this. For instance, a healing spell might use Scrabble letters to spell out the word "EVIL" for the illness, and then rearrange the letters to spell "LIVE."

By choosing a name that matches your Birth Number, you are then aligning yourself with the same associations as those of the day you were born, and thus doubling the power of your own special number. This is your "Lucky Number," and you can use it to note magickal syncronicities when that same number comes up in your life.

Lesson 4: Perfect Bodies

The concept of *Perfect Bodies* was defined by Greek geometricians. The notion of "perfectness" reflects their belief that geometry, of all sciences, is closest to the essence of things, expressing the rules set by the Gods in the creation of the Universe. A *polygon* (many angles) is a two-dimensional shape with straight edges. Multi-sided three-dimensional objects are called *polyhedrons* (many-sided). A *Perfect Body* is the polyhedron built from identical regular polygons, such as an equilateral *triangle,* a *square,* and a *pentagon.* It may appear that one could build an infinite number of such bodies yet, as it turns out, there are only five constructions possible. These five shapes were defined and classified by Euclid (325–265 BCE).

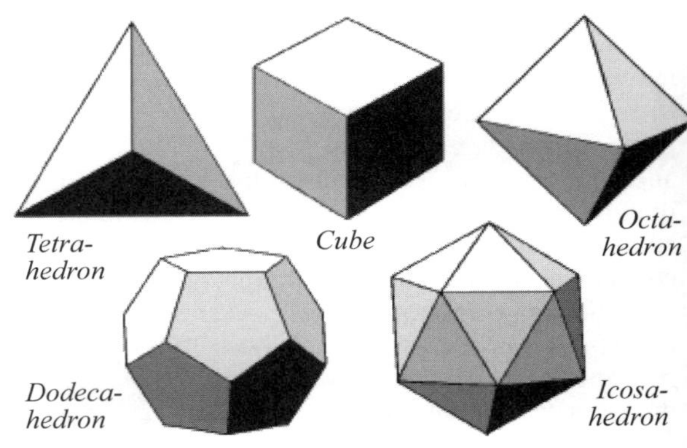

The *tetrahedron,* which is built of four triangles, is the simplest. The *cube* is made of six squares. The other Perfect Bodies are the *octahedron* (8 triangles), the *dodecahedron* (12 pentagons), and the *icosahedron* (20 triangles). These all currently appear in the forms of the dice used in board games.

In 350 BCE, the great Greek philosopher Plato (427–347 BCE) postulated that the four Elements—Earth, Water, Air, and Fire (thought by the Greeks to make up the world)—are composed of tiny particles, which cannot further be divided. Thus the concept of *atoms* ("undividable" in Greek) was born. Atoms were thought to be perfect geometric constructions like the Perfect Bodies.

According to Plato, **Earth** atoms are cubes, thought to be the most solid of these bodies. **Water,** that which rolls most easily, is represented by the icosahedron. **Air** is octahedral. And the simple tetrahedron represents **Fire,** the most rarified of all the Elements.

With Four elements and five perfect bodies, the correspondence between nature and geometry required an added constituent, and it was suggested that the dodecahedron represented the entire Universe. Some modern Wizards, however, associate the dodecahedron with the Fifth Element—**Spirit.**

Perfect Bodies in Nature

Nature of course knows all these rules, and shapes such as described above occur in nature. Microscopic radiolarians obeying these rules create complex structures based on Perfect Bodies. These are structurally the strongest constructions while at the same time very light. This feature has been used by modern architects as stronger materials became available.

As Plato predicted 2,350 years ago, we find such geometric constructions in the world of atoms and molecules, where the building blocks are held together with chemical bonds. These strict geometrical rules, expressing symmetries involved with the electronic distributions in atoms, create the bond formation. Such constructions occur involving many different atoms, such as methane, which is tetrahedral in shape. The electron bonds make an angle of approximately 109°, which is the most fundamental angle in chemistry.

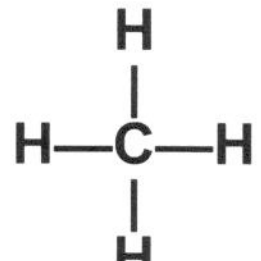

Solids can be thought of as networks of atoms built using these bonds as a glue to hold the atoms together. Bcause we ourselves are carbon-based life-forms, consider, for example, solids built entirely of carbon atoms. We know of two variations: diamond and graphite. The natural arrangement that obeys the symmetry of the local bonds, 109°, is a diamond, a three-dimensional tightly-bound network of carbons. The angle related to the bond in graphite is also close to this natural angle. In graphite the carbon atoms form sheets of strongly-glued atoms that do not interact much with those in the next layer. This small difference in the chemical bonding results in vastly different properties; compare the prices of the two versions!

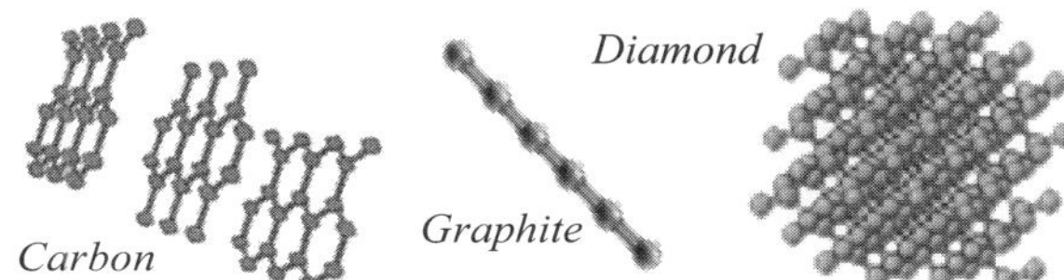

This we knew for centuries. It was therefore a great astonishment when a third form of carbon—C_{60}—was discovered in 1996. Called the *Buckyball* in honor of Buckminster Fuller (1895–1983), its geometry is exactly as drawn by Leonardo da Vinci (1452–1519), with 12 pentagons and 20 hexagons. The actual arrangement is the same as the sections of a soccer ball! Two other modifications can also be prepared by increasing or decreasing the number of hexagons. Surprisingly the most perfect of the three is the most likely to be formed.

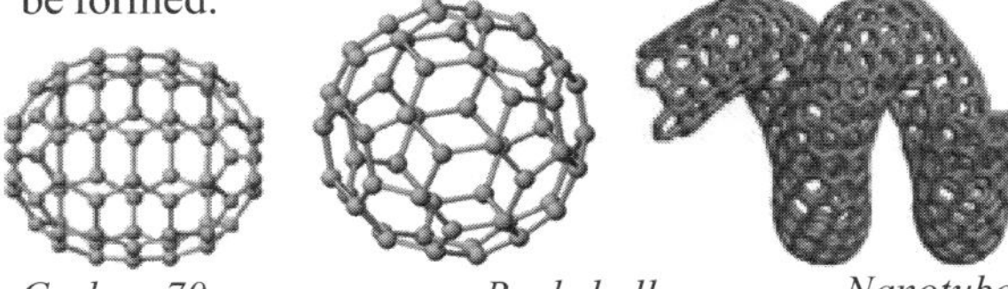

Carbon 70 *Buckyball* *Nanotube*

With these new carbon molecules, nanotubes can be constructed, providing fibers hunderds of times stronger than steel. Applications will transform our world! We could even build an orbital elevator....

Lesson 5: Sacred Geometry

"Let proportion be found not only in numbers and measures but also in sounds, weights, times, positions, and whatever force there is."
—Leonardo da Vinci

In Nature, we find geometrical patterns, designs, and structures from the tiniest particles to the greater Cosmos. These are also symbolic of the underlying metaphysical relationship of the part to the whole—"As below, so above; as within, so without." It is this principle of underlying oneness that permeates the geometrical architecture of all form in its myriad diversity. These principles of interconnectedness, inseparability, and union provide us with a blueprint for the sacred foundation of all things and a continuous reminder of our own relationship to the whole Universe.

> *Life itself is inextricably interwoven with geometric forms, from the angles of atomic bonds in the molecules of the amino acids, to the helical spirals of DNA, to the spherical prototype of the cell, to the first few cells of an organism which assume vesical, tetrahedral, and star (double) tetrahedral forms prior to the diversification of tissues for different physiological functions. Our human bodies on this planet all developed with a common geometric progression from one to two to four to eight primal cells and beyond.*
>
> *Almost everywhere we look, the mineral intelligence embodied within crystalline structures follows a geometry unfaltering in its exactitude. The lattice patterns of crystals all express the principles of mathematical perfection and repetition of a fundamental essence, each with a characteristic spectrum of resonances defined by the angles, lengths and relational orientations of its atomic components.*
>
> —Bruce Rawles, *Sacred Geometry*

The Fibonacci Sequence

Discovered in the year 1202 by Italian Leonardo Pisano Fibonacci (1170–1250), this is a very important series of numbers in which each one is the sum of the two previous ones: **1, 1, 2, 3, 5, 8, 13, 21, 34, 55, 89....** The Fibonacci numbers go on like this infinitely. Any two consecutive numbers in this series, expressed as a ratio or fraction, define practically all ratios and relationships found in Nature—that is, **1:1, 1:2, 2:3, 3:5, 5:8**... or **1, 1/2, 2/3, 3/5, 5/8**....

If you know how to look, you can find the Fibonacci sequence in pinecones and poems, sunflowers and symphonies, ancient art and modern computers, family trees, and the stock market. This sequence is the mathematical Key of the Universe!

Fibonacci ratios appear in the ratio of the number of spiral arms in daisies, in the chronology of rabbit populations, in the sequence of leaf patterns as they twist around a branch, and a myriad of places in nature where self-generating patterns are in effect. The sequence is the rational progression towards the irrational number embodied in the quintessential *Golden Ratio,* or *Golden Mean.* This most aesthetically pleasing proportion, called *phi,* has been utilized by numerous artists since (and probably before!) the construction of the Great Pyramid.

The Golden Mean

One of the most important numerical relationships noted by the ancient Greek geometricians was what they called *The Golden Mean.* This refers to a ratio of 1.618034… rounded to 1.62—a number called ***Phi*** (Φ). The Golden Mean is related to the Fibonacci sequence. For an explanation, take the ratios of the following successive numbers from the Fibonacci series:

1/1 = 1	**Φ**	**13/8 = 1.625**
2/1 = 2		**21/13 = 1.615**
3/2 = 1.5		**34/21 = 1.619**
5/3 = 1.66		**55/34 = 1.617**
8/5 = 1.60		**89/55 = 1.618**

As the Fibonacci numbers get larger, their ratio approaches the 1.62 ratio of the Golden Mean. This is not surprising if we look at the *Golden Rectangle,* in which the side of every square is equal to the sum of the sides of the next two squares. This is same concept that determines the Fibonacci sequence.

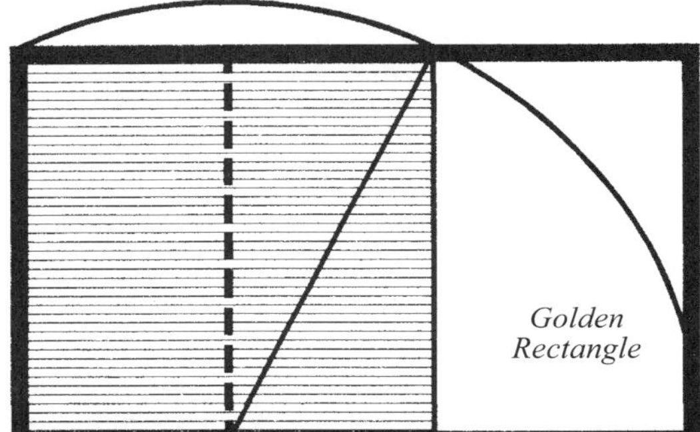

The Golden Mean (also called *Golden Ratio, Phi Ratio, Sacred Cut,* and *Divine Proportion*) is a fundamental measure that seems to crop up almost everywhere, including crops. It also governs all body proportions, such the respective lengths of your fingers, upper leg to lower, etc. (The actual ratio is about 1.618033988749894848204586834365638117720309180....) The Golden Ratio is the unique proportion such that the ratio of the whole to the larger portion is the same as the ratio of the larger portion to the smaller. As such, it symbolically links each new generation to its ancestors, preserving the continuity of relationship as the means for retracing its lineage.

As scholars and artists of eras gone by discovered, the intentional use of these natural proportions in art of various forms expands our sense of beauty, balance, and harmony to optimal effect. The most famous building of Classical Greece, and one of the Seven Wonders of the ancient world, was the Parthenon in the Acropolis at Athens. Its proportions are all based on the Golden Rectangle. Other buildings in ancient Greece contain a similar height to length ratio.

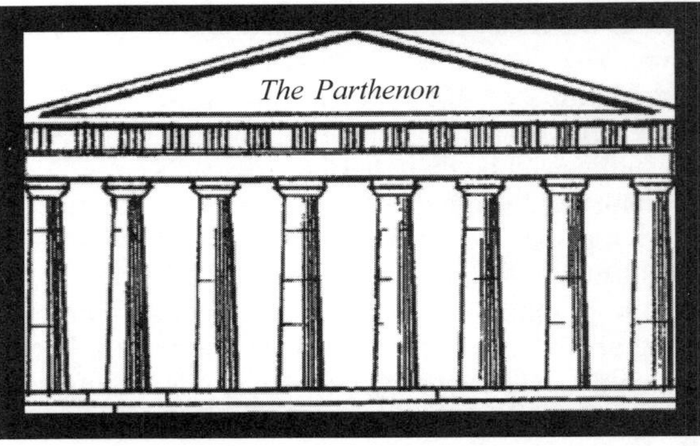

The Golden Spiral

We can make another picture showing the Fibonacci Sequence if we start with two small squares of size 1 next to each other. Above of both of these draw a square of size 2 (=1+1).

We can now draw a new square—touching both a unit square and the latest square of side 2—so having sides 3 units long; and then another touching both the 2-square and the 3-square (which has sides of 5 units). We can continue adding squares around the picture, each new square having a side which is as long as the sum of the last two squares' sides. This set of rectangles whose sides are two successive Fibonacci numbers in length, and which are composed of squares with sides which are Fibonacci numbers, are called *Fibonacci Rectangles.* However many you make this way, they always add up to a Golden Rectangle.

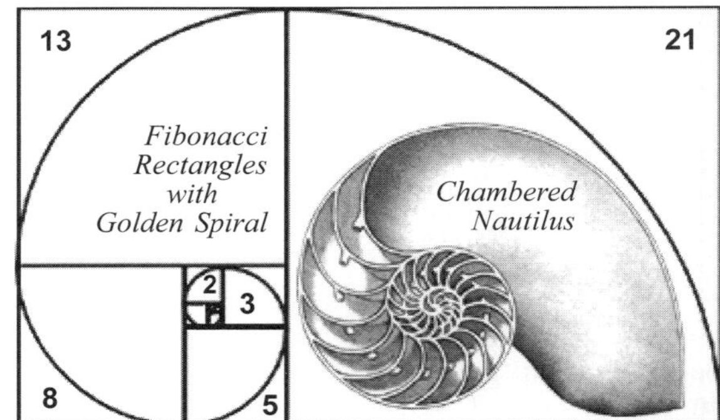

Now we can draw a spiral by putting together quarter circles, one in each new square. This is the *Fibonacci Spiral.* A similar curve to this occurs in nature as the shape of a snail shell or some seashells. Whereas the Fibonacci Rectangles spiral increases in size by a factor of *Phi* (1.62) in a *quarter of a turn* (i.e., a point a further quarter of a turn round the curve is 1.62 times as far from the centre, and this applies to *all* points on the curve), the spiral curve of a chambered nautilus shell takes a *whole turn* before points move a factor of 1.62 from the centre.

We can also see similar spirals from the atomic

level to the shape of gigantic spiral galaxies. In all cases these forms are associated with evolutionary growth, should it be a new layer of atoms in a crystal, a living organism, a tropical storm, or a galaxy.

Fibonacci Petals on flowers: On many plants, the number of petals is a Fibonacci number. Here are some examples:

3 petals: lily, iris (often lilies have 6 petals formed from two sets of 3)
5 petals: buttercup, wild rose, larkspur, columbine
8 petals: delphiniums
13 petals: ragwort, corn marigold, *cineraria*
21 petals: aster, black-eyed susan, chicory
34 petals: plantain, pyrethrum
55 or 89 petals: michaelmas daisies, *asteraceae* family.

Some species are very precise about the number of petals they have, but others have petals that are very near those above, with the average being a Fibonacci number.

Lesson 6. Dimensions

by Dragon Singing

One very important concept for a Wizard to understand is the physical concept of *dimensions.* While whole volumes of mathematics and physics have been devoted to the study and understanding of dimensions, the easiest way to think about them is as *directions of possible movement.*

Mathematicians (who are their own kinds of Wizards, make no mistake) begin their thoughts about dimensions by imagining a **zero-dimension** object, which would be a ***Point.*** You know how people talk about "a point in space"? Well, that's exactly what it is: a location, like an infinitely tiny dot. A Point has zero height, zero width, zero length. It can't move anywhere.

If you have two Points, you can draw a ***Line*** between them. A Line is a **one-dimensional** object. A Point on a Line can only move forward and backward along the line: not side to side, not up and down.

When you think about it, we're already in territory that's pretty mysterious: because a Point has no width, length or height, no matter how short a Line is, there is always space for an *infinite number of Points* between any two Points. So how does anyone ever get anywhere? You start from New York and head for California (or, for that matter, from one side of the room to the other), and there are an infinite number of points between. How do you ever cross them all? But you do...

But wait: it gets better.

If you add another Point (one which isn't exactly lined up with the other two, which would just extend the Line), you add another direction of possible movement, creating a **two-dimensional** object known as a ***Plane***, like the surface of a sheet of paper. Just the surface, mind you: no thickness, none at all. A Point on a Plane can move left, right, forward, backward...any direction except up and down.

Add another dimension, and we're almost in the situation we humans live in. **Three dimensional** objects have *volume,* and are known as ***Solids.*** A solid can be a ball or a cube or anything that has height, width, depth and thickness.

Now we're getting somewhere! But the day-to-day world as we know it doesn't exist just in three dimensions. You don't just move up, down, sideways, forward and backward: you also move *forward through* ***Time,*** which is the **fourth dimension.** I won't go into why Time only goes forward here: there's a reason, but it's complicated, and if you're interested, you should go investigate and find out (researching arcane knowledge is one of the most *basic* skills a Wizard must master!)

But there you have it: the Universe as we know it exists in four dimensions: three of **space,** plus **Time**. And the Universe, as we have learned, is expanding... which means that there must be a *fifth* dimension for it to expand into!

There are many physicists who now believe that our Universe may have extra dimensions as well, which have been compressed into subatomic spaces so small that we are never aware of them. The more we understand about our Universe, the more we come to see that there may very well be alternate layers of reality: other Universes, other versions of reality.

Moëbius Strip

There are very strange and fascinating things you can do with the concept of dimensions. Take, for example, the ***Moëbius Strip.*** It's easy to make: just take a strip of paper, put in a half-twist and tape the ends together. No big deal, right?

Wrong! Take a pencil, put it down at any point on the paper strip, and draw a line along one side. How many sides does the strip have? That's right! *Only one. The* ***Moëbius Strip*** *is a two-dimensional, one-sided object. It's all one surface.* But wait, there's more!

Cut the strip down the middle. What happens?

Now cut the strip down the middle *again.* Surprise!

The Moëbius Strip is an example of how there are strange exceptions to what we think of as "normal" reality: exactly the kinds of loopholes and anomalies that a Wizard exploits, through knowledge, to enact change through the exertion of his (or her) Will.

Klein Bottle

The Moëbius Strip has a single surface and a single edge. If you could somehow get rid of the edge, so there is only a single surface, you would have an "impossible" three-dimensional object called a ***Klein Bottle.*** At least, it was said to be impossible until I (Oberon) made the one shown here.

I made it out of two donut-shaped clear plastic rings, which I cut to fit and glued together with clear silicon. If you can find such rings, you can make one, too. It's a fun thing to pass around at parties!

"Flat space"

Curved Space

As the Moëbius Strip warps two dimensions into a continuum, so does the Klein bottle warp a three-dimensional object into a single continuum. By the same token, Albert Einstein (1879–1955) proposed a mathematical model for the warping of space itself into a curving continuum. This concept provides a basis for his theory of gravity, as well as a foundation for such things as wormholes connecting one part of the universe with another.

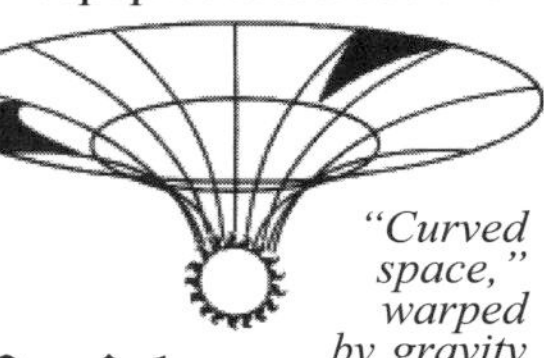

"Curved space," warped by gravity

Lesson 7: Chaos Magick

(by Ian "Lurking Bear" Anderson)

In recent times, mathematicians have devised a study known as *Chaos Theory.* We Wizards have recognized in it what many of us knew intuitively all along. One aspect of Chaos Theory tells us that there are horizons of knowledge in a complex, changing system, and that we can never know every detail about it. This knowledge horizon exists even if all the pieces follow predictable rules, which they don't.

Another aspect of Chaos Theory is that it shows how tiny changes in a chaotic system can cause large, unpredictable differences in the pattern that emerges. This is the famous "Butterfly Effect," so named because Edward Lorenz, a meteorologist, asked, "Does the flap of a butterfly's wings in Brazil set off a tornado in Texas?" Weather is a classic example of a chaotic, unpredictable system, and even the mightiest computers cannot predict the weather correctly.

Chaos Theory also describes times when systems break down into seeming randomness and emerge into new patterns in unpredictable ways. It is in these times that the Butterfly Effect can be especially potent, where crisis and opportunity intersect.

The entire biosphere is a chaotic system, and society and culture also are chaotic. It is in the chaos of the biosphere that new forms arise spontaneously and unpredictably, and evolution occurs. The Butterfly Effect gives the Chaos Magician the lever to influence huge systems, to choose carefully those cusps in unfolding patterns, and through small actions influence a larger sphere. Simply planting some plants in a recovering ecology, or a short speech at a key meeting can trigger a cascade of events that determines the pattern of a new emerging order.

Whenever a system has sufficient size and complexity, the extremely improbable becomes statistically inevitable. Chaos magick is the magick of the exceptional circumstance, the freak occurrence, the outlandish. The Chaos Magician rides the fencelines between different realities.

As usual, with that power comes responsibility. Make sure that herb you plant is not the next kudzu invasion, or that speech at a meeting doesn't just help trigger endless cycles of grief and conflict. Naturally, the Chaos Magician doesn't really control anything and can't really predict what exact effects a chaos working will have. The Chaos Magician can only help nudge things in desired directions with a very careful choice of time and place of action.

Another form of chaos magick is *Discordian* or trickster magick. Many cultures have trickster deities such as Coyote or Eris. The value of the trickster is in breaking down destructive orders such as oppressive governments, hidebound academic theories, or corporate monopolies. Where systems are broken down and things are stirred up, opportunities for change arise. We can act as tricksters in our lives and make many changes in the world around us. Tricksters can be found among modern activists, baffling and befuddling the keepers of systems they resist. A trickster is not afraid of seeming ridiculous and is willing to be a "holy fool" in service to the universe. The trickster is willing to call into question what is normal, think the unthinkable, and speak the unspeakable.

There are dangers to the trickster path. Trickster deities are not necessarily ethical, and we must stand for what we believe is ethical, or trickster spirits can run roughshod over us. Being a rule-breaker and trouble-maker all the time, no matter where you are, can be destructive and useless. There are some boundaries best left untested, some old traditions turn out to be a good idea, and some rules are there for sound reasons. At this time on the Earth, there is no shortage of destructive order in the world, so Trickster Wizards today shouldn't lack for creative, worthwhile outlets for their energies.

Class IV: Ceremonial Magick (White)

1. Introduction: Magicians

INCE MAGICK IS THE ART OF USING your Will to change things, *Ceremonial Magick* is the art of working with ceremonies to make the changes—magick—you want to occur. Ceremonial Magicians frequently wear robes and use a wide battery of tools to both control and direct magickal energy. Sometimes amazingly elaborate, such tools can also act as symbolic spurs to the imagination. Ceremonial Magicians may often use magickal recitations as part of their ceremonies to achieve their goals.

Many Ceremonial Magicians work with their inner energy combined with the spiritual energy of Gods, Archangels, Angels, and other spirits to achieve their magick. Sometimes it is attuning with or simply asking an Angel for help. Other times a more general spiritual energy might be used to create artificial "Elementals," make talismans and amulets, invoke and evoke various spirits, etc.

High and Low Magick

Many Ceremonial Magicians make a distinction between "High" and "Low" magick. Different Magicians give different meanings for the terms. For some, *High Magick* specifically refers to rituals in which an *Entity,* or Spirit Being, is conjured into visible appearance. This Entity is then directed to perform some task, or asked for assistance, information, divination, etc. The Magician *commands* the Entity, and remains in charge of the ritual throughout.

Low Magick, in contrast, does not require the conjuration of any specific Entities, and even if they are called upon, such Entities are not expected to actually *appear* in a visible form. This is by far the most common form of magick practiced, and includes Sympathetic and Imitative magick as well as religious services of all kinds. "Low Magick" does *not* mean negative or "black magick." Whether a ritual is done for positive or negative purposes depends on the intention of the practitioner; the magick itself, like electricity, is morally neutral.

Many of the preparations for High Magick involve mini-rituals of various sorts which are actually Low Magick. A well-rounded magician does both High and Low Magick with equal facility, as the situation requires.

Orders and Lodges

Ceremonial Magick was developed into its present form in the 17th and 18th centuries within secret magickal Orders and Lodges such as the Freemasons and the Rosicrucians. The teachings are based upon the *Qabalah* and the *Hermetica,* along with Neo-Platonism, Gnosticism and Oriental doctrines. In its ultimate sense, Ceremonial Magick is a transcendental experience that awakens the magician to his inner Divinity, taking him into mystical realms and into communication with the Higher Self. The ultimate objective of these practices is to attain union with the Divine Universal Consciousness, or God.

The greatest and most influential system of Ceremonial Magick was developed by the *Hermetic Order of the Golden Dawn* (O∴G∴D∴), founded by three Rosicrucians in 1888. It was said to be the outermost Order of the *Great White Brotherhood* of mystics.

Lesson 2. The Qabalah

The *Qabalah* (also spelled *Cabala* or *Kabbalah*) was originally a collection of ancient Jewish magickal lore said to contain the keys to interpreting the mystical symbolism of the *Torah* (the first five books of the Bible). The word Qabalah is based on the Hebrew *gibbel* ("to receive"), and refers to received (or revealed) wisdom. Regarded as the foundational system of all magick, the Qabalah is a set of beliefs and practices (some of which differ from one group of Qabalists to another) with many books explaining them. It has been studied by scholarly Jews throughout the ages, and has been adopted by magicians of all races and nations.

The Qabalah explains how the world came into existence as a series of emanations from the Divine Will. According to its tenets, all races and religions are descended from one original Source. The legendary chain of transmission goes like this: God taught the Qabalah to the Angels, who passed it on to Adam, the first man. From Adam through Noah, the secrets reached Abraham, who revealed them to the Egyptians. Moses learned the hidden wisdom in Egypt, and included it in the first four books of the Torah. Eventually the Qabalah reached King Solomon, who became the greatest Wizard in Jewish history. Solomon was said to have mastered the mysteries of the Qabalah, and to have written *The Key of Solomon, The Lesser Key of Solomon,* and other magical texts.

The Qabalah teaches that Divinity is both *immanent* (within) and *transcendant* (without). God is all things, both good and evil. The worlds came into being not by being "created" or made, but as "emanations" flowing out from the Infinite Prime Source of Divine Universal Consciousness. All things make up the whole of an organized universe, and letters and numbers are the keys to unlockings its mysteries. The cosmos is divided into four Worlds: *Atziluth,* the divine world of archetypes, from which arise all forms of manifestation; *Beriah,* the world of angels and creation, in which ideas become patterns; *Yetzirah,* the world of the planets and formation, in which the patterns are expressed; and *Assiah,* the material world of action which we perceive with our physical senses.

The supreme and central Mystery of the Qabalah is the Holy Union or "Sacred Marriage" between the male and female aspects of the Divine—or the unification of God. The Qabalistic Goddess is called *Shekinah,* and she was the guardian of the Tree of Life in the Garden of Eden. After the Fall, she became separated from her husband, *Yahweh.* Only on Friday nights, the eve of the Sabbath, are they briefly reunited before being forced apart again. Not until all the original light of creation has returned to its Divine Source will the Divine lovers be permanently reunited. Every act of love and compassion brings the cosmic couple closer together. Thus life may be seen as a great love story in which we all participate, as we seek the Lover from which we have been separated. The very fate of the Gods is in our hands!

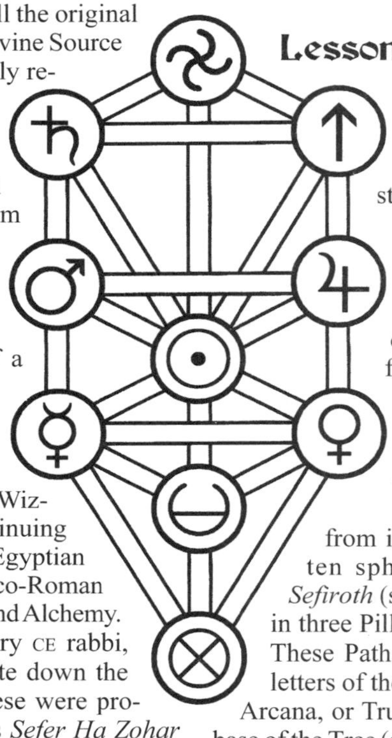

Books of the Qabalah

The Qabalah now consists of a number of books from different sources, most of them written down in several distinct sections between the 9th and 13th centuries CE. It is the collected wisdom of many ancient Wizards and magicians, as well as a continuing assimilation of occult writings from Egyptian magick, Middle Eastern magick, Greco-Roman magick, Judeo-Christian mysticism, and Alchemy.

Simon Ben Jochai, a 2nd century CE rabbi, seems to have been the first to write down the many Jewish Qabalistic myths. These were produced by his son, Rabbi Eleazor, as *Sefer Ha Zohar* ("Book of the Splendor"). The *Zohar* was introduced into Spain in the 13th century by Moses de Leon of Guadalajara, who is often claimed as its author. According to the *Zohar, An Sof* ("the Infinite"), the highest Holy of Holies, ruled the heavens with *Adni,* his Queen. Together they opposed *Samael Smal,* who was Evil Incarnate as the Angel of Death and Lord of the Devils.

The *Sefer Yezirah* ("Book of Creation") was written in Palestine or Babylon between the 3rd and 6th centuries CE. Its central theme is the mystical significance of letters and numbers. It may be considered a crossover book, linking the earlier Merkabah Mysticism and the later Qabalah.

The *Sefer Ha-Bahir* is considered the first book of "real" Qabalah; i.e., to employ the symbolism of ten *Sefiroth* as Divine Attributes (as distinct from *Seer Yetzirah*'s use of the term to designate numbers). It appeared in Provence, France, in the late 12th century.

The most important and lasting contribution of the Qabalah to magick and Wizardry was in establishing the first systems of *correspondences*, allowing things to be substituted or amplified by other associated representations. The *Sefer Yezirah*, for instance, classified everything in the universe under the 22 letters of the Hebrew Alphabet. Seven letters were for the days of the week and the Seven planets; 12 letters corresponded to the 12 months and Signs of the Zodiac. And the remaining three "mother letters" represented Air-Fire-Water. *Tables of Correspondence* are now an essential component of all grimoires.

Lesson 3: The Tree of Life

The foundation of the Qabalah is the diagram called the *Tree of Life.* This represents the underlying structure of the sacred Universe. From top to bottom, it reveals how the supreme consciousness of Divinity devolves into the material world and the self-consciousness of each individual person. In the same way, from the bottom up, the Tree shows the path by which we can ascend to unity with the Divine by removing those obstacles that limit our consciousness.

The Tree of Life grows downward from its Heavenly Source and consists of ten spheres, or *emanations*, called the *Sefiroth* (singular *sefirah*). These are arranged in three Pillars, with 22 Paths connecting them. These Paths have been associated with the 22 letters of the Hebrew alphabet and the 22 Major Arcana, or Trumps, of the Tarot. Starting with the base of the Tree (at the top of the diagram), the Sefiroth and their concerns are:

1. **Kether**—"Supreme Crown of Creation." Infinite bliss.
2. **Chokmah**—"Wisdom." The Great Father.
3. **Binah**—"Understanding." The Great Mother.
4. **Chesed**—"Love, Mercy, Greatness." The compassionate God.
5. **Geburah**—"Power, Strength, Rigor." The warring God.
6. **Tiphareth**—"Beauty, Harmony." The Messiah or Savior.
7. **Netzach**—"Victory, Force, Endurance." Love and the emotions.
8. **Hod**—"Splendor, Majesty." Intellect and reason.
9. **Yesod**—"Foundation." Sexual drives and creativity.
10. **Malkuth**—"Kingdom." Mundane preoccupations.

Table of Magickal Correspondences 10 – Sephiroth

SEPHIRAH	KETHER	CHOKMAH	BINAH	CHESED	GEBURAH	TIPHARETH	NETZACH	HOD	YESOD	MALKUTH
SPHERE	1	2	3	4	5	6	7	8	9	10
MEANING	Crown	Wisdom	Understanding	Mercy	Strength	Beauty	Victory	Splendor	Foundation	Kingdom
SYMBOL		↑	♄	♃	♂	☉	♀	☿	⊖	⊗
ELEMENT	Root of Air	Root of Fire	Root of Water	Water	Fire	Air	Fire	Water	Air	Earth
IMAGE	Old bearded King in profile	Bearded Patriarch	Celestial Queen Mother	Enthroned Priest-King	Armed Warrior in a chariot	Solar King, Divine Child	Naked Amazon	Herma-phrodite	Ithyphallic Youth	Veiled Maiden on throne
ACHIEVE-MENT	Divine union	Vision of God face-to-face	Vision of sorrow	Vision of love	Vision of power	Vision of harmony	Vision of beauty triumphant	Vision of splendor	Vision of celes-tial mechanism	Vision of Holy Guardian Angel
ILLUSION	Attainment	Independence	Death	Righteousness	Invincibility	Identification	Projection	Order	Security	Materialism
VIRTUES	Completion of Great Work	Devotion	Silence	Obedience, humility	Courage, loyalty	Devotion to the Work, integrity	Unselfishness, generosity	Truthfulness, honesty	Independence, competence	Discrimination, judgement
VICES	none	none	none	Tyranny, bigotry, hypocrisy, greed	Cruelty, destruction	Pride, self-importance	Lust, wan-tonness	Lying, cheating	Idleness, laziness	Avarice, inertia
KEY-WORDS	Unity, source, godhead, pure consciousness	Lifeforce, wellspring, creativity	Karma, time, space, death, law, limitation	Authority, vision, creativity, inspir-ation, leadership	Power, domin-ation, passion, courage	Harmony, inte-grity, balance, self-sacrifice	Empathy, sym-pathy, pleasure, sensuality, lust	Genius, medi-ation, reason, communication	Perception, imagination, emotion	Material, solid, nature, heavy
DIVINE NAME	Eheieh (I am)	Yahweh (Lord)	Yahweh Elohim (Lord God)	El (Him)	Elohim Gevor (Almighty Lord)	Yahweh Eloah va Daath	Yahweh Tzabaoth (God of Hosts)	Elohim Tzabaoth (Lord of Hosts)	Shaddai el Chai (Almighty God)	Adonai ha Aretz (Lord of Earth)
ARCHANGEL	Metatron	Ratziel	Tzaphqiel	Tzadkiel	Gamael	Michael	Haniel	Raphael	Gabriel	Sandalphon
CHOIR	Chioth Ha Qadesh	Auphanim	Aralim	Chasmalim	Seraphim	Malachim	Elohim	Beni Elohim	Cherubim	Ishim
MANIFEST'N	Galaxy	Zodiac	Saturn	Jupiter	Mars	Sun	Venus	Mercury	Moon	Elements
TAROT	Aces	Twos	Threes	Fours	Fives	Sixes	Sevens	Eights	Nines	Tens
CHAKRA	Sahasrara (crown)	Ajna (3rd eye)	Ajna (3rd eye)	Vissudha (throat)	Vissudha (throat)	Anahata (heart)	Manipuraka (solar plexus)	Manipuraka (solar plexus)	Svadistthana (genitals)	Muladhara (base of spine)
COLOR	White	Grey	Black	Blue	Red	Yellow	Emerald	Orange	Purple	Citrine
ANIMAL	Eagle	Man	Woman	Unicorn	Basilisk	Phoenix	Lynx	Jackal	Elephant	Sphinx
PLANTS	Flowering Almond	Amaranth	Cypress, poppy	Olive, shamrock	Oak, nettle	Acacia, bay, vine	Rose	Moly	Damiana, mandrake	Willow, lily, ivy
JEWEL	Diamond	Turquoise	Pearl	Amethyst	Ruby	Topaz	Emerald	Fire Opal	Quartz	Rock Crystal
INCENSE	Ambergris	Musk	Myrrh	Cedar	Tobacco	Olibanum	Sandalwood	Storax	Jasmine	Dittany

The Sefiroth can be understood as various facets of the Divine personality. The highest sphere, Kether, represents Divine Glory, and the lowest, Malkuth, is the material world. The Goddess of Malkuth ("Mother Earth") is the *Shekinah.* Below Kether on the Middle Pillar is an empty space where you would expect to find a Sefirah (much like the asteroid belt where you would expect to find a planet!). This space is called *Daath* ("knowledge"). It is the *Abyss,* or Void—the gulf that separates the finite from the infinite, and the manifest from the unmanifest. To reach Daath is to attain union with the Divine, the true goal of all mystics.

> *The first Sephira is the* pneuma (ruach *or* ruah) *["breath"] of the Living God. From the ruach comes forth Primordial Air, from which are born Water and Fire, the third and fourth of the Sefiroth. From Primordial Air, God created the 22 letters, from the Water he created the cosmic Chaos, and from the Fire, the Throne of Glory and the hierarchies of Angels. The last six Sefiroth represent the six directions of space.*
> —Gershom Scholem, *The Origins of the Kabbalah*

The *Bahir* deals with the Sefiroth, but not in terms of them being the Tree of Life. The earliest version of the relationship between the Sefiroth was as a set of concentric circles. The Tree of Life is part of the *Zohar,* and was later popularized by Isaac Luria.

Quest: Climbing the Tree of Life

Here is a ritual exercise of meditation and visualization that you can do if you wish, based on climbing up the Tree of Life from the material world to the Divine Realm. This sort of working is a foundation of much Ceremonial Magick. First, visualize the diagram of the Tree of Life mapped out upon your body as shown here.

You may find this exercise most effective if done naked before a full-length mirror, especially if you have just come out of the shower and are sparkly-clean.

(Malkuth) Visualize a lemon-yellow light around your feet. Say: "Lord of the Earth, establish your kingdom within me and teach me discrimination."

(Yesod) Visualize a purple light around your genitals. Say: "Almighty God, secure my foundation and teach me independence."

(Hod) Visualize an orange light at your left side. Say: "Lord of Angels, reveal to me your splendor and teach me truthfulness."

(Netzach) Visualize an emerald green light at your right side. Say: "God of Hosts, make me victorious against my foes and teach me unselfishness."

(Tiphareth) Visualize a pale yellow light surrounding your heart. Say: "Lord of Knowledge, grant me beauty and teach me integrity."

(Geburah) Visualize a scarlet red light at your left shoulder. Say: "Almighty Lord, with your strength, protect me and teach me courage."

(Chesed) Visualize a blue light at your right shoulder. Say: "Holy One, with your mercy, teach me obedience and humility."

(Binah) Visualize a black shadow above your left shoulder. Say: "Queen of Heaven, grant me understanding and teach me when to be silent."

(Chokmah) Visualize a light of all colors mixed together above your right shoulder. Say: "Heavenly Father, grant me wisdom and teach me devotion."

(Kether) Visualize a brilliant white light just above your head. Say: "Infinite Spirit, crown my life with the completion of the Great Work, and bring me into union with you."

Lesson 4: The Hermetica

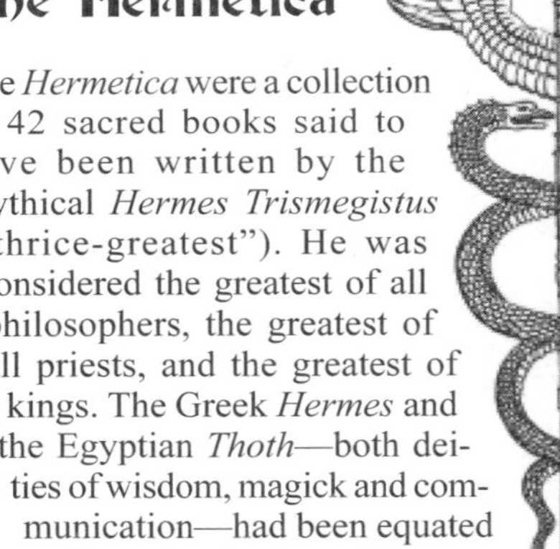

The *Hermetica* were a collection of 42 sacred books said to have been written by the mythical *Hermes Trismegistus* ("thrice-greatest"). He was considered the greatest of all philosophers, the greatest of all priests, and the greatest of all kings. The Greek *Hermes* and the Egyptian *Thoth*—both deities of wisdom, magick and communication—had been equated with each other by c. 500 BCE.

A third manifestation was the Hebrew Patriarch *Enoch,* "2nd Messenger of God." It was claimed that Hermes revealed to mankind the arts of medicine, chemistry, law, art, astrology, music, debate, magick, philosophy, geography, mathematics, the 365-day calendar, anatomy, and oratory (speech-making).

The most important Hermetic symbol is the *Caduceus,* Hermes's winged wand entwined by two serpents.

Although most of the Hermetic teachings are based on Greek philosophy—particularly Plato and Aristotle—the writings take the form of dialogues between Hermes Trismegistus; the Egyptian gods Thoth, Ammon, Isis and Horus; and the healing gods Asclepius (Greek) and Imhotep (Egyptian).

Their purpose is to convey an understanding of the relationships between the Gods, Humanity, and the Universe. The Hermetica teaches that because man combines a Divine and a mortal nature, he is superior to the lesser gods who are only immortal, and to other creatures who are only mortal. For the same reason, humans can create gods—those who live in statues and temples and derive their power from the worship of their devotees.

Written in Alexandria, Egypt, between the 3rd century BCE and the 1st century CE, these books have had an enormous influence on the development of Western magick. Sadly, most of the original Hermetic books were lost in the burning of the Alexandrian Library in 415 CE. Surviving fragments were translated by Arab scholars from Greek and Coptic manuscripts, and were introduced into Europe by the Spanish Moors in the 12th century.

The main body of Hermetic writings, however, was not translated into Latin until 1471, when Cosimo de Medici, the great patron of the Italian Renaissance in Florence, instructed Marsilio Ficino to translate Greek Hermetic manuscripts he had obtained from Byzantium. The newly invented printing press then made it possible for the Latin Hermetica to be spread quickly throughout Europe. The most important of these books are *The Divine Pymander* and The *Emerald Tablet.*

> *The impact of the Hermetica on Renaissance philosophy was enormous. Here was an ancient body of theological, magickal and medical writings of extraordinary beauty, intellectual power and spiritual authority, in which Jew, Christian and Muslim could find confirmations, amplifications and refinements of their own sacred teachings.*
>
> *In the Hermetica, the creation myth becomes a much richer, more detailed and expressive allegory, an awesome Alchemical process. Hermes describes man as "the great miracle," capable of achieving Godhood as an individual by transcending the stages of being that separate him from the Divine. Man is dignified as being truly made "in the image of God," being the microcosm that reflects the macrocosm. This is emphasized by Hermes' great dictum "as above, so below," with its correlate "as within, so without." Everything in creation finds its reflection in man. He therefore has at his disposal all the tools he needs to achieve his Divine Destiny, should he choose to accept it.* —Francis Melville,
>
> *The Secrets of High Magic*

The Emerald Tablet

Legend has it that the following words (in Greek) were originally carved in raised bas-relief on a single large emerald-green tablet (one ancient witness believed it had been cast in a mold, as molten glass). Hence this text is called *The Emerald Tablet.*

> *I. Truly, without deceit, certainly and absolutely—*
>
> *II. That which is Below corresponds to that which is Above, and that which is Above corresponds to that which is Below, to accomplish the Miracle of One Thing.*
>
> *III. And just as all things have come from One, through the Mediation of One, so all things proceed from this One Thing in the same way.*
>
> *IV. The Sun is its Father. Its Mother is the Moon.*
>
> *V. The Wind has carried it in his Belly. It is nourished by the Earth.*
>
> *VI. It is the father of every Perfected Thing in the whole World. Its Power is complete if it is converted into Earth.*
>
> *VII. Separate the Earth from the Fire, the subtle from the gross, gently and with great care.*
>
> *VIII. It rises from the Earth to Heaven, and descends again to the Earth,*
>
> *IX. And thereby receives Power from Above and from Below.*
>
> *X. By this means, you shall obtain the Glory of the whole World. All Obscurity will be clear to you. This is the strong Power of all Power. It overcomes everything subtle and penetrates everything solid.*
>
> *XI. In this way was the World created. From this there will be amazing Applications, of which these are the means.*
>
> *XII. Therefore am I called Thrice Greatest Hermes, holding three parts of the Wisdom of the whole World.*
>
> *XIII. Herein have I completely explained the Operation of the Sun.*

Lesson 5: Angels and Demons

Angels and Demons are common to the mythologies of Judaism, Christianity and Islam. In Qabalistic magick, *Angels* ("messengers") are considered to be Spirits or intelligences of the "higher" planes, whereas *Demons* ("evil spirits") inhabit the "lower" realms. (Humans, of course, are in the middle). Most of the rituals of "High Magick" are concerned with *summoning* (calling) or *conjuring* these Entities into visible presence, and commanding them to reveal certain information or perform assigned tasks. This is uncannily similar to the way we now use the Internet and the World Wide Web!

Both Angels and Demons are ranked in ordered levels of *hierarchies,* much like an army. Angels are by nature cooperative and wish to aid any worthy magician. Demons are shifty and uncooperative, and have to be threatened and coerced into helping. I will discuss Demons more fully in Class 6.6.3. In this Lesson, I wish to concentrate on the Angels of the Qabalistic tradition.

Angels are pure spirit, therefore they have no sexuality. They are free of the limitations of the material world, are incorporeal and immortal. They are fixed in their roles, have no free will, and do not change or evolve. Their functions and their objectives are to help us to know our true nature and purpose, and awaken our divine consciousness.

Groups of Angels are known as *Choirs.* Each Choir contains thousands of Angels, ruled by an *Archangel.* There are ten of these, each associated with a Sefirah on the Tree of Life. Here are the Angelic Choirs, ranked from the highest to the lowest. If you should decide to conjure up any of these Archangels, it's extremely important to pronounce their names correctly!

Chioth Ha Qadesh—This is the supreme Order of Angels, directly associated with the ultimate infinite Divine Spirit of *Kether.* They are known as the Holy Living Creatures, and they are led by Archangel *Metatron* (MET-a-tron) ("Angel of the Presence"). The King of all the Angels, and the youngest, he was once the Biblical Patriarch Enoch. Metatron is the link between God and humanity. His female counterpart is Shekinah (sheh-KEE-na).

Auphanim—These are the Whirling Forces. Associated with *Chokmah,* they are ruled by Archangel *Ratziel* (RAT-zee-EL) ("delight of God"), the Prince of knowledge of hidden things, who is called the Angel of Mysteries. The legendary *Book of Ratziel* is said to contain a secret coded key to the mysteries of the Universe unknown even to other Angels.

Aralim—These are the Strong and Mighty Ones. They are made of white fire and are associated with *Binah,* the Sefirah of Saturn and the Female Principle. Their ruling Archangel is *Tzaphqiel* (TZAF-kee-EL) ("contemplation of God"), the Prince of spiritual strife against evil.

Chasmalim—These are the Brilliant Ones. They are concerned with Justice and are associated with *Chesed,* the Sefirah of Jupiter. They are led by Archangel *Tzadkiel* (TZAD-kee-EL) ("justice of God"), Prince of mercy and beneficence who guards the Gates of the East Wind.

Seraphim—These are the Flaming Ones, the Avenging Angels of destruction. They serve *Geburah,* the Sefirah of Mars and the Fear of God. They are ruled by Archangel *Kamael* (KA-may-EL) ("severity of God"). As Prince of strength and courage, he bears the flaming sword.

Malachim—Also called the *Shinanin,* these serve *Tiphareth,* the Sefirah of the Sun. They govern all natural laws and are responsible for the motions and cycles of the heavenly bodies, as well as any miracles that break the laws of Nature. They inspire valor in heroes and virtue in saints. Their Archangel is *Raphael* (RAF-ay-EL) ("physician of God"), Prince of healing, with Michael as his lieutenant.

Elohim—These are the *pantheon* ("all Gods'), also known as the Choir of Principalities. They are associated with *Netzach,* the Sefirah of Venus. Their presiding Archangel is *Haniel* (HA-nee-el) ("grace of God"), Prince of love and harmony. His female counterpart, *Hagiel* (HA-gee-el), is a beautiful green-eyed Angel appearing exactly as the Goddess Aphrodite.

Beni Elohim—These are the Sons of the Gods, also known as the Choir of Archangels. They are associated with *Hod,* the Sefirah of Mercury. Their Archangel is *Michael* (MY-kay-EL) ("protector of God"), with Raphael as his lieutenant. Their province is art and knowledge.

Cherubim—These are the Guardian Angels of humanity; their name means "those who intercede." They serve *Yesod,* the Sefirah of action and the Moon. Their Archangel is *Gabriel* (GAB-ree-EL) ("strength of God"), most beloved of all the Angels. It was he who appeared to Mary with the Annunciation and dictated the Koran to Mohammed.

Ishim—These are the lowest order of Angels, assisting humanity directly. Also called the Blessed Souls and the Souls of the Just Made Perfect, they were once living saints and prophets. They are associated with *Malkuth*—the Kingdom of Earth and mundane concerns. Their Archangel is *Sandalphon* (san-DAL-fon) ("co-brother"), the twin of Metatron. He was once the Hebrew prophet Elias.

Lesson 6: Angelic Operations

If you haven't yet been working with the exercises in meditation and visualization I gave you earlier, you are certainly not ready to do Angelic operations. It's alright—there's no rush. Develop those skills, and then come back to this Lesson.

Angelic operations, like all conjurations of Spirits, require a quiet and private space where you will not be interrupted for at least an hour. If at all possible, you should be completely alone in the house, so you will not even hear other people's voices. Lock the doors and unplug the telephone. The temperature should be comfortable, and it helps to have a soft cushion to sit on. Have everything you might need within easy reach, and use the bathroom before you begin!

Don't eat spicy foods—especially things like beans or garlic that will give you stinky breath or farts—for at least 48 hours before your ritual! The only thing you want to smell is the special incense for the rite. Make sure you are well-rested. If you are tired or ill, don't attempt to do conjurations! Take a nice purifying shower or bath, and wear a clean white robe.

Here's a general plan for conjuration of an Angel:

First, you must become very familiar with the qualities and associations of the Angel you wish to contact. Study the various Tables of Correspondence in this Grimoire, and make up a little chart for this particular Angel. Below are some specific correspondences for the Archangels.

Second, you must have a very specific purpose in mind for this contact. Idle curiosity is just not good enough! Write down your Statement of Intent on a piece of parchment. Also make a checklist of all the items you will need. Prepare those that you have to make (such as incense), and have everything in place before you begin the operation.

The main special item you will have to construct for these conjurations is a plywood equilateral triangle with a round hole cut out of the center that your *Speculum* (Scrying Mirror) will fit into. You will need to make a brace for the back that will support it at a 45° angle. In the three corners, draw the appropriate sigils (see 4.VII.3: "Talismans of the Planetary Powers").

The other thing you will need to make is a Talisman appropriate to the Planetary Sphere. This can be painted or drawn on cloth or parchment in the appropriate color (again, see 4.VII.3 for details).

ARCHANGEL	DUTIES	OIL/INCENSE	STONE	COLOR
10. Metatron	Links human and Divine	Sage, Frankincense	Herkimer Diamond	White
9. Ratziel	Concealment, hidden knowledge	Geranium Eucalyptus	Fluorite	Smoky blue
8. Tzaphqiel	Answers prayers, intercession	Sage, Chamomile, Eucalyptus, Myrhh	Obsidian, Tourmaline	Black
7. Tzadkiel	Protect teachers, manifestation	Bayberry, Cedar, Nutmeg	Lapis lazuli	Blue, purple
6. Kamael	Strength, courage	Cinnamon, Gardenia, Cypress	Garnet	Olive, citrine
5. Raphael	Healing	Jasmine, Rose, Lilly	Rose quartz	Yellow, pink
4. Haniel	Artistic, creativity	Patchouli, Rose, Bayberry	Emerald, Malachite	Green
3. Michael	Protection, patience	Rosemary	Citrine, Calcite	Orange, peach
2. Gabriel	Messenger of God	Jasmine, Aloes, Sandalwood	Quartz, Moonstone	Purple
1. Sandalphon	Life, prayer	Sandalwood, Lemon, Carnation	Smoky quartz	Black, russet

Personal: Put on a tabard of the appropriate color over your white robe. Wear an appropriate gemstone on a pendant, a ring, or in your mojo bag. Anoint your wrists, temples, chest and third eye with the appropriate oil.

Ritual Space: Put an appropriate-colored light bulb in a lamp, and turn out all other lights. Mark a circle (you can use chalk, or a loop of string) large enough to sit in comfortably, and place a cushion in its center. Set up your scrying triangle outside the circle, in the East, with the mirror facing inward so you can see your face in it when you sit in the center of the circle. Set the Talisman in front of you, inside the circle. Have a little bell in the North—the best kind is one you can hit with a striker. In the West, set a Chalice of water. And place your Thurible and incense in the South.

Outside the circle, position 4 candles halfway between the compass quarters, all the same color.

The Operation: First, cast the circle in the usual fashion, but do not invoke the Elements. Then light the candles, and burn appropriate incense. Sit down on the cushion, and put yourself into a meditative state. Close your eyes and visualize a shining Angelic presence. When you are ready, open your eyes and gaze into the Speculum in the same unfocused fashion as when you are perceiving auras (or stereograms).

Continuing to gaze into the Speculum, strike the bell, and think silently the name of the Angel you wish to contact, as many times as their number. Strike the bell before each calling. Then do the same thing again, for the same number of times, only this time whisper the name softly. And finally, do a third repetition while intoning the name aloud in strong tones. At the conclusion, say: "I summon thee to appear before me!"

If you have prepared yourself properly, and have already acquired some skill in meditation and visualization, you should see the face of the Angel appear in your Speculum. With enough practice, you may become able to see his/her full figure rise up before you, as if your Speculum was a laser projector. Maintain your state of meditative calm, and ask the Angel for whatever you had previously determined according to your intention. You can be sure your prayers will be answered!

Finally, drink from your Chalice (you'll be quite thirsty!), thank the Angel, and bid him/her hail and farewell. After he/she fades from view, open your circle, put out the candles, and return the space to its normal use.

Class V: Lore Mastery (Grey)

1. Introduction: Lore Mastery

ORE MEANS “TEACHINGS,” AND LORE Mastery is the primary attribute of the Wizard. Throughout history, Wizards have studied and collected books and writings containing the wisdom of the ages, and many have assembled important libraries and museums. Perhaps the greatest female Wizard of all time was *Hypatia* (YIP-a-TEE-ah), who was a teacher, mathematician, astronomer, Platonic philosopher, and the last librarian of the great Library of Alexandria, Egypt, before she was brutally murdered and the library burned down by a fanatical Christian mob in 415 CE. Her father, Theon, also a great Wizard, was the last curator of the Alexandrian Museum.

Lore mastery is all about knowing arcane secrets and esoteric mysteries known to very few others. It is said that “knowledge is power,” and much of a Wizard’s true power comes from his vast knowledge. This is why many Wizards have been famed as wise teachers, mentors, guides and advisors—even to kings and queens.

Lore, however, is more than merely secrets and mysteries. A very important body of lore concerns myths and legends; a Lore-Master is also a storyteller, who can always come up with a tale to make any point.

I have always loved myths, legends and fairy tales. Before I even entered kindergarten, I had read Greek myths adapted for children in a set of books called *Childcraft* that my parents had gotten for me. I’ll never forget the very first story I learned to read—the tale of *Persephone* and *Hades* (only they used the Roman names of *Proserpine* and *Pluto*). All these classic stories have been very important in my life, and I have drawn upon them continually over the years. I have even created rituals and mystery plays to enact them in powerful and transformative ways for many people.

Lesson 2. The Bardic Arts

The Bardic Arts include poetry and storytelling, music and songs. In ancient Celtic tradition, Bards were part of the magickal Orders that were headed by the Druids. Bards were the poets, musicians and singers of the epic songs and tales that conveyed the history and lore of the People. At a time when very little was written down, a Bard was expected to memorize enormous amounts of poetry, songs and stories.

Modern Bards continue this tradition, and Bardic “Loresingers” are highly respected and honored throughout the magickal community, performing live at gatherings as well as producing recordings. Many of our magickal Bards have also become famous in the mundane world, and they can be heard in concerts and on the radio.

Bardcraft has always been so important to the life of the people that various cultures have even assigned patron (or matron) deities to *inspire* (“breathe into”) their Bards. In ancient Greece these were the *Muses,* goddesses of the arts and sciences. Our word “music” comes from their name. Before any performance, or in the throes of creation, or when seeking inspiration, Bards would invoke the appropriate Muse. The movie *Xanadu* features Olivia Newton John as a Muse, with the wonderful theme song, “You’ve got to believe we are magic!” The Muses were daughters of *Zeus,* the king of the gods, and *Mnemosyne* (NEM-oh-SY-nee), the goddess of memory. Here are their names and domains:

Calliope (kah-LYE-oh-pee) (“beautiful voice”)— Epic poetry and rhetoric. She holds a tightly-rolled scroll.

Clio (KLEE-oh) (“to celebrate fame”)— History. She is shown reading from a half-opened scroll.

Erato (er-AT-oh) (“passionate”)— Love poetry and marriage feasts. She is shown playing a lyre.

Euterpe (yu-TER-pee) (“charming”) — Music and lyric poetry (songs). She is shown playing two flutes.

Melpomene (mel-PO-men-ee) (“to sing”)— Tragedy. She holds a sad mask, the club of Hercules, and a wreath of grape leaves.

Polyhymnia (POL-ee-HIM-nee-ah) (“many hymns”) — Sacred hymns to the gods. She is shown singing.

Terpsichore (TERP-si-KOR-ee) (“rejoicing dance”)— Dancing and dance music. She holds high a tambourine as she dances.

Thalia (THA-lee-ah) (“to flourish”)— Comedy and idyllic poetry. She holds a happy mask, a shepherd’s crook, and a wreath of ivy.

Urania (yu-RAN-ee-ah) (“the heavenly”)— Astronomy. She is shown holding a globe and a wand.

In Ireland, the goddess of poetry, music, and the creative arts is **Brigit.** As matron of the Bardic oral tradition, she is the Mother of Memory. She is also the Goddess of herbalism, the healing arts, metal-smithing, sacred wells, animal husbandry, and midwifery. Given those qualities, my Ravenheart Family has adopted Brigit as our matron goddess, and she has a special place on our family altar.

Lesson 3: Classic Myths

In the Western world, what are called the "Classic myths" are stories of mainly Greek origin that were adopted and passed down by the Romans when they ruled the world. After 21-year-old Cleopatra, the last Pharaoh, allied with Julius Caesar in 48 BCE, some Egyptian myths also found their way into Rome.

In Greece, Hesiod's *Theogony* ("birth of the gods"), written in the 8th century BCE, told of the origins of the gods and the establishment of the rule of Zeus. His account of the succession of generations of gods shows the influence of Near Eastern mythology, particularly Sumerian, Akkadian, and Hittite. Around the same time, Homer recorded the saga of the Trojan War and the 10-year journey of Odysseus in his *Illiad* and *Odyssey.* Other poets and playwrights expanded greatly upon this material over the following centuries.

In Rome, Ovid's *Metamorphoses* ("transformations"), written in 1 CE, collected about 250 mythic stories and became an instant popular hit. He translated and adapted many Greek legends into Roman versions, frequently changing the names and locales. Ovid's influence on Western art and literature cannot be exaggerated. He was a major inspiration for Dante, Chaucer, Shakespeare, Milton, and many others.

Common Themes

In the many hundreds of myths that have come down to us, several common themes are often repeated:

1. Prophecies that a child as yet unborn will someday show up and kill the ruler. Efforts made to thwart these prophecies inevitably ensure their fulfillment.
2. A mortal woman boastfully comparing her beauty or skills with that of a goddess invites divine retribution, as does a mortal man comparing himself with the gods.
3. Hospitality is a sacred obligation. Refusing it brings certain doom, whereas offering it generously is greatly rewarded by the gods.
4. A bastard son born to a women impregnated by the supreme God will grow up to be a great hero.
5. If you attempt to flee from your destiny, it will overtake you from behind and destroy you. The hero must face his destiny and embrace it; only then will he triumph. Making the choice gives you the power.

Throughout this ***Grimoire*** I have mentioned many of these stories to illustrate various lessons. Now, here are a few more of my personal favorites I'd like to share with you. If you enjoy these, there are many more awaiting your exploration!

Prometheus and Pandora

Prometheus (pro-MEE-thee-us) ("forethought") and *Epimetheus* (EP-ih-MEE-thee-us) ("afterthought") were two of the four sons of the Titan *Iapetus.* Prometheus was wise but Epimetheus was foolish. When the gods were creating living creatures, Epimetheus was given the task of assigning qualities to them. But when the job was done, Prometheus discovered that his foolish brother had given all the strengths, powers, weapons, protections, and defenses to the animals, leaving humans naked and defenseless.

To remedy this situation, Prometheus stole fire from the gods and gave it to humanity—the greatest power of all. Thus did Prometheus become the great benefactor and champion of humanity—in opposition to Zeus, who feared that humans might become too powerful and threaten his rule.

Zeus demanded that men offer up animal sacrifices as tribute to the Gods of Olympus. Prometheus divided the butchered parts of an ox into two piles and asked Zeus to choose a portion for the gods. In one pile Prometheus had wrapped the meat and edible organs up in the dry skin. In the other, he had hidden the bones and inedible parts under glistening fat. Zeus chose the second pile, and from that time, humans have burned the fat, bones and offal as offerings to the Gods, while keeping the meat and hides for themselves.

Angry over being tricked again, Zeus plotted revenge upon Prometheus and his pet humans. He had *Hephaestos,* the smith god, mold a woman of clay, and all the goddesses gave her some of their attributes. Thus was she named *Pandora* (pan-DORE-ah), meaning "gift of all." Zeus gave her a box which he warned her never to open, and had Hermes take her to Prometheus. But Prometheus knew better than to accept any gift from Zeus, and he refused her. Epimetheus, however, was so taken by her charms that he married her.

Eventually, of course, Pandora could no longer restrain her curiosity about the contents of the mysterious box, and she opened it, as Zeus knew she would. Out flew all the ills and evils, which would ever after plague humanity. Pandora closed the lid just in time to prevent the escape of Hope, which remains as a comfort in our most difficult times.

Prometheus knew that Zeus in his turn would someday be overthrown by a new god, but refused to tell who it would be. In a futile attempt to torture it out of him, Zeus bound Prometheus with chains to one of the Caucasus mountains, and sent his mighty vulture/eagle to tear at his liver every day. As Prometheus was an immortal, it grew back each night. Eventually, he was released from this agony by Heracles.

In my youth, I so identified with Prometheus that I took his as my first magickal name. His willingness to defy the tyrannical King of the Gods to benefit humanity has always had an irresistible appeal to me.

(Interestingly, the first safety matches, invented in the early 1800s, were called "Prometheans.")

Inanna and Dumuzi

Inanna (ih-NAH-nah) was the Queen of Heaven in ancient Sumeria. Known as *Ishtar* (ISH-tar) in later Babylon, she was the most important Goddess in Mesopotamia. Depicted as richly dressed or naked, Inanna is a Goddess of love, fertility, and war. She is also the personification of the planet Venus, symbolized by an eight-pointed star.

Her best-known story is called "Inanna's Descent into the Underworld." Deciding to extend her dominion over the lower world as she has the upper, Inanna passes through seven gates and must leave something behind at each one. She is stripped of her crown, her scepter, her powers, her jewelry, her girdle, her clothing, and finally even her name, entering *Aralu,* the Underworld, naked and nameless. When she finally gets there, her cruel sister *Ereshkigal* (air-ESH-ki-gol), ruler of the realm, sentences her to death, hanging her rotting corpse on a meathook.

With Inanna's death, however, nothing would grow on the Earth anymore. Wise *Enki,* high god of creation and medicine, who held the secrets of life and death, declared that Inanna could be reborn only if someone took her place. She chose her husband *Dumuzi,* god of vegetation, who from then on ruled the Underworld for half the year. At the Fall Equinox, the beginning of the Sumerian new year, Dumuzi returned to the Earth. His reunion with Inanna revitalized all Nature.

Isis and Osiris

Isis (IY-sis) was the Goddess most widely worshipped by the Egyptians, and later, throughout the Roman Empire. She was the Queen of Heaven and Earth, and also ruled on the sea. Her brother and husband was *Osiris* (oh-SYE-ris), the green god of the fertile fields, representing the principle of Good. His brother *Set* was the red god of the burning desert, representing the principle of Evil.

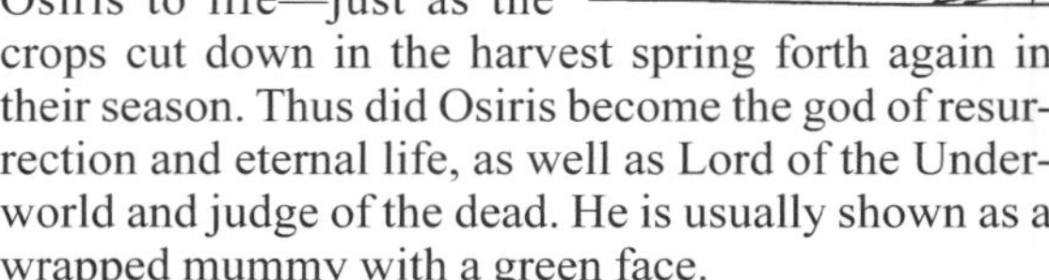

Once Set overcame Osiris, cutting his body into 14 pieces and scattering them all over Egypt. Over many months, Isis devotedly sought and collected all the pieces but one—his penis. She made him a new one of wood, and then performed special ceremonies with the other gods to join all the pieces together and restore Osiris to life—just as the crops cut down in the harvest spring forth again in their season. Thus did Osiris become the god of resurrection and eternal life, as well as Lord of the Underworld and judge of the dead. He is usually shown as a wrapped mummy with a green face.

Isis bore Osiris a son, named *Horus* (HORE-us). Commonly shown with the head of a hawk, he represented the life-giving power of *Ra,* the Sun-god. He fought and defeated Set, but lost an eye in the battle. This "Eye of Horus" became one of the most powerful symbols of magickal protection, known as the *udjat.*

Demeter, Persephone and Hades

Koré (KOE-ray) ("girl"), the flower-maiden, was the daughter of *Demeter* (de-MEE-ter), Goddess of agriculture. One day, when Koré was out picking flowers, she espied a beautiful black narcissus. But its roots went down to the Underworld. When she plucked it, the ground split open, and grim *Hadés* (HAY-deez), Lord of the Dead, rode out in his ebon chariot pulled by fire-eyed black horses. He seized Koré and carried her down to his dark realm of Erebos to become his bride and queen. There she she was known by her true name, *Persephoné* (pur-SEF-on-ee).

Demeter was so distraught over the disappearance of her daughter that she ceased attending to the fertility of the fields and wandered the world grieving in search of Koré. Meanwhile, the Earth grew barren and cold, as the first Winter settled over the land. The people were starving due to Demeter's neglect and were no longer able to make offerings to the Gods. Zeus appealed to Demeter to relent, but she insisted on the return of her daughter. So Zeus decreed that Persephone must be released—provided she had not eaten anything while in the Underworld.

However, Persephoné had already swallowed three pomegranate seeds, thus binding herself to the dark realm. So a compromise was reached: Persephoné would spend 1/3 of the year reigning with Hadés as Queen of the Dead, and the other 2/3 of the year upon the green Earth with Demeter. Koré's return each Spring with the flowers was a rebirth, erasing all memories of the previous cycle.

This story was enacted annually in the *Eleusinian Mysteries,* conducted as an 11-day festival from at least the 13th century BCE until 395 CE when Alaric the Goth demolished the temple at Eleusis. This was the most transformative ceremony of ancient times, and initiates were promised a special life in the Underworld after death. They were sworn to secrecy, and the inner rites were never revealed to non-initiates.

Athena and Poseidon

In order to thwart a prophecy that he would be overthrown by her son, Zeus swallowed his first wife, *Metis* ("counsel"), when she was pregnant. Instead of a son, she bore a daughter, *Athena* (ah-THEE-nah), who sprang fully grown and armed from Zeus's forehead. As Goddess of both war and wisdom, she fought in the great Clash of the Titans, and her brilliant strategies won victory for the gods. Athena became one of the greatest goddesses of Greece, presiding as well in peacetime as in war. She was the preserver of the state and of all the peaceful arts and trades, which she invented and taught to humankind.

After the Olympian Gods defeated the Titans, the first three brothers drew lots and divided the worlds among them. Zeus claimed the Heavens, *Poseidon* (po-ZY-don) received the Seas, and Hades got stuck with the Underworld. Not only did Poseidon rule the waves; he was also the master of horses, including the seahorses, or *hippocampi.*

Athena and Poseidon vied over who would become the patron deity of the capital of Greece. Zeus decreed a competition based on which one could offer the greater gift to the people—the winner to be determined by ballot in the first recorded election. Poseidon struck the ground with his trident, and a salt spring and a horse sprang forth. Athena offered the olive tree.

All the men and women of the city cast their votes. The men all voted for Poseidon, and the women all voted for Athena. However, there was one more woman than there were men, so Athena won the election by a single vote. Thus was the city named Athens, and thus was established the first democracy. However, the men were resentful at having been outvoted, so the first act of the new congress was to deny voting rights to women—even though their matron deity remained the Goddess!

Janet and Tam Lin

Janet was the independent daughter of a Medieval Earl. One day, she set off alone to explore the nearby forest of Carterhaugh. As she plucked a rose, a handsome young man suddenly appeared and challenged her, saying he was guardian of the woods. Janet replied that she meant no harm and asked who he was. He replied that he was *Tam Lin,* a notorious Elfin knight. But he had been born a mortal and had been captured by the Queen of Faerie when he fell sleeping from his horse. He longed to return to the mortal world, but was bound to Faerie by an enchantment.

The two fell in love, and Janet became pregnant. One day Tam Lin told her that night was Samhain, when the Fairie host rode out in the Wild Hunt, and he rode with them. With courage and love, she could win him away from the Elfin Queen. At midnight she must wait by the crossroads as the Elfin riders passed by. She must pull him from his milk-white horse and hold him tight, no matter what happened next.

Janet did as he told her. The Faerie Queen cast her spells upon Tam Lin, changing him first to a lizard, then to a snake, and finally to a red-hot block of iron. Still Janet held him fast, and would not let him go. Finally he returned to his own form as a naked man and Janet wrapped him in her green mantle. The Elfin Queen cried out bitterly that had she known the love of a mortal woman would take Tam Lin from her, she'd have torn out his heart and replaced it with a stone. And had she known he would be taken by Janet's beauty, she'd have torn out his eyes and replaced them with wood.

(This tale is sung in *The Ballad of Tam Lin.*)

Lesson 4: Heroes and Heroines

Gilgamesh (c. 2700 BCE)

Gilgamesh was an historical king of Uruk in Babylonia (modern Iraq). 2/3 god and 1/3 human, he was the strongest man who ever lived, and he oppressed his people harshly. They called to the goddess *Aruru* to help them. Aruru the Potter created a wild man, *Enkidu,* with the strength of a dozen wild animals to be a subhuman rival to the superhuman Gilgamesh. They fought furiously until Gilgamesh gained the upper hand. The two embraced and became devoted friends. After several adventures, Enkidu fell ill and died. Gilgamesh set out on a quest to find a cure for death. From *Utnapishtim,* the original Sumerian Noah, he learned of a plant of life that grew at the bottom of the sea. Gilgamesh recovered the plant, only to have it stolen by a snake, who thus gained immortality instead.

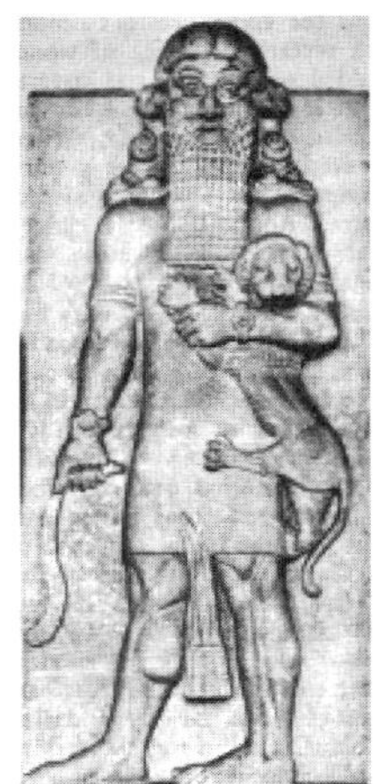

Perseus (c.1350-1310 BCE)

Perseus was the child of Zeus and the mortal woman *Danae,* to whom he had appeared in a shower of gold. In fear of a prophecy, her father cast the mother and child into the sea in a wooden chest, which was found by a fisherman to took them in. When Perseus was grown, the king (who desired Danae) tried to get rid of him by sending him on a quest for the head of the Gorgon *Medusa,* a cruel snake-haired monster so frightful that no one could behold her without being turned to stone.

From the *Graiae,* three ugly sisters who shared a single eye, Perseus obtained the winged sandals and crooked sword of Hermes, Hades' helmet of invisibility, and the bright shield of Athena. With these, he flew to Medusa's lair and, using the polished shield as a mirror to avoid looking at her directly, he cut off the Gorgon's head and stuffed it into a sack.

On the coast of Ethiopia, Perseus came upon the lovely princess *Andromeda,* chained to a rock, about to be devoured by a rampaging sea monster. He pulled forth the Gorgon's head and turned the monster to stone. He married the princess, and they lived happily ever after. He returned the gifts to the gods, including the head of Medusa, which Athena bore ever after upon her breastplate.

(The Perseus myth is well-told in the movie, *Clash of the Titans*)

Heracles (c.1303-1259 BCE)

Heracles (Roman name: *Hercules*) was the son of Zeus and Alcmene. He was the strongest man who ever lived, and Greece's most famous hero. Zeus' jealous queen, *Hera,* hated him from birth and made his life hell. She sent two serpents to attack him in his crib, but the new-born infant strangled them with his bare hands. When he was 18, he hunted down and killed a huge lion that was attacking the flocks of Mt. Cithaeron. Ever after, he wore its skin as a cloak, with the head and jaws serving as a helmet.

After killing the Cithaeron lion, Heracles went on to perform many more heroic deeds and won great acclaim and gifts from gods and kings, including a wife, Megara, who bore him three children. But his triumphs ended when Hera afflicted him with madness, during which he slew his family. In grief, he consulted the Delphic Oracle, who told him he could be purified only by a terrible penance: He must subject himself to his cruel cousin Eurystheus of Mycenae for 12 years and perform 12 brutal tasks at his command. These were the famous "Labors of Heracles," and he performed each of them triumphantly (see p. 291). Afterwards, he returned to Thebes to continue his heroic career. He married Deianeira, hunted the Caledonian Boar, and sailed on the Argo in quest of the Golden Fleece. He was finally killed by treachery with a poisoned cloak, and became one of the gods.

Theseus (c.1291-1233 BCE)

Theseus was the son of Aegeus, king of Athens, and of Aethra, daughter of the king of Troezene, where he was brought up. On parting from Aethra before the birth, Aegeus placed his sword and sandals under a large boulder, telling her to send his son to him when he became strong enough to roll away the stone and take them from under it. When he was 16, Theseus removed the stone with ease, and set out for Athens with the tokens.

In Athens, Theseus was acknowledged by his father, and declared his heir. At that time, the Athenians were paying a terrible tribute to Minos, king of Crete. Seven youths and seven maidens were sent every year to be devoured by the *Minotaur,* a half-bull, half-human monster. It was imprisoned in a maze—the *labyrinth*—so designed that whoever was put in it could never find his way out. Theseus resolved to deliver his people from this evil, or die trying. When the time came, he offered himself as one of the victims. The ship departed under black sails, which Theseus promised his father to change for white when he returned victorious.

When they arrived in Crete, the princess Ariadne fell in love with Theseus. She furnished him with a spindle of thread by which he might trace and retrace his way out of the labyrinth. He slew the Minotaur, escaped from the labyrinth, and taking Ariadne, sailed for Athens. On their way they stopped at the island of Naxos, where Theseus abandoned Ariadne. As the ship approached the coast of Greece, Theseus forgot to raise the white sails, and the old king, thinking his son had perished, took his own life. Theseus thus became king of Athens.

Theseus accompanied Heracles in his expedition to the Amazons. During their attack, he carried off Queen Hyppolyta's syster, Antiope, by whom he later had a son, Hippolytus. The Amazons in their turn invaded Greece. The final battle in which Theseus overcame them was fought in the very midst of Athens.

Jason (c. 1287–1247 BCE)

Jason's father was Aeson, the lawful king of Iolcus, whose half-brother, Pelias, had usurped the throne. He imprisoned Aeson and would have murdered Jason at birth. But Jason's mother, Alcimede, deceived Pelias by mourning as if the baby had died, secretly sending him away to Mt. Pelion to be raised by the wise Centaur, Chiron. When Jason turned 20, he returned to Iolcus intending to restore his father to his throne. On the way, he carried an old woman across a swollen stream, losing a sandal in the torrent.

An oracle had warned Pelias to beware of a stranger wearing one sandal, so when Jason showed up to claim his throne, Pelias plotted to get rid of him. He commissioned Jason to embark on a heroic quest to bring back the legendary Golden Fleece from Colchis (see below). Jason succeeded, bringing back not only the Fleece, but also the princess Medea as his wife. Medea, a sorceress, arranged the death of Pelias, then she and Jason fled to Corinth.

After many years, Jason left Medea to marry Glauce, daughter of Corinth's King Creon. Medea wreaked a terrible vengeance, killing the bride and Creon, and murdering her own children. She escaped in a chariot pulled by winged dragons, leaving Jason to mourn his losses. A broken old man, Jason was eventually killed by a falling timber as he was sleeping under the prow of his famous ship, the Argo.

Atalanta (c. 1285–1255 BCE)

Atalanta's father, King Iasus of Arcadia, wanted a boy. When a girl was born, he exposed her in the mountains were she was suckled by a mother bear sent by the goddess Artemis. A group of hunters found her and raised her to womanhood. Atalanta became a famously skilled archer and, like Artemis, loved to hunt.

Atalanta sailed with the Argonauts in quest of the Golden Fleece. She was wounded in battle with the Colchians and was healed by Medea. Atalanta also participated in the Calydonian Boar Hunt. Other male hunters objected to her presence, but *Meleager,* a fellow Argonaut and leader of the hunt, admired Atalanta and insisted she be allowed to join. Atalanta's arrow was the first to draw the boar's blood, so when Meleager finally killed it he gave her its hide and head.

King Iasus then proudly claimed Atalanta as his daughter and wanted her to marry. However, Atalanta had been warned by the Oracle not to marry, so she came up with a clever plan. Knowing no one could outrun her, she offered to race the suitors, agreeing to marry the man who could beat her. *Melanion* loved Atalanta and called upon Aphrodite, Goddess of love, who gave him three golden apples. During the race, whenever Atalanta would get ahead of him, Melanion would toss one forward. Atalanta could not resist stooping to pick up each apple, giving Melanion the advantage he needed. He won the race and Atalanta's hand in marriage.

Odysseus (c. 1260–1190 BCE)

Mortal grandson of Hermes, "wily" *Odysseus* (*Ulysses* in Latin) ruled the island kingdom of Ithaca. He was one of the most prominent Greek leaders in the Trojan War, famed for his cleverness and cunning, and for his eloquence as a speaker. As one of the original suitors of lovely Helen, he proposed the pact whereby her husband would be chosen by lot, and all the others would pledge to defend his marriage rights. This pact led to the Trojan War when Helen left her husband, Menelaus, and ran off with Paris of Troy.

After ten years of war (1220–1210), Odysseus came up with the idea of the Trojan Horse by which the Greeks were finally able to take the city of Troy itself. But Odysseus is most remembered for the saga of his ten-year voyage to return home to his own kingdom of Ithaca, his faithful wife, Penelope, and his son, Telemachus. This tale was immortalized by Homer as *The Odyssey* (see below).

Cuchulain (72–101 CE)

Cuchulain (ku-HOO-len) was the greatest hero of Ireland. His father was the Sun-god Lugh, and his mother, Dechtire, was the sister of Conchohar I, King of Ulster, Ireland (r.71–92). Named Setanta at birth, he

he killed the fierce hound of Culain the smith, which had attacked him. He then promised to guard Culain's forge until he could find a new dog, thus earning him the nickname of *Cuchulain* ("Hound of Culain"), by which he was known for the rest of his life.

By 17, Cuchulain was the greatest warrior of Ulster, bringing back the heads of three enemies on his first day of battle. A handsome and powerful youth, he courted Emer, daughter of Forgall the Wily, who opposed the marriage. Hoping he would get killed, Forgall sent Cuchulain off to learn battle skills from Scatbach, a renowned female warrior. But he was an apt pupil, and returned safely to marry Emer and become one of the 12 Champions of the Red Branch, the warriors of Conchobar.

Once, a giant named Terror challenged any hero to chop off his head, provided he grant Terror the same blow the next day. Only Cuchulian accepted, cutting off the giant's head in a single blow. But Terror picked up his head and axe and left the hall, to return the following morning. Cuchulian honorably laid his head on the cutting block. The blow of the giant's axe fell harmlessly beside his ear, whereupon Terror revealed himself as the wise Druid Curoi of Kerry, and proclaimed Cuchulain the bravest Champion of the Heroes of all Ireland, and Emer first among all the women of Ulster.

Cuchulian defended Ulster single-handedly against the armies of Queen Maeve in the famous "Cattle Raid of Cooley." Attacked by a dragon, he thrust his arm down its throat, and tore out its heart. At 29, Cuchulain finally met his end after a battle in which he displayed his usual gallantry but was overcome by treachery. Emer flung herself into his grave and died of grief.

King Arthur (466-537 CE)

In 410 CE, the Romans withdrew from Britain. Vortigern claimed the throne, inviting in Saxon mercenaries. The Saxons turned to marauding, and Uther Pendragon, fighting against them, rose to kingship. Disguised by the Wizard *Merlin* as Gorlois, Duke of Cornwall, Uther seduced his wife, Igraine, begetting *Arthur*. Arthur grew up at the castle of Sir Ector and was tutored by Merlin. After the death of Uther in 481, 15-year-old Arthur pulled a legendary sword from a stone and was proclaimed High King (*Artorius Roithamus* in Latin). After routing the Saxons, he conquered the Picts, Scots and Irish.

As peace flourished, Arthur married *Guinevere*, receiving a great round table as a wedding gift from her father. Arthur initiated the first order of Chivalry, holding his magnificent court at Camelot. Men from all nations answered the call to join the Knights of the Round Table, who were sent off on the legendary Quest of the Holy Grail. Merlin served as court Wizard and advisor, and Britain rose to new levels of culture and wealth.

Eventually, however, tribute demands from Rome drove Arthur into battle in Gaul, entrusting his kingdom to the Queen and his bastard son, Modred. During Arthur's absence, Mordred revolted, forcing Arthur's return to engage him. Arthur was mortally wounded and carried off to the mystical Isle of *Avalon* (Glastonbury), where he died and was buried. On his tombstone (excavated in 1190), the inscription read: "Here lies interred in the Isle of Avalon the renowned King Arthur." Legend says that he will return in England's hour of need: "The Once and Future King."

Robin Hood (1160-1247)

Born in the village of Locksley in Yorkshire, England, *Robin Hood* was an outlaw who lived and poached in the royal forest of Sherwood, in Nottinghamshire. Some say he was Robin Fitzooth, son of the Earl of Huntingdon, who returned from the 3rd Crusade to find his land stolen by the Sheriff. He championed the needy and oppressed and robbed and fought those who represented the corrupt power and wealth of government and Church—especially the Sheriff of Nottingham and cruel Prince John, his sworn enemy. Robin's outlaw band of "Merry Men" included Little John, Will Scarlet, Alan-a-Dale and Friar Tuck. His true love was Maid Marian. Some of the best-known stories and ballads tell of how Robin met each of these, and recruited them into his company.

At that time, King Richard the Lionhearted was away fighting in the 3rd Crusade, leaving his wicked brother, John, in charge of the kingdom. John outlawed and confiscated the lands of all who stood against him. Richard died in 1199, and John became king of England, which only increased his tyranny. The rebellion begun by Robin of Locksley spread through the noble houses, eventually forcing John to sign the *Magna Carta* ("Great Charter") in 1215, granting certain rights to other nobles and ending the absolute rule of the king by "Divine Right."

Lesson 5: Legendary Journeys and Adventures

The Epic of Gilgamesh (c. 2700 BCE)

King Gilgamesh proposed to his friend Enkidu a journey to the great Cedar Forest in southern Iran to cut down all the trees. In an epic battle, they killed the monstrous Guardian, *Humbaba* the Terrible, who cursed Enkidu with his dying breath. Gilgamesh and Enkidu cut down the cedars and made a great gate for the city of Uruk.

Gilgamesh's fame attracted the attention of the goddess Ishtar, who offered to become his lover. Gilgamesh refused, listing all the mortal lovers that Ishtar had and their dire fates. Insulted, Ishtar returned to heaven and begged her father, Anu the sky-god, to let her have the Bull of Heaven to wreak vengeance on Gilgamesh and his city. But together, Gilgamesh and Enkidu slew the mighty bull.

Then Enkidu fell ill after having ominous dreams; he learned from the priests that he had been singled out for vengeance by the gods. After suffering terribly for twelve days, he finally died.

Gilgamesh was grief-stricken by the death of his friend, realizing that he too must die. Deciding that he couldn't live unless granted eternal life, he undertook the journey to *Utnapishtim* and his wife, the only mortals to whom the gods had granted immortality. Utnapishtim had been a great king before the Flood and the two of them were the only humans to survive it.

After a long and perilous trip over land and water, Gilgamesh arrived at a distant shore and found Utnapishtim, who recounted the story of the Great Flood and told him of a secret "herb of life" growing at the bottom of the Underworld sea. Gilgamesh tied stones to his feet, sank to the bottom, and plucked the plant. On his way back to Uruk, he stopped to bathe. A snake slithered up, grabbed the magic plant and crawled away into a hole. Thus can snakes shed their skins and renew themselves, but humans must grow old and die.

The Labors of Heracles (c. 1281–1269 BCE)

Here are the 12 heroic tasks that Heracles performed for his cousin Eurystheus to atone for accidentally killing his own children in a fit of Hera-induced madness:

1. The Nemean Lion: The valley of Nemea was plagued by a ferocious lion. Eurystheus ordered Heracles to bring him its skin. After his club and arrows proved useless, Heracles strangled the beast with his bare hands and carried its body back on his shoulders.

2. The Lernean Hydra: The monstrous Hydra (a giant squid?) had nine heads, of which the middle one was immortal. Each time Heracles struck off one head, two new ones grew in its place. Ingeniously, his nephew and companion, Iolaus, burned the severed stumps with a torch, and they buried the immortal head under a rock.

3. The Arcadian Stag: With golden antlers and bronze hooves, this stag was sacred to Artemis, goddess of the Moon and hunt. Heracles pursued it for a full year before finally wounding it with his arrow, enabling him to bring it back to Eurystheus alive.

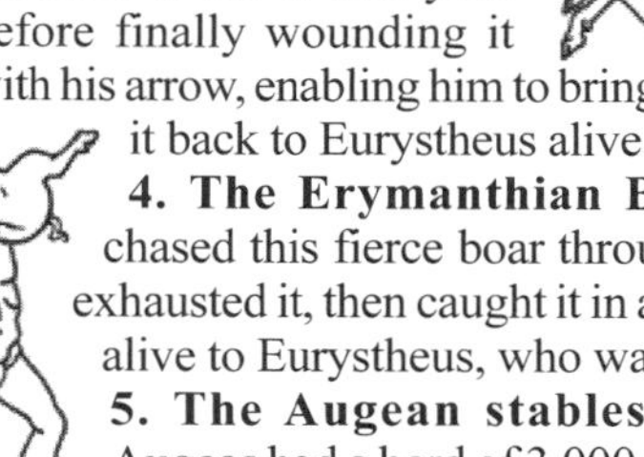

4. The Erymanthian Boar: Heracles chased this fierce boar through deep snows, exhausted it, then caught it in a net to take back alive to Eurystheus, who was terrified of it.

5. The Augean stables: King Augeas had a herd of 3,000 oxen. He stabled them in a large cave, which had not been mucked out for 30 years. Heracles diverted two rivers through the caverns and cleansed them thoroughly in one day.

6. The Stymphalian Birds: Reared by Ares, god of war, these were man-eating monsters with brass beaks, wings and claws, and feathers they could shoot as arrows. Heracles frightened them from their nests with a brass rattle and shot them as they flew off.

7. The Cretan Bull: King Minos had asked Poseidon to send him a bull for sacrifice. But the snow-white bull that rose from the waves was so beautiful that Minos decided to keep it for himself. Poseidon punished him by causing his queen to fall in love and mate with the beast, bearing the monstrous *Minotaur*. Heracles bested the bull and took it back to Mycenae, where he set it free.

8. The Wild Mares of Diomedes: King Diomedes of Thrace had a stable of fierce mares he fed on human flesh. Heracles captured them, killed Diomedes, and fed him to his own horses, after which they became docile. Eurystheus set them free.

9. Hippolyta's Girdle: Eurystheus's daughter wanted the belt of the queen of the Amazons, a nation of warrior women. Queen Hippolyta agreed to give it to him. But Hera persuaded the other Amazons that the stranger was

abducting their queen. The Amazons instantly attacked. Thinking Hippolyta had betrayed him, Heracles killed her and took her girdle back to Eurystheus.

10. **The Oxen of Geryon:** Eurystheus ordered Heracles to bring him the oxen of Geryon, a three-bodied monster living in Spain. The oxen were guarded by the giant Eurytion and his two-headed dog, but Heracles killed them both and brought back the oxen.
11. **The Golden Apples of the Hesperides:** Heracles went to Africa, where Atlas, father of the Hesperides, was condemned to bear on his shoulders the weight of the heavens. Heracles took the sky upon his own shoulders and sent Atlas to get the apples. He returned with them, took up his burden again, and Heracles carried the apples back to Eurystheus. On the way, he freed Prometheus.
12. **Cerberus:** Heracles descended into the Underworld and obtained permission from Hades to carry off *Cerberus,* the three-headed guard dog, provided he could do it unarmed. He seized the struggling beast, carried him off to Eurystheus, and afterwards brought him back to Hades.

The Argosy (c. 1264 BCE)

Because of a prophecy that Jason would someday do him harm, King Pelias of Iolcus sent him away on a seemingly impossible quest to bring back the legendary *Golden Fleece* from distant Colchis, at the eastern end of the Black Sea. Jason assembled a crew of the greatest heroes from all over Greece, and the shipwright Argus built for them the largest ship ever constructed, the Argo. Thus the voyagers were called the *Argonauts* ("sailors on the Argo"). These included *Heracles, Theseus, Atalanta, Castor,* and *Pollux,* and many others.

On the voyage to Colchis, the Argonauts had

many adventures. The *Sirens* (lovely bird-women whose singing was irresistibly seductive) lured some of the crew to leap into the sea. Jason freed the blind seer Phineus from the curse of the *Harpies*—disgusting bird-women who tormented him and befouled his meals. In gratitude for driving the creatures off, Phineus told Jason how to pass safely through the *Symplegades* ("clashing rocks"), which smashed anything caught between them. They released a dove, which flew between the rocks faster than they could clash, and when they opened again, the Argonauts rowed swiftly through.

When they arrived at Colchis, King Aeetes agreed to let Jason have the Fleece, provided he could accomplish a series of impossible tasks. First, he must yoke a team of savage, fire-breathing bulls to plow a field. Then he must sow dragon's teeth in the field and defeat the armed warriors who sprouted from these "seeds." Finally, he must overcome the never-sleeping dragon who guarded the Golden Fleece itself. Jason accomplished all these tasks with the magic aid of the sorceress princess Medea, who had fallen in love with him.

Having won the Fleece, Jason sailed back to Iolchus with Medea. On their return voyage, the Argonauts overcame Talos, the giant bronze guardian of Crete, by removing a plug at his ankle, letting his animating fluids drain out.

The Odyssey (1210–1200 BCE)

After the plunder and burning of Troy, Odysseus set sail for his far-off home on the island of Ithaca. But unfortunately he offended Poseidon, god of the sea. His homeward journey was to last 10 years, and it has been mapped around the eastern Mediterranean according to the descriptions of various places. The ship was first blown off course to North Africa, land of the Lotus-Eaters, whose opium-drugged food caused all who ate it to forget home and family. Odysseus had to drag his men back to the ship.

In Crete, they sought sanctuary in the cave of the one-eyed Cyclops, *Polyphemus,* son of Poseidon, to whom Odysseus gave his name as *Nemo* ("no-one"). But Polyphemus rolled a huge boulder across the cave entrance, trapping the crew and eating two of them. Odysseus got him drunk, and when the Cyclops passed out, Odysseus blinded him with a spear. When his Cyclopean neighbors came in response to his screams, Polyphemus cried out: "No one has wounded me!" so they went away. Odysseus and his remaining men clung to the bellies of Polyphemus' sheep, escaping when he rolled the boulder aside to let them out in the morning.

(Heraclion, Crete (AP-1/29/2003)—Researchers on the southern Greek island of Crete have unearthed the fossilized tusk, teeth and bones of a Deinotherium Gigantisimum, *a fearsome elephant-like creature that might have given rise to ancient legends*

of one-eyed cyclops monsters. Their skulls have one large central opening for the trunk, and look exactly like giant one-eyed human skulls.)

On the island of Corfu, the enchantress Circe changed his crewmen into pigs. But Odysseus, who was protected by the holy *moley* herb (mandrake) given him by Hermes, seduced her, and she helped him by directing him to the Oracle of the Dead. There the ghosts of his mother, the blind seer Tiresias, and other departed shades advised him on the remainder of his journey.

With this knowledge, Odysseus steered his crew safely past the Sirens by stopping the sailors' ears with wax and having himself tied to the mast. Although losing six men, they also survived the twin perils of *Scylla* (a monster with six heads on long necks; apparently a giant squid) and *Charybdis,* a whirlpool in the straits of Messina (between Italy and Sicily).

Becalmed on the island of the sun-god, Apollo, the crew disregarded all warnings and ate his cattle, so Zeus sent a thunderbolt that smashed the ship. Only Odysseus survived, as he had not participated in the slaughter and feasting. He was cast ashore on the island of Ogygia, home of the nymph *Calypso,* who made him her lover and refused to let him leave. Finally, after seven years, Odysseus sailed away on a raft, only to be shipwrecked by another storm. He swam ashore on the island of Phaeacia, where he was feasted and entertained. After telling his story, he was, at long last, escorted home to Ithaca.

During Odysseus' 20-year absence, his wife, Penelope, had remained faithful, but she was under great pressure to remarry. A host of obnoxious suitors had moved into her palace. Odysseus arrived disguised as a ragged beggar, and observed their insolent behavior and his wife's fidelity. With the help of his son, Telemachus, he slaughtered the suitors and regained his kingdom.

Lesson 6. Future Lore

by Ian Lurking Bear Anderson

Creating Lore

One of the most important aspects of lore mastery is mastering the power to create lore for the future. Through writing, poetry, story telling, song and other arts we can all add something to the lore of the future. Take the time to record your visions, develop your own invocations of the divine, draw pictures, and tell stories about your spiritual journey or your quest for magic. Even the humblest notebook can become the source of great, enduring lore. You are limited only by your own power to drink in the creative energy that flows through the universe all around you.

Computer Magic

This is a recent field in magical practice that has flowered tremendously. Computers are useful for creating illusion on the screen and conveying information. It is important to remember that everything that appears on the screen is an illusion, even if sometimes a useful one. These illusions can be used to broadcast dreams and ideas, to keep culture alive and growing. Just remember that visions of other worlds on the computer screen are no substitute for your own inner journeys, and scenery on the screen is no substitute for real Nature contact.

Computers are the enemy of secrecy, and anything that appears on a computer network can be considered possibly known by unwanted persons. Never put oathbound or secret material into email or on the web, even in encrypted form. This lack of secrecy has its positive side too. Any information broadcast over the Internet is very hard to destroy as it spreads from place to place. Knowledge, recipes, songs, paintings, political rants, alternative news, and crackpot theories can be transmitted by computers until there are many duplicates, and that information cannot be repressed by the authorities.

Thanks to the World Wide Web, we all have access to something like the old library at Alexandria that was destroyed by religious fanatics long ago. A staggering amount of art and literature is available as well as the inevitable torrent of half-baked dreck. It'll be up to you to figure out which is which. This new library is more changeable and chaotic than the old one, but it contains a vast wealth of material. If you find valuable material on the Web, you may want to keep your own copy. Web pages are discontinued, storage formats go out of date, empires and civilizations all crumble someday, and the web itself will not last forever. Those of you who enjoy using the web may wish to compile a grimoire of printouts of material you find especially worthwhile. Pick the good stuff and don't waste trees printing second-rate pages!

This great library is kept up by many librarians, and what keeps it going is that people put good stuff into it. When you are ready to, contribute to this library. Put your own creative work into a website, or create a website about one of your favorite topics, and do your part to enrich the library. This is your chance to join in the traditions of those who have written down and passed on lore and culture even when it involved long hours of writing by hand. Now that it is so much easier to transmit information, we would be foolish to pass up the opportunity. And check out *www.GreySchool.com*

VI. The Dark Arts (Black)

1. Introduction: "Black Magick"

HE SIMPLEST FORM OF LOW MAGICK is *sorcery,* in which a certain physical act is performed to achieve a particular result. For example, a wax image is melted over a fire to make a victim die; blood is scattered over a field to ensure a bountiful harvest in the next growing season; knots are tied in a cord to store wind for a sea voyage. Sorcery forms the bulk of folk magick, and is often popularly referred to as "Black Magick" or "the Black Arts."

One of the reasons for this color association is that much of such magick originated in Egypt, called *Khem,* meaning "black." This is because the fertile flood-deposited soil of the Nile Delta was black, in contrast to the barren sands of the surrounding deserts, which were red. In Egypt, therefore, black was good, and red represented evil. Also, black is the skin color of many peoples who live in equatorial latitudes, such as Africa, India, Australia, the Caribbean, etc. Many Egyptians were dark-skinned, reinforcing that color association with their land. So the magick of the "Black Country" became referred to as "Black Magick."

It is the *intention* of the magician which determines the purpose and alignment, not the color of the magick. Black Magick itself is not necessarily evil, any more than any other color. Fundamentally, this color of the magickal spectrum is about *power* and *control*—power to *do* things, power to control the world, and power to dominate others. And just as weapons may be used either in aggression or defense, Black Magick is also the color of *protection.*

All that notwithstanding, however, when people today talk about "Black Magick" and the "Dark Arts," they are generally referring to magick used for selfish purposes rather than *altruistic* (helpful to others) ones. In particular, dominating and manipulating people against their will; compelling people to do things they do not wish to do; working against the best interests of others; intentionally inflicting harm on others; threatening, oppressing, controlling, power-tripping, ripping off and screwing over—all these are considered practices of the Dark Arts. And those who practice magick with such purposes are known as "Black Magicians" and "Sorcerers." True Wizards, by definition, simply do not use magick in this way.

Lesson 2. Sorcery & Sorcerers

Sorcery is also sometimes called *sympathetic magic,* based on the principle that all things are linked together by invisible bonds (the "Law of Sympathy"). Sympathetic magick includes two types, which are often combined in actual use: *Homeopathic* and *Contagious.* Homeopathic magick holds that like produces like: a melted wax image, for example, causes death. Contagious magick holds that things once in contact can continue to exert influence on each other, even at a distance: blood, hair or clothing from a person may be used in spells to affect them.

While all magickal folk practice some forms of sorcery, few actually identify themselves as "Sorcerers." Those who do are generally engaged in attempting to control others and rule the world. The primary distinction between a Sorcerer and a Wizard thus lies in the realm of service *vs.* dominion: A Wizard desires to be of service to others; a Sorcerer desires to be served *by* others. Here's a simple test: is the person trying to do something for *you,* or are they trying to get you to do something for *them*—particularly something you really don't want to do? If it's the latter, stay away from them!

Often, powerful Wizards and Sorcerers will find

themselves standing in opposition as each other's *nemesis* (ultimate enemy). In the stories, Merlin, Gandalf, Obi-Wan Kenobi, and Albus Dumbledore are *Wizards*. Morgan laFey, Saruman, Darth Vader, and Lord Voldemort are *Sorcerers*.

> *Sorcerers are the performers of black magic and dark spells, who can call up the spirits of the dead and the Underworld. Above all, sorcerers seek unlimited knowledge, with a lust for power, control and mastery of the universe. They wish to use their powers to make them, in essence, gods. For some, the knowledge gained through the intense study of occult books and secret tracts is sufficient. For others, the cabalistic learning is used to summon up demons and spirits to do their bidding. Often a pact is signed with the Devil in exchange for earthly omnipotence and omniscience. Sorcerers do not worship Satan nor work on his behalf; instead, they seek to dominate and to control the powers of evil in an attempt to become divine themselves.*
> —Tom Ogden,
> *Wizards and Sorcerers,* p. ix

Lesson 3: Satanism

Whenever there are two clear sides in a conflict, some people will choose one, and some the other. Medieval Christianity conceived a notion (originally called the *Manichaen heresy*) that *Jehovah* ("God") and *Satan* ("The Devil") were equally powerful deities of Good and Evil, engaged in an eternal struggle for dominion over humanity and the universe. The Devil ruled this world, and God ruled the hereafter. The existence of the Devil as an actual entity was officially declared by the Church's Council of Toledo in the year 447 CE.

The Medieval Christian Church, calling itself *Catholic* ("universal"), rose to full political power after the sack of Rome in 455, the Pope replacing the Emperor. For the next thousand years—until the Renaissance and Reformation—"The Holy Roman Empire" was the sole "superpower" in the Western world. Declaring relentless war on all "heretics" and "unbelievers," including Jews, Witches, Pagans, and Moslems, the Church made a lot of enemies. Because the Church of the Crusades and Inquisition claimed to be on the side of God, some of those it persecuted inevitably decided to throw their lot in with God's proclaimed opponent, Satan. Hence was born a counter-cult of Satanic devil-worship, coming into being as the *antithesis* ("opposite") of a corrupt Christianity and all it stood for.

Unfortunately, what that meant for many was rejecting the excellent moral and ethical teachings of Jesus as well, which, in any case, were inaccessible to most people, as the Church maintained a tight monopoly on literacy; and the Bible (written only in Latin) was confined within the Church monasteries to be read only by *celibate* (that is, having nothing to do with women) priests.

So Satanists reveled in all that the Church declared to be wicked, sinful, and accursed. Defrocked Catholic priests performed inverted "black masses" and "black magick." All manners of evil were glorified, including the desecration of sacraments, sexual abuse, and even infant sacrifice. Satanism became the blasphemous parody of Christianity, mocking its most sacred rites and tenets. In the 18th century, Satanic "clubs" were formed, achieving a certain public notoriety and attracting jaded young noblemen who enjoyed throwing wild parties and riding around at night scaring people. (This is called "Freaking the Mundanes....")

In the late 20th century, several Satanic Churches were legally incorporated, adopting the image of Satan as the archetypal "rebel-against-authority." Most of these, however, dogmatically *dis*believe in his actual existence and automatically expel members caught breaking the law.

At the same time, an entire genre of Satanic movies and Fundamentalist Christian literature came into being, resurrecting the old Medieval mythology of Satan vs. God, war between Heaven and Hell, pacts with the Devil, demonic possession and exorcism, the "Anti-Christ," Apocalypse, and Armageddon. A new generation of sick, twisted psychopaths—called "self-styled Satanists"—began using this mythos as a justification and model for demented criminal behavior.

I have included this information out of a sense of responsibility to put out a "warning label" for you. Satanism is the darkest of the "dark arts," and has nothing whatsoever to do with Wizardry or Witchcraft. Satanic "ethics" are entirely self-serving and manipulative, and most Satanists will routinely lie about their intentions, actions, and objectives to gain control over others, whom they consider as cattle. Do NOT trust such people! If you should encounter any of them, avoid them like the plague!

Lesson 4: Demonology

Demonology is a form of sorcery popular in the Middle Ages and Renaissance, in which the aid of Demons is enlisted by the magician. Believed by such magicians to be powerful intelligences, Demons have been catalogued and ranked into complex hierarchies since at least 100 CE. Although thought to be easier to control than Angels, Demons can be dangerous and malicious, and the old Grimoires contained detailed instructions for conjuring and controlling them.

> *Even wizards thought demonologists were odd; they tended to be surreptitious, pale men who got up to complicated things in darkened rooms and had damp, weak handshakes. It wasn't like good clean magic. No self-respecting wizard would have any truck with the demonic regions, whose inhabitants were as big a collection of ding-dongs as you'd find outside a large belfry.*
>
> *Any wizard bright enough to survive for five minutes was also bright enough to realize that if there was any power in demonology, then it lay with the demons. Using it for your own purposes would be like trying to beat mice to death with a rattlesnake.* —Terry Pratchett, *Eric*, p. 30-31

Demons & Djinn

> *Demons have existed...for at least as long as the gods, who in many ways they closely resemble. The difference is basically the same as that between terrorists and freedom fighters.*
> —Terry Pratchett, *Eric*, pp. 34-35

Demons are usually considered to be evil by nature. However, the word actually means "replete with wisdom." It comes from the Greek *daimon* ("divine power"). Good ones are called *eudemons,* and evil ones are *cacodemons.* In Greek myth, *Daimonia* were intermediary spirits between humanity and the gods. While *cacodemons* could lead people into trouble, *eudemons* were like guardian angels, whispering good advice and ideas into one's ear. This image was recreated in the old Disney cartoons when Donald Duck would have a little devil on one shoulder and a little angel on the other, each trying to persuade him to take contradictory actions. Now people talk about "hearing the voice of conscience," or say "the Devil made me do it!"

In Arabic mythology, malicious and powerful demons are called *djinn* (JIN), from which we get the word *genie.* Though normally invisible, a *djinnee* could take any shape. According to the *Koran,* King Solomon tamed and controlled the djinn with a magic ring of power, set with a living gem. They served him, building his palaces, gardens and fountains. Djinn are born of fire and are mortal. There are five classes, each with different powers—all ruled by *Iblis,* the Prince of Darkness.

In Christian mythology, demons are believed to be fallen angels who were cast down into Hell after the great War in Heaven, in which the rebellious Lucifer was defeated by Jahveh (compare this story

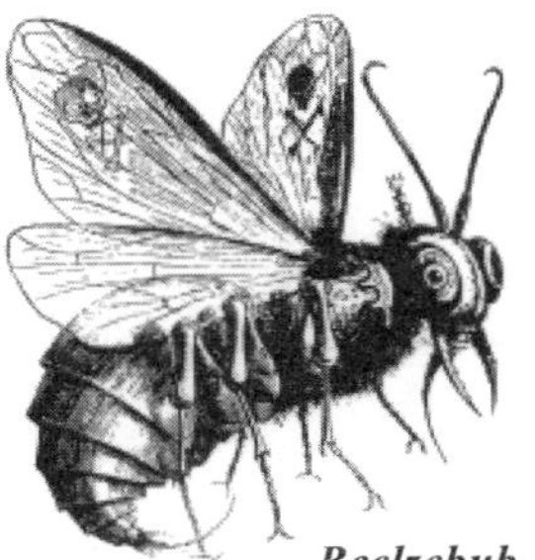

Beelzebub,
Lord of the Flies

Behemoth,
demon of animal strength

Asmodeus,
demon of lust and anger

Abraxas, *whose name is associated with* abracadabra

with the Clash of the Titans in the next Class). Their purpose is to tempt humans into sin and damnation, and to torture the damned eternally in Hell. Medieval Christian artists loved to show such terrifying images, depicting the demons as grotesquely hideous creatures. Those above were illustrated by L. Breton in Collin de Plancy's *Dictionaire Infernal* (1863). As the new religion spread, the gods and spirits of many peoples became assimilated as demons into Christian myth.

The Qliphoth

As described in the *Lemegeton vel Clavicula Salomonis Regis* ("Lesser Key of Solomon the King"), the Jewish Qabalistic Tree of Life has a mirror-image negative counterpoint called the *Qliphotic Tree of Death.* Just as the Tree of Life depicts progressive evolution towards reunion with God, the Tree of Death represents progressive degeneration and disintegration. Ten demonic *Qliphoth* ("shells") counter the ten angelic Sephiroth of the Tree of Life. Ten Orders of Demons are each ruled by an Arch-Demon. On the next page is a short Table of Correspondences for the Qliphoth.

Christian demonologists of the 16th and 17th centuries catalogued demons into hierarchies of Hell, assigning them each their individual seal, properties, associations and duties. The *Goetia* ("howling") lists the names, Orders and titles of 72 demon kings and princes, said to command *legions* totaling 7,405,926. Demonologists would evoke a particular demon

Qliphah	Meaning	Order of Demons	Arch-Demon	Planet	Tarot Trump
1. Shahul	Grave Hell	Thaumiel (Twins of God)	Satan & Moloch	Galaxy	The Fool
2. Shahul	of Supernals,	Chaigidel (The Hinderers)	Beelzebub	Stars	The Magician
3. Shahul	Triple Hell	Sateriel (The Concealers)	Lucifuge Rofacale	Saturn	The World
4. Abaddon	Perdition	Gamchicoth (The Smiters)	Astaroth	Jupiter	Wheel of Fortune
5. Tythihoz	Clay of Death	Golab (The Arsonists)	Asmodeus	Mars	The Tower
6. Baraschechath	Pit of Destruction	Tagaririm (The Hagglers)	Belphegor	Sun	The Sun
7. Tzakemoth	Shadow of Death	Harab Serapel (Ravens of Death)	Bael	Venus	Judgement
8. Sha'arimrath	Gates of Hell	Samael (Poison of God)	Adramelech	Mercury	Hanged Man
9. Giyehanim	Hell	Gamaliel (The Obscene Ones)	Lilith	Moon	High Priestess
10. Giyehanim		The Five Accursed Nations	Nahema	Earth	The Empress

for a particular purpose. For instance, Valefor teaches how to steal; Amdukias makes trees bend and fall; and Bael makes men invisible and gives wisdom. Barbatos teaches all sciences; reveals past, future, and treasures hidden by magic; and reconciles estranged friends.

Lesson 5: Necromancy: the Dead and the Undead

Another form of "Black Magick" is *necromancy,* in which the spirits of the dead are conjured up for consultation. This is what happens in a *séance,* where a *medium* goes into a trance, summoning and allowing spirits to temporarily inhabit her body and speak through her mouth. This is most often done at the request of a living relative who may wish to question the departed soul regarding some important matter, or even just seek reassurance that they are happy in the Afterlife.

The term *necromancy* commonly refers to the use of the dead for the magician's own purposes, without necessarily obtaining permission from the deceased. Such magickal workings are considered highly unethical, and therefore "Dark Arts."

Interestingly, the Greek word *nekros* ("corpse") has in the past been confused by the ignorant with the Latin *nigr* ("black"), and in Middle English (1200–1500), the word *nigromancer* was used to mean someone skilled in the Black Arts. Sometimes you will still encounter the word *necromancer* mistakenly used with this meaning.

Ghosts

Ghosts are considered distinct from other spirits by reason of having once been living beings who have died, yet still exist as *discarnate* ("having lost a body") entities in the Astral Realm. They can be seen by cats, dogs, and people who are especially psychically sensitive or trained; seeing ghosts is pretty much like seeing auras. More commonly than being seen, ghosts may be heard or "felt"—as a chilling invisible "presence" that makes the hair on the back of your neck stand up and goose bumps run down your arms.

There are several categories of "ghosts." Some are the souls of people who have died suddenly, as in an accident or murder, and are stuck between this world and the "Other Side." Some, called *phantoms* or *apparitions,* may be someone who has just died, and is paying a final farewell on their way to the Afterlife. Some departed spirits—such as ancestors, parents, or other family members—may take on roles of spirit guides, protectors, and "Guardian Angels" to those they were close to in life. Animal spirits may also appear as ghosts. And ghosts may appear in dreams as well as in waking.

Some "ghosts" are not even conscious spirits at all, but are more like a psychic impression or "recording" of some traumatic event, such as a violent death, that just keeps playing over and over at the place where it happened. These are called *haunts,* and hauntings may even involve completely imaginary beings, such as powerful characters created by a novelist. Throughout the 1930s and 40s, journalist and magician Walter B. Gibson, using the pen name Maxwell Grant, wrote 282 novels featuring a mysterious cloaked avenger known as *The Shadow.* After Gibson died in 1986, a shadowy cloaked apparition was frequently encountered by visitors to his studio, and even photographed!

And then there are *poltergeists* ("noisy ghosts") which make weird sounds and bumps in the night, throw things around, create messes, or even cause physical injuries. These are not actually "ghosts" in the sense of being the spirits of the once-living; true spirit ghosts cannot affect the physical world at all. "Poltergeist" is a *psychokinetic* manifestation usually caused by a living person who has experienced or is going through severe trauma—especially involving sexuality.

Vampires

Vampires are soulless "undead" with no life of their own, who sustain themselves by sucking life-essence from the truly living. There are essentially two types: those who suck your blood, and those who suck your soul. Victims of vampires gradually lose energy, decline, and wither. Although vampires are basically loners, sometimes in big cities they may frequent certain hangouts, like vampire bars

Vampires are creatures of the night who recoil from the light of the Sun, which burns their skin. Having no souls, they cannot see their reflection in a mirror. They can't come into your home (or your life) unless you invite them in. They are repelled by holy symbols and (except for the Italian ones) raw garlic. And they die if you drive a wooden stake through their heart (well, who wouldn't?). But they cannot turn into bats, except in fiction. And contrary to popular myth, real vampires are not super-strong, but tend to be frail and weak.

Blood-sucking Vampires are popular figures in literature, movies, and TV shows, and have been the subject of folklore for millennia. In former times, people who had fallen into a cataleptic paralysis or coma were often declared dead and entombed. Sometimes they would awaken in their coffins with severe mental impairment and struggle forth from their crypts to take up a nocturnal "undead" existence, preying on the living, and returning at dawn to sleep in their sarcophagi.

In 1985, Dr. David Dolphin, a biochemist at the University of British Columbia, proposed that vampires were afflicted with a genetic disease called *porphyria:*

> *This malfunction in the body's chemistry makes the skin sensitive to light, which explains why sufferers tend to avoid the sun....*
>
> *The disease can also cause retraction of the gums, making them so taut that the teeth, although no larger than ordinary, jut out in a menacing manner akin to something more animal than human.... And the disease may explain why vampires, or porphyria victims, might well have been afraid of garlic, in accord with mythology. Garlic, Dolphin says, contains a chemical that exacerbates the symptoms of porphyria.*
>
> *Dolphin also notes that one treatment for the disease is an injection of a blood product,* heme. *Since that treatment did not exist in the Middle Ages, when the myths originated, he speculates that victims might have instinctively sought heme by drinking blood.* —Roger Highfield,
> *The Science of Harry Potter,* pp. 188–89

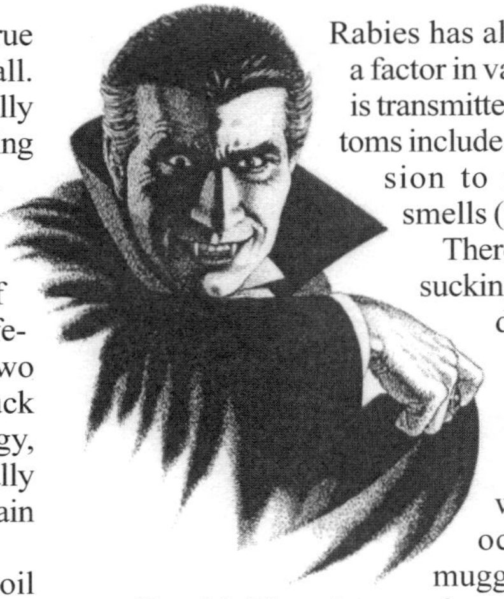

Rabies has also been suggested as a factor in vampirism. The disease is transmitted by biting, and symptoms include insomnia and an aversion to mirrors and strong smells (like garlic).

There are few actual blood-sucking vampires around today, and they present little threat to magickal people. They mostly get their blood from blood banks or willing volunteers, and occasionally prey on muggers and derelicts.

Psychic Vampires are far more common, and less easily recognizable—often not until too late. These soulless creatures are always needy, and fasten onto you like a leech, sucking your soul and draining your vitality with their never-ending demands. They appear as hopeless neurotics or junkies, with no real lives, and all they really care about is vainly trying to satisfy their own unquenchable needs.

During the course of your life you will undoubtedly encounter some of these creatures. Most appear to be fairly normal people, physically; however, their psychic nature will become apparent in the way they treat you and others around them. They will attempt to manipulate you to meet their needs—often in ways that are harmful to you either physically or emotionally. The psychic vampire is often known by other names: sexual predator, manipulative girl/boyfriend, co-dependent enabler. These are destructive people whom those who care about you have probably warned you to stay away from.

Zombies

Zombies are also called "the living dead." The word comes from the African Congo *nzambi* ("spirit of a dead person"). Pretty much confined to the Caribbean island of Haiti, these are people who have died and whose bodies have then been exhumed from the grave and "re-animated" to turn them into soulless slaves of evil *bokors* (Voodoo sorcerers).

Zombies are created by administering a powerful poisonous drug that induces total paralysis and a state of apparent death. After the victim is buried, the bokor digs him up and feeds him another concoction, which causes confusion and hallucinations. Giving the zombie a new name, the bokor puts him to work. Zombies need little food, but may recover if they eat salt.

The formula for the zombie death drug was determined by Harvard *ethnobotanist* (one who studies plants in a cultural context) Wade Davis in 1982. Of a long list of foul and poisonous ingredients, the essential element is the puffer fish, containing the deadly poison *tetrodoxin,* of which a tiny drop is fatal.

But there is much more to the zombie process than the potions. The bokor also captures the soul of the victim, keeping it in a bottle. Thus he commands not only the body of the "living dead," but also the "zombie astral"—a ghost or spirit the bokor can send forth to do his bidding, like a *fetch.*

Werewolves

"Even a man who is pure of heart,
And says his prayers by night,
May become a wolf when the wolfbane blooms,
And the Moon is full and bright..."
—*The Wolfman* (movie)

Werewolves are also "Children of the Night." A werewolf will seem to be an ordinary person during the day, but at night—especially (or only) during the full Moon, they will become, to all intents and purposes, a ferocious beast, attacking and even killing like a wild animal. In the morning, they generally have no memory of their depredations of the night before. Their main vulnerabilities are wolfbane (herb) and silver (metal of the Moon). Silver bullets will kill a werewolf as effectively as anyone else, and silver jewelry will protect you from attack by a werewolf.

Werewolfery is a recognized psychiatric disorder called *lycanthopy* ("wolf-man-ism"). A sufferer has a "split personality," like Dr. Jekyll and Mr. Hyde, in which one phase is an inhuman wild beast. Wolves are the most well-known, but *lycanthropes* may also be leopard-men, bear-men, cat-people, or other fierce predators. The shift is usually triggered by the appearance of the full Moon.

Compounding lycanthropy is a rare congenital disease called generalized *hypertrichosis,* in which a pelt of long hair grows all over the person's body and face, just as in animals. Some of these people have become famous working in circuses as "ape-men," "dog-faced boys," and "werewolves." In 1984, this condition was formally described in a Mexican family by José María Cantu of the University of Guadalajara, but its gene has not yet been isolated. All known cases are genetically related.

Hans Weiditz, from Die Emeis *(The Ants), 1517*

As with vampires, porphyria may also be a factor, as some victims become very hairy (probably to protect their skin against painful sunlight) and venture forth only at night. And rabies would explain transmission of the disease by biting. Imagine someone with all those conditions at once!

It is said that a person whose eyebrows grow together, whose middle two fingers are the same length, who has hairy palms or yellow eyes, may be a werewolf. Dogs and cats always recognize them and will not come near them—their hackles will rise, and they will hiss, growl and snarl at a werewolf even in human phase.

Lesson 6. Defense Against the Dark Arts

There are many forms of "Dark Arts" that may not be so obvious or conscious as the above, and yet can be incredibly destructive in your life. In High School, you will have to face and overcome the challenges of such negative forces as:

- Peer pressure
- Gang recruitment
- Procrastination
- TV/video game hypnotism and addiction
- Poisonous and addictive substances (tobacco, alcohol, various nasty drugs)

The magical work of grounding, centering, shielding, intention and becoming the best person you can be are your best defenses. As there are numerous circumstances in which you may encounter danger, there are several categories of magickal defense you should know. In escalating degrees, these are:

1. **Precautionary:** Avoid doing stupid and life-threatening things. Take reasonable precautions, like wearing seatbelts and bike helmets, and not walking alone through bad neighborhoods. Don't go anywhere alone at night. Don't ride in a car with a driver who is drinking or on drugs. Use common sense, and stay alert at all times!
2. **Protective:** Set up wards and shields around yourself and your space, like a series of shells, all with a mirrored outer surface. Carry protective amulets and wear protective jewelry. Walk with a sense of purpose and learn to project an aura of invincibility.
3. **Defensive:** Actively deflecting attacks, whether psychic or physical. Enroll in a good Martial Arts program, which will train you in defense of both

kinds. Learn to use your body and your mind as finely-honed weapons of defense.

4. **Retaliatory/offensive:** Fighting back. Taking your opponent out of action, so that not only can they not hurt *you* any more—they can't hurt anyone else either. If you are abused, molested, assaulted or attacked, by anyone, in any way (physical or mental), report them immediately to a responsible adult you trust. Don't put up for a second with abusive behavior!

As a Wizard, there are various things you can do to protect yourself and use in conjunction with the defenses you have learned from your mundane teachers. All magical defenses should be used to strengthen your mundane skills. Even highly-skilled magicians hike or swim with a friend, avoid dark alleyways and unlit parking lots, and refuse unhealthy, destructive or illegal temptations. Psychic shielding, amulets and charms, totem animals and spirit guides used with a healthy dose of common sense and routine safety procedures should keep you safe from harm. Eat lots of garlic, wear your silver pentacle prominently, keep a lodestone in your mojo bag, and get plenty of sunshine!

Accidents

Accidents will happen. You can reduce their chances of happening to *you* by not being stupid. Protect yourself. Plan ahead, think things through, and take reasonable precautions.

Stupidity

"Against stupidity, the gods themselves contend in vain." —Friedrich von Schiller (1759-1805)

No amount of education or intelligence can overcome sheer stupidity. This is what wisdom is for. If you are going to insist on doing truly stupid things, no one will be able to save you, and eventually you will probably manage to kill yourself. Many people do.

To get some idea of the astonishing stupidity of which people are capable, check out the "Darwin Awards" at: *http://www.darwinawards.com.* These *postumous* ("after death") honors celebrate Charles Darwin's theory of evolution by natural selection. Darwin Awards are bequeathed to idiots and jackasses who contribute to the improvement of our gene pool by removing themselves from it in truly stupid (and often grotesquely humorous) ways.

Stupidity consists largely of doing things without considering the consequences, like lighting a match to see how much gasoline is in the tank, or slugging a police officer. I shouldn't have to tell apprentice Wizards not to do life-threateningly stupid things, but I've certainly done my share in my life, and I've had to learn some lessons the hard way! So just to give you a heads-up, here are a few rather obvious idiocies which seem to be fairly popular, by which countless people kill or maim themselves each year:

- Smoking cigarettes.
- Not wearing seatbelts, helmets, safety goggles, etc.
- Swimming or hiking alone.
- Hanging out or walking alone in bad neighborhoods.
- Underage drinking of alcohol.
- Using addictive drugs (especially "speed").
- Driving drunk or stoned.
- Having unsafe sex.
- Being involved with violent or psycho friends.

Do I really have to explain *why* any of these things are a dumb idea? You know! Just don't do them, OK? I promise you from the bottom of my heart and a lifetime of experience—years from now, if you're still alive, you will deeply regret having done any of these. But at the end of a long life, you will never regret *not* having done any of them—for you will have doubled or quadrupled your life expectancy, and survived to become a happy old Wizard like me!

Or not. As always, the choice is up to you.

Psychic Attacks

Psychic attacks may be conscious and intentional, where someone is actively working to do you harm; or they may be unconscious, where someone simply hates you and projects constant malevolence towards you. If you feel you are under psychic attack, talk to someone you trust right away. Some of the symptoms can be:

- Feeling totally confused and unable to pull yourself together;
- Suddenly becoming incredibly clumsy;
- Having everything seeming to go wrong, no matter how hard you try;
- Constant misunderstandings whenever you try and communicate with others;
- A sense of desperation and panic;
- Or—the very worst, on top of all the rest, your Familiar becomes sick, or even dies.

When doing defensive spells against psychic attacks, set them to send any negative energy right back to where it came from. The best kinds of protection and defense magick are mirrored wards and shields. These involve throwing up a protective field around yourself and your space which will repel unwanted energies. The perfect metaphor is the energy fields/shields used to protect the Starship Enterprise from phaser fire and photon torpedoes.

"Harden" the outer shell of your auric field into a psychic shield. Stand strong, feet apart, and close your eyes. Do a grounding, as in 4.IV.4. Then move your hands, palms flattened and fingers spread wide, up, down, and all around your body at arms' length, while visualizing that you are shaping and pressing against the inside of a "Teflon-coated" shell all around yourself.

Now open your eyes and expand that shield around your entire room, strengthening it into an impenetrable shell, reflectively mirrored on the outside. Use visualization as well as an actual hand-held round mirror as you circle around your room, holding your hands up as if against an invisible wall. That's a Shield.

Tape small mirrors to the insides of your windows, reflecting side out. In addition, hang fresh garlic cloves around your room, and place cut halves of onions on the windowsills. When they no longer make your eyes water, slice off another section to keep the surface fresh. Finally, drive a few large iron nails into the ground in front of each doorway into your house, and, if you can get one, hang a horseshoe or hex sign over the door.

Warding, Blessing or Protection Ritual

(by Katlyn Breene)

Purpose: To protect, charge, or bless anything you hold dear, whether that be a person, place, or object.
Needed: A hand-held mirror, acrylic paint, and a candle. A dimly lit room.
Method:

1. Write down your exact intent before you begin.
2. Create Sacred Space; cast a Circle.
3. Call whatever Gods you wish to witness the work and lend their aid to the Ritual (your own words, straight from your heart, are probably the best way of doing so).
4. Paint the Pentagram (or magick symbol) upon the mirror's face.
5. Light the candle and hold the mirror before it so that the light reflects on the glass. Direct the light onto the person or object that you wish to be protected or blessed. See how the shadow of the Pentagram is emblazoned on it.
6. State that the person, place or thing is now blessed or protected. Not that you *wish* it to be protected, *but that it **is** protected.* In your mind, it should already be done. Again, your own words are probably best.
7. Thank the Gods for being there and helping with the working; then release the circle.

NOTE: This warding can also be done outdoors on a sunny day, reflecting the light of the Sun onto what- or whomever you wish to protect.

Laughter

Ultimately, the most powerful counter-defense against evil is laughter. Don't take it seriously; don't even take your*self* seriously! If you can find a way to make a laughingstock of your attacker, you can destroy his or her influence far more effectively than any amount of physical damage you could possibly inflict. Imagine sneaking up behind Lord Voldemort when he's being all scary, and pulling his pants down, or slapping a big "kick me" sign on his back! Telling jokes about some bully, or drawing cartoons featuring him, or making up a silly little jingle, can be devastating.

Political cartoonists have brought down powerful and corrupt officials and evil bastards. So have stand-up comics, parody songwriters, *Mad Magazine,* and *Saturday Night Live.* But be careful to not overdo it, as you can make dangerous enemies. You want to just pull their fangs enough to render them impotent, not enrage them to a blind and revengeful fury. When they back off, you must also.

A Word to the Wizardly Wise

(by Abby Willowroot)

We live in magickal times, but also dangerous ones. Be aware that predators lurk online and in the everyday world praying on the young and inexperienced. Some folks are very dangerous and may try to take advantage of you, or harm you. These dangerous folks often appear benign and are present in the everyday world, and sometimes they also haunt the magical community.

Do not blindly trust a person just because he appears powerful, or are in the magickal community, or claim to have powers and special insights. Never allow yourself to be coerced sexually, financially, or in any other way by someone promising to teach you, or give you powers. Wise Wizards are courageous, but they are also cautious, rational, and don't take foolish risks. Strangers are strangers and the same rules that apply to everyday encounters with strangers also apply when venturing into the magical community.

Never meet with strangers alone, or in a secluded place. Do not give your phone number or address to strangers. If someone asks you to keep a friendship secret, beware. If someone promises to initiate you for a large amount of money, beware. If someone tells you sex is necessary to become a part of their magick circle, beware. The first responsibility of a Wizard is to guard your personal safety. Stay alert, stay safe, and use common sense on your journey.

Course Seven: Lore

Course Seven: Lore

Class I: The Other Worlds

Modern humans go about their business in the mundane sphere as if the world were as it appears at first glance, having been assured that the notion of a realm beyond is merely a primitive, superstitious leftover from the foolish childhood of our race. Yet lurking beyond the façade of conventional reality, Faerie is still there, connected to all things, uncontrollable, and pervasive. What modern civilization has discarded like a forgotten child's toy is a mighty secret, a power that will blow the lid off the narrow "rational" worldview.
—Ian Lurking Bear ("Gateways to Faerie")

1. Introduction: Other Worlds

E LIVE IN A MULTIVERSE OF INFINITE worlds and possibilities. In addition to the Mundane world we inhabit with our physical bodies and share with each other, there are non-physical or *astral* realms of Dream, Myth, Imagination, and Story. Some of these are also shared with others, and some we may have all to ourselves. Nonetheless, these worlds are as real to us as we believe them to be. For when it comes right down to it, we each really live alone in a tiny room, and everything we see, hear, know, and experience of what's outside that room has to be piped in to us. What we "see" is what we get.

In this Class, I would like to introduce you to some of the non-physical worlds that are shared by many people. They each have their denizens and rules, and some of them have even been mapped. The world of Tolkein's Middle Earth is an example of such a realm, created by one man, but now shared by millions. I'll bet you can close your eyes and see the Shire or Rivendell as clearly as any other place you have lived or visited—I know I can!

Lesson 2. The Dreaming

The greatest astral country we can access directly is called *The Dreaming* because we enter it through our dreams. Australian *Aborigines* ("natives") call it the *Alcheringa,* or "The Dreamtime," and psychologists call it "The Collective Unconscious." We share this psychic realm with all other dreamers throughout the world, and it has a certain well-established geography shaped over the ages by the morphogenic fields—like well-worn pathways—of all who ever have visited there.

Within the Dreaming are gateways to the countries of Faerie, the Afterworlds of all faiths, the realms of gods, spirits, and ancestors, and all the fantasy-worlds of myth and story—such as Phantasia, Wonderland, Oz, Never-Never-Land, and Middle-Earth. As you learn to explore and become familiar with the landscape of The Dreaming, you will gain access to these other realms as well. Sometimes a portal to another realm is as simple as passing between two ancient trees.

Every species of sentient creatures on Earth and throughout the Universe dreams, and thus each species also has a Dreaming of their own. As we are cells in the great body of Gaea (Mother Earth), and planets are but cells in the greater body of the Galaxy, and so on—so are our dreams part of The Dreaming, and The Dreaming is part of the Dream of Gaea—and so on it goes, in ever-wider concentric realms.

Lesson 3. Faerie

> *Beyond conventional space and time, glowing through the physical world like a Chinese lantern, the raw, fundamental power of consciousness and desire in the universe pulses and dances, feral and exhilarating. To touch this power is to touch the secret truth of who we really are, of the nature of our being, outside life and death, beyond ego and attachment.* —Ian Lurking Bear

Faerie is the closest realm to ours, bordering on both The Dreaming and the mundane world. Faerie is also close to the realm of the dead, to the voices of the ancestors, and it is connected to the divine aspect of ourselves. Through Faerie we may contact sacred power more directly. We enter into a realm where gods and goddesses are quite real and may speak to us.

Gateways to Faerie are found not only in The Dreaming, but also in enchanted glens and forest clearings, mushroom rings, ancient stone circles, hollow mounds, raths, barrows, and overgrown ruins. In such places, all you need do to pass through is enter a trance or fall asleep—especially on Beltaine Eve or Samhain, when "the veil between the worlds" is particularly thin and the misty gates are open. Any time you are caught in a thick fog, you may find yourself in Faerie when it clears. Faerie is "as close as a prayer, as distant as the stars," says Faerie Shaman Victor Anderson (1915-2002).

Faerie is a twilight realm, lit only by the bright stars, candles, fireflies, and the auras of all living things (which are very visible there). Neither the Sun nor the Moon shines in Faerie, yet everything is illuminated. The inhabitants of Faerie (faeries, or the *fay*) dwell in fine halls and chambers beneath the ground, underwater, or high up in great trees. They also have exquisite crystal castles and aerie courts high in the mountains and deep in the forest glades. The only real city in Faerie is called *Tyr na Nog.*

However, in all of these places, a glamour of seeming magnificence is but an illusory veneer. For Faerie shares the same natural features and landscapes as our world, but without the artificial works of humankind. For instance, the Faerie Isle of *Avalon* corresponds to Glastonbury in the mundane world. In fact, Faerie can best be understood as a kind of "parallel dimension" to ours, connected by the aforementioned gateways, which appear the same from both sides.

Faerie is governed by rigid rules and formulae, and anyone entering this enchanted realm would be wise to learn them. The most important rule—which also applies to the Underworld—is *never eat or drink anything in Faerie* that you haven't brought with you! The fae are repelled by iron—especially if it is magnetized—so don't even think of entering Faerie carrying that metal! By the same token, keeping a lodestone in your mojo bag will protect you against unwilling abduction. And should you find yourself in Faerie and wish to leave, all you need do is take your shirt off, turn it inside out, and put it back on again—thus rendering yourself invisible to the Fae. Also turn your pockets inside out. But whatever else you do in Faerie—you must take care to be extremely courteous to the fae at all times! They are easily insulted, and their offense can be terrible!

Lesson 4. The Three Worlds

There is a saying that "Common sense is what tells us the world is flat." For most of human history, the vast majority of people believed this to be the case, and old maps depict the Earth not as a globe, but a disc. Medieval Christian maps showed Jerusalem, the "Holy City," at the center of the pancake, which encompassed the entire world known to the *cartographers* ("map-makers") of the time.

Above the world-disc, the vaulted arch of the Heavens formed an inverted bowl that could also be clearly seen and mapped, and so "the World Above" became the logical abode of the gods and angels. And the presence of caves, mines, wells, geysers, and volcanoes similarly indicated the existence of a hidden "World Below." It made equal sense to assign that dark realm deep beneath the Earth to the dead and

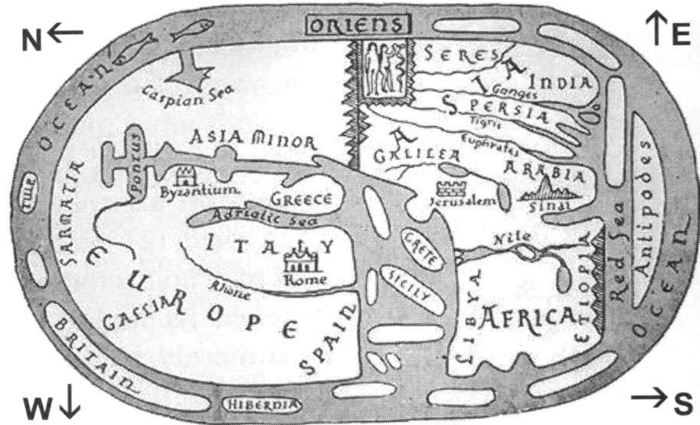

Medieval world map by Beatus of Liebana, 776 CE

populate it as well with monsters and demons—ruled over by gods of the "Underworld."

And so our mortal world, sandwiched between these supernatural realms like a hamburger in a bun, was naturally thought of as "Middle Earth," or *Midgard,* as the Vikings called it. Indeed, the Norse developed this concept into a rather elegant structure, portraying an ancient cosmology of multiple worlds that still informs the basis of many religions, including Christianity.

Yggdrasil

The Norse envisioned a complex system of nine worlds altogether, of which the main three are *Asgard* (above), *Hel* (below), and, of course, *Midgard* in the middle. These are arranged in various ways depending on which version you read. The current general favorite is to lay them out in a way similar to the Qabalistic Tree of Life, except that our world is in the middle

Midgard, held in the branches of the world-tree, Yggdrasil

instead of at the bottom. All these are held like *flets* (tree-platforms) in the roots and branches of the vast cosmic world-ash-tree, *Yggdrasil* (IG-dra-sil), which is aligned with the Earth's axis of rotation so that the tree's crown points to the North Star.

Asgard (home of the Aesir gods) is at the top, and *Ljosalfheim* (home of the bright elves) is usually placed below it. Then comes Midgard. Niflheim (Mist-home) is to the north, slightly below Midgard, and *Muspelheim* (land of fire giants) is in the south. Most modern writers place *Jotunheim* (home of the frost giants) in the east and *Vanaheim* (home of the Vanir) in the west. Below them is *Svartalfheim* (home of the dark elves or dwarves) and then *Helheim* (realm of the dead). A rainbow bridge, called *Bifrost,* spans the sky from Asgard to the judgement seats of the gods by the *Well of Wyrd,* which is below one of the roots of the Tree. Surrounding the land of Midgard was the great outer ocean, which reached to the edge of the disc. There it washed against the scales of *Jormungand,* the vast Midgard serpent, who circled ceaselessly, holding his tail in his mouth to prevent the sea from spilling off into space. Beyond the serpent were the realms of fire and ice.

Turtle Worlds

Although the Norse imagined the worlds being supported by a great tree, many tribes thought of the land as being carried on the back of a giant turtle swimming through an infinite sea. This is why North America is sometimes referred to as "Great Turtle Island." In India, the disc of the Earth was thought to be supported on the backs of four colossal elephants, and they, in turn, stood on the shell of a mighty turtle, swimming eternally through space. Terry Pratchett has written dozens of delightful satirical novels set on such a world, called the "Discworld." These books are favorites among magickal people (they feature some memorable Wizards and Witches), and a couple have been made into animated films.

The Discworld by Oberon

Lesson 5: Realms of the Gods

I am not aware of any peoples in the history of the world who did not acknowledge the existence of a spirit realm populated by entities we call "gods." Each of these heavenly abodes is like a separate country, inhabited by its own *pantheon* ("all gods") or family of gods.

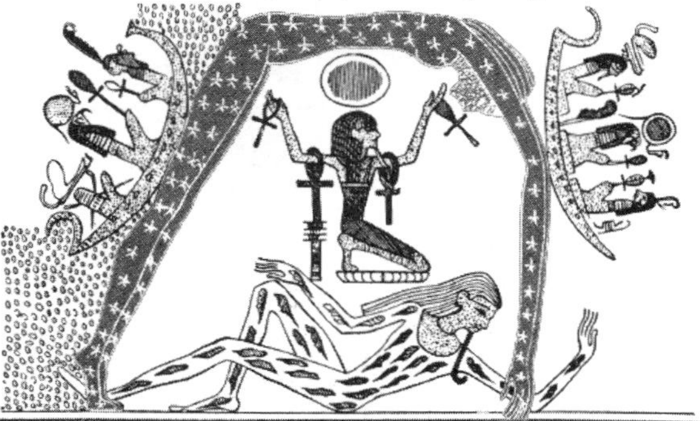

Manjet and Mesektet

The gods of Egypt dwell both in the heavens and in the natural world. In the beginning, or "First Time," they lived on Earth among humans. That was a Golden Age in which justice reigned over the land. Their houses were the great temples, each dedicated to a single host deity. However, every Egyptian temple honored and served all the Gods with subsidiary chapels and altars.

Departing each morning from *Manu,* the hill of sunrise, the gods also ride through the daytime sky high above the Earth on the great solar barge *Manjet,* identical (though, of course, on a larger scale) to those which plied the Nile River from the delta to the first *cataract* (falls). During the night, they sail the waterways of the Underworld on the boat *Mesektet,* the "Barque of a Million Years." So the realm of the Egyptian gods is like a luxurious cosmic cruise!

Mt. Olympus

In Greece, the main abode of the gods is *Mt. Olympus,* a real 10,000-foot-high mountain in Thessaly. However, like Faerie, the actual divine realm exists in a kind of parallel dimension and cannot be reached merely by climbing the mountain. Entrance to Olympus is barred by a gate of clouds, guarded by the *Horae* ("Hours" or "Seasons"). Each of the gods lives in his or her own palace, built of their corresponding metals. For relaxation, the gods listen to the lovely music of Apollo and the Muses—the official Olympian band. They are intensely interested in the affairs of mortal humans, which for them comprise a great ongoing game—sort of "sim-humanity." The gods feast on *ambrosia* (honey and poppies) and the golden apples of immortality (oranges) brought each day from the Garden of the Hesperides on the shore of the ocean in the far West. Although they enjoy the wine of Dionysos, their particular sacred beverage is *nectar* (honey wine).

Olympus

As in Egypt, the Earthly palaces of the gods were magnificent temples whose splendor indicated their relative status among worshippers. The Parthenon of Athena in Athens, the Temple of Zeus at Olympia, the Temple of Artemis at Ephesus, Apollo's temple at Delphi, and the Temple of Demeter at Eleusis are some of the most famous of these, and two (Artemis' and Zeus') were counted among the "Seven Wonders of the World." The central feature of each of these temples was an enormous statue of the god or goddess.

Asgard

As mentioned above, the Norse gods of the Germanic and Scandinavian peoples dwell in *Asgard,* high amid the branches of the great world-tree, Yggdrasil. There are two races of gods, the *Aesir* and the *Vanir.* After a long conflict, the two groups made peace and intermarried. The Vanir came to live in *Vanaheim* ("home of the Vanir"). Asgard itself comprises two areas—*Gladsheim* for the gods and *Vingolf* for the Goddesses. Many of the gods and goddesses have their own splendid homes, such as Thor's hall *Thruthheim* ("strength-home"), and Freya's *Sessrumnir* ("the many-seated"). Odin is chief of all, and lives with the *valkyries* (warrior maidens) at *Valhalla,* the hall of dead heroes, where he holds his court. There gods and heroes feast on wild boar and *mead* (honey wine).

Heaven

Jewish and Christian mythology conceives of *Heaven* as a divine region of golden light above the sky and beyond the stars. The stars themselves have been seen as little holes in the ceiling of the sky that the light of Heaven leaks through (the word "ceiling" comes from the Latin *caelum,* meaning "sky"). To traditional Jews, Heaven is solely the abode of the supreme (and only) God *Jahweh,* and myriads of Angels, known as the "Heavenly Host." The food of the angels is *manna.* Only a very few exalted saints and prophets were admitted into Heaven by being made angels (just as a few Greek heroes were deified and allowed entry to Olympus). Such "Blessed Souls" joined the ranks of the *Ishim,* the lowest order of angels.

Jahweh rules Heaven from a great golden throne, passing judgement on all who come before him. From beneath the eternal throne flow rivers of liquid fire. Four archangels surround the throne. On the right is Michael, the heavenly scribe, who records the actions of men and nations. Gabriel stands to the left with his sword of justice. The other two archangels are Raphael the Healer and Uriel, absentee ruler over Hell. In Christian tradition, on Yahweh's right sits his son Jesus, and on his left sits Mary, Mother of Jesus. Christianity opened the gates of Heaven for the departed souls of all who were "saved" by accepting Jesus as their *messiah,* or savior.

*Jahweh on Heavenly throne (*Malleus Malificarum, *1510)*

The great Temple in Jerusalem was considered to be Jahweh's literal dwelling-place on Earth. It was originally built by Solomon in 950 BCE, demolished by Nebuchadnezzar of Babylon in 587 BCE, rebuilt in 515 BCE, and finally destroyed by the Roman General Titus in 70 CE. It has not been rebuilt since. However, countless Jewish synagogues and temples, churches of Jesus, and cathedrals in honor of "our Lady" Mary have been erected throughout the world as these faiths have spread.

Lesson 6. Lands of the Dead

As universal as belief in spiritual realms inhabited by the gods are concepts of an afterlife, Underworld, or land of the dead, inhabited by the departed spirits of those who have died. In some mythologies, departed souls simply go to join the gods, and in others they *reincarnate,* returning to the mortal world to be reborn in new bodies.

Burial rites have been traced at least as far back as the Neanderthals and seem to a universal feature of the human species. The careful burial of people in ritual positions, dressed in their finest clothes, accompanied by food, personal belongings, and other "grave goods," implies that the deceased were expected to awaken into another life beyond the grave. Eventually, *sarcophagi* (coffins) and tombs were created—along with methods of mummification—to house and preserve the bodies for all eternity. Burial chambers commonly had "doors" sculpted or painted on the walls for the spirits to pass through into the Underworld. And elaborate descriptions of what they would encounter in that realm formed the foundations of most of the world's religions.

One of the strongest reasons for belief in an afterlife is the desire for justice. Life is often unfair. Many good people die young or suffer in poverty and illness. Many evil people lead rich, long, rewarding lives. Most religions offer an afterlife that provides the justice not found in this one. If there is a final judgment after death, and if some people go to Hell and others go to Heaven, then evil will be ultimately punished and goodness will be rewarded. The scales of justice will finally be balanced.

Egypt: Weighing of the Heart

As described in the Egyptian *Chapters of Coming Forth by Day*, often called *The Book of the Dead*, the *ka* ("double" or astral body) of a dead person passes from the burial chamber to wander in darkness through tunnels and passages under the Earth. At last he (or she) enters *Amenti,* the vast "Judgement Hall of the Dead." *Osiris*, Lord of the Dead, sits on a great elevated throne at the far end. In his hands he holds symbols of fertility: a flail (for grain) and crook (for herds), symbolizing his power to restore all life.

In the center of the hall is a shrine with a set of scales. The ka must recite a standard 42 "Negative Confessions" of sins and evils he did not commit in life, saying before each, "I have not...." These must satisfy the 42 divine judges (one for each *Nome,* or district of Egypt) seated around the chamber, each of whom the confessor addresses in turn. This is to assure the gods that the soul has been truly born again, transfigured into one who could not have committed these sins. Then jackal-headed *Anubis* (guardian of the dead) places the dead person's heart upon the scales, weighing it against the ostrich feather of *Ma'at,* goddess of Truth and Justice. Ibis-headed *Thoth* (god of writing) records the results.

If the deceased has spoken truly and followed the concept of Ma'at during his life, then his heart will be as light as the feather.

Passing this test, he is allowed to go on to the heavenly afterlife, *Sekhet-Aaru* ("Field of Reeds")—a lovely world with fertile fields and lakes, much like Egypt itself. There the blessed dead dwell forever in the favor of Osiris, feasting with the gods on the food of immortality. But if a person's sins in life weigh heavily upon his heart (if he had lied, cheated, killed, or done anything against Ma'at), they will tip the balance. If the person has not been transformed, he or she is no better than food for animals, and that is his or her fate. His heart will be fed to a horrible monster that waits beside the shrine. A composite of hippopotamus, cheetah, lion, and crocodile, she is called *Ammut*—Devourer of the Dead. From this final death there is no appeal, and no further existence.

Erebos, Tartarus, and the Elysian Fields

The third brother of Zeus and Poseidon was assigned rulership of the Greek Underworld, which is often called by his name, *Hades.* His Queen is *Persephone,* who rules by his side for half of the year, returning to the upper world as the Flower Maiden for the other half. Hades's realm is divided into several regions, which are well mapped in myth and replicated in several underground oracles. Except for those few heroes whom the gods chose to deify and invite to Olympus, all who die on Earth descend into the Underworld. The dead can still eat, drink, speak, and feel emotions. However, their bodies are nothing but shadows; hence they are called *shades.*

The entrance to the Underworld is in the West, and it is separated from the world of the living by several rivers. The first of these is *Acheron,* River of Woe, across which the newly dead are ferried by *Charon* the boatman. He requires a passage fee of the two coins that have been placed over the eyes of each corpse (sometimes a third is placed between the lips). Any who cannot pay the fee must wander the shore for 100 years. The Acheron joins the River *Styx,* by which the gods swear unbreakable oaths.

Disembarking from Charon's ferry, the dead enter the region

of *Erebos.* Here they pass *Lethe,* the River of Forgetfulness. If they drink of its dark waters, they are relieved of their shameful deeds but lose all memory of their former lives. At last the shades reach the gates of Hades's hall. These are guarded by the three-headed dog *Cerberus*, who greets all newcomers happily but refuses to allow any to leave. Grim Hades and stern Persephone sit on their great thrones, amid the wealth of gold and jewels from the depths of the Earth.

In the Hall of Hades, the dead are judged by kings *Minos, Rhadamanthus,* and *Aeacus,* who decide where each should go. Heroes and good people who did wonderful things in life go to the *Elysian Fields.* This is a place of eternal bliss where they are reunited with their loved ones. Souls who are not good enough for Elysium are sent to the *Fields of Asphodel,* where they drift unthinking and unfeeling like zombies. People who had been particularly wicked in life, such as *Tantalus, Sisyphus,* and *Ixion,* are consigned to *Tartarus* to endure an eternity of ironically appropriate punishment.

Tartarus is the deepest and most ancient part of the Underworld, as far beneath the Earth as the Heavens are above. It is a dank, gloomy pit surrounded by a wall of bronze, and beyond that a three-fold layer of night. Tartarus is a prison for the defeated Titans, who are guarded by the hundred-handed Hecatonchires. The *Cocytus,* River of Tears, and *Phlegethon,* the River of Fire, surround Tartarus and flow into the Acheron.

Annwfn and the Summerland

Annwfn, the Celtic Otherworld, is like an archipelago of separate islands in a mystical sea. These contain many different beings, gods and spirits, as well as the dead. The three major regions are *Caer Wydyr, Caer Feddwid,* and *Arran*. *Caer Wydyr* ("castle of glass") is a dark, gloomy place inhabited only by silent lost souls. It is the least desirable place to end up after death. *Caer Feddwid* ("castle of revelry") is ruled by Arianrhod of the Silver Wheel. The air is filled with enchanting music, and a fountain flows with magick wine that grants eternal youth and health. *Arran* is a land of eternal Summer, with grassy fields and sweet flowing rivers. In Arran is found the Cauldron of Plenty, which is linked to the Holy Grail. Only those who are pure of heart are allowed to enter here. This is the "Summerland" most identified with modern Wicca.

Different gods or lords ruled in various national regions of the Celtic Otherworld. The most ancient of these is *Cernunnos* ("horned one") who rules over all the Celtic dead. He is also known as *Herne the Hunter,* leading the Wild Hunt on Samhain Eve. A similar hunter god is *Gwynn,* who preys on souls, claiming them for Annwfn. *Donn* ("brown one") is the Irish god of the dead. His realm is a small rocky island off the southwest coast of Ireland called *Tech Duinn* ("house of Donn"), where he welcomes his descendants, the people of Ireland, to come when they die.

Pywll was a Welsh prince who chanced to meet *Arawn,* king of Annwfn, and the two of them agreed to exchange kingdoms for a time in each other's bodies. Each ruled the other's land well and was pleased with the arrangement when the time was completed. *Mider* is a benevolent god of the Gaelic Afterworld. His wife is *Etain.* He is a just overlord whose realm is a place of tedium and sorrow rather than pain and torture. *Bilé,* on the other hand, is an evil ruler whose kingdom is a vast wasteland of crushed spirits and broken bodies who must pay him eternal homage. *Bran* was a mortal hero in Welsh mythology. He angered the gods, was beheaded, and then banished to rule in the Underworld as punishment. Bran's kingdom is filled with failed heroes who must spend eternity in regret.

Valhalla and Hel

(by Diana Paxson)

In the North, beliefs about the afterlife varied from time to time and place to place. There were a number of options. Fierce Viking heroes who die in battle are received by one of Odin's *Valkyries,* or "choosers of the slain." These beautiful warrior maidens ride through the air and over the sea on flying horses, following the progress of every battle. They kiss the fallen heroes and carry their souls to Odin's great hall of *Valhalla.* There the warriors spend their days fighting over and over the glorious battles in which they had died and thus won eternal fame. Each night they feast on wild boar and drink mead to their heart's content. Women who died might go to Freya's hall. Kings were often believed to live on in their burial mounds, where they received offerings and blessed their people. Some families lived on inside sacred hills, and some continued to watch over their descendents as *alfar* (male) and *disir* (female) guardian spirits.

However the "default" destination was *Hel,* which is the general home of the ancestors. Like most places, it has both good and bad neighborhoods. The hall where Balder feasts is cheerful, with plenty of ale and mead. The part called *Nastrond,* on the other hand, is a terrible prison for oath-breakers and other criminals, its walls woven from snakes whose poison flows along the floor. This region is ruled by *Hella,* daughter of the trickster *Loki* and the giantess *Angurboda,* and sister of the *Fenris Wolf* and the *Midgard Serpent.* Hella is half black and half white, both alive and dead. Hella's domain is so far below Midgard (the Earth) that it takes Odin's eight-legged horse *Sleipnir* nine days and nights to reach it. It is surrounded on all sides by the river *Gioll* and steep walls impassable to the living. Hel lies on the other side of the treacherous Echoing Bridge, where souls trying to cross are challenged by the giantess *Modgudh.* The foul-smelling entrance *Gnipahelli* is guarded by the fierce dog *Garm*. However, there is another gate at the East through which Odin enters to ask for prophecies from the spirit of the ancient seeress.

Heaven, Hell & Purgatory

The Roman Catholic Church teaches that there are two main possible afterlives. Almost everyone will spend eternity in either *Heaven* or *Hell.* Heaven is a seven-tiered paradise of eternal joy and bliss, which comes from being close to God, among the angels. Hell is a fiery pit of eternal torment and punishment, ruled by the Devil (Satan or Lucifer) and filled with demons who were originally rebel angels cast down ages ago after losing the great "War in Heaven."

One's eventual destination is determined by their salvation status at the instant of their death. Newborns are believed to be afflicted with "original sin." An infant can be redeemed from this state only by the Church's rite of *baptism.* Once a person reaches the age of accountability, any mortal sin can cause them to lose their salvation, so that they would be "damned" and sent to Hell. However, by confessing their sin to a priest, one's salvation is restored. The souls of children who die before reaching the age of accountability, as well as other worthy people throughout history who died without receiving salvation, go to a happy place called *Limbo.* There they must wait until the *Final Judgment,* when they will be admitted to Heaven.

*Hell (*Le grant kalendrier et compost des Bergiers, *1496)*

Saints and those who have attained perfect piety are taken immediately to Heaven upon death. But most people go first to *Purgatory*, where they are systematically tortured with fire until they have become sufficiently purified to enter Heaven. People who have committed a mortal sin that has not been forgiven or those who have rejected God go straight to Hell where they will be tortured by demons forever without any hope of relief or mercy. The Catholic Hell is a vast pit with nine concentric descending rings, and the damned are consigned to different levels and punishments according to their sins. The capital city of Hell is called *Pandemonium* ("place of all demons").

Other denominations of Christianity present variations on these visions of the Afterlife, but almost all include the opposing concepts of Heaven vs. Hell. Most, however, dispense with Purgatory. Many envision Heaven as a glorious city, its streets paved with gold and a mansion for everyone. St. Peter sits before the Pearly Gates with a great book in which is recorded all the deeds of applicants, and he assigns them their places accordingly. They become angels, with wings, robes, haloes, and harps.

Other Afterworlds

According to the *Koran, Paradise* ("walled garden") is for devout *Moslem* men only. It is a splendid oasis, with gardens, rivers, and trees. Men wear silken robes and lie about on luxurious couches, with unlimited succulent fruits and wines. Bevies of beautiful, black-eyed, soul-less *houris* serve eternally the pleasures of the faithful. All other men are consigned to a Hell modeled after the Christian version. Moslem women, believed to have no souls, simply die.

In both *Buddhism* and *Hinduism* the numerous realms of the afterlife are stages in the never-ending cycle of birth, death, and rebirth that the soul must undergo in its spiritual evolution towards eventually escaping altogether from the "wheel" of incarnations. At each death the soul goes to a paradise or hell corresponding to the way the person has behaved in their last life. After a period of reflection, they are reincarnated into a new life—either better or worse than the last one, depending on how they handled it and the lessons they learned.

The *Tibetan Book of the Dead* says that after death each soul goes before *Yama,* Lord of the Dead, who holds up a mirror in which the person's deeds in life are reflected. Yama's mirror is the soul's own memory, and so Yama's judgment is actually that of the deceased themselves. Each person pronounces their own judgement, thus determining their next rebirth.

Class II. Gods of All the Nations

Oh hear my song, o gods of all the nations
A song of peace, for their lands and for mine!
—Finlandia (Finnish national anthem)

1. Introduction: Theagonies

HERE ARE *THINGS:* MOUNTAINS, LAKES, and rivers. Forests, fens, and fields. The crashing ocean, the fertile lands, the burning desert. The Sun, the Moon, and the wheeling stars. The broad Earth. Stonehenge, the Pyramids, Ankhor Wat. Animals and humans. And there are *events:* volcanoes erupt, eclipses darken the Sun and Moon, comets appear in the sky, meteorites crash into the Earth, earthquakes destroy cities, glaciers and floods cover the land. Tides ebb and flow, the seasons change, and some days, it just rains.

And then there are the *stories* we tell about things and events. Most of these are by way of explanation: How did things come to be in the first place? What happened long ago? How did things get to where we find them now? Who are we? Where did we come from? And where are we going? Some stories are meant to convey lessons, teaching by example—both positive ("Do like wise so-and-so did.") and negative ("Don't be like foolish so-and-so!"). Some stories explain why we repeat certain customs ("And that's why, ever since, we...")

Creation Myths

The foundation stories of every people are what we call *creation myths*. The simplest ones tell how the people came into being, and the really ambitious ones account for the world and the Entire universe. Each of these is different and unique, as seen from the perspective of those telling them. While they all express certain Truths in a metaphoric sense, none of them can be taken as "true" in a literal sense—especially since nearly all of them presuppose an Earth-centered cosmology, with the Sun, Moon, and stars coming into being later on!

However, the subsequent generations of gods, and eventually people, are mythically linked in each culture with the original Creation from which they all proceed. So it's important to know these stories. There are far more than I can tell here, of course; I only have room to mention a very few. There are many wonderful books of myths and legends, and you can also find them on the Web.

World Ages

Just as modern archaeologists refer to the Stone Age, the Bronze Age, and the Iron Age, many peoples have divided their conception of history into a sequence of *World Ages.* Unlike our modern notion of "pro-gress," however, these usually begin with a vision of a perfect utopian world in its original creation, with a progressive deterioration over the ages to the present time of woe and misery. Ages are often ended by a great cataclysm, such as a flood, asteroid impact, glaciation, or volcanic destruction. A typical example of such a sequence of World Ages is the Greek version:

The Golden Age—A time of perfect innocence and happiness, when Truth and Justice prevailed. War was unknown, and the gods walked among immortal humans in an eternal Spring (perhaps corresponding to the Neolithic, c.8500-5000 BCE).

The Silver Age—A time of harsh seasons, suffering, hardship, and mortality. The gods withdrew from the Earth, and men had to labor hard tilling the soil and building homes (perhaps corresponding to the Copper Age, c.5000-3000 BCE).

The Bronze Age—A time of war and violence, in which powerful men destroyed each other (c.3000-1500 BCE).

The Age of Heroes—The Greeks inserted here a period of demigods and heroes, culminating in the Trojan War (c.1500-1200 BCE).

The Iron Age—A time of labor and toil, with rampant crime. Positive ideals are stifled while greed, deceit, hatred, and war rule people and nations (from 1200 BCE...until ??).

Pantheons

The word *pantheon* means "all the gods." The pantheon of each culture is its own particular "family" of gods and goddesses who are honored and worshipped by that people. Each culture has its own pantheon, just for them, and no one pantheon is for everyone. The deities of each people are anchored in the right cerebral hemispheres of all the people in that tribe and are actual personalities as distinct as those of the individual humans. Thus they can be both immortal and omnipresent. This is very important to understand: The gods are *real*—as real as you and I.

The actual origins of the gods are lost in the mists of time, and all we have are the myths that have been passed down. But all cultures include traditions of exemplary mortals who were deified after death. Some scholars believe that entire pantheons, such as those of the Norse, Greeks, Egyptians, Celts, Hindus, Tuatha de Danaan, etc. may once have been living people who exerted a great impact during their lives on Earth, and continued to do so long after their mortal demise.

In this Class, I have selected only a few of the many pantheons in the world. Gods of India, the Orient, the Americas, the Balkans, Pacific islands, and many other countries had to be left out simply because of space. To explore the myths and gods of other nations, I recommend checking out the *Encyclopedia Mythica* online at: *www.pantheon.org/mythica.html.*

Successions

The longer a culture lasts, the more its pantheon evolves and changes. In many areas of the world, successions of new peoples moved in, invaded, conquered, and intermarried with the previous inhabitants. The old Neolithic agricultural civilizations in India, Iran, Mesopotamia, Greece centered on a worship of the Earth Mother Goddess with her sons and daughters as minor deities. These peoples were conquered some 3,500 years ago by the patriarchal nomadic Indo-European warrior tribes, who mainly worshipped male divine ancestors.

Each of these new waves brought their own gods, requiring adjustments in the myths to account for them. Most of the immediate pre-Christian religions were syncretisms between Indo-European ancestor worship and Neolithic goddess worship. Some, such as the Neolithic *Vanir* and the Indo-European *Aesir* in Scandinavia, reached a peaceful accord, both pantheons being merged. Others, such as in Greece, treated the new gods as generational descendants of the old (the *Titans*). Jewish, Christian, and Moslem myth regarded the old gods of the peoples they supplanted as fallen angels or demons.

Lesson 2: Mesopotamia

Mesopotamia ("land between the rivers") is the fertile plain of modern Iraq through which the Tigris and Euphrates rivers flow. From about 3500 BCE, this was the home of the Sumerians, Babylonians, Assyrians, and Chaldeans (in that order). The most complete stories we have are from the Babylonian period (612–538 BCE), but these built upon the older Sumerian mythology, as the Romans did with the Greeks.

In the Beginning...

Tiamet was the great dragon-serpent of the chaotic primordial ocean. After a great battle, she was slain by *Marduk.* He cut her body into two parts, thus creating Heaven and Earth. He set the stars and planets in the heavens, and established their motions. Then, on the advice of his father *Ea,* he created humanity. *Ninhursag,* the Earth Mother, planted the Garden of Eden, and in it the two trees of Life and Knowledge.

The Gods of Babylon

Adad (Sumerian *Hadad*)—God of thunder, lightning, and rain. His wife was **Shala.**

Allatu (Sumerian *Ereshkigal*)—Goddess of the Underworld. Her husband was **Nergal,** god of pestilence and destruction.

Anu—God of the heavens, and father of all the gods. Eldest of the gods, his was the North Star, and he ruled Destiny.

Asshur—God of war.

Ea—God of the waters: sea, springs, and rivers. He was also god of Air, Wisdom, and Life, and a potter who formed both gods and humans.

Enlil—God of the Great Mountain (Earth) and ruler of the Golden Age.

Girru—God of fire in all aspects.

Ishtar (Sumerian *Inanna*)—Queen of Heaven and goddess of love and war, she was the daughter of Anu. Her consort was **Tammuz,** god of vegetation.

Marduk—God of the Spring Sun, prudence, and wisdom. He was the son of Ea, and his wife was **Zarpanit.** He created the heavens and the Earth.

Nebo—Son of Marduk, he was the god of learning and inventor of writing.

Ninib—God of fertility and healing. His wife was **Gula,** the Great Physician and goddess of healing, who could restore life.

Shamash—God of the Sun, champion of justice, and giver of law. He was also a healer and life-giver.

Sin (Sumerian *Nannan*)—God of the Moon and son of Enlil. His queen was **Ningal.**

Zu—God of the storm. He stole the Tablets of Destiny from Enlil.

Lesson 3: Egypt

Isolated along the fertile Nile River, bounded by the sea at the north, the cataracts (falls) in the south, and burning deserts to the east and west, Egyptian culture was continuous for about 3,000 years before the Roman conquest.

In the Beginning...

In *Nu,* the world-ocean, existed *Neb-er-tcher* ("Lord to the uttermost limit"). Renaming himself *Khepri* ("creator"), he established a place to stand.

He then became *Ra,* the Sun God. Through union with his own shadow he begot *Shu* (dry air) and *Tefnut* (rain clouds). These two then united, bringing forth *Nut* (the heavens) and *Geb* (the Earth). They were held apart by Shu (air) during the day while Ra journeyed across the sky, but at night, Nut descended to rest upon the body of Geb. They became the parents of *Isis* and *Osiris, Set* and *Nepthys,* thus completing the *Ennead* ("the nine")—the basic pantheon recognized in every temple of Egypt.

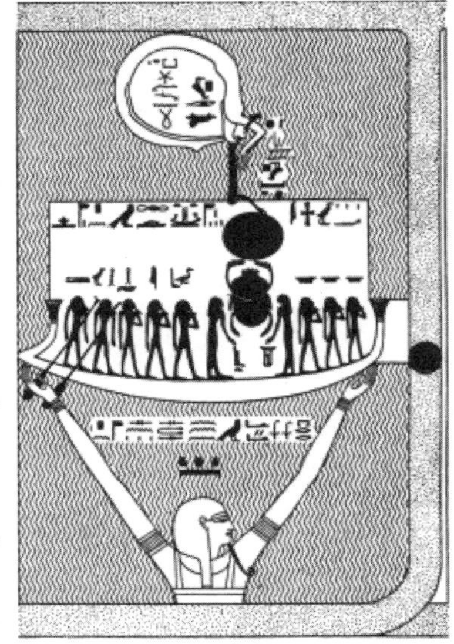

Creation of the cosmos

The Ennead

Khepri (Ra)—God of the Sun, patron deity of Egypt. His symbol is the scarab beetle rolling a ball of dung.

Shu—God of hot dry winds and the atmosphere, who holds apart the Heavens (Nut) and the Earth (Geb).

Tefnut—Goddess of cool moist afternoon breezes and gentle rains.

Geb—God of the Earth.

Nut—Goddess of night and the starry heavens.

Osiris—Lord of life, death, and rebirth. Ruler of *Amenti* (the Underworld) and husband of Isis. Their son is *Horus.* The Egyptian Dionysos, he is bread, beer, and wine. Deceased pharaohs were identified with him.

Isis—Great goddess of the Moon, she is the universal Goddess, both in Egypt and throughout the Roman Empire. Her symbol is a throne.

Set—God of chaos, darkness, the uncreated universe, and the burning red desert. He is the antithesis of Ma'at and nemesis of Osiris and Horus.

Nepthys—Goddess of the dead. Wife of Set and mother of *Anubis.*

Horus and Thoth binding together the thrones of Isis, Osiris, and Nepthys

Some Other Important Egyptian Deities

Ammon ("hidden one")—Chief god of upper (southern) Egypt, he represents the secret power that creates and sustains the universe ("The Force"). His wife is **Maut,** mother of the gods and mistress of the sky.

Anubis—Jackal-headed god of embalming and the Underworld, son of Nepthys and Set. Adopted by Osiris after Set's defeat by Horus, he become Osiris's messenger into the world of the living and our guardian during sleep and astral travel.

Bast—Cat goddess of the kindly warming rays of the Sun.

Hapi (Greek *Apis* and *Serapis*)—Represented as a sacred black bull, regarded as an *avatar* (incarnation) of Osiris. As the Greek *Serapis,* he is the god of healing.

Hathor—Cow-goddess of love and beauty, she is the Egyptian Aphrodite. Her symbol is the *sistrum.*

Horus—Hawk-headed Lord of Light, son of Isis and Osiris. The reigning pharaoh was worshipped as the living incarnation of Horus and personal savior of all Egyptians.

Khem—Lord of the harvest and patron of agriculture, he is the Egyptian Green Man. Represented as a mummy, his name is also that of Egypt itself. He eventually became subsumed into Osiris.

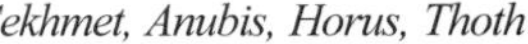

Sekhmet, Anubis, Horus, Thoth

Khnum—Lord of the sources of the Nile, he has a ram's head. He was the potter who fashioned all living things out of Nile mud.

Ma'at—Goddess of Truth and Justice, law and order, ethics and morality. Her symbol is an ostrich feather.

Neith—Goddess of outer space and mother of Ra. Also the Earth mother of the Nile Valley. Her husband is Khem.

Ptah—Master of artisans who made the Moon, Sun, and Earth. He was invoked in Memphis as the father of all beginnings.

Sekhmet—Ferocious lioness-goddess of the burning Sun, and protectress of women.

Selkhet—Scorpion goddess and guardian of tombs and mummies.

Tehuti (Greek *Thoth*)—Represented as an ibis or a hamadryad baboon, Thoth is the god of writing, wisdom, magick, arts and sciences; the patron god of all Wizards—the Egyptian Hermes.

Wadjet—Cobra goddess who protects the Sun and the royal family. She is represented by the *uraeus* symbol (a rearing cobra with spread hood).

Lesson 4: Greece and Rome

Achaean Greeks first settled into various areas of Greece around 2000 BCE. The Romans adopted the Greek gods pretty much intact, though giving them different names. The Greek versions of their origins and stories are found in Hesiod's *Theogony* ("birth of the gods") and in Homer's *Iliad* and *Odyssey.* The primary collection of the Roman versions is Ovid's *Metamorphoses* ("transformations").

In the Beginning...

> *First of all there came* Chaos, *and after him came* Gaea *of the broad breast, to be the unshakable foundation of all the immortals who keep the crests of snowy* Olympus, *and* Tartarus *the foggy in the pit of the wide-wayed Earth, and* Eros, *who is love.*
>
> *From Chaos was born* Erebos, *the dark, and black* Nix ("night").
>
> *But Gaea's first-born was one who matched her every dimension,* Ouranos, *the starry sky, to cover her all over, to be an unshakable standing-place for the blessed immortals. Then she brought forth the tall Hills, those wild haunts that are beloved by the goddess Nymphs who live on the hills and in their forests. She produced the barren sea,* Pontos, *seething in his fury of waves.*
>
> —Hesiod (*Theogony*)

The Titans

The *titans* were a race of godlike giants who personified the forces of Nature. The first titans were the six sons and six daughters of *Ouranos* (the Heavens) and *Gaea* (the Earth). The couples are: *Kronos* (Time) and *Rhea* (Nature); *Iapetus* (Order) and *Themis* (Justice); *Oceanus* (the outer Ocean) and *Tethys* (the fertile Sea); *Hyperion* (Sunlight) and *Theia; Crius* and *Mnemosyne* (Memory); and *Coeus* and *Phoebe* (Moonlight). These had many descendants over several generations, populating the entire natural world.

Ouranos hated all his children, and as they were about to be born he pushed them away into *Tartarus,* deep inside the Earth. Groaning in pain, Gaea called upon Kronos, her youngest, to take vengeance. With an adamantine sickle, Kronos castrated his tyrannical father, casting the severed organs into the sea. From the bloody foam was born *Aphrodite* ("foam-born"), the beautiful goddess of Love. Kronos claimed the throne, released all his brother and sister titans, and married Rhea.

The Gods of Olympus

Rhea bore Kronos, in order: *Demeter, Hades, Hera, Hestia, Poseidon,* and *Zeus.* To secure his dominion, jealous Kronos swallowed his children as soon as they were born; but Rhea managed to save the last, Zeus. She hid him in a cave on Crete and gave Kronos a stone wrapped in swaddling clothes, which he swallowed. When Zeus was grown, he overthrew his father in turn and made Kronos disgorge his immortal siblings. These became the Gods of Olympus, dwelling atop the 10,000-foot-high mountain in Thessaly.

Rhea and Kronos

Like the Titans, there were twelve Olympians. The six children of Kronos and Rhea were later joined by *Aphrodite, Ares, Apollo, Artemis, Athena,* and *Hermes*—the next generation, bringing the total number of Olympians to twelve. Other gods were admitted to Olympus over the years, as well as certain deified heroes, such as Heracles.

The 12 Olympians

Aphrodite and Ares

Aphrodite (Roman *Venus*)—Goddess of love, beauty, and sex. Husband: **Hephaestus**. Symbols: mirror and dove. Planet: Venus.

Apollo—God of the Sun, music, and prophecy. Twin brother of **Artemis**. Symbol: lyre. Planet: the Sun.

Ares (Roman *Mars*)—God of war. Symbol: spear and shield. Planet: Mars.

Artemis (Roman *Diana*)—Goddess of the Moon and the hunt. Twin sister of **Apollo**. Symbols: bow drawn like crescent Moon, deer, hounds. Planet: the Moon.

Athena (Roman *Minerva*)—Goddess of war and wisdom. Symbols: shield, spear, *aegus* (breastplate with head of Medusa).

Demeter (Roman *Ceres*)—Queen of the Earth, goddess of grain and all cultivated plants. Symbols: cornucopia, ears of wheat.

Hades (Roman *Pluto*)—Ruler of the Underworld, the dead, all things buried, and the wealth of mines. Wife: **Persephone.** Symbol: two-pronged scepter. Planet: Pluto

Hera (Roman *Juno*)—Queen of the gods, wife of Zeus. In charge of marriage, women, families. Symbol: peacock tail-feather.

Hermes (Roman *Mercury*)—Messenger of the gods. In charge of communication, magick, arcane knowledge,

Demeter

hidden things, thievery. He is the patron god of all Wizards. Symbol: caduceus. Planet: Mercury.

Hestia (Roman *Vesta*)—Goddess of hearth and home.

Poseidon (Roman *Neptune*)—Ruler of the seas: waves, tides, sea-monsters; also horses and earthquakes. Wife: **Amphitrite.** Symbol: three-pronged trident. Planet: Neptune.

Zeus (Roman *Jupiter*)—King of all the gods, ruler of the sky, clouds, thunder, lightning, judgement, authority. Wife: **Hera.** Symbols: thunderbolt and eagle. Planet: Jupiter.

Hermes

Some Other Important Greek Gods

Dionysos (Roman *Bacchus*)—God of the grapevine, wine, intoxication, and inspiration. Son of Persephone and Hades.

Eros (Roman *Cupid*)—God of love and the primal force of attraction in the Universe. Originally born of Chaos, he later incarnated as the son of Aphrodite.

Hephaestus (Roman *Vulcan*)—Smith god, son of Zeus. He is the great artisan, forging all the weapons and tools of the gods.

Pan—One of the most ancient gods, representing the wildness of all Nature. He is half-man and half-goat, and his symbol is the *syrinx,* or panpipes.

Persephone (Roman *Proserpina*)—Daughter of Demeter and Zeus, wife of **Hades,** and Queen of the Underworld. Her symbol is the poppy.

There are many other beings in Greco-Roman myth: the Muses, the Fates, monsters, nymphs, and half-human beings such as centaurs, satyrs, and mermaids.

The Clash of the Titans

The *Titanomachia* ("battle of the giants") was led by Zeus between the Olympian gods and the titans. It began when Zeus castrated and dethroned his father, Kronos. After ten long years of war, Zeus asked Gaea for help. She told him to release from Tartarus the giant one-eyed *Cyclopes* and hundred-handed *Hecatonchires*. The three Cyclopes ("round eyes") were giants with a single eye in the middle of their foreheads. They are the makers of thunder, lightning, and meteors. The three Hecatonchires ("hundred-handers") each had 100 arms and 50 heads, more fierce and powerful than even the mighty Cyclopes.

With the assistance of the Cyclopes and their meteoric thunderbolts, Zeus overthrew Kronos and the titans and became ruler of the cosmos. The defeated titans were bound in Tartarus where they are guarded for eternity by the Hecatonchires. In gratitude for the Cyclopes's help, Zeus allowed them to stay on Olympus as his armorers and assist Hephaestus, god of smiths. They also built the massive "cyclopean" walls of Tiryns and Mycenae.

Zeus

After the victory, Zeus was acclaimed King over all the gods, and the three Olympian brothers drew lots to divide up rulership of the worlds. Zeus became ruler of the Sky, with Hera as his queen. Poseidon ruled the Seas, with his queen Amphitrite. And Hades ruled the Underworld, eventually gaining Persephone as his wife and queen.

Lesson 5: The Norse

The Norse, or Teutonic peoples, originally lived in Germany and Scandinavia. In the 5th century CE the Anglo-Saxons moved to Britain, and later, in the Viking Age, Scandinavians raided and settled in Ireland, northern France, and Russia. Norse explorers also settled Iceland and Greenland. Our best source for their myths is the Icelandic *Eddas* and sagas that were transmitted orally until the 13th century. Northern lore is most familiar today through Richard Wagner's epic opera, the *Ring of the Nibelungs.*

In the Beginning...

In the beginning, there was only a bottomless chasm called *Ginungagap* ("emptiness"), and a realm of ice and snow called *Niflheim,* from which ran eleven rivers (the *Elivagar*) that filled the deep, freezing solid. Warm winds blew from *Muspelheim,* the southern region of fire, melting some of the ice into water and mist. Out of the mist appeared the first giant, *Ymir,* and a cow, *Audhumbla,* whose milk nourished Ymir. She sustained herself by licking salt and hoarfrost from the ice.

Out of the melting ice came the giants *Bor* and *Bestla,* parents of the first gods: *Odin, Vili,* and *Ve.* They slew Ymir and formed the worlds from his body. His blood became the sea, his bones the mountains, his hair the trees, his skull the heavens, and his brain the clouds. His eyebrows became *Midgard,* the future home of humanity. All of this was supported by the great ash tree, *Yggdrasil.*

Odin placed the Sun and the Moon in the sky. The gods made the first man, *Aske,* from an ash tree, and the first woman, *Embla,* from an elm. Odin gave them life and soul, Vili gave them reason and motion, and Ve gave them senses and speech.

The Vanir and the Aesir

There are two races of Norse gods, the *Aesir* and the *Vanir*. Some say that the Aesir attacked the Vanir, but it is also possible that the Vanir may have been the gods of a more advanced grain-raising people who moved into the territory of the worshippers of the Aesir, who mostly lived by herding cattle. In any case, after a long conflict, the two groups made a truce. To ensure this peace, they traded hostages and intermarried. The Vanir were given their own dwelling-place of *Vanaheim*.

The 12 Aesir

Balder—God of beauty, light, joy, purity, innocence, and reconciliation. His wife is **Nanna**.

Bragi—God of eloquence and poetry. His wife is **Idun**.

Forseti—God of mediation and justice, son of **Balder**.

Frigg—Wife of Odin, goddess of love and fertility, and patron of marriage and motherhood.

Heimdall—Watchman of the gods and guardian of the rainbow bridge, **Bifrost**.

Hod—Blind god of winter, twin brother of **Balder**.

Loki—God of fire and ally of the frost giants, he is crafty and malicious, always plotting against the gods. His wife is **Sigyn**.

Odin—God of wisdom, inventor of the runes, and chief of all the gods, he is called All-Father. He traded one eye for a drink from the Well of Wisdom. His two ravens *Hugin* (thought) and *Munin* (memory) bring him news from all the worlds. His wife is **Frigg**.

Thor—God of thunder, and strongest of the gods. Lightning flashes whenever he throws his hammer, Mjollnir. His wife is **Sif**.

Ve—Brother of Odin and co-creator of humans.

Vidar—Son of Odin, god of silence and revenge, the second strongest of the gods (after Thor).

Vili—Brother of Odin and co-creator of humans.

Thor

The Vanir

Freija—Goddess of love, beauty, fertility, prosperity, and magick. Daughter of Njordh and twin sister of Freyr, she likes love-poetry, but she also chooses slain warriors for her great hall, *Sessrumnir*.

Freyr—God of Sun and rain and the patron of bountiful harvests, son of **Njordh**. His wife is the beautiful giantess **Gerd**.

Idun—Goddess of eternal youth and keeper of the apples of immortality. Her husband is **Bragi**.

Freija

Nerthus—A Frisian Earth goddess whom many believe to be the sister-wife of Njordh and mother of Freyr and Freya.

Njordh—God of the sea, winds, fire, and the hunt. His wife is the giantess **Skadi**.

Sif—Golden-haired fertility goddess (some say giantess), wife of **Thor**.

Tyr—Original Germanic god of war and justice, the precursor of Odin.

Ullr—God of the hunt, famous for his skill in archery. He is the son of **Sif**.

Other Important Norse Deities (and Beings)

Dwarves—Skilled artisans, they live under the mountains and mine precious gems and ores.

Elves—Bright elves live in *Ljosalfheim* and are benevolent; malevolent dark elves and dwarves live in *Svartalfheim*.

Fenris—The huge and terrible wolf who will destroy the gods on *Ragnarök*.

Giants—Most live in *Jotunheim* and are generally hostile to the gods, but some are friendly and some have even married gods.

Hella—Goddess of the Underworld, daughter of Loki and sister of **Fenris**.

Mimir—Keeper of the Well of Wisdom.

Norns—Goddesses who determine fate. The three best known are *Urd* (what has been), *Verdandi* (becoming), and *Skuld* (what shall be). One's fate, or *wyrd,* was the result of what you were given at birth and the choices you made.

Valkyries—Daughters of Odin who select dead heroes and bring them to *Valhalla.*

Ragnarök

Norse mythology envisions the inevitable end of the world as *Ragnarök* ("Doom of the Gods"). It will be preceded by *Fimbulwintr,* the Winter of Winters, lasting three full years with no Summer. Fighting will break out everywhere, and all morality will disappear. Wolves will devour the Sun and the Moon, plunging the Earth into darkness. The stars will vanish. The Earth will shudder with quakes, and every bond will burst, freeing the terrible wolf *Fenris.* Frost giants, fire giants, and the dead from Hel will sail forth to battle the gods, who will lose. The nine worlds will burn, and the Earth will sink into the sea.

After the destruction, a new and beautiful world will emerge from the sea, filled with abundance. Some of the gods will survive, and others will be reborn. Wickedness and misery will be gone and gods and mortals will live happily together. And the thing is, all this has happened before, in previous cycles....

Lesson 6: The Celts

The gods of the Irish Celts were called the *Tuatha de Danaan* ("children of Dana"). *Dana* or *Danu* was Mother Earth, and her husband was *Bilé,* a god of the

Underworld. The Tuatha were a group of people who migrated into Ireland from their original homeland in the area of the Danube River. They were the fifth in a series of waves recorded in the Irish *Book of Invasions*.

The Six Invasions of Ireland

1. **Cessair** (or **Banbha**)— The first primitive race, all of whom perished in the Great Flood. They were led by *Banbha,* goddess of the land—or (in a Christian version) by *Cessair,* daughter of *Bith* (son of Noah).
2. **Parthlolons**— Descended from *Fintan,* sole survivor of the Flood, *Partholon* cleared four plains, created seven lakes, built lodges, and established laws. This race was destroyed by plague on the first of May.
3. **Nemeds** ("grove")— Perhaps the first Druid, *Nemed* cleared twelve plains and formed four lakes. After Nemed's death, the people were oppressed by the *Fomhoire.* Some fled to Greece, later to return as the *Fir Bolg.*
4. **Fir Bolg**— Returning to the isle of their ancestors, the Fir Bolg established the four cardinal Provinces of Ulster, Leinster, Munster, and Connaught, with Meath in the center. They also instituted the kingship. They were a small, dark race, later called *Picts.*
5. **Tuatha de Danaan**— The Tuatha were skilled in Druidry and magick. They arrived on May first and brought four sacred objects: the Sword of Nuada, the Spear of Lugh, the Cauldron of the Daghda, and the Stone of Fal. They defeated the Fir Bolg and won the kingship.
6. **Milesians** ("children of Mil")— These are the modern Gaelic people, who came to Ireland from Spain around 1000 BCE.

The Tuatha de Danaan

Angus— God of youth and love. He plays sweet music on his golden harp, and his kisses become little birds that hover around lovers.

Boann— Cow goddess, wife of Daghda. She bore him **Brigit**, **Angus**, **Mider**, **Ogma**, and **Bodb the Red**.

Bodb the Red— He succeeded his father, **Daghda**, as king of the gods.

Brigit— Goddess of fire, forge, hearth, poetry, inspiration, healing, sacred wells, and midwifery.

Camulus— War god who delights in battle and slaughter.

Daghda ("good god")— Father god of the Earth, who succeeded Nuada as king. His harp changes the seasons, and his cauldron is always full. Known for his prodigious appetites, his wife is **Boann**.

Dian Cecht ("swift in power")— God of medicine. He has a spring of health in which wounded gods are healed.

Goibnu— Metalsmith of the gods. He forges their weapons and brews a magick potion that renders them invisible.

Lugh— Grandson of Dian Cecht and god of the Sun. He is the master of all arts and crafts.

Lyr— God of the sea.

Manannan— The son of Lyr, he is the great Wizard of the Tuatha and patron of merchants and sailors.

Mider— A god of the Underworld whose wife, Etain, was carried off by Angus.

Morrigan— Goddess of battle.

Nuada— Son of Dana and chief of the Tuatha. He lost a hand in battle, and *Goibnu* made him one of silver.

Ogma— God of eloquence and literature, he invented the Ogham alphabet used in sacred writings.

Lesson 7. The Loa and Orixa

Afro-Caribbean religions are a mixture of Roman Catholic ritual elements from the period of French colonization and African theological and magickal elements brought to Brazil, New Orleans, Haiti, and Cuba by African slaves formerly belonging to the *Yoruba, Fon, Kongo, Benin,* and other tribes. These blendings created many regional variations, including *Voudon, Santeria, Candomble, Catimbo, Umbanda, Palo Mayombe, Batuque,* and *Xango.*

In Voudon, the *loa* are a group of African Nature divinities who are concerned with the lives of humans. Some loa protect certain places or areas, such as cemeteries, crossroads, the sea, etc., while others are ancestral deities. *Damballa* the snake god is the father and leader of all the loa. His wife is the rainbow goddess *Ayida Weddo.* The loa are invoked by *vévé* (magickal sigils) drawn on the ground and by singing and dancing, during which they may *possess* certain of their worshippers.

Oxun

There are seven main divinities represented—under various names—in all the Afro-Caribbean faiths. These are often called the *orixa* (oh-REE-shah), or "Seven African Powers." They come from the Yoruba pantheon.

Elegua

The Seven African Powers

Elegua (EL-ay-WHAH), **Legba, Exu** (eh-SHOO)— Orixa of crossroads, doorways, and gates, he is the messenger of the gods. He loves all things in excess: wine, spicy foods, singing, dancing, sex, and big cigars. His wife is **Bomba Gira**, the sacred whore

Obatala (oh-BAH-ta-LAH)— He is the creator God, of whom all the Orixa are but aspects. Bringer of peace and calm, and protector of the crippled and deformed, he drinks no alcohol.

Ogun (oh-GOON)— Metalsmith and warrior, he is the patron of civilization and technology.

Oxun (oh-SHOON), **Urzulie**— Beautiful River Queen of fresh waters, she is the goddess of love, sexual passion, sensuality, and luxury.

Oya (OH-yah)— Goddess of storms, tornadoes, lightning, and cemeteries. She epitomizes female power and righteous anger.

Xango (SHAN-go)— Orixa of lightning, dance, and passion, he is the epitome of all things masculine and the dispenser of vengeance on behalf of the wronged.

Yemaya (YEH-may-YAH), **Yemaja, Iemanja**— Loving sea-mother and goddess of the Moon, guardian of women and childbirth, fertility, and Witchcraft. She rules the subconscious and creative endeavors and is worshipped by millions in Brazil.

8. Some Archetypal Deity Correspondences

CULTURE→ *ARCHETYPE↓*	GREEK/ ROMAN	IRISH/ WELSH	ANGLO-SAXON	NORSE/ GERMAN	EGYPTIAN	SUMERIA/ BABYLON	CANAAN/ PHOENIC.	VEDIC/ HINDU
MOTHER EARTH	Gaea Terra	Ana Anu	Albion Don	Erda, Jörd Hertha	Neith, Isis, Geb *(m.)*	Ninhursag Enlil *(m.)*	Ashera	Prithivi, Maya
SKY FATHER	Ouranos Coelus	Dagda Bile		Aegir Alcis *(twins)*	Nuit *(f.)*, Anhur	Anu	Baal-Shamin	Dyaus-Pitar
FATHER SUN	Helios Sol	Grainne *(f.)* Lugh	Ludd Sun	Balder	Ra, Aten, Horus	Shamash Bel-Marduk	Baal-Moloch	Surya
SISTER MOON	Artemis Diana	Arionrhod		Mani Mon	Hathor, Khonsu *(m.)*	Nanna, Sin *(m.)*	Baal-ith, Tanit, Sin	Ratri Soma
MOTHER NATURE	Rhea Cybele	Dana Danu	Mother Nature	Nerthus	Neith, Isis, Mut	Nammu Mami	Baal-At	Aditi, Prisni
FATHER TIME	Kronos Saturn		Father Time		Neheh			Shiva, Kali *(f.)*
GREEN MAN *(vegetation)*	Adonis Florus	Robur Mabon	Jack-in-the-Green	Freyr	Khem, Osiris	Damuzzi Tammuz	Attis, Aleyn	Soma
GREEN MAID *(vegetation)*	Persephoné Flora, Ceres	Blodeuwedd	Litha, Habondia	Freya	Neith	Ashnan Hinlil	Ashera	Green Tara
RED MAN *(animals)*	Pan Faunus	Cernunnos	Herne	Loki	Apis	Enkidu Lahar		Pashupati
RED MAID *(animals)*	Artemis Fauna	Flidais Rhiannon	Elen	Artio	Bast, Hathor		Lilith	Manasa
SEAS & WATERS	Poseidon Neptune	Boann, Ler, Llyr	Dylan	Aegir, Ran, Njord	Nun, Nunet	Tiamet Ea, Apsu	Khusor, Asherat	Varuna
UNDER-WORLD	Hades Pluto, Dis	Donn Arawn	Math	Hel	Osiris, Anubis	Ereshkigal Nergal	Mot	Yama, Yami
DEATH	Thanatos Orcus	Arawn Tethra	Grim-Reaper	Odin, Hel	Nepthys, Set	Nergal	Azrael	Rudra
LOVE, SEX, BEAUTY & FERTILITY	Eros, Aphrodite Venus	Angus *(m.)* Creirwy Aine	Eostre, Ostara	Frigg, Sif, Freya, Freyr Gefion	Hathor, Min *(m.)*, Khnum	Inanna Ishtar Ninlil, Utu	Belitis, Mylitta	Lakshmi, Kama *(m.)* Indra
MAGIC & WISDOM	Hermes Mercury	Ogma, Dagda Manawyddan	Merlin, Cerridwen	Odin Bragi	Thoth, Ma'at	Enki Nebo	Latpon, Shehinah	Ushas
WAR & BATTLE	Ares, Athena Mars	Nuada Camulus Morrigan	Arthur	Tyr, Tiw, Tiwaz	Sekhmet, Septu	Inanna Ishtar, Asshur	Astarte Ninurta	Indra, Krishna, Kottavei
HEALING & MEDICINE	Hygeia, Aesculapius	Brighid, Dian Cecht		Freya	Serapis, Imhotep	Eshmun Gula, Ninib		Rudra, Asvins
SMITH-CRAFTS	Hephaestos Vulcan	Brighid, Lugh Gofannon	Wayland	Mime, Siegfried	Ptah	Ea Girru	Hiyon	Agni, Visvakarma
RAINS & STORMS	Zeus, Aeolus Jupiter	Taranis	Thor	Tefnut Donar	Zu, Enki Set	Baal-Hadad	Indra, Zebub	Agni

Class III: The Others

1. Introduction: Here There Be Monsters

TODAY THERE IS ONLY ONE SPECIES OF humanity on the planet—*Homo sapiens sapiens.* All humans throughout the world have less genetic diversity than can be found in a single troupe of chimpanzees. Samplings of mitochondrial DNA (passed only through the mother-lines) indicate that all people now living can trace our maternal ancestry to a single woman who lived in Africa about 200,000 years ago. Moreover, our species was reduced to only a few thousand about 65,000 years ago—possibly due to a huge volcanic eruption in Sumatra.

However, in former times there were other humanoid species as well —and some people consider that remnants may still survive in the form of *Sasquatch* ("Bigfoot") and *Yeti* (the "Abominable Snowman"). Indeed, *woodwoses,* or "hairy wild men," are frequently depicted in medieval art. Encounters with such creatures, as well as any of the great *anthropoid* ("manlike") apes, would be quite adequate to inspire stories of monstrous man-like beings such as trolls and ogres.

Woodwoses

But even among members of our own human species, there can be a greater range of physical forms than most people consider. "Little people" can be only two or three feet tall, while others may grow to be towering giants over eight feet (making great basketball players!). In ancient times (and even today), such people often formed communities of their own, if there were enough of them. And then there are the truly unusual and unique ones—people born with extra or fewer limbs, digits, or eyes; or two people fused together into one body, as with "Siamese twins." Some may have skin covered in scales, hair, or warts like a toad. Others may have hoofed feet, tails, or horns. To ordinary folk, these can appear *monstrous* (from the Latin *monstrum,* meaning "divine portent of misfortune"). Today, the mundane world considers such people as medical anomalies and mutations. But in ancient times, they were the stuff of legends, giving rise to many tales of "monsters." The stories told about them eventually evolved far beyond the reality, as myths are wont to do…

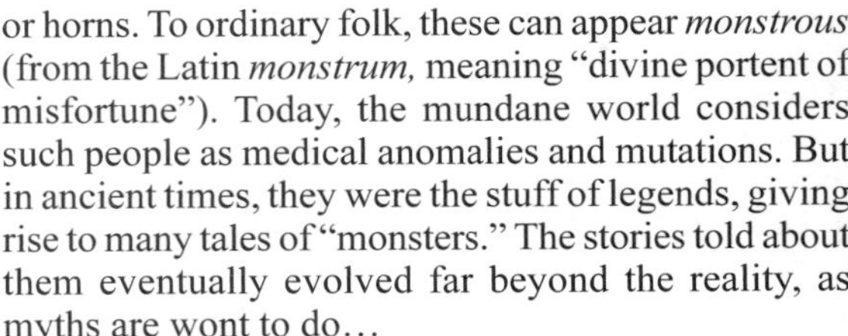

Lesson 2. Fauns, Satyrs & Sileni

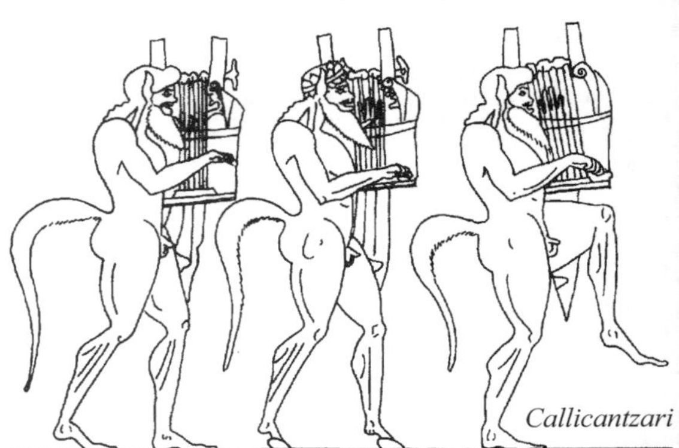

Callicantzari

Paintings and stories from ancient Greece, Rome, and other countries frequently describe people with tails. Sometimes they also have shaggy legs, hoofed feet, animal ears, and even horns. These are variously called *satyrs, fauns,* or *sileni.* Satyrs (called fauns by the Romans) are half-human and half-goat; and the sileni are half-human and half-horse. These are rural creatures associated with the fields and woods and are often shown sporting with Nymphs. In modern Greece and Crete they are referred to collectively as *callicantzari,* and they are popularly portrayed by costumed *mummers* during the 12 days following Christmas. Many people dismiss them as purely imaginary creatures, but I know better…

Many years ago, in the Summer of 1981, Morning Glory and I were on Chautauqua with one of our living unicorns (Bedivere)—traveling around the Pacific Northwest with a whole bunch of amazing performers from the Oregon Country Faire. One place we stopped for the night was a big hippie commune somewhere up in Washington, where we feasted and partied in a huge barn with stained glass windows. It was sometime in mid-July, and there was a full eclipse of the Moon that night.

That evening, a woman and her young daughter approached us outside in the silver moonlight. The mother said: "You have a magickal creature. My daughter is also a magickal creature, and she would like you to know..." Whereupon the little girl turned around and shyly lifted up the back of her dress to show us.

She had a long, beautiful tail—not a monkey-type tail, but more like a horse's tail, with silky blond hair reaching down below her knees. I've often wondered whatever became of her, and wished I could find her again....

Lesson 3: Giants, Ogres, and Trolls

There were giants in the Earth in those days ...
—Genesis 6:3

In all countries of the world, stories are told of giants in more-or-less humanoid form. They are enormous in size and strength and are often said to have created or rearranged the very landscapes. Islands are boulders they have dropped. Lakes are their footprints. Huge structures, such as Stonehenge (called the "Giants' Dance"), massive walls of ancient ruins, and unusual geologic rock formations (like the Giant's Causeway in Ireland) are said to be their doing. Myths tell of how all the old giants were killed off by gods and heroes.

The Bible refers to the giant races of Nephilim and Rephaim who once inhabited Palestine. Deuteronomy 3:11 states that the bed of Og, King of Bashan, was 14' long by 6' wide. Most famous of the Biblical giants was Goliath, champion of the Philistines, who was slain by David. During road construction in the Euphrates Valley of Turkey in the late 1950s, many tombs were uncovered containing giant human bones.

A Cyclopean Ogre from the adventures of Sinbad in a 19th-century edition of The Arabian Nights

The Lucerne Giant

Ogres are not only huge, they are also hideous in appearance, with horns, tusks, fangs, and bizarre clothes made out of skins, furs, twigs, leaves, and other natural materials. They usually carry an array of weapons—clubs, spears, forks, nets, and baskets in which to catch and carry off animals and people for dinner.

Trolls are often thought to be barely sentient. They are made of living stone, and if they are exposed to direct sunlight, they become frozen into rocky formations. Terry Pratchett, in his *Discworld* books, has ingeniously worked out an entire "natural history" for such silicon lifeforms, including the premise that their minds operate like the silicon chips in a computer, becoming more efficient at lower temperatures, and less so in the heat of day. This would explain why they normally live in the high frozen mountains, where their brains become super-conductors! It's only when they come to the warm lowlands that they dumb down.

The *golem* was a giant Troll-like figure made of clay, and magically animated by the Hebrew word *emeth* ("truth") on its forehead. Legend says it was created in 1550 by Rabbi Judah Loew (1520–1609) in Prague, Czechoslovakia, according to a formula given in the Qabalah. Soulless and mute, the golem was intended to serve and protect the Jews in the Prague ghetto, but it was too powerful and destructive, ran amuck, and had to be unmade. This was done by rubbing out the first letter to form *meth* ("he is dead").

All legendary giants are considered to be really stupid and easily outwitted by clever heroes. Sometimes they may be kindly and helpful, but mostly they are thought of as malevolent and dangerous—even preying upon humans to eat. Some people have considered that tales of these giants, ogres, and trolls may be based on late encounters with the last Neanderthals, who once inhabited the same countries from which these legends come down. Larger and more massive than our own *Cro-Magnon* ancestors, Neanderthals have bequeathed to us the red-haired gene. Perhaps they have left us with a genetic memory as well, preserved forever in myth and The Dreaming, where their lost race has grown into something huge and terrifying. Other bases for legends of ancient giants are the remains of prehistoric animals—especially mammoths, whose bones look very similar to human ones. Their skulls in particular look like gigantic hu-

Sicilian dwarf elephant

manoid skulls with a single eye-hole in the center of the forehead (see p. 292). The fossilized state of such bones supports the idea of giants being made of stone, as trolls are said to be. Peculiar rock formations are often said to be petrified trolls caught by the rays of the dawning Sun.

However, some humans do grow to enormous size. The largest documented giant I've heard of was named Gabbaras, and he was 9'9" tall! Pliny reported that he was brought from Arabia to Rome by Claudius Caesar (r. 41–54 CE). Roman Emperor Maximus ("the biggest") (r. 385–388 CE) was over 8' tall and of great bulk. He wore his wife's bracelet as a thumb-ring. Famous 18th-century giant Charles Byne (shown here) was 7'7" tall, and Robert Wadlow of Alton, Illinois, who died in 1940, was nearly 9' tall. And Chinese basketball star Yao Ming is 7'4" tall.

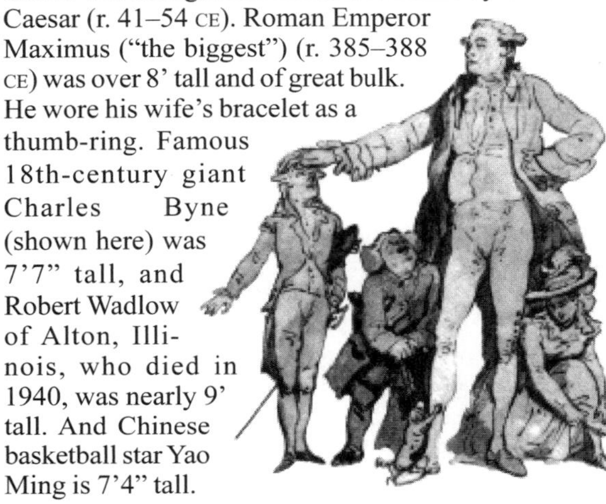

Lesson 4: Dwarves, Gnomes, and Leprechauns

I'm not entirely sure why *dwarves* are considered to be mythical beings—any more than Witches and Wizards. Dwarves are perfectly real—I know some personally, and many act in movies. They can range in size from 2 1/2' to 4' tall. Dwarves of old are said to have lived in large communities and to have excelled as miners, artisans, and craftsmen—ideal employment for such small people.

> *Archaeological and anthropological studies have produced evidence to justify the theory that the belief in dwarfs was based on reality rather than on imagination. Some of the first inhabitants of Western Europe were small, dark, shy people, dwelling among the dense forests which covered much of Britain, Brittany, western France and Germany...they were skilled in mining and smelting the metals which abounded in those regions.*
> —Sandy Shulman ("Dwarfs," p. 737)

Dwarves of legend had magnificent underground halls and kingdoms, and were highly organized under dynasties of noble kings. They lived to a great age and were endowed with special skills and wisdom far beyond those of ordinary men. In their smithies they forged wonderful magickal implements, weapons, armor, and jewelry, esteemed by gods and heroes alike. The secret wisdom attributed to Dwarves enabled them to foresee the future, become invisible, and assume other forms.

16th-century court dwarves

Dwarves are famous for their love of gold and other precious metals and for gathering great treasures under the mountains. Anyone treating them with kindness and courtesy was generously rewarded. Up to the 18th century, many dwarves occupied favored and trusted positions at the courts of Europe, often as tutors and playmates of the royal children.

Gnomes are Earth Elementals who are often regarded as a sub-race of Dwarves. They are guardians of mines and quarries, and of all the precious minerals under the Earth. This is why Gnomes appear in the Harry Potter stories as operating the Wizards' Bank of Gringotts! *Leprechauns* are the famous "little people" of Ireland. Less than two feet tall, they are dapper dressers who keep hidden hordes of treasure.

Lesson 5: Faeries, Pixies, and Goblins

The Fae

(by Ian "Lurking Bear" Anderson)

Small spirits inhabit every part of our world, animating it, driving the passionate dance of the atoms and all the myriad forms of evolving life. The process of evolution is so much more then a bizarre series of accidents. Great spirits animate the collective intelligence of forests, the oceans, the weather, our planet, and all the stars. Although these beings have threads of connection to physical matter, they do not live in the ego centered, highly attached manner most modern humans are used to. If we dare, we may grow to become more like they are, more attuned to the primal energies of our living world, and less walled up within ourselves, no longer entirely alone in our tiny rooms.

Nature spirits are associated with places, with powers of Nature, or with species. *Faeries, Dryads, Nymphs, Manitou, Kami, Devas,* and animal totems are examples of this phenomenon. Many of these beings will accept offerings of food, drink, or pretty baubles. These are also the easiest to contact, and many people report spontaneous experiences with them, especially in wild places or among the fringes of society. Faerie beings are to be approached with respect and caution. Their ethics are different from ours, and they may not be concerned about our little lives. They are of the ancient, primordial consciousness of the Earth and cosmos and not to be trifled with.

Faeries

There are countless varieties of beings called "Faeries" (or Fairies), and they are known throughout the world. They are small to tiny, often exquisitely beautiful, and usually shown with insect wings —especially those of moths and flutterbys. Sometimes, however, they appear just as little darting lights. There are many books of Faerie lore and much lovely artwork depicting them. In particular, Brian Froud has done several large art books and a deck of Faerie oracle cards. But my favorite book of Faeries is *Faery Call,* by Grey Council member Katlyn Breen.

Faeries or "The Fae" (also *Fay* or *Fey*) has become a generic term encompassing all varieties of Nature spirits, including Elves, Pixies, Goblins, Nymphs, Genii, Vila, Elementals—even old gods, Earthbound Angels, and ghosts of the dead. Some may be spirits of living or dead plants and animals. The word has roots in the Latin *Fatum* ("Fate"), the Goddesses of Destiny and also the Persian *Pari* or *Peri*—a sexy, heavenly nymph. Faeries, like their magickal realm, exist between the worlds of matter and spirit and are partly of each. Unlike other spirit beings, they can directly interact with the physical world, and they are famous for hiding things, moving stuff around, making messes, making gardens thrive, and even (if they wish to be helpful) doing little household chores. They are often seen (especially by children, cats, and dogs), and their appearance leaves quite an impression. They may be glimpsed as a sparkling glamour out of the corner of the eye.

Faeries are grouped into various categories. Nature faeries are classified according to the four Elements: *Air* (Sylphs, Peries, Winged faeries); *Fire* (Salamanders, Firedrakes, Genii); *Water* (Undines, Nixies, Lamias); and *Earth* (Gnomes, Kobolds, Brownies). Another major division is the *Seelie Court* of beautiful, friendly, and beneficent Faeries and the *Unseelie Court,* which are ugly and malign—such as *spriggans*, *boggarts,* and *hags*. Similarly, in Norse lore, beautiful White Elves live in *Alfheim* and are benevolent; ugly Black Elves live in *Svartalfheim* and inflict illness and injury.

It is considered rude to refer to Faeries directly or by name. In lands where they are well-known, they are called "The Good Folk," "Fair Folk," "The Gentry," "Good Neighbors," "Little People," "Wee Folk," or "Wee Ones."

Pixies, Brownies & Goblins

The *Fir Bolg,* legendary 4th people to inhabit Ireland, were a dark-skinned pygmy race. The Romans called them *Picts* for the elaborate pictorial tattoos with which they adorned their bodies. From that word, we get the name *pixies.* Other tiny human races are attested from every continent, and even from remote places like the Hawaiian Islands, where they were called *mini-huni* ("little people"). Of all these, only the Pygmies of Africa's Congo rainforest survive today as intact populations. With an average adult male height of 4'8", they have been known to the Western world since the Greek poet Homer wrote about them in the 8th century BCE.

Ancient writers seldom distinguish between Dwarves, Pygmies, Gnomes, and Elves, and perhaps all of these beings arose from a single source in those ancient small races. Modern writers routinely lump them all under *Faeries.* However, while they may have had a common origin, the mythical histories of these beings have certainly diverged.

The flint-knapping Picts were repeatedly conquered and greatly reduced by successive invasions of iron-bearing "big people:" the Tuatha, Milesians, Romans, Anglo-Saxons, and Normans. By the Renaissance, they were only a memory—and a myth. In spirit form now, they became known as *pixies, pucksies, pookas,* and *brownies.* Some became the mysterious swamp lights called *Will-o-the-Wisp,* leading travelers astray. Appearing as an ugly black horse, the Irish pooka ruined any crops left unharvested by Samhain. But the ancient "little people" were not simply exterminated by the big folk. Over the centuries there was a great deal of interbreeding. Many people today claim descent from "Faerie" ancestors, and the *Faerie Tradition* is well respected in the magickal community.

Many medieval Witches claimed that their lore and teachings came from the Faeries, and Witches and Faeries are often conflated in myth. A common profession of both was midwifery (helping mothers give birth). Deformed or unusual babies were considered to be *changelings*—a Faerie child substituted for the human infant. There is a genetic disorder called Williams Syndrome, first described in 1961, which affects about one in 20,000 births. Those who have it "are loving, caring, and sensitive to the feelings of others. Despite having low IQs, many are good storytellers and have a talent for music, notably perfect pitch. Most striking of all is their appearance. A relatively large number are short. They have childlike faces, with small, upturned noses, oval ears, and broad mouths with full lips and a small chin. They look and behave like the traditional depiction of elves." (Roger High-field, *The Science of Harry Potter,* pp. 192-193)

"Ollie" The House Brownie

Brownies are what J. K. Rowling calls "House Elves." In contrast to the fair-skinned faeries, brownies are covered with short curly brown hair and have wrinkled, brown faces. They are kindly household spirits and guardians, doing helpful little chores during the night. Farms are their favorite homes, and they will often move with their families. They delight in a bowl of cream and some bread left out for them, but are insulted by any gift resembling a bribe, and may even leave. In Germany they are called *kobolds,* and in Denmark, *nis.* The English call them *goblins* or *hobgoblins,* and in France they are known as *gobelins* or *lutins.*

Lesson 6. The Elven Sidhe & The Bean-Sidhe

The Tuatha de Danaan, or the *Sidhe* (SHEE), were the divine race who conquered the Fomor, the powers of Darkness, and their helpers the Fir Bolgs. These are the tall and beautiful Elves of Tolkein's Middle Earth, and they possessed Ireland until they were in their turn conquered by the Gaelic people and the Romans. Their physical bodies destroyed, they became spirit beings, making their homes in the hollow hills and barrow mounds of the ancients—much like ghosts who continue to haunt the places where they once lived.

Wights are *tutelary* ("protector") spirits and guardians of the land. As with the *barrow-wights* of Tolkein's *Fellowship of the Ring,* they dwell in ancient tombs and burial-mounds, as well as sacred trees and waterfalls. The *Bean-Sidhe* (BAN-shee, "woman of the faerie mounds") is a ghostly ancestor or household spirit who becomes so attached to a particular family that she wails grievously at the impending death of one of its members. The cry of the Banshee will chill the marrow in your bones!

Flint arrowheads dating from the Stone Age or Neolithic often turn up in gardens, especially after a rain. In Celtic countries these are called "elf-shot" or "fairy-arrows." Cattle afflicted by unknown diseases are said to have been wounded by such elfin arrows. With the coming of the Milesians from Spain, many of the Tuatha sailed away over the sea to a legendary western land that we now call North America. Their great white ships (built in Carthage) had sails of thin leather, upon which the salty sea spray crystallized. Hence they were called "crystal ships." The prows of these vessels were in the form of swans' heads (as the Viking ships were dragon-prowed). They are still remembered in the legends of the native tribes of America's eastern seaboard as the "great white birds" that arrived on their shores, bearing the "True White Brothers."

Julius Caesar encountered their entire fleet of 220 ships in June of 50 BCE, at the English Channel. But on that fateful day, no wind filled the great crystal sails, and the Roman galleys, under the command of Brutus, rowed alongside, threw grappling hooks into the riggings, and sank them all by fire and sword. This battle is recorded in detail in Caesar's 3rd book of the Gallic Wars. After the destruction of the crystal ships, no other vessels could cross the wide mid-Atlantic Ocean for the next 1,542 years (until Columbus), and the Western Lands, like the Elves themselves, passed into myth.

This largely forgotten sea battle was the pivotal point in the history of Western civilization. Had there been a wind on that day, Caesar and his forces would have been defeated. The Elves would have lived, and their ships would have continued linking Europe with the Americas. The Roman Empire would never have arisen, and never conquered Europe, Egypt, Greece, Britain, and Israel. Jerusalem and the Great Temple would never have been destroyed, and the Jewish Diaspora would never have happened. Christianity would never have been spread throughout the Empire and the world. There would have been no Dark Ages, no Crusades, no Inquisition, and no Burning Times. And the worlds of Magick and Mundane would never have become separated...

Lesson 7. Rules for Dealing with the Fae

—by Abby Willowroot

I was raised with a few traditional faerie beliefs. My Grandmother, Catherine Burke, came from the Aran Islands as an adult; she grew up on InishMor. Belief and knowledge of the Fae is strong to this day on InishMor. She taught her children and grandchildren how to stay safe and not offend the Fae, or the "Wee Folk" as she called them. Here are a few of the folk beliefs and "rules" that *must* be followed by those who do not want to court disaster.

1. *Never ever* call anyone SHE; never use the word as a pronoun. Always use the person's name when referring to him or her.
2. *Never* finish all the food on your plate. Always leave a bit of the best, tastiest, part and place the dish out of sight for time, about an hour or so. (Ellen Evert Hopman says: "I would like to add that in the Native American tradition I am trained in, if a piece of food or an herb or other good thing falls on the ground, especially during ceremony, it is supposed to stay there. It belongs to the spirits at that point.")
3. If you leave your house and realize you have forgotten something, do not go back for it; continue on your way without it. If you must immediately return to your house, you *must* make noticeable noise before entering, and upon entering the house, remove your shoes, and sit down in a chair for a few minutes. Then it is suggested you make a cup of tea, or eat a bit of something and return to the chair, or do some domestic activity. You may then leave the house again after at least 20 minutes has passed.

   The reason you must do all of these things is to establish your "ownership" of the space and right to be there. If you do this, no offense is taken by the Wee Folk. But, if you just burst back in unexpectedly, you have violated the space that was claimed by the Wee Folk for their own use in your absence. You are not welcome there; they feel you are not "entitled" to be there, and your presence is a grave offense.
4. A healthy plant is always kept by an open kitchen window, and you *never* sleep in a bedroom without an open window. To ignore either of these would be an offense to the Wee Folk and be seen as a sign that they were unwelcome in the house. Uppity humans are *not* appreciated, and this habit of taking offense at perceived human arrogance runs deep in all of these customs.

Ellen Evert Hopman adds:

I have had the privilege several times now of hearing the Faeries sing. They sing in three-part harmony, and they *love* music. They have their ancient songs, but they just adore humans who sing or play music for them, and they will immediately pick up the tunes and sing the words. They love laughter and celebration. They also like to have offerings of honey or other sweet things.

Everyone should have a little shrine for them somewhere in the garden. On holy days it is nice to put out a plate and specifically tell them that it is for them. Solstices, Equinoxes, and Cross Quarters are good times. In Scottish tradition, they "move house" on Solstices and Equinoxes and appreciate a wee bit of food. Milk and honey is easy, but they also like cooked oats with butter or mashed potatoes with butter, steaming hot. The butter symbolizes the sun and is something they can't get easily. The butter should be a big golden glob floating in the middle of the cooked oats or mashed potatoes.

Also, one must always save a bit of the beverage used in ritual and put it outside the Circle, after the rite has been finished, as a gift for the Faeries. The gift can be placed on a western windowsill or placed on the faerie altar in the garden. Every garden should have a place set aside where no human walks, for the use of the Faeries. If you find a solitary hawthorn tree, especially if it is on a small hill, or near water, an entrance to the Land of Faerie is nearby.

Class IV. The Magickal Bestiary

1. Introduction: The Physiologus and the Bestiary

HE *BESTIARY* ("BOOK OF BEASTS") IS A peculiarly Medieval phenomenon. Although ancient writers such as Pliny described and illustrated various animals, including many that were purely imaginary, the first to compile an "encyclopedia" of all the world's known creatures was an anonymous writer nicknamed *The Physiologus* ("naturalist") who lived between the 2nd-5th centuries CE. Although probably Egyptian, he wrote in Greek, and his book was so popular that it was translated into all the languages of Europe. Over the centuries, as travelers brought tales and reports from ever-more distant lands, each copier and translator of the *Physiologus Bestiary* added to it, filling in the blanks and expanding the number of creatures included on land, the seas, and the air. Though often distorted in descriptions and depictions, nearly all of the creatures listed are based on real animals. But the compilers had no way of making distinctions between actual or imagi-nary beasts—after all, the unicorn certainly appears no stranger than the hippopotamus, walrus, elephant, ostrich, kangaroo, pangolin, and giraffe—to say nothing of the platypus! And prehistoric creatures once walked the Earth that were far more bizarre than the wildest imaginings of myth.

The Physiologus and his successors, however, were less interested in the natural history of these beasts, birds, and sea-monsters than they were in allegorical symbolism that could be drawn from them to illustrate Christian values and morality. In presenting the animals I have chosen for this Class, I am omitting all those allegorical references. If you wish, you may find them in T. H. White's *Book of Beasts,* which is a translation of a late bestiary with copious notes. And I am not listing common and well-known animals, as in 6.I: "Beast Mastery." Rather, what you will find here are creatures of myth and legend. *Here be dragons!*

Lesson 2. Cryptozoology

Cryptozoology ("study of hidden animals") was coined by Dr. Bernard Heuvelmans in his personal corres-pondence among colleagues in the 1950s, after the 1955 French publication of his book *On the Track of Unknown Animals.* Cryptozoologists study reports and sightings from remote places of animals as yet unknown to science, attempting to discover and identify new species. These *cryptids,* as they are called, include not only the Loch Ness Monster, Bigfoot, and other "mega-monsters," but also many lesser-known mystery creatures. In the past century or so, many new species of large animals have been discovered, including the following:

Kodiak Bear [the largest bear] (1899)
Mountain Gorilla (1901)
Okapi [giraffid] (1901)
Mountain Nyala [antelope] (1910)
Pygmy Hippopotamus (1912)
Komodo Dragon (1912)
Andean Wolf (1926)
Bonobo [chimp-like ape] (1930)
Congo Peacock (1935)
Kouprey [forest ox] (1937)
Coelacanth [very ancient fish] (1938)
Chacoan Peccary [big pig] (1975)
"Megamouth" [huge shark] (1976)
Saola [Vu Quang ox] (1992)
Bili Ape [the largest ape] (2002)
"Colossal" giant squid (2003)
Orang Pendek [Sumatran ape] (2003)

Some of the most interesting cryptids long-reported but still unconfirmed include the following:

Bigfoot, Sasquatch, Yeti

While reports of giant, hairy, man-like creatures occur worldwide through-out much of recorded history, the vast majority of contemporary sightings come from America's Pacific Northwest, an unexplored wilderness over 125,000 square miles in extent. In this vast ter-ritory, these creatures are known as "Bigfoot" or *Sasquatch* (the Native American name). Similar, perhaps even identical, be-ings are called *kaptar* in the Rus-sian Caucasus, *chuhuna* in north-east Siberia, *almas* in Mongolia, *kangmi* in Tibet, *yowies* in Aus-tralia, and *yeti* in Nepal. In me-dieval Europe they were known simply as "hairy wild men" and were fre-quent subjects of illustration.

The "bigfoots" of the Pacific Northwest seem to average about eight feet tall and leave footprints about 18" long. The color of their hair ranges from reddish-brown through grey to black. Males, females, and in-fants are reported, often in family groups. They usually display shy, benign curiosity in contacts with humans, and they seem to be basically nocturnal, for which they have been designated *Homo nocturnus* ("night man"), a name originally set aside by Carolus Linnaeus (1707–1778) for just such a creature.

Although the main evidence for the existence of bigfoot has been in the form of footprints, there are also a few photographs, some video footage, hair samples, and—most compelling—a detailed examination of a frozen corpse viewed in 1968 by Ivan T. Sanderson (then president of the Society for the Investigation of the Unexplained) and Dr. Bernard Heuvelmans (president of the French Center of Cryptozoology). Sanderson's drawings and Heuvelmans's photographs of the so-called "Iceman" have been widely published. Shortly after this examination, however, the specimen was withdrawn from public display, and it has since vanished.

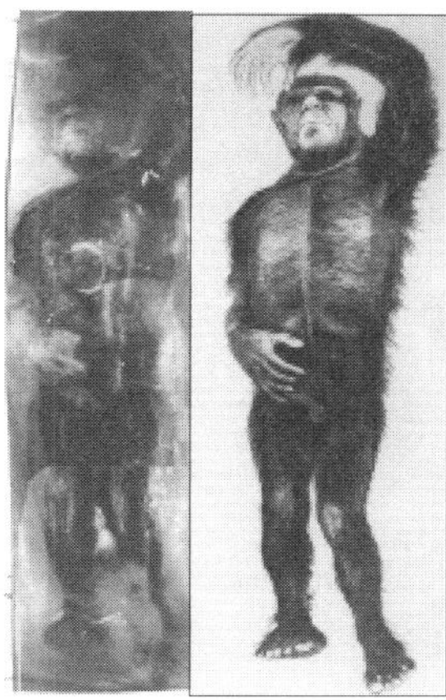

The "Iceman"

Loch Ness Monster

The large and as-yet-unidentified creatures inhabiting the murky depths of Loch Ness, Loch Morar, and other peat-filled lakes and bogs of Scotland, Ireland, Canada, and other countries have aroused both interest and controversy since 565 CE, when St. Columba, the first Christian missionary to Scotland, had a legendary encounter with "a certaine water monster" on the banks of Loch Ness. In 1975, the official name of *Nessiteras rhombopteryx* ("Ness wonder with diamond-shaped fins") was bestowed upon these creatures by Sir Peter Scott.

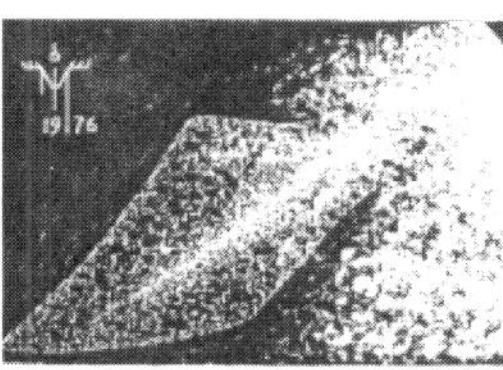

Nessie fin photographed underwater 8/9/72 by Academy of Applied Science

Popular conceptions of the phylogenetic identity of "Nessie" have invariably been based on *plesiosaurs* (long-necked Cretaceous marine reptiles). But any similarity between reports and photos of modern lake monsters and fossil forms is superficial at best. These creatures must breathe underwater, since surface appearances are rare. This ability is restricted to fish, some amphibians, and many invertebrates. However, they move in vertical undulations rather than horizontal, as do only mammals, birds, and invertebrates.

Sketch by Margaret Munroe of the animal she saw on Borham Beach, Loch Ness, on 6/3/34

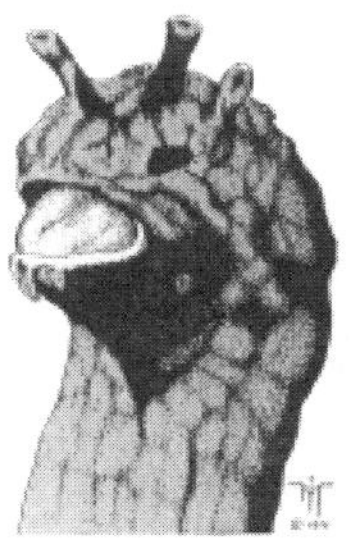

Nessie head from underwater photo taken 6/20/75 by Academy of Applied Science

The long neck for which they are noted precludes gills, which are an integral part of the skull and jaw structure; no gilled vertebrate has ever had a neck. Also, both eye-witness reports and underwater photos of the head have revealed extensible horn-like antennae similar to those of snails and slugs. Therefore I think that "Nessie," "Chessie," "Champ," "Morag," and the like are probably giant aquatic slugs, long-necked like the common garden snail. The small diamond-shaped fins for which they are named would be gill covers for openings in the normal position for slugs.

Photo taken Feb. 1976 by Mary F. on Falmouth Bay, Cornwall. She described the creature as 15–18' long at the waterline.

The Greek word *pteras* ("fin") also means "wing," suggesting a basis for legends of winged dragons. And ancient dragon lore frequently mentions that the bodies of slain orms or worms "melted away," leaving nothing but the teeth; thus explaining the lack of fossils or bones in the lochs.

Mokele-Mbembe, Sirrush

Are there still living dinosaurs in Africa? From the jungles of the central African countries of Congo, Cameroon, and Gabon come reports of a bulky animal with a long neck, a long tail, and rounded tracks with three claws. People of the Likouala swamp region call it *Mokele-mbembe* ("stopper of rivers"). When natives draw a representation of Mokele-mbembe in the dirt it looks like a *sauropod* dinosaur. Then when they are shown a picture of a sauropod dinosaur they say that is Mokele-mbembe. Its body size is somewhere between that of a hippopotamus and an elephant. The hairless skin is predominately reddish-brown ranging to grey. It's been reported to be 15'–30' long, with the neck and tail each being a third of the length.

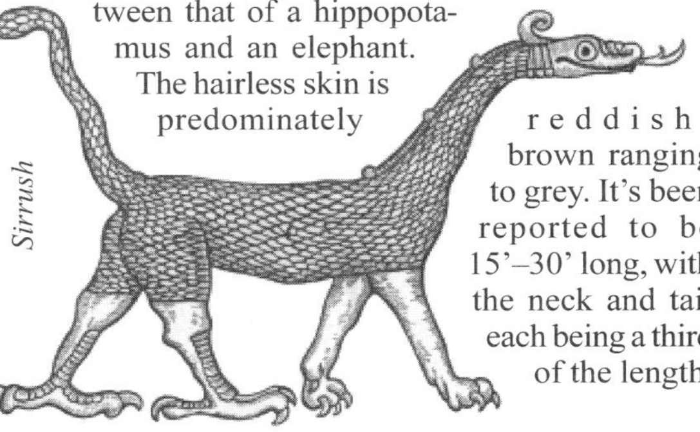

Sirrush

Sightings from Cameroon have reported Mokele-mbembe to be up to 75 feet in length. Some have described a frill on the back of its head like the comb of a rooster.

On the great Ishtar Gate of Babylon is depicted a similar creature. It has a scaly body with a long neck, long tail, and clawed feet. It is called the *sirrush* and is apparently intended to represent an actual animal. Other reports from the jungles of Africa and South America claim sightings of more prehistoric creatures, such as pterodactyls and plesiosaurs. These tales have inspired novels such as Arthur Conan Doyle's *The Lost World* and Edgar Rice Burroughs's *Tarzan* stories of the lost land of "Paul-u-don."

Lesson 3: An Illustrated Guide to Fabulous Beasts

Aspidodelone—A sea monster like a giant whale or turtle, so immense that when it is basking on the surface sailors mistake its back for an island and land on it. When they build a fire, however, the living "island" plunges into the depths, dragging the ship and crew to a watery doom.

Basilisk/Cockatrice—Half snake and half rooster; so poisonous that its very glance or breath paralyses. The basilisk is shown as a monstrous serpent crowned with a dramatic frill or crest. The cockatrice is depicted as a rooster with a dragon's tail and bat-like wings. Its enemy is the weasel or mongoose. In actuality, both derive from the Egyptian spitting cobra, which sprays poison from its fangs with great accuracy into the eyes of its victims.

Catoblepas (or **Gorgon**)—A bull-like creature of Ethiopia covered with scales like a dragon, tusks like a boar, and no hair except on its head. It is probably based on the gnu. The "Gorgon" name bears no relation to the Gorgons of ancient Greece, such as Medusa.

Centaur—Half man and half horse. Most were savage and lustful, frequently carrying off human women. But the centaur Chiron was a wise teacher who tutored many Greek heroes.

Cerberus—Guardian of the Greek Underworld; a great three-headed dog with the tail of a dragon. It was brought out of Hades's realm by Heracles, who apparently lost it in a bet to Rubeus Hagrid, who installed it at Hogwarts to guard the Philosopher's Stone....

Chimera—A composite monster with the body of a goat, the head of a lion, and the tail of a dragon. There was only one, slain by Bellerophon from the back of Pegasus, the flying horse.

Dragon—A giant reptile, often possessing bat-like wings and fiery breath. There are many varieties, living in all the Elements: Earth, Water, Fire, and Air. Wingless ones are called orms or worms. Eastern dragons are wise and benevolent creatures of clouds, rain, and bodies of water. Western dragons are more likely to be crafty and evil, and many were slain by various heroes and knights.

Gryphon (or **Griffin**)—Depicted with the hind body and tail of a lion and the head, wings, and foreclaws of an eagle, in actuality, it is the vulture-eagle, or *lammergeier* ("lamb-stealer"). A "mane" of long ragged feathers around its head and neck has given it the name of "lion eagle" or "bearded vulture." The largest and most powerful of all raptors, it is the eagle of Zeus.

Harpies—Foul and hideous creatures with the gnarled faces and withered breasts of old hags, and the wings, bodies and talons of vultures. Jason and the Argonauts encountered these on the quest for the Golden Fleece.

Hippocampus—An aquatic monster or sea horse, it has the head and forelegs of a horse with the body and tail of a fish. Its equine forefeet terminate in fin-like flippers rather than hooves.

Hippogriff—Similar to a gryphon, but with the hind parts of a horse instead of a lion. Harry Potter's friend Sirius Black has one called "Buckbeak."

Kraken/Hydra—A huge multi-tentacled sea monster. Heracles killed one whose

"heads," on long tentacle-necks, grew back two for every one that was severed. Scylla was such a monster who snatched sailors from the deck of Odysseus's ship. Vikings reported encountering squirming tentacles over acres of sea. This is actually the giant squid, of which the largest specimen recovered (April 2003) would have had an adult body bigger than a city bus! It was named *Mesonychoteuthis,* or "colossal squid." No giant squids have ever been captured alive, but a number of dead ones have washed up on beaches.

Lamia—A scale-covered quadruped of Libya with a woman's head and breasts. She has hooves, a horse's tail, and catlike forelegs.

Makara—A monstrous "elephant-fish" of India. From its depictions, it may be the same creature as the Loch Ness Monster. The elephant-like "trunk" could be a long neck and small head.

Manticora—A red lion-like creature of India with the head of a man, mane of a lion, tail of a scorpion, three rows of iron teeth, and a beautiful musical voice like a trumpet or flute. It is usually thought to be a tiger, but I believe it is actually the hamadryad baboon.

Mermaid/Merman—From the waist up, they are like humans, but their lower body is like a fish; tales say they longed for a soul. In actuality, the legends are based on the dugong, an oceanic mammal of Indonesia, which has a long sleek body, a large whale-like tail, and breasts (on the females) exactly like those of women.

Minotaur—A ferocious beast with the body of a powerful man and the head of a carnivorous bull. There was only one, the monstrous offspring of Crete's Queen Pasiphae and a beautiful white bull. King Minos kept it in the labyrinth and fed it on human prisoners. It was killed by Theseus.

Naga (male)/**Nagini** (female)—Serpent-people of India. They look human from the waist up, but are giant snakes from the waist down.

Pegasus—The magnificent winged white horse who sprang from the neck of the Gorgon Medusa when Perseus beheaded her. The only one who ever tamed and rode him was Bellerophon. See him in the movie *Clash of the Titans* (1981).

Phoenix—Sometimes called the *firebird,* she looks like a flame-colored cross between a peacock and a pheasant (though the name means "reddish-purple one"). Every 500 years, she lays a single egg in a nest of incense cedar, which bursts into flame, consuming her. When the egg hatches, warmed by the embers, she is reborn from the ashes. Albus Dumble-dore has one called "Faux."

Ruhk (or **Roc**)—A gigantic bird of Madagascar made famous in the stories of Sinbad and the journals of Marco Polo, said to be large enough to carry off elephants. In reality, it was the huge flightless "elephant bird" or *vouron patra (Aepyornis maximus)*, which reached 11 feet in height and weighed 1,100 pounds! Its 3'-circumference eggs, bigger than any dinosaur eggs, were the largest single cells to have ever existed on Earth. It was exterminated by sailors in the 16th century.

Salamandra—Named for Fire Elementals, these are brilliantly colored lizards or small dragons that can live in flames. Erroneously believed to be poisonous, they will actually put out fire. Fireproof asbestos fibers were said to be "salamander wool." The small colorful amphibians we call *salamanders* hibernate in dead wood, and often end up in the fireplace as they crawl out of the logs, awakened by heat. When frightened, they exude a harmless milky fluid that can extinguish a weak fire.

Sea Serpents—Any of a wide variety of huge serpentine sea-monsters that have been reported over the centuries by seafarers. Some appear to be giant snakes, huge eels, immense sea slugs, or even prehistoric creatures. Some may be based on seeing tentacles of giant squids. Although there have been many documented sightings, no specimens have ever been retrieved.

Selchies—Seal-people of Scotland. They can take off their sealskins and seem to be normal people, but they are really seals at heart.

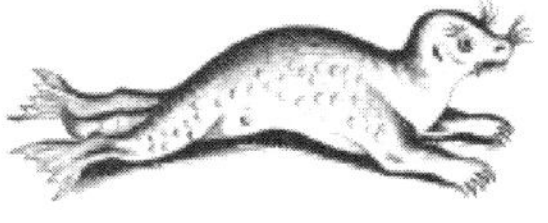

Sirens—These are depicted variously as part woman and part bird, part woman and part fish, or a composite of woman's body, fish's tail, and bird's feet. Their haunting voices lure sailors to their doom. Odysseus survived these by plugging his crew's ears with wax. It is believed that the song of the sirens is actually that of the nightingale bird, heard from the sea along the shore.

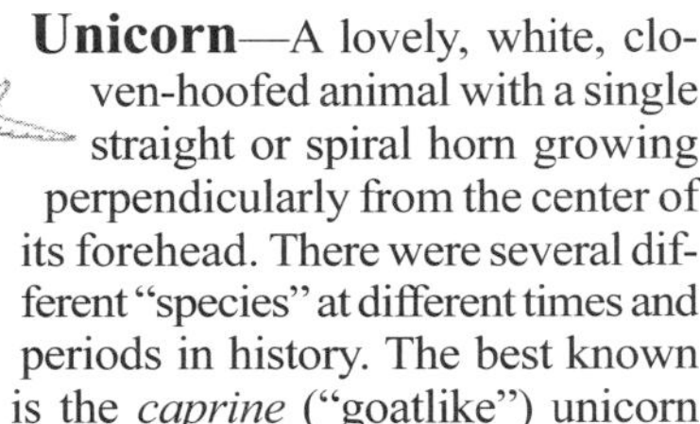

Sphinx— She had a lion's body and paws, and the head, breasts, and arms of a beautiful woman. The Greek Sphinx also had eagle wings, but the Egyptian version was wingless. She is famous for posing the following riddle to travelers: "What goes on four legs in the morning, two legs in the afternoon, and three legs in the evening?" If they answered correctly, they could pass; but if they failed, she would devour them. (Figure it out....)

Unicorn—A lovely, white, cloven-hoofed animal with a single straight or spiral horn growing perpendicularly from the center of its forehead. There were several different "species" at different times and periods in history. The best known is the *caprine* ("goatlike") unicorn depicted in a number of famous Renaissance tapestries. In actuality, these were real animals whose proto-horn buds were brought into fusion by a secret process that I rediscovered in 1976.

Wyvern—A kind of flying dragon with bat-like wings and two hind legs; basically, a large pterodactyl, like *Quetzelcoatlus.*

Lesson 4: "Creatures of Night Brought to Light"

Back in 1975, Morning Glory and I began researching the truth behind the legends of fabulous beasties. We intended to write a book, to be called *Creatures of Night, Brought to Light* (a line from Peter Beagle's wonderful novel, *The Last Unicorn*). But when we discovered the long-lost secret of the unicorn, we gave up on the book idea and set out on a magickal quest to bring real-life unicorns back into the world. It was through that work that I first became a true Wizard. Nonetheless, we have continued to gather lore, so here are a few more extensive entries on some of my favorite magickal beasties; I have sculpted images of each of these.

Dragons

The *dragon* is the primordial and archetypal monster of Western mythology. Dragons dominate each of the four Elements: There are wingless cave dragons, flying dragons, sea dragons, and fire-breathing dragons. Males are called "drakes" and females are "queens." All have been depicted in occidental legend as ancient, ferocious, and terrifying reptiles—symbolic of the raw, untamable, and even hostile power of Nature. Dragons are intelligent, crafty, cruel, and greedy. They have a passion for collecting vast hoards of treasure: gold, jewels, arms, and fabulous relics. These they pile together and sleep upon, guarding them jealously.

Tatzelwurm of the German Alps, by E. Topsell, 1607

Dragons know the speech of all living creatures, and a drop of dragon's blood tasted by the Teutonic hero Siegfried enabled him to understand the language of birds and animals. Possessing strong individual personalities, dragons have distinctive and magickal names that give power to those who learn them. Such names as *Vermithrax, Draco, Kalessin,* and *Smaug* have been given in stories. But *Velociraptor, Tyrannosaurus rex, Carnotaurus, Deinonychus,* and *Spinosaurus* are other dragon names in the Old Speech.

Winged dragons are of two basic types: the four-legged variety, with additional wings like those of bats or fins supported on extended ribs, and the two-legged *wyvern,* whose bat-like wings are formed of its forelimbs. These appear so much like prehistoric pterodactyls as to invite speculation as to the survival of such creatures into historic times.

There is a little 10"-long gliding lizard of the Malay Peninsula called *Draco volens* ("flying dragon"), which has fin-like rib-wings. Mummified bodies of these were taken to Europe and exhibited as "baby dragons"—proof positive of real flying dragons!

Draco volens

Although the biological basis of dragon legends no doubt include giant lizards, crocodiles, and fossil remains, I believe that the apparently authentic records of living dragons in medieval Europe derive from such invertebrate creatures as the Loch Ness Monster. At least this explanation would fit all those accounts in which the dragon is called a worm or orm. However, there is also Mokele-mbembe in Africa, which may be a genuine reptilian dragon!

But these are only poor vestiges of a once-mighty

order: the dinosaurs, or *Archosauria* ("ruling reptiles"). For 150 million years these true dragons ruled the Earth, in every size and form imaginable—until their reign came to an abrupt end with the impact of a giant asteroid. But such powerful spirits and intelligences that had existed for so long are not simply exterminated overnight. Just as the long-gone elves and little people live on as spirit beings of Faerie, so the souls of dragons continue their ancient lineage in the Dragonlands of The Dreaming, holding sway in our collective memories over the entire span of mammalian existence.

Gryphon

The mythological history of the *gryphon* goes back more than 5,000 years. The word *gryphon* in every language (French *griffon*, Italian *grifo,* German *greyff,* and English *griffin*) derives from the Greek *grypos*—"hooked"—because of its large predatory beak.

Matthäus Merian, 1718

The gryphon figures prominently in the art and legends of the ancient Sumerians, Assyrians, Babylonians, Chaldeans, Egyptians, Mycenaeans, Indo-Iranians, Syrians, Scythians, and Greeks. In medieval European heraldry, gryphons are frequently represented as a symbol of eternal vigilance, and in ancient astrology, they pulled the chariot of the Sun. According to legend, gryphons lived in the country between the *Hyperboreans,* the North-wind people of Mongolia, and the *Arimaspians,* the one-eyed tribe of Scythia. The favorite prey of the gryphon was horses, and its greatest enemies were the Arimaspians, who were continually trying to capture the vast hoard of gold guarded by the gryphons.

Although the gryphon is usually described as having the wings, head, and claws of an eagle with the body of a lion, it is actually based not on the eagle but on the *lammergeier, gypaetus barbatus* ("bearded vulture"), which measures four feet in length with a nine-foot wingspan. The powerful but rarely seen lammergeier (whose German name means "lamb stealer," from its habit of carrying off lambs) inhabits high mountain ridges in Southern Europe, Africa, and Asia. There is also a griffin vulture *(Gyps fulvus)* found throughout Southern Asia and South Africa.

Hippocampus

The mythical sea-horse or *hippocampus* (meaning

Konrad Gesner, 1551

"horselike water monster" in Greek) has the head and forequarters of a horse with fins instead of hooves, and the hindquarters of a fanciful fish. It is also known as the water-horse or horse-eel, and was a favorite art subject in Greco-Roman times, especially in Roman baths, where it is frequently found depicted in mosaic. In Roman lore the hippocampus was said to be the fastest creature in the ocean and thus, the favorite steed of Neptune, King of the Sea.

In Scotland the water-horse is called the *kelpie*. It haunts rivers and streams and, after letting unsuspecting humans mount it, will dash into the water and drown them. In Ireland the same creature is known as the *each-uisge* (ek-OOSH-kee) or *aughisky* (og-ISS-kee), where it inhabits seas and lochs and is far more dangerous. After carrying its victims into the water, it will devour them. If the aughisky is ridden inland, however, it is quite safe; but the sight or smell of the sea will doom the rider.

The water-horse may possibly be identified with the legendary Loch Ness Monster and its relatives, other lake monsters and sea serpents, which have been reported in dozens of locations throughout the world. The head and neck of these creatures is commonly described as appearing horse-like in profile, and they are frequently actually called "water-horses" by eyewitnesses.

Hippocampus is now the scientific name given to the curious little fish commonly known as the seahorse, of which the largest are no more than eight inches long.

Mermaid

The mermaid—a beautiful girl to her waist but a fish from the waist down—has always been a favorite creature of legend and romance. There has never been a time or place in nautical history in which mariners have not told of mermaids they encountered. The folklore of merpeople is ancient and widespread, crossing cultures, continents, and centuries. They have been called by diverse names—*sirens, selchies, tritons, undines, melusines, morgans, korrigans, lorelei, rusulki, nixies, nereids, naiads,* and *ningyos.*

The mermaid of tradition is seductive and dangerous. She personifies the beauty and treachery of the sea, especially of the shoals and rocks of the coastline. Her long hair is said to be composed of

Matthäus Merian, 1718

seaweed. For a sailor to see a mermaid is almost always a portent of disaster—storm, shipwreck, or drowning. Merfolk live in a kingdom on the bottom of the sea, ruled by Neptune, and they entice sailors to leap into the water with singing and lovely music.

The mermaid was believed real by both natural historians and explorers, who have reported many sightings and encounters over the centuries. Pliny the Elder (23–79 CE) was the first naturalist to record her in detail, in his monumental *Natural History.* In the mid-19th century, stuffed "Mermaids" (monkey-fish composites created by Japanese taxidermists) became spectacles in Victorian London. The most famous of these curiosities was the "Feejee Mermaid" brought to Broadway by P.T. Barnum in 1842.

Fiji Mermaid

The universality and vitality of the mermaid legend suggests a substratum of fact: an actual animal that may appear mermaid-like from a distance. Possible candidates have included *sirenians* (manatees and dugongs) and *pinnipeds* (seals and sea lions). In the early 1980s, off the coast of New Ireland, north of New Guinea, anthropologists reported seeing an unknown sea mammal. The natives called it a *ri* or *ilkai,* describing it as having a fishlike lower body and a humanoid head and torso, with prominent breasts on the females. In other words, a mermaid! This identification was reinforced by its Pidgin name: *pishmeri* ("fish-woman").

Dugong

In March of 1985, I led an ERA/ISC diving expedition to New Ireland to identify and video the ri. We discovered that the pishmeri was none other than the Indo-Pacific *dugong,* a rare sirenian exhibiting behavior unknown to marine biologists.

Unicorn

Out of the darkness of the Middle Ages, the legend of the *unicorn* ("single-horn") emerged as a bright and shining beacon, standing for beauty, strength, grace, and purity. The Physiologus describes him thus: "He is a small animal, like a kid, but exceedingly fierce, with one horn in the middle of his head...." He is invariably represented in medieval tapestries and woodcuts as being white in color, cloven-hoofed, with a high plumed tail and a goatee, flowing silken mane, and feathers of hair on the backs of his legs.

Because these characteristics are derived from goats, the medieval unicorn is also called the *caprine* ("goat-like") unicorn, to distinguish him from the bull-like *taurine* unicorns of the Bronze Age, the ram-like *arien* unicorns of the Iron Age, or the imaginary modern *equine,* or horse-like, unicorns.

Albertus Magnus, 1545

An animal is only called a unicorn when its single horn grows from the center of his forehead. As it grows, the medial horn alters the shape of the skull, enlarging the brain case and affecting the pineal and pituitary glands. The unicorn grows larger, more intelligent, more charismatic, and more capable of effective defense against predators. It becomes a superior herd leader and guardian. The unicorn thus became a symbol of royalty and eventually divinity; the Physiologus identifies it allegorically with Christ.

Unicorn horn was greatly valued as an antidote for poisons. Its medicinal values were vast, and a bit of powdered horn sprinkled upon suspect food or drink would counteract the effects of any poisons therein. One of the most famous legends of the unicorn is that of "water conning," whereby he purifies a polluted well or spring by dipping his magickal horn into the water.

Though always rare, unicorns have existed for more than 4,000 years. They were produced according to a closely guarded secret formula known only to a few tribes in North Africa and the Middle East. This secret was lost for centuries until Morning Glory and I rediscovered it in 1976, and we produced several living unicorns in the early 80s. Lancelot, the first caprine unicorn in more than 400 years, was born at Ostara of 1980 and later became the star of the Ringling Brothers/Barnum & Bailey Circus.

Lancelot, the Living Unicorn

Photo by Ron Kimball, 1981

Class V. Wizards of History

HERE HAVE ALWAYS BEEN WIZARDS, throughout all of recorded history and in every culture of the world—though seldom very many at any one time. The oldest profession is certainly that of the Shaman. The oldest cave paintings—dating back as far as 20,000 years, to the last great Ice Age—depict Shamans among the animals (and were probably painted by them as well). Shamans were the first artists, the first craftsmen, the first musicians, the first herbalists, the first midwives, the first healers, and the first Magicians. They were the first to take spirit journeys out of their bodies and explore the hidden realms of magick, The Dreaming, and the unconscious. And so the Shamans of the Age of Ice and Stone became the ancestors of all Witches and Wizards.

More than any other profession, the names and deeds of many Wizards have been recorded and come down to us. Even when the historical documentation has been lost, their legends have persisted in mythology. Here is a chronological list of a number of particularly famous Wizards who have lived and died through the ages. There is an overlapping continuity of schools and teachings, transmitted through a succession of Grimoires such as this one. Many Wizards have considered themselves to be re-incarnations of former adepts. This list ends with the 18th century and is continued in the next Class on modern Wizards. Those highlighted indicate biographies following.

- "Crooked Fox" (c.25,000 BCE)
- Cham-Zoroaster (c.7450 BCE)
- **Imhotep** (2635-2595 BCE)
- Dedi of Dedsnefru (c.2500 BCE)
- **Moses** (1668-1548 BCE)
- **Asklepios** (c.1600 BCE)
- **Solomon** (970-928 BCE)
- **Lao Tzu** (between 600-300 BCE)
- **Zarathustra** (630-553 BCE)
- **Pythagoras** (580-500 BCE)
- Aristotle (384-322 BCE)
- **Archimedes** (287-211 BCE)
- Maria the Jewess (3th century BCE)
- Vergil (68-19 BCE)
- **Apollonius of Tyana** (c.30-96 CE)
- **Simon Magus** (fl. 20-50 CE)
- Apuleius (c.124-172 CE)
- Zosimos of Panopolis (c.250-300 CE)
- Iamblicus (c.250-330 CE)
- **Hypatia of Alexandria** (370-415)
- **Merlin** (c.440-520?)
- Gwydion (6th century)
- Artephius (12th century)
- Michael Scot (1175-1235)
- Albertus Magnus (1206-1280)
- Roger Bacon (1210-1293)
- Honorius III (Pope 1216-1227)
- Raymund Lully (1235-1315)
- Peter of Abano (c.1250-1310)
- **Nicolas Flamel** (1299-1418)
- **Abramelin the Mage** (1362-1460)
- **Leonardo da Vinci** (1452-1519)
- Johannes Trithemius (1462-1516)
- **Heinrich C. Agrippa** (1486-1535)
- **Paracelsus** (1493-1541)
- **Nostradamus** (1503-1566)
- **John Dee** (1527-1608)
- Giordano Bruno (1548-1600)
- Giovanni B. della Porta (1538-1615)
- Simon Forman (1552-1611)
- Edward Kelly (1555-1593)
- Thomas Harriot (1560-1621)
- Sir Francis Bacon (1561-1626)
- **Robert Fludd** (1574-1637)
- William Lilly (1602-1681)
- Johann Rudolf Glauber (1604-1668)
- John "Aholiab" Dimond (1679-17??)
- Benjamin Franklin (1706-1790)
- **Saint-Germaine** (1707?-1784?)
- Giacomo Casanova (1725-1798)
- Alessandro Cagliostro (1745-1795)

Lives of Famous Wizards

Due to space limitations, I cannot include all the names listed above in the following biographies, but rather I have tried to concentrate on a selection of the most significant Wizards throughout the ages to whom I would like to introduce you. If you are interested in learning more about any of these fascinating ancestors, try doing a web search for their name.

Imhotep (2635-2595 BCE)

Many people know the name of *Imhotep* as the living mummy in the movies. He was thought to be a mythical figure until the end of the 19th century, but he actually was a real person. Revered as a god, *Imhotep* was the first and possibly greatest documented historical Wizard. He was the world's first doctor, as well as a priest, scribe, sage, poet, astrologer, and vizier to the great Pharaoh Djoser (reigned 2630-2611 BCE), the second King of Egypt's 3rd Dynasty. Imhotep may have served as many as four pharaohs. His titles included "Chancellor of the King," "First One Under the King," "Administrator of the Great Mansion," "Hereditary Noble," "Chief Sculptor," and "Chief Carpenter." He was also High Priest of Heliopolis—the religious capital of Egypt.

Imhotep is the first master architect we know by name. He built the first pyramid—Djoser's Step Pyramid complex at Saqqara, which remains one of the most brilliant architectural wonders of the ancient world.

Imhotep lived to the then-great age of 60, dying in the reign of Pharaoh Huni, the last of the dynasty. His yet-undiscovered tomb is believed to be at Saqqara, near the Step Pyramid.

Imhotep's best-known writings were medical texts. He is believed to have authored the *Edwin Smith Papyrus* in which more than 90 anatomical terms and 48 injuries are described. He may also have founded a school of medicine in Memphis, and he remained famous for 2,000 years.

Moses (1668-1548 BCE)

While *Moses* is most remembered for delivering the Ten Commandments and leading the Hebrews out of Egypt in the Exodus (1628 BCE), he is also famed for defeating the magicians of Pharaoh's court in the first magickal battle ever recounted. Moses and his brother Aaron went before Pharaoh to demand release of the Hebrew slaves. When challenged by Pharaoh to "Produce some marvel," Aaron threw down his staff, transforming it into a serpent. Then Pharaoh called forth the sorcerers of Egypt. Each threw his staff down and these also became snakes. But Aaron's serpent swallowed up those of the magicians (Ex. 7:9-12). When Pharaoh remained unmoved, Moses invoked a series of ten terrible plagues upon Egypt.

Moses and the Hebrews fled from Egypt and came to the shore of the Sea of Reeds, hotly pursued by Pharaoh's army. "Moses stretched out his hand over the sea… The waters parted and the sons of Israel went on dry ground right into the sea, walls of water to right and to left of them" (Ex. 14:21-22). When they pitched camp in the desert, Moses struck a rock, and water flowed from it for the people to drink. When they were plagued by vipers, he fastened a bronze serpent to his staff, which drove away the other snakes.

By the Middle Ages, Moses had thus attained a reputation as a powerful magician. It is said that the word *moses,* in its esoteric Egyptian sense, means "An initiate of the Mystery Schools of Wisdom who has gone forth to teach the will of the gods and the mysteries of life to the ignorant." Legend says Moses established a secret magickal school, the *Tabernacle Mysteries.* The first five books of the Bible (the *Pentateuch*) are known to Jews as the *Torah* ("Law"), and were believed to have been written by Moses himself. The elaborate rules and instructions, thought to be intended as allegories, with the keys to their symbolism as taught by the Tabernacle Mysteries, constitute the Jewish Qabalah—regarded by many Magicians as the foundational system of all magick.

Asklepios (c.1600 BCE)

The image of the physician in the Western world originates with the Greek god of health and father of medicine, *Asklepios* ("as-KLEE-pee-us"), often known by his more familiar Roman name, *Aesculapius* ("AS-ku-LA-pee-us"). According to the earliest known writings (c.1500 BCE), Asklepios was the son of the god Apollo and the nymph Coronis. Chiron, the wise centaur, taught Asklepios the knowledge of surgery, the use of drugs, love potions, and incantations. The goddess Athena gave him a magick potion made from the blood of the gorgon Medusa. With these gifts, Asklepios exceeded the limits of human knowledge.

Asklepios lived at Tricca in Thessaly (a country famed for its Witches). When the Triccans were stuck down by a plague, Asklepios advised them to go out into the countryside, gather all the snakes they could find, and release them under their houses and granaries. The snakes ate up all the rats whose fleas were the carriers of the plague. The custom of encouraging snakes to dwell among the people became established throughout Greece, Crete, and later, Rome.

Asklepios overstepped the bounds, however, when he brought the hunter Orion back to life after he had been killed by a scorpion. This act offended Hades, God of the Dead, who appealed to his brother, Zeus. Zeus struck down both men with a thunderbolt. But in acknowledgement of the good Asklepios had brought to humanity, Zeus placed him among the stars as the constellation *Ophiuchus* (the serpent-bearer).

Asklepios became the symbol of the healer in both ancient Greek society and later, the Roman Empire. Physicians were referred to as followers of Asklepios. His symbol, the *caduceus*—a staff with an Asclepian snake wrapped around it—survives to this day as the emblem of the medical profession.

Solomon (970-928 BCE)

Solomon was King of Israel and builder of the Great Temple. Renowned for his wisdom, wealth, and long and prosperous reign, Solomon flourished in legend as a master Wizard who controlled all demons by the power of his magick ring. It was said he employed these demons in building the Temple. *The Key of Solomon* and other magickal texts were attributed to him. Solomon's several political marriages to foreigners made him sympathetic toward their cultures and religious practices. Visits by foreign dignitaries—the most famous being the Queen of Sheba—also had a deep influence in Jerusalem and the royal palace.

According to Jewish Talmudic scholars, Solomon mastered the mysteries of the Qabalah. He was also an alchemist and necromancer (foretelling the future through communication with the dead). Talmudic legends claim he exercised dominion over the beasts of the field, the birds of the air, and assorted demons and spirits, from whom he gained much of his wisdom.

Solomon was called *Sulaiman* by the Arabs, who considered him the greatest Wizard of all time. The Islamic *Qur'an* relates that King Sulaiman's mastery of the languages of all creatures allowed him to regiment the hosts of humans, birds, and *djinn* ("Genie") under his command—particularly for his ambitious and demanding construction projects.

Lao Tzu (c.600-300 BCE)

The year of *Lao Tzu*'s birth is unknown. Legends vary, but scholars place his birth anywhere between 600 and 300 BCE. Lao Tzu is attributed with the writing of the *Tao-Te Ching,* (*tao* meaning "the way of all life," *te* meaning "the fit use of life by men," and *ching* meaning "text" or "classic"). Lao Tzu was not his real name but an honorific title meaning "Old Master." Lao Tzu believed that human life, like everything else in the Universe, is constantly influenced by outside forces. He believed "simplicity" to be the key to truth and freedom. Lao Tzu encouraged his followers to observe and seek understanding in the laws of Nature, to develop intuition and build up personal power, and to use that power to lead life with love, without force. Lao Tzu's wise counsel attracted followers, but he refused to set his ideas down in writing. He believed that written words might solidify into formal dogma. Lao Tzu wanted his philosophy to remain a natural way to live life with goodness, serenity, and respect. Lao Tzu laid down no rigid code of behavior. He believed a person's conduct should be governed by instinct and conscience.

Legend says that Lao Tzu, saddened in the end by the evil of men, set off into the desert on a water buffalo and left civilization behind. When he arrived at the final gate at the great wall protecting the kingdom, the gatekeeper finally persuaded him to record the principles of his philosophy for posterity. The result was the eighty-one sayings of the *Tao-Te Ching*—the world's most widely translated classic after the Bible.

Zarathustra (628-551 BCE; some claim c. 1300 BCE)

Called *Zoroaster* in Greek, *Zarathustra* was born in Iran and became a great prophet, teacher, priest, and Wizard. According to legend, he was trained by a sorcerer named Agonaces. Zarathustra founded the religion named after him, which survives today primarily among the Parsis of India. Freddy Mercury of Queen was a Zoroastrian. Zarathustra taught that there are two main deities: Ahura-Mazda, representing Light and Good (symbolized by fire) and Ahriman, representing and Darkness and Evil. These two forces are in perpetual conflict—both in the Universe and within the human soul. But humans have free choice, and therefore good will ultimately triumph.

Zarathustra proclaimed a universal message of equality for of all regardless of race, gender, class, or nationality. He insisted that leaders must be "chosen," thereby sowing the seeds of democracy. His simple message is contained in a small book of 17 songs or hymns called *The Gathas of Zarathustra.*

Zarathustra's cosmic teachings were held and practiced by priests called the *Magi,* from whence we get our words "magic" and "magician." Famed as astrologers and Wizards, the Magi were persecuted during the Persian Empire, around 500 BCE. Today, 70% of the world's 40,000 Parsis live in Bombay, India.

Pythagoras (580-500 BCE)

A Greek philosopher and mathemagician, *Pythagoras* was one of the most influential Wizards of ancient times. It is believed he was trained by a Scythian Wizard named Abaris.

Born on the Greek island of Samos, Pythagoras migrated to the Greek city-state of Croton in southern Italy about 530 BCE. There he established a commune and school of mystics who sought to discover through math the mysteries of the Universe—just as physicists do today. Pythagoras worked out the rotation of the Earth on its axis as the cause of day and night, and postulated that the planets are spaced apart according to musical intervals.

His teachings were not only scientific, however, but also ethical, religious, and mystical. He believed in an evolutionary form of reincarnation called *metempsychosis,* or transmigration of souls, in which souls progress upwards or downwards among animals and people according to the lessons they learn and their behavior during each lifetime. Because of this concept, Pythagoreans were vegetarians and did rituals of purification to gain better incarnations in their next lives. Pythagoras had great charisma, and legends attributed him with superhuman abilities and feats.

Archimedes (287-211 BCE)

Archimedes was an inventive genius similar to Leonardo da Vinci. He was born and lived in Syracuse, Sicily. He probably studied in Alexandria, Egypt, under the followers of Euclid. He worked out the principles of all basic machines, especially levers. He said: "Give me a lever long enough and a place to stand, and I will move the world." Archimedes invented compound pulleys, the water screw, the planetarium, and even the water organ. Regarded as the greatest scientist of antiquity and one of the greatest mathematicians of all time, he has been called the "father of integral calculus."

Archimedes discovered the measurement of volume by water displacement in a famous story: Asked by the king to determine whether a crown he'd commissioned was pure gold or a cheaper alloy, Archimedes had an epiphany when he got into his bathtub and the water sloshed over the side. Realizing that objects displace water according to volume rather than weight and that the volume of water displaced by the crown could be compared with that of an equal weight of pure gold, Archimedes leapt from his tub and went running naked down the streets to the palace, crying *"Eureka!"* ("I've found it!")

Archimedes invented war machines to help Syracuse defend itself against the Romans. His inventions included catapults and burning mirrors. In spite of his brilliant defenses, the Romans breached the walls and conquered the city. Archimedes was killed by a Roman soldier who did not even know who he was.

Apollonius of Tyana (c.30-96 CE)

Apollonius Tyaneus was the greatest Wizard of the first century. Francis Barrett declared him "one of the most extraordinary persons who ever appeared in the world." He witnessed the reign of eleven Roman Emperors. Born at Tyana in Asia Minor, Apollonius was educated at Tarsus and at the Temple of Aesculapius at Aegae. At 16, he became an adherent of Pythagoras whose discipline he ascribed to all of his life. In his desire for knowledge, he traveled through many Eastern countries.

According to legend, he performed miracles and reformed religious worship wherever he went. At feasts he astonished guests by causing exotic foods to appear at his bidding. Statues became animated with life, and bronze figures came down from their pedestals and performed the labors of servants. Gold and silver vessels with all their contents—and the servants—vanished in an instant. He is even said to have brought a dead girl back to life.

Apollonius was eventually brought before Emperor Domitian (r. 81-96 CE) at Rome, accused of being a sorcerer. His answers to the questions of his accusers were so wise that the Emperor acquitted him. Apollonius' death is a mystery. Most people did not even know he had died, and some believe he never did. A temple was built in Tyana and dedicated to him, and statues of him also reside in other temples.

Simon Magus (fl. 20-50 CE)

Simon Magus ("Simon the Mage") was a prominent Magician living in Sumeria at the same time as Jesus. Reference is made to him in the Acts of the Apostles, 8:9-24, and even Christians admitted that he performed genuine miracles. His fame was world-wide, and he had followers in every nation. Some even thought that he, rather than Jesus, was the true Messiah. Purported to have been the apprentice of a Wizard named Dosithesus, Simon became the center of possibly the first *Gnostic* religious cult (from the Greek *gnosis,* "knowledge"), a spiritual pursuit of divine wisdom. Writers of the early Church considered him the first heretic, the "Father of Heresies." His followers, however, variously referred to him as the First Aeon, the Emanation, the First Manifestation of the Primal Deity, the Word, the Paraclete, and the Almighty.

Simon was baptized into the community of early Christians, hoping to gain greater magickal power and thus increase his influence. Later, he had frequent "miracle-matches" with Peter to determine who had the greater power. It is stated in *The Acts of Peter and Paul* that Simon caused a brass serpent to move, stone statues to laugh, and himself to rise into the air—but he could not revive the dead. In a demonstration before Emperor Nero, he levitated in the Roman Forum, but the prayers of Peter and Paul (so they claimed) caused him to fall; he was severely injured and died soon after. His enemies cited this as proof of his association with demons. His magickal arts were continued by his disciples, the Simonians. Later Gnostics also practiced magick and sorcery.

Hypatia of Alexandria
(370-415 CE)

Hypatia was the daughter of Theon, the last head of the Museum at Alexandria. She was librarian at the great library and renowned for her wisdom, especially regarding astronomy. She wrote *The Astronomical Canon* and a commentary on *The Conics* of Apollonius. Hypatia was as articulate and eloquent in speaking as she was prudent and civil in her deeds. Wearing her philosopher's cloak, she walked through the middle of town, where she would publicly interpret Plato, Aristotle, or the works of any other philosopher to those who wished to listen.

Hypatia was beautiful and shapely but also chaste, and remained always a virgin. The whole city adored her, but Hypatia was both female and Pagan in an increasingly *misogynist* ("anti-women") Christian world. Cyril, the new Bishop, was so envious of her beauty, intellect, wisdom, and fame that he plotted her heinous murder. In the spring of 415, a mob of Christian monks seized Hypatia on the street, beat her to death, and dragged her body to a church where they flayed her flesh from bones with sharp oyster shells and scattered her remains throughout the city. They then burned down the great library—a tragic loss for civilization.

Merlin (Emrys Myrddhin Ambrosias)
(c.440-520?)

Perhaps the most famous Wizard of Western legend, *Merlin* is known primarily as the childhood tutor

Merlin and Nimué

and later advisor of King Arthur (465-537). A fatherless boy said to have been sired by a demon, young Merlin was brought before King Vortigern upon the advice of his court magicians. Vortigern had brought Saxon mercenaries into England to defend against the Picts and the Scots-Irish. The Saxons had taken control of the land, and Vortigern was attempting to build a tower to strengthen his holdings. But the construction kept collapsing, and Vortigern's advisors told him that only the blood of a fatherless boy would remedy this. But Merlin divined that the tower's instability was due to an underground pool of water, which was discovered upon excavation. This event secured his fame as a prophet.

About ten years later, with Vortigern dead and Uther Pendragon on the throne, Merlin arranged for the birth of Arthur by disguising Uther as the husband of Ygraine, Queen of Cornwall, whom Uther then seduced and impregnated. When Arthur was born, Merlin took him away for fosterage and tutoring. Upon Uther's death, Merlin arranged the contest of the sword in the stone; upon drawing it forth, Arthur became King of England. Merlin, then in his 40s, became Court Wizard. He is said to have established the Order of Chivalry with the Knights of the Round Table.

In his old age, Merlin was seduced by the enchantress Nimué, who learned his magick and turned it against him, trapping him, it is said, in a crystal cave, thorn forest, or oak tree. There it is believed he lives on still, resting until he is needed again.

Nicolas Flamel (1299-1418)

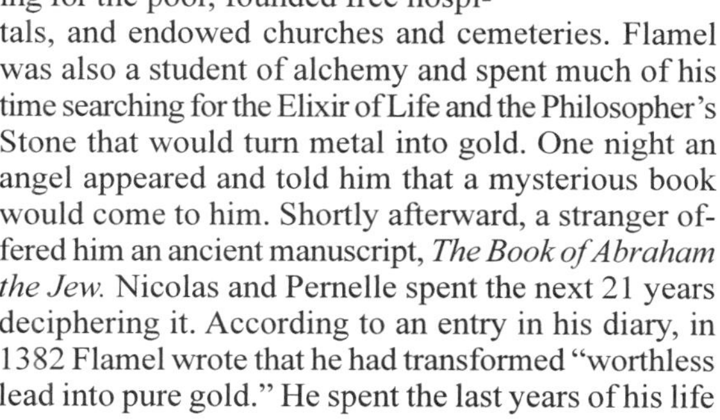

Nicolas Flamel, born in Pontoise, France, became a successful bookseller and philanthropist. At a time when most people were illiterate, he made his fortune as a professional scribe. With his wife Pernelle, he created low-income housing for the poor, founded free hospitals, and endowed churches and cemeteries. Flamel was also a student of alchemy and spent much of his time searching for the Elixir of Life and the Philosopher's Stone that would turn metal into gold. One night an angel appeared and told him that a mysterious book would come to him. Shortly afterward, a stranger offered him an ancient manuscript, *The Book of Abraham the Jew.* Nicolas and Pernelle spent the next 21 years deciphering it. According to an entry in his diary, in 1382 Flamel wrote that he had transformed "worthless lead into pure gold." He spent the last years of his life writing about alchemy, and died in 1418. *The Book of Abraham the Jew* has never been seen since.

Abramelin the Mage (1362-1460)

Abraham was probably born in Mayence, but traveled widely through Austria, Hungary, Greece, Palestine, and Egypt. At Arachi, on the banks of the Nile, a sage named Abra-Melin initiated him into magick. On returning to Wurzburg, Germany, he took the name *Abramelin* and began to practice alchemical research. He claimed to have learned his knowledge of magick from angels, who told him how to raise storms and conjure and tame demons into personal servants and workers. He said that all things in the world were created by demons, working under the direction of angels, and that each individual had an angel and a demon as familiars.

According to lore, Abramelin created 2,000 spirit cavalrymen for Frederick, elector of Saxony. He also is said to have aided an Earl of Warwick in his escape from jail and helped save the Antipope John XXIII (1410-'15) from the Council of Constance. At 96, he compiled his famous work, *The Sacred Magic of Abramelin the Mage*—three books originally written in Hebrew, dated 1458, which he left to the legacy of his son Lamech. Therein he specified details of the invocation of angelic forces and presented a series of rituals that required six months to perform.

Leonardo da Vinci
(1452-1519)

Leonardo was the greatest Wizard of the Italian Renaissance. His contributions to humanity were extraordinary—as an artist, inventor, writer, and thinker. His notebooks reveal explorations and examinations of everything in the known Universe, and some of his paintings (particularly the *Mona Lisa* and *The Last Supper*) are among the best-known artworks in the world.

Each subject that Leonardo studied, he made a field of scientific research. He studied human anatomy to better draw the human body; he studied botany and geology in order to accurately portray plants and landscapes. He became a geologist, physiologist, astronomer, and mechanical engineer. The many machines and inventions that he conceived are marvels of engineering—including his famous designs for a flapping-wing flying machine, or *ornithopter.* The thousands of pages of drawings and writings he has left us convey a new vision of unity that Leonardo sought to give the world. He spoke of science as the "knowledge of things possible in the future, of the present, and of the past." He wrote many of his texts in mirror image and is known for secreting coded symbols in his paintings.

Agrippa (1486–1535)

Heinrich Cornelius Agrippa von Nettesheim was a German mystic and alchemist. Born near Cologne, he studied both medicine and law at the University. In 1506, by the age of 20, he had established a secret society in Paris devoted to astrology, magick, and Qabalah and became court secretary to the Holy Roman Emperor. He went on to lecture on occultism in the French University of Dôle, where he set up a laboratory in the hopes of synthesizing gold. For the next decade or so he traveled Europe, making a living as an alchemist and conversing with important early humanist scholars. Hounded out of Cologne by the Inquisition, Agrippa set up a medical practice in Geneva, and in 1524 became personal physician to the Queen Mother at the court of King Francis I in Lyons. When the Queen Mother abandoned him, he moved to Antwerp, but he was later banned for practicing medicine without a license. Agrippa then became historiographer at the court of Charles V.

Agrippa wrote on a great many topics, including marriage and military engineering, but his most important work is the three-volume *De occulta philosophiae* ("Of the Occult Philosophy"), a defense of "hidden philosophy" or magick, which draws on diverse mystical traditions—alchemy, astrology, and Qabalah. This book had a profound influence on the development of Western magick. Agrippa embraced astrology, divination, numerology, and the power of gems and stones. It was said that he practiced necromancy, conjured various demons, found the Philosopher's Stone, and even traveled to the New World. Knowledgeable in law, theology, medicine, and philosophy, he spoke eight languages and has been called the Renaissance Man of the occult world.

Paracelsus (1493–1541)

Philippus Aureolus took the pseudonym of *Theophrastus Bombastus von Hohenheim.* After receiving his doctorate from the University of Ferrara, he called himself *Paracelsus* ("alongside Celsus"—the ancient Roman physician). He was a Swiss physician, scholar, and alchemist who studied with an abbot known for his writings on the Qabalah. Paracelsus's interest in alchemy and metallurgy took him to many mines in Germany, Hungary, and other countries, where he was often employed as an analyst. He was the first to describe zinc, and he developed the use of such minerals as mercury in healing potions for his medical practice. It is said that Paracelsus learned the secret of the Philosopher's Stone from an Arabian Wizard in Constantinople. He owned a *speculum* (magick scrying mirror), and he gave detailed instructions for making one. Believing that the stars and planets influenced life, he made and used talismans inscribed with planetary sigils on various appropriate metals.

In 1536, Paracelsus published his medical discoveries and theories in a book called *Die Grosse Wundartzney* ("The Great Miraculous Medicine") wherein he linked good health with living in harmony with Nature. Other writings, such as *Liber Azoth* ("Book of Azoth"—tincture of Mercury) and *Archidoxa* ("Ruling Doctrines") have had a great influence on occultists, alchemists, and mystics.

Nostradamus (1503–1566)

History's greatest prophet, *Michel de Nostredame* was best known by the Latin version of his last name, *Nostradamus* ("Our Lady"). His Jewish family claimed descent from the Issachar tribe, noted for prophecy. His grandfather taught him Greek, Latin, Hebrew, math, and astrology. Nostradamus studied philosophy in Avignon and received his medical license from the University of Montpelier.

Possessing a seemingly miraculous ability to heal the incurable, Nostradamus treated sufferers of the Black Plague. In a tragic irony, his first wife and two children died of the plague, and the Inquisition then accused him of heresy. For the next six years he wandered around France, caring for plague victims and studying the occult. In 1546, he married again and had six children. Using water scrying, Nostradamus was able to receive visions of the future. Starting in 1550, he issued an annual *Almanac* of predictions, and in 1556, he published *Centuries,* his famous book of prophecies from his time to the end of the world in 3799. He became famous throughout Europe for his predictions, and the French Royal Family asked him to come to Paris to prepare their astrological charts. He saw that all seven sons would gain the crown, and all would die.

Near the end of his life, Nostradamus was welcomed at the court of Catherine de Médici, where he continued making predictions, including that of his own death, which occurred exactly as he described it. His enigmatic quatrains have been reinterpreted by each generation since, and more than 40 are believed to have already come true.

Dr. John Dee (1527–1608)

Called "the last royal magician" for his services to Elizabeth I, *Dr. John Dee* became well-known as an astronomer and astrologer with many people seeking his advice. After being imprisoned under "Bloody Mary," his fortunes turned around with the accession of Elizabeth, who consulted with him to pick a propitious day for her coronation. Elizabeth was so impressed with Dee that she had him give her lessons in astrology.

Dee studied occult theories and practiced alchemy. In 1581 he began to experiment with scrying, using a crystal ball, a mirror, a clear pool of water, or any transparent object. He soon discovered he had no talent for scrying and sought a medium to work with. Dee found him in notorious con artist Edward Talbot/Kelly, who claimed to receive all kinds of messages from a host of "angels," including a 26-character Angelic (or *Enochian*) alphabet. With this material, Dee wrote *The Book of Enoch* and *48 Angelic Keys* to summon spirits.

After spending four years in Poland with Kelly, Dee returned to his home in England, where he continued his fruitless search for the Philosopher's Stone. Taking pity on his poverty, Elizabeth posted him as chancellor of St. Paul's Cathedral in London, and later gave him the wardenship of Manchester College, which he held until he retired in 1603. He died in extreme poverty at the age of 81.

Despite his delusions, John Dee was one of the keenest minds of his time. He is credited with making the calculations that enabled England to use the Gregorian calendar; he championed the preservation and collection of historic documents; and he was noted for being a great astronomer and mathematician. It could be said that Dr. Dee was the one of the first modern scientists, as well as one of the last serious alchemists, necromancers, and crystal gazers.

Robert Fludd (1574–1637)

A Wizard, philosopher, and physician in Elizabethan England, *Robert Fludd* received his degrees from Oxford. On the Continent, his studies in medicine and chemistry led him into Paracelsian medical circles (using mineral tinctures). He also developed a keen interest in Rosicrucian philosophy. He established a medical practice in London where he was successful enough to maintain his own apothecary and laboratory to prepare his secret potions and remedies, as well as carry on his alchemical experiments. The success of his practice was due not only to his medical skills, but also his magnetic personality and mystical approach (diagnosis using patients' horoscopes). Fludd also conducted some questionable experiments with human cadavers in his quest for the mystic bloodstone described by Paracelsus.

Over the years, Fludd became more involved in alchemy and Qabalistic magick. He joined a school of medical mystics who claimed to hold the Key to Universal Sciences; he wrote a two-volume *History of the Macrocosm and Microcosm,* exploring the nature of God and humanity, and surveyed various forms of divination. He defended the dark arts in *Mosaical Philosophy* and *Summum Bonum* ("All Good Things"). Initiated into the Rosicrucians by Michael Maier, he wrote a famous treatise defending the Order. Fludd also wrote scientific, medical, and alchemical books, reflecting his dual life as a physician and metaphysician in a time when the world of science was being separated from the world of magick.

Comte de Saint-Germaine (1707?–1784?)

Court Wizard of French King Louis XV, *Saint-Germaine* was a skilled violinist, harpsichordist, composer, and painter. Fluent in a dozen languages, he had a complete and detailed knowledge of history. His best-remembered occult treatise is *La Très Sainte Trinosophie* ("The Most Holy Triple Philosophy"). Only a single copy of the lushly-illustrated manuscript survives.

A skilled Qabalist, Saint-Germaine was famed for his amazing skills in medicine and alchemy, especially for transmuting metals into gold. He made a living from the trade of jewels, having a secret technique for removing flaws from diamonds. He claimed to possess the Philosopher's Stone and to have discovered the Elixer of Life, stating that he was more than 2,000 years old—though he always looked about 40. In 1762, Saint-Germaine was in St. Petersburg, deeply involved in the conspiracy to make Catherine the Great Queen of Russia. He returned to Paris in 1770, then settled in Germany where he studied the "Secret Sciences" with Charles of Hesse. He was said to have died in 1784, but he was allegedly seen in Paris in 1789, during the French Revolution. Since then, Saint-Germaine has been claimed to have been seen all over the world.

Saint-Germaine is a figure of mystery whose legend has grown in the 220 years since his supposed death. Because he rarely ate in public, always dressed in black and white, and was said to be able to render himself invisible, some even claim he was actually a vampire prince from Transylvania whose true name was Francis Ragoczy.

Class VI: Modern Wizards

1. Introduction: Wizard's Work

HE EARLIEST RECORDED WIZARDS, such as Imhotep, were advisors to kings. The word *Wizard* is related to the Arabic word *vizier,* meaning "advisor." For example, you are certainly familiar with Merlin, the archetypal Wizard and advisor to King Arthur. In Celtic times, every king or queen had a Druid/Wizard at their side, in order to give them advice and assistance. The kings were warriors and were not learned in the ways of magick, nor were they wise in the ways of the law. The presence of a wise Wizard ensured that the ruler would be just with his or her subjects.

From the Middle Ages through the Renaissance, Western Wizardry was dominated by alchemy and the search for the Philosopher's Stone. In the 17th and 18th centuries, the Scientific Revolution brought a shift in focus for many Wizards to a greater emphasis on science, Hermetics, Qabalah, and secret societies such as the Freemasons and Rosicrucians. With the Industrial Revolution in the 19th century, prominent Wizards were often involved in the proliferation of occult orders, practicing ceremonial magick. The mid-20th century saw the revival of Witchcraft and Paganism as the Old Religion, and many Wizards since then have been involved in the work of restoration and teaching. These include the members of the Grey Council.

2. Wizards of the 19th-20th Centuries

James Murrell (1780-1860)	**Arthur Edward Waite** (1857-1947)	Cecil Hugh Williamson (1909-1999)
Francis Barrett (19th century)	Charles Walton (1871-1945)	**Stewart Farrar** (1916-2000)
Eliphas Levi (1810-1875)	**Aleister Crowley** (1875-1947)	**Victor Anderson** (1917-2001)
George Pickingill (1816-1909)	**Gerald Gardner** (1884-1964)	Alex Sanders (1926-1988)
Charles Godfrey Leland (1824-1903)	Austin Osman Spare (1886-1956)	Leo Louis Martello (1931-2000)
S.L. MacGregor Mathers (1854-1918)	Francis Israel Regardie (1907-1983)	**Gwydion Pendderwen** (1946-1982)
	Arnold Crowther (1909-1974)	Scott Cunningham (1956-1993)

Francis Barrett (19th Century)

Little is known about *Francis Barrett* beyond his authorship of *The Magus,* a landmark compendium of occultism and magick published in London in 1801. Barrett, an Englishman, claimed to be a student of chemistry, metaphysics, and occult philosophy. He was an eccentric man, giving lessons in the magick arts from his apartment and spending long hours meticulously translating Qabalistic and ancient texts into English. *The Magus* dealt with the natural magic of herbs and stones, magnetism, talismanic magic, alchemy and other means of creating the Philosopher's Stone, numerology, the elements, and biographies of famous adepts from history. But the book gained little notice until it influenced Eliphas Levi.

Barrett was passionately interested in reviving interest in the occult. Using *The Magus* as an advertising tool, he formed a magick circle, and turned Cambridge into a center for magick.

Eliphas Levi (1810-1875)

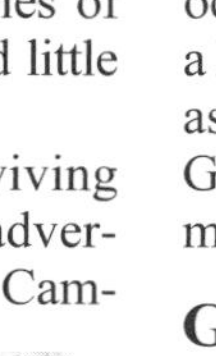

Eliphas Levi was the pseudonym for *Alphonse Louis Constant*, a French occultist credited for reviving interest in magick in the 19th century. He was considered more of a commentator on the subject than an adept, even though he professed to have practiced necromancy—conjuring up the spirit of Apol-lonius of Tyana. Constant became a follower of an eccentric old man named Ganneau, who claimed to be a prophet and the reincarnation of Louis XVII. He also learned arcane mysteries from the Polish mystic Hoëne-Wronski. He took the name of *Magus Eliphas Levi*, the Hebrew equivalents of his first and middle names.

Levi's first and most important work was *The Dogma and Ritual of High Magic*. It was followed by *A History of Magic*, *Transcendental Magic*, *The Key of Great Mysteries*, and other occult books. Levi was inspired by Francis Barrett, and in turn, he influenced occult author Sir Edward Bulwer-Lytton. They formed a London occult group which studied scrying, magick, astrology, and mesmerism. The Hermetic Order of the Golden Dawn, founded in London in 1888, adopted much of Levi's magick.

George Pickingill (1816-1909)

"Old George" Pickingill was a legendary English cunning man. Claiming descent through a line of hereditary Witches dating back to the 11th century, he was the oldest of nine children, born in the "Witch country" of Essex. Pickingill was vehemently anti-

Christian and collaborated with ceremonial magicians, Witches, Rosicrucians, and Freemasons in hopes of spreading beliefs of "the Old Religion" that would overthrow and replace the Church.

Called "Master of Witches," Pickingill terrorized the local farmers. He had Romany kin and was raised as a Gypsy, learning many practices and rituals imported from medieval Europe, including worship of the Horned God. Over 60 years, Pickingill established the "Nine Covens" in Essex, Hertfordshire, Hampshire, Norfolk, and Sussex, choosing leaders with hereditary Craft ancestry. Aleister Crowley was initiated into one of these in 1899 or 1900. Although most covens included both men and women, all rites were performed by the women. One of his covens, the Seven Witches of Canewdon, was all-female. Another was the New Forest Coven, into which Gerald Gardner was initiated.

Charles Godfrey Leland (1824-1903)

C.G. Leland was an American folklorist who wrote several classic texts on English Gypsies and Italian Witches. As a child, Leland learned Irish fairy tales from immigrant maids and Voudon from black kitchen servants. He spent summers with American Indians, learning their spiritual lore. Leland studied magick with the curiosity of a scholar and practiced it with the enthusiasm of an initiate. He was called Master by the Witches and Gypsies. He translated *The Divine Pymander of Hermes Trismegistus*.

In 1870 Leland moved to England, where he studied Gypsy culture. He developed a trusting friendship with the Gypsy King, who taught him *Romany,* the language of the Gypsies. Accepted as one of their own, Leland wrote two classic works on the Gypsies and became the founder and first president of the Gypsy Lore Society. In 1888, in Florence, Italy, Leland met a "fortune-teller" he would only refer to as "Maddelena." Learning that she was a Witch, he employed her in gathering material for his research of Italian Witchcraft, or *Stregheria.* The result of this collaboration was the publication in 1889 of *Aradia: The Gospel of Witches.* It was the first book to record specific Witchcraft spells, folklore, incantations, and lore, and it formed a basis for much of the 20th century revival of Witchcraft, particularly in America.

S. L. MacGregor Mathers (1854-1918)

Mathers was one of the most important occult figures of the late 19th century. Born in London, *Samuel Liddle Mathers* added "MacGregor" to his name to honor his descent from the Scots clan. Mathers married a clairvoyant, Moina Bergson. Moving to Paris, they founded an Ahathoor Temple and celebrated "Egyptian Masses" in honor of the goddess Isis. Together they translated an arcane manuscript on Qabalah and Tarot, publishing it as *Kabbalah Unveiled.* Mathers dedicated the book to his mentor, Dr. Anna Kingsford, leader of the Hermetic Society. Due to her influence, he became a vegetarian, non-smoker, anti-vivisectionist and women's rights activist.

Mathers claimed to have received his teachings from a group of superhuman adepts, the "Hidden and Secret Chiefs." With a letter of authorization from Fräulein Stein, an adept in one of the German Qabalistic orders, Mathers co-founded the Hermetic Order of the Golden Dawn in 1887. He wrote its rituals and became its "Visible Head." But an ego-battle and power struggle with his apprentice, Aleister Crowley, resulted in the break-up of the Order in 1900.

Able to read English, Hebrew, Latin, French, Celtic, Coptic, and Greek, Mathers translated and edited several important magickal texts. These included the *Key of Solomon* and *The Book of the Sacred Magic of Abra-Melin the Mage*, perhaps the most significant of all the medieval grimoires. But his greatest contribution lay in his establishment of a tradition of ceremonial magick—the Golden Dawn—that has become the wellspring for all Western occultism ever since.

Arthur Edward Waite (1857-1947)

A.E. Waite was born in New York but raised in London by his impoverished unwed mother. He dabbled with spiritism and Theosophy but was most influenced by the writings of Eliphas Levi, which inspired him to begin a lifelong career in the scholarly examination and popularization of occult and mystical philosophies.

Waite joined the Golden Dawn in 1891. He continued his occult writings, translating alchemical manuscripts and editing an occult journal. When the Golden Dawn broke up in 1900, Waite became a Mason and also started his own Orders: first the Rectified Order of the Golden Dawn in 1904, then the Fellowship of the Rosy Cross in 1915. Waite spent the rest of his life researching and writing on various occult and hermetic subjects, specializing in the history of Freemasonry. He was instrumental in the development of the famous Rider-Waite Tarot deck, and wrote numerous books that are still popular today.

Aleister Crowley (1875-1947)

Born the day Eliphas Levi died, *Aleister Crowley* believed himself to be the reincarnation of Levi, Cagliostro, Edward Kelly, and Pope Alexander VI. The most controversial figure in magickal history, he has been both idolized as a saint and vilified as a sorcerer. He had an enormous thirst for knowledge and power, coupled with an insatiable appetite for sex, drugs, and sensual pleasures. He joined the Golden Dawn in 1898 but was soon locked in a bitter power struggle with its founder, S.L. MacGregor Mathers, resulting in his expulsion and the breakup of the Order.

Crowley traveled widely, climbing mountains in India and studying Buddhism, Tantric Yoga, Egyptian magick, Qabalah, and Dee's Enochian magick. In 1904, his wife Rose channeled a spirit called "Aiwass," which Crowley identified as the Egyptian god Set. Through Rose, Aiwass dictated *The Book of the Law*. Its core is the *Law of Thelema* ("will"): "Do what thou wilt shall be the whole of the law." From 1909 to 1913, Crowley published the secret rituals of the Golden Dawn in his magazine *The Equinox,* infuriating Mathers and other Golden Dawn members. He lived in the U.S. from 1915 to 1919, then moved to Sicily, where he founded the notorious Abbey of Thelema. For a time he headed the *Ordo Templi Orientis*, before being deported in 1923 due to scandal as "The Wickedest Man in the World"—a title he relished, calling himself "The Great Beast 666."

In his final year, Crowley met Gerald Gardner and contributed some material to Gardner's *Book of Shadows.* A brilliant writer and poet, his several books include *Magick in Theory and Practice* (1929), considered by many to be the best book ever on ceremonial magick. In it, Crowley introduced the now common spelling of "magick" to "distinguish the science of the Magi from all its counterfeits."

Gerald Brousseau Gardner (1884–1964)

Born into a prosperous family in England, *Gerald Gardner* claimed several Witches in his family tree. In 1906, Gerald went to Ceylon as a cadet in a tea planting business. There, in 1909, he was initiated into Freemasonry. In 1912, he moved to Malaya to become a rubber planter. When the price of rubber fell in 1923, he joined the Malayan Customs & Excise Service. There he befriended the Sea Dayaks, a Malayan tribe from whom he learned their folk magic.

Returning to England in 1936, after retiring from the Service, Gerald and his wife Donna eventually settled in the New Forest region in 1939. There he joined an occult group called the Fellowship of Crotona, a Co-Mason lodge (both men and women) with three associated magickal groups: Rosicrucian (who also put on esoteric plays for the public), Theosophical, and Witchcraft reconstruction according to the ideas of Margaret Murray. Some claimed to be hereditary Witches, and "Dafo" (Elsie Woodford-Grimes), their high priestess, initiated him in 1939. She became his magickal partner for the next 15 years.

In 1946, he met Cecil Williamson, founder of the Witchcraft Research Center and Museum of Witchcraft. A year later, Arnold Crowther introduced him to Aleister Crowley. From materials obtained from Crowley, fragmentary elements from the New Forest Coven, Leland's *Aradia,* and his own collections and researches, Gardner compiled his *Book of Shadows.* Much of it he published as fiction in a novel, *High Magic's Aide* (1949). After Britain's anti-Witchcraft law was repealed in 1951, Gardner purchased Williamson's Museum. In 1953 he initiated Doreen Valiente, who substantially reworked the Book of Shadows, giving more emphasis to the Goddess. Out of this collaboration grew the Gardnerian Tradition. In 1954 Gardner published *Witchcraft Today,* supporting Murray's disputable theory of Witchcraft as the surviving remnant of old European Paganism. The book made Gardner famous and launched new covens all over England.

Gardner's last book was *The Meaning of Witchcraft* (1959). He met and initiated Raymond Buckland in 1963, just before sailing to Lebanon for the Winter. He died aboard ship on the return voyage the following Spring. Buckland brought Gardnerian Witchcraft to the United States, where it has blossomed into the Wiccan religion.

Victor Anderson (1917–2001)

Co-founder of the Feri (previously Faerie) Tradition, *Victor Anderson* was born in New Mexico and grew up in Oregon. As a child, he contracted an ailment that left him nearly blind for life—and a psychic seer. He claimed a mystical initiation at the age of nine by an old Faerie Witch woman, who introduced him to her coven of mostly Southerners. They honored "The Old Gods" and "The Old Powers," and emphasized harmony with Nature, magick, celebration, music, and ecstatic dancing.

Victor married Cora, an Alabama woman whose Christian family practiced folk magick, and they moved to the San Francisco Bay area. In 1959, they initiated a neighbor boy who later took the name Gwydion Pendderwen. Inspired by the rise of modern Witchcraft, Victor and Gwydion wrote beautifully poetic rituals for the Faerie Tradition, named for Victor's childhood Witches. It combined their "Faerie" Witchcraft with Hawaiian Huna, Vodoun, and Celtic folklore. Over the years, a number of remarkable people were trained by Victor, including Alison Harlow, Starhawk, Francesca De Grandis, Ian "Lurking Bear" Anderson, and my own beloved Morning Glory. Through these illustrious folks, the influence of the shamanic tradition now called "Feri" has been enormous.

Victor wrote a lovely book of mystical poetry, called *Thorns of the Blood Rose.*

Stewart Farrar (1916-2000)

Born in Essex, England, *Stewart Farrar* was raised as a Christian Scientist. In 1947, he embarked on a long career as a journalist and author. In 1969 his magazine, the weekly *Reveille,* assigned him to attend a press preview of the film, *Legend of Witches*, for which Alexander and Maxine Sanders, who had given technical advice, were present. Alex invited Stewart to a Witchcraft Initiation. He found the ceremony moving and wrote a feature story on it, which gained him Sanders' favor. Alex introduced Stewart to the publisher of his own biography, *King of the Witches,* whereupon Stewart got the contract for *What Witches Do*. He begun attending Sanders' training classes, and in 1970, Maxine initiated him into the coven, where he met and eventually married the vivacious Janet Owen.

In 1970, the Farrars formed their own London coven. *What Witches Do* clearly established Stewart as a voice who promoted the Wiccan community, resulting in many queries from people wishing to join the Craft. After nine years of running a coven and giving advice, the Farrars co-authored two books of ritual and non-ritual material: *Eight Sabbats for Witches* (1981) and *The Witches' Way* (1984). They also wrote *The Witches' Goddess* (1987), *Life & Times of a Modern Witch* (1987), and *The Witches' God* (1989).

Gwydion Pendderwen (1946-1982)

California-born, *Tom DeLong* met Victor Anderson at the age of 13 and was initiated into his magickal practices. Tom changed his name to *Gwydion Pendderwen,* as he was known for the rest of his life. He majored in theater in college and was a superb actor and dramatic reader. But he much preferred ritual drama, sacred poetry, and music, which he created for the Faerie Tradition that he and Victor developed. Gwydion was very active in the Society for Creative Anachronism (SCA) in its early years and became Court Bard. In 1975, he produced the magickal community's first music album: *Songs of the Old Religion.* About the same time, he purchased 55 acres of forest he called *Annwfn* (the Welsh Underworld) on Greenfield Ranch in Mendocino County, NorCalifia. I'd met Gwydion in 1972, so when Morning Glory and I moved onto the adjacent *Coeden Brith* ("speckled forest") in 1977, we all became deeply involved in creating a magickal community together on the land.

Gwydion began holding annual New Year's tree plantings to reforest the logged-over land, and these, along with Sabbats, soon grew to over 100 people. He chartered Forever Forests as a subsidiary Order of the Church of All Worlds to sponsor these events. In 1976, Gwydion traveled to the British Isles, where he met Alex Sanders and Stewart Farrar and was honored at the *Eistedffodd* (bardic assembly) in Wales. His second album, *The Faerie Shaman,* was produced in 1982, just before his tragic death in a car accident at Samhain.

3. Living Wizards & Wise Women: The Grey Council

"I am Grey. I stand between the candle and the star. We are Grey. We stand between the darkness and the light." (Delenn, B5, before the Grey Council, in "Babylon Squared")

"The Grey Council" is the legendary Council of Wizards, Mages, and Sages that has been a recurring theme through many tales and histories of Magick and Wizardry. The "Grey" in the name connotes both the notion of encompassing all shades of Magick (rather than just black and white), as well as the grey in our hair and beards that would seem to be a requisite for the experience and wisdom we bring to this Council!

Membership in the Grey Council is not fixed, but varies according to the projects and work we are doing together at any one time. At this point in history, there are more Wizards and Wise Women alive and practicing than ever before. I cannot possibly begin to list all of them. Members of the Grey Council are not just elders of the magickal community; we are also all teachers and mentors. Those indicated in bold, with bios following, have specifically participated in the creation of this Grimoire, contributing our best lessons as we pass them on to our own students and apprentices.

Current Members of the Grey Council (early 2004)

Frederic Lamond (1931-)
Raymond Buckland (1934-)
Nybor (1936-)
Nelson White (1938-2003)
Oberon Ravenheart (1942-)
Nicki Scully (1943-)
Richard Lance Christie (1944-)
Abby Willowroot (1945-)
Amber K (1947-)
Morning Glory Ravenheart (1948-)
Luc Sala (1949-)
Andras Corban-Arthen (1949-)
P.E. Isaac Bonewits (1949-)
Raven Grimassi (1951-)
Donald Michael Kraig (1951-)
Ellen Evert Hopman (1952-)
Lady Pythia (1952-)
Katlyn Breene (1953-)
Jesse Wolf Hardin (1954-)
Herman B. Triplegood (1958-)
Ian "Lurking Bear" Anderson (1959-)
Jeff "Magnus" McBride (1959-)
Trish Telesco (1960-)
Todd Karr (1965-)

Frederick Lamond (1931–) has worshipped Nature since the age of 12 when he lived in French Switzerland. At 23, he had a mystical experience in the arms of his first fiancée, and in February 1957 he was initiated into Gardnerian Witchcraft in the presence of Gerald Gardner himself. He is probably the longest continuously-practicing Wiccan in the world. He is also a member of the Fellowship of Isis and the Church of All Worlds, active in Inter-Faith activities, and attended the 1993 and 1999 Parliaments of World Religions in Chicago and Cape Town (South Africa), as well as the first Gathering of the Elders of Ancient Traditions and Cultures in Mumbai (India) in 2003. In addition to numerous articles in Pagan and Wiccan publications on both sides of the Atlantic, Frederic has written two books: *The Divine Struggle* (1990) and *Religion without Beliefs* (1997). He is currently working on *Wicca at 50, a Personal Retrospective.*

Raymond Buckland (1934–), known as "The Father of American Wicca," was the first to introduce Gardnerian Wicca to the U.S. in the early 1960s. He was born in London of Romany (Gypsy) descent. His spiritual quest led him to the works of Gerald Gardner. Buckland began serving as Gardner's spokesman in the U.S. and was initiated into the Craft shortly before Gardner's death in 1964. In the mid-1970s he founded the Saxon tradition, Seax-Wica, now practiced in countries around the world. He was also instrumental in helping spread the solitary practice of PectWita, a form of Scottish Witchcraft. He has had more than 30 titles published, including *The Witch Book* and *Buckland's Complete Book of Witchcraft.* Raymond is the *Fæder* of Seax-Wica and a member of the International Guild of Sorcerers and the International Society of Independent Spiritualists. *www.raybuckland.com.*

Nybor (Jim Odbert) (1936–) A graduate from the Minneapolis School of Art, Nybor has owned and operated art studios in Minneapolis and New York City and is most renowned for his black and white science fiction art, including book and magazine covers and interiors. In 1985, he gave up the tie, tails, and "cocktail crowd" for a humbler, more peaceful life in the West Virginia mountains where he could dedicate himself to creating the art he wanted to create. When you look at the detailed and colorful works of Nybor, you would never know that this 67-year-old artist has been colorblind since birth. *www.oakgrove.org/nybor/Nybor.html.*

Nelson White (Frater Zarathustra) (1938–2003) was active in the southern California occult scene for more than 20 years, and was instrumental in the formation and operation of several esoteric churches and magickal orders. For more than 15 years he published *The White Light,* a quarterly magazine of Ceremonial Magick. He operated a religious supply and bookstore in Pasadena for over 17 years, writing more than 125 books on Magick and other topics. Dr. White taught in a number of junior and senior high schools and was knighted by the *Alter Souveräner Templer Orden,* based in Vienna, Austria. Retired from NASA's Ames Research Center, he was a private pilot and ham radio operator, and sang in The Richmond Choir. He died just as this *Grimoire* was being completed.

Oberon Zell-Ravenheart (1942–) See p. 372 for bio and photo.

Abby Willowroot (1945–) is an archetypist, metalsmith, Goddess artist, writer, priestess, and mother and has been a practicing Pagan since the mid-1960s. Foun-der of the Goddess 2000 Project, Spiral Goddess Grove, and Willowroot Real Magic Wands, she is dedicated to putting Goddess and magickal imagery and consciousness into contemporary culture. Since 1965, Abby has been a professional Pagan and Goddess folk artist. Self-taught, she learned to follow her own muse at an early age. Abby lives and works in northern California. Her art and writing have appeared in books, museum shows, *WomanSpirit, SageWoman,* and Llewellyn publications. Nine pieces of Ms. Willow-root's jewelry are in the permanent collections of the Smithsonian Institution. *www.realmagicwands.com.*

Amber K (1947–) is a Wiccan Priestess of the Ladywoods Tradition, from the Pagan Way Tradition, out of the Gardnerian Tradition. She has served the Goddess and the Horned God for more than 24 years, in various roles: as priestess, as National First Officer of Covenant of the Goddess, as editor of Circle Network News, as a faculty member of RCG's Cella program, and currently as Executive Director of Ardantane Witch College and Pagan Learning Center in New Mexico. She is the author *of True Magick, Covencraft, Moonrise, The Pagan Kids' Activity Book, Candlemas,* and *The Heart of Tarot*. She lives and works with her partner Azrael Arynn K in among the red mesas and high desert of the Jemez Mountains, the home of Ardantane. *www.ardantane.org.*

Morning Glory Zell-Ravenheart (1948–) is a Witch, Priestess, and Goddess historian—famous for her rituals, songs, poetry, and her large collection of Goddess figurines. She met her soulmate, Oberon, at the 1973 Gnostic Aquarian Festival in Minneapolis, and they were married the following Spring. She helped produce *Green Egg* magazine and the living unicorns. She founded Mythic Images, producing museum replicas and original interpretations of ancient goddesses and gods. Morning Glory has created ceremonies of every kind and scale, from simple rites of passage to spectacular events, such as the 1979 solar eclipse at the Stonehenge replica in the Oregon Dalles. Her journeys have taken her to the Blue Mountains of Australia, the depths of the Coral Sea, the jungles of New Guinea, the ruins of ancient Greece, the caves of Crete, and the Taoist temples of China. *www.MythicImages.com.*

Luc Sala (1949–), Mage of Amsterdam, holds office in the Kalvertower at his MySTeR temple of kindness. He has been very visible in the Mundane world with his own television channel and many activities in the computer world, but also roams the other worlds under the name of *Lucifar.* He believes that "a bit is only information if it bytes" and that the science of Magick is about investigating what really touches us. Information is beyond mere data, even beyond the concept of transmitting a message; it is when we open ourselves up to that magickal realm of connectedness. The world we experience is just superficially governed by the laws of causality and reason; at a deeper level, the laws of Magick rule. Luc sees the revival of Magick and the acceptance of the consciousness dimension(s) as the major work for this century. Sala@euronet.nl.

Raven Grimassi (1951–) is the author of nine books on Witchcraft and Wicca, including the award-winning titles *The Wiccan Mysteries* and *The Encyclopedia of Wicca & Witchcraft.* Raven has been a practitioner and teacher of Witchcraft for more than 30 years. He is a popular lecturer and speaker at Pagan conventions and festivals throughout the U.S. Raven is currently the director of the Arician Tradition of Witchcraft and co-director of a Mystery school known as The College of the Crossroads. It is Raven's life work to preserve and teach the pre-Christian European roots of Pagan religion. He lives in southern California on a ranch in the countryside where he maintains a sacred grove to the Goddess and God of the Old Religion and a shrine to Ceres, the Goddess of the Mysteries, on whose festival day he was born. *www.stregheria.com.*

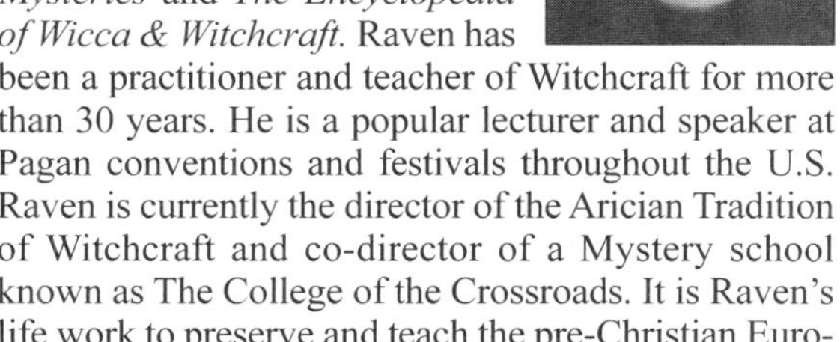

Donald Michael Kraig (1951–) graduated from UCLA with a degree in philosophy. He also studied public speaking and music at other colleges and universities. After a decade of personal study and practice, he taught courses in southern California on topics including Kabbalah, Tarot, Magick, and Tantra before writing his best-known book, *Modern Magick*, a step-by-step introduction to practical magick. His other books include *Modern Sex Magick* and *Tarot & Magic*, and his writing has appeared in numerous magazines, journals, and books. Donald has given lectures and workshops all over the U.S., has been a member of several spiritual and magickal groups, and is an initiated Tantric. He has been a professional musician, taught computer skills at USC, is a member of Hollywood's Magic Castle, and is currently studying for a doctorate in clinical hypnotherapy.

Ellen Evert Hopman (Willow) (1952–) is a Pagan author, a master herbalist, and a Druid Priestess. She is the author of several books and videos on herb craft and Druid wisdom including *Tree Medicine—Tree Magic* (on the herbal and magickal properties of trees), *A Druid's Herbal* (Druid medicine and lore of herbs), *Being A Pagan* (with Lawrence Bond, a book about what it means to be a Wiccan, a Witch, or a Druid in the world today), and *Walking The World In Wonder—A Children's Herbal* (a book of herbal formulas and recipes suitable for children of ALL ages). Her videos *Gifts From the Healing Earth,* Vol. I and II will teach you the basics of herbal healing and her video "Pagans" covers the eight festivals of the Pagan Wheel of the Year. *http://saille333.home.mindspring.com/willow.html.*

Marybeth Witt (Lady Pythia) (1952–) is an elder of the Craft and Covenant of the Goddess, having acted as a past national officer. She is a published poet, former university English teacher, and singer/songwriter (Earth Magick, Moon Magick). In serving as the High Priestess of the former Coven of the Floating Spiral, she has devoted her life to the pursuit of knowledge, compassion, and wisdom as a Witchmage in service to the Goddess and Gods and all of the children of Mother Earth. Lady Pythia has participated in many political workings for Mother Earth, including both ecological and anti-war activism throughout the country.

Katlyn Breen (1953-) has been creating sacred art, dance, and ritual for over 27 years. Her art is a manifestation of her beliefs and can be seen in places of worship around the world. She is currently the owner and creator of Mermade Magickal Arts, which makes fine hand-blended incense and oils, and she is the author and illustrator of many books on spiritual arts and folklore. She is also the co-founder/creator of the "Road to Eleusis," an initiatory and transformational retreat based on the Mysteries of ancient Greece at Eleusis (since 1991). Now in Nevada , Katlyn is the founder and Priestess of Desert Moon Circle—a spiritual community based on the Mysteries of the Sacred Wheel. Katlyn serves as an advisor to the Firedance gathering and holds degrees in several different traditions. She and her husband Michael, known as Zingaia, create techno-tantra-trance music dedicated to sacred lovers and to the Goddess in all Her many aspects. www.HeartMagic.com

Jesse Wolf Hardin (1954-) is a Gaian Wizard, contemporary spiritual teacher, artist, musician, and author of numerous books, such as *Full Circle* (1991) and *Kindred Spirits: Sacred Earth Wisdom* (2001). His two decades of public appearances have helped birth both a new Gaian theosophy and ecological ethic, resulting in recordings of spoken word and music including *The Enchantment* by GaiaTribe. Wolf's artwork and articles have united the principles of primal mindfulness, Earthen Spirituality, and personal activism like none before. He was a core columnist for *Green Egg* and currently appears in *Magical Blend, Circle Nature Spirituality Quarterly,* and *Talking Leaves*. Most of each year, Wolf is home on his enchanted New Mexico wildlife sanctuary, an ancient place of power where he teaches students, resident interns, and apprentices the art of practical magick, wildlands restoration, and Earth-centered spiritual practice. www.concentric.net/~earthway

Jeff "Magnus" McBride (1959-) For the past 30 years, Jeff has traveled the world as a performance magician and educator in ritual theater. He is especially known for his extensive magical work with masks. Jeff has been seen on many TV specials, including ABC's *Champions of Magic,* NBC's *Worlds Greatest Magic,* and PBS' *The Art of Magic,* and also on the Discovery Channel's *Mysteries of Magic,* where Jeff served as a consultant on shamanism and ritual magic. Jeff has been voted Magician of the Year by Hollywood's Magic Castle. He is also founder of The Mystery School of Magic, a yearly conference for the advanced study of magical arts. Jeff has been facilitating ritual theater events at festivals throughout the world for the past decade. www.McBridemagic.com

Ian "Lurking Bear" Anderson (1959-) says: "It has been a good life so far. I have escaped Muggle reality and I have danced with wild Witches in the moonlit hills. I have played harp in forest glades and wandered the mossy rainforest of Alaska. I have walked among ancient standing stones and climbed mountains. I have marched and taken action for causes I believe in and hitchhiked across vast distances. I am a poet, computer programmer, chaos musician, opportunistic trickster, mountain man, and spiritual explorer. My essays and poetry have appeared in *Green Egg, Green Man, Enchante,* and *Witch Eye.* I currently lurk in the mountains of far northern California."

Trish Telesco (1960-) is a mother of three, wife, chief human to five pets, and a full-time author with numerous books on the market. These include *Goddess in my Pocket, How to Be a Wicked Witch, Kitchen Witch's Cookbook, Little Book of Love Magic, Your Book of Shadows, Spinning Spells: Weaving Wonders,* and other diverse titles, each of which represents a different area of spiritual interest. Trish considers herself a down-to-earth Kitchen Witch whose love of folklore and worldwide customs flavor every spell and ritual. While her Wiccan education was originally self-trained and self-initiated, she later received initiation into the Strega tradition of Italy, which gives form and fullness to the folk magick Trish practices. Her strongest beliefs lie in following personal vision, being tolerant of other traditions, making life an act of worship, and being creative so that magick grows with you. www.loresinger.com

Todd Karr (1965-) brings a magickal sense of design to the lavish books he creates through his company, The Miracle Factory. Collaborating with artist Katlyn Breene, he has published an acclaimed series of elegant books for magicians with sales worldwide. After studies at the Sorbonne and USC, Todd wrote for the *Los Angeles Times* before moving to Paris as a full-time magician. Todd is also author of *Backyard Magic* (1996), a unique children's book of magick with nature. www.miraclefactory.org

Epilogue: Commencement

WELL, YOU'VE MADE IT ALL THE WAY THROUGH THIS GRIMOIRE, and I trust you have learned well the lessons contained therein. Congratulations! You have completed your Apprenticeship, and are now ready to begin your next phase as a Journeyman Wizard. Now I would like to offer you a few final words of wisdom from various members of the Grey Council and others, who have been your teachers throughout these lessons. Think of these as "graduation ceremony speeches"...

And to continue and deepen your education in Wizardry, as well as meet other students, go to the ***Grey School of Wizardry*** website at: http://www.GreySchool.com

Choices

By **Oberon Zell-Ravenheart**

Live each moment as if it's a scene in the movie that will someday be made of your life—for it is. When an adventure comes knocking at your door to invite you along, go for it!

Realize that great achievements involve great risk. Never forget: "With great power comes great responsibility." Make every act you do a planting of seeds. And someday you will reap the harvest... For a true Wizard always sees and keeps in mind the wider perspective, the long view—the "Big Picture."

Never stop learning. Everyone and every thing is your teacher. Especially, learn the rules so you'll know how to break them properly!

When you realize you've made a mistake (and you will!—we all do), take immediate steps to correct it. It takes true greatness to admit when you're wrong, apologize and atone. This is how we learn, and grow.

Make your decisions based on whether or not this will be something you will be proud to tell your own children someday, when they are your age. Consider—would you be proud of your own father (or mother) for doing this? Ask yourself: "Will I later regret doing this; or will I later regret *not* doing it?"

Base your choices not upon your fears, but rather your hopes. Not on what you *fear* might happen, but on what you *hope* will happen. This is the secret of living a magickal life.

The answers to life's questions lie within you. All you need to do is look within, listen to your heart, and trust in your own magick. Most often, the answer is "Yes!"

I, the Grey Council, and countless generations of Wizards before us, have provided you with knowledge and tools to change the world into a better place than you found it. Go forth now, and do so.

The power is yours. And so are the choices of how to use it.

Companions

By **Abby Willowroot**

Congratulations on selecting this book and following the lessons contained herein. You are on your way to realizing your Wizardly gifts and developing your skills. As you walk the path of a Wizard you will have essential companions on your journey. Companions who must be fed, protected and listened to. These companions are your courage, your compassion, your curiousness and your generosity. Keep yourself in the company of these fine companions, respecting and honoring them, so they can grow and become stronger each day, and you will be well on your way to becoming a Great Wizard.

Skill in the Magical Arts is essential for a Wizard, but it is in combining your skills with your companions of courage, compassion, curiosity and generosity that you will find the deeper magic that beckons the Universe to reveal its secrets to you. Listen with all your senses, See with every cell in your body, and Touch gently the true essence in all things.

Magical Blessings!

What it Takes

By **Herman B. Triplegood**

To be a High Magician, a True Wizard, a Hermetologist and Philosopher of Nature, a Mathemantician and a Thaumaturgist, I say, believe in yourself. Believe in the Power of your Threefold Magickal Action. It takes that engagement to the Kryptic Play, which follows with the Kryptic Edge of the Mytho-mantic Weave that preceded it, the Weave by which you now emerge as the Wizard that you are meant to be. All it really takes to be a Wizard is to act like one.

The Divine Fool

By **Ian Lurking Bear Anderson**

The Tarot Fool is typically shown stepping over the edge of a cliff blithely disregarding consequences or warnings. This may seem crazy, but it is an essential step in the Wizard's path. Somewhere in there, if we truly wish to live not confined by everybody else's sense of reality, we must take the fool's step into the unknown, indeed, the unknowable. There are times in the Wizard's path to be cautious, to meditate, to study, to seek visions, but these alone will not suffice to make you a true Wizard until you are ready to take the Fool's step. It may be a step outside the bounds of what has been socially acceptable, it may be a step outside of what is scientifically respectable, it may be a step outside of making enough money, or a step through any of the other boundaries we put around ourselves, sometimes without knowing.

The wise fool is able to see through the walls of illusion and walk through them. However, the Divine Fool is not merely the idiot, and it is important to have the developed intuition and magical sense to know when and where to step into the unknown. Magic by its very nature steps outside the bounds of conventional reality, and every act of true magic contains something of the unknowable, the eternally surprising, and carries some echo of the fool's step.

Graduation?

By **Raymond Buckland**

We none of us ever graduate. Even at what is termed "death" we do not finish—we move on to other dimensions and further progress. But that is the joy of life; the joy of living. There is always something new just over the horizon. Nurture your curiosity. Don't let it grow into simple idle curiosity but develop it into enquiry; investigation; experience; learning...all those things that will continue to expand your consciousness and move you ever farther along the path of life.

As a child I was a voracious reader. I read every book I could lay my hands on. But I didn't stop there. I would turn to the backs of those books and absorb the bibliographies; the lists of other works on the same and similar subjects. Then I would seek out and read those books...which, in turn, contained their own bibliographies! Life is a little like that—one thing can lead to another; one interest can spark a dozen more. One word of caution, however: don't spread yourself too thin. Don't scatter your energies too far or too fast. Learn to pace yourself. Yet the human mind is an incredible machine and can absorb and make use of far more than we could ever imagine.

This book has been a wonderful entry for you into the world of wizardry. I wish I had had access to such a book when I was a child. With the knowledge you have acquired from this work, you will always be one step ahead of your fellows. Be happy about that. Be satisfied with that. Don't flaunt your knowledge. Don't belittle those less fortunate. Modesty and a quiet self-satisfaction are always preferable to boasting and blustering. You have graduated from this book's work. You deserve a period of rest and relaxation. But then it's onward! You, me, and the rest of the Grey Council of Wizards—such as us will never rest. But that unease—that constant searching—is our life's blood. Know it, and enjoy it. Welcome to life!

The Future

By **Lady Epona**

You are the future of the Earth and the Universe beyond. While we have led you along the path of Wizards' Wisdom, we know that you will see things from a different perspective than that of your Elders. You will experience Magick in different dimensions from what we have experienced; for perspective and dimension are the constructs of Time. We give you what we have learned, it is up to you to take this knowledge into the Future.

Love and Respect the Earth and Her creatures;
Be true to Yourself;
Love one another;
Live Long and Prosper;
and Above All Else—LAUGH!

Bright Blessings upon you,!

The Real Secret

By **Luc Sala**

The path of the Wizard looks like a glorious one, gaining understanding of the deeper processes and interactions of mind and nature and achieving some kind of mastery over reality. This however, is only the surface. The deeper lesson one learns on this path is that of humbleness, of not being different. The simple farmer, the beggar, the stranger that smiles at you, might be a far greater magician than you if he or she has mastered the magic of happiness and love—the greatest art of all.

The powers of the mind as liberated, focused and harnessed by visualization, ritual and concentration are awesome, but don't abuse them and don't claim them as yours. You are only the channel, the vessel, and if you really look around you will notice that there is magic all around you. Becoming a magician is mostly becoming aware and conscious of what is already there, discovering the connections and correspondences between the inner and outer worlds and forever bridging them anew. It's a never-ending path and I'd like to share its most important lesson:

I am only different, as I have not yet learnt to be the same. For being the same, overcoming the barriers, connecting and loving is the real secret of the Craft.

Living the Magick

By **Donald Michael Kraig**

I invite you to pause and take a breath. If you have followed this course of study through to the end, if you have successfully done all of the assignments, if you have completed each task, you deserve high praise. For the truth is, many will start down this road, but few will finish it. As one of the few, you deserve to bask in the glory that is rightfully yours and feel pride in your accomplishments. Pause and breathe while you feel the accolades. Dream about it tonight.

And then you will wake up tomorrow. You will still have that "other" school to attend. You'll still have to deal with friends who want to dump their problems on you, with some teachers who do not treat you with respect, with others who tell you what to do without giving you a valid reason. You still will have to deal with a world that at times seems hostile and cruel.

But now, you have a powerful technology for dealing with this. The techniques you have learned, the magick you have mastered, will let you be at peace and feel balanced when others seem to be crazy. If you use these techniques and live the life of a Wizard, you will have the ability to study more effectively, relate to people more easily, and even deal more readily with the onerous tasks you sometimes have to do.

The course of study you have followed through to the end is absolutely useless...unless you put it to use. Not on a festival day. Not on a weekend. Not when you have the time. It is only useful if you use it. Every day. When you do, you will discover that magick really isn't something you *do,* it's something that you *are.* The way you walk, talk, think, and act will be magickal.

Friends and people you meet will become amazed by the power you have. And you will have learned a big secret. It is useless to strive for power over others. It is far more important to have power over yourself. When you have such power—power to achieve whatever you want while harming none and taking nothing from them—you will truly be strong, independent, and free.

Those are the indications of a real Wizard.

Gifts

By **Ellen Evert Hopman**

Now that you have read this book my hope is that you will use its wisdom to deepen your awareness of the mystery of life that is all around you. The elements of Earth, Air, fire, Water and Spirit are found in different combinations in everything you see and touch on this planet.

You are continually surrounded by life, from the smallest insects, algae and mosses, to the largest whales, elephants and oak trees. Nature has surrounded you with everything you need; with natural remedies for your health and with wild foods for your stomach. She has given you clean air to breathe and clear rivers to drink from. My hope is that you will always appreciate these gifts with reverence and awe.

May you never forget the Land Spirits who toil throughout the year to bring you these miracles, nor the Great Spirit that encompasses all of life, all lives, in the universes.

Blessings on your reading, blessings on your journey, blessings on your future work.

"To Know, to Will, to Dare, to be Silent"

by **Raven Grimassi**

You begin your Path now, carrying with you the knowledge that has been shared, passed, and entrusted. But know that there is a difference between knowledge and realization. Knowledge allows you to see, and it provides you with options. But it does not compel one to action. You can sit on a railroad track with the knowledge that a train is coming, and still take no action. But once you realize that if you don't move then the train is going to run you over, you will be overwhelmingly compelled to take action. Therefore, understand that knowledge and realization operate in two distinct ways. Knowledge allows consideration and reflection, but realization calls for action.

As you journey from this day forward it is my hope, and my wish, that the tools you have honed through your studies will bring you to many realizations. You have heard that the axiom "to know, to will, to dare, to be silent" are the words of the Magical Master. To possess knowledge you must do more than satisfy mere curiosity. To satisfy knowledge you must study not only the concept but those things that relate to the concept. To will, you must endure without yielding to defeat or discouragement. You must discern your path and then walk it despite its obstacles. To dare, you must be willing to accept the risks of disfavor and mistreatment that others will seek to burden you with. You must remain true to the path you walk regardless of whether the road is smooth or covered with pits and jagged rocks. To be silent, you must simply speak your truths without pretension or vanity.

So I encourage you to realize who and what you are. I encourage you to be a Wizard, not just in mind or intellect, but also in heart and spirit. In every Age there are those who make a difference. As you walk this noble Path, bring this difference to others and to the world. I envy you the days ahead; it shall be a glorious adventure!

The Path of the Mage

By **Lady Pythia**

The life of a Mage is one of eternal questioning—How do things work? Who am I? Why am I here? What is my true reason for studying magicks?

I offer you the motto that was carved upon the entrance to the Oracle of Delphi— This Maxim is one of the most important in the study of all of the Magicks, and a guide through all of the Magickal Paths:

"KNOW THYSELF"

Within these two simple words is the greatest guide for your studies, not only here, but in all of life...for they relate to another of Magick's greatest sayings:

"AS ABOVE, SO BELOW"

To that, you can extrapolate, as within, so without. You will find the universe within you. This book has given you many tools which you may use upon your journey, but eventually, even the tools will become just sacred extensions of ways you will think and relate to the world, manners in which you will learn not only cause and effect, but also the great responsibility which comes from how all people, magickal or mundane, use their personal power.

We are here not just to serve ourselves, but to serve humanity. When we forget that, and use power over others without regard for how it will affect them, the Law of Return guarantees that we will learn what it is to be treated in the same manner. We ask that you always remember the spark of the Divine, the principle of Life within all persons and beings, and within all of Nature.

May you learn, as all of us have, that every time you think you've "got" it, that the universe will remind you that you have ever so much more to learn. And what a joy THAT is!! We are all eternal scholars, for the pursuit of knowledge of all the Magicks, and the world, of Nature and her Elements, is endless.

Be humble in your path, which doesn't mean being a doormat. Learn when compromise is essential—do not let pride be a shield behind which you hide your human vulnerabilities and fears of inadequacy—for true pride is silently acknowledging what you are and are becoming—not how much "Power" you or others believe you have. And Compassion will be one of your most powerful tools for seeing into the heart of things, including yourself.

Keep alive the Child within you, for that child-self will allow you to be ever curious and filled with joy and wonder at new discoveries!

Above all, we are here to serve in the evolution of human consciousness, beyond the study of the mind and its abilities—a field which is growing incredibly in your lifetime. We are merely the Forerunners of those who are yet to come.

You may be one of those for whom our Paths have been readying the ever-changing world. As you examine the different planes, and imagine yourself holding this delicate and beautiful swirling blue planet, hold Her gently. May you be a caretaker for Mother Earth, for She greatly needs all of us—and She is in your hands, more so than all the other worlds and layers of reality you will explore. Stay connected to and cherish the roots you send into Her, even as you travel afar on the Planes.

May you come to Know Yourself. It is a lifelong journey, and may the Guardians of Wisdom that inhabit the Astral, and the Planes of Magick, guard your questing spirit as you journey to discover the Universe and its mirror within your own Heart, Mind, Soul, and Body. Never forget that laughter banishes fear, and is a necessary tool in life and Magick! You are on a wonderful journey! Treasure all of it, even the hard times—for you may gain your greatest strength from those lessons!

And as you age, and grow, may you know love, a most sacred gift of being human. Enjoy! Drink Deeply! And may you never hunger or thirst upon your journey as the Fool, the first card of the Tarot—who becomes, at the end of the Major Arcana, The World, the Universe, the Multiverse!! Study them, and you will see the path of the Mage!

Blessed Be!!

Crossroads

By **Morning Glory Zell-Ravenheart**

When you picked up this book and began to read it, a Gateway opened between the Worlds of the Magickal and the Mundane. This is the book that you always wished for, containing the genuine knowledge possessed by great Wizards. Now that you possess some of this knowledge for yourself, and you have completed the First Level, a challenge lies before you—because all the knowledge in the world is completely useless without action and experience.

You stand at the Crossroads of Initiation into the Mystery. With your mind's eye, look down and you will see a Magickal Blade lying in the center of the road. Pick it up. This Knife represents Choice and it is your birthright. It will always be yours. You cannot even throw it away because "not choosing" is still a choice. This Knife is subtle; having two edge, it cuts both ways.

To wield this Knife effectively, you must hone your Magickal Will by practicing the lessons learned in this book. To use the Blade wisely, listen to your heart and your dreams. But most of all, remember to allow Love to be a part of each conscious choice that you make. Because ultimately, when you use the Knife of Choice to divide this from that, and to cut away the stuff that doesn't really matter, you will find that it is Love which lies at the Heart of every true Mystery.

Expect a Miracle

By **Jesse Wolf Hardin**

Wizardry is not only an escape from the oppressiveness of the ordinary and "normal." It is reengagement with self and Spirit, purpose and place— the beginning of a lifelong assignment.

Magic isn't about indulging the self, but transforming the world. Likewise, responsibility isn't obligation— it's the willingness and ability to respond.

You have dreams you hardly share with anyone. Now it's time to live those dreams!

Every moment is a decisive moment, and our future is a blank canvas. The only things standing in the way are those habits we're attached to, and the fears we deny. No one is in charge of your life but you! The wand is in your hand....

Having toys is not the same as having fun. Focus on sports where you actually get to play. Swim in chemical-free water, and in places where you're "not supposed to be." Walk barefoot through clover. Cry, laugh and sing. Hug and howl!

Nothing is accomplished by avoiding new experiences. Taste the many diverse flavors of life, being sure to spit out the bad.

Try to remember that "making a living" isn't the same as really living. Find work that reflects not only your skills, but also your beliefs. Watching adventure stories on the television is a poor substitute for having adventures yourself. There are just so many hours between birth and death... spend them carefully, on what matters most. Ideally you will discover, and then fulfill your most meaningful purpose.

The point isn't to gather riches, but for us to have a richer life. Watch out for any solutions that can either be sold or bottled, and any intermediary standing between you and the experience of Gaia, God and Goddess.

Travel and explore as much of the world as possible. This will not only make you familiar with other bioregions and other kinds of lifestyles, but it will also help you appreciate any place you ever call home.

Never take anything for granted— not your health, your home or your family. Never say "whatever," because it means that you don't care, and you know very well you do! Neither our problems or the problems of the world, are caused by feeling too much. Rather, they're caused by us feeling too little! By opening up to the pain of conscious existence, we open ourselves up to the experience of joy.

Bravely explore anything and everything that increases the depth of sensation and the totality of Spirit, leading you through empathy into true connection and power. You are a part of the seamless universe as much as your hand is a part of your arm. All of creation is sacred, and thus so are you.

It would be wise to avoid any drugs, careers or lifestyles that deaden your awareness, or that impair your crucial and timely response. Be suspicious of anything that requires fossil fuels, brags about being "disposable," admits to having been artificially colored or flavored, or pretends to be something it's not. And pay attention, for goodness sake! Focus solely on your sweetheart when you're with him or her, and on no other food than that food which you're eating. Remember that nothing is worth anything, unless it's authentic!

All events, both good and bad, are valuable lessons we should be grateful for. Avoid stubbing your toe on the same rock twice. And don't fritter away too much precious time explaining your mistakes. Just learn from them, and go on!

Develop a personal wizard code of honor, and then live up to it! Promise your allegiance to your friends, your family, your community, your cause, and the land you love. And always keep your promises.

All the world is a great gifting cycle. Learn to give all you can. And just as importantly, learn how to graciously accept every gift that comes your way.

Take time to "be little" even if you think you're at an age when you need to be "wise" or "cool." Crawl around on the ground after interesting bugs, look for animal shapes in the clouds, and don't worry if you get grass stains on your clothes!

Find divine Creation and your place in it in every blade of grass, in every home's backyard. But don't forget to make pilgrimages to truly wild places. Open up to the information and inspiration they provide, and subject yourself to the solitude that teaches we're never truly alone.

Expose every harmful illusion or lie. Whatever is real and good, protect and nourish with all your might.

There is no one who will do the vital work for you, and thus there's nobody else to blame! Both the responsibilities and the rewards are yours. Take credit! Then give thanks....

Remember that it's never "too late," so long as you start right now.

Expect a miracle. That miracle is you.

So Mote It Be!

Appendix A. History of Magick Time-Line

BCE (Before Common Era)

800,000 Acheulian "Venus" figurine is oldest known sculpture—a stone female image, made by Neanderthals.

75,000 Earliest human (Neanderthal) altars reveal evidence of cave bear, wolf, and other animal cults.

60,000 Huge volcanic eruption in Sumatra reduces entire global human population to only a few thousand.

30,000 "Venus" of Willendorf is sculpted of limestone and stained with red ocre, becoming the prototype for a whole new art form lasting over 20,000 years.

23,000 "Crooked Fox" or "S'Armuna," a Shaman, lives and dies in a little village of mammoth-hunters in the present Czech Republic. Her skeleton, portraits, beads of ceramic and shells, bone flutes, her totem animal (arctic fox), the last firing in her kiln (the first known, filled with small animal and "Venus" figurines), even her fingerprints in the clay, are all preserved.

15,000 Cro-Magnon Cave paintings throughout France and Spain depict animals, hunters, and handprints.

c.8500 Riss Ice Age comes to an abrupt end with an asteroid impact in the Bahamas. Melting of the ice raises sea levels 400 feet, causing vast flooding worldwide. All coastal communities drowned. This event is remembered in legend as the destruction of Atlantis.

c.8000 Jericho, oldest known Neolithic city, settled. Harappan culture begins in Northern India along the Saraswati River.

c.6000 Cave drawings in Catal Huyuk (modern Turkey) depict hunters draped in leopard skins.

c.5150 Still-rising sea levels cause the Mediterranean to spill into and fill the Black Sea. The sudden flooding raises water levels by over 500 feet, and inundates 60,000 square miles of inhabited land. This event is remembered in legend as the *Deluge*—the Flood of Noah and Utnapishtim.

c.5000 Oldest known male fertility statue (Germany).

c.4800 Oldest known megalithic monument (Brittany).

c.3500 Beginning of Sumerian Civilization.

c.3000 Beginning of Egyptian Civilization. Accurate calendar based on stellar observation devised.

c.3000–2500 Height of Harappan culture, covering over 300,000 square miles. Population of city of Sindh is as big as all Egypt. Practices include astrology, *feng shui,* herbalism, medicine, magick.

c.2900–2600 Callanish stone circle built in Scotland.

c.2800 First pyramids begun in Egypt.

c.2700 Gilgamesh rules in Uruk, Sumeria, on the Euphrates River. *Epic of Gilgamesh* tells his story.

2630 Imhotep, the world's first doctor, as well as priest, scribe, sage, poet, astrologer, architect and Wizard.

c.2500–1628 "Minoan" Civilization in Crete and Cyclades. Snake Goddess/Priestess at Knossos.

c.2400 Construction of Stonehenge begins in England.

c.2000 Founding of Gaea's Oracle of Dodona in Greece, at the foot of Mt. Tomaros. Planting of Sacred Oak.

1628 Moses goes before the Pharaoh of Egypt to demand release of the Hebrew slaves. The Exodus follows.

1628 Volcanic Island of Kallisti (now known as Thera) **north of Crete, explodes,** ending the high Bronze Age in the eastern Mediterranean. This event is conflated with the impact c.8500 to create a "Legend of Atlantis" involving elements of both.

1628–1618 "War in Heaven;" "Battle of the Titans."

15th Century Aryan Invasion; ascension of Sky-Gods.

1478 23-day Kurukshetra war between the Kauravas and Pandavas (India), described in *Mahabarata.*

15th C. Saraswati river dries up. Harappan culture disappears.

13th Century Zeus becomes established as patron deity at Oracle of Dodona.

1367–1350 Pharoah Akhnaten introduces monotheistic worship of the Aten (Sun) into Egypt.

c.1264 The Argosy—Jason's Quest of the Golden Fleece.

1220–1210 Trojan War. Mycenaean Greeks sack Troy.

1210–1200 The Odyssey (voyage of Odysseus from Troy to his home in Ithaca, Greece).

c.1000 Etruscan civilization arises in Italy. Etruscans are famed throughout the world for their knowledge of magick, divination, and philosophy.

c.1000 Milesians come to Ireland, conquer Tuatha.

950–928 Solomon reigns as King of Israel. He flourishes in legend as a master magician, comanding the *Djinn.*

850 Carthage founded by Elissa, princess of Tyre.

753 Founding of Rome by twins Romulus and Remus.

700 Celtic civilization emerges in Austria; the so-called Hallstatt culture. Emergence of Celtic language.

551 Birth of Confucius in China. Buddha and Lao Tzu are contemporaries.

500 Brythonic Celts reach Britain. Druids emerge as a religious and intellectual caste.

500–450 End of Halstatt Era, Beginning of La Tène: Heroic Age Celts. Era of many mythologies.

460–429 Reign of Pericles of Athens: "Golden Age of Greece"—philosophers and playwrights flourish.

420 Cult of Asklepios, God of health and father of medicine, is introduced to Athens by Sophocles.

387 Celtic Gauls defeat Romans at Alia. Brennus' Sack of Rome.

325 Alexander the Great (356-323) conquers entire known world, establishes Macedonian Empire; Greek culture expands into Italy, Egypt, Persia, India.

280 "Pyrrhic Victory." Pyrrhus, King of Epirus in Greece, defeats Romans in battle at Heraclea.

279 Celts invade Greece, through Macedonia, and plunder Temple of Delphi.

264–241 1st Punic War between Rome and Carthage.

214 Construction begun on Great Wall of China.

186 Bacchanalia, Roman version of Greek Dionysia, is outlawed by the Senate due to its licentiousness.

168–165 Maccabean Revolt of Jews against the Greeks.

167 Greece: In retaliation for Pyrrhic Victory of 280, Roman Consul Lucius Aemilius Paulus burns 70 cities of Epirus in 3rd Macedonian War, including ancient Oracles of Dodona and Necromantaeon.

61 Julius Caesar (100-44) conquers Brigantium, breaks

Celtiberian resistance.

51–50 Caesar pacifies Gaul, then destroys 220 "crystal ships" of the Celtiberian Alliance in great sea battle.

4 Zoroastrian *Magi* make pilgrimage from Persia to Bethlehem to offer gifts to the newborn Jesus.

CE (Common Era)

29 Crucifixion of Jesus; dawn of Christianity.

43 Roman Invasion of Britain. From 43-409 Rome dominates Britain and parts of Wales.

30–97 Apollonius Tyaneus greatest Wizard of 1st century.

50–60 Simon Magus, prominent "miracle-worker," has magickal contests with the Apostle Peter.

61 Druid strongold at Anglesey destroyed by Romans; Suetonius Paulinus defeats Iceni (Boudiccea's Rebellion).

63 Joseph of Arimathea comes to Glastonbury on first Christian mission to Britain, bringing Holy Grail.

70 Romans destroy Jerusalem, level great Temple. Jewish Diaspora begins.

122–128 73-mile-long Hadrian's Wall erected across northern England to mark Roman frontier.

150 Celts conquered by the Romans. Britain and Gaul come under Roman rule.

c.250 Saxons begin raiding east coast of Britain.

313 Constantine (r. 312-337) legalizes Christianity in Roman Empire.

c.350 Christianity reaches Ireland.

361 Paganism is outlawed in Roman Empire.

361–363 Emperor Julian the Apostate attempts to revive Pagan religion in Roman Empire. He is defeated.

392 Sacred Oak of Zeus at Dodona cut down and Oracle closed by Christian Emperor Theodosios.

394 Theodosios closes Oracle of Delphi; prohibits cult of Apollo and celebration of Pythian games.

395 Alaric the Goth demolishes Demeter's temple at Eleusis, ending the annual celebration of the Eleusinian Mysteries after 1,600 years.

410 Roman withdrawal from Britain. Emperor Honorius tells the British they're on their own.

415 Martyrdom of Hypatia and burning of the great Library of Alexandria, Egypt.

432 Arrival of Padraig (St Patrick) in Ireland.

445 Vortigern comes to power in Britain.

455 Rome sacked by Vandals. End of Western Empire.

460–470 Ambrosius takes control of pro-Roman faction and British resistance effort; leads Britons in years of fighting with Saxons.

481 *Artorius Roithamus* (Arthur) (465-537) becomes High King of Britain. He is 15, and his mentor and counselor is the Wizard Myrddin (Merlin).

485–496 Saxon incursion stemmed by King Arthur in 12 battles. Arthur finally defeats Saxons at Mount Baden.

537 Arthur is killed at the Battle of Camlann, and buried in Avalon (Glastonbury).

540 Small comet or asteroid collides with Earth, ushering in the Dark Ages. Records in Europe coincide with those in China, reporting winter conditions that envelop the world for 18 months.

622 *Al Hajira,* "the flight;" start of Moslem era.

c.790 Raiding and colonization of British Isles by Vikings begins.

900 *Canon Episcopi*—most important legal document of early Middle Ages re: Witchcraft.

1014 Battle of Clontarf: Vikings are expelled from Ireland by Brian Boru. They withdraw from Celtic nations everywhere soon thereafter.

1054 "Great Schism" divides Roman and Eastern churches.

1066 Battle of Hastings. Normans under William the Bastard invade and conquer England.

1095–1244 Crusades

1095–1099 1st Crusade; Godefroi captures Jerusalem.

1099 Priory of Sion founded in Jerusalem by Godefroi.

1145–1148 2nd Crusade; meets with defeat.

1187 Pope Gregory VIII announces 3rd Crusade.

1189 Richard crowned king of England.

1199 Richard the Lionhearted killed in the 3rd Crusade. His brother, John, becomes king.

1215 King John forced to sign the *Magna Carta* ("Great Charter"), ending "Divine Right of Kings."

1227–1736 "The Burning Times"

1227 Pope Innocent III issues a bull to establish the Inquisition.

1233 Germany: Law introduced to encourage conversion rather than burning of Witches.

1233 Pope Gregory IX issues a bull decreeing that Inquisitors would be answerable only to the Pope.

1244 Combined force of Turkish and Egyptian Muslims recaptures Jerusalem. End of Crusades.

1258 1st Papal bull against black magick issued by Pope Alexander IV.

1311 Pope Clement persuaded by Philip IV of France to suppress the Order of the Knights Templar.

1324 An Irish coven led by Dame Alice Kyteler is tried by the Bishop of Ossory for worshipping a non-Christian god. Kyteler is saved by her rank but her followers are burned. Her servant, Petronella de Meath, is executed in Ireland's first Witch burning.

1331 Pope John XXII issues 4th Witchcraft bull.

1390 First documentation of the Masonic Fraternity in the Regius Poem.

1431 Joan of Arc, accused as a Witch, is officially condemned and burned at the stake as a heretic.

1471 Marcilio Ficino translates *The Hermetica* from Greek into Latin. Its impact on Renaissance philosophy is enormous.

1484 Pope Innocent VIII's Bull against Witches.

1486 German monks Heinrich Cramer & Jacob Sprenger publish *Malleus Maleficarum* ("The Witch Hammer") providing detailed instructions for the horrific persecution of Witches.

1506 Cornelius Agrippa founds secret society devoted to astrology, alchemy, magick and Qabalah.

1563 England: A new statute against Witchcraft, ordering death penalty for Witches, enchanters, and sorcerers issued under Elizabeth I. John Dee is Court Wizard.

1588 Invading Spanish Armada is sunk off English Channel by a sudden storm raised by Witches of England.

1584 *The Discoverie of Witchcraft,* by Reginald Scott.

1597 James VI of Scotland publishes his *Daemonologie.*

1604 Elizabeth I dies; James I ascends the throne. He repeals 1563 anti-Witchcraft law, replacing it with a stricter statute which remains in effect until 1736.

1600s Some European Pagans flee to the New World, ally with Native Americans whose practices and beliefs are similar to their own. Many settle in Appalachia, begin "Pow-Wow" traditions.
1611 *The Tempest,* by William Shakespeare (1564–1616).
1623 Paris, France: Order of the Rosy Cross (Rosicrucians) established.
1627 Quincy, Mass: Thomas Morton (1579–1647) celebrates first Beltane (May Day) in America with 80-foot Maypole and Pagan festivities at Ma-re Mount settlement. He is immediately arrested by Puritans.
1634 Father Urbain Grandier found guilty of bewitching nuns in Loudoun, France ("Devils of Loudoun").
1641 Massachusetts General Counsel enacts bill to give "more particular direction in the execution of the laws against Witchcraft." It remains in effect until 1695.
1659 Massachusetts Bay Colony Puritans ban Christmas celebrations as too Pagan.
1662 Royal Academy established in England; declares separation of "science" from "magick."
1692 The trial of a Livonian werewolf, an old man in his 80s, takes place at Jurgensburg.
1692 Infamous Salem Witch Trials in Massachusetts. 141 innocent people are arrested; 20 of them are executed on bogus charges of Witchcraft.
1696 Official Confession of Error by jurors of Salem Witch Trials.
1717 Ancient Druid Order of the Universal Brotherhood founded by John Tolland.
1717 Four of the "old" Masonic Lodges meet in London on June 24 to form first Grand Lodge of England.
1736 The 1601 Witchcraft Act is replaced by the English Witchcraft Act, based on premise there were no such things as magick and Witchcraft, and anyone claiming such powers was a fraud.
1776 Order of the Illuminati formed in Bavaria. Ben Franklin and George Washington are members.
1787 Final Witchcraft laws repealed in Austria.
1792 First Druidic/Bardic *gorsedd* is established by Iolo Morgannwg (Edward Williams). This leads to the founding of Bardic/Druidic *Eistedfoddau* in Wales.
1875 The Theosophical Society is founded by Helena Blavatski, Henry Steele Olcott, and others.
1888 Hermetic Order of the Golden Dawn is formed.
1889 C.G. Leland publishes *Aradia, Gospel of Witches.*
1889-1990 Aleister Crowley is said to have been initiated into one of Pickingill's Nine Covens.
1893 1st Parliament of the World's Religions in Chicago.
1900 Crowley breaks into Golden Dawn temple and steals documents, catalyzing demise of Golden Dawn.
1904 *Ordo Templi Orientis* (OTO) is founded.
1904 Crowley's wife, Rose, channels a spirit called "Aiwass," who dictates *The Book of the Law.*
1908 Winston Churchill is initiated into the Albion Lodge of Druids.
1909 George Pickingill, legendary English Cunning Man, dies, having established the Nine Covens over 60 yrs.
1921 Margaret Murray publishes *The Witch Cult in Western Europe,* which later inspires Gerald Gardner.
1924 Aleister Crowley is elected head of the OTO.
1925 OTO splits over the issue of accepting Crowley's *Book of the Law* as authoritative.
1925 *Secret Teachings of All Ages,* by Manly Palmer Hall.
1938 The Long Island Church of Aphrodite is founded by Rev. Gleb Botkin. First Pagan church in U.S.
1939 Gerald Gardner is initiated by claimed hereditary Witches who meet in the New Forest.
1940 17 Witches (men & women) meet in the New Forest to repel a wartime invasion by Hitler (Aug. 1).
1947 Aleister Crowley meets Gerald Gardner, contributes to his *Book of Shadows*, then dies.
1947 Paul Foster Case publishes *The Tarot.*
1948 Robert Graves publishes *The White Goddess.*
1949 Gerald Gardner publishes *High Magick's Aid.*
1950 The Great Oak Forest Celtic College of Broceliande founded by Goff ar Steredennou.
1951 The English Witchcraft Act is repealed, and replaced with the Fraudulent Mediums Act.
1954 Gerald Gardner publishes *Witchcraft Today,* inspiring many, including Victor Anderson.
1958 Frederick Adams founds the Hesperian Fellowship.
1961 Order of Bards, Ovates and Druids founded in England.
1961 Robert A. Heinlein publishes germinal science-fiction novel, *Stranger in a Strange Land.*
1962 Inspired by *Stranger in a Strange Land*, Tim Zell and Lance Christie found a water-brotherhood called Atl—antecedent to the Church of All Worlds (April 7).
1962 First Gardnerian Witchcraft coven formed in America by Ray and Rosemary Buckland.
1962 Reformed Druids of North America (RDNA) founded at Carleton College.
1962 *A History of Secret Societies*, by Arkon Daraul.
1963 Total eclipse of Sun across central US (July 20).
1964 *Bewitched* debuts on ABC-TV, introducing lovable Witch Samantha Stevens.
1964 *The Waxing Moon* begins publishing in England.
1966 Church of Satan founded by Anton LaVey.
1966 Society for Creative Anachronism (SCA) founded.
1966 Gene Roddenberry launches *Star Trek* on NBC-TV.
1967 Church of All Worlds (CAW) becomes first modern group to adopt the designation "Pagan."
1967 Frederick Adams founds Feraferia ("Wild Festival").
1968 Church of All Worlds (CAW) incorporates in MO. Founder Tim Zell begins publishing *Green Egg.*
1968 Gavin & Yvonne Frost found Church & School of Wicca.
1968 Sybil Leek publishes *Diary of a Witch.*
1968 The Council of Themis is formed by Tim Zell of CAW and Frederick Adams of Feraferia. It is the first Pagan ecumenical council, with 12 member groups.
1968 New Reformed Orthodox Order of the Golden Dawn (NROOGD) founded at San Francisco Univ.
1969 Pagan Way founded by Joseph Wilson, Tony Kelly, Ed Fitch, John Scorer, and a few others, to provide an accessible Wiccan Tradition with no formal initiation or membership requirements.
1970 Total eclipse of Sun across central U.S. (March 7).
1970 First Earth Day (April 22).
1970 First public Witch-In held by Witches International Craft Associates (WICA) in NYC's Central Park.
1970 Church of All Worlds becomes first Pagan church to

receive religious 501(c)(3) exemption from IRS.

1970 Egyptian Church of Eternal Source is founded.

1970 24-volume *Encyclopedia of Man, Myth & Magic,* edited by Richard Cavendish.

1970 John Scorer and Doreen Valiente found British Witchcraft Research Association, subsequently renamed the Pagan Federation in 1971.

1970 Paul Huson publishes *Mastering Witchcraft.*

1970 On Sept 6, Tim Zell has profound Vision of Gaea; writes "TheaGenesis: The Birth of the Goddess."

1971 Patricia Crowther's radio show, *A Spell of Witchcraft,* airs in Britain.

1971 Isaac Bonewits publishes *Real Magick.*

1971 William Gray publishes *Magical Ritual Methods.*

1971 Susan Roberts publishes *Witches U.S.A.*

1972 *Asatru* is officially recognized as a religion by the government of Iceland.

1972 Llewellyn begins publishing *Gnostica News.*

1973 Ray Buckland founds Seax-Wicca Tradition.

1973 Alison Harlow purchases *Coeden Brith,* a 220-acre Pagan sanctuary in NorCalifia.

1974 Adoption of *The 13 Principles of Wiccan Belief* by the Council of American Witches at Gnostic Aquarian Festival in St. Paul, MN. Tim Zell & Morning Glory are married in public ceremony.

1974 Circle Network founded by Selena Fox & Jim Alan.

1974 *WomanSpirit* magazine begins publishing.

1974 Zsuanna Budapest arrested in Los Angeles and later convicted for fortune-telling. Z publishes *The Feminist Book of Lights and Shadows.*

1975 Covenant of the Goddess is founded.

1975 Glainn Sidhe Order of Witches founded in Mass. by Andras Corben-Arthen.

1975 Fellowship of Isis established by Lawrence & Pamela Durdin-Robertson and Olivia Robertson.

1975 Gwydion Pendderwen establishes *Annwfn,* a 55-acre Pagan sanctuary adjacent to Coeden Brith. A great bard, he also produces the magickal community's first music album: *Songs of the Old Religion.*

1975 Michael Aquino breaks from Anton LaVey's Church of Satan, founds Temple of Set for black magick.

1976 Midwest Pagan Council formed.

1977 Zells move onto Coeden Brith for next 8 yrs.

1978 Blue Star Wiccan tradition founded in Pennsylvania by Frank "The Wizard" Dufner & Tzipora Katz.

1978 1st Goddess Conference at UC Santa Cruz, CA.

1978 Abby Willowroot creates Spiral Goddess figure.

1979 Largest magickal ritual in modern times celebrates total Solar eclipse (Feb. 26) at Stonehenge replica in Washington state, attended by over 3,000 people. Rites are conducted by Tim & Morning Glory Zell, Isaac Bonewits, Anodea Judith, Margot Adler, Alison Harlow, others. Zell takes the name "Otter."

1979 Margot Adler publishes *Drawing Down the Moon,* first full history of the modern Pagan resurgence.

1979 Starhawk publishes *The Spiral Dance.*

1979 Circle Sanctuary founded by Selena Fox & Jim Alan.

1979 Aquarian Tabernacle Church founded in Seattle by Pete Pathfinder Davis.

1979 First Rites of Spring festival in Mass.

1980 Lancelot and Bedivere, the first modern living Unicorns, created by Otter & Morning Glory Zell.

1980 Reclaiming Tradition founded in San Francisco by Starhawk & Diane Baker.

1980 Selena Fox begins publishing *Circle Network News.*

1980 First Pan-Pagan festival.

1980 First Starwood festival by ACE near Cleveland, OH.

1981 First Pagan Spirit Gathering sponsored by Circle.

1982 Goddess Rising conference in Sacramento, CA.

1983 *Ar nDraiocht Fein* (A Druid Fellowship) founded by Isaac Bonewits.

1984 Otter Zell mounts diving expedition to New Guinea to solve mystery of local Mermaids, called "Ilkai."

1985 Witchcraft is legally recognized in the US. District Court of Virginia rules that Witchcraft falls within a recognizable religious category and is therefore protected by the Constitution.

1986 *Buckland's Complete Book of Witchcraft,* by Ray Buckland.

1987 Anne Niven begins publishing *Sagewoman* magazine.

1988 Otter Zell resurrects *Green Egg* after 11 years hiatus.

1988 Adoption of Morning Glory's *Earth Religion Anti-Abuse Resolution,* with over 100 signatory groups.

1990 20th anniversary of Earth Day (April 22) results in significant participation by Pagan groups.

1992 Church of All Worlds becomes first non-Christian Church to be legally recognized in Australia.

1993 2nd Parliament of the Worlds Religions held in Chicago. Many Pagan representatives attend.

1994 Otter Zell is given new name of Oberon.

1995 Several rural Pagan sanctuaries founded: Camp Gaia, Brushwood, Mother Rest Sacred Grove, Heartspring, Four Quarters Farm.

1996 The Witches Voice (www.witchvox.com) goes online, founded by Fritz and Wren Walker.

1997 J.K. Rowling writes *Harry Potter & the Philosopher's Stone,* beginning a seven-book (& movie) saga.

1998 "Pagan Pride Day" established by Cecylyna & Dagonet Dewr. It soon becomes a national event.

1998-2001 "Goddess 2000 Project" founded by Abby Willowroot, unites over 20,000 Pagans from 52 countries in creating sacred Goddess Art.

1998 Oberon Zell creates The Millennial Gaia statue.

1999 Total Solar eclipse across Europe (Aug. 11).

1999 3rd Parliament of the Worlds Religions held in South Africa. Many Pagan representatives attend, meet and ally with traditional African shamans.

1999 "Petition for Papal Apology" sent to Pope John Paul II with 6,000 Pagan signatures.

2000 Pope John Paul II conducts "Mass of Pardon" at St. Peter's Basilica on March 12. He acknowledges that "Christians have often…violated the rights of ethnic groups and peoples, and shown contempt for their cultures and religious traditions."

2000 *Green Egg* ceases publication after 135 issues.

2001 "Pagan Summit" held in Indianapolis; 35 Pagan leaders attend harmoniously and productively.

2002 Total Solar eclipse (Feb. 4) in Australia.

2003 Oberon Zell-Ravenheart assembles Grey Council, writes *Grimoire for the Apprentice Wizard.*

2004 Oberon founds online Grey School of Wizardry.

Appendix B. The Wizard's Library

Here are a number of favorite books recommended by members of the Grey Council for the personal library of the young Wizard. I have grouped them into the kinds of categories in which my own Wizard's Library is organized. Within each category, books are alphabetized by author's last name, and titles are listed either by dates of publication, or in serial order.

I. Fantasy Novels & Series

Isabel Allende—
City of the Beasts (2002)
Peter S. Beagle—
The Last Unicorn (1968)
Emma Bull—
The War of the Oaks (2001)
Susan Cooper—The Dark is Rising:
Over Sea, Under Stone (1965)
The Dark is Rising (1973)
Greenwitch (1974)
The Grey King (1975)
Silver on the Tree (1977)
Tom Cross—
The Way of Wizards (2001)
John Crowley—*Little, Big* (1981)
Diane Duane—Tale of the Five:
Door Into Fire (1979)
Door Into Shadow (1984)
Door Into Sunset (1993)
Door Into Starlight (2004)
—Young Wizards series:
So You Want to be a Wizard (1996)
Deep Wizardry (1996)
High Wizardry (1997)
A Wizard Abroad (1999)
The Wizard's Dilemma (2002)
A Wizard Alone (2002)
The Wizard's Holiday (2003)
Lyndon Hardy—5 Magicks trilogy:
Master of the Five Magics (1984)
Secret of the Sixth Magic (1988)
Riddle of the Seven Realms (1988)
H.M. Hoover—
Children of Morrow (1985)
Madelyn L'Engle—Time Quartet:
A Wrinkle in Time (1962)
A Wind in the Door (1973)
A Swiftly Tilting Planet (1978)
Many Waters (1986)
Ursula K. LeGuin—Earthsea trilogy:
A Wizard of Earthsea (1968)
The Tombs of Atuan (1971)
The Farthest Shore (1972)
Cormac MacRaois—
—The Giltspur trilogy:
The Battle Below Giltspur (1988)
Dance of the Midnight Fire (1990)
Lightning Over Giltspur (1992)
Ruth Nichols—
A Walk Out of the World (1969)
Pat O'Shea—
The Hounds of the Morrigan (1988)
Tamora Pierce—
—Circle of Magic quartet:
1. Sandry's Book (1997)
2. Tris's Book (1998)
3. Daja's Book (1998)
4. Briar's Book (1999)
—The Circle Opens:
1. Magic Steps (2000)
2. *Street Magic* (2001)
3. Cold Fire (2002)
4. Shatterglass (2003)
Elizabeth Pope—
The Perilous Gard (1974)
Terry Pratchett—
Equal Rites (1986)
Mort (1987)
Sourcery (1989)
Small Gods (1991)
Terry Pratchett & Josh Kirby—
Eric (1990)
Philip Pullman—His Dark Materials:
I: The Golden Compass (1995)
II: The Subtle Knife (1997)
III: The Amber Spyglass (2000)
J.K. Rowling—Harry Potter series:
The Sorcerer's Stone (1997)
The Chamber of Secrets (1998)
The Prisoner of Azkaban (1999)
The Goblet of Fire (2000)
The Order of the Phoenix (2003)
The Half-Blood Prince (2005)
—with one more to come!
Mary Stewart—The Merlin quarto:
The Crystal Cave (1970)
The Hollow Hills (1973)
The Last Enchantment (1979)
The Wicked Day (1983)
J.R.R. Tolkein—Lord of the Rings:
The Hobbit (1937)
The Fellowship of the Ring (1954)
The Two Towers (1954)
The Return of the King (1954)
T.H. White—
The Sword in the Stone (1963)
Jane Yolen—*Wizard's Hall* (1991)

II. Magickal Practice

Robert Adzema & Mablen Jones—
The Great Sundial Cutout Book (1978)
Anton & Mina Adams—
Wizard's Handbook (2002)
The World of Wizards (2002)
Freya Aswynn—
Northern Mysteries & Magic (2002)
Rae Beth—
The Wiccan Path: A Guide for the Solitary Practitioner (1990)
Raymond Buckland—
Practical Color Magick (1983)
Buckland's Complete Book of Witchcraft (1997)
Pauline & Dan Campanelli—
Wheel of the Year: Living the Magical Life (1989)
Ancient Ways: Reclaiming Pagan Traditions (1991)
Pagan Rites of Passage (1994)
Deepak Chopra—
The Way of the Wizard (1995)
Scott Cunningham—
Earth Power (1983)
Wicca: A Guide for the Solitary Practitioner (1988)
The Complete Book of Incense, Oils & Brews (1989)
Spell Crafts: Creating Magical Objects (1997)
Scott Cunningham & David Harrington—
The Magical Household (1987)
Spell Crafts: Creating Magical Objects (1997)
Gerina Dunwich—
Candlelight Spells (1988)
The Magick of Candle Burning (1989)
Anodea Judith—*Wheels of Life: A User's Guide to the Chakra System* (1987)
Amber K—*True Magick* (1990)
Gillian Kemp—
The Good Spell Book (1997)
Janice Eaton Kilby—
The Book of Wizard Craft (2001)
Edain McCoy—
The Sabbats: A New Approach to Living the Old Ways (1994)
Francis Melville—
The Secrets of High Magic (2002)
Diana Paxson—
Taking up the Runes (2005)
Silver Ravenwolf—

Solitary Witch: The Ultimate Book of Shadows for the New Generation (2003)

Starhawk—
Circle Round: Raising Children in Goddess Traditions (2000)

Patricia Telesco—
Futuretelling (1998)
A Kitchen Witch's Cookbook (1998)
Magick Made Easy: Charms, Spells, Potions & Power (1999)
The Teen Book of Shadows (2004)

Arthur Edward Waite—
The Pictorial Key to the Tarot (1971)

Marion Weinstein—*Positive Magic: Occult Self-Help* (1985)

Valerie Worth—
Crone's Book of Words (1971)

III. Mythology

Lucius Apuleius—*The Golden Ass* (Robert Graves, trans.) (1998)

Padraic Colum—
The Children's Homer: The Adventures of Odysseus and the Tale of Troy (1982)
The Golden Fleece and the Heroes Who Lived Before Achilles (1983)
Children of Odin: The Book of Northern Myths (1984)
The King of Ireland's Son (1997)

Hilda Davidson—*Gods & Myths of the Viking Age* (1982)

Hallie Eagleheart—
The Heart of the Goddess (1990)

Robert Graves—
Hercules, My Shipmate (1945)
The Greek Myths (1955)
Greek Gods & Heroes (1965)

Roger L. Green—
Tales the Muses Told (1965)
Heroes of Greece & Troy (1970)
Tales of Ancient Egypt (1996)
King Arthur & His Knights of the Round Table (1995)

Stefan Grundy—*Rhinegold* (1994)

Edith Hamilton—*Mythology* (1942)

Barbara Leonie Picard—
Lady of the Linden Tree (1954)
Three Ancient Kings: Gilgamesh, Hrolf Kraki, Conary (1986)

Mary Renault—
The Bull from the Sea (1962)
The King Must Die (1988)

Robert Silverberg —
Gilgamesh the King (1984)

R.J. Stewart— *Celtic Gods, Celtic Goddesses* (1990)

Hyemehost Storm—
Seven Arrows (1985)

Rosemary Sutcliffe—
The Hound of Ulster (2002)

IV. Life, the Universe & Everything

Larry Gonick—
The Cartoon History of the Universe Vol. 1 (1990); *Vol. 2* (1991); *Vol. 3* (2002)

V. Nature Wild & Tame

Galen Gillotte—
Sacred Stones of the Goddess: Using Earth Energies for Magical Living (2003)

William Hillcourt—
The Boy Scout Fieldbook (1978)

Jesse Wolf Hardin—*Gaia Eros: Reconnecting to the Magic and Spirit of Nature* (2004)

Ellen Evert Hopman—
Tree Medicine—Tree Magic (1991)
A Druid's Herbal For the Sacred Earth Year (1995)
Walking The World In Wonder—A Children's Herbal (2000)

John Martineau—
A Little Book of Coincidence (2001)

Melody—*Love Is In the Earth* (1995)
Mineralogical Pictorial: Treasures of the Earth (2003)

Elizabeth Pepper & John Wilcock—
The Witches' Almanac (annual)

Peterson Field Guides

H.A. Rey—
Find the Constellations (1954; 1988)
The Stars: A New Way to See Them (1962; 1980)

Jamie Sams & David Carson—
Medicine Cards (1988)

Stanley Schuler—*How to Grow Almost Everything* 1965)

Patricia Telesco—*Gardening With the Goddess* (2001)
Animal Spirit: Spells, Sorcery & Symbols from the Wild (2002)

Herbert S. Zim, Ed.—
Golden Nature Guides (dozens of great books...1950s-on)

VI. Conjury

Walter B. Gibson—*Professional Magic for Amateurs* (1974)

Todd Karr—*Backyard Magic* (1996)

Henning Nelms—
Magic and Showmanship: A Handbook for Conjurers (1969)

Bill Tarr—*Now You See It, Now You Don't* (1976)

VI. Mythic Beings & Creatures

Katlyn Breene—*Faery Call* (1997)

Joseph Nigg—
The Book of Dragons & other Mythical Beasts (2002)

Barbara Ninde Byfield—
The Glass Harmonica: A Lexicon of the Fantastical (1967)

Brian Froud— *Faeries* (1978)
Good Faeries/Bad Faeries (1998)

John A. Keel—
The Complete Guide to Mysterious Beings (1970; 1994)

White, T. H.—
The Book of Beasts (1954; 1984)

IX. Reference Books

Raymond Buckland—
The Witch Book: Encyclopedia of Witchcraft, Wicca, & Neo-Paganism (2002)
The Fortune-Telling Book: Encyclopedia of Divination & Soothsaying (2003)

Scott Cunningham—
Cunningham's Encyclopedia of Magical Herbs (1985)
Encyclopedia of Crystal, Gem & Metal Magic (1987)

Raven Grimassi—*Encyclopedia of Wicca & Witchcraft* (2000)

Rosemary Guiley—
Encyclopedia of Witches & Witchcraft (1989; 1999)

Rudolf Koch— *The Book of Signs* (1955)

Carl G. Liungman—
Dictionary of Symbols (1994)

Carl McColman—*The Complete Idiot's Guide to Paganism* (2002)

Tom Ogden—
Wizards & Sorcery (1997)

Herbert Robinson & Knox Wilson—
Myths & Legends of All Nations (1976)

Patricia Telesco—
Seasons of the Sun: Celebrations from the World's Spiritual Traditions (1996)
The Language of Dreams (1997)
Ghosts, Spirits & Hauntings (1999)
The Magick of Folk Wisdom (2000)

Elizabeth & Allan Zolan Kronzek—
The Sorcerer's Companion: A Guide to the Magical World of Harry Potter (2001)

Appendix C. Credits and References

COURSE ONE: WIZARDRY

Class I: Concerning Wizards

Adams, Anton and Mina, *The World of Wizards*, Lansdowne Publ., 2002

Chopra, Deepak, *The Way of the Wizard*, Harmony Books, 1995

Guiley, Rosemary, *Encyclopedia of Witches and Witchcraft*, Facts on File, 1989; 1999

Highfield, Roger, *The Science of Harry Potter,* Viking Penguin, 2002

Rowling, J.K., *Harry Potter and the Sorcerer's Stone,* Scholastic, 1997

Class II: Becoming a Wizard

LeGuin, Ursula, *A Wizard of Earthsea,* Bantam Books, 1968

Class III: Foundations of Magick

Melville, Francis, *The Secrets of High Magic,* Quarto Books, 2002

Ogden, Tom, *Wizards & Sorcery,* Facts on File, 1997

Pratchett, Terry, *Lords and Ladies,* HarperTorch 1992

Telesco, Patricia, *The Magick of Folk Wisdom,* Castle Books, 2000

Class: IV: Magickal Arts

Brandon, S.G.F., *Milestones of History,* Newsweek, 1970

Guiley, Rosemary, *Ibid.*

Class V: Magickal Talents

Pratchett, Terry, *Witches Abroad,* HarperTorch, 1991

Class VI: Perchance to Dream

Buckland, Ray, *Buckland's Complete Book of Witchcraft,* Llewellyn, 1997

Highfield, Roger, *Ibid.*

Telesco, Patricia, *Ibid.*

Complete Book of Fortune Telling, Studio London, 1996

COURSE TWO: NATURE

Class I: Natural Mysteries

Chardin, Teilhard de, *The Phenomenon of Man*, 1955; Harper & Row, 1975

A Correlated History of Earth, Pan Terra, Inc., 1994; 2000

Dewey, Edward R., *Cycles: The Mysterious Forces that Trigger Events,* Hawthorn Books, 1971

LeGuin, Ursula, *The Farthest Shore,* Bantam Books, 1972

—, *A Wizard of Earthsea (op. cit.)*

Class III: The Elements

Fox, Farida Ka'iwalani, "Elemenetal Self-Healing" (series), *Green Egg* #89–92, 1990–91

Hall, Manley Palmer, *The Secret Teachings of All Ages,* Philosophical Research Society, 1928

Class IV: Back to Nature

Hillcourt, William, *Boy Scout Fieldbook,* 2nd edition, Boy Scouts of America, Workman Publishing, 1967; 1978

Ormond, Clyde, *Outdoorsman's Handbook,* Berkeley Windhover, 1974

Pratchett, Terry, *Moving Pictures,* HarperTorch, 1990

Rombauer, Irma and Rombauer Becker, Marion, *Joy of Cooking,* Signet/New America Library, 1931; 1974

Class V. Adventures in Nature

Friedl, Catherine, "The Role of Water in Human Evolution," March 2000, *www.wf.carleton.ca/Museum/aquatic/cont.htm*

Morgan, Elaine, *The Aquatic Ape Hypothesis,* Souvenir Press, 1997

Pratchett, Terry, *Ibid.*

Class VI: Your Magickal Garden

Goodpasture, W.W., *The Complete Book of Gardening,* Dell, 1954

Llewellyn's Magical Almanac, Llewellyn Publishing (annual)

Pepper, Elizabeth and Wilcock, John, *The Witches' Almanac* (annual)

Rodale, Robert, *The Basic Book of Organic Gardening,* Ballantine, 1971

Schuler, Stanley, *How to Grow Almost Everything,* Pocket Books, 1965

COURSE THREE: PRACTICE

Class I: Ethics of Magick

LeGuin, Ursula, *A Wizard of Earthsea (op. cit.)*

Pratchett, T., *Lords and Ladies (op. cit.)*

Thompson, Gwen ("Wiccan-Pagan Potpourri," *Green Egg,* 7:69 (Mar. 21, 1975)

Class II: Tools of Magick

Buckland, Raymond, *Ibid.*

Huson, Paul, *Mastering Witchcraft,* Perigree Books, 1970

LeGuin, Ursula, *The Tombs of Atuan,* Bantam Books, 1971

Zell, Oberon, "Tools of Magick," *How About Magic?,* #6–11, 1991–92

Class III: Your Magickal Regalia

Pratchett, T., *Witches Abroad (op. cit.)*

White, T.H., *The Sword in the Stone*, Bantam Books, 1963

Class IV: Your Sanctum Sanctorum

Melville, Francis, *Ibid.*

White, T.H., *Ibid.*

Class V: The Magickal World

Darling, Diane, "Elven Chess: A Game for All Seasons," *How About Magic?,* 1:3, Mar. 21, 1990

Class VI: Correspondences

Bran th' Blessed, "An Exploration of Circle Symbolism," *HOME Cooking,* 1997

Whitcomb, Bill, *The Magician's Companion,* Llewellyn, 1993

Zell, Oberon, Ed., *HOME Cooking: Rites & Rituals of the CAW,* 1997

Class VII: Signs and Symbols

Buckland, Raymond, *Ibid.*

Hall, Manley Palmer, *Ibid.*

Shlain, Leonard, *The Alphabet versus the Goddess,* Penguin/Compass, 1998

Strachen, Francoise, *Natural Magic,* Black watch, 1974

Telesco, Patricia, *Ibid.*

COURSE FOUR: RITES

Class I: Practical Magick

Attig, Sheila, "Why Study Magick?" ©1987, all rites reserved, Wicca: The Twin Paths: *www.geocities.com/WiccanTwin Paths/ymagick.htm* (used by permission)

Bonewits, P.E.I., *Authentic Thaumaturgy,* 2nd edition, Chaosium, 1978

Buckland, Raymond, *Ibid.*

Dunwich, Gerina, *The Magick of Candle Burning,* Citadel Press, 1989

Frazer, Sir James, *The New Golden Bough,* Mentor Books, 1890; 1959

Levi, Eliphas, *Dogma and Ritual of High Magic,* 1856

Magnus, Olaus, *Historia de Gentibus Septentionalibus,* 1555

Pratchett, Terry, *Moving Pictures (op. cit.)*

Zell, Oberon, *Ibid.*

Class II: Ritual Spaces

Mayfire, David, "Mazes and Labyrinths," *Green Egg,* Vol. XXVI, No. 101, Summer 1993

Vickers, J. Rod, "Medicine Wheels: A Mystery in Stone," *Alberta Past* 8(3):6–7, Winter 1992–93

Zell, Oberon, *Ibid.*

Class III: About Rituals

Gabriel, Liza and Zell, Oberon, "Sacraments in the CAW," *Church of All Worlds Membership Handbook,* 3rd Edition, 1997

Inglehart, Hallie, "Creating Rituals," *HOME Cooking,* 1997

Judith, Anodea, "Ethics of Magick & Ritual;" "Questions to Ask in Planning Ritual," *HOME Cooking,* 1997

Hunter, Wendy and Littlewolf, Eldri, "Circle Lore & Etiquette," *HOME Cooking,* 1997

Moonoak, Paul, "Rites of Passage," *Church of All Worlds Membership Handbook (op. cit.)*

Zell, Oberon, *Ibid.*

Class IV: Conducting a Ritual

Judith, Anodea, "The Magick Circle," *HOME Cooking,* 1997

Zell, Oberon, *Ibid.*

Class V: Magickal Times

Goudsmit, Samuel and Clayborne, Robert, *Time,* Life Science Library, 1966

Graves, Robert *The White Goddess,* Noonday Press, 1948

Foxtales, "Celtic Tree Calendar," *How About Magic?,* 3:12, Aug. 1, 1992

Pepper, Elizabeth and Wilcock, John, *Witches All,* Pentacle Press, 1976

Class VI: The Wheel of the Year

Hussey, Leigh Ann, "The Fire Festivals," ©1993 (used by permission)

Zell, Oberon, "The CAW Wheel of the Year," *Church of All Worlds Membership Handbook,* 3rd Edition, 1997

Class VII: Spellcraft

Buckland, Raymond, *Ibid.*

Dunwich, Gerina, *Candlelight Spells,* Citadel Press, 1988

Grammary, Ann, *Witches Workbook,* Pocket Books, 1973

Kemp, Gillian, *The Good Spell Book,* Little, Brown & Co., 1997

Kidd, D.A., *Collins Latin Gem Dictionary,* Collins, 1957; 1970

Telesco, Patricia, *Ibid.*

Whitcomb, Bill, *Ibid.*

Worth, Valerie, *Crone's Book of Words,* Llewellyn, 1971

COURSE FIVE: SPECTRUM I

Class I: Meditation (Aqua)

Buckland, Raymond, *Buckland's Complete Book of Witchcraft (op. cit.)*

Stewart, C. Nelson, "Astral Body," *Man, Myth & Magic,* Marshall Cavendish Corp., 1970

Class II: Healing (Blue)

Buckland, Raymond, *Ibid.*

—, *Practical Color Magick,* 1983

Harris, Benjamin, F., *Kitchen Medicines,* Natura Publications, Worcester, MA, 1961

Hopman, Ellen Evert, *A Druid's Herbal For the Sacred Earth Year,* Inner Traditions/Destiny Books, 1995

—, *Tree Medicine—Tree Magic,* Phoenix Publishers, 1991

—, *Walking The World In Wonder—A Children's Herbal,* Inner Traditions, 2000

Judith, Anodea, *Wheels Of Life: A User's Guide to the Chakra System,* Llewellyn, 1987

Quelch, M.T., *Herbal Medicines,* Faber & Faber Ltd., London, 1946

Class III: Wortcunning (Green)

Cunningham, Scott, *Cunningham's Encyclopedia of Magical Herbs,* Llewellyn, 1997

Gerard, John, *The Herball, or General Historie of Plants,* London, 1597; Dover, 1975

Harris, Benjamin, F., *Ibid.*

Hopman, Ellen Evert, *Ibid.*

Quelch, M.T., *Ibid.*

Rowling, J.K., *Ibid.*

Class IV: Divination (Yellow)

Adams, Anton and Mina, *Ibid.*

Crowley, Aleister, *The Book of Thoth,* Samuel Weiser, 1969

Doane, Doris Chase and Keyes, King, *How to Read Tarot Cards,* Funk & Wagnalls, 1967

Gardner, Richard, "The Tarot for Life," *The Fortune Tellers,* Black Watch, 1974

Howe, Ellic, *"Astrology," Man, Myth & Magic (op. cit.)*

Ogden, Tom, *Ibid.*

Peschel, Lisa, *A Practical Guide to the Runes,* Llewellyn, 1995

Rakoczi, Basil Ivan, *"Palmistry," Man, Myth & Magic (op. cit.)*

Sheridan, Jo, "How to Read Hands," *The Fortune Tellers,* Black Watch, 1974

Telesco, Patricia, *Ibid.*

Waite, Arthur Edward, *The Pictorial Key to the Tarot,* Rudolf Steiner, 1971

Williams, Athene, "The Runes," *The Fortune Tellers,* Black Watch, 1974

Class V: Conjury (Orange)

Gilbert, George and Rydell, Wendy, *Great Tricks of the Master Magicians,* Golden Press, 1976

Hay, Henry, *The Amateur Magician's Handbook,* Signet, 1950; 1972

Karr, Todd, *Backyard Magic,* Scholastic Inc., 1996

Nelms, Henning, *Magic and Showmanship: A Handbook for Conjurers,* Dover, 1969

Scot, Reginald, *The Discoverie of Witchcraft,* 1584

Tarr, Bill, *Now You See It, Now You Don't,* Vintage Books, 1976

Class VI: Alchemy (Red)

Biedermann, Hans, "Alchemy: A Secret Language of the Mind," *Man, Myth & Magic,* Marshall Cavendish, 1970

de Givry, Grillot, *Witchcraft, Magic & Alchemy,* Bonanza Books (no date or copyright indicated)

Hall, Manly Palmer, *Ibid.*

Kronzek, Allan Zola and Elizabeth, *The Sorcerer's Companion,* Broadway Books, 2001

Lionel-Porter, *Chemical Magic,* Lionel Corp., 1952

Melville, Francis, *Ibid.*

Ogden, Tom, *Ibid.*

Pratchett, T., *Moving Pictures (op. cit.)*

Raglan, "Alchemical Ritual Enhancements," *Green Egg,* 32:135, Sept.–Oct. 2000

Whitcomb, Bill, *Ibid.*

COURSE SIX: SPECTRUM 2

Class I: Beast Mastery (Brown)

Colombrano, Rosemarie, "Pet Briefs," *USA Weekend,* June 13–15, 2003

Pratchett, T., *Lords and Ladies (op. cit.)*

Sams, Jamie and Carson, David, *Medicine Cards,* Bear & Co., 1988

Telesco, Patricia, *Ibid.*

Class II: Cosmology (Violet)

Adzema, Robert and Jones, Mablen, *The Great Sundial Cutout Book,* Hawthorn Books, 1978

Arp, Halton, *Quasars, Redshifts and Controversies,* Interstellar Media, 1987

Bell, Cathy, "The Mythology of the Constellations," *www.emufarm.org/~cmbell/myth/myth.html*

Bergamini, David, *The Universe,* Time-Life Books, 1962; 1967

Bryson, Bruce, "Quarks to Quasars: Powers of Ten," *www.wordwizz.com/pwrsof10.htm*

Powers of Ten: *http://micro.magnet.fsu.edu/primer/java/scienceopticsu/*

powersof10/index.htm
Davies, Paul and Gribbin, John, *The Matter Myth*, Simon & Schuster/ Touchstone, 1992
LaViolette, Paul, *Beyond the Big Bang: Ancient Myth and the Science of Continuous Creation*, Park Street Press, 1995
Lerner, Eric, *The Big Bang Never Happened*, Vintage Books, 1992
Martineau, John, *A Little Book of Coincidence,* Walker & Co., 2001
NASA, *www.nasa.gov*
Rees, Martin and Natarajan, Priyamvada, "A Field Guide to the Invisible Universe," *Discover,* 24:12 (Dec. 2003)
Rey, H.A., *Find the Constellations,* Houghton Mifflin, 1954–1988
—, *The Stars: A New Way to See Them,* Mariner Books, 1962–1980
Space Science Institute, *www.spacescience.org*
Editors of Time-Life Books, *Voyage Through the Universe* (series), Time-Life Books, 1988
Van Flandern, Tom, *Dark Matter, Missing Planets & New Comets*, North Atlantic Books, 1993
Zim, Herbert S., *Stars,* Golden Press, 1960

Class III: Mathemagicks (Clear)

Bergamini, David, *Mathematics,* Life Science Library, Time-Life, 1963
Hall, Manly Palmer, *Ibid.*
Rawles, Bruce, *Sacred Geometry: www.intent.com/sg/*
Sacred Geometry & Math: *www.crystalinks.com/math.html; www.crystalinks.com/sacred_geometry. html*

Class IV: Ceremonial (White)

Gigon, Olof, "Hermetica," *Man, Myth & Magic (op. cit.)*
Hall, Manly Palmer, *Ibid.*
Kronzek, Allan Zola and Elizabeth, *Ibid.*
Melville, Francis, *Ibid.*
Ogden, Tom, *Ibid.*
Whitcomb, Bill, *Ibid.*
White, Nelson, *Secret Magick Revealed,* The Technology Group, 1995
—, *The Wizard's Apprentice,* The Technology Group, 1995
—, *Working High Magick,* The Technology Group, 1995
Zwi Werblowsky, R.J., "Cabala," *Man, Myth & Magic (op. cit.)*

Class V: Lore Mastery (Grey)

"'Cyclops'-like remains found on Crete," Associated Press, 1/29/2003
Encyclopedia Mythica, www.pantheon.org/mythica.html
Galadriel, Lady and Athenor, Lord, "The Quest for the Holy Grail," *Green Egg,* 25:98 (Fall 1992)
Graves, Robert, *The Greek Myths,* Penguin Books, 1955
—, *Hercules, My Shipmate,* Creative Age Press, 1945
Hesiod, *Theogony,* trans. Richmond Lattimore, University of Michigan Press, 1959
Homer, *The Odyssey,* trans. W.H.D. Rouse, Mentor Books, 1937
Online Mythology Guide: www.online-mythology.com
Pincent, John, *Greek Mythology,* Hamlyn Publishing, 1969
Renault, Mary, *The Bull from the Sea,* Pantheon Books, 1962
Robinson, Herbert Spencer and Wilson, Knox, *Myths and Legends of All Nations,* Littlefield, Adams & Co., 1976
Silverberg, Robert, *Gilgamesh the King,* Bantam Books, 1984
Skidmore, Joel, "Odysseus;" "Jason & the Argonauts," *Mythweb*, 1997, *www.mythweb.com/heroes*
Wright, Allen W., *Robin Hood, Bold Outlaw of Barnsdale and Sherwood, www.geocities.com/puckrobin/rh/*

Class VI: The Dark Arts (Black)

Cavendish, Richard, *The Black Arts,* Putnam, 1967
Davis, Wade, *The Serpent and the Rainbow,* Collins, 1986
Fortune, Dione, *Psychic Self-Defense,* 6th ed., Samuel Weiser, 1982
Frew, Don Hudson, "A Brief History of Satanism," *Witchcraft, Satanism & Occult Crime: Who's Who & What's What,* Green Egg pubs., 1989
Guiley, Rosemary, *Ibid.*
Hefner, Alan G., *The Mystica: www.themystica.com/mystica/pages/people.htm*
Highfield, Roger, *Ibid.*
Ogden, Tom, *Ibid.*
Pratchett, Terry, *Eric,* HarperTorch, 1990
Ravenwolf, Silver, *Teen Witch: Wicca for a New Generation,* Llewellyn Publications, 2000
Savedow, Steve, *Goetic Evocation: The Magician's Workbook, vol. 2,* Eschaton Publications, 1996
Stewart, R.J., *Celtic Gods, Celtic Goddesses,* Blandford, 1990
Summers, Montague, *Witchcraft and Black Magic,* Dover Publications, 1946; 2000
Whitcomb, Bill, *Ibid.*

COURSE SEVEN: LORE

Class I: The Other Worlds

Anderson, Ian Lurking Bear, "Gateways to Faerie," *Green Egg,* Vol. 27, No. 111 (Winter, 1995)
Breene, Katlyn, *Faery Call,* Mermade Magickal Arts, 1997
Briggs. K.M., "Fairies," *Man, Myth & Magic,* Marshall Cavendish, 1970
Bruyere/Sin, "The Shift from the Otherworld to the Underworld in Northern Europe," Chronicles of Hell, *www.geocities.com/SoHo/Museum/5999/hell/celtic.html*
Budge, Sir Wallis, *Egyptian Religion,* Bell Publishing, 1900
Firefall, Fiona, "The Egyptian Mythos: Creation Tales and the Sacred Pantheon," *Green Egg,* Vol. 30, No. 124 (Sept.–Oct. 1998)
"The Greek Underworld," *http://members.tripod.com/shs_odyssey/underworld.htm*
Ions, Veronica, *Egyptian Mythology,* Hamlyn Publishing, 1965
MacCana, Proinsias, *Celtic Mythology,* Hamlyn Publishing, 1970
Pincent, John, *Ibid.*
Pratchett, T., *Lords and Ladies (op. cit.)*
Religious Tolerance.org: *www.religioustolerance.org/afterlife.htm*
Robinson, Herbert Spencer and Wilson, Knox, *Ibid.*

Class II: Gods of All the Nations

Alternative Religions, http://altreligion.about.com/
Budge, Sir Wallis, *Egyptian Religion,* Bell Publishing, 1900
Encyclopedia Mythica, Ibid.
Firefall, Fiona, "The Egyptian Mythos: Creation Tales and the Sacred Pantheon," *Green Egg,* 30:124 (Sept.–Oct. 1998)
Ions, Veronica, *Ibid.*
Pincent, John, *Ibid.*
Robinson, Herbert Spencer and Wilson, Knox, *Ibid.*
Stewart, R.J., *Ibid.*
Wayne, Phil, "A Brief Introduction to the Orixa and Their Fellow Travelers," *Green Egg,* 29:114 (July–Aug. 1996)

Class III: The Others

Anderson, Ian Lurking Bear, *Ibid.*
Breene, Katlyn, *Ibid.*
Briggs. K.M., "Fairies," *Man, Myth & Magic (op. cit.)*
Froud, Brian, *Good Faeries/Bad Faeries,* Simon & Schuster, 1998
—, *Faeries,* Harry N. Abrams, Inc., 1978

Highfield, Roger, *Ibid.*
Robinson, Herbert Spencer and Wilson, Knox, *Ibid.*
Shulman, Sandy, "Dwarfs," *Man, Myth & Magic (op. cit.)*
Werblowsky, R. J. Zwi, "Golem," *Man, Myth & Magic (op. cit.)*
Wosien, Maria-Gabriele, "Giants," *Man, Myth & Magic (op. cit.)*

Class IV: The Magickal Bestiary
Byfield, Barbara Ninde, *The Glass Harmonica: A Lexicon of the Fantastical,* MacMillan Co., 1967
Cohen, Daniel, *A Natural History of Unnatural Things,* McCall Publishing, 1971
Costello, Peter, *The Magic Zoo,* St Martin's Press, 1979
Ellis, Richard, *The Search for the Giant Squid,* The Lyons Press, 1998
Keel, John A., *The Complete Guide to Mysterious Beings,* Doubleday, 1970; 1994
Ley, Willy, *Exotic Zoology,* Viking Press, 1959
Melillo, Elizabeth G., "Medieval Bestiary," 1966: *www.geocities.com/Paris/3963/bestiary.html*
Michell, John & Rickard, Robert, *Living Wonders,* Thames & Hudson, 1982
Norman, Scott T., "Mokele-mbembe: The Living Dinosaur," 1996–2003: *www.mokelembembe.com/*
White, T. H., *The Book of Beasts,* Dover, 1954; 1984

Class V: Wizards of History
Adams, Anton and Mina, *Ibid.*
Cahill, Robert Ellis, *New England's Witches & Wizards,* Old Saltbox Publishing, Salem, MA, 1970
Damascius, "The Life of Hypatia," *Life of Isidore*, *The Suda*, trans. Jeremiah Reedy, Phanes Press, 1993
Dilworth, John, "The Count of Saint-Germaine," The Mystica *(op. cit.)*
Golden Dawn Website: *home.earthlink.net/~xristos/GoldenDawn*
Guiley, Rosemary, *Ibid.*
Knight, Russell W., "Wine, Women & Witchcraft," *The 'Headers In Life & Legend,* Marblehead Magazine, 1989
Hefner, Alan G., *Ibid.*
Leonardo da Vinci, Reynal & Co., 1956
Ogden, Tom, *Ibid.*
Van Helden, Albert, "Giordano Bruno," 1995: *http://es.rice.edu/ES/humsoc/Galileo/People/bruno.html*
W., Sharon M., "Doctor Robert Fludd," The Alchemy website: *www.levity.com/alchemy/fludd1.html*

Class VI: Modern Wizards
Adams, Anton and Mina, *Ibid.*
Deese, Patrick, The Biogaphy Project: *www.popsubculture.com/pop/bio_project*
Golden Dawn website, *Ibid.*
Grimassi, Raven, *Encyclopedia of Wicca & Witchcraft,* Llewellyn, 2000
Guiley, Rosemary, *Ibid.*
Kheper: *www.kheper.net/topics/Hermeticism*
Hefner, Alan G., *Ibid.*
Ogden, Tom, *Ibid.*

Art Credits

Beatus of Liebana *(776)*: 304
Daniel Beard *(1889)*: 112, 290
Daniel Blair-Stewart: 29, 35, 37, 46, 51, 83, 87, 199, 252, 253, 316
Daniel Bloomfield: 258, 259, 260, 285, 289, 292
Jean Jacques Boissard *(1597)*: 244
Katlyn Breen: 63, 65, 66, 86, 189, 190, 192, 193, 194, 195, 238, 321, 322
Raymond Buckland: 205
Gustav Doré *(1873)*: 327
Dirk Dykstra: 124
Jim Fitzpatrick: 290
Scott Fray: 4, 225, 287
John Gerard *(1597)*: 219, 220, 221, 222, 223, 225
Konrad Gessner (1551): 329
Karl Gjellerup *(1893)*: 68
William Giese, Rhana Janto: 240
Claude Gillot *(c.1700)*: 2
Ernst Haeckel *(1904)*: 272
Ron "Ash" Hiscock: 205
Jesse Wolf Hardin: 350
Johann Georg Heck *(1851)*: 82, 85, 86, 120, 121, 228, 263, 264
Lars Hernquist, Volker Springel: 269
Hero of Alexander: 238
Bernard Heuvelmans: 324
Scott Hollander: 154, 328
Amber K: 97, 209, 211, 219, 225, 300, 346, 347, 349
Ron Kimball: 330
Christopher M.: xii
Albertus Magnus *(1545)*: 330
Oläus Magnus *(1555)*: 155, 156, 326
Matthäus Merian *(1718)*: 326, 327, 328, 329
Christopher Marlow *(1631)*: 30
Jeannine Masiello-Stuhmer: 316
Denys de Montfort: 327
Nybor: 62, 327, 342
Paracelsus *(1536)*: 69
Thomas Perkins: 305
Louis Rhead *(1912)*: 290
Paulus Richius *(1516)*: 29
W. Roberts: 143, 287, 307, 313, 314, 315, 327, 332
Paul B. Rucker: 150
Ivan Sanderson: 325
William Savage: 286, 306
J. Schliebe *(1846)*: 336
Reginald Scot *(1584)*: 146, 238
Susan Seddon-Boulet: 62
Carol Shugart: 125
Moria Starbuck: 197, 198
Jacobus de Teramo *(1473)*: 27
Edward Topsell *(1607)*: 326, 327, 328
Basile Valentin *(1413)*: 245, 250
John W. Waterhouse *(c.1900)*: 66, 257, 323
Hans Weiditz *(1532)*: 24, 299
Kathryn White: 30, 68, 180, 250, 348
Howard W. Wookey *(1928)*: 68
Mary Ann Zapalac: 137, 212
Oberon Zell-Ravenheart: iii, vi, viii, 1, 7, 8, 9, 12, 16, 22, 33, 34, 36, 37, 40, 42, 43, 44, 45, 46, 49, 50, 52, 55, 59, 60, 61, 62, 64, 65, 66, 69, 70, 71, 72, 73, 76, 77, 78, 80, 84, 89, 91, 94, 98, 104, 105, 106, 107, 108, 109, 110, 111, 113, 114, 115, 116, 117, 118, 120, 122, 127, 128, 131, 133, 135, 142, 143, 145, 146, 147, 151, 154, 159, 160, 161, 162, 165, 166, 175, 176, 177, 178, 179, 184, 187, 188, 200, 201, 202, 203, 204, 208, 214, 216, 226, 242, 243, 246, 247, 262, 263, 266, 267, 268, 269, 272, 274, 276, 278, 280, 283, 291, 292, 305, 322, 325, 326, 327, 330, 332, 344

Appendix D. Index

About the Author

Oberon Zell-Ravenheart (1942-) is an elder in the worldwide magickal community. In 1962, he co-founded the Church of All Worlds, a Pagan church with a futuristic vision. Through his publication of *Green Egg* magazine (1968-'75; 1988-'96), Oberon was instrumental in the founding of the modern Pagan movement, which he so named. In 1970, he had a profound Vision of the Living Earth that he published as an early version of "The Gaia Thesis." Oberon is an initiate in several magickal traditions and has been involved in many interfaith projects. He is a thealogian and ritualist, creating and conducting rites of passage, seasonal celebrations, Mystery Initiations, Earth-healings, and other large rituals. He has worked as a grade school teacher and a family and youth counselor. Oberon has traveled throughout the world, celebrated solar eclipses at ancient stone circles, raised unicorns, and swum with mermaids in the Coral Sea. He also sculpts altar statues of gods and goddesses. Living with wife Morning Glory in NorCalifia, Oberon is Headmaster of the online Grey School of Wizardry: *www.GreySchool.com.*